Architecture

Celebrating the Past, Designing the Future

Architecture

Celebrating the Past, Designing the Future

Edited by Nancy B. Solomon, AIA

Visual Reference Publications Inc., New York

The American Institute of Architects, Washington, D.C.

First published in the United States in 2008 by
Visual Reference Publications, Inc.
302 Fifth Avenue • New York, NY 10001
Tel: 212.279.7000 • Fax: 212.279.7014
www.visualreference.com

©2008 The American Institute of Architects
1735 New York Avenue, NW
Washington, DC 20006
www.aia.org

The information in this book has been obtained from
many sources. The American Institute of Architects
has made every reasonable effort to make this reference
work accurate and authoritative, but does not warrant or
assume any liability for the accuracy or completeness of
the text, or its fitness for any particular purpose.

ISBN: 978-1-58471-162-9   ISBN: 1-58471-162-0

Design and composition
Group C Inc, New Haven
(BC, MKH, SJ, KM, CS, LT)

Prepress
Bright Arts (H.K.) Ltd

Printing
Toppan Printing Company America, Inc.

Printed and bound in China

Cover photo
St. Louis Gateway Arch
©Walter Bibikow/JAI/Corbis

Distributors to the trade in the
United States and Canada
Watson-Guptill
770 Broadway
New York, NY 10003

Distributors outside the
United States and Canada
HarperCollins International
10 East 53rd Street
New York, NY 10022-5299

The paper on which this book is printed contains
recycled content to support a sustainable world.

viii Acknowledgments
      Nancy B. Solomon, AIA

 ix   Preface
      George H. Miller, FAIA

  x   Coordinated Creativity
      Christine McEntee
      AIA Executive Vice President/CEO

 xi   Prelude to the Possibilities
      RK Stewart, FAIA

  1   Introduction: The Power of Design
      Robert Ivy, FAIA

      GOLD MEDALIST, 1993
 10   **Thomas Jefferson**
      Richard Guy Wilson, Hon. AIA

      GRASS ROOTS
 11   **AIA Abroad: International**
      Achievements and Prospects
      Thomas Vonier, FAIA, RIBA

      HISTORY
 12   **100 Years of Changing**
      Architectural Ideals:
      The AIA Gold Medal
      Richard Guy Wilson, Hon. AIA

      HISTORY
 14   **The First 150 Years of the**
      American Institute of Architects,
      1857–2007
      Tony P. Wrenn, Hon. AIA

Part One : Vision

 1   18   The Need for Architecture
          Karsten Harries, PhD

          GOLD MEDALIST, 1960
     31   **Ludwig Mies van der Rohe, FAIA**
          Dietrich Neumann, PhD

          GOLD MEDALIST, 1971
     32   **Louis I. Kahn, FAIA**
          Susan G. Solomon, PhD

          GRASS ROOTS
     33   **Victoria Beach:**
          Architectural Ethics in Action
          Kira Gould, Assoc. AIA

 2   34   Architecture as a Reflection of Evolving
          Culture: The American Experience
          James Steele, PhD

          GOLD MEDALIST, 1978
     55   **Philip Cortelyou Johnson, FAIA**
          Robert A.M. Stern, FAIA

          GOLD MEDALIST, 1989
     56   **Joseph Esherick, FAIA**
          Andrew Brodie Smith, PhD

          GRASS ROOTS
     57   **Visionary American Architecture**
          Jeff Stein, AIA

          GRASS ROOTS
     58   **Sharon C. Park, FAIA:**
          The Art and Science of Technical
          Preservation Services
          Sara Hart

          VIEWPOINT
     59   **History of the Preservation Movement**
          in the United States
          Jack Pyburn, FAIA

          VIEWPOINT
     60   **The Architect as Rebel**
          Thom Mayne, FAIA

          VIEWPOINT
     61   **Great Buildings Lost, Saved,**
          and Threatened
          George C. Skarmeas, AIA

          VIEWPOINT
     62   **The Role of the Critic**
          Robert Campbell, FAIA

          VIEWPOINT
     63   **Struggling for Diversity**
          Kathryn H. Anthony, PhD

 3   64   Engaging the Public,
          Seeking Common Ground
          Sharon Egretta Sutton, PhD, FAIA

          GOLD MEDALIST, 1969
     78   **William Wilson Wurster, FAIA**
          Andrew Blum

          GOLD MEDALIST, 2004
     79   **Samuel Mockbee, FAIA**
          Andrea Oppenheimer Dean

          GRASS ROOTS
     80   **Architecture for Humanity:**
          How to Give a Damn
          Kira Gould, Assoc. AIA

          GRASS ROOTS
     81   **A Blueprint for America**
          Anthony J. "Tony" Costello, FAIA

          GRASS ROOTS
     82   **Charles Harper, FAIA:**
          Disaster Responder and Civic Leader
          Barbara A. Nadel, FAIA

          GRASS ROOTS
     83   **Discovering the Power of Youth**
          Sharon Egretta Sutton, PhD, FAIA

          VIEWPOINT
     84   **Rebuilding Ground Zero**
          Paul Goldberger, Hon. AIA

          VIEWPOINT
     85   **An Architect in Politics:**
          A Personal Reflection
          Richard N. Swett, FAIA

 4   86   Ensuring a Healthy
          and Prosperous Future
          Thomas Fisher

          GOLD MEDALIST, 1977
     97   **Richard J. Neutra, FAIA**
          Lauren Weiss Bricker, PhD, and Judith Sheine

          GOLD MEDALIST, 1994
     98   **Norman Foster,**
          Lord Foster of Thames Bank, Hon. FAIA
          Helen Castle

          GRASS ROOTS
     99   **Committee on the Environment**
          Kira Gould, Assoc. AIA

          GRASS ROOTS
    100   **Dignity by Design:**
          Ron Mace, FAIA, and the Center
          for Universal Design
          Kira Gould, Assoc. AIA

          VIEWPOINT
    101   **Universal Design**
          Wolfgang F. E. Preiser, PhD

          VIEWPOINT
    102   **What's the Difference?**
          Michael Sorkin

          VIEWPOINT
    103   **Building Security:**
          Design Strategies for a
          Safer Environment
          Barbara A. Nadel, FAIA

Part Two : Knowledge and Implementation

5   104   Education and Practice:
              The Architect in the Making
              Harrison S. Fraker Jr., FAIA

          GOLD MEDALIST, 1959
   118   **Walter Gropius, FAIA**
              Michael James Meehan, AIA

          GOLD MEDALIST, 2001
   119   **Michael Graves, FAIA**
              Kristen Richards

          GRASS ROOTS
   120   **Freedom by Design**
              Brad Buchanan, FAIA

          GRASS ROOTS
   121   **Solar Decathlon**
              Susan Piedmont-Palladino, PhD

          GRASS ROOTS
   122   **Mentor, Teacher, Professional:
              Laura Lee, FAIA**
              John A. Loomis, FAIA

          VIEWPOINT
   123   **The Design Studio:
              The Heart of Architecture Education**
              Harrison S. Fraker Jr., FAIA

          VIEWPOINT
   124   **Performance-Based Criteria**
              Harrison S. Fraker Jr., FAIA

          VIEWPOINT
   125   **American Institute of
              Architecture Students**
              Jonathan Bahe, Assoc. AIA

6   126   Reflections on Architectural Research
              Daniel S. Friedman, PhD, FAIA

          GOLD MEDALIST, 1964
   134   **Pier Luigi Nervi, Hon. FAIA**
              Fred Bernstein

          GOLD MEDALIST, 1970
   135   **R. Buckminster Fuller, FAIA**
              Vernon Mays

          GRASS ROOTS
   136   **McDonough Braungart
              Design Chemistry**
              Deborah Snoonian

          GRASS ROOTS
   137   **KieranTimberlake Associates**
              Sara Hart

          VIEWPOINT
   138   **Research on Neuroscience
              and Architecture**
              John P. Eberhard, FAIA

          VIEWPOINT
   139   **Collaborative, Practice-Based Research**
              Stan Allen, AIA

7   140   Material Matters
              Lance Jay Brown, FAIA

          GOLD MEDALIST, 1952
   153   **Auguste Perret, Hon. FAIA**
              William Richards

          GOLD MEDALIST, 2002
   154   **Tadao Ando, Hon. FAIA**
              Fred Bernstein

          GRASSROOTS
   155   **Sheila Kennedy, AIA:
              Portable Light Project**
              Deborah Snoonian

          VIEWPOINT
   156   **Improvements in Glazing Technologies**
              Sara Hart

          VIEWPOINT
   157   **New Building Material from Plastics**
              Sara Hart

8   158   The Design Process:
              Catching the Third Wave
              Kyle V. Davy, AIA

          GOLD MEDALIST, 1968
   170   **Marcel Breuer, FAIA**
              Stanley Abercrombie, FAIA

          GOLD MEDALIST, 1999
   171   **Frank O. Gehry, FAIA**
              Vernon Mays

          GRASS ROOTS
   172   **Creative Leadership over Three
              Generations: Ratcliff Architects**
              Kyle V. Davy, AIA

          GRASS ROOTS
   173   **Blurring the Boundaries between Design
              and Construction: The Beck Group**
              David Dillon

9   174   Architecture Practice:
              The Eye for Success
              James P. Cramer, Hon. AIA

          GOLD MEDALIST, 1957
   181   **Louis Skidmore, FAIA**
              Richard Guy Wilson, Hon. AIA

          GOLD MEDALIST, 1995
   182   **César Pelli, FAIA**
              Kristen Richards

          GRASS ROOTS
   183   **Steed Hammond Paul's
              Schoolhouse of Quality**
              James P. Cramer, Hon. AIA

          GRASS ROOTS
   184   **LS3P's Client Strategies**
              James P. Cramer, Hon. AIA

          VIEWPOINT
   185   **Designing an Integrated Practice with
              Building Information Modeling**
              Norman Strong, FAIA

          VIEWPOINT
   186   **Globalization and the
              Practice of Architecture**
              James T. Fitzgerald, FAIA

          VIEWPOINT
   187   **A Return to Design-Build Delivery**
              Martin Sell, AIA

13 240 Design Excellence:
Building a Public Legacy
*Edward A. Feiner, FAIA,
and Marilyn Farley, Hon. AIA*

GOLD MEDALIST, 1986
254 **Arthur C. Erickson, Hon. AIA**
Andrew Blum

VIEWPOINT
255 **Engaging the Public,
One Person at a Time**
Randi Greenberg

14 256 Building the Foundations
for Education:
C. C. Sullivan

GOLD MEDALIST, 1947
271 **Eliel Saarinen, FAIA**
C. C. Sullivan

GOLD MEDALIST, 1985
272 **William Wayne Caudill, FAIA**
Andrew Brodie Smith, PhD

GRASS ROOTS
273 **From Mouse House to DoodleOpolis:
Architecture in the Schools**
Randi Greenberg

15 274 A Model of Health
Robin Guenther, FAIA

GOLD MEDALIST, 1963
290 **Alvar Aalto, Hon. FAIA**
William Morgan

GRASS ROOTS
291 **The Logic of Green: Sustainable Practices
in Health Care Design**
Deborah Snoonian

16 292 Architecture for Arts' Sake
John Morris Dixon, FAIA

GOLD MEDALIST, 1979
310 **Ieoh Ming Pei, FAIA**
Nancy B. Solomon, AIA

GOLD MEDALIST, 1997
311 **Richard Meier, FAIA**
Fred Bernstein

GOLD MEDALIST, 2000
312 **Ricardo Legorreta, Hon. FAIA**
Luis E. Carranza

GRASS ROOTS
313 **Canstruction: An Architectural Feast**
Jen DeRose

Part Three: Results

10 188 Residential Architecture:
Shaping Our Homes and Communities
Michael Pyatok, FAIA, and Ralph Bennett, AIA

GOLD MEDALIST, 1949
200 **Frank Lloyd Wright**
Anthony Alofsin, PhD, AIA

GOLD MEDALIST, 1991
201 **Charles W. Moore, FAIA**
Avigail Sachs

GOLD MEDALIST, 2006
202 **Antoine Predock, FAIA**
Kristen Richards

GRASS ROOTS
203 **The Social Art of Architecture:
Good Design for All**
Kira Gould, Assoc. AIA

11 204 Innovation in Office Design
Vivian Loftness, FAIA

GOLD MEDALIST, 1944
219 **Louis Henri (Henry) Sullivan, FAIA**
Richard Guy Wilson, Hon. AIA

GOLD MEDALIST, 1992
220 **Benjamin Thompson, FAIA**
Andrew Brodie Smith, PhD

GOLD MEDALIST, 1993
221 **Kevin Roche, FAIA**
Andrew Brodie Smith, PhD

GRASS ROOTS
222 **Meet Me in Downtown St. Louis**
Jen DeRose

VIEWPOINT
223 **Third Spaces**
Roy Abernathy, AIA, and Clark Malcolm

12 224 America on the Move
David A. Daileda, FAIA

GOLD MEDALIST. 1962
236 **Eero Saarinen, FAIA**
Jayne Merkel

GOLD MEDALIST, 2005
237 **Santiago Calatrava, FAIA**
Vernon Mays

GRASS ROOTS
238 **Designing the Washington Metro**
Zachary M. Schrag

GRASS ROOTS
239 **The Fort Pitt Bridge Project**
Ingrid Spencer

17 314 Architecture for the Spirit
Michael J. Crosbie, PhD

GOLD MEDALIST, 1923
335 **Henry Bacon, FAIA**
Richard Guy Wilson, Hon. AIA

GOLD MEDALIST, 1990
336 **E. Fay Jones, FAIA**
Allen Freeman

GRASS ROOTS
337 **Partners for Sacred Places,
Texas Regional Office**
Ingrid Spencer

18 338 Creating Community
in the Midst of Diversity
David Dixon, FAIA

GOLD MEDALIST, 1956
354 **Clarence Stein, FAIA**
Allen Freeman

GRASS ROOTS
355 **Five Points Community
Revitalization Charrette**
Gregory Walker, AIA

19 356 City Limits
Douglas Kelbaugh, FAIA

GOLD MEDALIST, 1961
374 **Le Corbusier, Hon. FAIA
(Charles-Édouard Jeanneret)**
William Richards

GRASSROOTS
375 **The China–U.S. Center
for Sustainable Development**
Deborah Snoonian

20 376 The Experience of Place
Diane Georgopulos, FAIA

378 Endnotes

384 Contributors

380 AIA Presidents

386 AIA Honors and Awards

382 AIA150 Campaign Donors

382 Index

Acknowledgments

Nancy B. Solomon, AIA

Books, like architecture, are the product of teamwork. And this one is no exception. More than 100 people contributed to this endeavor in a very condensed period of time. The authors of the various essays, profiles, and sidebars that follow are clearly evident, but many other team members, although hidden from the reader's view, were also instrumental in shaping, fine-tuning, and illustrating this volume. Without the assistance of each and every one, this ambitious project would never have materialized. Although it would be impossible to list every name, I would like to thank all who added their voices and their talents in so many ways to this effort.

In particular, recognition must first go to the AIA150 Oversight Committee, chaired by George Miller, FAIA, who understood that the 150th anniversary of the Institute was a milestone worthy of such a comprehensive book. George, plus several members of his committee—Roy Abernathy, AIA, Diane Georgolopus, FAIA, and Michael E. Willis, FAIA—dedicated extra hours to this important and time-intensive undertaking. Special credit goes to Diane, who remained steadfast in her vision of a publication that would capture the breadth and depth of the profession at this pivotal period in its history. In addition, as the AIA leadership team member overseeing the entire AIA150 celebration, Helene Dreiling, FAIA, provided unwavering support and encouragement.

Numerous people, within and without the AIA, helped identify potential authors. I would like to highlight a few of them, including Andrea Oppenheimer Dean; Ellen Delage, Assoc. AIA; Daniel Friedman, FAIA; Kira Gould, Assoc. AIA; Beverly E. Hauschild-Baron, Hon. AIA; Brenda Henderson, Hon. AIA; Jayne Merkel; Barbara A. Nadel, FAIA; Andrea Rutledge; Deborah Snoonian; Terri Stewart; and Richard Guy Wilson, Hon. AIA.

Some chapters would not have seen the light of day if not for Sara Hart, who helped transform several rough drafts into polished gems. At the AIA, the research, writing, and editing talents of Pamela James Blumgart and Andrew Smith, PhD, were indispensable. Tony P. Wrenn, Hon. AIA, prepared the timeline entries on the history of the AIA. Raymond Rhinehart, PhD, Hon. AIA, graciously wrote several pieces and provided good advice.

Carol Highsmith generously provided her extraordinary photographs *gratis*. And, in addition to designing this beautiful book, Brad Collins and his staff at Group C Inc. have attended to the book's every detail and constantly pushed us to make it better. Their partnership on this project has been invaluable.

Yet others went beyond the call of duty to help locate photographs, write captions, obtain copyright permissions, and undertake other necessary tasks. This list includes Kathleen Daileda, Hon. AIA; Pam del Canto; Anne H. Dow; David Downey, Assoc. AIA; Mary Felber; Nancy Hadley, Assoc. AIA; Christopher Kieran; Cindie Kyte; Robin Lee, Hon. AIA; Pauline Porter; and Meagan Sweeney. Numerous firms and agencies helped out as well. Marilyn Farley, Hon. AIA, former director of Design Excellence and the Arts at GSA, and Taylor Lednum, audiovisual program manager of the Design Excellence program, were particularly helpful in obtaining up-to-date images and facilitating contact with some very busy practitioners.

I want to extend my deepest appreciation to Janet Rumbarger, director of AIA150 Special Projects, who served as the managing editor for this book. Through thick and thin, Janet undertook the myriad tasks required to pull this volume together—from writing author contracts and acquiring photographs to caption writing, copyediting, and proofing. She heroically handled all the administrative details, freeing me up to focus on editorial content. It is not hyperbole to say that, without Janet, this book would never have reached fruition.

On a personal note, I must thank my young sons—Aaron and Isaac—who allowed me to work intensively on this manuscript even though they sorely missed my attention. And, finally, I would like to dedicate this book to my father, Morris Abraham Solomon, whose ongoing search for both joy and justice shaped my life, influenced my career path, and resonates throughout this book.

Preface

George H. Miller, FAIA
Chair, AIA150 Oversight Task Group

It has been an honor and a pleasure to serve as chairman of the AIA150 Oversight Task Group, the AIA leadership team charged with guiding the initiatives undertaken by the Institute in celebration of its 150th anniversary in 2007. This book is the capstone project of a highly successful sesquicentennial year. Early in the planning stages of the anniversary celebration we wondered out loud if the public and the profession would respond. There was not much precedent to draw upon, as there are few national organizations in America, let alone professional societies that are as old as the AIA. To our delight and gratitude, the response to AIA150 programs has been enormous. The year's initiatives have included the "Blueprint for America," in which architects, civic leaders, and the public have worked together to develop plans for making our communities healthier, safer, and more sustainable. AIA chapters large and small across the country have undertaken more than 150 community service Blueprint projects. And thousands of people participated in the selection of "America's Favorite Architecture," celebrating the best of 150 years of American architecture. An exhibition of the selected projects is touring the nation, and people worldwide have visited the AFA Web site, dedicated to the iconic contributions of architects to the American landscape.

In addition to the customary celebrations, the AIA also has undertaken two other significant projects in its 150th year. Plans are underway to renovate the headquarters of the AIA to be an example of the new 21st-century workplace. In addition, we are planning a "Shape of America" series that focuses on memorable architectural and design achievements across the nation. Our capital fund-raising campaign in support of public service and outreach programs has been overwhelmingly successful. Taken together, these initiatives have helped to remind the public and the profession of the critical role that architects and the AIA have played in designing America's communities.

Architecture: Celebrating the Past, Designing the Future is precisely about those historical accomplishments and our collective vision of the future. With contributions from nearly 100 architects, educators, and friends of the profession, the book speaks with many diverse voices about the broad sweep of the profession. Many of the authors you will recognize as distinguished names in their fields; others you will be hearing from for the first time. Yet they are united by a tremendous belief in what architects have done and can do in service to humanity. The strength of the book lies not in any single contribution but in its collective whole—introducing us to the extraordinary men, women, organizations, and ideas that have helped shape our communities, our society, and, yes, our world.

I would like to thank the members of the AIA150 book subcommittee chaired by Diane Georgopulos, FAIA, along with Michael Willis, FAIA, and Roy Abernathy, AIA, for their hard work and imaginative ideas in helping to create this seminal volume. I would also like to thank our editor, Nancy B. Solomon, AIA, and the staff of the AIA for their devotion to this effort. I would like particularly to thank Janet Rumbarger for her tireless efforts and exceptional contributions. Without her, this book would not have been possible.

I would also like to thank the entire AIA150 Oversight Task Group, including subcommittee chairs Anthony Costello, FAIA, Tommy Cowan, FAIA, and Skipper Post, FAIA, for their inspired leadership and commitment to this yearlong initiative. Finally, a heartfelt thank you goes to the AIA staff for their dedication to all of the AIA150 efforts. The leadership of Christine McEntee, Norman Koonce, FAIA, Helene Dreiling, FAIA, Robin Lee, Hon. AIA, and David Downey, Assoc. AIA, and their associates has been exceptional, and on behalf of the AIA's 83,000 members, I extend our heartfelt appreciation. Their leadership has ensured the success of many programs honoring the 150-year legacy of the Institute and its members, including this fine book.

Coordinated Creativity

AIA Executive Vice President/CEO

Speaking on the eve of the Institute's centennial year, AIA President Leon Chatelain Jr. delivered this message to the approximately 12,000 members of the American Institute of Architects: "Of the future we know only this: that its pressures and the sum of the daily hungers of its people will pull us into a frenzy of coordinated creativity."

"Coordinated creativity." The words seem contradictory. Isn't creativity the sudden, breakthrough shout of "eureka!" while you're sitting alone in the tub? Yet President Chatelain was on to something, something that explains the enduring relevance, vigor, and, yes, the coordinated creativity of the American Institute of Architects—the power of collective action.

More than a century before President Chatelain delivered his message—in fact, decades before the AIA itself was founded—a 25-year-old Frenchman spent nine months touring this young nation, taking the pulse of a republic that had been created only 50 years earlier. Had there been sufficient time, he wondered, for the people and institutions of this new democracy to develop traits that were distinctly "American"?

What Alexis de Tocqueville discovered continues to be uncannily relevant to 21st-century America: the power of religion in public life, the relatively small role tradition plays in our lives, the high value placed on self-reliance and antielitism, and the art of association or group action outside of government. Americans instinctively form associations when action that cannot otherwise be accomplished is required in their personal affairs or on behalf of their community: "An association unites into one channel the efforts of divergent minds and urges them vigorously towards the one end which it clearly points out" (Tocqueville's *Democracy in America*, vol.1, chap. 12).

In other words, "coordinated creativity." The AIA's founders would have understood the point President Chatelain was making when they wrote the AIA's first mission statement, which began with the words "to unite in fellowship." It then went on to explain the purpose of this union: "To advance the art and science of architecture and to be of ever-increasing service to society." Unwavering fidelity by succeeding generations of AIA members to this mission has been a force for constant renewal within the profession. This and the AIA's investment in providing its members the tools to enhance their value have ensured one of America's oldest professional associations its continuing relevance.

But what of the AIA's future and the profession with it? The opportunities to advance the art and science of architecture and to be of service to communities around the world have never been greater. Consider some of the issues raised in this book: the mitigation of natural disasters, the stemming of global warming, and the ongoing improvements in building security, health care, affordable housing, information management, sustainability, and transportation. These are not simply matters in which architects enjoy professional competence; these are matters that will shape the destiny of our planet.

As never before, the creative genius of architects and their training intersect with society's needs. Never has the opportunity, not to mention the need, of coordinated creativity between architects and the society they serve been clearer. Coordinated creativity offers us our best chance for a world not of more of the same, but better.

Everyone who played a role in bringing this book to light—and there were many—deserves to be congratulated. In particular, I want to thank the members of the AIA150 Blue Ribbon Panel and the AIA150 Oversight Task Group, both under the leadership of George H. Miller, FAIA; AIA Presidents Eugene Hopkins, FAIA, Douglas Steidl, FAIA, Kate Schwennsen, FAIA, and RK Stewart, FAIA; as well as those members of the AIA's national component staff who kept this project on track and ensured that it would be a valued resource to present and future generations of readers.

I intentionally began this preface by quoting only a small excerpt from President Chatelain's speech to the 12,000 members of the AIA in 1957. Fifty years later, the nearly 83,000 members of the AIA and, yes, everyone else who also cares about the fate of this planet, would do well to recall the rest of what he said: "We have neither time nor balance to stand still, to contemplate our past. In the year of our centennial, let us look with care where we are going—into the future. We are needed there."

Yes, the future: We are indeed needed there.

As I take some time at 38,000 feet to fire up my laptop to tap out this essay, the American Institute of Architects' national component is in the midst of its annual strategic planning process. There's a nice symmetry between these two realities: the AIA's planning process and this book commemorating the AIA's 150th birthday. How so? Because the perspective of both this book and our strategic planning efforts directly addresses the future, not the past.

RK Stewart, FAIA, 2006-07 AIA President

Of course we must not ignore our past, certainly not a past that created and sustained the very idea of an architecture profession in this country. Before the AIA was founded in 1857, no architecture profession as we know it today existed in America: no architecture schools, no licensing laws, no system to advance the art and science of architecture, no standard contract documents, no architecture libraries to research the knowledge of an industry being completely transformed by the Industrial Revolution. Nothing. The actions of the AIA's founders and those members who followed in their footsteps changed the profession and the nation.

We are the grateful inheritors of values that guide our profession and that have withstood the test of time: the vision of fellowship among those who ply our chosen craft; a determination to advance the art and science of this profession; and a commitment on behalf of society to create communities that are safer, healthier, more productive, and more beautiful than those our ancestors bequeathed to us. These values are the foundation for everything we have done right. They will continue to be the source of our credibility for all we hope to achieve in the future.

My interest in the AIA's past is now quite personal. While I have been privileged to serve as president during this anniversary year, the presence of those who have held this office in past years is always with me. Their legacy of wisdom, commitment, and boldness inspires me each day. As the 83rd president of the Institute, I know that part of my job is to inspire our members to reach a bit higher, dream a little bigger, and see a bit farther, a job made both easier and more challenging precisely because of the breadth and strength of the shoulders I stand on.

As together we reach, dream, and see the future from our vantage point at the beginning of the 21st century, I am also aware of the already vast and still growing distance that separates the AIA's 13 male founders from the nearly 83,000 AIA members, men and women of all colors, who are today's AIA. As I write this, I can imagine AIA founder Richard Upjohn penning his hopes and dreams for the AIA's future from his New York office. After the inevitable editing and preparation of clean copy, his pages would have been gathered, proofed, typeset, proofed again, printed, and distributed on the small island of Manhattan.

It takes only a moment of reflection to see the chasm that separates a printing press with wet ink from the cut, paste, and spell-check functions of my laptop. The power of technology allows me to send a file electronically around the world for production wherever printing is, at this moment, most efficient and economical. Like the advances in telecommunications, the architecture profession is moving forward at an ever-increasing speed.

How Upjohn and his collaborators responded to the technical and social issues of the 19th century was critical to developing the values and reputation that are the inheritance of America's architects. How we, the grateful beneficiaries of this legacy, respond to the technical and social issues of the 21st century will be equally decisive in determining the legacy we leave to those who come after us.

This is no small challenge. The stakes are higher than in Upjohn's day. For the first time in history, human beings are coequals with nature in determining the destiny of our planet. That said, the possibilities of making a substantial contribution toward realizing a better world are likewise greater than ever if we act with purpose, forethought, and a deep commitment to be of service. As never before, the AIA and we, its members, must engage in the public discussion about the most pressing issues affecting our communities and our planet, inform the debate, and envision the solutions most likely to improve the quality of life for people everywhere.

While I'm pleased and proud to lead the AIA's celebrations of its 150th birthday, these festivities are only a prelude to pursuing the truly amazing possibilities that lie before us. Realizing those possibilities on behalf of the profession and the society we serve will be a direct consequence of the foundation we build today. If, as the great visionary architect Daniel Burnham is reported to have said, the past is truly prologue, the AIA's astonishing legacy is both the evidence and the inspirational incentive to do as good a job as those who gathered in Upjohn's office 150 years ago. Are we up to the challenge? For my part, I can't wait to see what the future holds!

1791
*Pierre-Charles L'Enfant presented
his plan for Washington, D.C., to
President George Washington*

1792
*George Washington chose Irish-born
architect James Hoban to design
the "President's House," officially
renamed the "White House" by
President Theodore Roosevelt*

1793
*Construction of the U.S. Capitol began;
William Thornton, Benjamin Henry
Latrobe, Charles Bulfinch, Thomas U.
Walter, Montgomery C. Meigs*

Introduction

The Power of Design

Robert Ivy, FAIA

Architecture, the art of building, traces its ancestry back to the primordial fire within the cave of early man. The sparks of this well-placed flame not only warmed the occupants but also lit the walls so that—through the visual arts—they could communicate. Pragmatism and poetry were integrally linked even in this most primitive form. Through the centuries architecture has evolved and matured, producing myriad artifacts—the structures and experiences that have been well described and documented in text and imagery. But the architect's role remains more elusive.

Perhaps part of the ambiguity lies in the fact that this role has evolved over time and across cultures. This book, written on the occasion of the American Institute of Architects' sesquicentennial, is intended to shed light on this much-admired calling within the American context. It does so in three parts. The first explores the overriding sociopolitical framework within which American architects have worked and that has shaped their goals and values. The second presents the training and tools of these practitioners plus the methods by which they best serve their clients. And the third describes the contributions of these architects through the evolution of some of the most common types of projects.

(Opposite) Once they acquired the ability to make fire, early humans began to take control of their environment—the essence of architecture. Indigenous peoples found warmth and safety in cave dwellings and other basic shelters. Inside, they were also motivated to produce early forms of art. *Richard Cummins/Corbis*

1

(Opposite) By and large, history did not begin to record the names of individual architects until the Renaissance. We know, for example, that Michelangelo designed the Piazza del Campidoglio in Rome. Planned in 1538, it was not completed for centuries. Michelangelo's original designs were recorded in 16th-century engravings by French architect Étienne Dupérac. *AA World Travel Library/Alamy*

At a time when lines were thinly drawn between the divine and the material, ancient holy shrines — such as an Egyptian pyramid or a Japanese temple — became the physical representation of the cosmic. The names of the people who designed and built these sacred structures are generally unknown. *Steve Allen/Corbis (temple); Dallas and John Heaton/Corbis (pyramid)*

(Right) Throughout the Middle Ages, the creators of Europe's great cathedrals remained anonymous. The local population is said to have volunteered to carry stones from five miles away to help build the Cathedral of Our Lady of Chartres. The French Gothic structure was erected during the 12th and 13th centuries on the foundations of a Romanesque church that had been destroyed by fire. *Bildarchiv Monheim GmbH/Alamy*

To more fully illustrate the multifaceted work of today's architect, and to honor the efforts of so many dedicated men and women in the field, each chapter highlights the work of at least one recipient of the AIA's Gold Medal—the Institute's premiere award for individual achievement, which celebrated its own centennial in 2007—and profiles at least one architectural organization, firm, or initiative that has contributed to the profession or society as a whole. These vignettes demonstrate that, although the field certainly has its share of well-known personalities, its success largely depends on the contributions and talents of many.

It's worth considering the historical backdrop to this comprehensive portrait of today's American practitioner. While the building arts may have begun with indigenous dwellings and basic shelters, they were quickly elevated to a higher plane by the human desire to understand our place in the universe. The physical "action" or "making" (the meaning of *ar*, the Indo-European antecedent of the word *architect*) of an Egyptian pyramid, a Japanese temple, or any other ancient holy shrine involved the concrete representation of the cosmic at a time when lines were thinly drawn between the divine and the material. The mediating position of constructing tangible links between earth and sky became architectural. The mediator—the one who captured the spark of the divine and infused it into the material world—remained unknown and unsung. The architect was merely the conduit of this heavenly inspiration.

The status of the architect did not change for hundreds of years. The authors of Europe's great cathedral complexes of the 12th and 13th centuries also worked largely in anonymity. Perhaps the act of building these great houses of worship was satisfaction enough. But, by the Renaissance, the architect enters the dramatis personae. Personalities begin to appear in association with major projects, such as Brunelleschi's design of the dome for Santa Maria del Fiore in Florence, dedicated in 1436, and Michelangelo's Piazza del Campidoglio in Rome, planned in 1538 although not completed for centuries. The masters of the craft of building were beginning to shift allegiance from god to king. Such individual designers would grow in prominence and expand their clientele to include nobility, the bourgeoisie, and the state. Creativity was becoming more and more the province of individuals, serving the needs of fellow citizens.

1817
Construction began on
the University of Virginia,
designed by Thomas Jefferson
(1817–26)

(Opposite) The Hearst Tower, designed by Foster + Partners and completed in 2006, is the first new office building in New York City to receive LEED gold certification. The structural diagrid pattern, derived by advanced computer software, enables the tower to use 20 percent less steel than a conventionally framed high-rise. *©Chuck Choi*

Through a life that fully embraced design and a personality that radiated control, Frank Lloyd Wright represents the apex of the architect as uber-hero. He designed not only the buildings themselves but also the interior details—from tables and chairs to floor lamps—for his clients. He even designed his own clothing. *Courtesy the Frank Lloyd Foundation, Taliesen West, Scottsdale, Arizona*

(Far right) Santiago Calatrava, 2005 Gold Medalist, sees architecture as a kind of culmination of all the arts. In addition to his well-known architecture and engineering talents, he is an active sculptor, painter, and music lover. His work can be found throughout Europe, in the United States, and elsewhere. *©Nathan Beck*

David Childs (second from left) and Daniel Libeskind (third from left) with World Trade Center leaseholder Larry Silverstein (fourth from left) at Ground Zero. Following September 11, 2001, individual architects became prominent in public conversation as people turned to them to express a collective memory in physical form. *Susannah Shepherd/McGraw-Hill*

Michael Graves, 2001 Gold Medalist, is popularly known for his domestic designs sold at Target stores. Along with architects such as Frank Gehry and Richard Meier, Graves's image has become a marketing tool. *©Andre Souroujon*

Ironically, it was shortly after Richard Upjohn and others gathered in New York to found what would become the AIA—a group of architects who recognized the value of professional association—that architecture's largest personality was born. Following on the heels of the rise of Romanticism and the cult of human genius, Frank Lloyd Wright represents the apex of the architect as uber-hero. Through a life that fully embraced design and a personality that radiated control, Wright fashioned a semihermetic world in which all objects within the architecture reflected his hand. This design philosophy defined a way of life at Taliesin Fellowship—the school that he and his third wife Olgivanna founded, based in Wisconsin in the summers and Arizona in the winters—and was presented as an enlightened offering to the rest of the world. The architect becomes a kind of high priest. Rarely again would architecture seek such an all-encompassing reach.

Despite some diversions toward Utopian communities along the way, a strong push for social housing by the Bauhaus in Europe, and increased legal statutes by state and local authorities to ensure health, safety, and welfare standards for all, U.S. architecture practice from the early to mid-20th century remained largely autonomous and independent. The lone shingle on the street was a kind of shorthand for this individualism. Gary Cooper as Howard Roark in the 1949 film version of Ayn Rand's *The Fountainhead* epitomized the architect to the broader public at that time: creative and at odds with the status quo.

The archetype represented by the real-life Wright and the fictional Roark, however, turned out to be circumscribed. To be sure, there are still solo practitioners, and some magnetic personalities that often take center stage: Among the profession, for example, Gold Medalist Santiago Calatrava represents an almost unattainable ideal—artist, engineer, architect, music lover—with a roster of sculptural and increasingly ambitious international projects. And, abetted by international media, other so-called stars are drawing increasing attention from the public. Following September 11, 2001, prominent architects lurched into public conversation and notice: Suddenly everyone knew Daniel Libeskind. Frank Gehry, arguably the most famous architect in the world, achieved such prominence following the debut of the Guggenheim Museum in Bilbao, Spain. His ascension to fame now involves advertising campaigns, a movie with the director Sidney Pollock, and a line of signature jewelry at Tiffany's. Richard Meier, the architect of the Getty Center in Los Angeles, among other signature projects, finds his name employed as a marketing tool for developers eager to acquire tenants for high-rise residential development.

But with the increasing complexity of design and construction in the latter half of the 20th century, many individual practitioners began to organize themselves into partnerships and small firms, and small firms into larger companies, to manage the knowledge explosion and the spiraling pace of global change. The exponential boom in international architecture opportunities, which began at the end of the past century, continues to fuel these varied partnerships and teams. And practitioners within all types of firms—small or large, local or international—increasingly rely on the resources made available through industry, professional associations, universities, and other collective think-tanks.

Advances in digital technology, for instance, are creating better tools for communication and analysis. Today, building information modeling (BIM) provides a method by which all elements are coded in a common way, allowing multiple team members to examine and address a project simultaneously, no matter where they are located. What a contrast to the builders of the Tower of Babel, who had to give up because they couldn't understand each other. And sophisticated software provides architects with powerful new ways of seeing and representing the world. As an example, stress diagrams produced by engineers can color code physical tensions and compressions on a building façade, giving the designers a way of converting what was once purely mathematical, or ideal, into material reality. The diagrid pattern, recently made evident by Sir Norman Foster's 30 St. Mary Axe (see page 98) in London and Hearst Tower in New York, was generated in this way. Digital technology has also provided a greater number of architects a way of exploring theoretical ideas to a degree not possible in the past.

Practitioners have also broadened their design scope. Keenly aware of the effect buildings have had on the natural environment, many architects are working holistically—considering all aspects of the building process—to achieve a sustainable society. Now they are literally channeling heavenly light to warm our homes and brighten our offices, among many other environmentally friendly techniques. Although rooted in modern science and common sense, there is something sacred about the sustainable agenda, as architects try to protect the natural world for generations to come.

In the process, architects are increasingly working across disciplines—with engineers, material scientists, and even biologists—to develop and implement revolutionary building materials and systems. Computer-controlled building envelopes, for example, can open and close fenestration in relation to wind flows; membranes can literally transmit light, electrical charges, and therefore information. Architects are engaged in these efforts, seeking new ways of integrating scientific advancement with human need—again as a kind of mediator, seeking a proper balance between what is possible and what is best for larger society.

In this secular age, architects nonetheless continue to translate the ephemeral, such as shared values or community bonds, into physical form. Many architects have come to the assistance of those who have suffered from natural disasters, including Hurricanes Katrina and Rita. These storms brought devastation on an unprecedented scale, destroying 300,000 houses and laying one major American city, New Orleans, to waste. Eager to aid in the rebuilding process, practitioners have designed replacement housing as well as redefined and replanted institutions, such as public schools, throughout the region. And although affordable housing remains an intractable problem for many in the United States, and demands solutions that exceed the architectural agenda, architects have routinely volunteered for nationwide programs like Habitat for Humanity. In addition, schools of architecture, including those at the universities of Washington, Texas, and Auburn, have been particularly noteworthy in fostering socially engaged design studios.

Whether working solo, in partnership, as a collective, or as a "star," architects typically maintain the central position as organizing authorities in a project, most often serving as the interface with clients. In other words, they have retained their historic role as translators and mediators. But other people now routinely help make architecture happen. The list is daunting, as the primordial cave has become so complex: In addition to the elements of three-dimensional design necessary for architecture (including pattern recognition, iconography, spatial perception, among others), teams routinely add expertise on structural and topographical engineering, landscaping, climatic systems, lighting design, social and political processes, construction information, specifications, and business fundamentals such as contract law, budgets, and human management.

SmartWrap

1835
Founding of the Royal Institute of
British Architects (RIBA)

1836
American architects formed the
short-lived "American Institution
of Architects"

All this must be orchestrated by the architect. Practitioners routinely combine these pragmatic and temporal requirements with the ineffable—call it creativity—that results in the educated power of synthesis. Something concrete, a project, emerges out of this mystery. Although we no longer associate this design process with the divine, it nonetheless remains a powerful force in our lives.

Design helps to set architects apart from the other professions. Architecture's defining characteristic has been to assimilate knowledge and translate those ideas into projects that represent a new vision. The world witnessed this recently and profoundly as architects grappled with the appropriate response to the site of the World Trade Center. Fascinated by schemes that incorporated human memory into physical fabric, the public sought some solace from architects as they channeled their powers of design.

In an era in which we continue to listen for voices from deep space and probe the smallest elements of the nanosphere, new ways of seeing—of understanding—our world still await us. Some answers to our questions may arise among painters, or poets, or digital artists, or even video game designers. But the three-dimensional core of our built environment—the only spatial language that incorporates human form and physical reality within the context of society—remains exclusively the realm of the architect. ●

(Opposite) Recent natural disasters have destroyed hundreds of thousands of houses and other buildings. The widespread devastation of the Gulf Coast by Hurricane Katrina in 2005 has called for the assistance and creativity of architects to design efficient replacement housing and redefine institutions in the rebuilding process.
©Neil Alexander Photography

Architect Maurice Cox (right) at the Biloxi Model Home Fair on August 19, 2006. The Model Home program gathered 12 teams of architects to showcase housing designs as part of its program to provide design services and financial assistance for families affected by Hurricane Katrina. *Tracy Nelson/Architecture for Humanity*

The Rural Heritage Center in Thomaston, Alabama, was designed by two teams of students from the Rural Studio between 2002 and 2004. This design-build studio, run by Auburn University, encourages aspiring architects to work as volunteer citizens. Other architecture schools, such as those at the universities of Washington and Texas, have similar socially engaged programs. *©Timothy Hursley*

Thomas Jefferson

Richard Guy Wilson, Hon. AIA

French sculptor Jean-Antoine Houdon's 1789 bust of Jefferson is on display in the parlor at Monticello.

Thomas Jefferson (1743–1826) was awarded the Gold Medal in 1993 on the occasion of the 250th anniversary of his birth. It affirmed not just his important political role in the creation of our nation but also his far-reaching contributions to this country's architecture profession. Jefferson, after all, was the only architect to have served as the president of the United States; he gave our then-fledgling country an official architectural image and created one of the greatest American architectural masterpieces of all times. (In 1976 a national poll conducted by the AIA ranked Jefferson's drawings for the University of Virginia as the single most important design done by an American.)

Thomas Jefferson has been called a Renaissance man for his varied interests, which included farming, gardening, philosophy, literature, anthropology, and music, along with his career as an American statesman (major author of the Declaration of Independence, governor of Virginia, ambassador to France, secretary of state, and vice president, in addition to president). He is sometimes labeled an amateur or gentleman architect because he had no formal training (even though architecture education was rare in the 18th century) and because he never received any reimbursement for his designs (Jefferson, for the most part, designed out of necessity as the head of a large plantation). But he observed: "Architecture is my delight, and putting up and pulling down one of my favorite amusements." Jefferson bemoaned the low state of architecture in the new country, and he advised James Madison that public buildings should be models of "study and imitation."

Jefferson's architectural accomplishments were considerable. He assisted in the design of at least seven houses for his friends, in addition to creating his own well-known residences—Monticello in Charlottesville, Virginia, and Poplar Forest in Bedford, Virginia. But his real influence lay in the public realm. The Virginia State Capitol in Richmond, designed by Jefferson in conjunction with the French architect, Clèrisseau, was the first public building in the new nation after the Revolution and set a classical precedent for those that would follow. And, as secretary of state in George Washington's cabinet, Jefferson proposed a scheme for public walks and buildings in the area that would become the National Mall for Washington, D.C., upon which Major Pierre-Charles L'Enfant expanded in his plan of 1791. Our third president also submitted designs for the U.S. Capitol and the Executive Mansion; although these two proposals were rejected, he was intimately involved in the selection of the eventual architects and in ordering many changes and alterations to both structures over the next several decades.

Back in Virginia, after his presidency ended in 1809, Jefferson designed several county courthouses and, between 1814 and 1826, the campus (or the "grounds") for the University of Virginia, which he also founded. Jefferson creatively combined rows of buildings and colonnades around a central space—known as "the lawn"—and focused them on the Rotunda (a reduced version of the Roman Pantheon) to create a composition that symbolizes the hierarchy of learning with a democratic spirit of openness and individuality. He displayed a respect for the past while offering original solutions—such as the varied facades of the professors' pavilions, which undercut the symmetrical order of the central axis. For Jefferson, architecture was not just form, space, and image, but a container for life and an educational instrument that should inspire.

Work on Jefferson's house, Monticello, near Charlottesville, Virginia, stretched over a long period, beginning in 1769; remodeling and enlarging of the house began in 1796 and was complete by 1809. *Courtesy Dan Addison/U.Va. News Services*

Symbolizing his faith in human reason, Jefferson placed a library (and not, as was common, a chapel) at the head of his plan for the University of Virginia. *Courtesy Dan Addison/U.Va. News Services*

1848
Cornerstone laid for
Washington Monument,
designed by Robert Mills

AIA Abroad: International Achievements and Prospects

Thomas Vonier, FAIA, RIBA

Architects in North America have always had close ties to foreign countries and to practitioners abroad. Many founders and early members of the AIA spent their formative years studying and working in Europe — mainly in France, Italy, and England — and some were born there. Long after the United States developed its own well-respected institutions of education and practice, links to architects in Europe continued to flourish, later expanding to practitioners in Latin America and East Asia.

As the representative body of the architecture profession in the United States, the AIA has fostered international relations through numerous initiatives. The AIA, for example, has been a leading force in the International Union of Architects (UIA). A democratic body, the UIA is a nongovernmental organization founded in Lausanne, Switzerland, in 1948 to unite architects throughout the world, regardless of nationality, race, religion, or architectural school of thought. The UIA represents more than one million architects around the world through national architecture organizations, such as the AIA, which form UIA member sections. Through the UIA, the Institute has helped shape the practical and ethical standards expected of architects worldwide. For example, the AIA has guided efforts of the UIA Professional Practice Commission and, with the People's Republic of China, headed development of the *Accord on Recommended International Standards of Professionalism in Architecture Practice*, which the UIA adopted in 1999.

In addition, the AIA has actively encouraged sustainable principles in the design and construction industry worldwide. The Institute has adopted standards for reductions in carbon dioxide emissions and fossil fuel consumption, and it supported the creation in 1999 of the World Green Building Council, a not-for-profit organization composed of national GBCs that work to transform the building industry by supporting and encouraging sustainable practices. Two important missions of the World Green Building Council are development of market-based environmental rating systems and recognition of global leadership in sustainable design.

The AIA has also worked with foreign counterpart organizations and within the UIA to develop standards and core competencies related to health, safety, and welfare and to promote lifelong continuing education programs.

Since 1952, some 481 architects from 61 countries have been named Honorary Fellows of the Institute, the highest honor bestowed upon foreign professionals by the AIA College of Fellows. Tens of thousands of foreign nationals have been educated and become licensed as architects in the United States, joining the AIA as a commitment to professionalism. Many of those who subsequently decide to return to their native countries choose to maintain AIA membership.

With the advent of unprecedented levels of global trade and business in the late 20th century, AIA members have ranged beyond Europe into the Middle East, the republics of the former Soviet Union, and throughout the Pacific Rim. Consequently, the Institute itself has become more firmly rooted abroad. AIA London/UK, chartered in 1993, was the first international chapter, followed by AIA Continental Europe (1994), AIA Hong Kong (1997), and AIA Japan (2005).

In 2006 the Institute appointed the first international director to its board to represent the large contingent of AIA members working and living abroad. As overseas membership continues to grow — as more AIA members work abroad and more foreign architects associate with the Institute — offshore members look toward the creation of an overseas region to join fully in AIA policy making and governance.

The coming years are certain to bring new requirements, challenges, and opportunities as established markets change, older resources dwindle and new ones emerge, and demands of the world's growing populations take form. New methods and materials will be needed, requiring extraordinary collaboration across disciplines *and* across borders.

More than ever, the world needs professionals who can work effectively in foreign settings and with foreign counterparts, improving the physical environment and helping to meet the profound social and technical challenges ahead. The AIA is well positioned to help architects lead the way.

Membership in AIA International Components*

AIA London/UK	118
AIA Continental Europe	166
AIA Hong Kong	181
AIA Japan	47
AIA members abroad unassigned to an international component	673
Total	1,185

*2007 data

AIA's International Partners

Professional organizations
African Union of Architects (AUA)
Architects' Council of Central and Eastern Europe (ACCEE)
Architects' Council of Europe (ACE)
Architects Regional Council of Asia (ARCASIA)
Architectural Society of China (ASC)
Colegio de Arquitectos de Costa Rica (CACR)
Federación de Colegios de Arquitectos de la República Mexicana (FCARM)
Federación Panamericana de Asociaciones de Arquitectos (FPAA)
Japan Institute of Architects (JIA)
Korean Institute of Architects (KIA)
Royal Institute of British Architects (RIBA)
Royal Australian Institute of Architects (RAIA)
Royal Architectural Institute of Canada (RAIC)
Sri Lankan Institute of Architects (SLIA)
Union of Architects of Russia (UAR)
International Union of Architects (UIA)

International elements of allied U.S. professional organizations
National Council of Architectural Registration Boards (NCARB)
National Architectural Accrediting Board (NAAB)
Association of Collegiate Schools of Architecture (ACSA)
American Institute of Architecture Students (AIAS)

International elements of U.S. government organizations
U.S. Department of State
U.S. Trade Representative
U.S. Department of Commerce

HISTORY

100 Years of Changing Architectural Ideals: The AIA Gold Medal

Richard Guy Wilson, Hon. AIA

On the obverse of the Gold Medal are the profiles of the three creators of the Parthenon in Athens: the painter Polygnotos, the sculptor Phidias, and the architect Ictinus. A standing eagle with upraised wings representing the unity of the arts adorns the reverse side of the medal.

The name of each AIA Gold Medalist is chiseled into a granite wall in the lobby of the AIA's national headquarters. *Douglas Gordon, Hon. AIA*

The AIA commissioned the great turn-of-the-century muralist Edwin H. Blashfield to illustrate the cover of the 1907 program for the banquet in honor of the Institute's 50th anniversary and the occasion of the presentation of the first Gold Medal. Blashfield murals are in many public buildings throughout the country, including the rotunda of the main reading room of the Library of Congress. *AIA Archives*

The American Institute of Architects' Gold Medal was most succinctly characterized by I. M. Pei (1979*) as "the greatest architectural honor in America." Established in 1907, it was the brainchild of Charles McKim (1909), a leading New York architect who wanted to demonstrate that the United States and its architecture had come of age. He modeled the AIA's medal program on European precedents, in particular the Royal Institute of British Architects' Gold Medal, established in 1848. The AIA Gold Medal's purposes were several: to commemorate the 50th anniversary of the founding of the AIA, to recognize individual architects for their accomplishments, and to increase the public's awareness of the profession. Over the years, these overall intentions have remained remarkably consistent. Yet, the names of all the Gold Medalists, inscribed on the black marble wall at the AIA headquarters in Washington, D.C., provide an illuminating look at what professional architects have admired at different periods in history.

The Medal
The noted sculptor A. A. Weinman designed the medal with the help of McKim and George B. Post (1911), another important New York architect of that era. On the obverse are the profiles of the three creators of the Parthenon in Athens (from left to right, the painter Polygnotos, the sculptor Phidias, and the architect Ictinus) above the symbols of their respective crafts (modeling tool, brush, and triangle and compass) along with the AIA's name and founding date (1857) in Roman numerals. The reverse bears an American eagle pulling a laurel branch from a rock labeled "AIA," along with Weinman's name and the date of the AIA's 50th anniversary (1907), also in Roman numerals. On the rim is placed the name of the recipient and the date of the award. For the first award, given to the British architect Sir Aston Webb in Washington, D.C., in 1907, the prominent muralist Edwin W. Blashfield designed the program cover with Liberty wrapped in an American flag and holding both a laurel branch and the Gold Medal. McKim had hoped it would be named the "President's Medal" and bestowed by the occupant of the White House; however, his friend, Theodore Roosevelt demurred, not wanting to tie future presidents to an award. Nonetheless, several medals have been presented by the sitting president.

Presentation
The actual presentation of the Gold Medal usually involves a ceremony, although none as lavish as that of 1923, when Henry Bacon was so honored. Those festivities took place at his recently completed Lincoln Memorial in Washington, D.C. Architects, members of learned societies, and representatives of trade and crafts unions—all dressed in colorful robes and carrying banners and standards—gathered along the steps of the memorial. Bacon and his collaborators, the sculptor Daniel Chester French and the muralist Jules Guerin, plus then-AIA president William Faville, sat in a barge at the far end of the Reflecting Pool. Architecture students pulled the flat-bottomed boat across the pool while trumpeters from the U.S. Marine Band played a joyous processional, "Walter's Prize Song" from Wagner's *Die Meistersinger*. William Howard Taft, chief justice of the U.S. Supreme Court and former president of the United States, met Bacon at the bottom of the steps and presented him to President Warren G. Harding, who bestowed the Gold Medal. After the ceremony, the participants dined al fresco on the grounds of the Lincoln Memorial.

Selection Process
The decision for the Gold Medal is the prerogative of the AIA's Board of Directors, although in the early years a vote by those attending the annual convention ratified the award. The usual procedure is for a member of the board to submit a name to the full board. Then by a vote, the field is reduced to three; a discussion and in some cases presentation of the candidates takes place before a final vote. At times, AIA members have proposed nominees, such as in the case of Frank Lloyd Wright. An outspoken critic of what he called the "arbitrary institute of appearances," Wright never joined the AIA. To many architects, however, he was a true American original—one of the few internationally known American designers. After Wright received the British Gold Medal in 1941, pressure grew from some members to award him the Gold Medal. The award to Charles Maginnis (1948), a noted but conservative architect, prompted a petition to the board that resulted in Wright receiving the medal in 1949. At the acceptance speech in Houston, Wright in top form blasted American architecture as "being in the gutter." Yet he added: "I don't think humility is a very becoming estate from me, but I really feel touched by this token of esteem from the home boys."

Although the medal was intended to be awarded every year, a lack of agreement can result in no medal; it has also been suspended during times of war. Very rarely are two medals given in one year, and in most cases dual awards came from odd circumstances, such as the death of a favorite son in 1925 with the double award to Edwin Landseer Lutyens and the recently deceased Bertram Goodhue or on the 100th anniversary of the AIA in 1957, when Ralph Walker received the "Centennial Medal" and Louis Skidmore the Gold. The other exception was the 250th anniversary of Thomas Jefferson's birth in 1993, when Kevin Roche was also recognized.

Range of Recipients
From the very first presentation to Webb, the medal was intended to be an international recognition. Those who have practiced in the United States, however, dominate the list. The internationalization of practice will undoubtedly change this in years to come.

Of the 62 Gold Medalists to date, 32 were born in the United States, and 30 were born abroad. Some, including Eero Saarinen (1962), Louis Kahn (1971), and Frank Gehry (1999), came as youths or, in the case of Pei, for architectural training and remained. Paul Cret (1938), Pietro Belluschi (1972), Romaldo Giurgola (1982), and César Pelli (1995) arrived as young, trained architects, but made their reputations here. About 17 of the Gold Medalists, such as Auguste Perret (1952), Willem Dudok (1955), Alvar Aalto (1963), Kenzo Tange (1966), Arthur Erickson (1986), Norman Foster (1994), Tadao Ando (2002), and Santiago Calatrava (2005), were foreign born and made their primary reputations abroad. Some architects, such as Eliel Saarinen (1947), Walter Gropius (1959), and Ludwig Mies van der Rohe (1961), came to the United States with established reputations, but the Gold Medal really honored their American accomplishments.

Changing Styles
What the Gold Medal has recognized over the years has varied widely. Most of the early Gold Medalists—including Webb, McKim, Post, Jean Pascal (1914), Victor Laloux (1922), and Lutyens—made their mark as classically oriented designers. Beginning in the mid-1920s, a new wind blew and a more Romantic imagery with traces of Art Deco began to reign, as exemplified in awards to Goodhue, Howard Van Doren Shaw (1927), Ragnar Östberg (1933), Cret, Eliel Saarinen, and Dudok. Architectural history in general and the Gold Medal program in particular, however, do not move as parallel lines: the awards to Maginnis and William Adams Delano (1953) recognized traditionalist architects whose major accomplishments, for the most part, lay years prior (although Delano had recently supervised the "restoration" of the White House under Harry Truman). The more radical Modernism that eschewed all applied ornament had been under development back in the 1920s, but its Gold Medal recognition comes in a wave 30 years later with Gropius, Mies, Le Corbusier (1961), Marcel Breuer (1968), and Richard Neutra (1977).

From a stylistic point of view, Modernism has dominated since 1957, though in many varieties: from the structuralism of Pier Luigi Nervi (1964) and the low-key abstraction of Belluschi to the more corporate imagery of Wallace K. Harrison (1967) and Roche and the sculptural forms of Gehry. Recognition of a regionalist response to design is evident in the medals bestowed on Bernard Maybeck (1951) and William Wurster (1969), who developed what is called the Bay Area Style, and the Canadian Arthur Erickson, whose work draws on local materials and forms. Whether Postmodernism ever will be recognized as a style is still debated among historians and critics, but the medal has gone to leaders of the revolt that began in the 1960s against abstract Modernism: Philip Johnson (1978), Charles Moore (1991), Pelli, Michael Graves (2001), and Antoine Predock (2006). And some architects have stood alone, developing unique idioms, such as Wright, E. Fay Jones (1990), and Ricardo Legorreta (2000).

Other Contributions
Style is but one way of understanding the Gold Medal. While most all the medalists are associated with major buildings, they also have other accomplishments. Technological advances are apparent in medals to Perret and Nervi for their innovative work with concrete, Richard Buckminster Fuller (1970) for his experimental structures, and Calatrava for his suspension systems. Another important area recognized by the Gold Medal is education and theory: the teaching and philosophical musings of Kahn, for example, shaped a generation of architects. Also honored for their commitment to education were Graves, Laloux, Pascal, Cret, Gropius, Mies, Wurster, Belluschi, Josep Lluis Sert (1981), Joseph Esherick (1989), Jones, Moore, Pelli, and Samuel "Sambo" Mockbee (2004).

While much of architecture practice involves a single building or a complex, the medal has also gone to community and city designers, such as Leslie Patrick Abercombie (1950), Clarence Stein (1956), Nathaniel Owings (1983), Benjamin Thompson (1992), and Mockbee. Some Gold Medalists also served the AIA and advanced its mission as president, such as McKim, Post, Milton Medary (1929), Maginnis, and Walker. Another area has been the transformation of architecture practice and the rise of the large firm, to which the awards to Louis Skidmore (1957), John Wellborn Root II (1958), Harrison, Owings, and William Wayne Caudill (1985) all attest.

The Gold Medal was intended to honor living architects, and in most cases the handful of medals that were awarded posthumously were decided before the recipient's death (McKim, Shaw, and Medary) or came as a genuine outpouring of respect for the recently departed (Goodhue, Eero Saarinen, and Mockbee). A few posthumous medals represent a rethinking of history: The architectural contributions of both Louis Sullivan (1944, 20 years after his death) and Thomas Jefferson (1993, 168 years after his death) were largely unrecognized at their deaths (for different reasons), but scholars had, over the years, resurrected them as critical figures without which no history of American architecture could be written.

A Few Tarnishes
What has the Gold Medal missed or ignored? Two answers seem obvious: cultural diversity among American-based designers (no African-Americans have been awarded) and female practitioners. A list of important American and foreign designers whose names are not engraved on the Gold Medal wall can easily be assembled. And, although the myth of the "superstar" designer still seems to rule much of the architecture media, the reality is that, more than ever, architecture is a multidisciplinary enterprise involving many hands. In recognition of this, the AIA created a separate Architecture Firm Award in 1961 and, subsequently, other national AIA awards to highlight more targeted contributions to the field.

The Gold Medal presents an interesting kaleidoscope of what the American architecture profession has seen fit to recognize. From Bill Caudill's programming studies and school designs to Richard Meier's elegant white boxes and Fay Jones's rural chapels, it has highlighted many important facets of architecture and has illustrated how the profession can both inspire and transform.

*The year the Gold Medal was awarded appears in parentheses after the name of the recipient.

(Top to bottom) AIA Gold Medalists
Sir Aston Webb, Hon. FAIA; Kenzo Tange, Hon. FAIA (left);
Frank Lloyd Wright (right) and 1947–49 AIA President Douglas
William Orr, FAIA; Antoine Predock, FAIA. *AIA Archives*

The First 150 Years of the American Institute of Architects, 1857–2007

Tony P. Wrenn, Hon. AIA

Richard Upjohn was one of the central figures in the founding of the AIA and served as its first president (1857–76). His name is synonymous with the Gothic Revival movement in the United States, and he is best known for his Trinity Church in New York. Upjohn's granddaughter, Anna Milo Upjohn, painted this portrait of him.
AIA Archives

In the first half of the 19th century, architecture was not an organized profession. Architects were isolated from each other, no architecture library existed to serve them, no American school existed to train them, they seldom met to swap ideas, and the public knew little about them or what they did. The founding of the Royal Institute of British Architects (RIBA) in 1835 spurred a handful of American architects to meet in New York in 1836 to form a similar institute for America. Although they agreed on the need, the method eluded them. Almost two decades later, on November 5, 1852, the American Society of Civil Engineers and Architects was formed, and an architect was elected as its vice president, but engineers and architects were not ready for equality, and the "and Architects" was soon dropped from the group's name.

Nonetheless, some American architects still wanted to establish a professional association. Thirteen of them, all New Yorkers, met on February 23, 1857, in the New York office of Richard Upjohn to study "the propriety of organizing a Society of Architects." They agreed that a society should be formed with "as little delay as possible" and subsequently invited 11 other architects, not all from New York, to join them at a second meeting. Thomas U. Walter, of Philadelphia but serving in Washington, D.C., as architect of the expanding U.S. Capitol, was among them. Although they initially talked of a New York Society, Walter suggested "The American Institute of Architects" (AIA), and that name was adopted. In the next five weeks, these men wrote and adopted a constitution and bylaws, and incorporated under the laws of New York. They invited other practitioners to a gala meeting in

New York on April 15, 1857. On that day, the constitution was presented to the attending architects, and 49 architects ultimately signed it. Upjohn was elected president that day, Walter vice president.

At regularly scheduled meetings in New York, members attended lectures, shared ideas, and discussed problems of design and practice. The advancing Civil War, however, forced them to suspend meetings on November 16, 1861, but Walter and his plans for the U.S. Capitol kept the public aware of architects and their work.

In Washington, Walter's great cast-iron Capitol dome took shape before Union soldiers, who were camped around the building, and the public, which came daily to view its construction. Whatever the fate of the Union in battle, work on the dome continued. With fitting ceremony and thousands present, the Statue of Freedom was raised atop the Capitol's completed dome on December 2, 1863: The crowd watched anxiously during her 20-minute ascent. As Freedom was bolted into place, Union artillery fired 35 volleys, one for each of the states, and each of the 11 forts around the capital echoed with 35 firings. The dome, which had become a Union icon, appeared on magazine and newspaper mastheads and was printed on all manner of stationery and souvenirs, which made their way around the nation and world. Walter's awe-inspiring dome demonstrated what architects could do, no matter the circumstances. By March 1864, the AIA felt that the Union, and their profession, was secure enough to resume meetings.

Recognizing that the Institute discussed architectural matters of general, but not local, interest, the AIA Board approved constitutional

Construction of Thomas U. Walter's cast-iron dome for the U.S. Capitol continued during the Civil War. The dome was completed in 1863. Walter served as the AIA's second president (1876–87).
AIA Archives

revisions on January 16, 1867, to authorize the creation of local professional associations as part of the Institute's overall organizational structure. The term *branches* was suggested for these local groups, but *chapters* won out because it seemed less subordinate in tone. On March 19, 1867, Boston architects notified the AIA Board that they were "about to organize." Immediately after the board meeting that day, New Yorkers formed a New York Chapter, the Institute's first. The Bostonians had evidently spurred them to action.

The AIA pushed for schools of architecture and soon several were founded. The Massachusetts Institute of Technology opened America's first, in 1868; Cornell followed in 1871; and the University of Illinois in 1873. Existing publications—*Crayon, The American Architect and Building News,* and *The Architects and Mechanics Journal*—carried news of AIA meetings, discussions, and national conventions, the first of which was held in New York in October 1867. This was followed by two more conventions in New York, then a move to Philadelphia in 1870, Boston in 1871, and Cincinnati in 1872.

In spite of the growing number of AIA members from the West, Midwest, and South, many architects felt that the AIA remained too much of an East Coast and New England club. In 1884 some 100 architects from 14 Midwestern states, many of them already AIA members, met in Chicago and organized a Western Association of Architects (WAA). Their goals were the same as those of the AIA, but they offered only a single class of membership. They frowned on the tiered membership of the AIA, which, with board approval, could advance associate members to the higher class of Fellow.

Recognizing their identical interests, the two organizations agreed in 1887 to consolidate. Two years later, both met in Cincinnati: the WAA dissolved into the AIA, accepting its name, founding date of 1857, and incorporation in New York, while the AIA accepted the WAA's classless membership. All AIA and WAA members became Fellows. It would be 1898 before the AIA reinstated a tiered membership for those who joined after that date. Meanwhile, the consolidated organization pushed for architectural licensing laws, and in 1897 Illinois became the first state to enact one.

The 1893 World's Columbian Exposition in Chicago advanced architects in the public mind even more than had Walter's Capitol expansion and dome. In less than a year, Daniel H. Burnham; John W. Root; Richard Morris Hunt; McKim, Mead and White; George Brown Post; Peabody & Stearns; Van Brunt and Howe; Adler and Sullivan; and W. L. B. Jenney, plus landscape architect Frederick Law Olmsted, put together an exhibition whose buildings were dubbed the "White City."

The exposition, which became an immediate international success, changed the manner in which the public viewed architecture, landscape architecture, city planning, and other arts. In addition, it ushered in the City Beautiful movement, which influenced urban planning for years to come. RIBA President MacVickar Anderson called it "the most wondrous development that international exhibitions have ever reached, or perhaps, are ever likely to attain." RIBA was enthusiastic enough to give its 1893 Gold Medal to Richard Morris Hunt, who had studied in France, was well known to Europeans, and had designed the fair's Administration Building. RIBA followed two years later with a Gold Medal to Charles Follen McKim, also well known abroad and

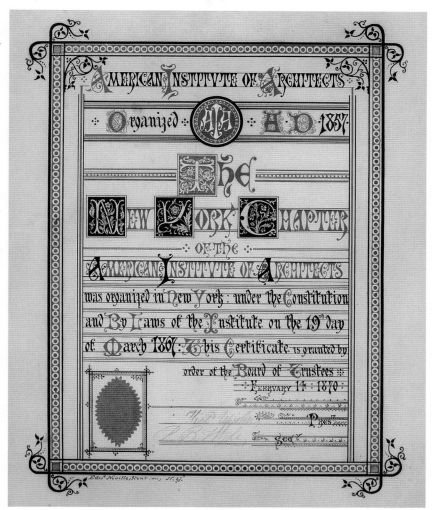

The first chapter of the AIA was chartered in New York in 1867. *AIA Archives*

Attendees at the 1883 AIA convention gathered with President Thomas U. Walter for a photograph on the steps of the First Baptist Meeting House in Providence, Rhode Island. Walter is the tall, white-haired man, center left, standing on the second step. This is the earliest known convention photograph. *AIA Archives*

Louise Bethune was the first female member of the AIA and the first woman to become a Fellow, in 1889. *AIA Archives*

Richard Morris Hunt, a founding member and third president (1887–88) of the Institute, as he was depicted in an 1891 bas-relief by sculptor Karl Bitter. *AIA Archives*

another Chicago fair architect. Those medals would help inspire the creation of an AIA Gold Medal, the first of which was given in 1907 to, appropriately enough, a British architect, Sir Aston Webb.

In the last decade of the 19th century, the AIA still had national offices in New York, but its members, in chapters that now stretched from coast to coast, routinely discussed moving the headquarters elsewhere. The AIA Washington Chapter, organized in 1887, petitioned the 1889 AIA convention to move the Institute's main offices to the Octagon in Washington, D.C. The house had served as the temporary residence of President James Madison and first lady Dolley Madison after the burning of the White House during the War of 1812. The Treaty of Ghent, ending that war, had been signed there, and it was considered second only to the White House as a historic Washington dwelling. The move was approved in 1896, and the Octagon leased in 1897. On January 1, 1899, the Octagon officially became the AIA's headquarters. In 1902 the AIA purchased the building. The move not only provided the AIA with a nationally recognized building located one block from the White House but also gave the organization access to congressmen and other government officials who were instrumental in awarding contracts for government buildings, the largest single source of construction in the United States.

Glenn Brown, a Washington architect, was elected AIA secretary in 1898. Given broad duties and powers under the constitution and bylaws adopted that year, he immediately set out to ensure restoration of the Octagon and reestablishment of Pierre L'Enfant's plan for the nation's capital. The 1899 convention in Washington, D.C., had authorized publication of the *Quarterly Bulletin*. It began publishing in April 1900. *The Quarterly Bulletin* became a powerful voice for the City Beautiful movement, epitomized in Washington by the 1901 McMillan Commission, which was staffed by AIA members Burnham and McKim and honorary AIA members Augustus Saint Gaudens and Olmsted. The McMillan Commission Plan followed recommendations of the 1900 AIA convention session on "Grouping of Government Buildings, Landscape and Statuary in the City of Washington." Though never officially adopted, the

McMillan Commission Plan became the instrument for clearing the Mall of obstructions; building the Federal Triangle and the Lincoln, Grant, and Jefferson memorials; and reaffirming L'Enfant's 18th-century plan for the city.

In 1902 the AIA was able to wrest control of the project to enlarge the White House from the Army Corps of Engineers and, under President Theodore Roosevelt, oversee its restoration. Charles McKim, then president of the AIA, served as architect, and AIA secretary Glenn Brown as supervising architect on site.

Between 1901 and 1910, the AIA organized several major Washington exhibitions on architecture, sculpture, and the McMillan Plan; lobbied for government to build within the concepts of the plan; moved L'Enfant's body from an obscure grave in Maryland to a public one at Arlington; and helped secure the 1910 establishment of a U.S. Commission of Fine Arts (CFA). President Roosevelt, as he prepared to leave office in 1908, wrote the AIA, asking the Institute to maintain "a perpetual 'eye of guardianship' over the White House to see that it is kept unchanged and unmarred from this time on."

President William Howard Taft proved to be no less a friend of architects than Roosevelt, joining with the AIA in insisting, against stiff opposition from Congress and the highway lobby, that the Lincoln Memorial, designed by Henry Bacon, be built on the Mall site recommended by the McMillan Commission. The memorial was dedicated in 1923 and its architect recognized in what has been called the greatest architectural pageant of modern times.

The Institute weathered World War I but was hard hit by the Great Depression. In the 1920s the AIA Press had published some of the most beautiful and important art and architecture books of the 20th century, including Louis Sullivan's *Autobiography of an Idea* and *A System of Architectural Ornament*. The Press also published the *AIA Journal*, a monthly that took the place of the *Quarterly Bulletin* in 1913. The *Journal* published the first work of Lewis Mumford and hired Clarence Stein as associate editor, but the Great Depression forced it to change from a fine arts journal to *The Octagon*, a magazine of Institute news.

The AIA moved its headquarters from New York City to the Octagon, in Washington, D.C., in 1899. The house, designed by architect William Thornton, the first architect of the U.S. Capitol, was the residence of President James Madison and Dolley Madison after the White House was burned during the War of 1812. *AIA Archives*

In 1934 AIA member Charles Peterson envisioned a Historic American Buildings Survey, which would find and list historic buildings and record them through text, measured drawings, and photographs. Under a tripartite agreement among the AIA, the Library of Congress (which agreed to house the drawings), and the National Park Service (which agreed to oversee the program), hundreds of out-of-work architects and draftsmen were hired, with federal funds, to carry out the survey. It continues today, some 73 years later, but has been broadened to include engineering and landscape landmarks. Its collection of documents on historic buildings, structures, and sites is one of the largest in the world.

In 1940, in need of additional space, the AIA built a two-story office building that wrapped around the back of the Octagon. It was immediately taken over by the federal government, used throughout World War II, and not recovered by the AIA until 1948. By that time the Institute needed even more space, so planning began for a larger building that could provide both offices for the Institute and rental income. A 1963 competition for a building "of special architectural significance, establishing a symbol of the creative genius of our time yet complementing, protecting and preserving a cherished symbol of another time, the historic Octagon" was won by the Philadelphia firm of Mitchell/Giurgola. The original design proposal was twice redrawn to satisfy

increased AIA space requirements, the acquisition of additional property on which to build, and the recommendations of the CFA. After the plan was twice rejected by the CFA, Mitchell/Giurgola withdrew, and the AIA chose The Architects Collaborative (TAC) of Cambridge, Massachusetts. The TAC plan won CFA approval, and the building was dedicated in 1973. It wraps around the Octagon and its garden, respects the historic building's setback from the street, and echoes its shape—while presenting a two-story glass center entrance that reflects the image of the Octagon and, from the interior, invites views of the red-brick mansion.

The Institute works to stay abreast of scientific, technological, social, and political developments, from the information revolution and the growing concerns of global climate change to socially conscious planning and issues of equality. Its members participate in planning, historic preservation, and care for the environment at all levels of government and provide assistance teams to help with disaster recovery around the globe. Its national and local award programs are widely publicized and well respected by the design and planning communities as well as the public.

Although the players have changed, the architects who met in New York on February 23, 1857, would still recognize the problems and possibilities that the AIA and its members, 150 years later, deal with daily.

Washington-area architect Glenn Brown served as the secretary of the AIA from 1898 to 1913. More than any other figure, he was responsible for relocating the AIA to Washington, D.C., and involving the Institute in federal policy discussions on city planning and beautification efforts. *AIA Archives*

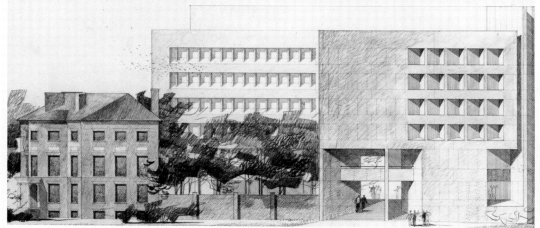

Mitchell/Giurgola of Philadelphia won the 1963 competition to design the new AIA headquarters building in Washington, D.C., but withdrew after the design (top left) was twice rejected by the city's Commission of Fine Arts. The building was ultimately designed by The Architects Collaborative (TAC), with Norman Fletcher and Howard Elkus as lead architects (bottom left). Dedicated in 1973, the AIA building (above) wraps around the Octagon and echoes its shape. Today, the Octagon houses the American Architectural Foundation. *AIA Archives*

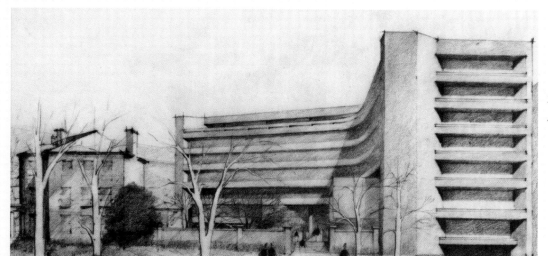

1857
Founding of the American Institute of Architects. Richard Upjohn elected president, Thomas U. Walter, vice president

Elisha Graves Otis installed the first passenger elevator, in a New York City office building

1

The Need for Architecture

Karsten Harries, PhD

"Architecture" names, first of all, the art of building and, second, any structure raised in accordance with the rules of that art. Figuratively, it also refers to anything that has been set on a firm foundation and well constructed. Philosophers, especially, have found it useful to invoke architectural metaphors, and no one more so than the Frenchman René Descartes, who, convinced that reason was sufficient to raise a conceptual edifice that would allow human beings to understand the world and their place in it, compared his method to that used by architects. But if the edifice his reason raised—his "spiritual architecture," if you will—remains a presupposition of the science and technology that have shaped our modern world, including our built architecture, his expectation that the progress of reason would provide human beings not only with physical but also spiritual shelter went disappointed. The conviction of the Enlightenment and of its heir, Modernism, that reason would lead humanity toward an ever-brighter future, has been shattered by the horrors of holocaust, war, terror, and environmental catastrophes.

Architecture, too, is caught up in such disenchantment. Do we still expect it to build an environment that will provide not just the body but also the spirit with adequate shelter? How will the world look as our children and grandchildren make their way? No doubt, buildings will still be part of that world: we would have to rid ourselves of our bodies to eliminate the need for physical shelter. But will there still be a need for architecture? Just what task remains for architecture today?

Even to ask that question is to presuppose that "architecture" is not to be equated with "building." To be sure, every work of architecture is also a building, but it is more. How is this "more" to be understood? A first answer is suggested by the traditional understanding of architecture as one of the arts. In *The Ten Books on Architecture*, the first and still most famous treatise on architecture, the Roman architect Vitruvius demanded that the architect build "with due reference to durability, convenience, and beauty."[1] Ever since, thinking about architecture has tended to take this demand pretty much for granted.

Dreams of Beauty

Consider, for example, the way in which architectural historian Nikolaus Pevsner begins his influential *An Outline of European Architecture* with the seemingly self-evident observation: "A bicycle shed is a building; Lincoln Cathedral is a piece of architecture." What distinguishes works of architecture from mere buildings, according to Pevsner, is that they are "designed with a view to aesthetic appeal." In the light of that distinction, our initial question could be rephrased: what need will there be for functional buildings that also succeed as aesthetic objects? For many, this revised question is answered by the very conception of the aesthetic object as that which gives pleasure simply because it is what it is, not because it is good for anything. Prize-winning writer, critic, and philosopher William Gass illustrated this point of view when he celebrated the way one of Peter Eisenman's houses turns its back on the world and the everyday cares and concerns of individuals: "Thank God, I thought. This house has no concern for me and mine, over which it has no rights, but displays in every aspect and angle and fall of light the concern for the nature and beauty of building that is the architect's trust and obligation."[2] But does such an aesthetic response provide us with a key to the responsibility of the architect or do justice to either beauty or architecture?

(Opposite) In attempting to distinguish architecture from utilitarian buildings, historian Nikolaus Pevsner cites Lincoln Cathedral as an exemplar. The original Romanesque structure, consecrated in 1092, was damaged in 1185 by an earthquake and subsequently rebuilt in the Gothic style. *©Steve Vidler/SuperStock*

The AEG Turbine Factory (1908–10) in Berlin, designed by architect Peter Behrens with engineer Karl Bernhard, was pivotal in the development of German Modernism. Eschewing ornamental motifs from the past, Behrens and other Modernists preferred a streamlined aesthetic to more accurately reflect the culture within which they practiced. *Bildarchiv Monheim GmbH/Alamy*

In 1908 Adolf Loos wrote "Ornament and Crime," in which he argued for pure, undecorated forms. He used traditional local idioms and building materials in this mountain villa (1930), designed for Paul Khuner on the Kreuzberg, Payerbach, Austria. *©Roberto Schezen/Esto*

Austrian architect Otto Wagner believed that the architecture of his day should not try to imitate the past but rather respond to and celebrate engineering advances. This evolution, however, could be subtle: The composition of his Austrian Postal Savings Bank, or Postparkasse, built in Vienna around 1905, is undoubtedly classical, but the simplified façade gains visual interest from the pattern formed by new technology—metal bolts that secure stone panels to the structure. *E.J. Baumeister Jr./Alamy*

Human beings have always dreamed of a more beautiful world. The urge to decorate dwellings and tools—indeed the human body—is as old as humanity. But the goal was rarely to create beauty for beauty's sake. Across centuries and cultures, human beings have yearned to experience the presence of spirit in the things that surrounded them in order to feel at home in the world. Ornament had an animating function. When experienced as just an aesthetic addendum, decoration loses this aura.

The aura that gives a building such as England's Lincoln Cathedral its special weight is threatened as soon as architects take their primary responsibility to be the creation of aesthetic objects. For what is "aura"? German critic and philosopher Walter Benjamin understood the experience of aura as an experience of spirit incarnate in matter. The observer's identification with some thing, say a coconut with the look of a human face, gives it a special aura, lets it appear as more than just mute matter. But is this ever more than an appearance, an illusion, read into things by the observer?

Is the experience of aura then, at bottom, self-deception? A child may experience rocks and animals as animate, endowed with the power of speech, and fairy tales preserve traces of an older magical experience of the aura of all things. But the commitment to objectivity that is a presupposition of our science and technology banishes spirit from matter. To us moderns, things do not speak, except perhaps as echoes of our own voice. Such echoes leave us alone and homeless. Has what we today call "beauty" not lost the aura beauty once possessed? Our answer depends on how much we allow our commitment to objectivity to limit our understanding of what deserves to be called "real."

German philosopher Friedrich Nietzsche's answer to the question "What is the beauty of a building today?" speaks to this threatened loss: "The same as the beautiful face of a woman lacking spirit: something mask-like." His metaphor helps us better understand his distinction between two different kinds of beauty: When the subject is a human being, we can more readily distinguish a beauty that is still experienced as the incarnation of spirit in matter from a made-up, masklike beauty—even if this latter beauty may be more "perfect" in its presentation.

Crucial here are the different ways in which beauty relates to what is beautiful. The first beauty invites the metaphor of a veil that conceals even as it calls attention to what lies beneath, be it face, body, or something sacred. Such a veil does not want to be appreciated for its own sake but as a boundary and a bond with what remains concealed, a threshold both separating and linking the sacred and the profane, the inner and the outer, the spiritual and the material. The second beauty would have us forget what is beneath. Such superficial beauty gains special importance in a world in which all too much invites such forgetting. This beauty offers an escape from reality into a world of simulacra.

Returning to our example of Lincoln Cathedral, do we capture the special aura of such a work when we understand it as a functional building overlaid with aesthetic intentions? The beauty of this church allowed the building to speak of life on this earth, of death, of community, and of the promise of happiness—the profound issues that mattered most to those who built it. Into the ground of everyday buildings, the cathedral inserted a figure of utopia. This form of beauty provided spiritual shelter. In stark contrast, beauty that is enjoyed only for beauty's sake lets us forget the burdens of our everyday existence.

Nietzsche's remarks on the beauty of architecture appear in a section of *Human, All Too Human* that bears the title: "Stone is more stone than it used to be."[3] But are not stones what they always were? Of course, the earlier reference to our modern commitment to objectivity already hinted at what has changed.

The contrast Nietzsche had in mind would seem familiar to all of us and to hold not only for architecture: Perceived meaning often veils the materiality of the things we encounter. To better understand this, consider some printed page. Matter, in the form of ink on paper rather than stone, is meant to communicate. And when we get caught up in some story, we may hardly be aware of the paper, the ink blackening our fingers. Our mind is focused on the ideas communicated by the printed words and our reactions to them. Here, in an obvious way, meaning veils matter. And do not buildings, too, have meaning in this sense, meaning that allows us to liken them to texts? When we enter a railroad station or a bank, what we see is not an assemblage of stones but shapes and surfaces that suggest the purpose or importance of the place and invite a certain behavior. In all architecture, meaning veils the materiality of the material of which buildings are made.

The stones of architecture thus speak to us, although we may want to add that it is really human beings who endow these stones with meaning, as both those who build and those who live in and with these buildings bring to them their expectations and understanding of what purposes buildings should serve and what they should look like. In that sense, buildings cannot help but speak to us. But how then are we to understand Nietzsche's claim that "stone is more stone today than it used to be"? In what sense had the buildings of his day lost their ability to speak?

Nietzsche was thinking of Neo-Gothic churches and Neo-Renaissance city halls, of apartment houses given the look of Baroque palaces, of banks built in the image of Greek temples. In the way they appropriated past styles, such buildings did of course speak, but the original significance of the styles that were appropriated could no longer be understood.

The architecture of the second half of the 19th century offers ready illustrations of the masklike beauty Nietzsche had in mind. Functional buildings were dressed up aesthetically with borrowed ornament, whose former spiritual significance was no longer understood. In the first decades of the 20th century, just about every progressive architect, critic, or writer shared Nietzsche's dislike of such architecture. This sense that architecture had become a masquerade provoked many a Modernist to demand a more honest architecture that was responsive to our modern reality and, in particular, to our science and technology.

But have we today not returned to the "decorated sheds"—to borrow a term from the authors of *Learning from Las Vegas*[4]—of the 19th century, if in a new key? Consider Frank Gehry's Frederick R. Weisman Art Museum in Minneapolis (1991–93). I would not deny this museum's distinctive beauty. But almost self-consciously, with its folded façade of brushed stainless steel, this architecture brings to mind Nietzsche's remark on the masklike beauty of today's architecture, here made conspicuous by the loose fit between glittering cladding and a quite ordinary shed. Whenever such a building lifts or drops its mask, the material beneath presents itself all the more insistently as the mute material it is, in this case terra-cotta-colored brick and concrete.

Does the aesthetic approach not demand of the architect attention to certain visual qualities that help make his or her work aesthetically appealing—if not beautiful, then at least interesting? Such concern with aesthetic appeal, however, denies architecture the aura that once belonged to it: "Originally everything on a Greek or Christian building had a meaning, with an eye to a higher order of things: this aura of an inexhaustible significance surrounded the building like a magical veil."[5] Our modern approach to architecture is governed by a very different understanding of the task of the architect: The architect is asked, among many other

Through software originally designed for the aeronautics industry, architect Frank Gehry has explored novel techniques to design and fabricate highly sculptural facades such as the Frederick R. Weisman Art Museum (1993) at the University of Minnesota. ©*Carol Highsmith*

This essay was written in the Langhorne Pavilion (1996), a modest structure in Vieques, Puerto Rico, designed by Edward F. Knowles. The pavilion's relationship to earth and sky answers to at least some of the author's dreams. *Courtesy Karsten Harries*

requirements, to create buildings that succeed as aesthetic objects—but the more successful the practitioner is in this regard, the more completely does the aesthetic object ornament and finally smother the building itself, transforming it into a megasculpture. The resultant beauty is experienced as but a mask, leaving what lies beneath pretty much untouched—and leaving us dreaming of a very different kind of architecture.

Dreams of the Complete Building

That architecture has difficulty rising to the purity found in modern painting or sculpture is evident. Reality, with its own demands, places too many restraints on the architect. This shows itself in the disjointed appearance of countless decorated sheds. But should great architecture not overcome that tension by embracing that reality more completely, instead of hiding it beneath some beautiful mask? Valéry's definition of poetry as "an effort by one man to create an artificial and ideal order of a material of vulgar origin,"[6] the material in this case being ordinary language, invites application to architecture: architecture is an effort by one individual to create an artificial and ideal order out of a material of vulgar origin, the material now furnished by all the requirements of building. Frank Lloyd Wright's dream of an organic architecture that would make it "quite impossible to consider the building as one thing, its furnishings another and its setting and environment still another" points in this direction: "The very chairs and tables, cabinets and even musical instruments, where practicable, are of the building itself, never fixtures upon it."[7] Those living in such a house would be expected to behave, perhaps even to dress and eat, in ways that would preserve the integrity of the aesthetic whole.

Such dreams invite an aestheticization of life, and because the physical and social environment, too, are to be incorporated into the aesthetic whole, an aestheticization of politics. Architects and theorists have long dreamed of architectural concepts that might gather some multitude into a genuine community. As religion proved less and less able to offer effective spiritual shelter, such dreams gained a new actuality: Why should some genius not be able to create a city that would once again allow individuals to discover their vocation as parts of a greater whole? Presupposed is the conviction, articulated by Nietzsche, "that the human being has value, meaning only in as much as he is a stone in a great building."[8]

Nietzsche knew that this kind of dream is likely to strike most of us as a nightmare. We are too committed to the autonomy of the individual, too preoccupied with the self, to furnish suitable material for such an architecture. But this does not mean that many of us do not dream now and then of it. Those spiritually at sea may well long for some architecture strong enough to bind or crush freedom. (In the absence of Moses, they may call for Aaron and the golden calf.)

Many a Modern architect has been seduced by this dream. Walter Gropius invited the students of the Bauhaus to see themselves as part of a new elite, from which would grow a new belief, "a universally great, enduring, spiritual-religious idea," that would find its expression in an architecture worthy to take its place beside the great cathedrals. Projecting the "miracle of the Gothic cathedrals" into the future, Gropius dreamed of an architecture that once again would be "the crystalline expression of man's noblest thoughts, his ardour, his humanity, his faith, his religion!"[9]

We may wonder whether architects like Paul Ludwig Troost and Albert Speer did not come closer to realizing the dream of a new cathedral than did the Bauhaus, although, like German philosopher Martin Heidegger, Nazi architects preferred the paradigms furnished by the Greek temple, transposed into a cold monumentality that reduces the individual to insignificance. As long as nostalgia looks to architecture to furnish human beings with spiritual shelter, it will also feed dreams of Babel's tower. All dreams of the complete building are shadowed by that tower.

Dreams of Freedom

Does the kind of edifying architecture represented by Lincoln Cathedral still have a place in our modern world? Does it not belong, as German philosopher Friedrich Hegel insisted, to a never-to-be-recovered past—where Hegel would have us affirm the death of architecture in its highest sense as part of humanity's coming of age, no more to be mourned than the loss of the magic the world held when we were children? Perhaps the only spiritual shelter that can adequately protect us moderns is a conceptual architecture raised by reason.

The French writer Victor Hugo suggested that the printing press killed the cathedral. Has the car not similarly rendered the place-establishing city obsolete, where the car is but one manifestation of a way of life that has brought us physical and spiritual mobility and, thus, a freedom that by now seems an inalienable right? How will the electronic revolution and all it stands for transform our sense of space and the need for architecture? Many today dream of a post-architectural future. And with good reason: Must an ever more vigorous commitment to the freedom of the individual not make us suspicious of all place-establishing architecture? In aesthetics, the shift from the beautiful to the sublime testifies to that change, where beauty has long been linked to the establishment of bounded wholes, while the sublime demands open space. Freedom, democracy, and the promise of open space go together. There is tension between the call for a place-establishing architecture and the value we have placed on freedom. French writer George Bataille was not alone in suspecting a prison in every work of architecture.[10]

Similarly, this desire for freedom will rebel again and again against the rule of reason. In his short novel *Notes from Underground*, Russian writer Fyodor Dostoevsky succinctly portrays this seemingly deep-rooted need to oppose modern society's reliance on the authority of reason. One of his characters acknowledges that, "Twice-two-makes-four is, in my humble opinion, nothing but a piece of impudence. Twice-two-makes-four is a farcical, dressed–up fellow who stands across your path with arms akimbo and spits at you. Mind you, I quite agree that twice-two-makes-four is a most excellent thing; but if we are to give everything its due, then twice-two-makes-five is sometimes a most charming little thing, too."[11] Recent manifestations of such contrarian thinking can be found in the architectural movements known as "deconstructivism" and "anarchitecture." Influenced by the French philosopher Jacques Derrida, the former has liked to challenge well-established expectations about what a work of architecture should look like by playing with fragmentation, distortion, dislocation of familiar architectural elements, and surprising geometries, where the computer has greatly facilitated such play. By now, such gestures have descended from elite architecture into the vernacular and become a familiar part of everyday postmodern building practice.

The neologism *anarchitecture* suggests buildings that rise without the architect's art. It's not a wholly new concept: the Austrian architect Bernard Rudofsky's *Architecture Without Architects*, published in 1964, was a "frankly polemical" celebration of Old World vernacular building. But in the work of architectural historian Robin Evans and architects Gordon Matta-Clark and Lebbeus Woods, the word speaks with a different, more oppositional voice: for them, *anarchitecture* is not a product of anonymous builders supported by the collective wisdom of generations in tune with the rhythms of nature, but very much the expression of

Anarchitecture as practiced by American-born architect Lebbeus Woods challenges viewers to question assumptions and explore alternatives. This drawing is part of a series titled Berlin Free Zone (1991), in which Woods reflected on possible shifts in the city's social fabric once the infamous wall came down. *Courtesy Lebbeus Woods*

individuals responsive to our rapidly changing cyber-world, ever on the verge of slipping out of our control. *Anarchitecture* here means cuts, ruptures, insertions, and intrusions into the body of architecture that challenge its often all-but-overlooked rule over our lives, inviting more thoughtful consideration of architecture and its ruling ethos. Anarchitecture invites us to fantasize about very different environments, very different ways of life. (Gordon Matta-Clark, on the occasion of the 1973 dedication of the Twin Towers, in fact called for their erasure, unable to even suspect that terror would all too soon realize what was meant only as a thought-provoking comment. Of course, 9/11 has made words such as *deconstruction* or *anarchitecture* more difficult to use and invites weightier and more difficult reflections concerning the future of architecture.)

Anarchitecture can be seen as a recent species of "fantastic architecture," which has long communicated the tension between the generally accepted function of architecture (to provide us with physical and spiritual shelter by bounding space) and our unruly imaginations that, moved by desire, fear, pleasure, or disgust, give birth to fanciful apparitions, fictions, and dream-visions, none of which rests on solid ground. Fantastic architecture belongs with utopia, this land which lies somewhere beyond our all-too-familiar earthbound world with its place-assigning order. Utopia, in fact, possesses two faces: eutopia, that imaginary realm where reason coexists with freedom and happiness, and dystopia, a realm where pain drowns freedom and mocks pretentious reason. Visions of paradise, Jerusalem, or the City of God—realms where human beings, no longer bound by the spirit of gravity, are finally free to fly and where buildings will seem to float, immaterially, in boundless space—are thus shadowed by versions of the labyrinth, Babel, or hell—dark suffocating spaces in which lurk minotaur and devil. The seductive appeal, not just of eutopic visions but also of dystopic ones (think of Piranesi's *Carceri*) invites consideration: while it does not lead to an architecture fit for earthbound mortals, it should make our building more thoughtful.

Dreams of Nature

Suspicion of architecture has attended thinking about architecture from the very beginning: in paradise there was no need for building; in this garden, Adam and Eve were at home. And might artifice not recover what pride is supposed to have lost? Both English philosopher Francis Bacon and Descartes thus dreamed of paradise regained on the basis of science and technology. We are not done with that dream. Our architecture shows that the Cartesian promise, that reason will render us the masters and possessors of nature, was not idle. But the history of the 20th century demonstrates that the possession of such power has not brought us wisdom. The shadow of Babel's tower, which today so easily blurs with the shadow cast by fascist architecture, darkens many a Modernist dream of architecture and invites very different thoughts. Was it not Cain who built the first city? Convinced that our true home is not to be established by human artifice, painters thus liked to place the Nativity in some fantastic ruin.

(Opposite) Trees grow from inside rooms, their branches extending from windows, in Vienna's Hundertwasser Haus (1986). The project was designed by the artist Friedensreich Hundertwasser, who believed that buildings should not be subjugated to the hegemony of "straight lines," and implemented by architects Joseph Krawina and Peter Pelikan. *©Murat Ayranci/SuperStock*

Animal architecture is completely at home in nature. Termite mounds, for example, are sited and designed to drive air circulation inside. Some mounds have indoor gardens of carefully tended fungus. *©age fotostock/SuperStock*

To ensure a livable environment far into the future, we must develop a less oppositional relationship between architecture and nature. Consider the Arthur & Yvonne Boyd Education Center (1996–99), Riversdale, New South Wales, designed by Glenn Murcutt in collaboration with Wendy Lewin and Reg Lark. The building collects rainwater, is naturally ventilated, and is built of recycled timber. ©John Gollings/Esto

(Opposite) German architect Stefan Behnisch's Genzyme Corporation headquarters, completed in 2003 in Cambridge, Massachusetts, received the U.S. Green Building Council's premier LEED platinum rating. The design features, among many other sustainable strategies, roof heliostats that move with the sun to bounce light into the building's interior atrium. ©Anton Grassi/Esto

The same distrust of an architecture ruled by an all-too-human reason let the painter Friedensreich Hundertwasser call "the air raids of 1943 a perfect automatic lesson in form; straight lines and their vacuous structures ought to have been blown to pieces, and so they were." He admonishes us to "strive, as rapidly as possible for total uninhabitability and creative mouldering in architecture."[12] In this connection, the decision by architects of the 18th century to actually build ruins deserves consideration, as does the related decision by Romantic painters to represent still-intact buildings as ruins.[13]

Related is the dream of buildings in the image of the architecture of animals. Juhani Pallasmaa has suggested that what makes their architecture so beautiful "is its total integration into the life pattern of its builder, and to the dynamically balanced system of nature."[14] Its beauty figures what is denied to us: a dwelling completely at home in nature, in tune with its rhythms.

Today, such dreams have gained weight and been given a special urgency by ever-more-pressing environmental concerns. Green architecture has become much more than just a slogan: it is demanded by a still expanding humanity on a collision course with finite natural resources. How should environmental problems, of which the energy crisis is only the most visible manifestation, affect the look of the built environment? How will they transform our still prodigal use of space? Will there be gardens on the roof of every building? Everyone who builds, no matter how modest the work, bears responsibility for how those who come after have to live with it. To meet that responsibility, architects must be able to meet the challenges presented by the environment and by the needs of still-unborn generations.

Common sense tells us that, in light of these environmental pressures, much of what we call development today is in fact irresponsible. Not just this country but the entire world remains caught up—despite numerous warnings, prophecies of doom, and modest efforts to remedy the effects of waste and pollution—in a process that, if not checked by a changed attitude to this earth, will lead to disaster or, rather, disasters. The list is long and sobering: a deteriorating environment that will make clean water, air, and soil—not to mention relatively unspoiled nature—a thing of the past; wars over dwindling resources; mass starvation; and moral disintegration that could lead to the self-destruction of humanity itself. To ensure a livable environment for future generations, we must learn to consider physical space a scarce resource; to develop different, much denser settlement patterns; and to imagine a less oppositional relationship between architecture and nature.

Such efforts, however, are unlikely to be successful without a change of heart. If shortsighted, selfish interests are allowed to continue to shape the built environment, we can only expect its further deterioration. Also needed is what German poet and philosopher Friedrich Schiller called an aesthetic education. Decisions to give a high-rise the look of a turning torso, as Santiago Calatrava did in Malmö, or an apartment building the look of a dancing couple, as Frank Gehry did in Prague, may lead to interesting aesthetic objects but make no contribution to such an awareness. Needed is architecture that transforms our understanding of how we should live. A high standard of living measured by per capita income does not necessarily mean a high quality of life. What kind of life do we want for our children and our children's children? A greener architecture is needed, not just to address ever-more unavoidable environmental problems but, more fundamentally, to help bring about a change of heart.

The Responsibility of the Architect

William Gass called "concern for the nature and beauty of building" the architect's "trust and obligation." Much depends here on how the nature of building and its beauty are understood. In the late 1950s the philosopher Paul Weiss, writing very much in the orbit of aesthetic Modernism, defined architecture as "the art of creating space through the construction of boundaries in common-sense space."[15] Like William Gass, he thought it important that the architect's creativity not be fettered by "judges, critics, clients, and problems relating to engineering, city planning, and scales." So he called on architecture schools to encourage students "to experiment with the building of all sorts of space, in all sorts of ways, with all sorts of material. They should have periods in which they do not care that their work may not interest a client or that no one may ever build it or that it may not fit in with prevailing styles.

Nine five-story cubes, rotating a cumulative 90 degrees from the ground floor to the topmost segment, make up Santiago Calatrava's Turning Torso building (2005) in Malmö, Sweden.
Ann Johansson/Corbis

The towers of Frank Gehry's Nationale-Nederlanden building (1996) in Prague have been nicknamed "Fred and Ginger" after dancers Fred Astaire and Ginger Rogers. *©age fotostock/SuperStock*

Not until they take seriously the need to explore the possibilities of bounding spaces in multiple ways will they become alert to architecture as an art, as respectable, revelatory, creative, and at least as difficult as any other."[16]

But while such thinking has led to the creation of countless striking aesthetic objects, their often undeniable beauty resists inhabitation and contributes little to the creation of a successful built environment. Like all aesthetic objects, such works invite admiration simply for what they are. If we demand that architecture provide both physical and spiritual shelter, the creation of such aesthetic objects fails to meet the architect's special responsibility. Instead of shelter, it offers distractions. A different kind of beauty is needed.

Benjamin's understanding of aura points toward such a beauty. Why does aura matter? An answer is suggested when Benjamin links the experience of aura to the experience of a person as a person: "Looking at someone carries the implicit expectation that our look will be returned by the object of our gaze. Where this expectation is met (which, in the case of thought processes, can apply equally to the look of the mind and to a glance pure and simple), there is an experience of the aura to the fullest extent."[17] To experience the distinctive aura of the other is to experience an incarnation of spirit in matter so complete that there is no distance between the two. Although Benjamin is describing an interaction between two people, something of the sort is present in every experience of aura.

Benjamin claimed that works of art have to lose their aura in the age of mechanical reproduction. Does this not also hold for works of architecture? Jean Nouvel points to what awaits us: "From the moment an office building is made on the basis of an existing typology, whose technology and price and the conditions for its realization are known, we can duplicate the building and have it constructed without paying for a new design."[18] In the

French architect Jean Nouvel's Monolith, a monstrous presence born of the desire to "create holes, interstices, voids, et cetera, in the metastatic fullness of culture," floated on Lake Murten in Switzerland as part of Expo.02. *Prisma/SuperStock*

same conversation, French social theorist Jean Baudrillard had this to say about the then still-standing Twin Towers: "These two towers resemble two perforated bands. Today we'd probably say they're clones of each other, that they've already been cloned."[19] To experience a work of architecture as a simulacrum is to experience it as unbearably light. (This observation of their design, of course, does not in any way take away from the unbearable weight we feel for the destruction of these two towers and the subsequent loss of so many lives.)

In this age of the computer, the very concept of aura may seem to betray nostalgia for something that lies irrecoverably behind us. But without some experience of aura, we feel alone and homeless. That is what makes the increasing loss of aura in the age of technical reproduction so frightening: Are not even human beings today in danger of losing that special aura that distinguishes persons from their simulacra? What in principle distinguishes a person from a robot with a computer brain? The loss of an experience of aura threatens the loss of our humanity.

That threat is recognized by Baudrillard when, in his discussion with Nouvel, he takes the task of art today to be that of tearing away the masks that aesthetics and culture have placed over our suffocating artificial world, where the virtual threatens to displace the real. Art, he insists, should preserve the "enigmatic side" of things, should break open modern culture, which today is "everywhere . . . a homologue of industry and technology . . . A work of art is a singularity, and all these singularities can create holes, interstices, voids, et cetera, in the metastatic fullness of culture."[20] Why such emphasis on singularity? At issue is the distinction between what artifice can produce and what is given. Whatever artifice can produce can, in principle, be reproduced. But the simplest thing, say a rock or a leaf, is infinitely complex, a unique given that resists full comprehension and therefore reproduction. What is at issue is related to the question: Why does aura matter? What allows us in this age of the technical reproducibility, not just of works of art, but increasingly of everything, to hold on to a fundamental distinction between the aura of human beings, works of art, and natural objects? The threat that reproduction poses to our experience of the aura of things is also a threat to our own human essence. This makes it important to open windows in the conceptual architecture raised by reason, windows to dimensions of reality that resist comprehension and therefore cannot be reproduced. A successful work of art should have something of the enigmatic presence we experience in the face of a person. That, it seems to me, is a test that architecture, too, must meet if it is to continue to provide us with spiritual shelter. At stake is nothing less than our humanity. ●

Emily and Joseph Pulitzer selected Japanese architect Tadao Ando to design the Pulitzer Foundation for the Arts (2003) in St. Louis. A building resulted that possesses something of "the enigmatic presence we experience in the face of a person."
©David Sundberg/Esto

GOLD MEDALIST, 1960

Ludwig Mies van der Rohe, FAIA

Dietrich Neumann, PhD

When the German Pavilion at the International Exposition in Barcelona was opened on May 27, 1929, critics unanimously celebrated the small building at the heart of the exhibition grounds as the beginning of a new epoch in architecture. One of them described it as "space-in-itself, architecture as a free art, the expression of a spiritual commitment." The low-slung, open pavilion was almost entirely empty. It only contained a few of the architect's Barcelona chairs and a statue in an enclosed water basin by Georg Kolbe. With supreme elegance, it juxtaposed walls of polished marble with tall glass panels, a white-stuccoed ceiling, travertine floors, and eight slender, cruciform columns appearing immaterial under their reflective chromium skin.

The pavilion's creator was the 43-year-old Ludwig Mies van der Rohe, one of Germany's most prominent architects at the time, despite the fact that he had executed only a handful of modern residential commissions and two housing blocks. His breakthrough to modernity and to national acclaim had come in 1922 with his unexecuted design for a soaring, glass-clad skyscraper in the heart of Berlin. Other visionary designs soon followed. Mies's designs and famously terse statements ("less is more") were part of a broad and vocal avant-garde movement in Germany after World War I, which succeeded, at least for a while, to convincingly align innovative forms with leftist political convictions and found the broad support of local social democratic governments.

From 1930–33, Mies served as director of the Bauhaus, Germany's most important design school. Less politically engaged than most of his peers, Mies applied Modern architectural language, originally based on notions of practicality and economy of means, to luxurious dwellings for clients across the political spectrum. Nevertheless, the new Modernist idiom appealed only to a minority in Germany, and the Nazi government after 1933 fiercely opposed it because of its alleged left-wing political connotations.

In 1938 Mies accepted an offer to head the architecture school at the Illinois Institute of Technology (IIT, then called Armour Institute) in Chicago. With a string of important commissions in the following years, Mies van der Rohe redefined Modern architecture. The elevated glass cube of the Farnsworth House (1950) in Plano, Illinois, took ideas of open, simple interior spaces to their extreme. The pristine steel and glass towers of the Lake Shore Drive Apartments (1951) in Chicago were hailed as perfect new renditions of this building type, and the Seagram Building (1958) in New York was viewed as the prototypical new skyscraper. The custom-designed, ornamental I-beams adorning the facades of his high-rises were subtle attempts at rendering the load-bearing structure hidden inside the building readable on the outside. Mies also developed "large span" interiors, such as at IIT's Crown Hall (1956), in which many functions could be accommodated.

The AIA awarded Mies the Gold Medal in recognition of his lifelong contributions as both teacher and practitioner. Not all of the countless architects whose work Mies van der Rohe inspired were equally skillful in their handling of spaces, proportions, light, and material. While their efforts have defined much of postwar American architecture to this day, the precision, formal beauty, and minimalist intelligence of Mies van der Rohe's work stands as a reminder of what made Modern architecture fascinating and compelling from the outset.

The elegant, exquisitely detailed German Pavilion, designed by Mies for the 1929 International Exposition in Barcelona, received unanimous approval from the critics and ushered in a new epoch in architecture. *Courtesy Dietrich Neumann*

Although never built, Mies's design for the glass-clad Friedrichstrasse skyscraper in Berlin brought him national acclaim. *Digital image ©The Museum of Modern Art/Licensed by SCALA/Art Resource, NY.*

Louis I. Kahn, FAIA

Susan G. Solomon, PhD

(Below) The design of Trenton Bath House (1955), Ewing, New Jersey, was pivotal in clarifying Kahn's thinking about the integration of "servant" and "served" spaces. *Louis I. Kahn Collection, University of Pennsylvania and the Pennsylvania Historical and Museum Commission*

(Below bottom) The Kimbell Art Museum (1972), Forth Worth, Texas consists of 16 rectangular vaulted elements. The gallery spaces, however, are not confined within individual vaults but flow from one to another. *Marshall D. Myers, Architectural Archives, University of Pennsylvania*

(Below right) Kahn's Yale University Art Gallery (1952), considered his first architectural masterpiece, represented a sharp departure from Yale's Gothic-inspired campus. The building, recipient of the AIA's Twenty-five Year Award in 1979, was restored by Polshek Partnership Architects in 2007. *Elizabeth Felicella, ©2006 Yale University Art Gallery*

The AIA Gold Medal, capped more than three decades of acclaim for Kahn's work. While earlier praise honored Kahn (1901–74) for his design of private and public housing (many carried out in the 1940s with partners George Howe, Oscar Stonorov, or both), later distinctions recognized his more sublime achievements, such as the Salk Institute for Biological Studies. The Gold Medal citation expanded on these accolades by identifying Kahn's role as a gifted teacher, first at Yale and then at the University of Pennsylvania. It extolled Kahn as "a man whose architectural genius is equaled only by his tireless generosity in sharing his wealth of ideas with colleagues and students."

Kahn, who graduated from the University of Pennsylvania in 1924, fulfilled the educational aspirations of his Jewish family, which had emigrated from Estonia to Philadelphia when he was a small child. Trained in the Beaux-Arts method, Kahn used a Modernist vocabulary and elegant problem solving for a variety of government-sponsored projects during the first decades of his career. He inaugurated his own firm in 1947 and began to reassess building for postwar America. By the early 1950s, following his personal confrontations with ancient ruins in Europe and the Near East, Kahn began to implore architects to uncover the elemental human purpose and use of each commission. Kahn's quest for the singular character of institutions became the hallmark of his mature career.

Kahn's search for "beginnings" and his supporting belief that "architecture is the thoughtful making of spaces" were attempts to strengthen Modernism. He believed that architects would be able to tackle the changing needs of the 20th century by unearthing the history of human activity, thereby rescuing Modernism from being just another "historical style." He maintained that practitioners who followed this approach had the capacity to ennoble individual behavior and forge greater interaction among users. Kahn, by trusting architects to seek the meaning of each building and arrive at their own open-ended conclusions, demonstrated profound faith in his own profession.

Describing himself as someone who wanted to blend Classicism and Modernism, Kahn achieved a successful paradigm when he designed the Trenton Bath House (1955). This small structure, housing the changing rooms of the outdoor pool at the Jewish Community Center in Ewing, New Jersey, illustrates how Kahn employs humble materials to produce Beaux-Arts grandeur in order to fashion a new building type, the suburban swim club. He crafts finite spaces and creates "servant and served" hierarchies at the same time that he cherishes Modernism through the use of geometric clarity and the integration of natural light and gardens within a building.

Aided by Anne Tyng, Kahn offered an inventive solution. Bold square pavilions define the space where the mundane act of changing clothes becomes an exalted ritual. In his first successful integration of "servant" and "served" space, Kahn shows that infrastructure should never be hidden but rather celebrated as evidence of how architects construct buildings and of how people conduct their lives. Kahn demonstrates his true passion for nature in the empty space between the walls and the roof. Using this simple void, he shapes natural light, infuses the room with fresh air, and offers swimmers a view of the sky and trees.

During the following two decades, at buildings such as the Kimbell Art Museum, Kahn attained more refined and poetic results. His mature works are timeless buildings that were meant to evoke ancient human actions to satisfy the evolving requirements of contemporary life.

Victoria Beach: Architectural Ethics in Action

Kira Gould, Assoc. AIA

It was the mid-1990s when architect Victoria Beach began to notice how little design attention was paid to "everyday" projects, especially in disadvantaged neighborhoods. At that time, Beach was teaching design and ethics at Harvard Graduate School of Design, was a fellow at Harvard's Edmond J. Safra Foundation Center for Ethics, and served as chair of the Ethics Forum, an academic colloquium for design professionals. In addition to being an outspoken advocate for ethics in architecture, she saw a connection between the profession's ethical lapses and the frustration of young practitioners going under-utilized at their jobs. "Many firms believe intern designers are not ready to do the real work," she says, "but I was seeing tremendous potential and passion—and then attrition." The leadership structure at most firms means that only senior leaders enjoy what Beach calls the "holistic exposure to a project—what our discipline is about."

In 1996 Beach started Design Foundations to create field-training opportunities for intern designers and to fulfill some of the profession's ethical responsibilities by promoting community service for groups that cannot afford to pay practitioners and often cannot attract funding for facility needs. A grant from the Echoing Green Foundation got her started. Each year, Beach identified a Boston-area project—teen center, nature trail, playground, athletic facility, or school yard—and assembled teams of architecture interns, guided by licensed architects, to tackle the job. "The interns get a chance to take leadership roles in real-world projects—something that would take years to achieve in private practice." And the communities received pro bono design services for projects that otherwise might never have occurred. In most instances, the initial efforts of Design Foundations attract other in-kind services, construction materials,

and necessary funding to turn hypothetical projects into physical constructs.

In 2004, for example, members of Design Foundations worked with the P. A. Shaw School, a public elementary school in Boston's Dorchester neighborhood, to plan the transformation of its yard into a safe, attractive, and engaging place for learning and play. Intern Christian Stainer helped lead several community workshops, which included staff, students, parents, and neighboring residents, through schematic design and design development. The team meticulously documented the process; a resulting book recommended a series of projects and paths to implementation. "This process helped the client and the community plug into the design process in a deep way," Beach says. "They were excited to see the physical environment as a manifestation of their own pedagogy." The new school yard opened in the fall of 2005.

Beach now teaches at the California College of the Arts in California's Bay Area and is planning to reestablish Design Foundations on the West Coast. Today, Beach is part of a socially responsible architecture "subculture" that includes Design Corps (established by Bryan Bell and Victoria Ballard Bell in Raleigh, North Carolina, in 1999), Architecture for Humanity (Cameron Sinclair and Kate Stohr, New York City, 1999), and Public Architecture (John Peterson, San Francisco, 2002), among others. "What we've learned over and over again is that the design process and its visual artifacts are absolutely riveting to most people," Beach says. "A good design exudes the architect's affection and care for a place and its citizens. Once people see that, they seem to care, too, and the resources flow from there."

Victoria Beach
Courtesy Design Foundations

With help from Design Foundations, the school yard at the P. A. Shaw School was refurbished in 2005. The sketch resulted from workshops with residents of Boston's Dorchester neighborhood to discuss new possibilities for the school.
Courtesy Design Foundations

1863
Construction completed on
Thomas U. Walter's dome
for the U.S. Capitol

2

Architecture as a Reflection of Evolving Culture
The American Experience

James Steele, PhD

Architecture is not mere construction: It functions as a tangible manifestation of a specific social ethos, offering a three-dimensional record of cultural attitudes. While a work of architecture can be enjoyed at a purely experiential or aesthetic level, its significance cannot fully be appreciated without understanding the dreams and struggles of the society in which it was designed and constructed. The architecture of the United States, like that of all cultures, can be read as a textbook of history, providing profound insights into who we are as a people.

(Opposite) Monticello, Thomas Jefferson's home in the foothills of southwestern Virginia, is the perfect mirror of the characteristics and aspirations of a young nation. The house also reflects the ingenuity of its architect-owner: Monticello is grand and pragmatic at the same time. *©Buddy Mays/Corbis*

Creating a National Identity

Like other nascent world powers making their debut before it, the United States initially appropriated authority by using the architectural forms and symbols it knew best and coveted most—most notably British Neoclassicism. But as a product of the late 18th-century Enlightenment—a philosophical and intellectual movement that expounded upon the ideals of freedom, justice, and human rights—the young nation borrowed these Neoclassical prototypes with the hope that their Periclean origins would best convey the new country's democratic intentions to the rest of the world.

Thomas Jefferson, who so eloquently described the aspirations of the new nation in its Declaration of Independence, capitalized on his knowledge of architecture to promote a national image of stability, equality, and innovation. Although Jefferson participated in the planning and design of many projects, his intention to reinterpret the subliminal message of Palladian Classicism from a colonial metaphor to a symbol for freedom from foreign rule is most evident in the design of his own home, Monticello, the centerpiece of his 5,000-acre plantation near Charlottesville, Virginia. Its name alone, which means "little mountain" in Italian, reflects his broad, independent, international view. In the house itself, Jefferson domesticated—through both scale and detail—what had previously been a stuffy formal Georgian style in Britain. His audacious use of Classical elements clearly conveys his intention to be as stylistically free of past architectural constraints as he wanted his new nation to be politically free from its colonial master. Monticello, like America itself, was a work in progress from the start. Construction started in 1768, but its signature dome and portico, inspired by the Pantheon in Rome as well as several Palladian villas that Jefferson had seen in his travels, was only completed in 1809.

The White House by James Hoban, completed in 1801, and the U.S. Capitol by William Thornton, Benjamin Latrobe, and Charles Bulfinch, finished 30 years later, are also overtly Neoclassical. Today, these two edifices remain closely associated with the focal point of U.S. power, but Monticello more accurately represents the true spirit of the nation's youth and its attempt to establish proud traditions of its own.

President George Washington chose James Hoban, an Irish-born architect living in South Caroline, to design the "President's House." Hoban based his design for the White House (1801) on Dublin's Leinster House, today the seat of the Irish parliament. *©Carol Highsmith*

Industry and Institutions

In addition to inspiring American independence, the Enlightenment also promoted scientific investigation, which ultimately resulted in the Industrial Revolution. This dynamic period of social upheaval began in earnest in the United States at the beginning of the 19th century. It was first evident in the Northeast, with the start-up of textile factories in Massachusetts similar to those in cities throughout the United Kingdom. This second, economically based revolution quickly expanded into other products and regions, producing a wealthy upper class and a demand for social and residential settings deemed appropriate for its luxurious new lifestyle. The Industrial Revolution also produced burgeoning middle and lower classes and, as cities grew, a parallel need for civic institutions to represent an expanding population. In this environment, architects were faced with the unprecedented challenge of designing new building types, such as city halls, railway terminals, department stores, and warehouses.

Americans once again turned to European precedents, particularly those provided by the Ecole des Beaux-Arts in Paris, to satisfy these new social needs. The Ecole, which represents the first organized attempt at architectural education, was founded during the ancien régime to provide a convenient pool of designers for royal projects. The design curriculum was based almost entirely on classical principles, and the few students admitted in the beginning had aristocratic backgrounds. After the French Revolution, Napoleon rejected demands from those who called for the abolition of the Ecole des Beaux-Arts because of its royal associations, deciding instead to make it more accessible. Although admission was made easier, the program became more rigorous, so that many students dropped out after the first year.

The Ecole was opened up rather late and only selectively to foreign students, including several Americans who went on to become famous proponents of its approach. These included Henry Hobson Richardson and Julia Morgan. Richardson's Trinity Church (1877) in Boston typifies the grandiose, eclectic, historicist characteristics of the Beaux-Arts tradition. His trademark, however, is his skill in seamlessly synthesizing recognizable stylistic influences from the past into an imposing new presence. For example, his Marshall Field warehouse (1887) in Chicago, derived from a Florentine palazzo layered with various Italianate elements, set the precedent for the massive bases of office buildings that would soon be erected in cities all over the country.

Julia Morgan's achievements—of being the first woman admitted into the Ecole, surviving its rigorous requirements, and then opening and managing her own firm in the San Francisco Bay Area—cannot be overestimated, especially considering when she accomplished them. She also managed to successfully cope with extremely demanding clients such as William Randolph Hearst, miraculously making the Hearst Castle in San Simeon, near San Francisco, reflect her own aesthetic as well as that of the notorious press baron.

Julia Morgan's work on William Randolph Hearst's San Simeon ranch began in 1919 and continued for the next 28 years. He asked her to design "something that would be more comfortable" than the platform tents he used on the site. *Marc Wanamaker/Bison Archives*

H. H. Richardson's design for Trinity Church (1872–77), Boston, embodied a unique style, radical for its time, that became known as Richardsonian Romanesque. *©Wayne Andrews/Esto*

In his 1896 essay "The Tall Office Building Artistically Considered," Louis Sullivan stipulated that a skyscraper should "soar," breaking free of the purely pragmatic concerns of his contemporaries. His intentions are most clear in the Carson Pirie Scott store constructed in Chicago in 1899. This building represents an elegant resolution of all the issues that had preoccupied those involved in designing this form during the previous 20 years. *Copy of historic photo, Historic American Buildings Survey, Library of Congress*

The first step toward the skyscrapers of today was taken after the Civil War by William Le Baron Jenney, who devised a fireproofing method for use in tall buildings. Underwriters endorsed two Jenney designs erected in Chicago using this method; pictured is the Second Leiter Building, built in 1891. The insurers' acceptance of these buildings instigated a boom in steel tower construction. *Cervin Robinson, Historic American Buildings Survey, Library of Congress*

(Opposite) In the final two decades of the 19th century, Chicago was a vibrant testing ground for new ideas that would eventually result in the uniquely American typology of the skyscraper. Burnham and Root's Reliance Building, completed in Chicago in 1895, is the epitome of the new steel towers made possible by advances in engineering. *Copy of photogrammetric plate, Historic American Buildings Survey, Library of Congress*

A Race for the Sky

Economic differences between states above and below the Mason-Dixon line developed because of different attitudes toward the introduction, pace, and application of technology as opposed to the continued use of human labor, which had been institutionalized as slavery. These differences led to civil war and "reconstruction" in the South. Industrial development continued unabated in the North, however, as did the westward expansion of the American frontier. The latter was fueled by the transcontinental railroad, which rapidly increased the growth of cities such as Chicago, St. Louis, Kansas City, and San Francisco. The headlong pace of change, as well as the brash, edgy attitude that it inspired, encouraged invention—and architects and engineers put convention aside to join in the fray. James Borgardus, who was initially apprenticed to a watchmaker, invented a chronometer, cotton spinner, grinding mill, and engraving machine before turning his attention to the potential of cast iron. His five-story factory, built entirely of this material in New York City in 1847, one of the first metal structures of its kind in the world, eventually led to the use of his cast-iron system throughout the country.

It soon became apparent, however, that such buildings were just as prone to destruction by fire as wooden structures. In fact, they were even more dangerous because their increased bearing capacity and the invention of the Otis elevator in the late 1800s allowed greater height. Disastrous fires in Chicago and San Francisco intensified interest in a solution to the problem of fireproofing tall cast-iron and, later, steel buildings, which quickly began to replace cast-iron structures once the Bessemer process of mass-producing steel had been perfected.

Civil War veteran William Le Baron Jenney devised a way of wrapping steel columns, girders, and joists in ceramic tile. This fireproofing method received underwriter endorsement in the first and second Leiter Buildings, two department stores built between 1879 and 1891 in Chicago. Its acceptance unleashed a frenzy of steel-tower construction, culminating in the Reliance Building of 1895 by Daniel Burnham and John Root in the same city. The entire evolution of the building type is visible in another Chicago landmark, the Monadnock Building. Designed and built in two phases, the proto-skyscraper's northern half (by Burnham and Root, 1889–91) features load-bearing walls that are 6 feet 4 inches thick at street level; its southern half (by Holabird and Roche, 1891–93) was erected with a steel frame that eliminates the need for such a massive base. By the time Louis Sullivan had realized his iconic Carson Pirie Scott department store in Chicago in 1899, the technological knowledge to build tall buildings was finally at hand. Using steel frame and spandrels, flat white cladding, and what has come to be called the "Chicago window" (a long triptych of two casement units flanking a central fixed-glass panel), Sullivan resolved many issues that had been involved in development of the skyscraper and, as a result, created a truly American building type.

A Righteous Reaction

The extreme and highly visible social cost of industrialization in England included dislocation due to rural-urban migration, poverty and homelessness, alcoholism, drug addiction, prostitution, crime, and disease. A slow but eventually vigorous and passionate response was finally organized by Victorian intellectuals such as A. W. N. Pugin, Thomas Carlyle, John Ruskin, and William Morris. Their respective stances appeared in the mid- to late 19th century, primarily in books and lectures. Each of these men approached the problem of social injustice differently, but they agreed on the idea that human identity was sacrosanct and that the physiological well-being of the worker was paramount in the manufacturing process. They also agreed that handcraft must play a fundamental role in industrial production, so that laborers would not just be babysitters to machines.

Although the same economic and social issues that these British reformers were battling contributed to the Civil War in the United States, the theoretical and subsequent architectural response to such conditions was not as virulent here. Company towns and garden cities were built in the United States, to be sure, but not to the extent they were in Britain. In addition, the American versions lacked the moralistic and socialistic framework of a Port Sunlight or Letchworth in England. There is a distinctly free, unfettered flavor to the architecture produced by those sympathetic to the Arts and Crafts movement in America. Poet Ralph Waldo Emerson and other proponents of American Transcendentalism echoed the movement's ideals, which received an enthusiastic reception, especially in areas farther away from the heavily industrialized East Coast.

Louis Sullivan and his protégé, Frank Lloyd Wright—two leaders of the Chicago School—championed the Arts and Crafts approach and attempted to find a balance between mechanization and nature, progress and tradition. At Carson Pirie Scott, for example, Sullivan insisted on using his trademark castings of organic, vegetal patterns on the street-level elevation before shifting, on the upper floors, to what is now considered the most advanced rendition of its time of an emerging Modern aesthetic.

Wright picked up where his "Liebermeister" had left off, in the design of his own overtly Arts and Crafts house and studio in Oak Park, Illinois, in the late 1880s. This was followed by the controlled evolution of what he called the Prairie Style house, based on a Japanese teahouse he and Sullivan had seen at the 1893 World's Columbian Exposition. The teahouse initiated Wright's lifelong relationship with Japan. In selecting such a prototype for his residential model, Wright aligned himself with Charles Rennie Mackintosh and Mackay Hugh Baillie Scott. These British Arts and Crafts architects were equally impressed by the effortless affinity with nature represented by this Asian tradition, which was introduced to the West after Admiral Perry's opening of Japan for trade in the 1880s.

Architects in the Bay Area, including Bernard Maybeck and Julia Morgan, were also influenced by the ideals of the Arts and Crafts. The Japanese influence of the movement had an obvious effect on Southern California architects Charles and Henry Greene, evinced in such exquisitely handcrafted examples as the Blacker (1907) and Gamble (1908) houses, both in Pasadena. Greene and Greene's eloquent renditions along the West Coast demonstrate the pervasive impact this hybrid style had in the United States by the end of the 19th century.

(Opposite) There are no better examples of the pervasive influence of the British Arts and Crafts movement in America than the work of California architects Charles and Henry Greene, and the Gamble House is their masterpiece. This hand-carved redwood jewel, built in 1908, clearly reflects the interest in traditional Japanese architecture that resulted after trade with Japan was opened in the late 19th century. The warm, dry climate of Southern California prompted the Greene brothers to use wide, overhanging eaves and deep verandas, blurring the boundary between inside and outside. *Ezra Stoller/©Esto*

Frank Lloyd Wright's Arts and Crafts–inspired house and studio, built in Oak Park, Illinois, in the late 1880s, was a step in the development of what he called the Prairie Style. *Philip Turner, Historic American Buildings Survey, Library of Congress*

The Renewed Promise of Progress

French influence, which began with bedrock Enlightenment ideals in America and was later reinforced by Ecole des Beaux-Arts institutional and educational models, continued in the popularity of the Art Deco style immediately following World War I. This trend, named after the Exposition des Arts Décoratifs held in Paris in 1925, provided a refreshing alternative to the recent experience of the horrors that technology could cause. When combined with the compelling image of speed suggested by its streamlined design, the style's angular energy reminded people of the initial promise of scientific progress, making it exciting once again.

The Paris exposition was held in the middle of the roaring '20s, a hedonistic time in which pre–World War I social restrictions seemed pointless in light of the unprecedented death and destruction of the war. Taking their cue from the sinuous, natural forms of the earlier Art Nouveau style, the curators of the exposition collected work that captured the spirit of the times, seductively amalgamating individual freedom of expression with a machine aesthetic.

At the same time, the 1922 discovery of the tomb of King Tutankhamen in Luxor, Egypt, with its virtually intact artifacts, caused an international sensation that whetted the public's appetite for the exotic and influenced the organizers of the exposition. Architects, as well, were inspired to adopt motifs from this ancient world, whose luxurious and pleasure-loving side had only recently come to light.

Although wonderful examples of the Art Deco style are scattered throughout the United States, four classic case studies are located on the East Coast. The Chrysler Building (1928) in New York City, by William Van Alen, epitomizes the movement's egalitarian appeal; owner Walter Chrysler worked his way up from the machine-shop floor to found one of the largest auto companies in the nation. The skyscraper's arched, radiating sunburst spire, hood-ornament gargoyles, and hubcap friezes are a nostalgic reminder of a time when the idea of progress had real meaning. New York's Empire State Building (1931), by Shreve, Lamb and Harmon, also has sunburst motifs as well as the metalwork and curving forms we now identify with Art Deco. In addition, its interior lobby walls are covered with murals that glorify human endeavor through scientific advancement.

The best example of the application of Art Deco design principles at an urban scale is also in New York City. Planned by Raymond Hood between 1932 and 1940 but added to up through the 1970s, Rockefeller Center is a civic contribution of incomparable skill. Composed of 19 buildings that create an intimately scaled series of open spaces among them, the center is an attempt by its planner and his philanthropic client to prove that modernity and humanity need not be mutually exclusive—and it succeeds in doing so.

George Howe and William Lescaze managed to convey this same delicate balance in their Philadelphia Savings Fund Society building in 1929. From the time of its construction until the early 1980s—a period during which an unspoken agreement was honored not to build higher than the hat of Alexander Milne Calder's William Penn atop City Hall—the gently curving profile of the PSFS tower had a civic stature almost equal to that of Calder's sculptural masterpiece nearby. But pent-up commercial pressure to build higher finally proved too strong: new, taller towers, along with its extensive conversion into a hotel, have severely weakened the symbolic, streamlined power of this Art Deco icon.

The stock market crash of 1929, followed by the Depression and World War II, put an abrupt end to optimism about the future and the Art Deco style that symbolized it. A concerted effort by the leaders of the Modern movement in Europe, followed by those in America, would be required to bring back faith in progress.

(Opposite) The frenetic growth of American industry in the decade or so after World War I saw numerous rags-to-riches stories. The saga of Walter Chrysler, who began on the machine-shop floor and later founded one of the most successful automobile companies in America, has become entrenched in national mythology. It is appropriate that architect William Van Alen, designer of the Chrysler headquarters in New York City, expressed Chrysler's success using Art Deco forms, as the style was closely associated with industrial and scientific progress. *©Carol Highsmith*

Rockefeller Center in New York City, planned by architect Raymond Hood during the Depression, is a showcase of Art Deco design principles on an urban scale. The complex, ultimately 19 buildings connected by a series of intimately scaled open spaces, was intended to demonstrate that modernity could be executed on a human scale. Pictured is the GE Building (originally the RCA Building), built in 1931–33. *Samuel H. Gottscho, Gottscho-Schleisner Collection, Library of Congress*

Modernism: American Precedents

The reductivist and semiotically anonymous style that we now refer to as High Modernism was arguably introduced in the United States by German émigrés, such as Walter Gropius and Ludwig Mies van der Rohe, just before World War II. But history, of course, is never that simple. In truth, a healthy, homegrown variant was already well established when they arrived. The indigenous strain started in the late 19th century with the construction of steel skyscrapers and the recognition of a unified, technologically based ethos tempered by humanistic concerns. This approach spawned the aforementioned Chicago School, which was thriving when the foreign influence arrived.

Rudolf Schindler built the Kings Road House in West Hollywood for himself, his wife, and another family. Completed in 1922, the house integrated indoor and outdoor space and contributed to the development of a unique California residential style.
©*Tim Street Porter/Esto*

The evolution of Frank Lloyd Wright's architecture reflects the same transformation of Arts and Crafts principles into Modernist values that took place in Britain and Germany in the middle of the 20th century: A reformist reaction to industrial production became a deliberate decision to amalgamate craftsmanship with mechanical fabrication. Wright referred to this antithesis as "Art and the Machine," and his entire *oeuvre* may be characterized as his personal attempt to come to terms with it.

This American version of Modernism reached its peak in 1936 with Wright's **Fallingwater**, near Pittsburgh. Here, Wright balanced the artistic side of the equation, represented by the stone that was taken from the site and applied to all vertical elements, with the mechanical side, which took the form of the dwelling's horizontal, reinforced concrete decks.

Wright also played an important part in promoting the careers of two other, earlier proponents of Modern architecture in America, although his motive in doing so was not entirely altruistic. Viennese architect R. M. Schindler immigrated to the United States in 1914 and worked for Wright in Oak Park and at Taliesin in Spring Green, Wisconsin. In December 1920 Wright sent him to Los Angeles to supervise construction of the Hollyhock House for Aline Barnsdall. Richard Neutra came to the United States in 1923, worked for Wright at Taliesin in 1924, and arrived in Los Angeles in 1925 at Schindler's invitation. Wright promoted the work of both young architects until around 1930, when, without much work himself, he felt that Schindler's and Neutra's successes were beginning to eclipse his own.

The extent of Rudolf Schindler's influence on the course of early Modernism along the West Coast is only beginning to be fully understood. Soon after his arrival in Los Angeles, he designed a two-family house on **Kings Road** for himself and his wife, Sophie Gibling, and for engineer Clyde Chace and his wife. Inspired by Yosemite, which he and his wife had recently visited, Schindler wanted to reproduce in microcosm the feeling of being at one with nature. He accomplished this by providing an exterior garden component of comparable size for each of the four main spaces in the house (individually allocated to one of the four co-owners). This balance of inside and outside space and the repetitive L-shaped plan, which accommodated sufficient privacy, became a model for many other West Coast Modernists.

Soon after Fallingwater was completed and Wright's intentional *riposte* to Le Corbusier's Villa Savoye had appeared on the cover of *Time* magazine as a singular American achievement, messianic émigrés Walter Gropius and Ludwig Mies van der Rohe arrived in the United States. Gropius had relocated from Germany to become chairman of the Graduate School of Design at Harvard in 1937 and remained there until 1952. During that time, he completely revamped the curriculum to conform to a more ahistorical, antithetical educational model based in Modernist theory. His compatriot, Mies van der Rohe, accepted an equally influential post at the Armour Institute, later the Illinois Institute of Technology (IIT), in Chicago in 1938, where he remained until 1958. From these two powerful positions, Gropius and Mies subsequently redirected the course of American architecture.

High Modernism's European Roots

The Modernist credo that Gropius, Mies, and other German disciples brought with them to the United States had been fueled by industrial competition between European countries. As early as the 1890s, a powerful faction in the German government began to believe that Germany would be able to surpass the manufacturing prowess of the United Kingdom if it could emulate the principles of the Arts and Crafts movement. German envoy and architect Hermann Muthesius maintained that Arts and Crafts architects such as Charles Rennie Mackintosh had succeeded in synthesizing the reflexive or automated character of industrialization with the humanistic ethos of a more idyllic, preindustrial age, thereby allowing the British to fully exploit the new means of production.

(Opposite) Fallingwater, a weekend house near Pittsburgh, is the perfect realization of Frank Lloyd Wright's long search for a way to integrate architecture with nature. The house remains one of the best examples of the balance between artistry and technology that embodies the concept of organic architecture espoused by Wright and others.
Jack E. Boucher, Historic American Buildings Survey, Library of Congress

Gropius, along with Muthesius and others, was instrumental in launching a government-sponsored association, called the *Werkbund*, to help make Germany more competitive. The long-term goal was to systematically educate all citizens so they would be involved in some aspect of industrial design or at least become an informed consumer.

The house Mies van der Rohe designed for Dr. Edith Farnsworth in Plano, Illinois, completed in 1951, is an icon of Modernist domestic architecture. *Jack E. Boucher, Historic American Buildings Survey, Library of Congress*

The structure that Gropius conceived to house the *Werkbund* was symbolically anonymous, deliberately free of anything that might be interpreted as a historical style. Its Arts and Crafts roots, however, are evident in his determination to have form follow function, to use materials in ways that are true to their essential character, and to demonstrate craft through detailing. The moralistic implications inherent in the Arts and Crafts approach became more crystallized in this streamlined iteration; its transformation into Modernist principles required the adoption of metaphorical neutrality to fully erase any signs of social status. Rather than fondly regarding historical style as a tangible record of cultural tradition, Modernists disdainfully viewed it as irrefutable evidence of the exploitation of the poor by the rich because, they argued, only the upper class could afford to build durable monuments that would survive the ravages of time and remain as a historical record of the past.

Industrial materials were believed to offer a neutral means of architectural expression, appropriate for a bright, new, egalitarian future free of stratified economic associations. Telluric materials, such as timber, brick, and stone, were shunned because they were reminders of the past. Glass was singled out as especially symbolic of the Modernist ideals of equality, transparency, and social well-being.

Immediately after World War I, in which both Gropius and Mies fought, the *Werkbund* experiment was reconfigured into the Bauhaus, first based in Weimar in 1919 and then moved to Dessau. Gropius was its founder and first director. His mission, now more focused than before the war, was to use this institution to improve the lot of his fellow citizens by helping to rebuild his defeated nation through industrial development and design excellence. This vision, which had its own political implications, is evident in the manifestos he published to accompany the founding of the Bauhaus. In the school's first catalog, for example, Gropius wrote: "Together let us desire, conceive and create a new structure of the future, which will embrace architecture and sculpture and painting in one unity and which will one day rise toward heaven from the hands of a million workers like the crystal symbol of a new faith."

Back in the United States: Minimalism without Ideology

The structure Gropius was referring to, of course, was political, and Modern architecture was to be the phalanx in the epic struggle to build a new political order. This ideological implication, however, was not readily apparent to many of the American architects who so readily adopted the physical aspects of Modernism or to the students faced with the new educational doctrine that quickly replaced existing Beaux-Arts curricula. Many were simply attracted to the freedom that Modernism represented: Its minimalist simplicity was a welcome relief from prewar social conventions and the traditional architectural forms and materials that represented and sustained them. The cataclysmic events witnessed abroad by veterans returning from both world wars and the sacrifice, anxiety, deprivation, and tragedy experienced by those who had remained behind fed a national desire for change.

The period just before and immediately after World War II was a heady time for Modernists in America. Philip Johnson was in the center of the action, taking on the role of tastemaker, a role he would not relinquish until his death, at 99, in 2005. Johnson, director of the department of architecture at the Museum of Modern Art in New York, and architectural historian Henry-Russell Hitchcock believed they had discovered a groundswell of support in Europe and America for Modernism, based on formal similarities they had identified in a group of architects from both continents. They gathered such projects together for a 1932 MoMA exhibition, which was accompanied by a publication titled *The International Style*. The name stuck.

After receiving a BArch degree from Harvard in 1943, Johnson built a house for himself on his estate in New Canaan, Connecticut. Built in 1949, it was called the Glass House because of its extensive use of that material to create complete transparency. This, along with the 1951 Farnsworth House in Plano, Illinois, by Mies van der Rohe, and the 1958 Seagram Building in New York City, on which the two collaborated, may be considered the apogee of High Modernism in America. Lever House, designed by Gordon Bunshaft of Skidmore, Owings & Merrill in 1952, was also pivotal, as it marked the beginning of the standardization of the style in its high-rise tower format and its acceptance by corporate America as a symbol of businesslike efficiency.

The 1958 Seagram Building owes its elegant profile to a strategic approach to New York's zoning restrictions. Philip Johnson and Ludwig Mies van der Rohe were able to make this Modernist tower higher by convincing the Bronfman family to give over a major portion of this expensive Park Avenue site to public use. *Ezra Stoller/©Esto*

1867
AIA New York, the first AIA
chapter, chartered on March 19

First formal AIA convention, from
which all other conventions are
numbered, held in New York City,
October 22–23

Gordon Bunshaft was responsible for many of Skidmore,
Owings & Merrill's outstanding works in the early years of the
firm. The Lever House, however, stands out as his most important
contribution. The design of this International Style skyscraper,
completed in Manhattan in 1952, marks the point at which corporate
America adopted Modernism. Bunshaft's treatment of the blue-
green glass skin as a curtain wall gives the tower a crisp, clean
image. *Peter Mauss/ ©Esto*

Late Modern: Louis Kahn and the Philadelphia School

By the end of the 1950s, the strict dogma that once surrounded the Modern movement had begun to erode. While several important architects, including Philip Johnson, William Pereria, and Paul Rudolph, may be identified as representative of what is now referred to as the late Modern phase of the movement, Louis Kahn figured most prominently in this transitional period.

Although the number of buildings Kahn actually completed was relatively small, his contribution to the history of American architecture was substantial. He alone is now seen as the protean challenger to the enormous influence of leading Modernist Le Corbusier. Both architects had initially paid their metaphorical Modernist dues by adhering to the purist, scientific side of the rationalist tradition within the movement. Both had conscientiously tried to improve the general social welfare by taking on prototypical projects to help the less fortunate. Each also had the opportunity to plan a large capital city in a developing nation, although Le Corbusier's intentions for Chandigarh, India, eventually progressed much further than Kahn's hopes for Dhaka, Bangladesh.

What separates these two great architects, however, is Kahn's profound love of history. It is true that Le Corbusier made lyrical references to the Parthenon, the Hagia Sophia, and other ancient buildings in his influential book *Towards a New Architecture*, published in 1923, in which he showed how he had extrapolated key proportional principles from them. Nonetheless, his worldview essentially aligned with other early European Modernists who viewed history as an embarrassing, tectonic record of class struggle. His plans for Paris (1925) and for St. Dié (1946–48), for example, are each based on the complete destruction of major parts of existing, historically significant cities.

Perhaps because of his background, Kahn was more sensitive to the significance of the past. He was born in Estonia, and his family immigrated to Philadelphia when he was very young. He did not return to Europe until 1928, after he graduated from the University of Pennsylvania in his early twenties. His copious sketchbooks and notebooks from subsequent trips show that he reacted to everything he saw with the objectivity and enthusiasm of someone coming from a young culture but also with a deeper, preexisting set of sensibilities. Greece and Italy especially impressed him, inspiring what was to become a lifelong, almost mystical exploration of the characteristics of natural light. He also found he had an affinity for massive structures, such as ancient Roman theaters, bathhouses, and aqueducts. When Le Corbusier announced in the mid-1950s that the time had come for a movement away from purism and minimalism in Modern architecture toward monumentality, Kahn was not far behind.

Lured away from Yale by G. Holmes Perkins, dean of what was then the School of Fine Arts at the University of Pennsylvania, Kahn returned to his alma mater to teach in 1955. A Modernist visionary, Perkins had previously served as chair at Harvard when its architecture program was still based on the Beaux-Arts system. There, he implemented a cross-disciplinary curriculum in which students were exposed to an equal number of courses in architecture,

By the mid- to late 1950s, Modernism had run its meteoric course in America. The style had become devalued: complex details, once custom crafted, became standardized in the hands of less talented designers. When Louis Kahn's Richards Medical Research Building (1957–61) appeared in Philadelphia, it gave Modernism a fresh, more substantial face. The design of the laboratory towers adheres to principles such as the unmistakable expression of function and structure, which Kahn clarified by separating elements into what he called "served and servant spaces." At the same time, historical references to Italian towers and use of brick give Kahn's structures a strong appeal. *Bettmann/Corbis*

In his design for the Salk Institute in La Jolla, California, built from 1959 to 1965, Louis Kahn foreshadowed the Postmodernism that took over soon after his death. The Salk demonstrates his idea of layering, a concept at odds with the Modernist rule that form follows function. *Ezra Stoller/©Esto*

1868
America's first school of
architecture opened at MIT,
under William Robert Ware

Highest class of AIA
membership—Fellow of the
American Institute of Architects—
established on June 2

landscape architecture, and urban planning. He believed that professional integration would promote Modernist ideology, which would, in turn, trigger comprehensive social change. Perkins implemented this same idea at Penn, also a Beaux-Arts institution when he arrived. The appointments Perkins made, representing all design disciplines, now read like a who's-who of Modernist leadership in America at the time.

Perkins continued as dean of the Graduate School of Fine Arts at Penn until 1971; Kahn died in 1978. During the roughly two decades that each was in a position of prominence at the school, it achieved the stature that Perkins had sought: Penn became the hotbed of what the press dubbed the Philadelphia School. If the Chicago School had centered around Frank Lloyd Wright, this later, East Coast counterpart was equally identified with Kahn.

Paving the Way for Postmodernism

Kahn's position as a modern rationalist is fairly well understood, but his role as an enabler of the Postmodern movement that was to crest soon after his death is less so. The social upheaval that occurred in America in the 1960s—fed by the profound coincidence of several factors, such as the Cold War, Civil Rights movement, Vietnam War, and increasing awareness of the growing threat of environmental degradation—was paralleled by an upheaval in architecture. Postmodernism marked the beginning of the loss of innocence in America—the point at which idealism was replaced by cynicism and sincerity became infected by irony. A growing distrust of authority and institutions was magnified by an increasingly prevalent media. This attitude was accompanied by, or symptomatic of, an increasing acceptance of plurality in the nation as well as a concomitant rise of interest in origins.

Kahn's background and multivalent passions made him the perfect arbiter of change. His Richards Medical Research Laboratory, completed between 1957 and 1965 on the University of Pennsylvania campus, clearly demonstrates his love of history: Its soaring vertical forms are inspired by the hill town of San Gimignano, which he had visited on successive trips to Italy. Further prompted by historical precedents as well as his strong interest in modulating natural light, he introduced the idea of layering, which he called "wrapping ruins around buildings," in the library for Phillips Exeter Academy (1972) in Exeter, New Hampshire; the Salk Institute (1959–65) in La Jolla, California; and Sher-e-Bangla Nagar (1962–83) in Dhaka, Bangladesh, among other examples. This design approach countermanded a basic Modernist rule that the skin of a structure should be as transparent as possible so as not to obscure the building's function.

Seeing the potential of aligning this idea of layering with subliminal communication, Robert Venturi took it further. His 1964 house for his mother, Vanna, in Chestnut Hill, near Philadelphia, continues Kahn's use of historical reference. Venturi, however, referred to American sources as the paradigm of shelter, such as McKim, Mead and White's Low House, rather than foreign ones. But more significantly, the Vanna Venturi House marks one of the first attempts to use surface as a message board to establish a dialogue between architect and viewer. Defining his approach as a "decorated shed," Venturi and his partner Denise Scott Brown made a case for inclusivity rather than aloofness. In collaboration with Steven Izenour, they made the then-iconoclastic proposal in *Learning from Las Vegas* (1972) that—rather than rejecting it outright—architects should try to learn why the popular taste epitomized by Las Vegas appeals to the public. Their instincts were reflected in a growing realization that Modernism was too hermetic and, as a result, had alienated people.

Sher-e-Bangla Nagar (1962–83), the capital complex in Dhaka, Bangladesh, also exhibits layering, which Kahn called "wrapping ruins around buildings." ©Roberto Schezen/Esto

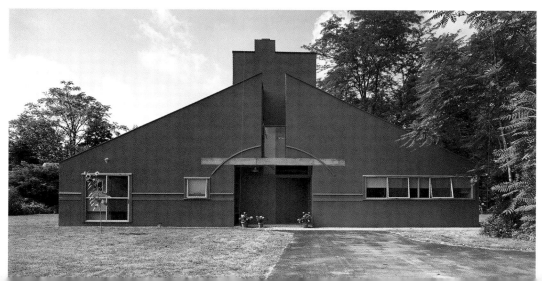

Sited at the end of a quiet street in the upscale Philadelphia community of Chestnut Hill and backing up to Fairmount Park, the house Robert Venturi designed for his mother typifies his idea of a "decorated shed." The elevation facing the street, with its triangular gable form and chimney, is like a diagram of elemental shelter reminiscent of "a child's drawing of a house." From the park side of the house, it is apparent the facade is just a billboard signifying domesticity, with a much smaller house hiding behind it. ©Bill Maris/Esto

1869
*Founding of the Philadelphia and
Chicago chapters of the AIA*

The Whites versus the Grays

The rift that Venturi and Scott Brown opened was formalized in a taking of sides in what has subsequently become known as the battle of the Whites, or Modernists, against the Grays, or Postmodernists. The Whites, who took their name from their affinity with Le Corbusier and his hue of choice, were led by Peter Eisenman, Michael Graves, Charles Gwathmey, John Hejduk, and Richard Meier. These five were canonized in a book titled *Five Architects*, which focused on their collective belief in Corbusian principles, including his five-points system of grid, free plan, free elevation, strip window, and roof garden. The Grays were led by Venturi and Scott Brown. Clearly differentiating them from the purist approach, their moniker also alluded to the gray, cardboard-like quality of the surface of Vanna Venturi's house, which had come to symbolize their position.

During this period of schism, which lasted from the mid-1960s until the late 1980s, there were several notable defections—most notoriously Michael Graves of the New York Five and Philip Johnson, the Modernist proselytizer himself. When Graves's highly decorated Portland Public Service Building appeared in Oregon in 1982, criticism was widespread among architects, who bemoaned its historicism and eccentricity. But, when Johnson's AT&T building was completed six years later—with its so-called Chippendale-chair roofline— outrage was replaced by resignation: If the person who had introduced Modernism and the International Style to the United States said things should change, then they must. Following this unmistakable sign of conversion, Johnson generated several more equally discursive projects: Transco Tower (Houston, 1983), inspired by Amsterdam town houses; RepublicBank Center (Houston, 1984); and PPG Place (Pittsburgh, 1984), both of which were informed by the Gothic cathedral.

Deconstructivism: A Growing Distrust in Communication

But the Postmodern experiment, too, would run its course. By 1990, there was a growing conviction that it had failed to realize its proponents' objective of restoring historical authority and humanity to architecture. In an article titled "Plus Ça Change," Robert Venturi declared that Postmodernism had been unable to communicate with the public, ending instead as an in-joke among architects.

Venturi's disappointment in the inability of Postmodern architecture to meaningfully connect with the public was followed by an even more negative reading of society's current condition by Peter Eisenman of New York Five fame. Eisenman, who identified the work of philosopher Jacques Derrida as having the power to express that failure best, spearheaded the Deconstructivist movement, which dominated the architecture scene throughout the 1990s.

Derrida disputed Structuralist linguistic theory, which held that all human beings, regardless of cultural background, have the internal capacity for common communication. Instead, his theory of deconstruction proposed that perfect communication is impossible and that people must use other techniques, such as the interpretation of body language and reading between the lines of what someone says or writes, to determine true meaning. Eisenman's Wexner Center (1989) in Columbus, Ohio, is intended to be a physical interpretation of Derrida's linguistic theory.

(Opposite) Some architects criticized Michael Graves's Portland Public Service Building in Oregon for its historicism and eccentricity. The building, completed in 1982, came at the end of a two-decade controversy among prominent architects—those who clung to the tenets of Modernism and those who took up the banner of Postmodernism. ©*Peter Aaron/Esto*

Peter Eisenman intended his 1989 design for the Wexner Center for the Visual Arts at Ohio State University to be a literal translation of Deconstructivist theory as defined by French theorist Jacques Derrida, who maintains that all communication is flawed and destined for misunderstanding. In Eisenman's skillful and intentionally imperfect translation, a fragmented structural grid intervenes between two existing institutional structures, apparently leading nowhere. ©*Herb Levart/SuperStock*

The ethics of the New Urbanist movement are clearly revealed in the 80-acre community of Seaside, Florida, designed in 1989 by architects Andrés Duany and Elizabeth Plater-Zyberk. New Urbanist principles call for the development of design guidelines that stem from a particular community's vernacular architecture. For Seaside, this meant adopting ideas from historic houses in the nearby town of Grayton Beach, as well as from relevant regional influences such as Charleston, South Carolina; Key West; and the French Quarter of New Orleans. The relatively small community, which began with 350 detached houses and 300 additional dwelling units, was one of the first New Urbanist initiatives. *Peter Aaron/Esto*

(Opposite) At Pugh + Scarpa's 2004 Solar Umbrella House, Venice, California, passive and active solar design strategies make the house energy neutral. Recycled, renewable, and high-performance materials were used throughout. The project received a 2007 Institute Honor Award for Architecture. *Marvin Rand, courtesy Pugh + Scarpa Architects*

The Death of Theory

Following the abstract, theory-based adventure of Deconstructivism, which seemed nihilistic to many, architects have turned once again to more positive, socially beneficial approaches, enthusiastically embracing possibility and diversity. In addition, many architects seem to be pushing back against the commodification cycle, in which *isms* become *wasms* with increasing speed, by rejecting brands and labels.

Several promising directions are now being followed, in stark contrast to the restrictions enforced by stylistic dictates in the recent past. One of these is sustainable design, which is free of theoretical interpretation because it is relevant as a real-world alternative to the rapidly growing problem of environmental degradation. Several innovative architects, such as the Los Angeles firm of Pugh + Scarpa, are moving past stereotypical installations of energy-saving devices such as solar panels to find new and exciting applications for them. Another is New Urbanism, which began as an entirely American initiative and now has thousands of signatories to its manifesto from all over the world. The New Urbanists have attacked urban degradation and suburban sprawl, as well as the environmental repercussions of each, by working to revise segregated zoning laws that prevent mixed use and promote commuting. In doing so, they have addressed the root cause of isolation at the level of politics and policy. Most recently, in the wake of the destruction caused by hurricane Katrina in 2005, the leaders of several affected Gulf Coast cities, including Biloxi, approached the New Urbanists to help plan and rebuild their devastated cities. The New Urbanists' first steps were to hold charrettes in each of the affected cities, involving as many citizens as possible, and to develop a pattern book based on past vernacular typologies to guide future design. Like sustainable design, New Urbanism has also endured because it has effectively answered real needs, even though its founders' proclivity for historical typologies has been controversial.

In addition, the digital revolution has profoundly changed the way in which architects work, helping to feed the vitality and multivalence that is so palpable in the field today. Frank Gehry has described computer technology, and the digital tools that dramatically improve efficiency and accuracy, as a second chance for architects to reclaim the leadership role they were in danger of forfeiting by becoming too effete and unrealistic.

Nearly two centuries since Jefferson completed Monticello, idealism seems respectable once again, after being denigrated by the *fashionistas* for so long. Proof positive of its return is the high regard with which architecture students and professionals alike hold the efforts of Samuel Mockbee and the Rural Studio, which he cofounded with Dennis K. Ruth at the Auburn University College of Architecture. The home base for the studio is 160 miles from the campus in the small town of Newbern, in Hale County, Alabama, one of the poorest regions in the United States. The studio is based on the premise of providing students with hands-on involvement in the building process while working within a severely restricted budget to help the most disadvantaged. Mockbee also wanted to return architecture to its community roots, believing that when people are given priority, economic considerations are somehow dealt with. He used materials at hand, such as salvaged wood and metal and similar bits and pieces that other architects would not consider suitable, to help the poor families in that region. For example, car windows were reused in the main elevation of the community center the Rural Studio designed for tiny Mason's Bend, Alabama. Mockbee did not believe that his choice of materials justified a lowering of aesthetic standards but rather that it made a higher level of inventiveness necessary.

The United States is a nation in flux, and the diversity of its contemporary architecture is testimony to that. Social values are rapidly changing, due in large part to the unparalleled growth of new technology and a rise in technical skills. No longer is a single, dominant style capable of representing such plurality, so architects are now completely free to exercise their aesthetic and creative abilities in many ways. Jefferson's wish, for a nation in which each citizen could freely pursue an individual version of happiness, finally seems to have prevailed in the profession he loved so much. ●

The community center in Mason's Bend, Alabama, designed by the Auburn University College of Architecture Rural Studio and constructed in 1999–2000, exemplifies the ideas of Samuel Mockbee, who believed in putting the needs of people first in the design of buildings. Mockbee raised $20,000 from the Potrero Nuevo Fund in San Francisco for the community center, designed and built as a thesis problem by fifth-year students at Auburn. The walls are made from earth from the site, and most of the wood for the roof timbers came from cypress trees on the property. Car windows salvaged from a junkyard in Chicago serve as glazing. ©Timothy Hursley

Philip Cortelyou Johnson, FAIA

Robert A.M. Stern, FAIA

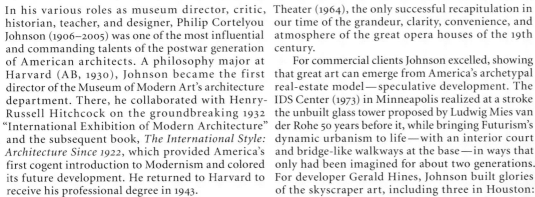

In his various roles as museum director, critic, historian, teacher, and designer, Philip Cortelyou Johnson (1906–2005) was one of the most influential and commanding talents of the postwar generation of American architects. A philosophy major at Harvard (AB, 1930), Johnson became the first director of the Museum of Modern Art's architecture department. There, he collaborated with Henry-Russell Hitchcock on the groundbreaking 1932 "International Exhibition of Modern Architecture" and the subsequent book, *The International Style: Architecture Since 1922*, which provided America's first cogent introduction to Modernism and colored its future development. He returned to Harvard to receive his professional degree in 1943.

In an age obsessed with self-referential object making, Johnson, who was nothing if not an object maker, committed the cardinal sin of not being self-referential. He was one of the few of his generation who made a genuine effort through his work as an architect to connect to and comment on the past, the work of his contemporaries (and rivals), and his clients' goals.

Johnson dared to see architecture as it was always seen before the Modernists—as a service. When monarchies ruled, this service was to the king, but in Johnson's era of democratic capitalism, it was to rich patrons and developers. And Johnson served his clients—and the public—very well with buildings that were outstanding exemplars of their genre. His work for the Rockefellers included the best urban garden of our time at the Museum of Modern Art (1953; 1964) in addition to one of our era's great public places, the plaza at Lincoln Center (1966). This plaza was set in front of Johnson's New York State Theater (1964), the only successful recapitulation in our time of the grandeur, clarity, convenience, and atmosphere of the great opera houses of the 19th century.

For commercial clients Johnson excelled, showing that great art can emerge from America's archetypal real-estate model—speculative development. The IDS Center (1973) in Minneapolis realized at a stroke the unbuilt glass tower proposed by Ludwig Mies van der Rohe 50 years before it, while bringing Futurism's dynamic urbanism to life—with an interior court and bridge-like walkways at the base—in ways that only had been imagined for about two generations. For developer Gerald Hines, Johnson built glories of the skyscraper art, including three in Houston: Pennzoil Place (1976), Transco Tower (1983), and the Republic Bank (1984). For the Pittsburgh Plate Glass Company (1984), he designed a magnificent piece of symbolic and literal advertising—a virtuosic display of just about everything you could do with the company's product. And for the telecommunications conglomerate AT&T (1984), Johnson produced an epochal work of Postmodern Classicism: no building did more to destroy the nihilism of the unadorned glass box.

And for himself (and now for all of us because it is open to the public), Johnson incrementally realized, over more than 50 years, an environmental autobiography on 40 acres in New Canaan, Connecticut. Here, the 1978 Gold Medal recipient brilliantly showcased his evolving talent: each new building opened up a new direction of architectural inquiry, beginning with his Glass House (1949), a consummate work of 20th-century architecture.

Philip Johnson, 1983 ©Wolfgang Hoyt/Esto

The 56-foot-by-32-foot Glass House (1949), New Canaan, Connecticut, is generally considered one of the great works of 20th-century architecture. *Ezra Stoller/ ®Esto*

1871
*Cornell University opened the nation's
second school of architecture, headed by
Charles Babcock, a founder of the AIA*

Great Chicago Fire

GOLD MEDALIST, 1989

Joseph Esherick, FAIA

Andrew Brodie Smith, PhD

Joseph Esherick, FAIA. Environmental Design Archives, University of California, Berkeley

California Bay Area architect Joseph Esherick received formal training in the Beaux Arts style at the University of Pennsylvania, where he studied with Paul Cret. While appreciative of the rigors of this curriculum, Esherick was ultimately drawn to the Modern movement as embodied in Philadelphia by such architects as George Howe and William Lescaze. He was also inspired by sculptor and furniture-maker Wharton Esherick, his paternal uncle.

Shortly after finishing his education, Esherick moved to San Francisco where he fell in with the inheritors of the Bay Area architectural tradition, particularly Gardner Dailey and William Wurster. After a stint in the Navy during World War II, Esherick opened his own architecture practice. His residential projects won acclaim for the way in which they integrated tenets of Modernism with the region's vernacular style.

Despite his Modernist inclination, Esherick converted an old canning factory in San Francisco into a delightful retail space, The Cannery (1968). The project would prove to be a model for other efforts in the adaptive use of buildings.

Esherick joined the architecture faculty at the University of California, Berkeley, in 1952 and remained there until his retirement in 1985. He was a cofounder of Berkeley's College of Environmental Design and a codesigner of its campus home, Wurster Hall (1964). In 1982 he was awarded the AIA/ACSA Topaz Medallion for Excellence in Architectural Education. His firm, Esherick Homsey Dodge and Davis, received the AIA's Architecture Firm Award in 1986. And, in 1989, the Institute honored him with its Gold Medal. Esherick died in 1998 at the age of 84.

Esherick won acclaim for his residential designs, which married Modernism with the Bay Area's vernacular style. The Bermak House (1963) is located in the hills of Oakland, California. *Environmental Design Archives, University of California, Berkeley*

At the Monterey Bay Aquarium (1984), on historic Cannery Row in Monterey, California, window walls with industrial sash provide views of the bay. *©Nik Wheeler/Corbis*

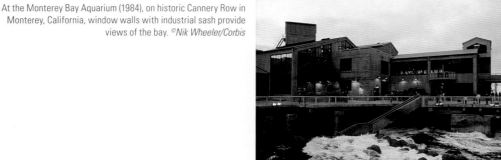

Visionary American Architecture

Jeff Stein, AIA

Visionary when coupled with *architecture* implies something fantastic, imaginative, at the periphery of professional practice. More than merely innovative, the word suggests provocative, critical work that not only explains present conditions but reveals a preferred—sometimes astonishing—future.

The United States—only 80 years older than the American Institute of Architects—is itself a visionary project. It is only natural, then, that this country would have its own visionary architecture, informed by the country's vast landscape and independent people.

From Thomas Jefferson onward, visionary American architects have always responded to reality, not by designing more of what is but by giving us a taste of what could be. And what is the peculiarly American quality that separates the work of these visionary architects from that of their European counterparts? Simply put, *construction*. Visionary architecture, as it comes to us from Europe, nearly always implies *paper* architecture—seldom realized, impossible to build, and largely free from the constraints of earthly life. In the United States, we actually build the stuff.

Many of the brightest lights in American architecture may be called visionary. This list includes Daniel Burnham, Frank Furness, Bernard Maybeck, Hugh Ferriss, Charles Eames, Louis Kahn, Bruce Goff, Buckminster Fuller, James Wines, Moshe Safdie, Frank Gehry, and more. Some were born or trained elsewhere, but once here, their work expressed a spirit synonymous with America. Conjoining optimism with pragmatism, their buildings dot the American landscape.

A lineage born in the middle of the country forms the historic center of American visionary architecture: Louis Sullivan, Frank Lloyd Wright, and Paolo Soleri. These three—in succession teachers and students to each other—represent a mythic independence of mind that most architects, American or otherwise, only dream of handing down through the ages. Their work is about *what ought to be*. Their drawings, buildings, books, movements, and schools have given new generations reasons to become architects.

Louis Sullivan began formally rethinking the tall building in the 1880s, as the corporation became the organizing force of American society, therefore requiring expression. Rather than stack short buildings on top of each other, as others had done, Sullivan created a new aesthetic, pulling vertical elements to the surface of his designs for corporate headquarters and recessing horizontal ones. His Wainwright Building (St. Louis, 1891), Guaranty Building (Buffalo, 1895), and others so transformed architecture that by 1896 he could write of the tall office building, "It must be every inch a proud and soaring thing, rising in sheer exultation," and Americans knew what he was describing.

Frank Lloyd Wright, beginning practice near the end of Sullivan's career and continuing past the mid-20th century, developed entirely new house forms that grew out of the horizontal landscape of the mid-American prairie. His "Broadacre City" in the early 1950s created a template for suburban growth that has lasted until today. Translating the idea of democracy into architecture and documenting the cult of the individual in American society, he understood his work thusly: "An organic architecture means more or less an organic society."

Paolo Soleri, after spending time with Wright at Taliesin, chose the Arizona desert in which to create an "urban laboratory." The resulting community, Arcosanti, may yet reinvent urban form. In work that presaged the current "sustainability" movement by a generation, he makes architecture that connects its inhabitants to each other and to the realities of sun and seasons. Soleri's concept of arcology—understanding architecture and ecology as a single entity—raises the spiral begun by Sullivan as *organic ornament* and continued by Wright as *organic architecture* to a higher level, positing buildings and even entire cities as *organisms* themselves.

Visionary architects have appeared at critical times in our culture, inspiring us toward change. We are at one of those times now. Confronted by issues of energy, climate change, and a shifting global economy, we eagerly await the inspiration of new visionaries.

Paolo Soleri received the 2006 Lifetime Achievement Award from the Cooper-Hewitt National Design Museum.
Michel Sarda, courtesy Cosanti Foundation

The vaults at Arcosanti serve as a public plaza, used by residents and visitors for work and play.
Yuki Yanagimoto, courtesy Cosanti Foundation

1872
Opening of Central Park,
New York City, designed by
Frederick Law Olmsted
and Calvert Vaux

Central Synagogue,
New York City,
Henry Fernback

GRASS ROOTS

Sharon C. Park, FAIA: The Art and Science of Technical Preservation Services

Sara Hart

"Our mission is twofold. We manage the Historic Rehabilitation Tax Credit Program and publish technical information to support 'best practices' in historic preservation," says Senior Historical Architect Sharon C. Park, FAIA, who has served, since 1997, as chief of the Technical Preservation Services (TPS) branch of the Heritage Preservation Services Division of the National Park Service.

The tax credit program is a huge responsibility: it fosters private-sector rehabilitation of historic buildings, thereby helping to promote economic revitalization. It also provides a viable alternative to government ownership and management of these structures. Properties must be held for the production of income and be rehabilitated according to strict standards set by the secretary of the interior (in conjunction with the Internal Revenue Service) to qualify for a 20 percent tax credit. Annually, private investors spend $3 billion rehabilitating their respective properties according to these requirements. Since it began in 1976, the program has made possible the preservation and, in many cases, adaptive use of more than 100,000 buildings in the United States.

In addition to administering this large, complex financial initiative, Park manages the publication of *Preservation Briefs*, a resource for architects, public building administrators, specialists, and owners—in fact, anyone interested or involved in the maintenance and preservation of historic buildings. Topics include accessible design, affordable housing, historic building codes, and sustainable design. There is no shortage of issues to explore, as new concerns are constantly emerging. "Today, interests range from seismic retrofit to window replacement in historic buildings to graffiti removal," she explains. "And, of course, building security and antiterrorism

strategies are top priorities." Since its inception in the early 1970s, TPS has produced more than 150 publications and has sold and distributed over five million copies.

TPS briefs are intended to provide guidance and technical information to encourage best practices. "[Best practices] are those that preserve the original materials and the architectural character of the building and ensure that new construction is compatible with the existing building," Park explains. These publications are neither restrictive nor prescriptive. Guidelines take into account extenuating circumstances and assume thoughtful decision making on the part of the parties involved. To prepare these pamphlets, Park and her highly trained, 20-person staff spend considerable time in the field, evaluating, for example, what maintenance techniques work best under which circumstances. Park sees the task as both art and science. "The goal is to match the appropriate technique with the specific project," she explains. For example, cleaning historic facades is a delicate matter, and conditions must be carefully evaluated to avoid damaging the materials with abrasive agents. No one formula that can be applied to every situation.

Park has written or edited many of the *Preservation Briefs* herself, in addition to writing or coauthoring more than 50 other publications. She also shares her accumulated knowledge outside of the office as a member of several associations and serves on the advisory group of the AIA Historic Resources Committee. She is not a mere bureaucrat with a professional specialty but an architect who has applied her talents and devoted her career to public service, and, as a result, she deserves to be acknowledged as a guardian of many of the country's historic buildings.

Sharon C. Park, FAIA
Courtesy National Park Service

Albert Loeb, for a time president of Sears, Roebuck Company, built Castle Farms, Charlevoix, Michigan, in 1918. The present owners purchased the farm in 2001 and restored it under the rehabilitation tax credit program. It now serves as a meeting and banquet center.
Courtesy Castle Farms

"The history of civilization and the world is traced by the character of its buildings and its architecture, and the degree of civilization of peoples is determined by the monuments they have left."

This statement of 1890 by Richard M. Upjohn, founding member and first chair of the then newly created AIA Committee on Conservation of Public Architecture, set the foundation for what is known today as the AIA Historic Resources Committee,[1] the Institute's oldest standing committee. But long before this committee was even conceived, American architects had demonstrated an understanding of the value of protecting their young country's built legacy: the earliest evidence of an architectural conservation effort in the United States was architect Robert Mills's 1812 attempt to reconstruct the steeple on Independence Hall in Philadelphia.[2] The AIA's purchase of the Octagon House (1799) in 1903 and its integration into the Institute's headquarters in 1973 are manifestations of the profession's commitment to preservation as an important component of both the present and the future built environment.

Architects are not alone in their interest in maintaining the works of their predecessors.Few efforts define the preservation movement in the United States better than the tenacity demonstrated by the Mount Vernon Ladies' Association of the Union. The first preservation organization in the country, it was founded in 1853 to protect and restore George Washington's estate. Following in the footsteps of these women, private citizens have since undertaken much of the work required to safeguard America's architectural heritage. In modern times, no person better represents this grassroots advocacy than Jane Jacobs in her fierce battle to preserve Greenwich Village in the 1950s in the face of a crosstown expressway proposed by New York City's powerful planning commissioner, Robert Moses.

The preservation movement has had many notable milestones over the years. The Historic American Buildings Survey, for example, was created in 1933 to document buildings significant to our nation's history. In 1949 the National Trust for Historic Preservation was chartered by the U.S. Congress to facilitate public participation in the preservation of sites, buildings, and objects of national significance. The National Park Service established the National Historic Landmarks program in 1960, and the first graduate-level preservation program at a U.S. university began at Columbia University in 1964.

The 1966 National Historic Preservation Act continues to be the centerpiece of preservation legislation in the United States. It provided for the establishment of an expanded National Register of Historic Places and the Advisory Council on Historic Preservation, plus a critical grant-in-aid program to support preservation at the state and national levels. The 1966 act also promulgated *The Secretary of the Interior's Standards for the Treatment of Historic Properties* as overarching guidance in support of sound preservation stewardship. The 1976 Tax Reform Act provided highly successful tax incentives to encourage private building rehabilitation.

Despite its name, preservation is not a static endeavor. The value of the movement, for example, has grown in light of increasing environmental concerns. Advocates of green building include preservation as an important strategy, acknowledging the natural resources already embodied in existing structures. And the regional planning movement known as "Smart Growth" recognizes preservation as a successful means of creating a rich community life. In addition, as society has gained a greater appreciation for the history and meaning expressed by the buildings of past generations, designers of today have learned better ways of preserving the old as they accommodate the new. Important research has been supported by agencies such as the National Center for Preservation Technology and Training and disseminated by organizations such as the Association for Preservation Technology, International.

Preservation is entering a new century with new challenges and opportunities. The number of structures eligible to be considered historically significant due to age will increase exponentially over the next several decades. The range of materials preservation professionals will be required to address is also increasing at a significant rate. And the Modern movement of the mid-20th century, the perceived nemesis of preservation efforts of that time, is now being considered for its historic significance, causing a reconfirmation of preservation values as inclusive of all history. A new generation of preservation professionals is taking a leadership role with new perspectives and creative approaches to both the old and new challenges before them. In their hands, the future holds great promise for our past.

History of the Preservation Movement in the United States

Jack Pyburn, FAIA

Jane Jacobs and Vincent Scully at the National Building Museum, after she received the museum's Scully Prize (2000). Jacobs, author of *The Death and Life of Great American Cities* (1961), was a fierce advocate for livable cities and the preservation of dense urban neighborhoods. *Liz Roll, courtesy National Building Museum*

The Mount Vernon Ladies' Association, founded in 1853 to protect and restore George Washington's estate, is the oldest preservation organization in the United States. Mount Vernon was designated a National Historic Landmark in 1960.
Hal Conroy, courtesy the Mount Vernon Ladies' Association

VIEWPOINT

The Architect as Rebel

Thom Mayne, FAIA

Among the arts, architecture and filmmaking share a parallel dilemma when ivory tower meets commerce. Inordinate investments of time and capital are required, both of which carry elements of risk for producers/clients/developers. And in recent years the distance between the creative and business sides of these two fields has been narrowed. We now have films made by MBAs, buildings made by committee—both typically resulting in bland, repetitive, and unimaginative outcomes. The studio system, once supportive of artistic integrity, no longer produces films worth the price of admission. Independent filmmakers, the bad boys of cinema, have risen to fill the void. Although there is no guarantee that a truly great film (or building) will come from a stance of independence, it is nearly impossible for one to occur without it.

Architect as rebel? Yes. This is part and parcel of our training. As a young architecture student in the late 60s, I felt in sync with the world. One of the outcomes of this period of cultural upheaval was a sense of power for our emerging generation. We fought against the war, we fought for civil rights, and we felt that we had prevailed. It was not a revolt—which would have been to refuse to obey the constraints of others . . . it would more accurately be described as a time of rebellion—in which we aspired to replace the constraints set by others with a set of our own making. In architecture school we are challenged to develop a critical stance: to question, to interrogate, to maximize inquiry. While the battles were intense, the mood was collegial and respectful. The toughness of the dialogue, the sparring, and the challenges were designed to develop a critical thought process that would result in outcomes that were open, flexible, and expansive as opposed to closed and a priori.

But what happens to the critical stance, so carefully nurtured at the university, when young architects enter the world of practice? When capital talks, it does not generally do so in patient dialogue. So as a young architect full of broad, humanistic ideas and with a battalion of heroic architects as models (including Kahn, Corbusier, Mies, etc.), I embarked on my career. Nuances in negotiation were sometimes lost as my focus remained firmly on the work and less on political considerations, but I quickly learned to differentiate between aspiration and reality—even as I continued to hold on to the belief in the power of architecture to transform people, institutions, culture. I was, and still am, astonished by my optimism (which my wife claims is a synonym for denial).

In school we were honored for achieving our objectives, for fighting it out, and for prevailing with ideas. But it was in the post-university world that the real fighting began. In the beginning this felt like a day-to-day, full-on assault that was both intellectual and emotional. I was fighting for autonomy—fighting to work within the ideals of my profession as I saw it—to resist becoming a person who sells a product. I was committed to remaining connected to the critical practice for which I had been so well trained. It was curious to me that the normative world would attach titles like "bad boy" to behavior that had been so hard earned and respected in the educational milieu. But for me, "bad boy" was far preferable to "good boy." I have yet to lose my conviction that architecture is a contact sport. It is clear to me, now 40 years into my career, that resistance to the ordinary is precisely what leads to work that is other than ordinary. Architects who do not have the stomach or the will to fight for the integrity of their creative ideas will not likely experience the satisfaction of achieving objectives that are worthy of discussion later. And curiously, I have come to understand now that there is an even greater satisfaction in taking one's clients along on the journey. Developing a patron is much more difficult than working in a service relationship—but this is precisely the transformation that can occur through critical dialogue with the client.

A curious symmetry exists at this point in my life. The training in critical thinking that served me well in school created some considerable challenges in midcareer. But now, with some years and a few buildings in the ground, that stance once labeled "difficult" is seen as the place from which artistic credibility derives. The decision to remain an outsider created the ground on which to develop authority. As in the world of film, it is imperative to stay out of the mainstream to produce excellent work. This is true precisely because authenticity of product requires independence and critical thinking—something not currently valued by the mainstream. We are trained to develop our voice, to learn the importance of our voice, and then to fight for that voice. One lives with the labels—it is the work that matters.

Morphosis' Hypo Alpe-Adria bank (2004), in Udine in northeastern Italy, rises out of the landscape at 14 degrees off vertical and overlooks an Italian bean field. The building is perhaps not what you expect for a bank headquarters but is evocative of Thom Mayne's belief that "resistance to the ordinary is precisely what leads to work that is other than ordinary." ©*Roland Halbe Fotografie/2007*

Historic buildings are threatened or lost almost on a daily basis. This fact is a reality of our culture today, and it is likely to continue to be true for a variety of economic and social reasons. Fortunately, though, a great number of historic structures, sites, districts, and towns are now being protected, preserved, and restored in a continuing effort to save our past for the future.

The first serious effort to protect an important part of American history took place more than 150 years ago, when Ann Pamela Cunningham formed the Mount Vernon Ladies' Association of the Union to save the home of the country's first president. This effort paved the path for a new movement that would focus on the protection of our historic, cultural, and architectural legacy.

Two of the most important milestones in the history of the preservation movement in the United States occurred less than a mile and several years apart in New York City. The first was the demolition, completed in 1966, of McKim, Mead and White's Classical Pennsylvania Station. An architectural tour de force and an early example of an intermodal transportation facility, the 1910 building was torn down for the Madison Square Garden complex. Galvanized by this loss, preservationists were much better prepared for the next major threat. In 1967 Penn Central Transportation Company proposed that a tower by Marcel Breuer be added atop Grand Central Station, despite its designation as a landmark two years earlier by the New York Landmarks Preservation Commission. When the company's application was denied, it sued the city. A line in the sand had been drawn, and the preservation forces waged a battle that would shape the future of historic preservation in this country. In 1978 the case reached the U.S. Supreme Court, which ruled in favor of the city. This historic decision upheld the legitimacy of historic preservation regulations and provided the framework for organizations, communities, and local governments to create the tools necessary to protect our built environment.

While these events were taking place in the public eye, another endeavor unfolding behind the scenes would subsequently define how architects actually undertake preservation projects. In the 1950s the late Charles F. Peterson, FAIA, assembled a team of bright, talented, and dedicated preservation architects to address the needs of Independence Hall in Philadelphia. By the end of the 1960s, his team had created a new model of professional practice that was systematic and scientific in its approach to preservation. Not only was this national treasure properly protected, but it was also designated a World Heritage Site, the highest honor that can be bestowed upon such a landmark.

Today, historic preservation is an integral and legitimate part of our culture. Yet we face new and different threats, which, quite possibly, have implications more far-reaching than the loss of individual structures. America's Main Street—the backbone of our most livable communities, villages, and towns—is fighting for survival as local merchants are forced to compete, often unsuccessfully, against national chain stores and big-box retail centers filled with low-priced inventory. Similarly, upscale shopping in wealthy areas introduces a new form of gentrification, which needs to be understood and managed to ensure the special qualities of these communities are not lost. And, finally, we cannot forget the need to protect architecture of the more recent past. The Modern movement in the United States has produced some of the most important buildings of the 20th century, including landmarks by Ludwig Mies van der Rohe, Eero Saarinen, Frank Lloyd Wright, Gordon Bunshaft, and other giants of our architectural pantheon. Some of these buildings have already been lost, and others face uncertain futures. Clearly, the preservation movement has come far, but there is still much work to be done.

Great Buildings Lost, Saved, and Threatened

George C. Skarmeas, AIA

McKim, Mead and White's grand, Beaux-Arts–style Pennsylvania Station (1910), New York City, was demolished (above) in the 1960s to make way for Madison Square Garden. The loss helped galvanize support for enactment of the city's first preservation statutes.
Historic American Buildings Survey, Library of Congress;
©Bettmann/Corbis (demolition photo)

The Role of the Critic

Robert Campbell, FAIA

My favorite definition of a critic is by the French author Anatole France. He wrote: "A good critic is one who describes his adventures among masterpieces." That's the ideal. A critic should be an enthusiast, someone who can waken readers to the wonder of the world as it is, and the wonder of how much better it could become.

Architecture criticism is different, however, from other kinds of criticism. Most critics are consumer guides. They help you decide what play or concert or exhibit or movie or restaurant to go to. But few of us buy tickets to a work of architecture. So what is the architecture critic for?

Having been critic for the *Boston Globe* since 1973, I think the goal is not so much to judge buildings as good or bad, as if they were merely works of art. The purpose, instead, is to stimulate and join an ongoing conversation in society about what makes good places for human beings to live and work in. No one person can or should decide that. But we can all learn to notice different examples of architecture and environment and ask ourselves whether they support the kind of culture and community we believe in. By "places," I mean everything we build. Architecture is best defined as the art of making places for human habitation: rooms, streets, squares, gardens, villages, cities. You have to inhabit it, move through it, maybe put it to use, before you can evaluate it. A painting may exist only to be appreciated, but a building exists for many other purposes.

Architecture criticism as now practiced in the United States was begun in the *New York Times* in 1963 by Ada Louise Huxtable. She had precursors, notably Montgomery Schuyler in the years around 1900 and Lewis Mumford in the mid-20th century. Huxtable began at a time when the Modern movement was still near its height, and her work was an endorsement of that style. When she won the first-ever Pulitzer Prize for criticism in 1970, and a MacArthur Fellowship in 1981, she solidified the status of architecture criticism as a beat for major newspapers.

Today the Modernist consensus no longer governs. New styles of architecture, or revivals of old ones, appear every few years and enjoy a run of fashion. They then usually fail to disappear, so that we now live in a world of competing taste cultures. We've seen, in recent decades, styles called Postmodern, Deconstruction, Blob Architecture, Modernist Revival, New Urbanism, and Neoclassicism. At Harvard, near where I live, its business school builds traditional Colonial Revival while its design school teaches the latest trend. Similar battles rage elsewhere. It's a lively time but sometimes a confusing one. The critic can be a helpful guide.

Architecture today enjoys more popular interest than at any time since, at least, the arrival of Modernism in the late 1940s and 50s. We now have the so-called starchitects, a few dozen figures worldwide who, having been elevated to celebrity status by the media, are given the opportunity to design many of the most significant buildings internationally. Although the starchitects are sometimes accused of becoming brand names, they've created some of the most daring and beautiful works in architectural history.

Today, architecture is, as always, moving forward to engage a changing and challenging world. There's intense interest in green architecture and its hope of conserving the earth's resources; interest in the computer and its ability to create new architectural shapes and new ways of building them; and interest in urbanism, the art of creating livable, walkable communities in a world that has sometimes been blown apart by the automobile. As always, critics will be needed to celebrate the successes, query the failures, demand better quality, and serve as informative go-betweens for the public and the architecture profession.

Lewis Mumford
AIA Archives

Ada Louise Huxtable
AIA Archives

Struggling for Diversity

Kathryn H. Anthony, PhD

In scores of American cities, what were once racial minorities are now majorities, and both people of color and women have assumed leadership roles. The demographic portrait of the architecture profession in these and other cities, however, remains predominantly white and male. As of September 2006, 4 percent of the licensed-architect members of the AIA were Asian Pacific, 2.6 percent Hispanic/Latino, 1.1 percent African-American, and 13 percent women (the AIA does not collect information on disability or sexual orientation). For reasons too complex to discuss here, this profession has had far greater difficulty—in comparison to its counterparts in medicine and law—achieving a distribution that reflects the American population. Yet, despite seemingly insurmountable difficulties, talented men and women have broken through many traditional barriers to become historic "firsts" as leaders in the architectural world. As well, professional groups have formed for support in the ongoing effort to achieve greater diversity. The profession has benefited from the contributions of these active individuals. This essay highlights just a few of these heroic individuals.

After entering the male-dominated profession through an apprenticeship at a Buffalo, New York, architecture office, at age 25 Louise Blanchard Bethune, FAIA, opened an office with her husband, Robert Armour Bethune. Louise Bethune became the first woman member of the AIA in 1888 and the first woman elected a Fellow of the Institute in 1889. Her well-known designs for the Lafayette Hotel and Kensington Church in Buffalo and the women's prison for the Erie County Penitentiary were accompanied by a steady stream of educational, commercial, and industrial projects. Sophia Hayden was the first woman to graduate in architecture from the Massachusetts Institute of Technology, in 1890. Hayden designed the Woman's Building at the 1893 World's Columbian Exposition. Julia Morgan was the first woman to graduate from the engineering program at the University of California, Berkeley (1894); to enroll in the Ecole des Beaux-Arts in Paris (1898); and to become a registered architect in California (1904). Her career spanned 47 years and approximately 700 buildings, including Hearst Castle in San Simeon, California.

Almost a century would pass after these pioneers began their architecture careers before women took on significant leadership roles in the profession. Blanche Lemco van Ginkel, Hon. AIA, of the University of Toronto served as the first woman president of the Association of Collegiate Schools of Architecture (1986–87). Diane Ghirardo was the first woman executive editor of the *Journal of Architectural Education* (1988–99). Seattle-based L. Jane Hastings, FAIA, principal of Washington's oldest woman-owned architecture firm, became the first woman chancellor of the AIA College of Fellows (1992). Susan Maxman, FAIA, principal of her Philadelphia architecture firm, became the first woman president of the AIA (1992). And Baghdad-born British architect Zaha Hadid became the first woman to receive the prestigious Pritzker Architecture Prize (2004).

In 1923 Paul Revere Williams, FAIA, of Los Angeles broke the racial barrier to become the first African-American member of the AIA and in 1957 the first African-American elected to the AIA College of Fellows. In his early career, Williams perfected a technique of rendering drawings "upside-down" so that his clients, some of whom may have been uncomfortable sitting next to him, could see his designs "right-side-up" from across the table. Throughout his 60-year career, Williams designed 3,000 projects, including schools, hospitals, churches, office buildings, and U.S. Navy bases. He became known as the "architect to the stars," designing homes for such luminaries as Lucille Ball and Desi Arnaz, Frank Sinatra, Betty Grable, and Cary Grant. In 1938 *Life* magazine named him one of "20 of America's most distinguished Negroes." Ironically, racial discrimination prohibited him from entering some of his own projects, including the Polo Lounge at the Beverly Hills Hotel.

In 1963 a controversial court order requiring racial integration allowed Harvey Gantt, FAIA, to gain admission to Clemson University. In 1965 he became the first African-American to graduate from that university. Since then, he has led a distinguished career as both architect and politician. Starting in 1984, Gantt served two terms as the first African-American mayor of Charlotte, North Carolina.

Norma Merrick Sklarek, FAIA, became the first African-American woman member of the AIA in 1966 and the first elected to its College of Fellows in 1980. She faced significant discrimination when she started her career. Although she had earned an architecture degree from Columbia University in 1950, she received no job offers after applying to more than a dozen offices in New York City. She subsequently worked at well-known Los Angeles architecture firms, however, and her built works include the U.S. Embassy in Tokyo and Passenger Terminal One at the Los Angeles International Airport.

In 1996 Raj Barr-Kumar, FAIA, became the first AIA president of color. In 2001 Gordon H. Chong, FAIA, became the first Asian American to assume that role. In 2002 Bradford Grant became the first African-American to serve as president of the Association of Collegiate Schools of Architecture. And in 2008 Marshall Purnell, FAIA, became the first African-American to lead the AIA as president.

(From top, left to right)
Sophie Hayden
Courtesy MIT Museum

Gordon Chong, FAIA
AIA Archives

Susan A. Maxman, FAIA
AIA Archives

Marshall E. Purnell, FAIA

Raj Barr-Kumar, FAIA

Zaha Hadid
Steve Double, courtesy Zaha Hadid Architects

L. Jane Hastings, FAIA

Norma M. Sklarek, FAIA

Paul R. Williams, FAIA
University of Southern California Archives

3

Engaging the Public, Seeking Common Ground

Sharon Egretta Sutton, PhD, FAIA

Architecture is both an art and the embodiment of a society's values at any moment in time. It involves negotiation between an artistic vision and the public's notion of the ideas and ideals it wishes to express through architectural form.[1] But who is included in the "public" has evolved over time, reflecting changing notions of democracy and its basic emancipatory thrust toward greater inclusiveness in decision-making processes.[2] Over the past 150 years of American history, forward-thinking architects have expanded their purview to address the needs of immigrants, low-income families, people of color, women, and disabled persons, as well as to protect the natural environment by responding to an exponential growth in development. Accordingly, their strategies for involving an increasingly diverse constituency around increasingly complex environmental issues have evolved from generating heroic design solutions top-down to greater engagement with the public in co-creating shared, environmentally sustainable visions of spaces and places. As this thrust toward democracy proceeds, today's architects, more than ever, are called upon to negotiate common ground among overlapping and often conflicting interests.

This chapter presents nine profiles, both historical and contemporary, of architects who have successfully orchestrated public decision-making processes. Collectively, their stories foretell the trajectory of a profession engaged in a 21st-century, socially constructed art.

Historical Leaders

Just as the perception of the American city has evolved from that of wicked immigrant enclave to a front line for achieving an inclusive democracy, so too have architects transformed themselves from elitist visionaries into social and environmental activists. Five historical profiles illustrate this gradual change from top-down decision making to an inclusive, participative approach.

Frederick Law Olmsted and the Gilded Age

Olmsted launched his career around the time of the Civil War, when the United States was rapidly changing from a rural, agrarian landscape into the world's leading urban industrial nation.[3] As lower-class American migrants and European immigrants crowded into disease-ridden slums,[4] many well-bred men, Olmsted included, perceived a serious threat to the cultural unity of a romanticized civic life.[5] Often, this reformist gentry sought to build character among the urban poor by *eliminating* inappropriate behavior, but Olmsted—taking the more idealistic stance of a designer—set about *creating*, through his urban parks, a context for social progress.

(Opposite) Olmsted advocated for public parks to promote national harmony and refine the national character, creating spaces such as this meadow in New York's Central Park.
©Photo collection Alexander Alland Sr./Corbis

Olmsted gained administrative experience during the Civil War as secretary general of the U.S. Sanitary Commission, which operated field hospitals, dispensaries, and hospital ships, and employed scores of surgeons, nurses, and health inspectors.
©Medford Historical Society Collection/Corbis

Olmsted's vision was informed by an eclectic background, including his first occupation as a gentleman farmer, pursued after he studied chemistry and scientific agriculture at Yale College.[6] Before beginning the design of Central Park at age 35, he had written travel reports to the *New York Times*, eventually published as three books;[7] served as executive secretary of the U.S. Sanitary Commission, working to integrate former slaves into the economy; and organized the Union League Club to foster a spirit of nationalism.[8] During this period, Olmsted, in association with other distinguished reformers, also launched *The Nation* and the American Social Science Association, both stressing the responsibilities of the well-to-do toward the less fortunate.[9]

As a park designer, Olmsted developed broad consensus among prominent decision makers, convincing them that the poor required rural scenery, cool breezes, and cleansing sunlight to counteract their diminished social bonds, deadened sensibilities, and dearth of opportunities for reflection.[10] He persuaded not only the gentry but also city officials and real estate tycoons—groups frequently at odds on urban issues—that his parks would inoculate uncultivated working people against the disease-laden vapors of the inner city.[11] According to Olmsted, parks managed by trained personnel and surrounded by posh residential neighborhoods would uplift those who lacked social responsibility, while imposing a calming sense of neighborliness.[12] In keeping with this outlook, Olmsted resisted poor and working-class demands for organized sports, seeing the artistic integrity of his designs as crucial to their moral uplift.[13]

Olmsted's effectiveness as a Gilded Age activist can be attributed to his vast technical, political, and administrative expertise—along with having the prerequisite social status for decision makers of this era. In short, he possessed the skills and social characteristics needed to influence other elite social reformers and political leaders, sharing their sense of urgency to find a physical form for the country's democratic ideals.

Daniel Hudson Burnham and the City Beautiful Movement

At the turn of the century, during what is known as the Progressive Era, social reformers became increasingly concerned about the moral destiny of the nation's largely immigrant cities. Dissatisfied with the outcomes of their piecemeal improvements to tenements, parks, playgrounds, and sanitation, they began promoting a fundamental restructuring of urban areas. Their concerns gave birth to the City Beautiful movement, a comprehensive approach to imposing social and aesthetic order on these areas. Burnham, the movement's principal exponent, wanted to transform America's industrial capitals into oases of harmonious neoclassical buildings and natural landscapes, which he believed would convey the orderliness of great European cities.[14]

Burnham first realized this concept of urban transformation through his design for the 1893 World's Columbian Exposition in Chicago, the nation's earliest large-scale city planning project.[15] Working with his partner, John Wellborn Root; the 71-year-old Olmsted; and Olmsted's partner, Henry Sargent Codman, Burnham chose Jackson Park as the exposition site. This site allowed him to juxtapose the project's sparkling white buildings and spectacular lagoon with Chicago's grimy industrial reality.[16] Through this and subsequent plans for the nation's capital, Chicago, and San Francisco, Burnham intended his monumental, symmetrical plans to express stability while also engendering loyalty and civic responsibility.[17]

For such massive undertakings, Burnham required backing from a broad constituency, beginning with the plan's sponsors, typically business or political elites, who would establish a planning commission. This group sought support from the public and the press through elaborate education campaigns, including lectures, exhibitions, publications, and even civics curricula for school children.[18] This top-down outreach program was accompanied by the formation of grassroots, voluntary associations that crusaded against blight, cleaned and landscaped streets, sponsored home beautification contests, and advocated for public art,[19] bringing Burnham's vision of beautiful cities to life in local communities.

Burnham, who completed the Columbian Exposition in less than two years, possessed talents both as an administrator and architectural impresario.[20] He thought on a grand scale, eloquently communicated the link between city planning and other moral reforms, and effectively bridged the concerns of Progressive Era reformers with upper-class economic interests. Like Olmsted, he benefited from his social status and the prevailing sense of urgency to find an appropriate form for the industrial cities of a democracy.

(Opposite) Dazzled by the architecture of the radiant "White City," 28 million visitors from all over the world attended the 1893 World's Columbian Exposition in Chicago. ©*Corbis*

The Commercial Club of Chicago commissioned this Jules Guerin painting depicting a plaza west of the Field Museum of Natural History, proposed in Burnham's 1909 master plan for the city. *Chicago History Museum*

Elisabeth Coit, FAIA, and the Great Depression

In the late 1920s, Coit was designing private homes,[21] a role typical among the nation's few women architects. Fears of the evil city had ameliorated as intellectuals, journalists, and the stars of an expanding entertainment media began to characterize the disharmonies of urban life as essential to its vitality.[22] The focus of attention had shifted from creating a uniform society to addressing the needs of the poor on their own terms. When the economy faltered and the country was plunged into the Great Depression, Coit had an opportunity to distinguish herself by articulating the needs of millions of laid-off workers.

Faced with widespread mass demonstrations, President Franklin D. Roosevelt introduced his New Deal reform program. Unlike the earlier reforms of the Gilded Age and Progressive Era, when the middle and upper classes spoke on behalf of the poor, FDR's initiative reflected the growing power of the poor and working classes to articulate their own needs. Yet, because his program provided only emergency relief, unrest spread—and became more violent—leading Roosevelt to undertake a second, more ambitious New Deal, which established, among other forms of social support, a permanent low-rent public housing administration.[23]

The Housing Act of 1937 set the stage for Coit's pioneering work. That year, at age 45, she received an AIA Langley Scholarship, which she used to survey low-income housing developments on the East Coast and in the Midwest. As a researcher, Coit projected herself into the tenants' lives, considering every detail of their surroundings, from small elements to entire building systems, and bringing to light the need for adaptability and flexibility. Her public housing guidelines, still useful today, appeared in professional journals in this country and were translated and published abroad. Coit spent the rest of her career working for federal and municipal housing authorities, where she conducted field investigations and used her findings to plan projects and educate the international architecture community about low-income housing needs.[24]

Coit advocated for the great masses of people who lacked decent, affordable housing at a time when few architects or builders had stepped up to produce the millions of dwelling units needed to secure the country's social health.[25] Working not with broad strokes but with the details of people's life experiences, she helped shape new roles for architects as researchers and advocates for the poor.

Elisabeth Coit (1892–1987) received a BS degree in architecture from MIT in 1919. Her landmark study of low-income housing, "Design and Construction of the Dwelling Unit for the Low-Income Family," was published in the *Octagon* (1941) and later in *Architectural Record* (1942).
AIA Archives

Coit's study of the needs of low-income housing residents led her to recommend designs that were adaptable and flexible.
Architectural Record, *April 1942*

ROOMS AS TENANTS USE THEM

Where the strenuous activities of family life must be compacted into a few not-too-large rooms, "normal" room uses get sadly confused. Under such circumstances, the tenant's most urgent desires as to room types might be summarized thus:

Living Rooms, little used as such by low-income families, are best designed if they serve these purposes:

    1. Reception room, kept neat for callers.

    2. Bedroom, (a) frequently as regular sleeping place for child or adult; (b) occasionally for a child with illness or "symptoms."

    3. Occasionally as dining room, but not as the only dining space.

Dining Space, whatever its location, should fulfill three requirements:
    1. Convenient place for frequent "staggered" meals.

    2. Space for whole family and guests.

    3. Light and ventilation.

Bedrooms, too often suitable only for sleeping, would be more effective if also used for:
    1. Quiet space for homework or hobbies, for both adults and children.

    2. Secondary living room space where club-age boys or girls can discuss their own affairs with their own friends.

Bathrooms are often called upon to relieve the over-used kitchen, particularly for laundry work, and might well be arranged and equipped for light laundering.

Kitchens, usually the busiest room by far in the whole dwelling, are called upon to accommodate several functions besides that for which they were designed:

    1. Some of the bathroom uses overflow into the kitchen; babies and small children are often bathed in the laundry tray, as the bathtub is too low.

    2. Even the "laboratory" type of kitchen has to be the small child's play space, and the family assembles where the mother is working.

    3. Kitchen is used for snacks, homework, sewing, mending, etc., and for many small tasks done while the stove is watched.

Through her study of how theories of housing design meshed with low-income clients' needs, Coit found that the kitchen was the most overloaded room, with far too little counter, storage, and eating space.
Architectural Record, *April 1942*

"Please! This is the work area, not the recreational area!"

1876
Thomas U. Walter elected
AIA president, succeeding
Richard Upjohn, who had
served for 19 years

Founding of American Architect
and Building News

Pennsylvania Academy of the Fine Arts,
Philadelphia,
Frank Furness and George Hewitt

Richard Buckminster Fuller, FAIA, and the Affluent Society

Undoubtedly influenced by his daughter's death from a disease contracted while living in a Chicago slum during the 1930s, Fuller's thinking must also have been shaped by the social climate of the late 1940s and 1950s. The national mood of the "silent generation" was one of anticommunism and conformity paralleled by prosperity, suburban growth, and a proliferation of cars and highways,[26] all made possible by wartime scientific advances. Within this context of conventionality and prosperity-driven growth, Fuller, a self-described nonconformist, set out to help improve human existence on a finite "spaceship earth," where infinite possibilities existed for ever-increasing standards of living.[27]

Ahead of his time, Fuller sought to advance the sustainability of the planet by making the best use of resources through technologically sophisticated designs. In particular, he advocated extensive science education for students of architecture so they would learn to sustain *all* of humanity without destroying the environment or putting anyone at a disadvantage.[28] Fuller's inventions, which included thousands of geodesic domes along with prototypes for a car and house, employed lightweight materials and structures, energy-conservation devices, and efficient methods of production and shipping.[29] They contradicted conventional thinking in architecture and engineering, exploiting new structural designs and the special properties of new materials.[30]

In addition to his professional practice, Fuller wrote 18 books, taught at Southern Illinois University in Carbondale and Black Mountain College in North Carolina, and lectured worldwide. Early in his tenure at Black Mountain, one of the country's most fabled experimental art schools, he improvised his first geodesic dome with sculpture student Kenneth Snelson, among others.[31] Later in life, this passionate educator traveled to some 500 universities and colleges, beseeching audiences to replace the prevailing compartmentalization of knowledge with systems thinking.[32]

Fuller placed civic activism within a global context, serving not only as architect, engineer, inventor, author, and iconoclast but also, most significantly, as educator-at-large. He deliberately ran against the grain and at the same time had a profound effect on architectural thinking and the public consciousness. Through thousands of lectures, Fuller forcefully nudged professionals, students, and citizens alike to "think outside the box."[33]

To promote his ideas of synergy and systems thinking, Fuller made 48 trips around the world and gave more than 2,000 lectures at colleges and universities. *Courtesy the Estate of R. Buckminster Fuller*

Fuller (far left) at Black Mountain College in the 1940s, where he designed his first geodesic dome with sculpture student Kenneth Snelson and others. *Courtesy the Estate of R. Buckminster Fuller*

Architecture students enrolled in Sharon E. Sutton's community-based design studio at the University of Michigan present recommendations to Detroit citizens and city officials for redeveloping a deteriorated residential neighborhood.
Courtesy Sharon E. Sutton

The participatory spirit that began with the Civil Rights movement and practitioners like Susana Torre continues: In the early 1990s, sixth graders worked with art teacher Janet Sygar and architect Joanne B. Yoshida to redesign and then refurbish a playground at Public School 110 in New York City. Hundreds of volunteer architects, local residents, and business owners helped with the effort.
Courtesy Sharon E. Sutton

Susana Torre and the Civil Rights Movement

Armed with an architecture diploma from the University of Buenos Aires, Torre arrived in New York City in 1968 at the pinnacle of the Civil Rights movement.[34] Congress had passed the Civil Rights Act in 1964 and even more aggressive Great Society legislation in 1965. Along with racial and ethnic minorities, many other disfranchised groups (including women) coalesced to call into question the entire structure of society, its institutions, professional/client relationships, and professional monopolies. Foremost on the agenda were economic opportunities, enabled by student loans and affirmative action, and the participation of low-income communities in decision-making processes.[35] As with other professions, this movement affected both the demographic makeup and practice of architecture.

Although attempts to advance architects of color faltered, the advancement of women blossomed, in part, because of the efforts of Torre and her colleagues at the Architectural League of New York. The group set out to document the work of women architects in 1973, when women composed just 1.2 percent of practicing architects and 8.4 percent of architecture students.[36] After cofounding the Archive of Women in Architecture to collect biographical and project data, Torre produced an edited book and an exhibition, which opened at the Brooklyn Museum and then toured the country.[37] Her project—along with the many other alternative professional venues (exhibitions, conferences, schools, organizations) for women that were bubbling up nationally—helped give birth to a new agenda of activism in architecture.

Although the issues of improving their own working conditions and uncovering the histories of women and minority architects took center stage, many of the women who were empowered by Torre's project also began exploring more culturally responsive approaches to design. Torre and other feminist architects encouraged design strategies that today are commonplace, such as including child-care facilities in building budgets, preserving sites significant in the history of women and people of color, involving architecture students in community-design activities, utilizing participatory planning and design processes, exposing inner-city youth to careers in the field, and exploring new spatial and social arrangements.[38]

Torre multiplied her knowledge and skills by bringing together other women—practitioners, scholars, and students—to debate how they could improve their own professional lives, as well as those of other marginalized groups. As a community organizer, Torre inspired a group of women architects who, in turn, helped articulate the needs of a previously unserved public.

Contemporary Leaders

Enriched by the cumulative effect of the reforms of the Progressive Era, New Deal, and Civil Rights movement, today's architects draw upon an array of leadership strategies to orchestrate the ever-more-complex processes of designing new or renovating old spaces and places in varying cultural contexts, whether small community projects or major ones of national and international significance. Four contemporary profiles illustrate some of the challenges today's civic-minded architects are tackling.

J. Max Bond Jr., FAIA

An internationally recognized architect, educator, and civic leader, J. Max Bond Jr. grew up in a family of prominent African-American educators and activists in the Jim Crow south, the Caribbean, and Africa, where his father served as president of the University of Liberia.[39] After earning a master's degree from Harvard at age 16, Bond worked briefly for Le Corbusier in Paris and then spent four years in Ghana. His first major public building was the Bolgatanga Library, in the upper east region of the country.[40] After returning to the United States, he helped establish ARCH (Architects Renewal Committee of Harlem), one of the country's first community design centers. In addition to providing technical assistance on building rehabilitation, community planning, and tenants' rights, Bond's volunteer staff offered precollege architecture training to inner-city youth. At the same time, he joined the architecture faculty at Columbia University, remaining there 16 years, including four as chair of the Division of Architecture. During his tenure, he served as adviser to minority students (this author included), actively pursued Columbia's divestment in South Africa, and advocated strategies to make the program less intimidating for entering students.[41] Later, as dean of City College's School of Architecture and Environmental Studies, he sought to empower the culturally diverse, primarily working-class student body by teaching them about the architectural contributions of various cultural groups and by encouraging democratically run design studios.[42]

In a New York practice that includes such important buildings as the Martin Luther King Jr. Center for Nonviolent Social Change in Atlanta, the Birmingham Civil Rights Institute in Alabama, and major university research laboratories, along with smaller projects such as a series of dormitories at Mary Holmes College in West Point, Mississippi, Bond seeks opportunities to affect the quality of lived experience.[43] A cofounder of Bond Ryder, which later merged with Davis Brody & Associates, Bond attempts to create an adaptable, flexible architecture that not only allows occupants to shape their own surroundings but also invites input from builders.[44] In the same way that his mother drew upon the utilitarian quilting skills of former sharecroppers to execute a dynamic collection of museum-quality American quilts,[45] Bond's designs consider the skills of the builders, the materials they use, and how large a contract they can undertake.[46]

Bond (far right), his partner, Don Ryder (back row, left), and members of the Bond Ryder staff, photographed in Central Park North in the late 1960s. *Courtesy Sharon E. Sutton*

From Bond's perspective, the post-1930s liberation movements have radically changed how architects work. No longer solo designers, they now function within a network of many players—other professionals, developers, financiers, community groups, future occupants, builders—all of whom contribute to the successful completion of projects.[47] This reality came to the fore during the design process for the Mary Woodard Lasker Biomedical Building, part of a four-block research facility for Columbia University in upper Manhattan. In 1983 when this largely Dominican area had deteriorated because of a crack cocaine epidemic, Columbia purchased a site for the facility that contained the abandoned Audubon Theater and Ballroom. Although not officially a landmark, the building was known as the place where, in 1912, William Fox began an entertainment empire that became 20th Century Fox and, more poignantly, where Malcolm X was assassinated in 1965.[48] When Columbia announced plans to demolish the structure, these two histories—along with the prospect of a biomedical facility in the neighborhood—sparked a decade-long confrontation among city and state agencies, university officials, area residents, black leaders, preservationists, and the family of Malcolm X.[49]

Although some preservationists and black leaders lobbied to turn the entire building into a cultural facility, Bond helped negotiate an architectural resolution to the conflict. His redesign preserved the most valuable aspects of the historic building (part of the ballroom where Malcolm X was shot and a spectacular polychrome terra-cotta façade) and expanded the program to include one space for a Malcolm X memorial and another for community use.[50] Bond accommodated the additional space without compromising the research functions by using the lobby and space above it for the memorial and the community functions.[51] His design also called for storefronts in the historic façade along the main street and placement of the more sterile biomedical facility on the side street.[52]

The restored historic façade of the Audubon Ballroom provides human-scale shopping along the avenue; the new six-story, aluminum and glass biomedical building, entered from the side street, is tucked behind. *Roy Wright, courtesy Davis Brody Bond*

Bond believes that negotiating with the various stakeholders resulted in a design that maintained the social significance of the building and made it an integral part of the community. The building's shops, along with a nearby park, have made the project a destination point.[53] Bond's many careers—as a practitioner, educator, and administrator—have been distinguished by his ability to address the social and political complexities of a project and to convey those complexities to his clients, colleagues, and students.

In his Lower Manhattan office, Bond discusses the placement of a mural honoring Malcolm X in the restored Audubon Ballroom. *Courtesy Davis Brody Bond*

Peter Steinbrueck, FAIA

Peter Steinbrueck's lifelong engagement in civic activism began at age six, when he worked alongside his architect father, Victor, to preserve Seattle's Pike Place Market and its historic districts. This boyhood activism continued during the Civil Rights movement and Vietnam War protests, but Steinbrueck's engagement in civic life began in earnest when he organized a citizens' committee that filed an initiative to require comprehensive planning, restrict building heights, and mandate design review for buildings over 50,000 square feet in Seattle. Voters approved this clarion call for better city planning in 1989, setting the stage for the state's growth-management legislation. After a short stint in private practice, Steinbrueck won a seat on the Seattle city council in 1995, where he now conceives his practice as one of designing the entire city.[54]

Guided by insights gained through his father's wisdom about what makes a good city, Steinbrueck characterizes himself as a public guardian who protects what people value about their community.[55] His work is also informed by an enduring commitment to civil rights, peace, and justice, which he focuses not just locally but nationally and internationally. To advance new legislation, he generates the research needed to convince skeptics of its viability and then builds broad-based community support. His achievements range from a computerized system that connects homeless Seattleites with a network of shelters and social service organizations to design excellence in the city's major public buildings. Because of his insistence that city-funded projects be designed as green buildings, every city-owned public building, as well as every public building in the state over 5,000 square feet, must now achieve a silver-level certification through the U.S. Green Building Council's LEED (Leadership in Energy and Environmental Design) rating system. These legislative successes make Steinbrueck one of the nation's foremost spokespersons for urban sustainability and the environment.[56]

However, Steinbrueck's most rewarding achievement grew out of the projected need to accommodate tens of thousands more people and jobs in downtown Seattle over the next 20 years. Given the expected increase in population, the mayor had proposed to raise building heights dramatically in the downtown area from those legislated by Steinbrueck's 1989 citizens' initiative. In promoting his plan, the mayor pointed to Portland, Oregon, and Vancouver, British Columbia, as precedents, but he failed to consider what made those cities livable; nor did he specify the appearance of buildings, the income levels they would serve, or the public amenities that would be created.[57] As chair of the council's urban development and planning committee, Steinbrueck stepped into the void, elaborating the mayor's prescriptive new zoning heights as a comprehensive plan for livability.

Steinbrueck speaks at a meeting of Seattle's urban development and planning committee in Council chambers.
Courtesy Seattle Municipal Archives

The downtown livability legislation advocated by Steinbrueck affects Belltown, Seattle's most densely populated neighborhood, adding family-friendly amenities to its trendy restaurants, boutiques, nightclubs, and residential towers.
Courtesy Seattle Municipal Archives

To get an objective, third-party perspective on the mayor's proposal, Steinbrueck convinced the council to engage the services of Vancouver's current and former planning directors, both widely credited with achieving the qualities the mayor had been trumpeting. The two planners faulted the proposal, especially with respect to attracting families to the center city,[58] suggesting that Seattle could tap the profits developers would reap from the up-zoning to pay for family-friendly amenities such as a park, school, and community center.[59] At their suggestion, Steinbrueck then convinced the council to commission two local real-estate experts—persons often employed by Seattle developers—to conduct a study of the economic implications of the mayor's proposal. The study showed that developers could comfortably contribute twice the amount the mayor proposed toward expanding affordable housing and the amenities that support family life.[60]

With these two studies in hand, Steinbrueck went to every constituency in the downtown and sought its support for transforming the mayor's "heights and density" plan into a "livability" plan.[61] Along with a 100 percent increase in contributions to an affordable housing fund from developers who build to the maximum, the plan increases the city's capacity to accommodate jobs and housing in the downtown area and provides an incentive for green buildings. It promotes a safe pedestrian environment by limiting aboveground parking, which precludes activity-generating uses. It brings more light and air into city streets by setting floor-area ratios that produce taller, more slender towers. It ensures the economic viability of historic buildings by allowing owners to sell more development rights. And it includes a resolution calling for more family-friendly amenities.[62]

Steinbrueck sees the downtown livability legislation, passed after a nine-month effort to improve the mayor's proposal, as the most important work of his eight years in office. Like the earlier citizens' initiative, this policy will shape Seattle's skyline, socioeconomic makeup, and quality of life well into the future. Although he advocated limits on building heights at a different moment in time, Steinbrueck recognized that the city's inevitable increase in population required a parallel increase in density. His legislation accommodates density in a gracious manner.

At Victor Steinbrueck Park, named in honor of his father, Peter Steinbrueck helps celebrate the centennial of Seattle's Olmsted park system; landscape architect Richard Haag is at left.
Courtesy Seattle Municipal Archives

Douglas Kelbaugh, FAIA

Lance Brown, FAIA (center), from City College in New York, one of the distinguished guests recruited for the 2000 Detroit charrette, and Kelbaugh (right) discuss a proposal with Senator Carl Levin.
Courtesy A. Alfred Taubman College of Architecture and Urban Planning, University of Michigan

Charrette team leader James Singleton depicted the Michigan Central Depot as a high-technology incubator, conference center, and high-speed transportation hub flanked by mixed-use loft buildings.
Ken Arbogast-Wilson

To his position as dean and professor of architecture and urban planning at the University of Michigan, Doug Kelbaugh brought a history of civic engagement that began in high school. At Princeton University in the 1960s, he was influenced by the student activism of the National Association of Student Planners and Architects (NASPA) and the work of ARCH in New York City. To realize his own activist agenda, Kelbaugh spent two years as a VISTA volunteer between undergraduate and graduate studies, when he established a community design center in Trenton, New Jersey. After earning a master's degree, Kelbaugh returned to Trenton to work for the city's department of planning and development. As the 1973 oil embargo heightened concerns about the use of nonrenewable resources, he designed one of the nation's first passive solar houses, launching a career focused on sustainable design and transit-oriented development.[63]

However, it was as chair of the University of Washington's architecture program that Kelbaugh became known as a champion of the academic design charrette, which he later transported to the University of Michigan.[64] These fast-moving events—which bring together students, faculty, government officials, citizens, and distinguished designers recruited from around the world—produce an array of creative approaches to environmental problems. Charrettes engage design teams in testing new public policies or design theories on specific sites, responding to needs defined by neighborhood groups or government agencies, and exploring topics of interest to the academy.[65] All told, several thousand people from across the country have participated in Kelbaugh's charrettes, and more than 10,000 people have attended the public presentations of the results. They usually attract significant media attention and result in such outcomes as follow-up presentations to community groups, design studios to study problems in greater depth, publications, the commissioning of consultant studies, and built projects.[66]

Because charrettes are short, explosive events, Kelbaugh prefers to study districts that lack residents or other strongly embedded constituencies so designers can work with broad strokes without causing undue displacement. On the other hand, some of his charrettes have dealt with mature neighborhoods where a more nuanced approach is required.[67]

A recent charrette in Detroit provides an example of combining district- and neighborhood-level interventions. The Detroit charrette took shape after a failed attempt by city officials to solicit proposals from developers for reusing Tiger Stadium as a multimillion-dollar loft-and-shopping complex. Faced with a dearth of ideas from developers, city officials were delighted when Kelbaugh organized a charrette to explore a greater range of possibilities.[68] The charrette study site eventually encompassed a large area with many stakeholders, including not only the stadium but also two neighborhoods (a middle-class historic one and a very low-income one),

1879
*James Renwick's St. Patrick's Cathedral,
New York City, opened for services*

a gambling casino, and a huge, deserted train station.[69] Over a period of five days, more than 80 designers, planners, artists, social historians, and community representatives—including students and faculty from four universities—worked in interdisciplinary design teams, using a space that overlooked the site as their design studio.[70]

Believing that elected officials and planners too often rely on megaprojects to rejuvenate Detroit, the teams proposed both large projects requiring significant public and private investment (such as a regional recreational center or cultural institution) and ones that could be carried out by community groups and small property owners (light industry, a communal organic farm, or loft conversions, for example). The teams also outlined the infrastructure (such as light rail, open space, green boulevards, or historic street lights retrofitted with solar panels) needed to sustain such projects.[71] Three hundred stakeholders and citizens attended a public presentation in a local union hall, including the mayor, who concluded the evening by making an extemporaneous and enthusiastic speech.[72] This dialogue continued in the following months as students studied the site in greater detail in their design studios.

Offered pro bono to the city, charrettes such as this one rely on support from universities, corporations, foundations, and individual donors, along with faculty and student sweat-equity and in-kind community contributions. Charrettes provide a public venue for discussing a city's future and also provide students with invaluable lessons in civic engagement.[73] According to Kelbaugh, charrettes nurture civic unity by bringing together a diverse mix of people who develop a sense of shared ownership and pride, producing a larger pool of ideas than conventional design consultations.[74] Such discussions have been essential to spurring the redevelopment of Detroit and other underutilized urban and suburban areas.

Design teams inspected the long-deserted Michigan Central Depot before the 2000 Detroit charrette. *Courtesy A. Alfred Taubman College of Architecture and Urban Planning, University of Michigan*

Ginny Graves, Hon. AIA

An educational consultant, Ginny Graves received honorary membership in the AIA for her landmark efforts to engage children and adults in improving their surroundings.[75] Graves's spirit of volunteerism began as a child observing her parents find ways to enrich art education in the public schools of rural western Kansas. Later, in 1969, Graves was searching for a way to strengthen the sense of community in Kansas City as more and more families moved to the suburbs. Her husband, Dean Graves, FAIA, was president of the local AIA chapter that year and noted that many architects were interested in introducing their craft to children as a way of nurturing future citizens who recognize good design. Together they developed "Box City," a curriculum that provides children with standardized materials for constructing an ideal city and exposes them to the vocabulary and processes of city planning.[76]

In 1983 with guidance from a network of architects, preservationists, and educators, Graves formalized the "Box City" concept as CUBE (Center for Understanding the Built Environment), an organization that links educators with community partners to advocate for urban environments that work for children as well as adults. Through CUBE, she helps children learn to value their surroundings, improve their problem-solving and social skills, and—more important—learn to take responsible action in their communities. Over the years, Graves and her entirely volunteer staff have augmented "Box City" with many other resources, including "Teach the Teachers," workshops and college-credit courses that introduce teachers to architecture; "Walk around the Block," which utilizes the neighborhood as a context for teaching basic skills; "Archi-Camp," a summer program offered annually for fourth- to eighth-grade students; and "Architivities," interdisciplinary community-based activities. To finance these activities, Graves and her staff channel all their honoraria back into the program. Over the years, they have exposed thousands of teachers and community partners to the value of architecture. In turn, these teachers and community partners have helped hundreds of thousands of young people appreciate design excellence and their power to demand it.[77]

Graves's generosity of spirit is not only directed toward children but also toward those adults who feel helpless to change what is happening around them or influence the city planning process.[78] For example, when a group of residents in the Washington Wheatley neighborhood of Kansas City wanted to change their circumstances, Graves adapted her curriculum to their needs. The neighborhood was suffering from typical urban problems: crime, drugs, prostitution, abandoned buildings, garbage-strewn streets, inadequate shopping, poor transportation, and lack of employment opportunities. To address these problems, members of a neighborhood-improvement association secured funding from housing and energy conservation agencies and then recruited experts—including Graves, Atlanta-based planner A. Hakim Yamini, and local architect Robert Berkebile, FAIA—to assist them in a community planning process. Under

Graves and the children take delight in the neighborhood being constructed from colorful Box City materials. She has conducted thousands of workshops over almost a quarter of a century.
Courtesy CUBE

their tutelage, residents, business owners, and agency representatives came together over a three-month period to create a Box City model of a major thoroughfare in the neighborhood. Graves designed the process with staff from an energy conservation agency, Yamini facilitated discussions on sustainable neighborhoods, and Berkebile turned the completed model into architectural drawings.[79]

Early in the process, participants learned about the characteristics of sustainable neighborhoods, viewed images of other communities, and considered what they wanted to preserve, change, and create in their own community. They toured the area, took photographs, and then used Box City tools—cardboard boxes and brown paper—to create a base model of the existing conditions. With this preparatory work in hand, about 100 participants gathered for an all-day session, which Yamini introduced by laying out a vision for a sustainable neighborhood. Invigorated by this vision, small groups collectively worked on "enhancing" the base model and then worked with Berkebile on land uses, road configurations, and landscaping. The conversation that occurred during the hands-on activities resulted in a planning document that outlines broad strategies for improving the community (such as encouraging transit and pedestrian activity, improving the safety and character of the area, and enhancing the sense of community) as well as the small details that affect people's day-to-day experience (for example, specifying restrictions on billboard advertising, calling for angled parking to form a buffer between pedestrians and vehicular traffic, and barring liquor sales except in establishments that sell more food than liquor).[80]

In many such participatory processes, architects maintain control over visioning tools that require skill to use. The beauty of Graves's Box City is that participants—without relying on architects to interpret their comments—can directly explore local issues and envision novel solutions. Whether the plans created ever come to fruition, these processes are empowering in themselves because they engage participants in learning about their communities and envisioning collective action. Graves demonstrates how today's architects can facilitate these important processes.

The Contributions of Activist Architects

This collection of historical and contemporary profiles provides a sample of the rich diversity of roles activist architects play—ones that are evolving as society continues along a path toward greater inclusiveness and social equity. Rather than attempting to achieve civic unity by imposing idealized spatial arrangements, today's architects nurture a spirit of collaboration, engaging citizens and public officials in mapping out common ground. In undertaking such dialogic processes, they draw on their enduring commitment to improve the nature of human existence on "spaceship earth," producing new and rehabilitated spaces and places that reflect a shared public consciousness. Architects use both broad-brush and nuanced methods to address people's lived experiences and reconfigure complex environmental relationships, incorporating culturally responsive design approaches and reusing scarce environmental resources. They encourage children and adults to care about the power of good design and then equip them with the tools to demand healthy and aesthetically pleasing housing and neighborhoods. And they shape the future of the global landscape, engaging in sustained policy making, inciting public debate, and inspiring the next generation of architects. Assuming varied roles—as visionaries, inventors, elected officials, administrators, educators, researchers, community organizers, facilitators, and practical problem solvers—today's architects draw on an array of skills to achieve design excellence in their socially constructed art. ●

Kansas City–based architect Bob Berkebile, FAIA, volunteered his expertise at the Washington Wheatley neighborhood planning session. *Kansas City Star*

Using paper and boxes provided by CUBE, participants proposed large and small interventions to make a sustainable neighborhood, the first such experiment in Kansas City. *Kansas City Star*

William Wilson Wurster, FAIA

Andrew Blum

Born in 1895 in Stockton, California, William Wilson Wurster studied architecture at the University of California, Berkeley. Following a European tour and a year working in New York, he opened his office in Berkeley in 1924. There, he began a quiet revolution that subsequently touched the lives of many Americans.

Wurster's work celebrated, and often defined, California living. Reflecting the vernacular of the region, his calculatedly modest—today one would say "shabby chic"—Gregory Farmhouse (1926–27) near Santa Cruz popularized the informal American home that many now take for granted. Describing the Bay Area regional style, which he helped advance, Wurster explained, "It is an architecture of *everyday use* rather than form or intellectual theory. Viewed as sculpture, it may disappoint, but if in a democratic society architecture is a social art, it may have some validity."

Wurster was equally influential in architecture education. As dean of architecture at Massachusetts Institute of Technology in the 1940s, he pioneered open critiques of students' work. He returned to Berkeley in 1950 to become dean and, in 1959, combined the departments of architecture, landscape architecture, and planning into the College of Environmental Design, a move that reflected his belief in the benefits of disagreement and discussion. Through open critiques and a multidisciplinary education setting, Wurster sought to make architecture studies reflect real-life situations, an impulse that foreshadowed the profession's increased political involvement in coming years. Wurster was awarded the Gold Medal in 1969 in recognition of his significant contributions to both design and education. He died in 1973.

Wurster's rustic, one-story Gregory Farmhouse (1926–27), Santa Cruz, is often cited as the prototype for the Bay Area–style ranch house.
Roger Sturtevant, Wurster/WBE Collection, Environmental Design Archives, University of California, Berkeley

Known primarily for his residential work, Wurster designed what he liked to call the "large small house." The Coleman House (1957) typifies many elements of his style: curved glass walls, intimate gardens, and breathtaking views of San Francisco Bay.
Environmental Design Archives, University of California, Berkeley

Samuel Mockbee, FAIA

Andrea Oppenheimer Dean

Larger-than-life, sixth-generation Mississippian Samuel "Sambo" Mockbee directed the Rural Studio—Auburn University's design-build studio—which has created more than 60 houses and community buildings in some of the poorest towns in southwestern Alabama. In a letter nominating Mockbee for the 2004 Gold Medal, Los Angeles architect Frank Gehry wrote, "There have been few programs as radical as the Rural Studio in helping students to believe in their role for the future." New York architect Peter Eisenman commended the studio for stressing "the ethical dimension of building." And another Los Angeles architect, Michael Rotondi, stated that "Mockbee represents all that we aspire to be as individuals and as a profession."

Mockbee, who studied architecture at Auburn, upheld the conviction that "everyone, rich or poor, deserves a shelter for the soul." He believed that architects should lead in procuring social and environmental change, but felt that the profession had lost its moral compass and needed reform. For Mockbee, education was the place to start: He wanted to get students away from classroom theory into what he called the "classroom of the community."

Mockbee's ideas and aesthetic evolved while he was in private practice. He described his architecture as contemporary modernism grounded in the culture of the South. He was inspired by vernacular sources: overhanging galvanized roofs, metal trailers, dogtrot forms, porches. "I'm drawn to anything that has a quirkiness to it, a mystery to it," he said. His designs tended toward asymmetry and idiosyncrasy, as seen, for example, in two award-winning residences: the Barton House in Madison County, Mississippi, and the Cook House in Oxford, Mississippi.

Mockbee, together with Auburn University's then-chair of architecture D.K. Ruth, founded the Rural Studio in 1992. He chose to plant the studio in Hale County, Alabama's second poorest, thereby forcing students to test their abstract notions about poverty by "crossing over into that other world, smelling it, feeling it, experiencing it," Mockbee said. The isolation, he believed, would concentrate their minds on building projects.

In addition to providing students with a hands-on education in both architecture and social welfare, the design-build studio encouraged the young designers to experiment with salvaged, recycled, and curious materials and to explore an aesthetic of place. "I want to be over the edge—environmentally, aesthetically, and technically," Mockbee said. His students used hay bales to enclose the studio's first house, worn-out tires for the walls of a chapel, and salvaged Chevy Caprice windshields for the roof of a community center.

The Rural Studio changed architecture education. While there were only eight or ten university-based design-build programs in 1992, they are common today—and much of the increase is ascribed to Mockbee's example. More important, the mere presence of the Rural Studio has served as an economic engine for Hale County. And the program has created buildings that are, in the words of District Judge William Ryan, "much more creative than what we could have received on the commercial market." Ryan says, "the students don't know you can't do things, and, therefore, things get done that normally wouldn't." At the same time, stresses the local resident, students at the Rural Studio are exposed to the realities of Hale County: "They see how people live in this forgotten part of the world."

Mockbee directed the program until his death in late 2001. A venture like the Rural Studio rarely flourishes after the loss of its prime mover, but Mockbee's endeavor continues to thrive—testimony to the validity of his ideas and the strength of his spirit.

The Rural Studio's Yancey Chapel (1996), Sawyerville, Alabama, is constructed of recycled tires, slate from a nearby riverbed, and timber recycled from an old house. *©Timothy Hursley*

The Hay Bale House (1994), so-called because its interior walls are of hay bales, is located in the tiny community of Mason's Bend, Alabama. It was the Rural Studio's first completed building. *©Timothy Hursley*

1882
San Francisco chapter of the
AIA, the first on the West Coast,
was organized

Crane Library,
Quincy, Massachusetts,
H. H. Richardson

GRASS ROOTS

Architecture for Humanity: How to Give a Damn

Kira Gould, Assoc. AIA

Is it the role of the architect to create the signature monuments that define and exalt our cultural and economic values? Or, is there an alternative path to building in the world today, one that engages people where they live and work and recognizes that sustainability is not a luxury but a necessity?
—Architecture for Humanity

London-born architect Cameron Sinclair was working at a large New York architecture firm in 1999 when he and Kate Stohr, a journalist and documentary producer, founded Architecture for Humanity (AFH). The mission of this nonprofit design organization, as outlined in its literature, is to "promote architectural and design solutions to global, social and humanitarian crises" by way of competitions, workshops, educational forums, and partnerships with aid groups. "We believe that where resources and expertise are scarce, innovative, sustainable and collaborative design can make a difference," declares AFH.

Volunteers and donors believe it too. AFH has been active in two of the largest natural disasters in recent years. Following the tsunami in December 2004, AFH helped raise funds and bring design services to the devastated areas of India and Sri Lanka. Since Hurricane Katrina, AFH has worked along the Gulf Coast to connect displaced families with architects and designers. The housing crisis in Kosovo—caused by war, not weather—motivated Sinclair and Stohr to organize a 1999 competition in which 220 teams from 30 countries designed living spaces for returning refugees. And the organization is currently developing mobile medical facilities to help combat HIV/AIDS.

"Chapters" weren't part of the original plan, but groups sprang up in two dozen cities; thousands of designers now work together on local projects under the AFH name. Many such initiatives, plus those by like-minded people who are applying design when and where it is needed most, are elegantly profiled in the AFH-edited book, *Design Like You Give a Damn* (Metropolis Books, 2006).

Metropolis editor-in-chief Susan Szenasy credits Sinclair and Stohr, who have since married, with helping architects refocus. "When they started AFH, the talk in the architecture community was about the stars," she says. "That is not going away, but there is a growing trend toward socially responsible architecture. Cameron is one of a few architects who are helping the profession get back to its humanist roots. Equally important, he has an impressive following among young architects looking to connect with something bigger than fleeting fame."

Robert Ivy, editor-in-chief of *Architectural Record*, agrees. "Cameron tapped into a wellspring of social consciousness and goodwill that, historically, has characterized architects," he says. "In succeeding in the larger culture, we have become almost myopic, perhaps by necessity. Yet we enter architecture to help people, and we understand it as a social art. We are hungry for opportunities to express that in a tangible way. Cameron has reached thousands who share his perspective, and he has given us an opportunity to contribute."

Ardent, articulate, and energetic advocates for solutions that are based on design, place, and community, Sinclair and Stohr believe that architects have an ethical responsibility to the neediest. Sinclair has written, "If you strip away the ego, the archi-lingo and the philosophies of design, the sole purpose of architecture is to provide shelter. Our profession embodies far more than creating inspiring spaces, it is about innovating and striving to achieve an ideal."

Chicago architect Jeanne Gang used vernacular elements in her entry for Architecture for Humanity's Biloxi Model Home Program, held in post–Katrina Biloxi, Mississippi.
Tracy Nelson, courtesy Architecture for Humanity

As part of its 150th anniversary celebration in 2007, the American Institute of Architects launched a multiyear initiative, the AIA150 Blueprint for America. This effort, which has truly inspired and engaged AIA members from across the country, could be considered the Institute's "call to community service."

In 2006 the AIA invited its 300 state and local components to work with local partners to identify opportunities to apply the Institute's overall vision of a livable and sustainable future. More than 175 responded with creativity, enthusiasm, and a strong sense of purpose. They proposed a diverse array of initiatives to address their respective communities' distinct issues and needs. And the AIA national component responded by awarding more than $1.4 million in supplemental funding to assist 157 chapters in these undertakings. Jack Ford, former mayor of Toledo, Ohio, concluded that this initiative was the AIA's "gift to America" on the occasion of its sesquicentennial celebration.

Beginning in 2006 and continuing throughout the anniversary year, thousands of AIA architects will partner with local government officials, allied professionals, not-for-profit entities, schools of architecture, and fellow citizens to achieve their goals. The scale of initiatives being undertaken varies greatly. Some will address regional issues associated with a river valley or major transportation corridor; others will focus on downtown and neighborhood revitalization, affordable housing, homelessness, sustainability, or adaptive use of historic structures. But all are tackling conditions that their respective communities have identified as being critical to the long-term quality of life. In 2008 participating components are expected to document their efforts so that they can serve as models for others.

In its ongoing effort to engage the public in a dialogue about the impact of architecture on our daily lives, the AIA has partnered with Google Earth to make Blueprint for America projects available to more than 200 million users. As a featured "layer" on Google Earth, the Blueprint reinforces the message that architects and local citizens are part of a growing global effort to create healthy, sustainable, livable communities.

In terms of its component participation, the Blueprint for America is certainly the most ambitious community-service initiative ever undertaken by the Institute, but it is by no means the first. In fact, since

it sent its first Regional/Urban Design Assistance Team (R/UDAT) to Rapid City, South Dakota, in 1967 to assess existing conditions and help develop a vision to guide downtown redevelopment, the AIA has built a solid record of community advocacy.

Now managed by the Institute's Center for Communities by Design, the R/UDAT program has, as of mid-2006, assisted 138 cities and towns. AIA architect-led teams of multidisciplinary professionals have responded to requests for assistance by community leaders from California to Massachusetts and Montana to Texas. Offered as a public service of the Institute, the R/UDAT program uses a charrette-style, visioning approach to provide a community with a fresh perspective on, and innovative solutions to, longstanding, seemingly intractable, problems. Emphasizing the engagement of all members of the community, the AIA team combines local resources and citizen participation with the expertise of professionals from across the nation in an intensive, four-day workshop held in their community. This approach—which can address social, economic, political, and physical issues—offers communities a powerful mechanism to mobilize local support and foster new levels of cooperation among the public, not-for-profit, and private sectors.

A second program that has also served as a model for the Blueprint is the Sustainable Design Assistance Team (SDAT), which began in 2005. Although patterned to some extent on the R/UDAT model, the SDAT program offers a broader assessment of a community's policies or design approach in the context of sustainable principles. SDATs bring teams of volunteer professionals (such as architects, urban designers, planners, hydrologists, economists, and attorneys) to work with community decision makers and stakeholders in a three-day charrette to help formulate a vision and framework for a healthy and economically viable future. In 2006, eight communities—from Guemes Island, Washington, to Syracuse, New York—were chosen to receive this technical assistance.

It is my sincere hope that when the Institute celebrates its bicentennial in 2057, the members will reminisce that it was the AIA150 Blueprint for America initiative that helped the public finally begin to understand that architects have the knowledge, skills, and unwavering commitment to work with communities to improve the quality of life for all.

Blueprint for America

Anthony J. "Tony" Costello, FAIA

AIA New York's Blueprint initiative, titled the "New Housing New York Legacy Project," is generating creative approaches to quality, affordable housing on a site in the South Bronx.
Phipps Rose Dattner Grimshaw, courtesy AIA New York

AIA Utah architects are helping to lay the groundwork for the future growth and development of Salt Lake City. Their "Downtown Rising" initiative envisions a more vibrant, dense, environmentally sustainable, mixed-use urban core. *Paul D. Brown*

AIA Lubbock architect-volunteers, along with neighborhood and business leaders, public officials, and Texas Tech architecture faculty, are tackling issues of rapid economic and population growth in the "North University Avenue Mercado" project. Conceptual design of the mercado addresses the community's needs; respects the area's Hispanic art, architecture, and culture; and emphasizes sustainable development. *Brian Griggs, AIA*

GRASS ROOTS

Charles Harper, FAIA: Disaster Responder and Civic Leader

Barbara A. Nadel, FAIA

Charles Harper, FAIA
Courtesy Charles Harper

Charles Harper has provided disaster response assistance to homeowners, businesses, public officials, and architects for more than 35 years. He has guided reconstruction efforts, shared technical expertise, and led his community. And his building assessment checklists and disaster planning guidelines have been published and read around the world. For these many accomplishments, Harper received the AIA's 2001 Kemper Award, the Institute's highest honor for service to the profession, the Distinguished Alumnus Award from the College of Architecture at Texas Tech University (TTU), and the TTU Distinguished Alumnus Award.

Harper's journey as an emergency responder began when he joined the AIA Urban Planning and Design Committee (UPDC) in 1967, as the Regional/Urban Design Assistance Team (R/UDAT) program started. In 1970, when Harper was Texas Society of Architects (TSA) vice president, a tornado struck downtown Lubbock and Hurricane Celia hit Corpus Christi. Architects in both cities called TSA for disaster recovery assistance, and Harper was appointed to lead a response committee, the first professional response group to help cities recover from natural disasters.

After the devastating 1972 flood in Rapid City, South Dakota, the mayor of that town asked Harper and UPDC to provide disaster recovery assistance. Immediate action was required, but R/UDATs needed six months to assemble, prompting formation of the national AIA Disaster Response Committee (DRC), designed for quick mobilization. Harper subsequently used DRC to train architects and state components in developing local response organizations.

Throughout the 1970s, Harper led many teams to sites of natural disasters and man-made accidents in the United States. Federal disaster response activities remained fragmented, however, because of the many public agencies involved. To streamline the process, Harper, along with DRC members and governors, lobbied Congress for a centralized federal approach. Eventually signed by President Jimmy Carter, a 1979 executive order merged separate disaster-related responsibilities into the new Federal Emergency Management Agency (FEMA).

In April of the same year, a large tornado struck Harper's hometown of Wichita Falls, Texas, resulting in more than 42 deaths and more than $400 million in damage. Harper organized disaster response efforts and, along with TTU colleagues, studied the damage. Their findings led to development of safe rooms, central spaces with reinforced walls designed to protect people during storms.

Harper was appointed chair of the Wichita Falls Tornado Reconstruction and Redevelopment Committee, where he strengthened regulations for contractors, inspections, and zoning; coordinated national and state assistance; and managed volunteer architects during rebuilding. In recognition of his efforts, the community elected Harper to its city council (1983–86) and later as Wichita Falls mayor (1986–88).

During this time, Harper maintained his practice at Harper Perkins Architects. He retired in 2004 but remains active with clients. Although he stepped down as DRC chair in 2005, after Hurricane Katrina hit, he has since made five trips to help architects in Louisiana and Mississippi. As a civic and professional leader, Harper has trained several generations of architects to apply their skills after disasters. His remarkable legacy has revitalized communities, engaged the public, and inspired others to provide emergency response services.

The April 1979 Wichita Falls, Texas, tornado destroyed everything in its path.
Courtesy Charles Harper

A multistory masonry building with one of the floating casinos that washed ashore after Hurricane Katrina (photo taken September 2005). *Courtesy Charles Harper*

Discovering the Power of Youth

Sharon Egretta Sutton, PhD, FAIA

I began working with youth quite by accident. As an architect and first-year doctoral student in environmental psychology, I had organized residents in a working-class neighborhood to protest a church congregation's plans to enlarge its parking lot. Instead of increased macadam and deserted areas for drug dealing, the residents asked church members to designate the property as a community garden. When the congregation agreed, workers were needed to construct the garden. The children who had been following me around as I went door to door organizing residents seemed my best option. Several years later, I passed by the site, and it was still in use as a community garden.

With that project in hand, I secured another assignment—this time to design and build structures with low-achieving black and Hispanic children in the yard of an overcrowded elementary school. Low test scores notwithstanding, the children proved imaginative designers. They also demonstrated proficiency in raising money and then specifying and purchasing construction materials. Compensating for limited manual dexterity with determination and patience, these 8- to 12-year-olds erected perfectly crafted structures. As I watched the exuberant commitment of so-called low-achievers, I became more and more convinced of the need for developing a view of achievement that would be supportive of the abilities I observed.[1]

Thus began my life's work to make the talents of disadvantaged children visible to the adults who have power over their lives. On the one hand, I try to convince educators, social workers, and psychologists, among other youth-development experts who typically view low-income youth as problem-laden clients, that this population can help eradicate the structural inequities in their lives and neighborhoods. On the other hand, I try to convince planners and designers, who typically see community development as the purview of adults, that youth not only offer an important perspective but also have a fundamental right to participate in decisions that affect them.

Recently I received a grant from the Ford Foundation to further the involvement of disadvantaged youth in community life. For two-and-a-half years, I oversaw a national team of senior and junior scholars representing the fields of art, architecture, anthropology, education, geography, landscape architecture, psychology, social work, urban design and planning, and women's studies. Our team studied 88 programs in 36 large cities, selected because their staffs have a commitment to treat disadvantaged youths, ages 12 to 28, as community resources rather than community problems. The research revealed the barriers to healthy development that the youths in these programs face. They live in horrid environmental conditions—enduring, for example, poor nutrition, substandard housing, and overcrowded, understaffed, and underfunded schools. They experience multiple forms of discrimination and harassment, from police misconduct to racial profiling and gay-bashing to relentless military recruitment. At the same time, many already shoulder adult responsibilities.[2]

Despite these circumstances, the research confirmed my belief in the resourcefulness of this population. The directors of the programs we studied report that, when given appropriate opportunities, the youths have successfully partnered with adults to shape their own development and that of their communities.[3] They may work directly to improve their surroundings through community planning, design, and construction, as well as through artistic productions and what is known as "participatory action research," in which residents (including youths) participate in researching a community problem and then acting to address it,[4] or they may demand that others improve those surroundings through direct actions such as campaigns, demonstrations, and letter writing. Some efforts concentrate on the schools, while others focus on neighborhoods or even an entire city. To all their work, youths bring special qualities that, along with the work itself, contribute to the rejuvenation of communities. Many staff not only express an appreciation of young people's energy, idealism, and playfulness, but they also insist that these traits sustain them and their organization. Such programs provide fertile ground for architects to enhance the social and spatial characteristics of disadvantaged communities while also spiritually enriching themselves and their profession.

Children in the inner city of Lancaster, Pennsylvania, construct a garden on property given over to community use by the mostly suburban congregation of a nearby church. *Courtesy Sharon E. Sutton*

A passerby admires the handiwork of the 8- to 12-year-olds who designed and built this structure, an outdoor history "museum," in the schoolyard of Public School 152, Brooklyn. *Courtesy Sharon E. Sutton*

Teens in a Massachusetts program develop leadership skills by farming 31 acres of urban and rural land, which produces nearly a quarter-million pounds of chemical-free crops. They donate half their crops to local shelters and sell the other half through farmers markets. *Greig Canna*

VIEWPOINT

Rebuilding Ground Zero

Paul Goldberger, Hon. AIA

Studio Daniel Libeskind's winning master plan for Ground Zero has been substantially compromised since its adoption in 2003.
Courtesy Lower Manhattan Development Corporation

The THINK team, led by architects Frederic Schwartz, Rafael Vinoly, and Ken Smith of New York, and Shigeru Ban of Tokyo, created a master plan for Ground Zero that was passed over in 2003 in favor of Studio Daniel Libeskind's proposal.
Courtesy Lower Manhattan Development Corporation

Architects Michael Arad and Peter Walker, in conjunction with associate architect Max Bond, designed "Reflecting Absence," the memorial marking the footprint of the World Trade Center towers and honoring those lost in the terrorist attacks of September 11, 2001, and February 26, 1993.
Courtesy Lower Manhattan Development Corporation

If the long and tortuous process of rebuilding Ground Zero has proven anything, it is that architecture is one thing, and architects quite another. From the morning of September 12, 2001, architectural issues were central to the public discussions about the future of the 16 acres where the World Trade Center once stood. There was more public interest in the future of this site than in any urban site in modern history, and unlike most public issues, the civic debate about redevelopment was cast in architectural terms. In the months following the terrorist attacks, it seemed not only as if architecture might actually be able to express the national ideals, but more notable still, that a piece of contemporary architecture might become a viable symbol of the national response to a great crisis.

Beginning with the call to architects shortly after September 11th from a gallery owner asking them to produce visionary designs for the trade center site—a call to which more than 60 architects, including such diverse figures as Zaha Hadid, Michael Graves, and Paolo Soleri, responded—and continuing with the critical role many architects played in several civic groups, most notably New York New Visions, which arose as vehicles to channel public engagement in the rebuilding process, architecture seemed in the public eye as never before. And when the official planning process under the jurisdiction of the Lower Manhattan Development Corporation produced, first, a series of studies by Beyer Blinder Belle and Peterson Littenberg in 2002, and then a master plan competition that included works by such figures as Daniel Libeskind, Rafael Vinoly, Frederick Schwartz, Norman Foster, Richard Meier, Charles Gwathmey, Peter Eisenman, Steven Holl, Greg Lynn, and Ben van Berkel, it seemed to assert that the nation was prepared to let the world's leading architects make significant decisions about land use.

The nation may have been willing, but the politicians were not, and all the attention given to the official planning process obscured the fact that the program for the site was essentially the same as the original program of the World Trade Center—several million square feet of office space—with a memorial and some cultural buildings respectfully thrown in. There was no room for truly visionary schemes. By the time the design process reached a climax in early 2003—when the proposals were narrowed down to one master plan by Libeskind and another by THINK, a team led by Vinoly, and these preeminent designers were invited to present their respective visions on national television—it was clear

that however much architecture had become central to the public dialogue, the role of architects would be severely constrained at Ground Zero.

Libeskind won the competition, but as soon as his master plan was adopted, it began to be compromised. The tall tower that Libeskind envisioned as the main symbol of his reconstructed Ground Zero remained in the plan, but Larry Silverstein, the developer who held the lease on the old twin towers and was planning to build the new buildings, wanted David Childs of Skidmore, Owings & Merrill, not Libeskind, to design it. The governor of New York, George Pataki, tried to broker a compromise between Childs and Libeskind, and the result was a building that represented neither architect's best work. Later, commissions for other Ground Zero buildings went to Santiago Calatrava, who was asked to design a transportation center; Frank Gehry, who was assigned a performing-arts building; Snohetta, a museum; and Norman Foster, Richard Rogers, and Fumihiko Maki, who were each asked to do individual office buildings. Libeskind received no building commissions, and his master plan was further compromised by the design of the memorial to the people who died on September 11, by Michael Arad and Peter Walker. The cultural buildings themselves were changed to accommodate financial and political pressures, and the dominant thrust of the project seemed increasingly to be the production of commercial office buildings.

It wasn't only a matter of real-world concerns compromising idealistic plans—that happens all the time, even though such compromises stood out in higher relief amid the powerful emotions that surround Ground Zero. The problem at Ground Zero was more complex, and more subtle. For the first year or two after September 11, it appeared as if politicians were looking to architects to create what would, in effect, be a calling card for the renewed city, and were willing to cede some authority to the profession in determining what kind of national symbol would be most appropriate at Ground Zero. But if architects were finally given a seat at the table, it soon became clear that its place was not, as many members of the profession had expected, at the head. Political and economic forces remained firmly in control. A planning process that began with high expectations for the profession has slipped, month by month and year by year, toward the ordinary. And Ground Zero now seems less likely to demonstrate the nation's architectural potential than to reveal the country's hesitation and uncertainty.

Love has played a central role in my life's choices. The first love was that of architecture. As an aspiring artist and the son of an engineer, architecture early on captured my heart as the perfect marriage of these two wonderful worlds. The second love was that of my wife, Katrina, a first-generation American daughter of Hungarian holocaust survivors, who instilled in me a more urgent sense to improve the world. These two loves led to my somewhat unorthodox career path from a designer of buildings to a designer of public policy to my current position as a developer of and consultant to large, sustainable real-estate and alternative-energy projects.

When I first ran for the House of Representatives in 1990, I chose to emphasize my unusual professional background for a congressional candidate with the catchy phrase, "Every good house needs an architect." When I was subsequently elected, becoming the first architect in the 20th century to serve in Congress (and the first Democrat in 78 years to serve in New Hampshire's 2nd District), I began to realize how true my slogan was. My architecture training provided me with a different toolbox than was possessed by many of my law-school-trained colleagues. The design process I had learned as an architect allowed me to be more inclusive and creative in solving problems.

One example of this designer's approach to legislation was the 1995 Congressional Accountability Act, which essentially required members of Congress to abide by the same laws that they pass for the rest of the country. My coauthor, Republican Congressman Chris Shays from Connecticut, and I sought to engage our colleagues as stakeholders in a cooperative design process, not as adversaries on the field of combat. For example, we met with various interested groups to brainstorm on blank paper, much as an architect would sketch a client's initial ideas. Chris and I then selected the best aspects and presented three "schemes" from which the stakeholders could choose. This approach contrasts sharply to the status quo: legislation is typically written by one member and offered to colleagues as a fait accompli, alterable only by amendment on the House floor. Our innovative methodology worked. Despite an institutional reluctance to lose any "privileges and immunities" of their office, the representatives passed the legislation and the bill was signed into law.

In 1998 President Bill Clinton asked me to serve as the American ambassador to Denmark. Not since Thomas Jefferson had an architect joined the U.S. Diplomatic Corps. Again, my professional background helped me provide the necessary vision and management skills for the Copenhagen staff. In large part due to my successful overhaul of this embassy's organizational structure, State Department Undersecretary Marc Grossman contacted me three weeks after 9/11, and less than three months after I had left Denmark, with an important request. He wanted me to assist Secretary of State Colin Powell in designing an organizational system to integrate information from embassies and consulates all over the world to be used in the federal government's efforts to build a global antiterrorism coalition.

I convinced the undersecretary to take the unusual step of convening a design charrette with senior State Department officials and some of the nation's most highly accomplished architects. The architects at this special work session, which I led in October 2002, were able to draw out the organizational needs of the officials to create a critical-path methodology that would help the country quickly and effectively build the needed coalition. Perhaps for the first time, "architectural thinking" was creatively applied in the fight against international terrorism.

Mark Twain once observed that if the only tool you have is a hammer, after awhile every problem begins to look like a nail. For too long our political leaders have been pounding at problems when far more subtle techniques were required. Architects have the vision, training, and tools to help us craft better solutions for the 21st century. It is my deep hope that, over the AIA's next 150 years, there will be many more successful "marriages" between architect-leaders and their communities.

An Architect in Politics: A Personal Reflection

Richard N. Swett, FAIA

Richard N. Swett, FAIA (middle), former congressman from New Hampshire and ambassador to Denmark, with President Bill Clinton (and unidentified man), 1994. *Courtesy Richard N. Swett*

1885
Poll by American Architect and
Building News *named H. H.
Richardson's Trinity Church the
most admired building in America*

*Home Insurance Building,
Chicago,
William Le Baron Jenney*

4

Ensuring a Healthy and Prosperous Future

Thomas Fisher

(Opposite) Aerial view of Central Park, New York, 1880s. Olmsted called such parks the "lungs of the city," providing relief from the noise and grime of industry. *Getty Images*

While all professions are licensed to attend to the public good, few of them have as broad a responsibility as architects. Medicine focuses on our health, law on our safety, and social work on our welfare, but architecture encompasses all three—the health, safety, and welfare (HSW) of people in buildings, where we all spend most of our time. In our hyperspecialized society, which rewards people according to how much they know about some very narrow subject, the public tends to undervalue the breadth of the architect's duties. But that is about to change.

Faced with HSW threats at a scale rarely seen before, modern industrialized culture stands at a tipping point. What we do over the next few decades will make all the difference in whether we thrive or barely survive as a civilization. This is not hyperbole: most of the HSW advances we have made over the past 150 years arose out of catastrophic events that had devastating effects within a relatively limited geographical area. The resulting evolution in building codes and regulations over that same period largely occurred on an equally limited scale, primarily locally and, more recently, nationally. Over the next 50 years, however, the threats we face are global, and their potential impacts are much more far-reaching than what we have experienced before. Hence, our thinking about HSW needs to expand accordingly. In that context, the very breadth of architects' visions will become the profession's most valuable asset.

Efforts of the Past

In terms of health and safety, the first regulation of buildings in the Western Hemisphere occurred in New York City in 1625, when the Dutch West India Company established rules for the type and locations of buildings and for public safety and sanitation. While primitive by modern standards, those regulations showed how new approaches to HSW arise when people confront new conditions. For these Europeans, who began to colonize North America during this earlier phase of globalization, rapid development, local building materials, and sometimes jerry-built structures demanded that trading companies establish building guidelines. Over the next two centuries, New York continued to improve its health and safety regulations: laws regulating construction safety, fire prevention, and public sanitation—all of which were in place by 1674—evolved to the point that, by 1761, they specified the types of construction materials and methods allowed in certain parts of the city.

Yet catastrophic events still occurred. In New York, the Great Fire of 1845 destroyed 300 buildings, leading the city to write the country's first comprehensive building code in 1850. Although that code improved the safety of buildings in New York by putting in place approval and enforcement measures, it did not benefit other jurisdictions. The Great Chicago Fire of 1871 destroyed 17,000 buildings, killed 250 people, and left 100,000 homeless. However, not until 1905 did the National Board of Fire Underwriters write the first national fire code, recognizing that all Americans deserved the same basic level of fire protection.

U.S. planners and politicians began to consider the human health problems associated with poor indoor sanitation and air quality around the middle of the 19th century, coinciding with the rise of the "sanitary movement" in public health. Landscape architect Frederick Law Olmsted helped lead the cause in this country. Olmsted, along with architect Calvert Vaux, had won the 1857 competition to design a new Central Park for New York on city-owned land. Such parks, Olmsted believed, were the "lungs of the city," providing a physical and psychological breath of fresh air within increasingly noisy and dirty industrial cities.

Landscape architect Frederick Law Olmsted designed Central Park and championed the cause of improved health and sanitary conditions for Union soldiers during the Civil War. Olmsted left his Central Park job in 1861 to lead the U.S. Sanitary Commission. *©Corbis*

New York's Tenement House Act of 1901, the nation's first comprehensive housing legislation, set standards for improved daylight, ventilation, and toilet facilities in tenements. *©Bettmann/Corbis*

Jacob Riis's famous 1887 photo of Bandits' Roost, an alley off Mulberry Street in New York City, helped galvanize public opinion for tenement reform. *Jacob Riis/©Hulton-Deutsch Collection/Corbis*

With the outbreak of the Civil War in 1861, Olmsted turned his attention to the physical and mental health of the Union soldiers. He, along with a group of doctors, theologians, and committed citizens, approached the federal government about the unsanitary conditions in military camps. After some initial resistance, they were given government approval to establish the Sanitary Commission. Olmsted became its first general secretary. The commission inspected the camps and made recommendations about a number of design issues, including the location of camps, provision for drainage and waste disposal, ventilation of tents, and storage and preparation of food.

The Sanitary Commission led to the founding of the American Red Cross 20 years later. But it also led—almost immediately—to a more holistic view of HSW in civilian life by showing how poor sanitation, bad indoor air quality, and unsafe site conditions can endanger people as much as jerry-built structures or combustible materials. Although periodic epidemics of smallpox and yellow fever got the most attention, chronic ailments such as tuberculosis, malaria, and respiratory and digestive diseases—widely accepted until the mid-19th century as part of everyday urban life—also became killers because of overcrowded conditions and bad sanitation. This changed, however, in large part because of the work of the Sanitary Commission during the Civil War.

In 1867 New York City enacted the nation's first tenement law to control unhealthy conditions in housing by limiting, for example, the placement of outdoor latrines. At the turn of the century, when the density in parts of New York City had reached 665 people per acre, a group of reformers held a two-week exhibition on Fifth Avenue that

1886
Dedication of Statue of Liberty,
New York City

Allegheny County Courthouse,
Pittsburgh,
H. H. Richardson

detailed the squalid living conditions of Lower East Side residents through photographs, charts, and maps. This exhibition prompted the city's prosperous population to pressure the state of New York to pass the country's first comprehensive housing legislation, the Tenement House Act of 1901. The act required features that we now consider essential to the livability of buildings, including daylight and natural ventilation in most spaces, the privacy and security of housing units, and the availability of adequate indoor plumbing.

This legislation sparked an uproar from some landlords, especially over the requirement that tenements have airshafts for interior rooms and water closets with sewer connections. Claiming that the new law violated their 14th Amendment right of property, the landlords took their opposition, on appeal from municipal and state courts, all the way to the Supreme Court. In 1906 the Supreme Court upheld, in *Tenement House Department of City of New York v. Moeschen*, the lower courts' decisions. In the wake of that ruling, cities and states around the country enacted similar housing laws, a major step in making HSW a national concern.

In 1909 the AIA passed its first code of ethics, which had, as its first principle, a clause that made it "improper [for architects] to engage in building." While challenged decades later for preventing architects from working as developers or in design-build companies, that prohibition sought to ensure that architects would look after the public good and not succumb to the temptation of tenement owners and builders in shortcutting HSW to increase profit.

The early 1900s also saw the establishment, in the United States, of three regional building codes: the Building Officials and Code Administrators (BOCA) code used in the East and Midwest, the Southern Building Code Conference International (SBCCI) code in the South, and the International Conference of Building Officials (UBC) code in the West. The regional codes recognized the need to balance national standards with local differences by including the input and advocacy of architects responsible for following them (something that remains true today, with the AIA's Codes Advocacy Program).

The 1906 San Francisco earthquake and fire, along with the 1925 Santa Barbara earthquake, led to the UBC's first seismic code, in 1927. This 1906 photo is of San Francisco's Market Street.
©*Ted Streshinsky/Corbis*

1887
Richard Morris Hunt elected third
president of the AIA

Founding of the Washington, D.C.,
chapter of the AIA

National Pensions Building
(National Building Museum),
Washington, D.C.,
Montgomery C. Meigs

Glessner House,
Chicago,
H. H. Richardson

Another catastrophe, in 1906—San Francisco's 7.8 Richter magnitude earthquake and the subsequent fire that killed some 3,000 people—took HSW concerns in a new direction. That event not only gave rise to modern earthquake science but also led, along with the Santa Barbara quake of 1925, to the first seismic code in the UBC in 1927, which focused on the structural stability of buildings and the safety of both inhabitants and passersby.

The early seismic codes signaled a trend that would emerge over the course of the 20th century—a focus on more specialized threats to a more diverse group of people. Although the Depression and World War II slowed construction and, with it, the evolution of HSW, the 1950s and 1960s brought new challenges as buildings became larger and more technically advanced, leading to the regulation of materials, assemblies, and uses unanticipated just a few decades before.

In the wake of the first Earth Day in 1970 and the oil price shocks of the mid-1970s, another new area of regulation arose: energy codes. Responding to wasteful practices in the building sector, which accounted for as much as 40 percent of the energy Americans consumed at that time, California took the initiative with its Title 24 regulations in the early 1970s, followed nationally by groups such as the American Society of Heating, Refrigerating and Air-Conditioning Engineers, Inc. (ASHRAE), with its Standard 90 in 1975, and the Council of American Building Officials, with its model energy code of 1986.

Toward the end of the 20th century, the design and construction industries began exploring other ways—in addition to building codes—to address energy and other growing environmental problems. The 1980s and 1990s saw a transition from focusing specifically on energy-saving strategies in buildings to looking more holistically at the sustainability of modern society in general. The AIA took the lead in this effort with information and best practices promulgated by its Committee on the Environment (COTE) through the *Environmental Resource Guide*. COTE members, among other architects, also helped establish the U.S. Green Building Council to write voluntary guidelines—Leadership in Energy and Environmental Design (LEED)—that give points for a wide variety of environmentally friendly decisions involving not just the design of buildings but also their operations, immediate surroundings, and access.

A parallel conservation effort occurred with the rise of preservation laws and codes. With the passage of the National Historic Preservation Act in 1966 and the writing of preservation-oriented building code provisions beginning in the 1970s, the reuse of old buildings became a mainstream part of American architecture practice. Unlike the energy codes, which allowed for uniform enforcement, the preservation codes required building officials to be flexible, depending on existing conditions. This approach created conflicts at first, but these codes eventually led HSW regulations to become more performance based and outcome oriented, and somewhat less prescriptive and absolute, thereby benefiting everyone. Special interests also found common ground in the codes: environmentalists, concerned with conserving energy, and preservationists, concerned with protecting physical remnants of our history, saw their goals converge around the growing awareness of the embodied energy that exists in all materials, new as well as old. By saving existing buildings, energy also is saved.

Slowly but surely, society also came to realize that the conservation of precious resources applied to people as well as buildings. Architects became sensitive to the physical barriers their buildings created for disabled people. This problem was viewed initially as a code issue, with the Architectural Barriers Act of 1968 requiring that the physical environment accommodate the needs of people in wheelchairs and with certain other handicaps. But with the passage of the 1973 Rehabilitation Act, the issue of physical barriers to disabled people was reframed as an act of discrimination, leading to more than a decade of debate before the enactment of the Americans with Disabilities Act in 1990. This legislation also brought on a sea change in how we think about people in buildings. With an aging population and the likelihood that almost everyone will, at some point in their lives, have some sort of physical impairment, the idea of universal design, which accommodates all levels of physical ability, has become more widely embraced. As has happened repeatedly in the evolution of our thinking about HSW, what began as a minority concern eventually became universally applied.

The same could be said for the codes themselves. By the early 1990s, with more architecture firms practicing nationally and even internationally, a greater need for coordination among the three major regional codes arose. As a result, the three model code groups formed the International Code Council in 1994, publishing the first International Building Code in 1997, which, by 2000, had replaced the three regional codes.

(Above and opposite) The embodied energy represented by the existing bricks in the Samuel T. Dana Building, built in 1903, is equivalent to the amount of fuel in about 135 tanker trucks. By renovating the building for the University of Michigan in Ann Arbor in 2002, the design team of William McDonough + Partners, Quinn Evans Architects, and Ove Arup & Partners saved this energy plus other natural resources.
Christopher Campbell, courtesy Quinn Evans Architects

The Challenges Ahead

By the turn of the 21st century, architecture had become well established as a global profession, with a growing number of U.S. architecture firms working in Europe and Asia and the best-known foreign firms working here. With that has come a standardization of building codes and practices, at least among the most developed countries. Despite that growing uniformity, however, the way in which particular countries deal with HSW reflects the prevailing attitudes of their respective cultures toward the balance among risks, rights, and responsibilities. The United States tends to be more averse to putting individuals at risk and more sensitive to individual rights, so regulations here have more stringent life-safety, accessibility, and air-quality requirements than those in other countries. At the same time, the American focus on the individual often leads to a downplay of social responsibility, so matters such as resource conservation frequently are handled through voluntary action rather than code compliance.

Cultural habits will no doubt continue to shape the ways in which individual countries approach HSW regulations. However, because of several looming problems, the scope of which we have never seen before, the codes of the future may need to look far past the borders of a particular nation—thus marking a major turning point in HSW laws. This will not be easy, because no global body has the power to regulate building codes internationally in the same way individual countries do internally. Unfortunately, as typical of HSW reform in the past, it may take a catastrophe to change this situation.

One phenomenon that may fuel such a calamity is the ongoing exponential growth of the world's population. Over the next 50 years, the human population will likely grow to a total of 10 billion people, 6 billion more than the population in 1974. Most of this explosive growth will occur in poor, overcrowded, unhealthy, and unsafe slums, which have been growing at a rate of 25 million people every year, according to the United Nations, thereby creating what author Mike Davis has called a "planet of slums" in his 2006 book of that title. This growth recalls the conditions that led to the first building code in New York City in 1850 (although 19th-century New York looked spacious in comparison to the densities of some of today's cities). And the same degree of outrage on the part of the well-to-do that led to the Tenement House Act of 1901 may now be required of wealthy nations before something is done about the untenable slums in poorer countries.

According to the United Nations, explosive population growth over the next 50 years is likely to occur in overcrowded, unhealthy, and unsafe slums, such as this one in Caracas, Venezuela.
Krzysztof Dydynski/Getty Images

Aided by global transportation and trade, diseases once limited to isolated regions now pose threats to populations worldwide. This map shows the spread of avian flu as of late 2006.
Courtesy World Health Organization

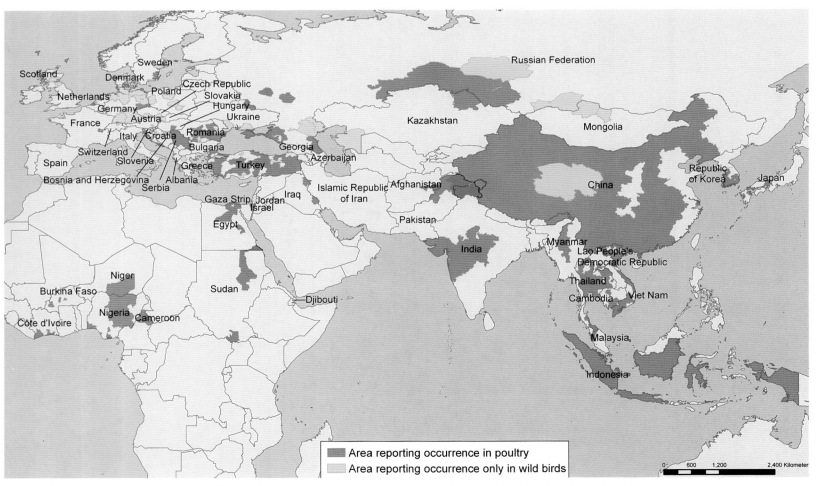

Area reporting occurrence in poultry
Area reporting occurrence only in wild birds

1888

*AIA, Western Association
of Architects, and National
Association of Builders jointly
issue first uniform contract*

*Louise Blanchard Bethune,
Buffalo, became first woman
elected to AIA membership*

*Fisher Fine Arts Library,
Philadelphia,
Frank Furness*

*Rookery Building,
Chicago,
Burnham and Root*

*Concertgebouw,
Amsterdam,
Adolf Leonard van Gendt*

Some may call these actions charity, especially when looked at individually, but they are really examples of human attempts to preserve our species. A main reason for New York's leadership in demanding water closets in tenements had to do with the fact that poor sanitation had turned the slums into breeding grounds for diseases—such as tuberculosis—that threatened rich and poor alike. The same is true today, even for slums located halfway around the world. Aided by global transportation and trade, once isolated diseases such as HIV/AIDS, SARS, and avian flu have become either epidemics or potentially deadly pandemics that, according to the World Health Organization, could become the "next black plague." We cannot inoculate ourselves against these threats today any more than New Yorkers could protect themselves a century and a half ago. The only solution is to deal with the problem at its source.

The World Bank spends billions of dollars on slum improvement every year, although it has often resorted to legal solutions—for example, giving slum residents title to their tiny plots of land—that do little to deal with the immediate dangers of poor sanitation, exposed wiring, unsafe drinking water, and combustible building materials. The lack of physical solutions may stem, in part, from the relatively few architects involved in this activity, despite the desperate need for our skills. This situation recalls the lack of design thinking in the military camps that Olmsted found at the beginning of the Civil War. We may soon need a global equivalent of the Sanitary Commission, in which the design and public health sectors work together synergistically to provide optimal shelter and sanitation now lacked by an estimated two billion people.

An exploding population affects not only the living conditions of billions of people but also the ability of the planet to meet rapidly growing needs for food, land, and resources. According to the research institute Redefining Progress, humans now need an earth one-third larger than the current planet to support our (highly unequal) standard of living. Just since 1992, the demand on the carrying capacity of the globe has increased by 10 percent. In addition, increased human activity and production in our industrial society over the past 150 years has increased the amount of CO_2 in the earth's atmosphere from 280 to 380 parts per million, with many scientists predicting that it could go up to 500 or 550 parts per million over the next 150 years—a higher and faster increase than at any time in the last 160,000 years, according to the ice-core record.

This tremendous increase in atmospheric CO_2 and the subsequent warming of the planet (the past eight years, globally, have been the six hottest on record) portend an unprecedented amount of instability in the global climate: from increasing severity and frequency of storms in some areas and droughts and unbearable temperatures in others to the melting of polar ice caps, which would lead to rising sea levels and the flooding of coastal cities worldwide.

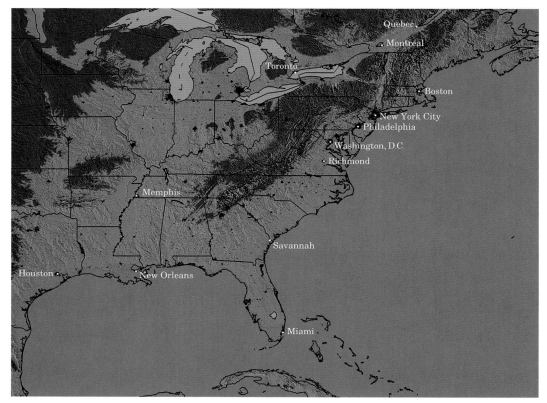

If the melting of polar ice caps causes a three-meter rise in sea level, Miami and New Orleans will be under water, as will many other areas along the East Coast of the United States and across the globe. *Map courtesy Dave Pape*

A green roof—which mitigates storm-water runoff, reduces the heat-island effect, and helps restore natural habitats in urban areas—was planted atop the new addition to the Sidwell Friends Middle School (2006) in Washington, D.C., designed by KieranTimberlake Associates. *Barry Halkin, courtesy KieranTimberlake Associates*

It is highly likely that these conditions will require new code provisions (both here and abroad) that address immediate threats, such as requiring structures to be more wind- and flood-resistant. Furthermore, to slow down if not reverse the increase of atmospheric CO_2, additional laws and building codes will have to be put into place that require, for example, the generation and storage of more renewable energy on-site and the creation of more compact communities close to food production. The United States—and American architects—have a particular responsibility in this looming crisis. While rapidly developing countries like China and India have contributed to the increase of CO_2 in the atmosphere in recent years, the United States still contributes the most—and far more than its share: this country generates 25 percent of the globe's greenhouse gases, although it represents less than 5 percent of the world's population. The AIA's recent commitment to a 50 percent reduction in the current consumption level of building- and construction-related fossil fuels by 2010 recognizes the crucial role of architects in designing a more energy-efficient built environment.

Increased population worldwide and predicted climate changes will likely be accompanied by the precipitous decline of other species. Biologists now predict that one-half of all the species currently alive on earth will be extinct within the next 100 years, leading some scientists to call the period we have now entered the world's "sixth extinction"—and the first one generated by humans rather than by natural forces. In creating human habitats for a bourgeoning population, the building industry has contributed to the constriction or outright destruction of the habitat of the planet's other species, upon which we depend for everything from food and medicine to the very oxygen we breathe. Even the most environmentally friendly buildings often begin with the virtual clearing of a site, the compressing of the soil, and the disruption of the ecology of a place. And the sheer amount of development has shrunk animal habitat so greatly that some species have been literally pushed off the planet by human beings, who have become the most invasive "weed species" the earth has ever seen.

As the ecologist Bill McKibben has observed, environmentalists have done amazingly well over the last century in establishing nature preserves and reducing certain types of pollution, but "none . . . were able to slow the economic juggernaut that rushed across this continent." The same could be said of the architecture community. It has embraced energy codes and sustainability guidelines with real commitment, but the profession has also fed the economic juggernaut, constructing more buildings ever faster and destroying places for plants and animals as we go. As a result, HSW codes in the future may require that, as we build for ourselves, we also provide habitat for other species, with elements such as green roofs, rain gardens, and even bird cotes.

With population growth and dwindling natural resources come new threats to our safety as well. While the global market has promised to spread wealth across the globe, the world's economy has a few very large winners—most notably China and India, with record (and probably unsustainable) rates of growth—and billions of people who remain stuck in dire poverty. According to the World Bank, the number of people living on $2 or less per day increased from 2.65 billion in 1990 to 2.74 billion in 2001. Some shrug off such numbers, but as the environmental historian Jared Diamond has documented, civilizations that overtax the environment and bring on their collapse also tend to have great inequality. The wealthy consume more than their share, and the poor consume whatever they can when available, often becoming violent when they become more desperate.

Global terrorism may be the first shot across the bow, the beginning of a struggle in which the world's poor fight back in ways that the wealthy have few defenses against. Terrorism has certainly affected the built environment, whether by causing increased surveillance of public places (and private transactions), hardening of perimeters of likely targets, or cumbersome security procedures in airports and, no doubt soon, all other transportation facilities. But no amount of homeland security can make the world safe from terrorism. The long-term solution may lie not in building security but instead in a transformation in how we use resources and how we define success. As Gandhi once said, "Live simply so that others can simply live," and that ethic may translate in our building or consuming not as much as we can afford but as little as we absolutely need. Such a shift would mark a return to a very old economic idea—thrift—and may be the only way in which our civilization can avoid collapse. As Diamond shows, those people who learned how to control excess and embrace moderation survived.

(Opposite) Sky gardens that spiral around the 53-story Commerzbank (1997) in Frankfurt, designed by Foster + Partners, bring daylight and fresh air into the central atrium. *©Ralph Richter/archenova/Esto*

The Role of the Architect

The health and safety of humans, in short, may come to depend on the welfare of all inhabitants of our planet. This inclusive attitude drove the accessibility codes of the past, based on the belief that we all benefit when those least able benefit as well. To do the same in the future, the HSW codes must lift the living conditions of an even greater number of people across a much wider geographical area.

Some people still say this would be too costly or too restrictive of their right to property, echoing the New York landlords who opposed water closets in their tenements for the same reason. But the history of the HSW codes shows that prosperity, not penury, follows the improvement in people's living conditions, creating new markets, new products, and new jobs. As happened over the past 150 years at a local and then national level, helping the poorest of the poor at a global level may be the only way to ensure everyone's health, safety, and welfare.

The AIA code of ethics, although continually modified since 1909, still focuses on our obligations to the public as well as to clients and colleagues. In the next 150 years, though, practitioners may need a broader sense of ethical responsibility to respond properly to the global threats that confront us. As Richard Neutra suggested in his prescient book, *Survival Through Design*, our long-term existence depends, in part, on our embrace of "biorealism," the term he used to describe the way in which the built environment affects others: other people, other species, and future generations. It is to them that our ethical responsibilities, and our codes of ethics, need to extend.

Issues of sustainability, for instance, should not be addressed just in one or two sections of the codes but as something woven into every part of them, so that architects are asked to consider the environmental impact of everything we design. And the codes may one day be much more demanding—requiring, for example, that we replenish the habitat that once occupied the site and conserve all of the resources within its boundaries. Such accounting for our actions may seem to us, now, as too complicated to calculate. But like the seismic and energy codes of the 20th century, changes in HSW codes lead to changes in technology that, in turn, enable us to understand and predict complicated phenomena.

We may even come to see buildings not as discrete physical objects but as the intersection of material and energy flows that have existed long before a building's completion and that will continue long afterward. And that realization may lead architects to design not only buildings and the environments inside and immediately around them but also the processes by which materials get mined, products get made, and orders get shipped—all with the goal of minimizing the environmental footprint of what gets put in place as architecture. At the same time, architects may design, in the future, the process of deconstructing, recycling, and repurposing everything in a building as well as the structure itself, in an effort to reap all of the embodied energy within materials and to maintain a balance of matter and energy so that we have enough of both to build in the future. This may sound like science fiction, but it has already begun to occur to varying degrees. Foster + Partners, for example, has shown the power of architects working closely with manufacturers to develop new products and processes, and with engineers such as Arup to minimize the use of materials and energy.

So we end where we began, with what the architect has to offer the world. We have, as a profession, two of the skills most needed if we are to achieve healthier and more prosperous lives for all. Architects regularly envision alternative futures in the design of buildings, and there may be no time in which the ability to do so will be more important than now, when the future of the globe seems cloudier than it has in a very long time. Architects also look holistically at problems to propose solutions that address the greatest number of requirements most effectively. This ability, too, is badly needed at a time when the problems we face seem almost insurmountable. In a world at a tipping point, when hazards that once threatened small or isolated groups of people now endanger entire populations of humans and other species, architectural thinking, applied on a planetary scale, becomes critically important. As it was for urban dwellers in the 19th century, fire victims in the early 20th century, and innocent and vulnerable populations in the late 20th century, so it will be for the health, safety, and welfare of every human being, and every other species upon which we depend, in the 21st century. ●

1889
Merger of AIA and the Western
Association of Architects; all
members of both organizations
became Fellows; membership
totaled 465

Washington, D.C., chapter presented a
convention resolution urging the AIA to
move its headquarters to Washington,
suggesting the Octagon, a ca. 1805
mansion designed by William Thornton

Eiffel Tower,
Paris,
Gustave Eiffel

Louise Blanchard Bethune became
the first female Fellow of the AIA

Johns Hopkins Hospital,
Baltimore,
John S. Billings

GOLD MEDALIST, 1977

Richard J. Neutra, FAIA

Lauren Weiss Bricker, PhD, and Judith Sheine

Born and educated in Vienna, Richard J. Neutra (1892–1970) worked for Erich Mendelsohn in Berlin and Frank Lloyd Wright at Taliesin before moving to southern California in 1925 to join his colleague R.M. Schindler. He later opened his own practice in Los Angeles. Neutra introduced International Style Modernism to southern California, gaining global recognition with the completion of the Lovell Health House in Los Angeles in 1929 for Dr. Phillip Lovell, a naturopath. It was the first documented steel-framed house in America.

Neutra's work in the late 1920s and through the 1930s—as exemplified by his own house and studio, the VDL Research House in Los Angeles (1932)— featured compact volumes in white or silver with thin stucco surfaces and bands of windows. By the end of the 1930s, his largely residential work emphasized indoor/outdoor living through one-story pavilions with flat roofs spreading into the landscape, with great expanses of glass shaded by deep overhangs. Notable examples include the Kaufmann House (1946) in Palm Springs and the Tremaine House (1948) in Montecito.

As his focus on environmental design evolved, projects of the 1940s through 1960s featured natural materials and innovative technology that responded to climatic conditions. In this period, he also received significant larger commissions, including the 600-unit, federally funded Channel Heights Housing (1942) in San Pedro, which demonstrated his progressive ideas about social housing, and a number of widely influential school projects that integrated indoor and outdoor spaces, such as Palos Verdes High School (1961). The AIA Gold Medal was awarded in recognition of his contributions to Modernism and environmental design.

Neutra at the VDL Research House II, Los Angeles, 1965–66. Neutra built the original VDL Research House in 1932 to serve as his home and office. It was named in honor of C.H. Van der Leeuw, the Dutch industrialist who gave the architect a loan to finance it.

At the Tremaine House (1948), Montecito, deep roof overhangs shade large expanses of glass. The landscape appears as part of the house itself. ©J. Paul Getty Trust. Used with permission. Julius Shulman Photography Archive, Research Library at the Getty Research Institute

1890
*Wainwright Building,
St. Louis,
Louis Sullivan*

*Auditorium Building,
Chicago,
Adler & Sullivan*

GOLD MEDALIST, 1994

Norman Foster, Lord Foster of Thames Bank, Hon. FAIA

Helen Castle

(Right) Foster's 30 St. Mary Axe (2004), an icon of 21st-century London, is naturally ventilated with fresh air drawn in through panels that open in the façade.
Nigel Young, courtesy Foster + Partners

(Below) A dramatic 10-story atrium and café space, cooled by a two-story waterfall, occupies the historic base of Foster's Hearst Tower (2006), New York City. Recycled steel was used for the interior diagonal columns and braces. ©*Chuck Choi*

At the Gold Medal ceremony in 1994, AIA President L. William Chapin II, FAIA, commended Norman Foster (1935–) for his "well-crafted work" that unites a "passion for technology" with "a delight in humanity." It was Foster's desire to harness new "appropriate technologies" in a manner that seeks "to improve the built environment for people" that marked him out for this lifetime achievement award.

From early in his career, the English architect's work was characterized by a cutting-edge modernity, redolent of industrial systems and the aeronautical. (Foster is a keen pilot and undertook his National Service in the Royal Air Force.) The first building he completed was the Reliance Controls Factory (1967), Swindon, which had an exposed steel frame and modular cladding. This he designed with Team 4, the practice he formed with his late wife and Richard Rogers in 1963, after they received their respective MArch degree from Yale. The aircraft-hangar aesthetic and finely honed detailing evident in this early project were further developed by Foster when he set up his own practice in London in 1967.

Foster's spectacular tower for the Hong Kong and Shanghai Bank (1986) made him an international name. With its three-stepped profile and distinctive exterior mast structures, the bank has come to symbolize modern Hong Kong. The external supports enable the bank to have a highly flexible floor plan and optimize daylight. Giant mirrors at the top of the atrium reflect sunlight downward to a public plaza.

Foster went on to create some fine buildings in Europe, including the Commerzbank (1997), Frankfurt. Hailed as the first green office tower, the Commerzbank furthered the ideas that Foster had developed with Buckminster Fuller in their theoretical project, "Climatroffice" (1971), which proposed a new synergy between nature and the workplace. Indoor gardens spanning multiple stories within Commerzbank aid in the circulation and oxygenation of air.

Foster's remodeling of Berlin's Reichstag (1999) propelled him to a premier position on the world stage. His dramatic, transparent dome provided an effective and sensitive icon for the newly reunited Germany. In addition, pioneering environmental features, including a means of fueling the structure with vegetable oil, were assimilated into the parliament building.

Around the same time, Foster was given the opportunity to build significant public and commercial buildings in London. The most recent, 30 St. Mary Axe (Swiss Re building, 2004), is popularly known as the "Gherkin" because of its iconic curved profile. As a naturally ventilated tall structure, Swiss Re furthers many of the ideas of Commerzbank: here, fresh air is drawn in through light wells that spiral up the building.

Foster's recent work includes two notable projects in the United States: the redesign of the courtyard for the Smithsonian American Art Museum and National Portrait Gallery (2007) in Washington, D.C., and the Hearst Tower (2006) in New York. The 42-story, glazed Hearst Tower, springing from an existing Art Deco base, rivals the "Gherkin" both as an eye-catching landmark in an urban context and as a green building. It is the first office building in New York City to be given a gold rating under the U.S. Green Building Council's LEED program.

Foster is certainly uncompromising in his attitude to sustainability; as he says, it is "about survival." His ability to seamlessly integrate sustainable features into buildings that are also socially responsive, adaptive, technologically advanced, and exciting in design continues to set him apart internationally.

Committee on the Environment

Kira Gould, Assoc. AIA

As designers of the built environment, architects have long played an important role in how humans interact with nature. The energy crisis of the early 1970s prompted the profession to assume a more active role in tackling one aspect of what would later be recognized as a host of interrelated environmental concerns that threaten the ability of societies to sustain themselves over time.

The AIA Research Corporation formed in 1973 and, with federal funding, directed significant research into climate, energy, building systems, human comfort, and more. At the same time, the AIA's Energy Committee participated in advocacy efforts to encourage the continuation of federal support for such research. Many people in the design community recall this period as a golden moment for building research in the United States, largely because solutions to the energy crisis were being sought through better design strategies as much as through new technologies. Unfortunately, by the 1980s, this sense of urgency and enthusiasm had waned, as most architects—along with the rest of the country—were generally lulled back into complacency by lower energy prices.

That decade held a reawakening for one practitioner, however, after a building disaster spurred him to rethink his own work. This wake-up call came on July 17, 1981, in Kansas City, Missouri: Walkways suspended above the lobby of the Hyatt Regency Hotel collapsed, killing 114 people. Bob Berkebile, FAIA, founding principal of BNIM, the architecture firm that had designed the hotel, rushed to the scene and stayed all night to help. Although the subsequent investigation ruled that BNIM was not responsible for the collapse, the failure nonetheless marked the beginning of his transformation. "After the tragedy of that event," he says, "I began to think in a new way about the real impact of our designs. I asked myself, 'Are our designs improving quality of life, well-being, and the quality of the neighborhood, community, and planet?'"

Believing that architects and the AIA had a special role to play in answering these questions, Berkebile set out to make changes. At the 1989 AIA convention in St. Louis, he and the Kansas City Chapter presented Critical Planet Rescue, a measure calling for the Institute to sponsor research and to develop a "resource guide" to enable architects and their clients to act responsibly in terms of how development affects the earth. The AIA board authorized a group to study the issue: in 1990 the Energy Committee was reshaped into the Committee on the Environment (COTE) to include the broadest array of environmental concerns. In addition to energy, recalls founding member Harry Gordon, FAIA, "We were talking about healthy environments for people. We were looking at waste, land use, ecologies, and water."

A story about Critical Planet Rescue found its way to the desk of Bill Reilly, the new director of the Environmental Protection Agency, which eventually put $1 million toward the committee's work. The founding Steering Committee, chaired by Berkebile, had 10 members, including people from outside the profession. "We knew we couldn't do this alone," Berkebile says. "We saw that this would have to be interdisciplinary and integrated."

That holistic understanding—plus EPA funding—drove the development of the Environmental Resource Guide, published in 1992. The following year, AIA President Susan Maxman, FAIA, presided over the first AIA convention to focus on sustainable design. At that event, 3,000 AIA members joined Maxman and Olufemi Majekodunmi, president of the Union Internationale des Architects, in signing the Declaration of Interdependence for a Sustainable Future, a document placing "environmental and social sustainability at the core of our practices and professional responsibilities."

Recognizing that practitioners need to study exemplars, COTE introduced the Top Ten Green Projects program on Earth Day in 1997 under the leadership of Gail Lindsey, FAIA. The program, which pioneered a blend of qualitative and quantitative assessment, is now in its 11th year. Today, 50 state and local COTEs are engaged in advocacy, education, and environmental leadership programs that parallel those at the national level.

The Ballard Library and Neighborhood Service Center in Seattle, by Bohlin Cywinski Jackson Architects, was chosen as a 2006 COTE Top Ten Green Project. ©*Nic LeHoux Photography Ltd.*

GRASS ROOTS

Dignity by Design: Ron Mace, FAIA, and the Center for Universal Design

Kira Gould, Assoc. AIA

It is negative in our society to say "I am disabled" or "I am old." We tend to discount people who are less than what we popularly consider to be "normal." To be "normal" is to be perfect, capable, competent, and independent. Unfortunately, designers in our society also mistakenly assume that everyone fits this definition of "normal." This just is not the case.

Ronald F. Mace, FAIA, delivered these words at the first international conference on universal design in June 1998, just ten days before he died suddenly at the age of 56. An advocate for design, equity, and good public policy, Mace coined the term universal design, founded the Center for Universal Design at North Carolina State University in Raleigh, and worked tirelessly to mainstream design for all. Recognizing that our abilities change over the course of our lives, Mace encouraged others to accept that reality and plan accordingly.

He inherited his determination from his parents, who refused to institutionalize him despite his doctors' advice after he contracted polio at age nine. They insisted he come home and remain part of his community, even though it meant carrying him up and down stairs at his primary and secondary schools. When older, Mace applied to the School of Design at North Carolina State University, although the dean of the architecture school tried to discourage him. And he completed his studio work in a trailer near campus, where he and his mother lived until he finished his degree in 1966 because both the student housing and design studios were inaccessible to him.

Mace worked for an architecture firm in Greensboro and then taught drafting in Fayetteville before he was hired by the state of North Carolina in 1973 to demystify accessibility issues in the building code by developing detailed technical illustrations and to train designers and builders on the subject. This led to the creation of his own architecture and consulting firm and, later, the university-housed organization, the Center for Universal Design. Mace and his staff subsequently helped shape significant legislation, such as the Americans with Disabilities Act of 1990, and the center remains a key voice in the ongoing discourse on inclusive design. Mace was active with the U.S. Access Board, among many other organizations. Colleagues recall his patience and tenacity, which were required for working with regulatory groups, in addition to his spirit and sense of humor.

According to Leslie Young, an architectural accessibility expert at the center, "Ron would never miss an opportunity to talk about design and universal design. He could put complicated ideas into a language that anyone could understand, and his powerful illustrations brought these issues to life for people." His product design and architecture, as well as books and illustrations, are still important references.

President George H. W. Bush presented the Distinguished Service Award to Mace in 1992. And the AIA awarded him a presidential citation in 1996. The latter reads, in part, "He has used his gifts to insist that no one is free unless we accord each other dignity and celebrate as one our common humanity."

Ron Mace, FAIA
Courtesy Center for Universal Design, North Carolina State University

Mace was the lead consultant for JCDecaux on the design and development of an accessible public toilet and newsstand for use on city streets.
Courtesy Center for Universal Design, North Carolina State University

Universal Design

Wolfgang F.E. Preiser, PhD

Historically, building and product specifications targeted one human body type above all others—that of the adult, able-bodied male. People who did not happen to fit that particular category—including children, women, and the elderly—managed as best they could. In the 20th century, largely because of changes in technology, public education, and demographic makeup, politicians and designers alike began to see that society could better serve the broader spectrum of its citizens.

In 1990 Congress passed the Americans with Disabilities Act (ADA), a civil rights law that states that all people, regardless of their abilities, should have access to goods and services provided by businesses. Subsequently, designers and business owners became responsible for providing facilities and spaces that are safe for the public to use. Yet accessibility advocates such as Ron Mace, FAIA, of the North Carolina State University, believed society—and designers—could do much more. These proponents envisioned an inclusive and nondiscriminatory approach to the shaping of the man-made environment that would go far beyond the minimum requirements stipulated by federal law. In fact, six years before the ADA was enacted, Mace had coined the term universal design to describe his ideal vision of the built environment.

As its name implies, universal design benefits everyone—able-bodied and disabled alike. In the United States alone, more than 50 million people are permanently disabled, and many others will experience some kind of mismatch between themselves and their environment at some point in their lives. Just consider the economic impact of ignoring the potential purchasing power of one-sixth of our population, not to mention the contribution this segment can make to the productivity of our nation. Given that people worldwide are living about 20 years longer—and therefore are more susceptible to the impairments commonly associated with increasing age—the need has never been greater to design public spaces, urban infrastructure, buildings, rooms, products, and information technology and telecommunications systems that can serve everyone.

Universal design can be applied at three different scales: products and amenities, building design, and urban planning. By considering each, architects have the tools to foster participation—which is, after all, the very basis of a democracy—at all levels of society.

Products and Amenities

These are technologies or treatments that can be specified for new construction and, in many cases, added to existing structures. They include automatic entry doors, accessible elevators, easy-to-use signage systems, accessible controls and devices, and floor-surface characteristics.

Building Design

When considered early on, accessibility can be woven seamlessly and attractively into the design of a building. So-called patio homes, for example, feature single-floor living with open floor plans, few doorways, wide hallways, main entries without raised thresholds, and floor surfaces that best accommodate wheelchairs. On a sloping site, side entrances to a commercial building may avoid the need for ramps of excessive length. And fire egress for persons with disabilities can be achieved in high-rise construction by designing twin towers connected by sky bridges.

Urban Planning

Accessibility at the civic level is primarily a function of proximity and good transit. A new generation of mixed-use buildings, which combine residential, hotel, office, retail, restaurants, and entertainment, is beginning to spring up in major U.S. cities. These adjacencies make it much easier for the public to reach both necessities and amenities. They are especially beneficial when well connected to public transportation and major urban spaces.

In the suburbs, greater effort is being made to create affordable communities with town centers, so that residents can reach whatever they need by foot or good public transportation.

Seven Principles of Universal Design

North Carolina State University's Center for Universal Design, in collaboration with universal design researchers and practitioners from across the United States and with funding from the U.S. Department of Education's National Institute on Disability and Rehabilitation Research, developed the following seven principles of universal design.

Principle One: Equitable Use
The design is useful and marketable to people with diverse abilities.

Principle Two: Flexibility in Use
The design accommodates a wide range of individual preferences and abilities.

Principle Three: Simple & Intuitive Use
Use of the design is easy to understand, regardless of the user's experience, knowledge, language skills, or current concentration level.

Principle Four: Perceptible Information
The design communicates necessary information effectively to the user, regardless of ambient conditions or the user's sensory abilities.

Principle Five: Tolerance for Error
The design minimizes hazards and the adverse consequences of accidental or unintended actions.

Principle Six: Low Physical Effort
The design can be used efficiently and comfortably and with a minimum of fatigue.

Principle Seven: Size & Space for Approach & Use
Appropriate size and space is provided for approach, reach, manipulation, and use regardless of user's body size, posture, or mobility.

What's the Difference?

Michael Sorkin

America is the land of the melting pot. Much of our national mythology is bound up in the promise that, if willing to surrender that which makes us different, we can emerge the same as everybody else. *E pluribus unum* is our motto. But America's offer is also that of free expression, the right to guard our private habits and beliefs: the Constitution predicates difference. Our politics are founded on this dialectic of the universal and the singular and the corollary balance of responsibilities with rights. The struggle over where to draw that line marks the condition of our democracy.

If both justice and liberty are to exist for all Americans, architecture must support diversity in all its forms—from cultural and artistic to economic and ecological. We need to be skeptical of all formalizations that purport to represent the whole truth, whether the International Style, the New Urbanism, or any other stifling codification of the universally correct. Architecture—which mediates between culture and nature and fixes our common memory and place—must change continuously, as we do, not by annihilating the past or clinging too tightly to it but by adding to our store of possibilities. To rise to this task, it must constantly reformulate the ever-shifting relationships among universal concepts (such as justice, equity, and love), universal facts (such as our own physicality and our dependence on clean water and air), our particular identities (as individuals, groups, and societies), and our places within a planetary environment that produces an infinite and shifting richness of species, habitats, and circumstances.

As architects, our first job is conservation, to preserve diversity by understanding and recognizing it, by interpreting it, by respecting its dynamism, and by acknowledging, with smart humility, the inevitable relativity of our own standards. This should yield a certain self-skepticism, tolerance for other forms of happiness, and a critical regard for ancestry. We must always give evolution the benefit of the doubt and be very cautious about our unique—and growing—capacity for catastrophe. This presumptive reverence applies equally to the snail darter, the skyscraper, the whooping crane, and the pueblo—to all the localized modes of perfection or balance that exemplify the integral bond between life and art. Like old growth forests, the brownstones of Brooklyn, the squares of Savannah, or the bungalow courts of L.A. represent forms at climax and demand preservation and respect.

Architects must also be intelligent designers, actively using their abilities and positions to enhance diversity on a global scale by working to eradicate slums (and, therefore, the misery and disease they harbor), halt global warming, and eliminate nuclear weapons. This means we must be intolerant of certain built forms that others may have found perfect—the lightless tenement, the sealed, energy-hogging tower, the share-cropper's shack, or the sprawling morphologies produced by the monoculture of the car. These local and large-scale struggles to make distinctions are vital both to life's ongoing development and to the growing complexity of knowledge itself, which is contingent upon the richness of its field of observation and interaction.

Our second role is to celebrate and contribute to the creative force that is so evident in the lush diversity around us. Diversity demands an ethics of respect and, in exchange, offers infinite points of inventive departure. At a time when globalizing culture increasingly assails the logic of difference, architecture must seek new means to reinforce the diversity of our people and places. This does not mean the dumb reproduction of forms that have been totally wrested from their originating contexts, the theme park approach that builds New England villages in Florida or Mediterranean villas in Maine, that claims that meanings are simply transportable in time or space. Rather, it suggests that new differences must emerge from the realities of local culture, from the specifics of bioclimate, and from artistic invention. Indeed, in a world where anything can be juxtaposed with anything, the role of imagination in securing the authenticity and vibrancy of local and regional differences is utterly crucial. The idea of region is not static but constantly remade.

Architecture is defined by a double duty: to shelter and protect us and our planet and to express and expand our hopes and dreams. For these tasks to be accomplished, we must all remember that human diversity is not the outcome of dumb biology but the embodiment of choices and imagination. If all our architecture is the same—its choices as reductive as those that would limit their view of human variety to matters of nappy hair or pale skin—both we and it are lost. Instead, we need works of architecture full of differences that reflect the authentic manifestation of private desire and imagination on a field informed by local conditions and defined by genuinely democratic consent. Human expression is not genetic expression. Architecture is not biology. And the world is more than a museum.

Terrorism, natural disasters, and crime are major threats that concern American society. Since the events of September 11, 2001, increased interest in building security has inspired architects and the public to leverage the power of design to enhance the built environment, minimize loss of life, and reinvigorate cities and communities.

The challenge facing architects and building owners is finding the balance between allowing access to facilities and protecting the public and occupants from threats. Those who fail to adequately address building security in the post-9/11 era may find themselves subject to liability concerns in the event of a catastrophe. Under such circumstances, victims, families, and the courts will likely scrutinize security and design decisions. Thus, it is important for architects and owners to understand the implications of security planning and design.

No one-size-fits-all security solution or code applies to every facility. Architects and owners must determine what they should do, versus what they are required to do, to protect people, facilities, and major assets. To stay current, architects must rely on various guidelines, standards, code changes, best practices, and professional resources.

Risk analysis and threat assessments should be performed on all facilities to determine appropriate security responses. Factors typically include location, owner, occupancy, and site-specific conditions. Replacement costs, cultural value, and historic significance are also relevant.

Security Design Issues

National landmarks, civic buildings, financial centers, and public venues with large numbers of people are typically considered terrorist targets because they are symbolic icons of democracy. The 1995 Oklahoma City bombing and the 1993 and 2001 attacks on the World Trade Center have frequently served as security design case studies.

After the bombing of the Alfred P. Murrah Federal Building in Oklahoma City, the U.S. General Services Administration and others evaluated how the overall building and its systems and materials had performed and how these elements could be improved. The study included site planning, vehicular circulation, hardening of building exteriors to increase blast resistance, building setbacks to mitigate damage from vehicular bombs, glazing systems to reduce fatalities from glass shards, and structural design to prevent progressive collapse. Findings from this analysis formed the basis of building-security planning and design standards for federal facilities. Private sector groups and other nonfederal public agencies often refer to these standards but are not required to use them.

In 1993 a truck carrying a bomb entered the underground parking garage of the World Trade Center and exploded. Below-grade emergency systems were destroyed, and 50,000 people evacuated the two 110-story buildings within four hours. After this event, underground parking was eliminated at the site. Redundant, above-grade emergency systems were installed, along with life safety upgrades. Evacuation drills were conducted every six months.

On September 11, 2001, these measures enabled many people to evacuate the twin towers within an hour after the two planes crashed into the buildings. However, the narrow exit stairs prevented first responders from ascending while occupants descended. The collapse of both buildings, just an hour after impact, raised more issues about egress, life-safety codes, building systems, and materials in commercial building design.

In 2004 New York City amended its building code to reflect the recommendations of 400 industry leaders. Known as Local Law 26, the amendment addresses security and fire safety, from exit signs, egress systems, wider stairs, and building materials to the use of photoluminescent strips in stairs and corridors.

Security in Architecture Education

Protecting future generations from security threats begins with training emerging design professionals now. Risk analysis, threat assessment, and security planning criteria should be added to all architecture, engineering, and construction management educational programs.

Building Security: Design Strategies for a Safer Environment

Barbara A. Nadel, FAIA

In response to the collapse of the World Trade Center towers on 9/11, New York City amended its building code to address security and fire safety measures. ©*Carol Highsmith*

Ross Barney + Jankowski designed the new building, shown here, that replaced Oklahoma City's Alfred P. Murrah Federal Office Building, destroyed by a bomb in 1995. In addition to security, sustainability and the urban context were important design considerations. ©*Timothy Hursley*

1893
World's Columbian Exposition
changed the public's view of
architects and architecture and
ushered in the City Beautiful
movement

RIBA awarded its Gold Medal
to Richard Morris Hunt, the first
American so honored

5

Education and Practice
The Architect in the Making

Harrison S. Fraker Jr., FAIA

The American architecture profession was founded 150 years ago, in 1857, yet surprisingly, no comprehensive history of architecture education has been written. The rich and evolving teaching philosophies, curricula content, and research traditions are only partially documented. And yet, in the past 75 years, no fewer than seven major studies and two major books have examined the conditions of education and practice.[1] From the 1932 publication of *A Study of Architectural Schools*, sponsored by the Association of Collegiate Schools of Architecture (ACSA), to the so-called Boyer Report of 1996, the critical issues identified seem to have a "continued force." Faculty and practitioners alike might be astonished to learn that the 1932 ACSA report criticized the dominance of design faculty over those specializing in construction, the prevalence of "paper architecture," the scarcity of "real research," and, therefore, the problems schools were having fitting into a university culture.[2] The reports are a "testimony to the depth and durability of the dilemmas that continue to confront architecture education and practice."[3]

Pedagogical Roots

It has been argued that the institutional framework of American architecture education can be understood as an "uneasy synthesis" of various European antecedents: the British model of apprenticeship; the French Beaux-Arts atelier within a centralized, state-certified system; and the German focus on empirical scientific research within a university system.[4]

In the 18th century, architecture education in the New World was primarily accomplished through apprenticeship (and was therefore practitioner dominated) or through self-teaching (as in the case of men like Thomas Jefferson). By the middle of the 19th century, in response to the need for more professionally trained architects, an atelier system was organized. While begun almost exclusively by American architects who had graduated from the Ecole des Beaux-Arts, the American atelier system was different in its plurality of settings. Some ateliers were associated with an architect's office (R.M. Hunt and H.H. Richardson, for example); some were linked to architecture clubs (Boston, New York, Philadelphia, Chicago, San Francisco); and some were established within universities (Massachusetts Institute of Technology, Columbia University, and University of California, Berkeley). The Society of Beaux-Arts Architects was founded in the United States to support the educational methods of the Ecole in this country. This advisory group of practitioners evolved into the Beaux-Arts Institute of Design (BAID), which served as the extra-collegiate arbiter of design education. Its influence can be measured by the fact that in 1929, 41 out of 52 U.S. collegiate schools (and an equal number of the architecture clubs and ateliers) relied on BAID members to judge their students' final designs. In other words, even though architecture education was equally divided between the universities and the professional ateliers and clubs, it was dominated by practitioners who developed the curriculum content and judged design quality.

The Great Depression brought an end to this balance between university and practice-based education. As architecture commissions dried up, most ateliers and architecture clubs were forced to close, and with few exceptions architecture education migrated into the universities, thereby creating a new context for its evolution.

(Opposite) Before the 20th century, it was common for aspiring architects to learn by doing, either by working in the building trades or apprenticing in an office. Shown is the atelier of Richard M. Upjohn, son of Richard Upjohn, a founder and first president (1857–76) of the AIA. The younger Upjohn learned the craft largely from his father and became a junior partner in his firm in 1853. *AIA Archives*

Architects at work in H. H. Richardson's studio, attached to his home in Brookline, Massachusetts.
Courtesy Shepley Bulfinch Richardson and Abbott

University-Based Education

Out of the 125 architecture programs, approximately half grant a five-year undergraduate professional degree (BArch) and the other half grant either two- or three-year graduate professional degrees (MArch). More recently, a few schools have approved a doctor of architecture degree (DArch) requiring seven or more years of study. These approaches primarily differ in their attitudes about the amount and type of liberal education and research necessary for practice. In all cases, more than 90 percent of these programs are conducted within the academic structure of a university. The curriculum involves prerequisites, required and elective courses, and a prescribed sequence and number of course credits to a degree.

The development of architecture education at the university was influenced in part by what department absorbed it. Many programs began in "mechanics arts," the early term for engineering, including MIT, UC Berkeley, University of Michigan, and University of Minnesota. Others began as part of fine arts clusters (Carnegie Mellon, Penn, and Yale) or in independent art schools (California College of the Arts, Cooper Union, Cranbrook, Philadelphia College of Art, Pratt Institute, Rhode Island School of Design, Savannah College of Art and Design, and Southern California Institute of Architecture), and yet others were incorporated into humanities departments (at Princeton, for example, the program was positioned in the department of architecture, archaeology, and art history).

Frequently, the architecture program emerged in contrast to the prevailing intellectual model. It was quite common, for example, for architecture programs within engineering to resist the scientific paradigm by focusing on the artistic content of buildings, while those within fine arts allied themselves with engineering schools to deliver much of their technical course content. In some cases, however, the architecture program flourished within its department: history and theory, for example, have been a distinguishing focus of the humanities-based program at Princeton.

Students work at drawing tables at the School of Applied Design, c. 1906, at Pittsburgh's Carnegie Technical Schools, which strove to combine the best aspects of France's Ecole Polytechnique and Ecole des Beaux-Arts. At that time, architecture education was fairly evenly distributed between private practices and universities. *Carnegie Mellon University Archives*

This photograph of the Tech Architecture Club at Carnegie Technical Schools was taken around 1915. As the student garb suggests—and despite the club's name—Carnegie's school of architecture began as part of a fine-arts cluster, as did those at Yale and Penn. In 1967 Carnegie merged with another institution to become Carnegie Mellon University. *Carnegie Mellon University Archives*

By and large, the early programs within existing university departments eventually grew and became independent departments or schools. While a few of these have remained freestanding units (including Princeton and Rice), most architecture programs are now clustered in some fashion with related disciplines. In 1959 UC Berkeley was the first school to bring architecture, city and regional planning, and landscape architecture together into one College of Environmental Design to collaborate on issues of the built environment. Other schools have since brought together their own mix of disciplines. It has taken almost 50 years for the potential of collaboration to be realized, but increasingly today's architecture students are involved in joint interdisciplinary studios. In addition, some now pursue joint degrees with, for example, schools of business, law, public health, or engineering. Although slow in coming, the opportunity for multidisciplinary approaches is undoubtedly one of the advantages of university-based architecture education, because students are exposed to multidisciplinary collaboration, which is essential to operate in today's practice environment.

Established in 1903, the department of architecture at the University of California, Berkeley, was the first such program west of St. Louis. Decades later, UC Berkeley was the first university to bring together the disciplines of architecture, city and regional planning, and landscape architecture. Its College of Environmental Design is housed in Wurster Hall (1964), designed by Joseph Esherick in collaboration with Donald Olsen and Vernon DeMars.
Robert Holmes/Corbis

Faculty Constraints

Almost every school has had, at some point in time, a major figure in architecture whose ongoing presence at the institution created its distinguishing identity. In fact, the history of architecture education could be told by the stories of such charismatic practitioners/educators. It would be hard to think of Harvard without acknowledging Gropius, Breuer, and Sert; of Penn without Kahn and Perkins; Princeton without Geddes, Graves, and Labatut; IIT without Mies; Minnesota without Rapson; Cranbrook without Saarinen; and Cooper Union without Hejduk — to name just a few. Many schools can point to multiple personalities who defined different eras of their institutions.

This phenomenon of associating a school with the work of an individual is more than an American fascination with the individual genius or singular artist. These personalities earned their status because they were exemplars of a way of thinking and making, of "reflective practice," or they assembled a faculty who were. As with many cultural figures, the stylistic content of their work was emulated, but it was their "design thinking," their process, that opened up innovative approaches to architectural design for students and, therefore, defined "the school."

Despite this historical template, very few such figures, if any, work within architecture education today. The most well known architects are now recognized for their practice, not for their role in education. It can be argued that the demands of maintaining a prominent national, let alone international, practice make teaching much more difficult if not impossible. These prominent figures do exert their influence on the schools, but in a different way. They participate, for example, through a much more developed school lecture circuit or, in some instances, by teaching studios that are arranged as short courses or with intermittent visits, made possible by prestigious endowments. Although these opportunities can have an important and invigorating impact on programs, they offer a plurality of approaches. The time when a singular personality defined a school is past; one of the current challenges facing schools is how to make the curriculum coherent and integrated despite these multiple voices.

This is not the first time, however, that the demands of practice have not fit neatly with the demands of the overall university's structure and requirements. Architecture schools have always had to be creative in using a full array of faculty appointments outside of the time-honored academic process of tenure in order to capture a broad range of skills and knowledge from professional practice. Adjunct professors and lecturers are enlisted to convey current professional knowledge by teaching specific subject areas, such as acoustics and building construction, plus special design studios.

Crown Hall (1950–56), designed by Ludwig Mies van der Rohe and located on the campus of the Illinois Institute of Technology, houses the IIT College of Architecture. Mies designed the master plan for the IIT campus and was head of the college from 1938 to 1958.
Todd Eberle, courtesy IIT

And for years, architecture schools struggled with the tenure track itself. Regular, full-time faculty whose research and creative production focused on building technology (such as building construction, building systems performance, and delivery systems), on the social sciences, or on architectural history and theory had an easier time presenting a case to faculty in other disciplines as to how their efforts measured against the tenure standards set by the educational institution because such work is recognized as similar to other, accepted university models.

The criteria and measures of excellence for design faculty, however, proved more problematic. Almost every school can point to at least one design faculty member who was lost because his or her design work could not meet the university's standards for tenure. Fortunately, by the 1980s and 1990s most architecture schools had developed a specific set of written guidelines and standards for promotion and tenure for all architecture faculty, including design faculty. Tenure for design faculty is usually limited to those who have demonstrated a clear record of design excellence and distinction but whose practice or work can be described as critical—in other words, that explores approaches that open up new or innovative design models. This standard is usually met not only by a record of design awards and exhibitions but also through reviews by architecture critics or the faculty member's own published theoretical writings.

In addition, a few schools have recently introduced a new type of appointment known as the professor in practice: this part-time, tenured position acknowledges that achieving distinction in practice does, in fact, require the time to practice.

The largest group of programs that operate outside a research university structure are those organized within independent art schools. These programs have the benefit of operating within an artistic tradition: Design exploration and design thinking are the "coin of the realm" and are therefore measured and justified by their own standards of excellence, not against those of scientific research. Most of these programs do not have the same kind of tenure system as research universities and can, therefore, hire the most innovative young and established practitioners. These programs have had periods of great influence, producing important work and practitioners: John Hejduk's work at Cooper Union, Daniel Libeskind's early work at Cranbrook, and Thom Mayne's early work at Southern California Institute of Architecture (SCIARC) are excellent examples of how a teacher/practitioner can benefit from a period of gestation at an independent art school, launching new directions in architecture thinking.

Cooper Union, founded in 1859 in New York City, focuses exclusively on preparing students for the professions of architecture, art, and engineering. A new academic building (rendering above), designed by Morphosis with Gruzen Samton, is expected to open in 2009. *Courtesy The Cooper Union (historic photo); Morphosis Architects 2006 (rendering)*

Scholarship versus Service

Often compounding the tensions between architecture education and practice is the position a particular educational institution takes on the role of research, scholarship, and creative production. A wide spectrum of opinion and models exists for how excellence is achieved in this domain. At one end of the spectrum, some argue that universities should maintain their critical independence from society—that the goal of research and scholarship is to comment critically about current practices, to conduct basic research that reveals hidden facts about how things work and that remains unbiased and "pure." This model, normally associated with the elite private universities, maintains the position that if one becomes an advocate for a specific position, one loses critical independence. At the opposite end of the spectrum is the service model, the idea that knowledge must be applied to real-world problems to test its validity and that research, scholarship, and creative production should be in the service to society. This model is normally associated with the "land grant" tradition of large public universities.

While these extremes exist conceptually, most universities fortunately embrace both models, with pure research associated more with the sciences and humanities and applied research with engineering and the social sciences. Following suit, architecture education has undertaken research, scholarship, and creative production that span this spectrum. Architecture education has taken seriously the responsibility of commenting critically about the current models of architectural production. At the same time, it has understood that schools are a place to generate and test new theories, models, and methods that are based on critical analysis and research. Using the discipline's traditions in postoccupancy evaluation, technical building performance, and empirical case studies, for example, architecture education is producing knowledge that both satisfies the highest standards of scholarship in institutions and responds to the profession's call for more knowledge-based practice.

That being said, the stance that individual faculty or a school may take about the production of knowledge may be at odds with the local professional community—in other words, it may be too critical or too disengaged from the problems of practice. This should not be surprising because architecture education's existence in an educational institution demands that its knowledge production be positioned to meet the highest standards of that particular institution.

Work versus Study

Although some schools have internship electives as part of the professional practice sequence and some schools require work experience (i.e., a number of hours) to graduate, faculties have been extremely reluctant to integrate office experience into the curriculum or give it credit. In addition to the ethical and compensation questions around giving course credit for professional work, the faculty would have no control of the content, and they are reluctant to give up studio time in school to practice because they feel the studio time—the heart of the architecture curriculum—is already too limited.

In spite of these obstacles, a few schools have integrated internship and work experience into curricular requirements. The University of Cincinnati is known for its innovative approach of alternating quarters in school and quarters in practice. Originally a BArch program, it was transformed in 2003 into an MArch degree that incorporates eight quarters of "critical" internship across six and one-quarter years of undergraduate and graduate experience. During the graduate years, a two-quarter internship is bracketed with two seminars, both under faculty supervision, the first to prepare a research question to be explored during the internship, the second to prepare a detailed report. Rice University is known for its Preceptorship Program, which requires one year of office experience between the fourth and fifth years of a BArch program, effectively making it a six-year BArch.

Rice and Cincinnati have solved the compensation and course credit questions by not giving credit for the professional work but having students compensated for their work experience. The extra time it takes to earn a degree is justified because the work helps pay for the cost of education, and students receive credit toward the three years of formal internship required by the National Council of Architectural Registration Boards (NCARB) to take the licensing exam. (Only by passing this exam can one actually call oneself an architect.)

The program of the Boston Architectural College—the only remaining architecture education program that retains vestiges of the original architecture club system of the 19th century—is designed so that architecture employees can work during the day and go to school at night, not unlike night or weekend MBA programs. Courses are taught almost exclusively by practitioners (similar to the atelier clubs). The college meets all the requirements for accreditation by the National Architectural Accrediting Board (NAAB). Some universities and art institutes, including Drexel and the Art Institute of Chicago, offer similar nighttime accredited programs.

1895
Reliance Building,
Chicago,
Daniel Burnham
and John Root

Boston Public Library,
McKim, Mead and White

Guaranty Building,
Buffalo,
Louis Sullivan

Biltmore House,
Asheville,
Richard Morris Hunt

Strengthening the Ties between Education and Practice

The relationship between architecture education and practice has been the subject of debate ever since education began moving into the academy in the latter half of the 19th century. It reached a height of rhetorical intensity in the mid-1990s when *Progressive Architecture* published an article titled "The Schools: How They're Failing the Profession," by Michael J. Crosbie, and *Architecture* magazine published a response by Reed Kroloff titled "How the Profession Is Failing the Schools."[5] The two essays outlined the pressures, attitudes, values, and behaviors in both realms that were contributing to an alleged "gap" between education and practice, as if they were isolated worlds. While each argument offered important insights, the emphasis on a supposed gap ignores the fact that the relationship between education and practice has been and continues to be complex, extensive, and profound in both directions. Indeed, as Princeton sociologist Robert Gutman has pointed out, most of the important new design directions in practice originated in the work of architects while they were teaching in the schools. Given that at least 25 percent of all faculty, including adjuncts and lecturers, have significant involvement in practice, the debate is really not between isolated worlds but is about how to coordinate and align the exchange between different parts of a historical couplet.

Nonetheless, the details of the debate triggered by these two articles brought sharp focus to bear on the assumption that "education" takes place predominately in school and precedes "training," which takes place predominately in practice during the required preprofessional internship period. The debates placed blame in both directions for the problems in this structure but begged the question of whether this split was the most productive structure. They revealed what has been described as the "double bind" of architecture education: "derided by the profession and disdained by the universities."[6] It can be argued that the articles, which appeared before the Boyer Report, initiated one of the most intense examinations of

The Knowlton School of Architecture (2004), Ohio State University, houses the disciplines of architecture, landscape architecture, and city and regional planning. The Atlanta-based firm of Mack Scogin Merrill Elam Architects, in association with WSA Studio, designed the building. *©Timothy Hursley*

1896
AIA convention approved the
Washington chapter's formal
petition to move the AIA from
New York to Washington

St. Luke's Hospital,
New York City,
Ernest Flagg

the relationship between education and practice. The impact of the debate, together with the Boyer Report, has produced significant responses by all five collateral organizations involved in the relationship—AIA, NCARB, NAAB, ACSA, and the American Institute of Architecture Students (AIAS)—and the transformations are ongoing.

The AIA Large Firm Roundtable was among the first to respond by initiating, in the late 1990s, a series of Deans Roundtables to explore the issues. One of the most open, candid, and productive exchanges about the pressures and constraints on education and the realities of practice, the Deans Roundtables, among other initiatives, led to the formation of the Case Study Working Group. This group has pioneered the use of the case study method as a bridging pedagogy among faculty, students, and practitioners. Architecture case studies, as adapted from the Harvard Business School model, take many forms but usually focus on telling the "story" of a specific project in a professional office, examining the multiple roles of the client, program, budget, approvals, design concept, technologies, contractor, etc. Case studies introduce students to the substance of practice and help build the knowledge base of the profession by shining a spotlight on the knowledge embedded in day-to-day practice. In turn, the Case Study Working Group led an AIA/ACSA–sponsored Cranbrook Teachers Seminar that examined the emerging best practices of the architecture case study method.

In 2001 the AIA College of Fellows made its own response by establishing the Benjamin Latrobe Research Fellowship, a $100,000 grant awarded biennially to support research on critical issues of practice. The first recipients, Stephen Kieran and James Timberlake, turned their research into the highly provocative and influential book *Refabricating Architecture*, which explores how new manufacturing processes are poised to transform the role of architects in building construction.[7] The three subsequent awards hold similar promise.

The NCARB Prize for the Creative Integration of Practice and Education in the Academy recognizes innovative courses, projects, and pedagogies in schools that weave the issues of practice into the curriculum. The award has not only celebrated but also promoted innovation and best practices in design-build courses, professional practice courses, and comprehensive studios. At the same time, the focus of ACSA's awards program has shifted dramatically to honor teaching and research that links education and practice.

NAAB has amended its list of student performance criteria to require "ability" in building systems integration and technical documentation through a "comprehensive design studio," modeled after the successful comprehensive studio at the University of Maryland. This change marks the first time that NAAB has required students to demonstrate technical ability in a design studio, forcing them to integrate knowledge from technical courses into design.

Largely due to the insistence of AIAS, the five presidents of the collateral organizations focused attention on shortcomings in the transition from school to professional licensure by sponsoring three Internship Summits. In preparation for the summits, position papers on issues were solicited from faculty, practitioners, and students. The meetings then examined the detailed experience of students, beginning with the level of preparation in school for practice, the internship experience in offices, and preparation for the licensure exam. The excellent materials developed and published from the summits have had a profound impact on improving, state by state, the Intern Development Program (IDP). However, the most substantive outcome has been the creation of the *Emerging Professional's Companion (EPC)*. This online AIA education tool provides curriculum modules, written by experts, for all the major subject areas covered in the licensure exam. The modules introduce the critical concepts and detailed exercises to develop application skills. The *EPC* filled a vacuum, giving both interns and their practitioner-mentors content and structure to help guide the internship experience.

By far the most profound change for architecture education in recent years emanates from the AIA leadership. In 2004 the AIA Board of Directors created a special Board Knowledge Committee to explore how to transform the Institute to support the development of a more knowledge-based profession. Moreover, the AIA has recognized that, to realize the potential of becoming a knowledge-based profession, it must partner with schools and industry to generate new knowledge. Each of its Knowledge Communities (AIA member groups, formerly called professional interest areas, that focus on particular building types or issues within a discipline) must identify and pose critical questions so that schools can apply their research capabilities to these concerns. This is a sea change in attitude. Rather than complaining about the inadequacies of architecture education, the profession is asking the schools not only to assist in research but also to prepare students to enter a knowledge-based profession with a focus on lifelong learning.

Carnegie architecture student Betsy Bell was the first-prize winner of the first small homes architecture competition for women at the National Association of Home Builders convention in 1950. Through such jury processes, architecture students refine their presentation skills, which are much needed in practice.
Carnegie Mellon University Archives

Current Directions in Education

Architecture schools today are animated by the challenge of finding appropriate responses to a rapidly changing world. The lines of adjustment are on multiple fronts, as evidenced by the following trends in education:

Renewed exploration of architecture as a material art

Today, building construction is recognized as a process that is a critical part of a designer's imagination. Building construction courses do not just look at materials and assemblies but also explore how building systems have been manufactured. They even investigate how new pieces might be fabricated to improve the performance of assemblies. In addition, almost 25 percent of schools offer some type of design-build studio, in which students realize their ideas in built form.

The effect of the digital process on architectural thinking and production

In many design studios, students are encouraged to be innovative in terms of analyzing and graphically representing phenomena. Students are also learning how preliminary design ideas can be represented digitally and explored with parametric programs, how building performance can be modeled, and how the digital process can lead directly to manufacturing. Design studios have begun to explore building information modeling (BIM) programs, and design-build studios are increasingly using CAD/CAM technology to manufacture building components for installation.

Reemergence of building performance as a focus of research and teaching

Faculty members are increasingly researching the how and why of our environments, from occupant responses to the energy performance of building systems and the track record of specific details. Such studies require knowledge of social science methods, including carefully constructed surveys, observation, and time-motion studies, plus sensitivity to the ethnographic differences of an increasingly diverse society. They also require knowledge of applied scientific method, from gathering data and information to constructing a physical model of how things work from which one can predict future performance. In courses and studios, case studies of built projects provide students with opportunities to investigate and draw conclusions from real-life conditions.

Expanded discourse on sustainability and whole-systems thinking

The threat of global warming requires that we understand and dramatically modify how our buildings, landscapes, and cities interact with nature. When as much as 60 percent of global CO_2 emissions can be attributed to the construction and operation of the built environment, we have more than a technological and policy problem—we have a whole-systems design problem. Buildings can no longer be conceived as isolated objects of art but must be seen as part of whole systems, whose interdependence is fragile and on whose dynamic balance we depend. These questions, once marginalized along the academic periphery, are moving front and center in courses, studios, and university research.

Ongoing discourse on and exploration of urbanism

How our cities have evolved and now operate continues to be a focus of analysis, criticism, and design inspiration. Students and faculty explore urbanism as a field of action for architecture, as a series of events, and as a complex set of man-made and natural processes. Today's designers must learn how to operate within this context, which condenses so many of the critical issues now facing society.

Modernism reconsidered

Criticism of modern architecture's positivist and technological determinism produced multiple reactions over the past 40 years in the form of postmodern historicism, "critical regionalism," and multiple forms of deconstruction. As these critical narratives have played out, some designers and teachers have returned to (or never left) the more subtle and nuanced trajectories of the modern project. At least two paths are discernible. One is an interest in the abstract construction of space, where designers are using a neutral framework as a foreground for the more sensuous, dynamic, and ephemeral qualities of materials, light, color, and transparencies. The other is a fascination with new spatial and structural configurations that were previously unimaginable without today's digital parametric programs.

1897
Illinois became the first
state to license architects

AIA Board of Directors
voted to lease the Octagon

Rewriting history

The perspective of poststructuralism has drawn attention to what is missing from previous historical narratives and has demanded a much closer reading and fuller account of a building's production. This has led to a greater emphasis on the cultural process of building—the social, economic, and political conditions that have fostered well-known edifices. Historians are also attempting to present in more detail the technical means by which social and aesthetic purposes have been achieved. What is emerging is a more complex and holistic history of architecture.

By the mid-1970s, when this photo was taken at Carnegie Mellon, women and people of color were enrolling in architecture programs in greater numbers than ever before. Although progress has been made, the profession itself is still not as diverse as the makeup of students aspiring to enter the field.
Carnegie Mellon University Archives

Questions about the Future

The Boyer Report and the debates of the mid-1990s fostered changes in the content, format, and process of the design studio, as well as the rethinking of theory seminars, history courses, and the pedagogy of many building technology and practice courses. The quality of those changes is marked in the ACSA teaching awards and the AIA education awards given out over the past 10 years. Even a cursory review reveals a commitment to innovative teaching at the highest level. The knowledge and level of inquiry developed in these best practices is the kind of preparation for lifelong learning and leadership that bodes well for the profession. When these teaching models are viewed with the best architecture research, conducted collaboratively with faculty, industry, and practitioners, architecture education is alive and well. The work is a tribute to a truly talented faculty. The question of whether this is enough remains, given that these are only quality adjustments to pieces of an education structure that has not changed radically since architecture education moved into the academy.

The answer could go either way, and the arguments for both sides are compelling. If yes, then architecture education needs to continue to evolve within its existing structure, only in a more strategically intelligent and carefully aligned trajectory with practice. Those in favor of evolving the existing structure are probably more realistic, given the time and effort required of overly committed faculty and market-driven practitioners. In fact, it could be argued that all that is necessary is a change in attitude, not structure. If faculty would collaborate with practitioners to focus on the "critical" needs of practice, they could strategically integrate those needs into architecture education's venerable structure of courses, design studios, and research efforts. In addition, if work experience was structured into the five- to seven-year period of education, formally or informally, and some of the faculty research agenda was arrived at collaboratively with practice and industry, would not this approach create the kind of strategic partnership between education and practice needed to build a more knowledge-driven design profession?

If no, then architecture education must completely rethink its assumptions about the integration of education and practice across the period from high school graduation to licensure and redesign this structure. The arguments for this more radical redesign start with the observation that, if the problems of architecture education have had "continued force"[8] over the last 100 years, then there must be internal problems with the structure that cannot be avoided any longer. This critique focuses on the fundamental assumption that education begins predominantly in school and training occurs predominantly in practice during the three-year apprenticeship period after graduation. It is argued that tenure-track faculty inevitably become isolated from practice and that their research has more to do with university expectations than with the knowledge needs of the profession. It is further argued that the training of graduates during their three years of apprenticeship is uneven at best, in spite of the progress made by IDP, and that those years and talent are largely wasted by the profession. The suggestion is that education and training must be more seamlessly integrated over the full eight to ten years from high school to licensure—that education and internship need to be thought of together.

If such a reconception were pursued, education and practice would have to forge a partnership to share in the responsibility for internship, ending its stepchild status. Both education and internship training could be dramatically improved by such a strategic alliance. Integrating the three-year equivalent of internship into the education stream would mean an expanded scope for architecture education, but the additional income students would earn during their internship work experience would help cover their increased costs. An important further outcome would be that licensure could occur immediately upon graduation.

The proponents of a more radical redesign of architecture education argue that the AIA's call for a more knowledge-based profession demands imagination and innovation in the creation of new collaborative research models. They propose that some research should be conducted in a hybrid territory between education and practice, where faculty and practitioners work together to set the agenda and conduct research. One could imagine this approach as a distributed concept: Each "institute"—allied with a particular AIA Knowledge Community— might be located either at a university or an independent research center. It could involve practitioners, industry partners, and faculty from around the country, thus capturing greater research and intellectual horsepower through open collaboration. The successes of medicine and engineering in creating a similar type of research landscape provide excellent models for analysis and adaptive implementation.

1898
Julia Morgan became the
first woman admitted to the
Ecole des Beaux-Arts, Paris

The Past Is Prologue

One hundred and fifty years ago, in its first decade of operation, the AIA engaged in a prolonged debate over the form and content of architecture education. Leopold Eidlitz, a founding member of the AIA, proposed that the AIA create and administer an independent, national school, the Grand Central School of Architecture. The Eidlitz program "encouraged students to 'build more and draw less,' focusing on the practical side of architecture, including materials and construction, before moving to aesthetics."[9] Eidlitz's program was opposed by William Ware, who had just established a program at MIT based on a Beaux-Arts atelier model in which design aesthetics were emphasized from the beginning. The themes of this debate form an important, overlooked chapter in the history of architecture education. The AIA ultimately voted to endorse Ware's university-based (and, thus, regionally driven) model in 1870. In hindsight, Eidlitz's program anticipated the separation from practice created by a university-based system, and his focus on the "art of building" as the core of study seems all too prescient, given the challenges facing architecture education today.

With the burst of innovative teaching and research in the schools and the profession's move to create a more knowledge-based practice, the time has never been more opportune for substantive change in the relationship between education and practice. Ten years after the Boyer Report and 150 years after the founding of the AIA, a truly integrated future seems achievable. Boyer's reflection that "the fascination with architecture education lies more in its possibilities than in its problems" is even more relevant today.[10] The question is, to what degree will architecture education and practice seize the moment? ●

In addition to drawing, architecture students explore design through three-dimensional model building. A class of Carnegie students in the 1950s is assembling their structures, which most likely will be included as part of their final reviews. Students and architects alike still work with physical models, now often in conjunction with computer modeling. *Carnegie Mellon University Archives*

Walter Gropius, FAIA

Michael James Meehan, AIA

Walter Gropius (left) with Pietro Belluschi, c. 1958.

Walter Gropius (1883–1969) was born in Berlin and studied architecture at the universities of Charlottenburg and Munich. He began his career in 1908 in the office of Peter Behrens, where he worked on the AEG Turbinenfabrik (1908; see page 19), an icon of Modern architecture. In 1910 Gropius left Behrens's office to form a partnership with Adolf Meyer. The following year, they designed the Fagus shoe-last factory at Alfeld, Germany, creating a seemingly weightless, transparent curtain wall stretched thinly over the structure's concrete frame. In their design for a model factory for the 1914 Werkbund exposition in Cologne, Gropius and Meyer further advanced their use of industrial forms and materials.

In 1919 Gropius became director of the Bauhaus in Weimar, where he emphasized the union of art and science. Students began their studies by experimenting with forms and materials for six months to unlearn artistic assumptions. Next, they undertook three-year apprenticeships in crafts such as carpentry, painting, and ceramics. Only after successfully completing their apprenticeship did the students begin formal architecture training, which often involved working on commissions with Gropius

or Meyer. The Bauhaus moved to Dessau in 1925, and the campus buildings, designed by Gropius, have become landmarks of Modern architecture. Gropius left the Bauhaus in 1927 to return to private practice in Berlin. The Nazis closed the school in 1933.

Gropius immigrated first to England in 1934, then in 1937 to the United States, where he joined the faculty of Harvard's Graduate School of Design. He was named chair of the department of architecture the following year and remained at Harvard until 1952. A teacher and practitioner, Gropius understood the role of collaboration in architecture. At a 1961 symposium at Columbia University on "Four Great Makers of Modern Architecture," he said that he viewed architects not as master builders but as master communicators, designers, coordinators, and leaders in the world community. He founded The Architects Collaborative (TAC) in 1946.

His Gold Medal citation noted that he had "held steadfastly to one purpose, the reunification of art and science." This vision, embodied in both his principles and practice, helped shape a generation of architects, including Philip Johnson and I.M. Pei, and made Gropius one of the most influential architecture educators of the 20th century.

The Bauhaus buildings at Dessau, designed by Gropius in 1925–26, reflect his belief in the union of art and science made possible only by modern technology and materials. ©*Wayne Andrews/Esto*

The Fagus shoe-last factory (1911), Alfeld, Germany, an early example of curtain wall construction, represents the creation of a transparent architecture of industrial materials.
©*Bildarchiv Monheim GmbH/Alamy*

1899
*AIA officially opened
its headquarters at
the Octagon, Jan. 1*

*Founding of the
American Society of
Landscape Architects*

Born in Indianapolis in 1934, Michael Graves earned a bachelor's degree from the University of Cincinnati in 1958 and an MArch from Harvard in 1959. But his two-year Prix de Rome fellowship at the American Academy had the most influence on his future work. "[Rome] is, for me, my teacher," Graves told the *Princeton Weekly* in 2001.

When he returned to the United States in 1962, Graves's first job was teaching architecture at Princeton University, where he remained until 2001. There is no telling the influence he had on the thousands of Princeton undergraduate and graduate students he mentored over those 39 years. Many are now prominent in both academia and professional practice. According to Patrick Burke, AIA, a former student of Graves and now one of his partners, "He inspired us to engage in architecture as a cultural act, as if it affected absolutely everything." At the same time, Graves has credited his teaching career with helping him define his own design direction: "You must find a way when you teach to explain to a student, and ultimately to yourself, why something might be deemed better than something else—that it's not just a personal reaction."

But teaching has not been his only vocation. Since founding Michael Graves & Associates in Princeton, New Jersey, in 1964, the indefatigable Graves has taken design to places it had never been before. Though he eschews the label "postmodernist" with his often-cited statement, "If I have a style, I am not aware of it," his controversial and provocative Portland Building (1982) in Oregon and Humana Building (1985) in Louisville, Kentucky, heralded the rise of Postmodern architecture. Graves's use

of ornament and color in these two buildings was a sharp departure from the stark, glass-box aesthetics of Modernism. His subsequent designs for the Swan and Dolphin Resort (1990) at Walt Disney World in Orlando, Florida, and the Team Disney Building (1991) in Burbank, California—for which he translated classical elements into playful yet sophisticated forms—introduced the world to his wit and whimsy.

This sense of humor—plus his desire to "democratize design"—has made Graves a household name. Introduced in 1985, his now-iconic Alessi 9093 kettle, with chirping red bird spout, became a must-have item in many kitchens around the world. Today, hundreds of other household gadgets and furnishings are available at Target stores under the Michael Graves Design label.

Even a spinal cord infection, contracted in early 2003, which left Graves paralyzed below the waist, does not keep him down. That same year, he turned his product design studio, Michael Graves Design Group, into a separate business that has since designed close to 2,000 consumer products for companies such as Tiffany, Steuben, Baldinger Lighting, Phillips Electronics, and Black & Decker. Now wheelchair-bound, he is developing medical equipment and a household product line for the disabled called Michael Graves Solutions.

Perhaps Graves's Gold Medal citation says it best: "Eloquent teacher, gifted artist, and inspired poet of memories and dreams, his is a hand skilled in the alchemy of place making . . . inviting the public, not as an observer or even a guest, but as a participant in his joyous celebration of life."

GOLD MEDALIST, 2001

Michael Graves, FAIA

Kristen Richards

Courtesy Michael Graves & Associates

(Below left) Introduced in the same year the Humana Building was completed, Graves's Alessi tea kettle was the first in a long line of product designs from Michael Graves Design.
George Kopp, courtesy Michael Graves & Associates

(Below) Although his Humana Building (1985) in Louisville was a harbinger of Postmodernism in architecture, Michael Graves does not see himself as a designer in any particular style.
Courtesy Michael Graves & Associates

1900
AIA issued its first serial publication,
the AIA Quarterly Bulletin; it continued
publication through 1912

GRASS ROOTS

Freedom by Design

Brad Buchanan, FAIA

As a whole, architects are problem solvers. Specialists in arranging disparate objects into harmony—chaos into order—they are always looking for a way to make a difference. Freedom by Design is no exception.

Buchanan Yonushewski Group started this volunteer program in 1999 in Denver in recognition of the overwhelming needs of low-income, disabled residents in the community. Architects, builders, and specialty trades were organized into more than 20 project teams that, over six months, created simple design and construction solutions that would radically improve the quality of life for many people. Whether the project was to eliminate one single step to open up a route to a bus stop for a woman confined to a wheelchair, thus making it possible for her to work, or the renovation of an entire kitchen and bath, Freedom by Design teams were up to the challenge.

At a 2003 meeting of the AIA national board in California, Wayne Mortensen, then president of the American Institute of Architecture Students (AIAS), attended a presentation about the Freedom by Design program. He thought it would be a good fit with his organization's student chapters, and he was right. Within 12 months the liaison between Freedom by Design and AIAS had created student volunteer programs in six AIAS chapters to design and construct projects that would afford local residents greater accessibility. Today, 25 such programs are in place around the United States. Through them, students are given a chance to lead a single-source project team from concept to punch list in a classic "master builder" style, all the while making a difference in their communities.

Freedom by Design teams undertake community service projects that affect the lives of low income and disabled residents. Here, a team from the University of Colorado, Boulder, designed and built an accessible ramp. *Courtesy AIAS*

In 1839, not long before the founding of the AIA, the seeds of photovoltaic science were being sown by French physicist Antoine-César Becquerel. Another 120 years passed, however, before Bequerel's pure science found its application in the development of the photovoltaic cell. Photovoltaic and solar hot-water panels were applied to houses in the 1970s in an early attempt to address fossil-fuel shortages. Today, much more advanced solar technology is often seamlessly integrated into a range of building types. Dramatizing this reality and further advancing the application of solar technology, is the Solar Decathlon, a university-based contest conceived by Richard King of the U.S. Department of Energy's (DOE) Solar Photovoltaic R & D Program. The first Solar Decathlon took place in 2002, the second in 2005, and a third in 2007.

DOE invites schools from across the country and around the world to organize teams of architecture, engineering, and design students, assisted by faculty and local practitioners, to design a small house that demonstrates a range of solar technologies. As part of the competition, each team must successfully transport and erect its structure and demonstrate its performance on the National Mall in Washington, D.C., during a week of competition. Judges from different design and engineering disciplines score the projects. Before the end of the event, tens of thousands of curious visitors tour the Solar Village, exploring, learning, and marveling at the students' creativity, ingenuity, and industriousness.

As the name of the competition implies, the teams compete in 10 categories. Nine of the contests yield a maximum of 100 points each, while the winner in the Architecture category gains 200 points. The Architecture and Dwelling contests are each evaluated by a separate panel of judges comprised of architects, designers, writers, and builders. Success in the Architecture competition depends on overall concept, integration of technology, quality of construction, and aesthetics. The Dwelling contest focuses more specifically on livability, the user-friendliness of the systems, buildability, and appeal. For the Documentation contest, staff from the National Renewable Energy Laboratory, the Decathlon managers, and outside professionals evaluate a series of process submittals and a set of as-built documents. For the Communications contest, a panel of marketing and communications professionals judges both written and Web-based informational materials, as well as each team's oral presentations for the public.

The houses have instruments that measure energy use from heating and cooling and household appliances, hot water efficiency, and lighting levels. These data are used to quantitatively score the contests for the Comfort Zone, Appliances, and Hot Water categories. Lighting is judged both quantitatively (foot-candle efficiency) and qualitatively (by a panel of lighting designers). Energy Balance and Getting Around, the final two categories, are scored quantitatively. Energy Balance is an all-or-nothing contest, with 100 points awarded only for houses that have produced a net gain of electrical energy. Getting Around is designed to demonstrate that solar power is abundant enough for both the house and an electric car for household errands. Teams are required to log miles for the six days of the contest.

Solar decathletes address a range of pragmatic needs and symbolic associations of house and home. This complex mixture of engineering performance and architectural accomplishment—which clearly challenges both the competing teams and their judges—also challenges the traditional boundaries of teaching and research at the participating universities. In fact, through this single project, the Solar Decathlon offers schools an opportunity to address many of the architecture education objectives identified by the Carnegie Foundation's 1996 report, *Building Community: A New Future for Architectural Education and Practice* (aka the Boyer Report), which called for promotion of "the value of beauty in our society; the rebirth and preservation of our cities; the need to build for human needs and happiness; and the creation of a healthier, more environmentally sustainable architecture that respects precious resources."

Labor and resource intensive, messy and boundary crossing, the preparation involved in undertaking a Solar Decathlon entry represents a compelling paradigm for architecture education in the 21st century. Tacit learning, described by philosopher Michael Polanyi as learning by doing rather than by didactic instruction, has long provided the pedagogical foundation for architecture's studio-based curriculum. The "doing," however, has tended to be limited to making representations of buildings rather than construction itself. The current interest in design-build, service learning, and sustainable building finds common ground in the Solar Decathlon, explaining the increasing popularity of this event.

Solar Decathlon

Susan Piedmont-Palladino, PhD

The Cornell University team, the second overall prize winner in 2005, installed an edible landscape to make use of the ultimate solar energy, photosynthesis. *U.S. Department of Energy*

The University of Colorado, first-prize winner in the 2005 Solar Decathlon, transported its bio-based house to the National Mall in Washington using biofuel. *U.S. Department of Energy*

1901
New York passed the Tenement
Housing Act, the nation's
first comprehensive housing
legislation

Boston Symphony Hall,
McKim, Mead and White and
Wallace Clement Sabine

GRASS ROOTS

Mentor, Teacher, Professional: Laura Lee, FAIA

John A. Loomis, FAIA

Laura Lee, FAIA

Great teachers are marked not only by great intellect but also by great humanity, and Laura Lee's humanity shines through all her many intellectual accomplishments and activities.

Lee is head of Carnegie Mellon University's School of Architecture, the institution where she has invested the major part of her professional career. She has also taught abroad, most notably at the Higher Institute of Architecture in Antwerp, the Royal Danish Academy of Fine Arts in Copenhagen, and the Swiss Federal Institute of Technology in Zurich. As a teacher, she is known for her passion for synthesizing information across disciplines and bringing this process into the design studio. At Carnegie Mellon, she was the 2002 recipient of the university's highest honor, the William H. and Frances S. Ryan Award for Meritorious Teaching. In the letters of recommendation for this honor, one student noted, "Laura is not only an excellent teacher, but also an amazing mentor and adviser. Her studio is well organized and demanding (in a very positive, motivated way). Her criticism is concise and honest, and she encourages students to make every minute in studio productive."

Lee is appreciated as much by her faculty as by her students. She is a mentor to junior faculty and takes the time to work with them on all aspects of planning and building their careers. In her years as department head, she has rapidly brought about significant changes, including new computer resources, a new wood shop, new pinup and gallery spaces, travel/study opportunities for all classes, and increased financial support.

One of Laura Lee's passions has been finding ways to improve connections and enrich the exchange between architecture education and the

profession. In this effort, she is recognized as a national leader, having played an important role in creating both the AIA Case Studies Initiative and the *Emerging Professional's Companion* (*EPC*). The case studies program, embraced by the AIA Large Firm Roundtable, is an ambitious project in which students work with a design firm to rigorously document and analyze a built project. The process offers an important learning experience, not only for the student but also for the practice, providing critical after-the-fact information and evaluation. The long-term objective is to create an open-access database of the best projects that will serve as both an educational and professional resource.

The *EPC*, an online resource that provides professional development exercises to help interns complete the Intern Development Program's training areas, grew out of the 2002 Internship Summit sponsored by ArchVoices at the University of Oklahoma. Lee and John Cary, Assoc. AIA, executive director of Public Architecture and cofounder of ArchVoices, cochaired the event and subsequently wrote "Architecture Internship: Everybody's Issue." Their work spurred leaders in education and the profession to streamline IDP and produce the *EPC*.

The Case Studies Initiative and the EPC involved the efforts of many talented and dedicated individuals, but in both cases, Laura Lee distinguished herself as a first among equals, one who provided critical informal leadership and lots of hard work. According to Harrison Fraker Jr., FAIA, dean of the UC Berkeley College of Environmental Design, who was involved in both efforts, "Neither of these important projects would have achieved the high level of quality they attained had it not been for the efforts of Laura Lee."

The Case Studies Initiative, a national program that Laura Lee helped develop, pairs architecture students with firms to document and analyze built projects. In one such study, students from the University of Nebraska joined with staff from Leo A Daly to study the firm's First National Tower in Omaha. The team prepared several diagrams for the case study, including one that shows the operation and location of the building's air-handling units and the chilled water and steam line connections. *Courtesy Leo A Daly*

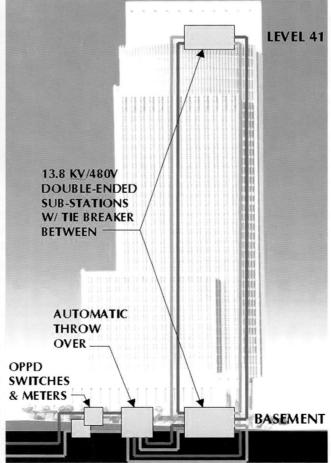

LEVEL 41

13.8 KV/480V
DOUBLE-ENDED
SUB-STATIONS
W/ TIE BREAKER
BETWEEN

AUTOMATIC
THROW
OVER

OPPD
SWITCHES
& METERS

BASEMENT

The design studio is the defining pedagogical model at the core of architecture education. In it, students are given a design problem that they must solve holistically through background research and explorations in two- and three-dimensional media. They present their data, analyses, and proposals, documented by drawings and models, for review and discussion at various points in the semester. A student in a professionally accredited degree program will take between six and eight design studios, often including a thesis. The design studio will dominate their credits and time by as much as 60–70 percent.

The studio dates to the 18th- and 19th-century atelier system of the Ecole des Beaux-Arts in Paris. Many details of this antecedent can still be found in the current structure of today's design studios. For example, a senior faculty member (the equivalent of the Beaux-Arts "patron") typically organizes a group of graduate teaching assistants or younger visiting lecturers (comparable to the "anciens," or seniors in the atelier), who teach individual sections of a large introductory studio to first-year design students ("les nouveaux"). Often, students are given a group of precedent buildings to analyze (the Beaux-Arts "analytiques") through plans, sections, and elevations, and they are expected to build scale models (today, of course, the drawings and models may be digital). More important, the students are asked to diagram the idea, or "parti," of the building. Thus, while today's students, like their Beaux-Arts forerunners, are learning from precedents (albeit contemporary ones), they are not only evaluated for their skill and mastery of the tools of representation but also by their ability to understand and articulate the formal, spatial, and material content of architectural ideas. And unlike the Beaux-Arts "juries," which were held in private, the final reviews are now open discussions, usually with distinguished outside practitioners, faculty, community representatives, and fellow students, about the ideas and learning discovered in the studio.

While remnants of the Beaux-Arts atelier system can be found in almost every school, the contemporary design studio is equally, if not more, influenced by the Bauhaus curriculum and Modernist philosophy that replaced it. Conversion to the Bauhaus curriculum began with the arrival of Gropius at Harvard in 1937, Mies at the Illinois Institute of Technology in 1938, and Laszlo Moholy-Nagy at the Institute of Design in Chicago in 1937. In contrast to the Beaux-Arts system, history was removed from the list of required courses, and the design studios emphasized more current building tasks based on careful analysis of the "program" rather than idealized monumental building types based on precedent. Technical courses emphasized new materials and processes as inspiration for innovative building forms, structure, and building assemblies. Courses in basic design explored abstract formal composition, inspired by new theories of perception from Europe. While elements of the Bauhaus system have been forgotten or lain dormant in schools, especially during the Postmodernist focus on historicism, fragments of its fundamental concerns have remained and are reemerging. It can be argued that over the last 50 years, faculties have developed an innovative and hybrid attitude about the studio's dual origins, experimenting widely with elements of both.

The design studio has proven to be a remarkably powerful and adaptable teaching model. It is the place where emerging issues in practice can be explored, where the implication of new theories can be examined, and where new digital techniques can be tested. It teaches students not only to explore alternative approaches to a design problem but also to build the arguments for a preferred solution. Graduates leave "well prepared as problem solvers,"[1] not in a narrow sense but in the expanded sense of "design thinkers." They become leaders and innovators within and beyond the profession.

In fact, during their study of architecture education, Ernest Boyer and Lee Mitgang became convinced "that the core elements of architecture education [read the "design studio"]—learning to design within constraints, collaborative learning, and the refining of knowledge through the reflective act of design—have relevance and power far beyond the training of future architects."[2] It should therefore come as no surprise that the design studio is now being recognized by other disciplines as a pedagogical model that creates an experience of real-world questioning and problem solving with great integrative power. Indeed, the design studio is being used more and more as an interdisciplinary crossover experience for students and faculty from multiple disciplines, including engineering, environmental sciences, business, and law.

Addressing real-world problems that do not recognize disciplinary boundaries forces students and faculty to bring the most critical knowledge from their different disciplines to bear on potential solutions. The process challenges the core of what we know and do not know, leading to new hypotheses and research questions. The design studio is being recognized for what it has always been: in building both empirical and discursive arguments for a proposal, the studio becomes a "search engine" for new knowledge.

The Design Studio: The Heart of Architecture Education

Harrison S. Fraker Jr., FAIA

The design studio has proven to be a powerful model for teaching real-world problem solving and collaborative learning. In these photos, students at the Yale School of Architecture participate in an urban design studio (top) and a final student critique.
©*Yale School of Architecture*

1902
AIA purchased the Octagon

*Flatiron Building,
New York City,
Daniel H. Burnham*

*White House restored and
enlarged by Charles F. McKim,
architect, and Glenn Brown,
supervising architect*

VIEWPOINT

Performance-Based Criteria

Harrison S. Fraker Jr., FAIA

Accreditation of architecture education began in 1897, when Illinois passed legislation regulating the practice of architecture. What began as separate state regulations evolved into a national standard with the founding of the Association of Collegiate Schools of Architecture (ACSA) in 1912, which required that schools meet a "standard minima" to be granted membership. In 1940 the ACSA, the American Institute of Architects (AIA), and the National Council of Architectural Registration Boards (NCARB) established the National Architectural Accrediting Board (NAAB) and gave it the sole authority to accredit U.S. professional degree programs in architecture.

The conditions and criteria for accreditation have evolved since then. The most important changes occurred in the 1980s, when NAAB established performance-based criteria to evaluate the coursework required of the student. The current 34 criteria cover not only the scope but also the level of performance deemed necessary "to assure the maintenance and enhancement of an appropriate educational foundation for the profession of architecture." While the criteria are established as minimum standards of performance, schools are encouraged to exceed them. The range of topics outlined by the criteria headings, listed here, convey the breadth of information covered in an accredited architecture education program.

1. Speaking and writing skills
2. Critical thinking skills
3. Graphics skills
4. Research skills
5. Formal ordering systems
6. Fundamental design skills
7. Collaborative skills
8. Western traditions
9. Non-Western traditions
10. National and regional traditions
11. Use of precedents
12. Human behavior
13. Human diversity
14. Accessibility
15. Sustainable design
16. Program preparation
17. Site conditions
18. Structural systems
19. Environmental systems
20. Life safety
21. Building envelope systems
22. Building service systems
23. Building systems integration
24. Building materials and assemblies
25. Construction cost control
26. Technical documentation
27. Client role in architecture
28. Comprehensive design
29. Architect's administrative roles
30. Architecture practice
31. Professional development
32. Leadership
33. Legal responsibilities
34. Ethics and professional judgment

Susan Lawrence Dana House,
Springfield, Illinois,
Frank Lloyd Wright

Carson Pirie Scott,
Chicago,
Louis Sullivan

Metropolitan Museum of Art
(central pavilion and main entrance),
New York City, Richard Morris Hunt

VIEWPOINT

American Institute of Architecture Students

Jonathan Bahe, Assoc. AIA

Since its founding in 1857, the American Institute of Architects has always considered the needs and concerns of those aspiring to enter the profession. But it wasn't until 1956 that a particularly active group of students decided to organize a disparate array of local, school-based programs into a collective voice called the National Architectural Student Association (NASA). In 1960 the organization was renamed the Association of Student Chapters of the AIA (ASC/AIA) and then became the American Institute of Architecture Students (AIAS) in 1985.

Today, AIAS is an independent, nonprofit, student-run organization. Its mission is to promote excellence in architecture education, training, and practice; foster an appreciation of architecture and related disciplines; enrich communities in a spirit of collaboration; and organize students and combine their efforts to advance the art and science of architecture. As the voice of all architecture students, AIAS advocates for issues important to students and empowers them to be active participants in their education. The national group has served members at every school of architecture across the country as well as numerous community colleges and even high schools.

Since its grassroots beginning in 1956, AIAS has functioned as an advocate for the rights and responsibilities of students and young professionals. In the early 1990s, for example, AIAS was instrumental in ensuring that students and interns working in architecture firms receive fair monetary compensation. Among other strategies, AIAS required that speakers invited to any of its events confirm in writing that their firms adhere to this policy. The AIA and the Association of Collegiate Schools of Architecture soon followed suit.

More recently, the AIAS brought the issue of studio culture to the forefront. In 2002 an AIAS task force released a report titled "The Redesign of Studio Culture." The design studio is a core part of architecture education through which students learn how to think holistically and critically about specific problems and apply this methodology to the design process. However, while the studio environment is intended to be one of thoughtful collaboration, integration, and experimentation, its intense demands all too often make it an all-consuming part of students' lives, leading to sleep deprivation, poor nutrition, and an unhealthy learning environment. This report, and the subsequent discussions, brought about positive changes to the studio environment, promoting the fundamental values of optimism, respect, sharing, engagement, and innovation among students, faculty, and administration.

Students are also committed to contributing to their communities. For example, through the AIAS Freedom by Design™ program (see page 122), students implement design-build solutions to help individuals with physical challenges while focusing on issues of life safety, dignity, and comfort. Simultaneously, Freedom by Design provides these young men and women with the real-world experience of working with clients and with mentorship from local architects.

AIAS celebrated its 50th anniversary in 2006. In the years ahead, the student-run organization foresees a stronger partnership with the AIA and its other collateral organizations to develop the architecture leaders of tomorrow.

AIAS leaders gathered in 2006 for their annual Grassroots leadership conference. *Courtesy AIAS*

6

Reflections on Architectural Research

Daniel S. Friedman, PhD, FAIA

Design reigns unchallenged as architecture's signifying epistemology. Properly speaking, it is the poetic synthesis of ethical and technical understanding. This helps explain why design in itself—uncoupled from commercial or contractual obligations—dominates all other branches of architectural understanding. In its essence, design is an intensely visual and uniquely autonomous form of research, supported by its own internal, naturally integrative grammars, methods, and procedures. Although schematic composition consumes a mere 10 percent of the total cost of building, design invariably absorbs the greatest amount of professional and educational interest, time, attention, and debate. Design is the root of architectural identity and as such is—in the broadest possible sense—the ultimate aim of all architectural research.

The Nature of Architectural Research

Research plies the space between theory and practice. It generates the tools that shape and focus both quantitative and qualitative outcomes—from injury rates, workplace productivity, and energy consumption to innovative forms, contextual fit, and even greater self-awareness. Although architecture has long benefited from research, the nature of that inquiry has varied not only with project needs but also with cultural imperatives.

Design depends on compositional principles, and compositional principles depend on research. Two thousand years ago, Vitruvius used research to help formulate *De architectura*, our oldest surviving written treatise on architecture. As architect Bernard Cache explains, "Vitruvius is *researching* a middle ground that anchors the concept of proportion in a wide variety of applications . . . mathematical, geometrical, formal, aesthetical, anthropological, religious, and physio-medical . . . [H]e seems to limit himself to collecting materials accumulated by other authors he does not understand entirely . . . but in any case he is a grand 'administrator' who most often preserves a critical eye. By building a theory of architecture, he delivers to us an architectonic of knowledge."[1]

Research also helped propel the great milestones of architectural history. It allowed Filippo Brunelleschi to dome Florence's cathedral and to represent three-dimensional space on a two-dimensional plane. It fueled Leone Battista Alberti's great civic treatises on family and architecture. And it guided the assiduous eye of Leonardo da Vinci, whose investigations into the forms of art and nature used the same methodology—drawing, *sapere verde*, "knowing how to see."[2]

By the end of the 18th century, Western civilization's growing reliance on rational analysis was increasingly subjecting traditional standards of composition to rigorous economic and quantitative evaluation. Custom and taste, while important, had less and less influence over agreed-upon standards of building production. As science and industry grew, performance and economy supplanted sensation and pleasure as the best measure of "beauty." Therefore, our current understanding of research, which flows from the Enlightenment, is based on philosophical convictions about the sovereignty of reason, experiment, and objective verifiability.

Modern industry and modern technology draw from this root, as does modern architecture. Yet despite the increasingly scientific character of contemporary architectural research, it remains uniquely and persistently preoccupied with the relationship between evidence and form.

Two 19th-century giants of research illustrate this point. The indomitable French architect and educator Viollet-le-Duc developed a novel analysis of Gothic engineering and construction that recast the French cathedral as an exemplar of structural reasoning. Supported by prodigious historical and visual analysis, Viollet-le-Duc argued for new principles of order more conducive to the integration of modern technology and materials, thereby helping to foster the structural rationalism that would later characterize 20th-century European architecture.

Likewise, the German architect and scholar Gottfried Semper employed empirical analysis to argue that architectural style derived from ethnological conditions that converge in endless variation around four primordial motifs: hearth (associated with clay and molding), partition (associated with fiber and weaving), frame (associated with wood and joinery), and mound (associated with stone and stacking). According to Semper, all architectural expression stems from these few immutable origins. Following his logic, forms that flow from looms and computers belong to the same "stylistic" genealogy. The influential Chicago architect John Wellborn Root translated essays by Semper for *Inland Architect* in the late 1880s; today, Semper's theory of *Bekleidung* (cladding, or wall dressing) still profoundly influences the development of curtain-wall construction and the discourse on structure and enclosure.

The 1893 World's Columbian Exposition in Chicago marked the shift from geography to technology for the American frontier. Industrial greatness presupposed a great culture, which helps explain why the fair's East Coast designers chose imperial classical imagery over the democratic compositions of Louis Sullivan. Nonetheless, rising out of the White City, as the fair was called, was an urgent question about the relationship between technology and form. No less in the 19th century than the 21st, what distinguishes research in our discipline from research in medicine, engineering, or physics is its enduring and indissoluble marriage to art—to form and the problem of its surplus value, to the gift of design, and to the surplus quality that remains when we subtract construction from architecture. Modern research entwines the empirical and poetic achievements of architecture, seeking to refine the principles of composition, elaborate the relationship between part and whole, improve the way buildings benefit people, and better understand the life of buildings and the spaces and places they create. The double obligations of architecture are perhaps best captured by Louis Kahn's most penetrating aphorism: "A great building . . . must begin with the unmeasurable, must go through measurable means when it is being designed, and in the end must be unmeasurable."[3]

(Opposite) Research allowed Filippo Brunelleschi to top the Santa Maria del Fiore Cathedral, Florence, Italy, with a dome, which was completed in 1461 after years of construction. ©*age fotostock/SuperStock*

The 1893 World's Columbian Exposition in Chicago marked the shift from geography to technology for the American frontier. Rising out of the "White City" was an urgent question about the relationship between technology and form. ©*Bettmann/Corbis*

1904
Larkin Building,
Buffalo,
Frank Lloyd Wright

New York Stock Exchange,
George B. Post

The Mechanics of Architectural Research

Almost all hypotheses in architecture flow from questions about how we make buildings, what they look like, how they work, how they affect us, and what they mean. Accordingly, contemporary research explores three adjacent and sometimes overlapping domains: the physical, the social, and the cultural. Each avenue of inquiry explores how buildings and spaces register across the spectrum of human experience.

Research into physical issues in architecture, which includes topics such as structures, building performance, and architectural technology, tends to employ methods and techniques common to engineering and mechanics. Research into social issues in architecture, including behavior, perception, and patterns of use, tends to employ methods and techniques common to psychology and sociology. Research into cultural issues in architecture arguably incorporates the greatest variety of methods and disciplinary orientations. This third domain covers, among many other topics, historical and theoretical analysis of the social, political, and economic context of building production; problems of representation, linguistics, and semiotics; and feminist theory and gender studies. Moreover, architectural theory and criticism has emerged as an autonomous branch of the humanities that tends to employ historiographic and philosophical methods, techniques, and nomenclatures.

In contemporary research, when architects refer to "knowledge-based practice" and "evidence-based design," they generally mean practice and design supported by methods of inquiry characteristic of the physical and social sciences. In this case, architects seek to use knowledge in the same way as doctors and engineers, shaping it with verifiable conclusions and measurable data that result from scientific methods. On the other hand, when architects speak of "history, theory, and criticism," they seek to use knowledge as literary critics and art historians do, shaping it with provisional interpretations and readings that flow from the indeterminable nature of "truth."

Much like that of other disciplines, the research process in architecture begins with a theory or hypothesis. Next, investigators undertake a series of steps or procedures—reviewing existing literature, gathering primary source material and data, and conducting experiments—in the course of which they record, describe, interpret, and predict phenomena or persuasively explicate and interpret texts, artifacts, trends, and events. These procedures invariably condition findings. Once investigators articulate these, they disseminate the fruits of their efforts in various narrative forms (statistical reports, historical analyses, and critical exegeses) to various readers and audiences.[4] New research often yields new standards of practice and performance, typologies, building products and techniques, policies, organizational models, pedagogies, design criteria, codes, and construction methods.

Notwithstanding different emphases and methodologies, every domain of architectural research seeks to refine and fortify core principles. First among these is the welfare of the public, in particular its health and safety. Codes and regulations that result from research into standards of performance increasingly influence architectural engineering, technology, and building product manufacturing. Perhaps the best example of the relationship between building and social welfare is the 1990 Americans with Disabilities Act (ADA). The ADA has substantially affected the design of buildings, cities, parks, and public transportation—all environments which, by law and civil right, must now be accessible to people with diverse motor, visual, and aural capabilities.

Sponsoring Institutions and Organizations

Rapid economic expansion and population growth after World War II fueled concern among architects and planners that traditional design methods and existing professional training were inadequate to meet the demands of increasingly complex environmental problems. Many in the design professions felt these challenges required a much deeper engagement with economics, behavior, and culture, which could only be obtained through a more rigorous system of architecture education and research. The number of accredited degree programs and post-professional master's and doctoral degrees in architecture steadily increased. For example, 23 American universities offered PhD degrees in architecture in 2006, roughly double the number available in 1980.

Also multiplying after the war was the number of academic associations established to address problems related to what architect and environmental theorist Amos Rapoport calls the "human aspects" of form.[5] These organizations include the Design Methods Group (1966), the Environmental Design Research Association (1969), the Architectural Research Centers Consortium (1976), and the Association for Computer Aided Design in Architecture (early

1980s). By the last quarter of the 20th century, research and theory proliferated. Publications, peer-reviewed journals, books, and conferences steadily multiplied, all broadcasting advanced discourse and analysis in theory, history, criticism, building science, environment-behavior studies, computing, and sustainable technology.

Over the past 60 years, the AIA has explored ambitious programs and initiatives designed to stimulate the knowledge base of the profession. These efforts have included the short-lived Department of Education and Research in 1945, the Research Advisory Council in 1960, and the AIA Research Corporation in 1972. Among other topics, studies undertaken by these entities focused on housing, health care design, schools, and energy conservation. Today, AIA staff researchers regularly monitor market trends, economic indicators, and the construction industry. In 1995 the AIA struck an alliance with the McGraw-Hill Companies (publisher of *Architectural Record, Engineering News Record*, and *Sweets Catalogue*, among other products and services), directly connecting the Institute to commercial research and data.

In 2003, as part of a millennial strategic plan, the AIA reorganized its professional interest areas into 22 "knowledge communities." To support these diverse specializations and interests, the AIA subsequently launched a series of special reports and research funding initiatives, addressing new developments in building information modeling, hazard mitigation, cost-benefit analysis, geriatric care, data management, and design methodology. For its part, the AIA College of Fellows introduced a major new grant program in 2000 intended to support cutting-edge research by leading practitioners and scholars. Renamed the Latrobe Prize in 2006, this biennial program awards $100,000 to a research proposal based on its potential for advancing professional knowledge in architecture. Since the program's inception, Latrobe recipients have undertaken research in the areas of technology transfer, the neurosciences, and health care design.[6]

In the most recent comprehensive study of architecture education, *Building Community: A New Future for Architecture Education and Practice*, Ernest L. Boyer and Lee D. Mitgang observe that traditional university standards of research productivity, in particular grants and publications, tend to exclude achievements in conventional practice, such as completed buildings and speculative design. The report recommended "widening the scope of scholarship beyond the old dichotomies of teaching and research" by expanding academic achievement to include a clinical category. This new form of "engaged scholarship" includes community design and planning initiatives, design-build projects, and critical and activist practices that emphasize discovery, integration, and application.[7]

Stimulated by digital technology such as building information modeling, fractal geometry, and animation software, methods research and theoretical analysis have greatly diversified. In addition, the use of computers has greatly accelerated both hermeneutical and positivist traditions, shaped over the last 30 years by robust innovations in contemporary philosophy — the writings of Jacques Derrida, Gilles Deleuze, and Félix Guattari, for example — and technology, as illustrated by the development of computer numeric-controlled rapid prototyping technology, software innovations adapted from the aviation and engineering industry, and computational fluid dynamics.

Research Highlights

Looking back at the last 150 years, it is tempting to try to name the most significant advances affecting American architecture during this period. A few that come to mind are electricity, mechanical equipment, fire safety, codes and zoning, the glass curtain wall, environmental psychology, computers, digital animation, sustainability, deconstruction, and virtual construction.

Theorists might argue that the most significant product of research in the past 25 years has been the shift in emphasis from static to dynamic building composition. While static composition tends to see the building as an object, organized around a hierarchy of axes within the gestalt of figure and ground, dynamic composition tends to see the building as an event, organized around an ecology of tangible forces within the indeterminate play of vector and field. Drawing from advancements in biology, mathematics, medicine, and economics, among other sciences, more and more designers and researchers conceptualize form as the consequence of intricate systems that "escape definitive control or closure" and "address the complexity of loosely structured organizations that grow and change with time."[8]

New insights into the behavior of structure and space suggest a steady shift away from plane and solid geometry toward "animated" forms, which embody the character of living organisms and biomes. Design pedagogies that use animation software to stimulate the exploration of dynamic form are increasingly commonplace. Most of these pedagogies stage formal exploration within a theoretical framework heavily influenced by the contemporary avant-garde and loyally documented by the popular press, which regularly showcases projects derived from advanced digital media.

Environmentalists might argue that the most significant research in the past 50 years belongs under the category of sustainability. Energy conservation and sustainable technologies increasingly influence policy in both the marketplace and the university. Green research supports sustainable principles by extending biological research, in particular biomimicry and ecology. This area of research is becoming more sensitive to the behavior and interdependence of dynamic networks across multiple scales of production. From films on glass to regional biocomplexity, researchers increasingly situate problems of design, construction, and development within an ecological matrix. Moreover, researchers in this area increasingly see their work within an ethical framework that places responsibility for the well-being of future generations on the shoulders of the current one.

Practitioners might argue that the most significant development in the past 100 years is building information modeling. Originally developed for the aeronautics and automotive industries, this technology can precisely simulate and specify the three-dimensional construction of an object or building in virtual space and time. It allows designers to manipulate data points that embody dimensions, specifications, material properties, structural behavior, scheduling, and cost in the same building information model (BIM). Together with research that explores the transfer and adaptation of manufacturing technologies from the automotive and aerospace industries to building construction, building information modeling promises to transform practice by substituting conventional representation (plans, elevations, sections, and digital and physical three-dimensional models) with highly precise virtual constructions. These virtual models, or BIMs, embody all the properties of "reality"; thus, the more operators know about how real things behave, the more they can optimize the models' compositional and economic benefits.[9] More significantly, however, building information modeling will transform the underlying organizational assumptions of the entire AEC industry—how we make and assemble buildings, who participates in their design and documentation, and how we distribute the risks and rewards.[10]

Behaviorists might argue that the most significant development in the past 150 years is the proliferation of literature that examines the fundamental relationship between people and space. Though more inquiry is needed, this research has had a powerful and lasting influence on housing and community development. It has significantly elevated the standards that shape affordable neighborhoods and generally increased the representation of diverse constituencies in urban and regional environmental policy. Springing from research about access for people with disabilities, for example, an international movement called universal design aims to extend these principles to the design of all products and environments for all people of all ages and capacities in all nations.

What does the future hold? Like every burgeoning epoch, the 21st century will place its own signature on research and practice. The interdependence between practice and applied research will surely intensify, as we have already witnessed in recent advances in digital imaging, virtual construction, and information design; developments in building science and sustainability; increased understanding of rapidly changing global economics; and new paradigms in architectural theory with new significance for practice. Undoubtedly, as research in architecture stimulates greater precision in our design, production, and management of the constructed world, it will increasingly influence our evolving professional identity. ●

Pier Luigi Nervi, Hon. FAIA

Fred Bernstein

Pier Luigi Nervi was born in Sondrio, Italy, in 1891 and received an engineering degree from the University of Bologna in 1913. He believed he could best explore what he called "the mysterious affinity between physical laws and the human senses" by personally supervising architecture, engineering, and construction. With a cousin, he formed Nervi and Bartoli, a contracting company in Rome, and began experimenting with ferro-cemento, a thin, pliable form of reinforced concrete in which metal mesh replaced the more "typical rebar. Nervi used the material to build formwork for his structural pours, opening up aesthetic possibilities beyond the flat surfaces of traditional plywood formwork. His engineering training allowed him to make large structures gloriously slender and graceful, often with roofs supported by ribs that closely resembled Gothic tracery.

Nervi's most dramatic prewar building was a 1938 airplane hangar in Orbetello, Italy, which featured endless diamond-pattern ribbing. His Palazzetto dello Sport, designed for the 1960 Olympics in Rome, seemingly lifted that city's ancient Pantheon into the air on angled pillars. In 1963 he designed New York's George Washington Bridge bus terminal, which makes explicit reference to the crisscross trusses of the bridge but in a far more fluid medium—as if he had abstracted a set of engineering drawings.

Nervi's Gold Medal recognized his explorations into the sculptural possibilities of poured concrete. As Ada Louise Huxtable wrote, "His uniquely personal, intricate structural logic has established a creative highpoint in 20th-century engineering and architectural design." Nervi died in Rome in 1979.

In a competition organized by the Italian Air Force, Pier Nervi designed an airplane hangar of reinforced concrete, several of which were built, including this one in Orvieto (1936). The Germans destroyed these hangars during World War II. *AIA Archives*

1906
San Francisco earthquake and fire
destroyed much of the city

Fairmont Hotel,
San Francisco,
Julia Morgan

No problem was too large, no idea too complex, for visionary Buckminster Fuller to tackle. Whether he was adopting the role of inventor, architect, engineer, poet, philosopher, or cartographer, Fuller expressed an unending faith in technology's ability to solve many of humanity's problems.

The world—or, as Fuller called it, "spaceship earth"—came along for the ride. While he is best known for his invention of the geodesic dome, Fuller focused public attention on issues such as housing, world hunger, transportation, and environmental stewardship decades before they became popular causes.

Born July 12, 1895, in Milton, Massachusetts, Richard Buckminster Fuller was the progeny of an influential New England family, but he found greater success in the U.S. Navy than as a student at Harvard, where he spent two troubled years. In the 1920s, he worked with his father-in-law promoting the Stockade Building System, masonry units built of cement and compressed wood shavings. When the company failed, Fuller was bankrupt and emotionally distraught. At age 32, with little to his name, he made a profound commitment to work for the betterment of mankind.

Described by *Fortune* magazine in 1946 as having "a mind that functions like a cross between a roll-top desk and a jet-propulsion motor," Fuller was one of the earliest proponents of renewable energy sources. In typically blunt fashion, he once claimed, "There is no energy crisis, only a crisis of ignorance." His belief in the need to conserve resources led to his design of the Dymaxion House, which afforded maximum design efficiency with minimal materials.

During World War II, Fuller adapted his idea of the Dymaxion House into a new form—the Dymaxion Deployment Unit. Using the technology of grain silos made by the Butler Manufacturing Company, Fuller developed a hybrid unit suited to the rapid deployment needs of the U.S. Army Signal Corps. He attempted to convert this prototype into a marketable alternative for postwar housing and won a commission from the Beech Aircraft Company to design the Wichita House, which was projected to sell for $6,500. But the project lost momentum before it got off the ground.

In 1947, while teaching at Black Mountain College in North Carolina, Fuller invented the geodesic dome, which he believed would herald a new era in housing. Composed of a web of interconnected tetrahedrons, Fuller's innovative dome gained worldwide attention. The Ford Motor Company commissioned Fuller in 1953 to design the Ford Rotunda Dome in Dearborn, Michigan. Later he designed "radomes" to house military radar antennas and, most famously, the 20-story dome housing the U.S. Pavilion at Montreal's Expo '67. He later proposed a dome two miles in diameter that would enclose midtown Manhattan.

Although he lacked a formal academic degree, Fuller was the recipient of 47 honorary doctorates in the arts, science, engineering, and the humanities. By the time he died in 1983, this practical philosopher—who was awarded 28 U.S. patents—had become one of the 20th century's most influential thinkers.

GOLD MEDALIST, 1970

R. Buckminster Fuller, FAIA

Vernon Mays

Among his many vocations, Fuller was a tireless educator, as seen here at Black Mountain College in 1948.

The Wichita House, otherwise known as the Dymaxion Dwelling Machine, never progressed beyond the prototype stage.
Courtesy the Estate of R. Buckminster Fuller

Fuller gained international exposure with the construction of his 250-foot-diameter geodesic dome at Expo '67 in Montreal.
Courtesy the Estate of R. Buckminster Fuller

McDonough Braungart Design Chemistry

Deborah Snoonian

By now, phrases such as "cradle to cradle design," "waste equals food," and "the next Industrial Revolution" are familiar to many eco-friendly architects. For William McDonough, FAIA, the man who coined them, they articulate the beliefs he has practiced for years—as a sustainable designer, innovator, and educator—and that form the basis for one of his most renowned ventures. In 1995, while dean of the school of architecture at the University of Virginia in Charlottesville (where he still runs an architecture firm), he teamed with chemist Michael Braungart to form McDonough Braungart Design Chemistry (MBDC), a multidisciplinary product design and consulting firm that works with companies to overhaul the way building materials and many other products are made.

MBDC's paradigm (elaborated in McDonough and Braungart's popular 2002 book *Cradle to Cradle*) is rooted in the deceptively simple concept that human activities should be modeled on natural systems—and need not damage them. The natural world teaches us that waste should not exist; instead, products should be made of safe materials that are reusable indefinitely, even after the original item is no longer needed. McDonough and Braungart define safe materials as those made of either biological nutrients, which break down naturally to nourish the soil without introducing persistent toxins, or technical nutrients, which can be reused over and over to fabricate high-quality goods. A safe product can be made of both biological and technical nutrients as long as the two types of materials can be properly separated at the end of the product's useful life. To achieve this sustainable model, revolutionary manufacturing and assembly methods are required—that's the next Industrial Revolution part—which McDonough says will create "short-term profitability and long-term prosperity" for both manufacturers and society at large.

This sustainable model sounds straightforward, until you think of what it would *really* take to disassemble and recycle, say, an office chair (all that plastic, fabric, and metal) or a window shade (all those small moving parts), let alone an entire building. The bulk of MBDC's work involves collaborative research and consulting with building product manufacturers like Steelcase, MechoShade, Herman Miller, and Milliken Carpet, as well as corporations like Nike, FedEx, and Volvo. They examine products in terms of how and with what they are made, with an eye toward eliminating materials and methods that harm the ecosystem. "Sometimes a process redesign can be as simple as using screws instead of toxic glues to assemble a piece of furniture," says Jay Bolus, MBDC's executive vice president for benchmarking and certification. The company has also worked with clients to design new products from the ground up.

In addition to developing new materials and methods, many MBDC clients have implemented programs for collecting existing products to recycle or refurbish them. "The challenge is the economics—right now it's cheaper to throw stuff away than to recycle it," says Bolus. He envisions a national network of third-party companies that would collect, recycle, and refurbish building products in local markets, thereby making reuse more cost-effective.

MBDC's definition of sustainability has evolved over time. "Originally we focused on the material chemistry—its toxicity or ability to be recycled," Bolus says. "Now we're including factors like how much energy it takes to make a product, how much water the manufacturing consumes, human elements like fair labor practices." These evolving definitions are captured in the company's three-tier Cradle to Cradle certification program, launched in 2005. To date more than 40 products have been certified. "This is a focus for our future," says Bolus. "Through the certification program, we want to recognize and reward companies for continual improvements."

MechoShade's EcoVeil solar shade system recently received Cradle to Cradle certification from MBDC for its environmentally friendly manufacturing and materials. *Courtesy MechoShade*

1907
The AIA celebrated its 50th
anniversary; the first AIA Gold
Medal was presented to Sir
Aston Webb of Great Britain

Blacker House,
Pasadena,
Charles and Henry Greene

Avery Coonley House,
Riverside, Illinois,
Frank Lloyd Wright

Union Station,
Washington, D.C.,
Daniel Burnham

GRASS ROOTS

KieranTimberlake Associates

Sara Hart

Historically, architects have depended on time-tested methods and materials to create buildings. While they improvise and customize, their role has rarely been that of innovator. The culture of design and construction is assumed to be too complex, segmented, and bound by the laws of economics to support experimentation beyond the occasional one-off exception that proves the rule. In 1984 Philadelphia-based architects Stephen Kieran, FAIA, and James Timberlake, FAIA, opened their office and—as a prelude to rethinking the methodologies for carrying out their firm's commissions—began to analyze this hegemonic and seemingly archaic system of making buildings. Their investigations led them to conclude that the insular cultures of design and construction, as practiced for more than a century, had created a system so linear and segregated that architects, in effect, were excluded from the craft of building—leaving them to focus primarily on appearance.

In 2001 the AIA College of Fellows awarded KieranTimberlake Associates the inaugural Benjamin Latrobe Research Fellowship. This biennial grant, arguably the most forward-looking endowment the AIA has ever established, funds research that will "increase the knowledge base of the architecture profession." Kieran and Timberlake took this opportunity to investigate transfer technologies (including design and manufacturing methodologies and new material applications) in the automotive, aerospace, and shipbuilding industries, among others. They discovered a parallel universe in which process is integrated, not segregated, and design is collaborative from conception to completion. With this knowledge, Kieran and Timberlake developed practical, cost-effective ways of bringing new methods and materials—including off-site fabrication, mass customization, component assembly, and the commercial application of new and composite materials—to the mainstream of architecture practice.

The architects have not limited their research to a theoretical critique of building industry hegemony but have advanced all their research toward commercial application through their own projects and in partnership with forward-looking manufacturers. The result is a growing body of work in which research is applied and, therefore, open to real-life scrutiny of performance and quality. Completed commissions have included an active, pressure-equalized, double-skin curtain wall for the engineering school at the University of Pennsylvania and prefabricated bathroom modules for Yale University residence halls.

KieranTimberlake's most futuristic experiment to date is probably its SmartWrap pavilion at the Cooper-Hewitt National Design Museum in New York in 2003. For the exhibition, the architects enclosed an aluminum-framed structure, measuring 30 feet tall and covering an area of 1,000 square feet, with SmartWrap, an advanced composite of microthin layers, which KieranTimberlake had begun to develop as an exterior cladding material in partnership with the material's manufacturer, DuPont. Embedded within the layers are a variety of microtechnologies that give the envelope its highly versatile attributes, including the ability to generate electricity that can provide illumination and informational displays on the walls and the ability to regulate the structure's internal temperature. The product offers a glimpse into the possibilities of the building envelope of the future.

Today the 54-person firm dedicates four professional staff members and 3 percent of its gross revenues to ongoing research. Kieran and Timberlake find that their commitment to research naturally brings innovation to every project and, thus, adds value for every client. At the same time, they are training the next generation of architects to reinvent the profession. The firm received the AIA's Architecture Firm Award in 2008.

The team at KieranTimberlake Associates

Working with DuPont, KieranTimberlake Associates developed SmartWrap, a very thin and versatile cladding material, shown here on a pavilion exhibited at the Cooper-Hewitt National Design Museum in 2003. *Barry Halkin*

Research on Neuroscience and Architecture

John P. Eberhard, FAIA

At the most fundamental level, all architecture is experienced by the human mind. The brain interprets the myriad signals it receives from our physical senses to understand, engage with, navigate through, and, one hopes, enjoy our surroundings. It follows, then, that the most advanced approaches to any kind of design for the built environment would take into account "why" our brains and minds respond the way they do.

Intrigued by this mind-body relationship, the AIA—along with the American Architectural Foundation (AAF), the College of Fellows, a number of architecture firms, and several other organizations—began in 1995 to support research on neuroscience, the science of the brain and mind. Many at the Institute believe that, over the next 50 years, such research will provide evidence-based knowledge for creating spaces that support the functions of their occupants, such as cognitive activity for students in classrooms, convalescence for patients in hospitals, and productivity for workers in offices.

In 1995 Dr. Jonas Salk proposed to the leadership of the AIA and the AAF that an exploration be mounted to better understand the research being produced by the neuroscience community. I was appointed director of discovery for the AAF and spent the next decade exploring the research publications of the neuroscience community, writing papers for architectural publications, and lecturing to the architecture community. In 2003 the San Diego chapter of the AIA created the Academy of Neuroscience for Architecture (ANFA) to develop intellectual links between neuroscientists and architects.

ANFA has organized a number of workshops designed to forge such links and to develop hypotheses about human experience in spaces for testing in neuroscience labs. These workshops have included explorations of interactions between patients and medical staff in health care facilities, the effects of K-6 classroom design on the cognitive activity of young children, human responses to sacred spaces, and the impact of laboratory design on the cognitive activities of neuroscientists. The workshops have resulted in a series of reports and more than 90 hypotheses that are ready to be tested in neuroscience laboratories once funding is obtained.

Recent research has examined how the design of school facilities affects students' academic performance. For example, studies show that natural daylight in classrooms has significant positive effects on student achievement.

Daylight floods a shared learning area at the Benjamin Franklin Elementary School (2005) in Kirkland, Washington, shown here. The Seattle-based firm of Mahlum Architects designed the school, which was chosen as a 2006 Top Ten Green Project by the AIA's Committee on the Environment. *©Benjamin Benschneider Photography, courtesy Mahlum Architects*

1908
Gamble House,
Pasadena, California,
Charles and Henry Greene

President Theodore Roosevelt asked the AIA to keep a "perpetual 'eye of guardianship' over the White House to see that it is kept unchanged . . . from this time on."

Farmers' National Bank, Owatonna, Minnesota, Louis Sullivan

VIEWPOINT

Collaborative, Practice-Based Research

Stan Allen, AIA

Research in architecture is a subject of great confusion, to both academics and practicing architects. The pressures of day-to-day practice rarely allow the luxury of time that research demands, and the profession has looked to the academic sector for readily available information that can be easily applied in professional practice. For its own part, the university has had a difficult time reconciling the intricacies of practice with the expectations of academic research.

It would seem that the more closely academics approach the protocols of university research—according to either a scientific or a humanities model—the more they distance themselves from the real concerns of active, creative practitioners. For example, the move in the 1960s and 70s among some schools toward applying sociological models and systems theory—in an effort to place design on a more secure "scientific" footing—failed to find widespread application in practice. The humanities-based research model—that is to say, theoretical and art historical research, which has been the dominant form in most schools of architecture until recently—is typically carried out by individual scholars; is disseminated through publications, conferences, or exhibitions; and is sometimes openly critical of normative practice.

Today, there is a renewed interest in collective, practice-based research, largely because clients are demanding innovation, not just service, in our knowledge-based economy. Architects are being asked to participate more fully in programming and development decisions, which require an understanding of social, economic, and cultural variables. Buildings today are expected to perform to, or exceed, increasingly higher environmental and energy-use standards, requiring both broader and deeper technical expertise on the part of the practitioner. In addition, designers must stay abreast of new materials and systems that continue to proliferate on the commercial market.

To remain competitive, architects are actively incorporating research into practice, and they are doing so in a collaborative way because of a growing awareness that today's complex design challenges can be effectively addressed only by an exchange of information among many disciplines. Architects have recognized that, with immense quantities of information now available to all, their ability to process, organize, and visualize such information is crucial. As a result, practitioners are increasingly serving as coordinators and synthesizers of diverse teams.

Practices embracing research include large firms such as SOM, which has recently inaugurated a materials and technology research arm, and Arup's Advanced Geometry Unit in London, to name only two of the many initiatives that blur the boundaries between academic and professional expertise. Through an active research presence, smaller firms can leverage limited resources to become more agile and entrepreneurial. Firms such as SHoP and ARO in New York engage in practice-based, applied research into materials, digital design technologies, and fabrication techniques that have enabled them to successfully execute larger and more complex projects, such as SHoP's East River complex or ARO's recent projects for academic institutions.

To be sure, we have to be careful not to confuse data gathering (which the Internet facilitates) with true research, which involves processing and analyzing that data to produce new knowledge. This is an appropriate role for the university, and many schools today have introduced a more experimental approach to urbanism, design, and technology that involves information sharing, moving the entire field closer to an "open-source" model of design research. The emergence of the new field of "landscape urbanism" is a good example of productive transfers of knowledge from one discipline to another under this model.

Looking forward, three areas offer productive venues for collaborative research involving academic and professional expertise: sustainability, urbanism, and digital technology. In addition to requiring informed design decisions, close attention to materials and systems choices, and precision in details and construction, a more environmentally sensitive architecture also necessitates the integration of multiple disciplines, such as site planning, landscape design, and mechanical systems. The problems of urbanization, infrastructure, and sprawl are also intrinsically interdisciplinary, involving the coordination of economic, political, technical, and architectural variables. Finally, digital design technology has emerged as a wide-open field where architectural expertise, technical innovation, and material creativity converge. These are all areas where a mixture of skills and knowledge, from a variety of interrelated fields, might productively intersect.

Sharples Holden Pasquarelli, known as SHoP, uses digital tools not only to generate the form of its buildings but also to streamline the entire building process, thereby minimizing labor hours and materials waste. SHoP, along with Ken Smith Landscape Architects, was chosen to design New York City's East River Waterfront Esplanade and Piers Project. *Courtesy SHoP Architects PC*

1909
Adoption of first AIA code of ethics, titled "Circular of Advice Relative to Principles of Professional Practice and the Canon of Ethics"

AIA membership reached 1,000

Victoria and Albert Museum, London, Sir Aston Webb and Ingress Bell

Charles Follen McKim, FAIA, received the AIA Gold Medal

7

Material Matters

Lance Jay Brown, FAIA

Simply put, the architectural process is a fusion of mind and matter. It begins as a collection of abstract ideas that are subsequently realized in physical form—bricks and mortar, if you will. In the best cases, the methods and materials employed to create buildings have an identifiable relationship to the ideas. Although architecture has always attempted to provide what Roman architect Vitruvius succinctly termed "firmness" (structural stability), "commodity" (social purpose), and "delight" (comfort and beauty), the material means to achieve these timeless goals has changed considerably over time. Following are very brief snapshots of the profession's ever-evolving and broadening palette. These are intended to provide an appreciation of the breadth of elements architects have to work with and the depth of technical knowledge required to give physical form to their visions.

(Opposite) Steel reinforcing bars, or rebars, are cast into concrete building components to provide tensile strength. Reinforced concrete, first developed in the mid-to-late 19th century, made it possible to design larger, more highly expressive structures in the 20th century. *©Kevin Burke/Corbis*

Indigenous Methods and Materials

When European settlers arrived in America in the early 17th century, they brought their building traditions with them. The unintended consequences were described by the late architecture critic and historian James Marston Fitch:

[T]he importation of building concepts and techniques developed in other climates and conditions . . . [was] not especially well suited to those occurring here. Two characteristic tendencies were thereby set in motion: the need for speedy invention and development of architectural forms suitable for New World conditions; and the necessity for the colonists to do all the work themselves. The result was an architectural tradition of immense plasticity, on the one hand, and a chronic shortage of labor, which drove toward rationalization, standardization and industrialization of the building process, on the other.

Early building was based primarily on available materials. Timber was abundant in most American colonies and could be easily hand-sawn and planed on site. Therefore, most buildings erected in the first 200 years in the New World were built of wood. (As a matter of fact, as recently as 1960, 85 percent of all housing in the United States was built primarily of wood.) When stone could be quarried locally, it was used for civic buildings. In regions where clay was abundant, it was molded and fired into bricks, a process that was fast and economical. However, when roadways, railroads, and canals made transportation of materials easier, the imperative to build with local materials faded.

The abundance of timber in most American colonies made wood construction expeditious.
DeWitt Historical Society/Morton Collection/Getty Images

Ferrovitreous Construction

Great Britain claimed its place as leader of the Industrial Revolution by mounting the Great Exhibition of 1851 in London. The centerpiece was the Crystal Palace, designed by Joseph Paxton and built in the city's Hyde Park. Paxton's design was enormous and expensive, consuming nearly 10,000 tons of cast iron and 25 acres of glass. While cast iron had been used in Europe before the Great Exhibition as an alternative to masonry, the Crystal Palace—due to its enormous scale and high profile—is the historical benchmark for ferrovitreous, or iron-and-glass, construction.

In the United States, cast iron was arguably the most important material development in the 19th century. Cast-iron machinery was critical to railroad expansion and development of city infrastructure such as water systems and street lighting. Known for its great strength in compression and its inflammability, cast iron changed the structure of buildings and their ornamentation. Cast-iron storefronts and structural framing became ubiquitous across the country.

In 1855 Sir Henry Bessemer patented a process in England for producing steel economically by introducing air into molten iron to remove carbon and make the iron malleable. The resulting steel was stronger (less brittle), had a higher melting point, and offered better ductility than the material made using other processes. Two years later, the "Bessemer process" was patented in the United States.

(Opposite) The Crystal Palace (1851), designed by Joseph Paxton for the Great Exhibition in London, was a benchmark in iron-and-glass construction. *Library of Congress*

Louis Sullivan was the only architect of Chicago's Columbian Exposition (1893) to reject the fair's Beaux-Arts palette. Instead, he chose a polychrome, protomodern scheme for his Transportation Building. *©Bettman/Solidos/Corbis*

1910
First AIA convention held
on the West Coast, featured
activities in San Francisco, Los
Angeles, and Santa Barbara

Congress approved establishment
of the U.S. Commission of
Fine Arts, first proposed by
the AIA some 30 years earlier

AEG Turbine Factory,
Berlin,
Peter Behrens

First Church of Christ, Scientist,
Berkeley,
Bernard Maybeck

Albert Lane Technical High School,
Chicago,
Dwight Perkins

Robie House,
Chicago,
Frank Lloyd Wright

Pennsylvania Station,
New York City,
McKim, Mead and White

Ideals versus Ingenuity

Steel would eventually become, both in the United States and abroad, the most important building material of the 20th century. In the late 19th century, however, the United States was struggling to come to terms with its identity and growing prowess, and the conflict was reflected in physical form. On the one hand, it was generally believed that the United States was heir to the ideals of classical democracy and humanism and that these ideals were best expressed architecturally by the style and materials of academic classicism. On the other hand, with its abundance of raw materials, seemingly endless fossil fuels, and an ever-expanding infrastructure of canals and rails, the country was industrializing at an enormous pace, and there was great national pride in its material and technological advances.

Perhaps nowhere did this dichotomy become more apparent than at the Columbian Exposition held in Chicago in 1893. Touted as a celebration of the 400th anniversary of Columbus's discovery of America, the fair was held at the height of what became known as the American Renaissance, the period between 1880 and 1914. Frederick Law Olmsted designed the expo fairgrounds, and Daniel Burnham, a partner in Burnham and Root, directed building design and construction. Richard Morris Hunt, Charles McKim with his partners Mead and White, George B. Post, and William Le Baron Jenney were among the prominent architects who accepted Burnham's Neoclassical palette and designed a collection of Beaux-Arts pavilions around the Court of Honor. This complex became known as the "White City" because it stood in stark contrast to the urban bleakness nearby. Louis Sullivan, however, rejected the formal restrictions of the palette for his Transportation Building in favor of a polychrome, protomodern scheme, which was consistent with his belief that buildings should reflect the structure and properties of the materials with which they were constructed. He correctly predicted that the Neoclassicism so enthusiastically pursued by the other architects would set architectural design back decades, and it did indeed remain the dominant style for years to come.

(Opposite and above) The Chicago exposition showcased a staggering array of inventions developed in the late 19th century. George Ferris's wheel was considered an engineering marvel, and General Electric's "tower of light" was one of many exhibitions devoted to electricity. *Waterman Company/ ©Corbis (Ferris wheel); Souvenir Photo Company/ ©Corbis (GE)*

Elisha Otis founded the Otis Elevator Company in 1853, pioneering the development of the safety elevator and leading the way to development of the skyscraper. *©Bettman/Corbis*

1911
AIA published first edition
of six standardized contract
documents, including the
first version of what became
A201

Fagus Factory,
Alfeld-an-der-Leine, Germany,
Walter Gropius

Taliesin,
Spring Green, Wisconsin,
Frank Lloyd Wright

(Opposite) The northern half (foreground) of the 16-story Monadnock Building, designed by Burnham and Root and built in 1891 in Chicago, is the tallest building to use masonry load-bearing wall construction. The southern half (background) was designed by Holabird and Roche and erected in 1893 with a steel frame. *©Bettman/Corbis*

It could be considered ironic that such traditional, conformist edifices actually housed some of the most unconventional, cutting-edge advances of the time. For example, George Bartholomew's demonstration of his new invention, concrete pavement, received a prize for engineering innovation at the exposition. As a result of this public validation, his paving technique found widespread adoption in the United States and abroad. In terms of sheer spectacle, bridge builder George Ferris's eponymous wheel was the overwhelming crowd pleaser. Weighing in at 1,200 tons with a diameter of 250 feet, the Ferris wheel's 45-foot axle represented the largest steel forging in the world. Erected on the Midway, a short distance from the main grounds, the wheel was held up by two 140-foot steel towers and powered by two 1,000-horsepower reversible engines. From the top, nearly 1.5 million riders were treated to spectacular views of Chicago and Lake Michigan during the fair's run.

In contrast to most of the buildings, the exhibits showcased at the Columbian Exposition more honestly reflected the staggering number of inventions being developed in the second half of the 19th century. "The [post–Civil War] period was lusty and inventive," Fitch wrote. Referring to Morse's telegraph, Bell's telephone, Otis's elevator, Westinghouse's transformer, and Edison's light bulb, he continued, "The cumulative impact of the work of these men, in the years between 1865 and 1900, completely transformed the character of both our buildings and the landscape in which they stood." Building infrastructure began to be of equal importance to structure and enclosure. Gas, electricity, running water, heating systems, sanitation systems, electric lighting, and communications systems all became part of the building equation.

William Le Baron Jenney's Home Insurance Building (1885), Chicago, was the first to use a load-bearing structural skeleton, making way for a new building type that would become known as the skyscraper. *©Bettman/Corbis*

1912
H. Van Buren Magonigle's
design for the AIA seal, the
basis for the seal still in use
today, was adopted

Woolworth Building,
New York City,
Cass Gilbert

Founding of the Association of
Collegiate Schools of Architecture

The Birth of the Skyscraper

Buildings taller than six stories were rare before the 19th century. But progress in the manufacture of steel, glass, reinforced concrete, water pumps, and elevators late in that century changed the American skyline forever. In *The Rise of an American Architecture* (edited by Edgar Kaufman Jr.), Winston Weisman develops a short history of the American skyscraper: There is little question that the "Chicago frame" (the first load-carrying structural skeleton, developed by William Le Baron Jenney for the Home Insurance Building of 1885) and the New York "skyscraper" led to the basic form of this entirely new building type. Today, a skyscraper is often defined as a building higher than 500 feet, whether it is a steel or reinforced concrete structure.

Burnham and Root's 16-story Monadnock Building, built in 1891, pushed the bearing wall to its limit. Afterward, it would be the steel frame that would reach for the skies, including their Reliance Building of 1895 (see page 39), also in Chicago, and Burnham's 1902 Flatiron Building in New York. Located on a triangular site, the northern facade of the Flatiron Building—the city's oldest skyscraper—narrows dramatically to a mere six feet. Legend has it that Burnham "supported" the building with a rusticated limestone base to give it visual weight, thus tempering fears that it was structurally suspect and prone to tipping over. In fact, the stone and terra-cotta panels are only a few inches thick and support only their own weight.

The Flatiron provides an example of how traditional perceptions of structural solidity linger in the face of technological advances. Once structure became independent of envelope, a debate over cladding materials emerged. Much analysis has focused on the development of the modern curtain wall, which has been the architect's largest canvas for more than a century.

In curtain wall construction, large expanses of glass are supported by steel mullions and held in place by tape and urethane sealants. On the exterior face of the mullions, a cap protects

(Opposite) Daniel Burnham's steel frame Flatiron Building (1902) is considered the oldest skyscraper in New York City. ©*Bettman/Corbis*

Pietro Belluschi's Equitable Building (1948) in Portland, Oregon, is a classic example of curtain-wall construction with glass cladding. *Ezra Stoller/©Esto*

The United Nations Building (1953) in New York, designed by Le Corbusier, Oscar Niemeyer, Howard Robertson, and others, is another influential example of glass curtain-wall construction.
©Carol Highsmith

the seals. Still unsurpassed in grace and beauty is Skidmore, Owings & Merrill's (SOM) Lever House (see page 47) on Manhattan's Park Avenue, completed in 1952. An expression of weightlessness was achieved with a cladding system consisting of the thinnest possible polished mullions embedded within a skin of different colored glazing. The Manufacturer's Hanover Trust Building (1954; see page 181) on 5th Avenue, also by SOM, is a classic model of the clear glass enclosure made possible by the invention of float glass in the 1950s.

As SOM explored sheets of glass, other firms were investigating sheets of metal. Aluminum and steel sheet-metal technology, advanced during World War II for the production of airplanes and vehicles, became a major influence on building technology and materials. Harrison and Abramovitz clad Pittsburgh's Alcoa Building (1953) completely in aluminum as a showpiece for the company's primary product. In 1956 the architects wrapped the Socony-Mobil Building in New York with 750,000 pounds of stainless steel, pleated to enable the wind to keep it clean. According to architectural historian Christopher Gray, "By using steel panels on the 1.6 million-square-foot building, the team gained several inches of floor space on the inside wall, greatly reduced labor costs on the skin, and saved weight—the panels weighed two pounds per square foot, as opposed to 48 pounds per square foot for brick." It remains the largest stainless-clad skyscraper in the world.

Despite the proliferation of glass and metal cladding for modern curtain walls, masonry continued to be used, albeit in a radically different form. Stone veneer dates back to the 1890s, when stone was sometimes cut to four inches thick and installed on the exterior, as on Burnham and Root's 1895 Reliance Building. Not until the 1960s did thin stone veneer begin to appear on high-profile buildings. In *Twentieth-Century Building Materials* (edited by Thomas C. Jester), thin stone veneer is defined as "stone that is cut to less than 2 inches thick and applied to a building façade in a non-load-bearing manner." The John F. Kennedy Center for the Performing Arts in Washington, D.C., designed by Edward Durell Stone and completed in 1971, is clad with marble veneer a mere one inch thick. Technological developments in cutting and installation since the 1980s have made even thinner veneers possible, increasing demand for this material dramatically.

(Opposite) Thin stone veneer began to appear on high-profile buildings in the 1960s. The John F. Kennedy Center for the Performing Arts (1971) in Washington, D.C., designed by Edward Durell Stone, is clad with a one-inch-thick marble veneer.
©Carol Pratt Photography

Mechanical Systems

The postwar development of the curtain wall paralleled the disappearance of the operable window. In 1969 Rayner Banham, the British historian and author of *The Well-Tempered Environment*, looked back 100 years to chronicle the evolution of artificial control of the interior environment. He argued that lighting, air-conditioning, and other mechanical and electrical utilities were of greater influence than enclosure on an occupant's experience of a building. Two years later, Fitch published his companion volume to *American Building: The Historical Forces That Shape It*, this one subtitled *The Environmental Forces That Shape It*. Clearly, developments in mechanical systems were coming to the fore.

Climate control of building interiors has evolved for longer than most people think. Willis Carrier designed the first air-conditioning system in 1902 for a printing firm in New York. Movie theaters became the first public places to have air-conditioning in the second decade of the 20th century. By the early 1920s, department stores also had such technology. The centrifugal chiller was created in 1922; it was manually controlled and allowed large fluctuations in temperature and humidity.

All of this invention eventually led to the hermetically sealed environment. This seemed like a good idea when there were fewer buildings and a seemingly endless supply of cheap energy. But times have clearly changed: According to the U.S. Department of Energy's Commercial Buildings Energy Consumption Survey, there were nearly 4.9 million commercial buildings in the United States in 2003, each with a voracious appetite for finite and increasingly expensive sources of energy. Buildings now consume 40 percent of the nation's energy, mostly from nonrenewable fossil fuel sources.

Manufacturers, responding to energy shortages, price fluctuations, government incentives, and the public's recent embrace of sustainable design, have developed new products and systems. Much of their research is conducted in collaboration with the Department of Energy's many agencies. For instance, new low-emittance coatings suppress infrared radiation transfer and provide additional thermal insulation. New panelized wall construction can include both operable or fixed window sashes, recessed night insulation, and integral solar shading, and it can be prefabricated in the ideal environment of a factory. In other words, today's innovations are focused on reversing the problems created by many of the past century's innovations.

Old and New Materials and Methods

As national priorities shift in response to global challenges, architects are exploring both old and new methods and materials simultaneously. The rediscovery of natural ventilation, linoleum, and green roofs is one course. Meanwhile, advanced technology has led to the development of new building components, giving architects access to a whole new design vocabulary. New materials range from the embedded to the prominent. Binders and mastics invisibly hold classic materials in new suspensions. At the same time, form meets function in carbon-fiber skyscrapers, stainless steel diagrids, and a new generation of plastics. In addition, more modern methods of prefabrication and unitized construction are replacing the slow, wasteful process of one-of-a-kind building on site.

The Digital Age has had an enormous impact on architectural form and engineering, as well as building materials. Frank Gehry became famous for his use of aircraft-industry software, Catia, to produce the complex surfaces and frames of his world-renowned cultural buildings. The change in design tools is so significant that it is generating heated debates about the nature and direction of design as it affects culture and the quality of life. Computer technology not only drives the design process but also has revolutionized material production. Laser cutting and computer numerical control (CNC) tools have allowed complex structural components and sheets to be fabricated to support the most extreme concepts.

It would behoove the 21st-century architect, whose palette is seemingly limitless, to learn from the past while embracing the future. Innovation releases extraordinary opportunities for creativity, but it also seems to make it easier to turn a blind eye to potential consequences down the road. What are the consequences of using new technologies to build even taller buildings? If computer modeling and advanced geometry make it possible to build any form, do we build whatever form someone designs? It remains to be seen if the proliferation of options is really the beginning of a yet-unnamed era in design. A Mies van der Rohe quotation from another time serves as a fitting reminder: "The long path from material through function to creative work has only one goal: to create order out of the desperate confusion of our time. We must have order, allocating to each thing its proper place and giving to each thing its due according to its nature." ●

Auguste Perret, Hon. FAIA

William Richards

Auguste Perret (1874–1954), the Brussels-born, French architect and planner, received the AIA Gold Medal on October 21, 1952, at the American Embassy in Paris at the age of 78. He was honored for his lifelong commitment to singular, fundamental design principles at a time when multiple and concomitant modernisms proliferated. Among these principles were the essential and timeless modes of proportion and craftsmanship. Perret's genius, however, was his expression of these principles in reinforced concrete, a relatively new building material at the beginning of the 20th century. Working with his brothers Gustave and Claude in their family-owned construction company, Perret Frères, Perret approached architecture as both a design discipline and a building proposition.

Notre Dame du Raincy (1922–23) is widely regarded as the architect's finest achievement. Within the sanctuary, the visceral weight of its molded concrete members is tempered by the fragile luminosity of its glazing. It is a concrete cage, to be sure, but one in which material richness holds us captive. Notre Dame du Raincy was a relatively inexpensive building to produce—in large part due to the material economy of concrete, which could accomplish multiple tasks to fulfill the program. Yet Perret's practical innovations for a post–World War I economy did not cause him to lose sight of formal qualities. To remember Perret, then, is to remember concrete's liberation from being a prosaic tool to a vehicle of variable brilliance.

Auguste Perret (right), with the Honorable James C. Dunn, U.S. ambassador to France, received the AIA Gold Medal at the American embassy in Paris.

At Notre Dame du Raincy (1922–23), Raincy, France, regarded as Perret's finest achievement, tall, thin columns support arched vaults, and prefabricated concrete units support the continuous wall of glass. *©Archivo Iconografico, SA/Corbis*

Perret headed a team to rebuild the heavily bombed city of Le Havre, France, after World War II. His work is known for its integration of the prewar pattern of the town and its historic structures with a modular grid of prefabricated, reinforced concrete buildings. *©Durand Patrick/Corbis Sygma*

GOLD MEDALIST, 2002

Tadao Ando, Hon. FAIA

Fred Bernstein

In his 40-year career, Tadao Ando has become associated with a single material (gray concrete) used in a singular way (with wooden formwork that infuses the concrete with grain and imperfection). With this method, even the heaviest concrete walls bear permanent reminders of Japan's ancient woodworking traditions.

Born in Osaka in 1941 and raised amidst the deprivations of the postwar era, Ando intended to become a boxer. Later, influenced by the work of Frank Lloyd Wright and Le Corbusier, he studied architecture by traveling the world and sketching what he saw. He never attended architecture school.

In 1969 Ando opened an office in a crowded section of Osaka and began building houses, using concrete walls as bulwarks against the burgeoning city. He was, says architectural historian Kenneth Frampton, "creating introspective microcosms to stand against the urban chaos." He perfected techniques for handling concrete—down to methods of "shaking" that produced the most uniform surface—as well as a vocabulary of forms that made even the heaviest walls appear to levitate. For example, as sunlight pours through a pair of intersecting slits at his Church of Light (1989) in Osaka, the concrete wall seemingly floats above a cross-shaped aura.

Ando experimented with glass block and wood construction as his buildings became larger, but he repeatedly returned to concrete, finding new ways to dematerialize large volumes, such as placing them in shallow pools of water or burrowing underground. Despite his identification with a limited palette, Ando's work is as varied as that of any of his contemporaries. Indeed, it is a sign of his genius that he has done so much with so little.

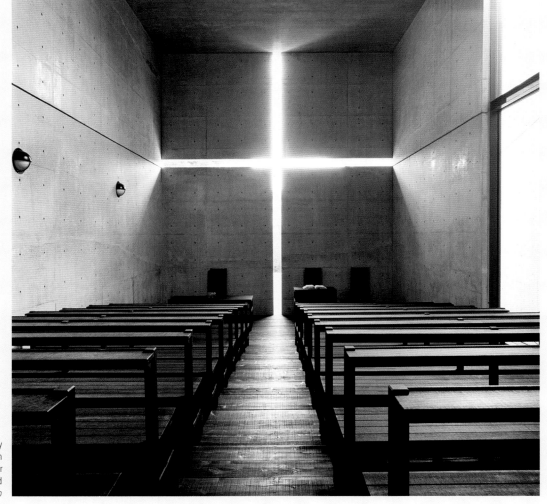

Ando's Church of Light (1989) in Osaka demonstrates his virtuosity as a designer in concrete. Light pouring through the cruciform cut in the east-facing concrete wall defines the chapel. Lumber used for scaffolding during construction was repurposed for the pews and floorboards. ©*Tim Griffith/Esto*

Worldwide, the number of people lacking access to electric light exceeds two billion—a figure that could be significantly reduced by the Portable Light Project, an interdisciplinary research effort begun by Sheila Kennedy, AIA, principal of the Boston architecture firm Kennedy & Violich Architecture (KVA). This unique venture brings architects, material scientists, anthropologists, students, and others together to create new models and technologies for implementing energy-efficient, decentralized power and lighting systems in developing countries.

The project launched in 2003 when MATx, KVA's research arm, began studying a new class of lightweight semiconductor materials, which allowed the designers to combine tiny photovoltaics (PVs) and light-emitting diodes (LEDs) into self-driven lighting systems. The PVs would convert sunlight into electricity, which would then power the LEDs. MATx began to assess performance issues, such as how much sunlight the PVs needed, how long the LEDs would glow, and how to integrate the systems into fabrics or other flexible media.

That same year, while traveling with friends in Mexico, Kennedy encountered the Huichol community, an indigenous, nomadic people with a long tradition of textile weaving and braiding. "I had a flash of insight that our work could help them," says Kennedy. Her research team began working with Huichol leaders to develop and field-test prototypes. In 2005 the project was run as a design studio at the University of Michigan's Taubman College of Architecture.

Besides bringing light to the Huichol and other native communities, Kennedy hopes that the Portable Light Project will inspire other architects to work across disciplinary boundaries and to help develop decentralized power sources worldwide. "We need to move away from top-down, grid-based schemes," she says, and adds that "architects have the skills to help solve such complex social and political problems."

Sheila Kennedy, AIA: Portable Light Project

Deborah Snoonian

Architect Sheila Kennedy, AIA, with a young girl at the Centro Huichol in Jalisco, Mexico. *Courtesy Stanford Richins*

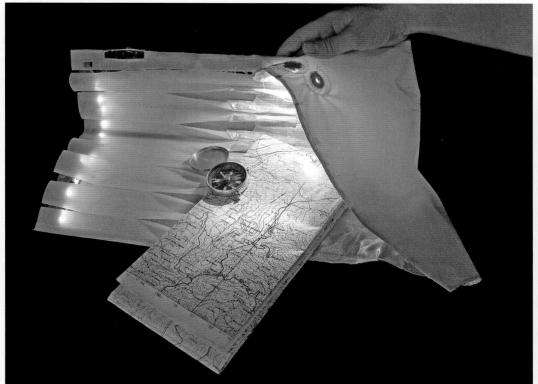

A Huichol woman in Santa Caterina, Mexico, examines a prototype of a portable-light reading mat. *Courtesy Stanford Richins*

(Left) A prototype of the portable light mat developed in summer 2006. *Courtesy Kennedy & Violich Architecture*

Improvements in Glazing Technologies

Sara Hart

Glazing has been the focus of continuous improvement, especially in the area of energy efficiency. Advances have yielded an ever-increasing selection of coatings from the now commonplace low-emissivity films, including spectrally selective systems, to the design-driven application of ceramic fritting and the emerging generation of "smart windows," which employ either active or passive chromogenic (optical switching) glazing.

However, progress moves beyond improvement to true innovation and even invention when the building envelope is considered as a single composite made up of many elements, including glazing. For example, when Rem Koolhaas designed the McCormick Tribune Campus Center (2003) at the Illinois Institute of Technology, he chose Panelite—a manufacturer of proprietary, translucent, honeycomb panels—to produce a noncombustible, exterior-grade, insulating glass unit that would meet both aesthetic and performance criteria. The result was a completely new product—Panelite IGU.

With regard to aesthetics, Koolhaas wanted the envelope to have directional transparency. In other words, when viewed straight on, the walls were to be completely clear. From other angles, however, the honeycomb construction created a luminous translucency that muted the view into the interior, creating some degree of privacy for the inhabitants. As an unanticipated added value, the clear, UV-stabilized, polycarbonate, honeycomb core provides high shading and solar heat gain coefficients without the need for tinted or reflective glass.

This example illustrates a new paradigm, one that suggests that collaboration between designer and manufacturer is a more productive way to stimulate product innovation than relying only on the incremental improvements of industry. In the public sector, the federal government is committing considerable resources to similar collaborations. The Department of Energy's Lawrence Berkeley National Laboratory, for example, conducts extensive research with representatives from the window and glass industries, and their efforts have resulted in new, energy-saving building technologies.

Rem Koolhaas's curtain wall for the McCormick Tribune Campus Center (2003) at the Illinois Institute of Technology led to the development of a new type of insulated glass unit, now a standard product of Panelite, a firm founded by two architects.
Richard Barnes/Illinois Institute of Technology

1915
The Octagon Monograph, *a folio of
measured drawings of the Octagon by
Glenn Brown and his son Bedford, set
standards for measured drawings and
historic structures reports*

New Building Material from Plastics

Sara Hart

The development of modern plastics (i.e., synthetic polymers, including textiles, films, and foils) will revolutionize architectural design by offering a wide range of materials and systems that will replace many traditional materials. For example, the thermoplastic ethylenetetrafluoroethylene (ETFE), developed in the early 1980s for the aerospace industry, is gaining widespread acceptance as an alternative to glass. The material is both low maintenance and environmentally friendly. It is unaffected by atmospheric pollution; does not harden, discolor, or deteriorate over time; and is 100 percent recyclable. As well, it is produced by an enclosed water-based process and lends itself to shaping novel architectural forms.

British architect Nicholas Grimshaw showcased the dramatic possibilities of ETFE foils when he used them to cover the giant, geodesic domes at the Eden Project, a large-scale botanical complex near Cornwall, England. Completed in 2001, the greenhouse domes at Eden are the world's largest self-supported transparent envelope, with individual panels measuring up to 860 square feet in area. Each panel is a sandwich of three sheets of foil welded together along the sides to form "pillows" that are inflated pneumatically. The forces generated by this air pressure, plus any external forces applied to the envelope, are transferred to the steel structural frame of the greenhouse. The insulation can be tuned, so to speak, by increasing the volume of air—the more air,

the greater the insulation, without any loss of light penetration. As a result, the domes can capture the maximum amount of daylight while maintaining the desired amount of passive solar gain. This control is important, as the greenhouses at Eden are used to simulate three different biomes with different average temperature ranges.

Evidence that ETFE is practical for all building types can be found at the Beijing National Aquatic Center, which will host the swimming competitions for the 2008 Olympics. Designed by the China State Construction Engineering Corporation, Australian architects Peddle Thorp Walker, and engineering firm Arup, the facility will be enclosed in 1.7 million square feet of ETFE foils. The ingenious design of the envelope's steel frame is based on the Weaire-Phelan structure, which describes the most efficient way to divide space and is demonstrated by the way soap bubbles form in foam. According to the engineer, the structure is so robust it would still hold its shape even if it were turned on its side.

In his book *Material Architecture: Emergent Materials for Innovative Buildings and Ecological Construction*, MIT professor John Fernandez predicts that the polymer industry will continue to expand by introducing better-performing applications. As the author concludes, "This convergence of technical advances and aesthetic interest calls for sustained attention from both research and design circles."

The geodesic domes of Nicholas Grimshaw's Eden Project (2001) are covered with three-ply pillows made of plastic foil, exemplifying the building opportunities offered by plastics. *Ben Foster/The Eden Project*

8

The Design Process
Catching the Third Wave

Kyle V. Davy, AIA

In his breakthrough book, *The Innovator's Dilemma*, Harvard Business School professor Clayton Christensen observes that technologies move through a performance life cycle that can be represented by an S-curve (see figure, top right). Early in its development, performance gains from a new technology are slow, but, as it is better understood and diffused, the rate of improvement accelerates. As the technology matures, progress once again slows, eventually reaching a natural limit where little additional performance improvement is possible. When technologies reach that point of maturity, they are ripe for overthrow by new, disruptive technologies.

When viewed as a technology, the current architectural design process has, after a 50-year run, reached maturity. Signs of disruptive change are increasingly evident across the field of practice. Architects are using new digital tools to imagine new building possibilities and to collaborate with project stakeholders in new ways. For the first time since R. Buckminster Fuller was practicing, many architects are actively involved in the design and development of new materials. Architecture firms are staging participatory design experiences in which project stakeholders cocreate the design. And architects are providing creative leadership for clients and communities struggling with increasingly complex social and environmental challenges.

The architectural design process is on the brink of a new wave of evolution in the way architects design and think. As it accelerates, the wave will transform where and how design takes place and who is involved, redefine the architect's role in the process, and shape a new theory of architectural design. This new process promises to quickly outperform the current model of practice, creating significant new forms of value for clients, communities, and society.

Gathering Momentum

Architecture practice in the United States has moved through two previous waves of evolution (see figure, bottom right). The first wave gathered through the middle of the 19th century and crested during the 1890s in Chicago, where Burnham and Root, Adler and Sullivan, and other architects transformed the city skyline as they invented and refined the skyscraper. From his studio in Oak Park, a young Frank Lloyd Wright was laying the groundwork for his Prairie Style of architecture. And, in 1893, Chicago's setting for the Columbian Exposition — the "White City" — dazzled throngs of Americans with new concepts of urban order, amenity, and aesthetics.

A second wave began to swell just before World War II with the arrival of European refugees such as Walter Gropius and Ludwig Mies van der Rohe on American shores. These immigrants brought with them a new approach to design that became wedded to a new model of practice pioneered by firms such as Skidmore, Owings & Merrill (SOM) and Caudill, Rowlett, and Scott (CRS). This wave held sway for the next 50 years. Styles might vary, from functional and Brutalist to Post-modern, but the underlying model of practice and design process remained relatively fixed.

Now, at the start of a new century, the architecture profession has reached another tipping point. Driven by the convergence of multiple disruptive trends, a third wave is poised to radically transform the way practitioners design and think. To better understand this next wave, it helps to examine how four basic components — setting, participants, roles, and process — were manifested in the first two periods and what these are beginning to look like today.

(Opposite) A team of designers works in the drafting room of the Chicago office of Skidmore, Owings & Merrill in 1952. The firm pioneered the second wave of U.S. practice. *Chicago History Museum*

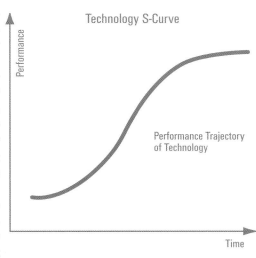

The performance life cycle of a technology, defined by Harvard Business School professor Clayton Christensen and illustrated by the "S-curve" in the top figure, also seems to apply to the life cycle of the architectural design process. As the bottom figure suggests, the profession is now entering a third model of practice. *Kyle V. Davy*

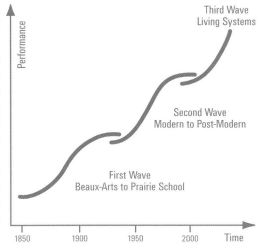

The ateliers of the late 19th century were the settings of the first wave of practice in America. A noted example was the Brookline, Massachusetts, office of architect H. H. Richardson, who was trained at the Ecole des Beaux-Arts. *Courtesy Shepley Bulfinch Richardson and Abbott*

Setting

Traditionally, architects have designed behind closed doors, in relative isolation from clients and other project stakeholders. During the first wave, the American Beaux Arts, the setting for design was the master's atelier. Architects were artists who worked in the creative isolation of their studios. Clients were patrons and beneficiaries of this public art and waited until the design composition was complete and ready for display. With the rise of the Modern movement during the second evolutionary wave, the setting for design shifted into the corporate studio or office, but the activity of design still took place out of sight. Although occasionally involved in programming activities, clients were not active participants in the design process.

As the third wave swells, design is moving to spaces—both literal and virtual—where architects, clients, and other project stakeholders can cocreate designs. These collaborative environments—including low-tech brainstorming and idea-generation spaces, "caves and dens" for individual reflection and synthesis, and high-tech workstations where digital models and simulations can be displayed and manipulated—support a wide range of creative team activities.

Participants

In the atelier, the architect-master was attended by a small number of acolytes. Design was an elite endeavor, confined to those who had been prepared either through extensive schooling at institutions like the Ecole des Beaux-Arts in Paris or through long apprenticeships to American masters. The ateliers of Richard Morris Hunt and H. H. Richardson were widely emulated by architects across the country. In the second wave, participation remained exclusive: design principals continued to lead a small team of gifted subordinates in development of the design, from programming through conceptual and schematic designs. As work progressed into design development and construction documentation, larger numbers of production-oriented architects could be engaged in the detailed design of building components and systems.

The third wave is opening up the design process to active participation by various project stakeholders, from clients and contractors to community representatives. Architects are beginning to act as creative leaders, facilitating movement of team members through collaborative design processes.

Roles

In the 19th century, the role of the architect in design was structured around the "artist-master" of Beaux-Arts instruction. By the 1950s that role had evolved, and the autonomous "design principal" was responsible for understanding the client's program, conceptualizing and elaborating the design scheme, and maintaining the integrity of the design ideas through subsequent construction documentation and building phases.

In the third wave, architects are evolving from being the "designer" to being the "creative leader" of a design team. As creative leaders, they facilitate growing numbers of team members through a collaborative design process; the design is cocreated by the team, not generated and controlled by a lone creative genius. The architect "designs the design process" and facilitates the team's work as it moves from defining goals and setting the vision through concept generation and design refinement. The creative leader also continues to share personal insights and to synthesize, express, frame, and develop key design concepts. However, the leader does so as an active team member, not the sole design authority.

Process

Adhering to Beaux-Arts principles of composition and method, the architectural design process in the 19th century was formal, artistic, academic, and hierarchical. The process moved from development of the basic "parti," or concept, to sketches and then to formally rendered plans, sections, and elevations. Construction documents were minimal; much of the design intent was communicated by the presence of a master-architect on site during construction. By the height of the Modern movement, the design process had evolved into a linear set of highly prescribed phases structured to take full advantage of an increasingly specialized workforce. Design— separated from drafting (whether by hand or by computer), construction, and administrative tasks—was to be substantially complete by the end of the design development phase. By contract, almost no design would happen during construction. The third wave, in contrast, is transforming architectural design into an iterative, participatory, and emergent process.

1917
No AIA convention was held
because of World War I

AIA issued the first
Owner-Architect Agreement

Founding of the AIA Committee on
Architecture for Education

Engulfed in Change

In the early 21st century, more project stakeholders are joining architects in increasingly collaborative design experiences. The process uses a mix of media—from traditional sketches and rough physical models to advanced 3-D and 4-D digital models—to help participants make critical design decisions. Phases of work are being replaced by continuous processes, enabled by building information modeling (BIM) and other digital software, that allow architects to program, design, and complete building instructions and specifications simultaneously. In this way of working, design can stretch from project initiation through construction. This evolutionary wave is being driven by the following four disruptive trends:[1]

New digital design tools and technologies

Exponential growth in computational performance, digital memory and storage, digital communication, and the Internet continue to disrupt and change society. These information technologies are also yielding a growing array of next-generation digital design tools. Digital modeling, prototyping, and simulating tools offer architects new opportunities to engage in what technologist Michael Schrage of MIT calls "serious play" as part of the design process.[2] Serious play occurs when individuals, teams, and organizations use digital technologies to spark creative thinking, foster new conversations and interactions, and energize team performance. Schrage has noted that "the most important raw material of innovation has always been the interplay between individuals and the expression of their ideas." Change the media, and you change the way people think, interact, and design.

In the past, architects relied on sketches and the occasional handcrafted model as the primary media for expressing and communicating design ideas. Now, equipped with a wide array of digital design and modeling technologies, including 3-D design, BIM, energy-use simulators, and quantity take-off and cost databases, architects are transitioning to new mixed-media design environments. The combination of traditional sketch techniques with these digital tools offers a potent new creative engine for architects and project teams.

The work of architect Frank Gehry is a powerful illustration of this combination. To turn his design vision into reality for projects ranging from the Guggenheim Museum in Bilbao, Spain, to the Disney Concert Hall in Los Angeles, Gehry married sophisticated digital modeling software and rapid prototyping tools to his idiosyncratic drawing style and use of physical models. The synergy of these techniques allows an iterative design and modeling process that supports both his personal creative search as well as his ongoing creative dialogue with members of his design team. Using digital models, he has extended the boundaries of the design process to include project stakeholders such as builders, subcontractors, and fabricators.[3]

Engineers supporting the architectural design process are also applying new digital modeling tools. The global engineering firm Arup has used a variety of software packages to help its staff devise solutions for the increasingly complex designs generated by the architects it works with. For example, by reprogramming software originally developed by the automobile industry for crash test simulations, the firm was able to help engineer solutions for complex seismic and vibration problems that could not be addressed by traditional structural engineering processes. For Renzo Piano's Maison Hermès in seismically active Japan, Arup engineers used this software to simulate their way to a base-isolation structural scheme that ultimately made possible the architect's design for a glass curtain wall.

More broadly, architects are on the verge of replacing 2-D CAD software with new 3-D BIM software. For the most part, 2-D CAD never made a serious contribution to the architectural design process because it was primarily used simply to shift production of construction documents from manual to digital drafting. BIM software, however, enables architects to design and document at the same time, opening up possibilities for reconfiguring the overall design process.

Since the 1950s, the design process has been defined by the five phases specified in the AIA owner-architect agreement, in which the bulk of design is completed during the first two phases (schematic design and design development), detailing and specifying the design is left to the construction documentation phase, and no design is supposed to occur during bidding and construction. By combining design and construction documentation efforts, BIM technologies can be used to move away from phases toward a continuous process. As a result, architects can spend less time on details and specifications, which can be handled by suppliers and fabricators, and more time on creating value through design. Digital tools are also being used to create new, integrated processes that provide end-to-end support for owners during the life of a project, starting with site acquisition and moving through programming, design, and construction and continuing into occupancy.

New materials and methods

The construction industry is witnessing an explosion of technologically enhanced building materials, equipment, and manufacturing processes, which are transforming both the "what" and "how" of building. New composite materials offer significant advances in structural strength while radically reducing weight. Processors embedded in materials and equipment improve monitoring and control of the performance of building structures and environments. New energy-conserving equipment and green building materials help clients achieve sustainability goals. And new computer-aided design and manufacturing techniques enable the mass customization and prefabrication of building products.

Architects are extending their design domain to include research, design, and development of new building materials and methods. They are embracing this expanded design role, both individually and in collaboration with other industry stakeholders, for specific projects and in independent product development efforts. Architects are reclaiming territory previously abandoned to manufacturers and contractors.

Architect William McDonough is at the leading edge of architects pushing a green design agenda through active engagement in the development of materials and methods that move beyond resource efficiency to eco-effectiveness. Along with environmental chemist Michael Braungart, McDonough cofounded MBDC in Charlottesville, Virginia, to design and develop eco-intelligent building products. In collaboration with manufacturers such as DesignTex, Rohner Textil AG, and Ciba-Geigy Ltd., MBDC has helped create a series of fabrics, carpets, and building products with a reduced environmental burden from their production, use, and disposal.

Boston-based Kennedy & Violich Architecture established MATx (short for materials), an applied research business to develop products and building systems that integrate energy-efficient, digital semiconductor materials into architecture, creating new ways to generate and distribute electricity. KVA's electroluminescent desk uses ultra-thin polymer films to carry electricity and data embedded into its plywood surface, eliminating external cabling and wiring. The Office for Metropolitan Architecture's New York studio has fashioned a series of products that help create unique shopping experiences for its clients' customers. For Prada, for example, the firm has developed a series of translucent panels of polycarbonate, colored resin, and porous-transparent polyurethane to highlight the retailer's products.

RDG Planning & Design, a Midwestern architecture and design firm, is capitalizing on this new attention to materials by folding artists and artisans directly into the firm. Merging the Dahlquist Art Studio into its operations has allowed RDG to offer a range of artwork and public art. Taking the process a step further, the firm is setting up new collaborations between its architects and artisans that, according to its Web site, "push the limits of design

(Opposite) The work of the global engineering firm Arup illustrates how new digital design tools and technologies can transform the design process. By reprogramming existing software, the firm was able to simulate a base-isolation structural scheme that made possible Renzo Piano's design for Maison Hermès (2001) in seismically active Japan. The 11-story building, located in Tokyo, is clad with more than 13,000 custom glass blocks. *Michael Denancé*

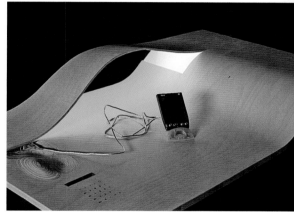

Boston-based Kennedy & Violitch Architecture established an applied research business, MATx, to develop products and building systems that integrate energy-efficient digital semiconductor materials into architecture. KVA's electroluminescent desk uses ultra-thin polymer films to carry electricity and data embedded into its plywood surface, eliminating external cabling and wiring. *Courtesy Kennedy & Violitch Architecture*

Rem Koolhaas and his Office for Metropolitan Architecture developed a series of products, including translucent panels of various materials, to transform the retail shopping experience of Prada customers. The company's flagship store opened in New York City in 2001. *Graziella Pazzanese/Esto*

by integrating new materials and techniques into every level of project development . . . from concept to fabrication and installation." RDG's efforts recall a time when architects and artisans were natural collaborators, such as when Louis Sullivan designed the hallmark terra-cotta tiles and bronze screens for the Chicago skyscrapers of the 1890s.

Architects are also engaged in the design and development of new ways of constructing buildings. In the past 20 years, manufacturers such as Dell have learned to deliver mass-customized products to their customers, combining the cost, delivery, and quality advantages of factory assembly with attributes tailored to specific customer preferences. Manufacturers serving the construction industry are collaborating with architects to move in the same direction, developing building components, systems, and entire structures around mass-customization concepts. Architects such as Stephen Kieran and James Timberlake in Philadelphia are working with manufacturers to develop prefabricated assemblies that can be used in a variety of project types. By taking advantage of factory-fabricated components, designs by KieranTimberlake Associates offer clients cost, schedule, and quality gains not possible when these elements are stick-built on site.[4]

On the West Coast, designer Michelle Kaufmann is working with Britco, a manufacturer of factory-built buildings in British Columbia, Canada, to create a new line of modular houses, including her popular Glidehouse™ and Sunset® Breezehouse™ styles. Customers can tailor modules to their particular site and customize materials, roof styles, floor plans, and finishes that turn these assembly-line products into premium housing, featuring a distinctive modern aesthetic and sustainable design components.

Architects such as Stephen Kieran and James Timberlake in Philadelphia are working with manufacturers to develop prefabricated assemblies that can be used in a variety of project types. The 27 modules for this Yale University dormitory, designed by KieranTimberlake Associates in 2004, were fabricated off site and then set by crane over four days.
Courtesy KieranTimberlake Associates

The rise of the experience economy

In their book *The Experience Economy*, Joseph Pine and James Gilmore argue that our economy is shifting toward a new class of economic offerings—memorable "experiences." According to Pine and Gilmore, experiences stand atop a hierarchy of economic value, which moves upward from commodities to goods, from goods to services, and from services to experiences. The willingness of consumers to pay top dollar for coffee concoctions served at Starbucks is an illustration of the power of experience to change the economic value of products and services. Many service companies, including retail, restaurant, hotel, resort, and hospitality operations, are using buildings and interiors designed by architects to create similar high-value experiences for their customers.[5]

The Glidehouse™, a modular, prefabricated structure by designer Michelle Kaufmann, is laid out according to sustainable design principles and features eco-friendly materials.
Courtesy Michelle Kaufmann Designs

Architects are also realizing that the design process itself offers an opportunity to create memorable experiences. The industrial design firm IDEO, based in Palo Alto, California, has pioneered the application of this concept, staging a variety of activities for clients as part of its product design and development process. Clients get "backstage" office tours to witness IDEO's unique approach to design and are invited to participate in the firm's Monday morning show-and-tell sessions and brainstorming events. Some clients, such as electronics giants Matsushita and Samsung, have sent their product design teams to work on-site in IDEO's offices for extended periods to absorb a new creative mindset that may enhance their corporate product development processes and organizational cultures.[6]

Participatory programming processes and design charrettes for clients and project stakeholders are being reconceived not only to generate a work product, such as a program or design, but to leave participants changed in some way—more knowledgeable about themselves or some issue central to the project. William McDonough + Partners offers a wide range of learning experiences that help clients not only implement eco-effective projects but also extend this green philosophy to other aspects of their businesses and operations. These events include facilitated visioning sessions that help industry leaders think outside the box about eco-effective design opportunities in their field, collaborative design processes to create new products and materials, and educational workshops about green design principles and practices for staff. As an example, McDonough set up a "peace room" (in lieu of a "war room") in the basement of Ford's Rouge River manufacturing plant to support the reinvention of that enormous, old factory site. It provided a place where representatives from all parts of the company could interact with the design team, help Ford set goals and strategies for the project, and learn more about sustainable design and the need for eco-effective design and manufacturing practices.[7]

Developments in creative leadership and adaptive work

Leadership and organizational development consultant Susan Harris, my coauthor for *Value Redesigned: New Models for Professional Practice*, has noted that rising social and technological complexity is driving a need for creative leaders who can help clients, communities, and society cope with escalating adaptive challenges. Architects are responding by moving beyond the limitations and mental models of traditional design work toward a new stance that recognizes the need for new leadership capacities. They are mobilizing clients and stakeholders to tackle tough problems and guiding them through the difficult adjustments necessary to respond to changing conditions.

In the mid-1990s Ronald Heifetz, who teaches leadership at the John F. Kennedy School of Government at Harvard, offered key insights into the need for a new type of leader. He redefined the work of professionals by directly linking their efforts and the value they create to the type of leadership challenges faced by their clients. Heifetz makes a distinction between two types of situations. The first, which he calls "technical work," involves problems that are easily diagnosed and fixed by professionals with little involvement by the client. The second type, labeled "adaptive work," arises when circumstances are significantly more complex, precluding both easy diagnosis and straightforward problem solving. Adaptive work requires the professional to assume a leadership role, guiding the client to confront, understand, and respond to the more difficult challenge in the best way possible.[8]

In the past 20 years or so, a significant portion of what used to be considered technical work for architects has migrated into the category of adaptive work, driven by growing complexity and interdependence in the client's social and technological environments. An airport terminal expansion provides a good example. Project definition, planning, and design efforts demand significant involvement and consultation with countless project stakeholders, including the airport authority, airlines, unions, vendors, the flying public, FAA and homeland security representatives, and the broader community. The situation demands creative leadership that inspires, mobilizes, and guides this social constellation through a long, involved project delivery process.

Beyond this type of collaborative leadership, architects may be able to assist clients who face situations where there really are no solutions. At best, clients in these cases can hope to learn more about the problem and better understand its different facets. Their only viable option may be to adapt and change deeply held values, beliefs, and behaviors. The role of the professional in this instance becomes one of transformative leadership, helping the client engage in and move through this difficult process.

The City of San Jose, California, and San Jose State University faced such an adaptive challenge when they decided to build the first joint-use library in the United States, combining a new public library for the city with a new academic library for the university. Both clients needed to build new library structures at the same time and in roughly the same location. They realized that by combining their resources into one project, sharing funding, and eliminating the duplication inherent in construction of two buildings, the resulting library could be bigger and better equipped than either party could afford separately. However, mixing public and academic library cultures was like mixing oil and water. To facilitate the planning and design of this joint operation, the coclients turned to Anderson Brulé Architects (ABA) of San Jose.

ABA designed and facilitated a process that included dozens of meetings involving hundreds of staff members from both organizations over a 12-week period. At the end of the process, ABA had helped the library staff not only define a "seamless" operations plan but also transform themselves into a single high-performance team, unified around shared vision, culture, and values. Although ABA would go on to be part of the architecture team that designed the library structure, which opened in 2003, the firm's greatest achievement flowed from the transformative leadership it provided to help the two clients design and create a new organization. Commenting on ABA's performance, one library leader stated, "ABA's process made the potential of a combined facility believable for staff members from both sides. . . . Its facilitation allowed staff to think outside the box and enabled participants to reflect more on real possibilities . . . and to understand staff concerns on each side . . . . The process improved communication and created stronger relationships." The process generated buy-in from staff at both libraries and supported a rapid evolution of the new organization, which paid significant operational dividends once the new building—Martin Luther King Jr. Library—was occupied.

(Opposite) The new Martin Luther King Jr. Library (2003), San Jose, California, needed to serve both as a public and academic library. To facilitate the planning of the building, Anderson Brulé Architects designed and managed a process that included dozens of meetings involving hundreds of staff members from the two client organizations. *©Timothy Hursley*

Architecture firm Lucchesi Galati
designed the Las Vegas Springs
Preserve and Desert Living Center to
create a place where residents can
"learn to achieve water conservation
and sustainable design in their daily
lives and to help them shift from being
'in' the desert to being 'of' the desert."
*Courtesy Las Vegas Springs Preserve
and Desert Living Center*

In some cases, the architect's creative leadership may not lead to either a design or a building. Rather, the architect may help the client identify other opportunities for change and organizational development that solve the client's problem without the need to build. The Las Vegas firm Lucchesi Galati worked with a public utility services division, which had come to it with a commission for a new warehouse facility. Before proceeding to the traditional architectural design process for which it had been commissioned, Lucchesi Galati convinced the client to open up its time and organizational boundaries to facilitate a 20-year analysis not only of the division but also of the city's entire public works department. This effort showed that operational improvements, staffing changes, and other efficiencies would allow the agency to satisfy its needs without building any new structures. The firm lost a design commission but gained credibility and the city's trust through this act of leadership, ultimately becoming the agency's exclusive design consultant.

Lucchesi Galati has also exercised creative leadership to grow beyond operational consulting into facilitating deep cultural shifts. Principal Ray Lucchesi observes, "Before you know what a client needs, you have to be able to get inside the organization, its group dynamic, its culture, and its relationship to its environmental context." For client R & R Partners, an advertising and public relations company, Lucchesi and Galati's approach involved "cultural stitching" to bring the client's organizational culture back together in a new office environment that enhanced both group and individual creativity. For the Las Vegas Springs Preserve and Desert Living Center, the solution was helping the city's water utility preserve a desert oasis and create a place where residents can "learn to achieve water conservation and sustainable design in their daily lives . . . to help them shift from being 'in' the desert to being 'of' the desert."

To engage clients from a cultural perspective, Lucchesi Galati has had to change its own culture. It has shifted deeply held mental models about the traditional practice of architecture toward a new stance focused on helping clients achieve their purposes, whether through architecture or by other means. The firm, for example, has added sociologists to its staff to improve its ability to understand organizational and community cultures. It has adopted new collaborative processes to engage project stakeholders and has learned to recognize their input as key to understanding the client's true needs.

A New Design Theory Inspired by Living Systems

Driven by powerful disruptive forces, the third wave is shaping a new theory of design for architecture practice. Early indications suggest this emergent design theory will be inspired and informed by a deep understanding of nature, life, and living systems.

During the Beaux-Arts wave, design theory was built upon a foundation of immutable artistic principles drawn from classical art and the great architectural monuments of classical Greece and Rome and Baroque Europe. In the second wave, Modern movement design theory was inspired by industrialization and built around a new machine aesthetic. Design emphasized planning, technical problem solving, and honest expression of materials. This new theory preempted, but did not entirely replace, the first wave's commitment to composition and artistic expression; the old design theory still existed in practice, residing in the shadows of a new dominant theory. With the advent of Postmodernism, the stylistic imperative of the Beaux-Arts theory resurfaced, giving architects renewed license to practice the art of design.

"Living systems theory" and parallel developments in chaos and complexity theory evolved as a reaction to the closed, Newtonian paradigm that has dominated much of scientific thinking.[9] Living systems theory is having profound effects on knowledge disciplines ranging from biology, ecology, and brain sciences to sociology, business management, leadership, the arts, and—now—architecture. As a result, we are beginning to understand the following:

- Buildings are nested within larger living systems, and design must serve those larger societal and environmental systems at the same time it satisfies the immediate needs of a particular client.

- Designers can draw inspiration from, and work in harmony with, nature, natural systems, and nature's economics.

- Living systems stay alive by partnering with and learning from their environments. Designers must fully engage and learn from the organization and environmental ecosystems surrounding their clients and communities.

- Living systems are most creative when on the edge of chaos, the "sweet spot" between order and disorder. Design can leverage the power of self-organization and emergence by moving to this edge and involving the client and other project stakeholders in new, collaborative, creative processes.

This new design theory will, once again, not entirely replace the old. Architectural design will continue to be informed by artistic and functional imperatives from the past. However, living systems theory will move to the forefront and directly link architectural design to stewardship of the larger societal and environmental ecosystems in which buildings exist. Empowered by this new design theory, architects of the 21st century can play a leadership role to help clients, communities, and society creatively deal with the increasingly serious adaptive challenges facing all of us. ●

GOLD MEDALIST, 1968

Marcel Breuer, FAIA

Stanley Abercrombie, FAIA

Marcel Breuer Associates

Hungarian-born Marcel Breuer (1902–81) became a student at the Bauhaus in 1920. After practicing architecture in Paris in 1924, he returned to the Bauhaus as master of its carpentry shop. There he pioneered modular cabinetry and furniture frames built of tubular steel, combining the tubes with leather straps in his 1925 Wassily chair and with hand-woven cane in his cantilevered 1928 Cesca chair. Breuer's furniture designs, intended for mass production, clearly illustrate his strong interest in incorporating innovative technologies into the design process.

Breuer worked with Bauhaus founder Walter Gropius as an architect in Berlin and then, fleeing Germany, as an architect and furniture designer in London. In 1937 he joined Gropius in a Boston architecture firm and in teaching at Harvard. In 1946 he opened his own firm in New York.

Breuer's residential work in the United States combined the machine aesthetic of the Bauhaus with the vernacular building materials of New England tradition, as evinced by the Caesar Cottage (1951) in Lakeville, Connecticut. His small, early masterpieces include the Robinson house (1948) in Williamstown, Massachusetts, and his own house (1948) in New Canaan, Connecticut. Larger institutional work followed, such as the 1958 UNESCO headquarters in Paris and the 1966 Whitney Museum in New York.

Throughout his career, Breuer maintained the investigative curiosity that had made him such an appealing teacher, always asking, "What if . . . ?" The results, although always rooted in function, allowed inclusion of the quirky detail, the homely material, and the unexpected inspiration. Of the early Modern giants, Mies's design was the most dogmatic and consistent, but Breuer's was the most idiosyncratic and full of character.

Like many of Breuer's residential designs, Caesar Cottage (1951), Lakeville, Connecticut, combined the vernacular building materials of New England with the machine aesthetic of the Bauhaus. *Marcel Breuer Associates*

Breuer collaborated with Pier Luigi Nervi of Italy and Bernard Zehrfuss of France for the design of the UNESCO headquarters building (1958) in Paris. *Yann Arthus-Bertrand/Corbis*

Frank O. Gehry, FAIA

Vernon Mays

It took only one building to secure Frank Gehry's place on the cultural map once and for all. With his design for the Guggenheim Museum in Bilbao, Spain—a twisting, restless form wrapped in a shiny titanium skin—this maverick of the architecture profession achieved wide acceptance among his peers and notoriety among the public. The universal acclaim heaped on the glistening building seemed to reward Gehry's inventiveness, creative risk taking, and persistent belief in his own way of making architecture. As critic Ada Louise Huxtable observed, "He takes chances; he works close to the edge; he pushes boundaries beyond previous limits. There are times when he misses the mark, and times when the breakthrough achieved alters everyone else's vision as well."

Born in Toronto in 1929, Gehry was raised in a hard-working family that moved to California to seek new opportunities. At 18, Gehry started taking night classes in fine arts at the University of Southern California. He graduated from USC with a degree in architecture in 1954. After brief service in the army, he studied city planning at Harvard University, but Gehry left Harvard disenchanted. He apprenticed in large firms in Los Angeles and then spent a year in France before returning to California, where he opened a small office in Santa Monica in 1962. Early commissions reflected his schooling in Modernism, but over time Gehry strayed from the teachings of his predecessors, whose emphasis on formal purity and functionalism produced what he considered cold and lifeless buildings. "I thought it was possible within the aesthetics of the day to find a way to express feeling and humanistic qualities in a building," Gehry said in a National Public Radio interview. "I got interested in a sense of movement."

Gehry had a strong affinity for the art scene and sought ways to express his own artistic bent. Early experiments produced the "Easy Edges" corrugated cardboard furniture. Next, Gehry unleashed his imagination on his Santa Monica residence, a nondescript Dutch Colonial that quickly became a national sensation with the addition of rippled aluminum walls and chain-link fencing.

By the time he received the Pritzker Architecture Prize in 1989, Gehry's design concepts were outpacing the ability of the construction industry to build them. Liberation came in the form of CATIA, a high-powered computer software discovered by staffer Jim Glymph in 1991. Developed for the French aerospace industry, CATIA could render surfaces with complex geometries. The software's first large-scale test came with the Walt Disney Concert Hall in Los Angeles. CATIA became essential to the design process at Gehry Partners, spawning other large-scale projects, including the Experience Music Project in Seattle, Stata Center at MIT, and the Jay Pritzker Pavilion on the Chicago lakefront. Yet Gehry's process remains, in a way, elemental, eschewing the computer at the beginning stage in favor of handmade models of wood and folded paper. This approach to design—reliance on means both tactile and technological—is synonymous with Gehry.

Critics have been quick both to credit and blame Gehry for the "Bilbao effect"—a rebirth of public interest in architecture coupled with a tendency among institutional clients to hire celebrity architects who can deliver the requisite "wow factor." But don't expect Frank Gehry to be hamstrung by his own success. For if his career demonstrates nothing else, it is that he will keep seeking new ways to breathe life into inert materials.

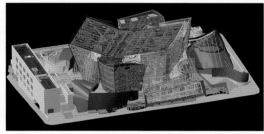

The Walt Disney Concert Hall (2003) benefited from the use of CATIA software, which enabled the building's complex design.
Courtesy Gehry Partners

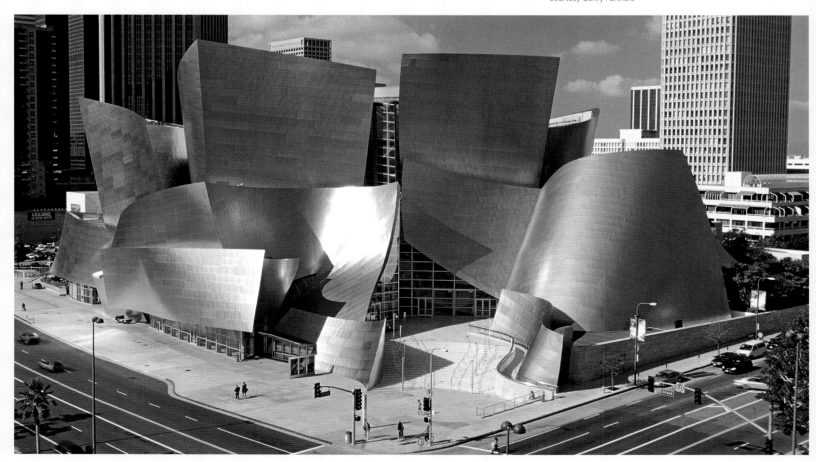

1922
*National Shrine of the Immaculate
Conception, Washington, D.C.,
Charles Donagh Maginnis*

*Kings Road House,
West Hollywood,
Rudolf Schindler*

*Imperial Hotel,
Tokyo,
Frank Lloyd Wright*

GRASS ROOTS

Creative Leadership over Three Generations: Ratcliff Architects

Kyle V. Davy, AIA

Second generation, 1945–80: Robert Ratcliff, educated at UC Berkeley, became inspired by Corbusier, Mies, and Gropius. Ratcliff's Modernist aesthetic is evident in his design for this Berkeley fire station. *Mark Citret, courtesy Ratcliff*

When he became president of his California firm in the mid-1980s, Christopher ("Kit") Ratcliff knew he had to both embrace and transcend a legacy of design and leadership dating back to the founding of Ratcliff in 1906. Overseen by three generations of his family, this century-old San Francisco Bay Area firm parallels the evolution of architecture practice in the United States.

In the first decades, the work of the firm's founder, Kit's grandfather, Walter H. Ratcliff, centered on creating a classically inspired architectural expression appropriate to individual clients and sites. With designs drawn from his collection of oversized, leather-bound portfolios, Walter Ratcliff populated Berkeley and Oakland with Classical Revival and Mannerist structures intended to be lasting in style, material, and technology. Projects executed by the firm's 10-person staff during this period included houses, schools, and academic buildings such as the Music Building at Mills College.

Kit's father, Robert Ratcliff, was educated at the University of California, Berkeley, in the classical orders and ink washes but, inspired by Corbusier, Mies, and Gropius, adopted the new Bauhaus style of architecture. During the middle decades of the firm's history, Robert Ratcliff's design philosophy centered on searching for and expressing the "big idea" that both satisfied client needs and served as the armature for a lasting work of architecture. Design emphasized a Modernist aesthetic, looking at form and light in new ways. At the same time, attention to pattern, decoration, and the use of durable materials reflected the firm's Classical Revival legacy. During his tenure, the firm's staff grew to 35 and executed projects throughout the East Bay communities. Work included residences, banks, libraries, and fire stations.

By the time Kit Ratcliff took the helm, the firm was taking responsibility for major health care, academic,

and civic projects across the western United States. Also trained at UC Berkeley, but at a time when larger social and environmental concerns were stressed, the youngest Ratcliff wanted to "invent and learn and be free to look beyond 'architecture,' . . . expanding the architect's role to see the larger issues."

Guided by Kit Ratcliff, the 75-person firm has expanded its services to address the entire life cycle of a facility, from helping owners articulate their mission and vision for a project to construction completion and postoccupancy operations. The firm has also pioneered collaborative processes in which the architect's creative role shifts from doing the design to facilitating the design process. For the four-building Science Complex (1990) at the University of Oregon, for example, Ratcliff—along with associate architect Moore Ruble Yudell—led a series of five workshops to address site use, building massing, departmental organization, spatial layouts, and image. Each workshop lasted two to three days and involved between 30 and 100 participants. Ratcliff designed the overall process and individual workshops, identified and engaged project stakeholders, guided teams through design workshop activities, identified differences among stakeholders, helped the group reach closure around key design ideas and decisions, and synthesized and crystallized design concepts in drawings. The result of this collaborative approach was a set of laboratory buildings that are adaptable, flexible, safe, productive, and enjoyable to work in, thereby enabling cutting-edge, interdisciplinary scientific research.

This type of creative leadership allows the Ratcliff firm to fulfill its stated mission: "to be explorers and discoverers of what is important and to be valued for creating extraordinary outcomes." Kit Ratcliff urges architects to see themselves as agents of change and "to evoke the world to which we aspire."

Third generation, 1980–present: Kitt Ratcliff has expanded the firm's services and adopted a collaborative design process, such as the one for the University of Oregon's Science Complex (1990). *©Timothy Hursley*

First generation, 1906–45: Walter Ratcliff populated Berkeley and Oakland with his Classical Revival and Mannerist buildings, including the Music Building (1928) at Mills College, Oakland. *McCullogh, courtesy Ratcliff*

The Beck Group prospered for decades as contractor of choice for Philip Johnson, I. M. Pei, Renzo Piano, and other well-known architects. Yet in the mid-1990s, president Peter Beck concluded that pure construction had become an economic dead end for all but a handful of megacontractors. Fees were shrinking, and competition had become cutthroat. His company's future, he believed, lay in providing seamlessly integrated design, construction, and development services. So, in 1996, Beck purchased the rights to a British software program and renamed it Destini, short for design, estimating, integration, and initiative, and three years later he bought the small Dallas firm Urban Architecture.

Destini, it turned out, could generate four-square, five-story concrete office buildings down to the window gaskets but was hopeless for designing schools, hotels, or any building with a curve. To make it a more versatile architecture tool, the firm rewrote the program and called it DProfiler. This proprietary software now allows Beck to offer clients integrated project delivery that combines 3-D modeling and quantity calculations (how many tons of steel or cubic yards of concrete, for example) with cost estimating linked to the firm's own database or one offered by RSMeans.

The software supports direct collaboration among architects, construction managers, and subcontractors through design development. Such teamwork has radically changed the type and timing of information needed by the firm's architects, allowing them to design more and draw less.

"The program is best for determining how to fit a building on a site and for testing various planning and design options," says Betsy del Monte who, with her husband, Rick, founded Urban Architecture. With the software, the firm can obtain real-time costs for each component, allowing clients to decide whether to go forward with the project or cut and run long before drawings are sent out for bids from contractors. "It takes the guesswork out of estimating," explains del Monte.

The Beck Group now employs 650 people, including 60 architects, in four offices. One-third of its projects are fully integrated, and it anticipates substantial revenue from the licensing of DProfiler to developers, contractors, corporate real estate departments, and architects. It also recently signed a joint marketing agreement with Gehry Technologies in Los Angeles to share client lists and make joint marketing presentations.

The integration of design and construction is changing the Beck culture, says del Monte: "We're blurring conventional boundaries. Our architects feel comfortable going into the field, and our construction folks want to be part of the design team. We think it's the future."

Blurring the Boundaries between Design and Construction: The Beck Group

David Dillon

The Beck team, left to right, Stewart Carroll, Doug Maiden, and Betsy del Monte. *Courtesy the Beck Group*

The rendering of this corporate office building in Dallas was generated by the Beck Group's DProfiler software. The software allows the firm to offer clients integrated project delivery that combines 3-D modeling and quantity calculations with cost estimating. *The Beck Group*

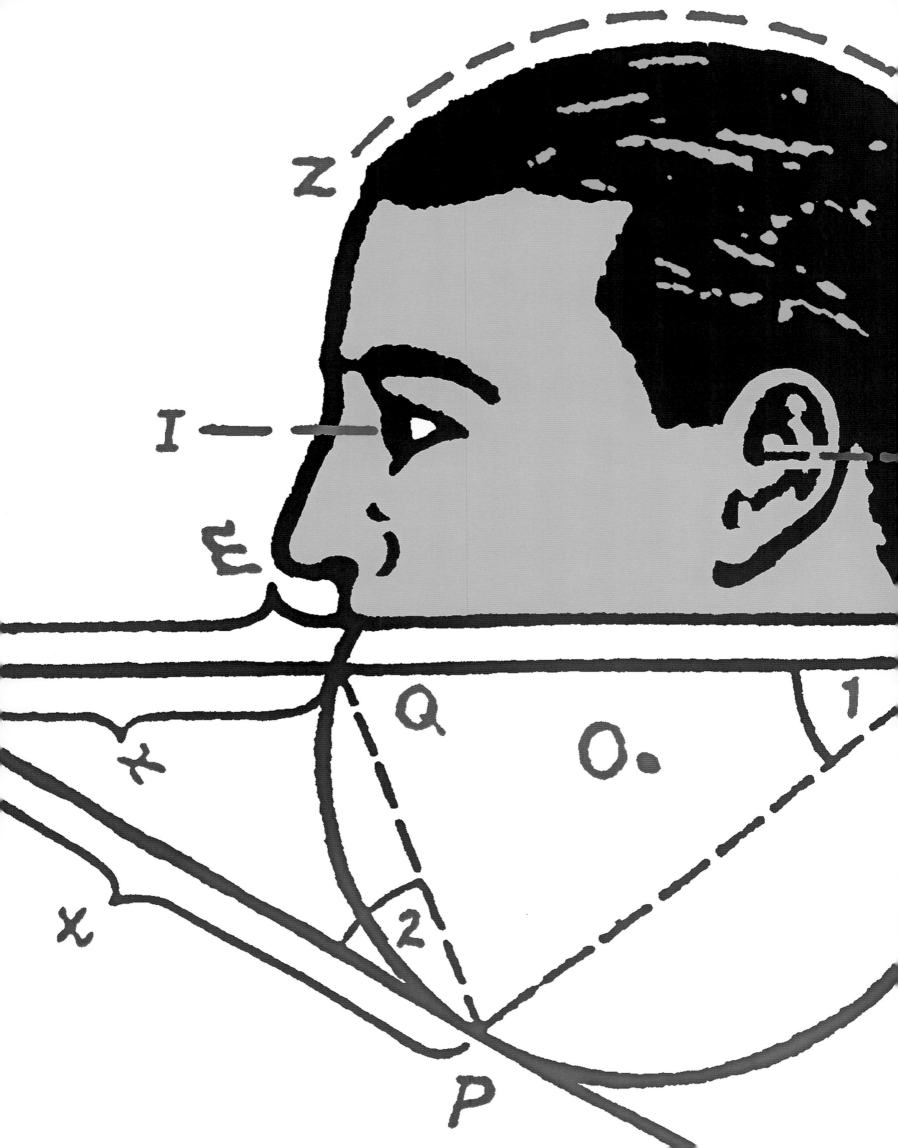

9

Architecture Practice
The Eye for Success

James P. Cramer, Hon. AIA

Architecture is both an art and a science, depending equally on creativity and constraint. A blend of the symbolic and the real—the ethereal and the tangible—it requires more than considerations of color, texture, material, and proportion. Successful architecture depends on strategy (what is being built and why), technology (what it is made of and how it is put together), economics (how much it will cost to build and maintain), and politics (what approvals are required and who will grant them). Architects have also come to recognize that, to successfully tackle the considerable challenges facing the profession today, excellent business practices are necessary to best leverage design talent. With appropriate business marketing and branding skills, practitioners are positioning themselves as relevant problem solvers in today's complex world.

Architecture, a constantly changing and challenging profession, is in the midst of a golden age unlike any other in history. New creative expansion is underway, many practitioners are experiencing new levels of personal satisfaction, and the nation's leading architecture firms are enjoying higher profits. It is also a field of increasing significance. Indeed, the architecture profession has become one of the most respected, admired, and—many would argue—most needed professions. With the planet under extreme stress, architecture is now a profession of hope.

Architects have begun to capture the "life force" of design and its transformative role in addressing critical issues in our society and on our planet. The scope of practice is expanding from designing buildings to designing community experiences, and herein lies the signal new-value proposition that will hasten development of a powerful, generational momentum within the profession.

While still a relatively small profession of approximately 110,000 licensed individuals, architects occupy diverse positions. They can be found in private practice (nearly 20,000 firms of all sizes), in corporations with large design divisions, in construction firms, and at all levels of government. And no matter where they are situated, these professionals influence the built environment of the United States, which currently boasts a trillion-dollar design and construction economy. At the same time, a healthy portion of architecture firms now exports services in a global architecture market well in excess of $3.5 trillion. In the past seven years, growth of international fees (those generated outside the United States) has averaged 18 percent at HOK and Cannon Design, 19 percent at Gensler, and 33 percent at Kohn Pedersen Fox.

(Opposite) Illustration by Mark Futz/Veer

1923
In an elaborate pageant at the Lincoln
Memorial, Henry Bacon, designer of
the memorial, received the AIA Gold
Medal; President Warren G. Harding
and Chief Justice William Howard
Taft attended

Paul Revere Williams became
the first African-American
member of the AIA

Boston Avenue Methodist Church,
Tulsa,
Bruce Goff

Notre Dame du Raincy,
France,
Auguste Perret

Four Fundamental Factors of Practice

Regardless of the size, geographic location, scope of influence, or area of specialty of an architecture firm, its performance depends on four essential components: marketing, operations, professional services, and finance. To the extent that these four factors are in balance, a practice will have far fewer constraints on its growth and success.

All projects start with successful marketing, which can be simply defined as the process by which a firm identifies, acquires, creates, and retains its clients and projects. Marketing should be seen as the essential connection between a firm's skill and the needs of the marketplace and society as a whole. It is how firms declare to all that "this is what we do, this is what we're good at, and this is how we can help you be successful." In marketing, architects design client relationships. Seen this way, marketing is the first step in the design process. Firms often carve out "brand equity" by capitalizing on media coverage or gaining cutting-edge recognition for designs of a particular building type. Renzo Piano's Building Workshop and HOK Sport + Venue + Event are two firms that have achieved distinct brand differentiation.

Operations refers to the processes by which the work gets organized. It creates the context in which good design can thrive and, like marketing, is very much a design activity. The digital revolution has enabled firms to organize themselves in ways that allow them to be far more productive. The human resources element of operations is key to success. Firms pay competitive salaries and bonuses to retain talent and invest money in ongoing training to stay at the top of their game. People, far and away a firm's most important and costly asset, account for more than 50 percent of all expenses in a typical architecture firm. Human resource functions that encourage productivity, along with rapport, respect, and admiration, can drive success and satisfaction.

Once a commission has been secured and workplace protocols established, the third success factor—professional services—kicks in. Simply put, this is doing the actual work, which goes far beyond drawing and modeling. It includes analyzing relevant data; researching rules and regulations; conceptualizing possible solutions; expressing design ideas in drawings and models (both tangible and electronic); coordinating the activities of various team members, both inside and outside the office; transmitting vast amounts of information; helping the client make key decisions; and, finally, bringing the process to closure on time and within budget. In fact, the architect's province is expanding, as successful leadership in today's real-estate life cycle requires the architect to coordinate a much broader range of issues, disciplines, and stakeholders for the client than ever before.

Finance, of course, is about collecting and managing money. This involves timesheets, expenses, invoices, payments to consultants, operational cost controls, and provision of feedback to everyone in the firm on measurements of value. The mythology of a profession not well versed in money is history. In fact, the language of business and the language of architecture are merging: The architecture profession is driving client strategies, and the profession's involvement in real estate and building life cycles is growing substantially. Architects understand that money (i.e., the economy) is a force that shapes the outcome of all projects and the quality of life in communities. To get the very best out of a design opportunity—to maximize all available resources—it is necessary to know what things cost. Thus, the use of money is strategic and very much a tool of the architect, along with pencils and CAD technology. Leading firms have devised methods for winning in today's fast-moving, hypercompetitive world

Transformative Trends

Although these four factors are critical to the practice of architecture today, they are not enough. Today's success also requires an architect to have foresight. We live in a time of flux and opportunity. Old solutions no longer work. Fortunately, architects are resilient and are moving into the future with great agility.

In my book *The Next Architect*, coauthored with Scott Simpson of the Stubbins Associates in Cambridge, Massachusetts, we outline the transforming trends identified in annual surveys taken by the Design Futures Council, a think tank in Washington, D.C. At the macro level, about 50 signal trends are affecting the success of professional practice today. Of these, a few stand out enough to be underscored: use of building information modeling, integrated service delivery, fast architecture, sustainable design, and life-cycle design.

Building information modeling is significantly changing the "product" of design services from lines on paper to a highly integrated digital database (a building information model, or BIM) that not only describes a building's design attributes but can incorporate other relevant

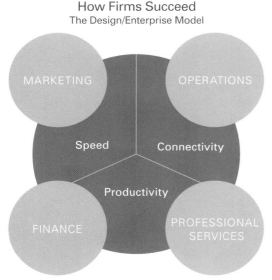

How Firms Succeed
The Design/Enterprise Model

MARKETING

OPERATIONS

Speed

Connectivity

Productivity

FINANCE

PROFESSIONAL
SERVICES

Reprinted with permission. James P. Cramer and Scott Simpson,
How Firms Succeed (2004).

Publication of Towards a New
Architecture, *by Le Corbusier*

Storer House,
Los Angeles,
Frank Lloyd Wright

Stockholm City Hall,
Sweden,
Ragnar Östberg

data, such as quantity take-offs, coordination of engineered systems, and cost. Building information modeling is a rich technology possessing a level of artificial intelligence that changes the game for everyone. It demands a higher level of sophistication from its users, which include not only the architect but the owner, engineers, and consultants, who are often working simultaneously on a project. Many in the profession are capitalizing on the technology to expand the definition and purview of the architect. SOM, for example, is using building information modeling exclusively on the Freedom Tower project in New York City. The software is more efficient and more productive than digital technologies of the past.

As owners seek more streamlined approaches to building development, they will increasingly turn to integrated service delivery, which contracts with a single entity to provide both design and construction services. This delivery method, in fact, may be the beginning of the end of the AEC industry—long characterized as factional and fractional—as we know it. The various players will have to find new ways of working in this collaborative model. Integrated service delivery places a premium on critical mass (because larger firms will be needed to provide the services required) and leadership (because these multidisciplinary teams must be managed effectively). The shift to integrated delivery will also substantially affect issues of risk management, because formerly competitive entities will be linked by a common contractual bond.

Another significant trend today is fast architecture. Speed matters—it has strategic value. How long does good design take? This is an uncomfortable question for architects who are accustomed to marinating and meditating design ideas until they are just right. But smart firms understand that speed is not necessarily the enemy of quality—often faster is better. Through the use of new technologies and management techniques, they are finding ways to greatly accelerate the pace of the design process, which is another way of saying they are producing more value in less time. Clients are demanding speed and will continue to do so. To respond to this trend, Stubbins Associates has developed a process called HyperTrack©, which provides an alternative to the traditional "sequential" project delivery process. Its benefits include better overall communication and coordination, faster decision-making, less redesign, accelerated construction schedules, fewer mistakes in the field, and lower capital cost for the owner. Other firms have approached the demand for faster delivery by using fast-track scheduling or developing integrated service delivery.

The past decade has seen a rapid adoption of green or sustainable design by most design practices. Three significant influences in the United States have been the creation and widespread adoption of the U.S. Green Building Council's LEED® (Leadership in Energy and Environmental Design) rating system, increased awareness of the "triple bottom line" benefits of sustainable design (economic, environmental, and social), and growing concern about climate change and availability of fossil fuels. The scope of green design has evolved significantly, from an energy focus after the oil embargo in the 1970s toward a comprehensive approach that spans a project's life cycle (from the earliest site and building concepts to final material selection, construction, and ongoing operations and maintenance) and works across disciplines (site, energy, materials, indoor environment, water, and waste) to seek synergistic solutions. Designers are recognizing that environmentally responsible design is not optional but rather a new qualification for good design.

The Gap headquarters campus (1997; see page 212) in San Bruno, California, by William McDonough + Partners was one of the earliest examples of a holistic approach to sustainable design. Inspired by the idea that a bird could fly over without recognizing a structure below, the building incorporates abundant natural light, natural ventilation, and green roofs. The EPA Environmental Research Center at Research Triangle Park, North Carolina, is another breakthrough project. Here, HOK introduced new levels of research into materials selection, focused carefully on indoor air quality and energy reduction, and instituted a method for recycling 90 percent of all construction waste.

Another significantly different trend in this new century is that of life-cycle design. A brand-new building starts changing from the moment the ribbon is cut. People move in and immediately begin adapting it to their needs. As people change, so do buildings. Equipment wears out and needs replacement. Finishes and furniture must be renovated and refreshed over time. Exteriors require short-term and long-term maintenance—everything from washing the windows to replacing the roof. Who better than the original design team to care for the structure over its entire lifespan? Taking care of buildings is a smart investment. Increasingly, architects will not only plan and design buildings but will also be involved in commissioning, management, renovation, restoration, and even deconstruction and recycling.

Leadership

The culture of a firm is determined by its leadership. Leaders in architecture practice are respected not only for their design abilities but also for their emotional and business intelligence, which includes the ability to make sound decisions, admit mistakes, assume accountability in day-to-day behavior, and prioritize the client's best interest ahead of personal ego. In short, today's architect leaders exhibit applied brilliance.

An individual's leadership skills and their effect on firm culture can be measured. The Greenway Group—my Atlanta-based design consultancy—has developed a diagnostic tool called LEAP®, an acronym for leadership, empowerment, accountability, processes. LEAP is divided into 12 categories, such as challenging processes, clarity of vision, development of rapport, and collaborative spirit. Each category has scaled subcategories that reveal the strengths and weaknesses in a firm. Firms can use this analysis method to chart their progress in establishing a culture of success and high performance].

Today, measuring and monitoring performance in all areas of professional practice is mandatory. And just as leadership can be measured, so can backlog, staff utilization ratios, profitability, and marketing success. Many professional firms now keep a dashboard, of sorts, to monitor their progress. Partners come together to review these reports and decide what to do differently once the metrics have been evaluated.

The most important number to monitor is the dollar amount of monthly billings, and today's benchmark target is a three-month blended average of 8.5 percent of the annual revenue goal. Other key benchmarks are 60 days or better for accounts receivable; 60–65 percent of staff utilization (i.e., the percent of billable time performed by all staff, not just technical); a backlog of 9–14 months; a marketing hit rate of 50 percent or higher, producing an average monthly increase of 10 percent; and 15 percent pretax, preincentive profits. Each firm monitors feedback differently, of course, depending on building specialties, other specializations, and geographic regions. As well, private work has somewhat different metrics than federal work.

Looking more broadly and further out in time, the leadership in the profession must also address another signal trend of the 21st century—a significant shortage of talent. While more students are entering design schools than ever (about 36,000 in accredited architecture schools and another 12,000 in preprofessional programs), fewer of them are pursuing traditional career paths upon graduation. This trend is both wonderful and worrisome: It goes hand-in-hand with

(Opposite and below) The sustainable design movement was still in its infancy when planning began in 1991 for design and construction of the EPA Environmental Research Center in North Carolina. HOK used the opportunity to research environmentally friendly materials, investigate ways to improve indoor air quality and reduce energy usage, and devise a method for recycling construction waste. *Courtesy HOK*

Greenway's LEAP Cultural Assessment

1. Challenging processes — continuing improvements
2. Vision clarity — ability to inspire others
3. Systematic priority planning, enabling others to succeed
4. Role model — stature in field
5. Boosts morale especially during times of stress
6. Builds financial resource strength

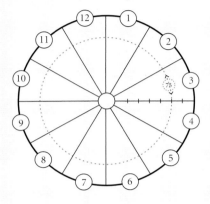

7. Communications are at exemplary levels
8. Collaborative spirit enriching the people and organizations
9. Steady and strong without alienating egotistic pride
10. Work ethic without micromanagement
11. Applied brilliance – intellectual power
12. Builds rapport, respect, admiration

Courtesy Greenway Communication

Best Practices for the New Millennium

- Hire and train the most talented people.
- Look for niches of specific business interest and return on investment.
- Select clients with great care.
- Develop strong communication skills.
- Nurture a culture of high standards and continuous improvement.
- Encourage strong knowledge management, collaboration, and efficiency.
- Strive to achieve profit goals year after year.
- Work to achieve growth goals in quantity and quality.
- Develop competence and leadership in sustainable design.
- Maintain turnover rates at 8–12 percent.
- Plan for transitions and have a backup plan.
- Know risks and protect the assets of the firm.

Adapted from DesignIntelligence/Design Futures Council, 2006

the expansion in the scope of the profession, but it also has the potential to create a brain drain in traditional practices. As baby boomers age, fewer younger staff are ready to step up and take their place. Tomorrow's successful firms must find new, creative ways to hire, train, and retain talent

Managing Constant Change

Creating good architecture is a complicated enterprise. It requires not only the ability to conceptualize and give physical form to the aspirations of the client but also the management skills to organize and choreograph the contributions and activities of a multitude of team members. As Scott Simpson says, "Architects must find ways to enable others to participate effectively in the design process, and this includes not only colleagues, but clients, consultants, and contractors as well." And let's not forget the public — the ultimate consumer of all this effort. The essential act of leadership is to unleash the power of the team. In this way, design can be embraced by all who are touched by it.

Architecture is made even more complicated by the fact that change — in technologies and processes — is ever present and has been particularly rapid beginning in the latter half of the 20th century. But change is also invigorating. "To dawdle is to die," says Simpson, reminding us that when architects communicate the same things and deliver their services in the same way over and over, their firms can stagnate.

The great majority of today's architects are responding to rapid change by becoming change agents themselves. They are using a positive vocabulary of motivation and action to pursue coalitions in which they can create value for individuals, companies, and communities. Today's profession is one of leadership. It is truly energized by what's ahead and willing to provide the focus, commitment, and inspiration to make the future better for our fragile planet. ●

1925
"Wassily" chair,
Marcel Breuer

Tribune Tower, Chicago,
John Mead Howells
and Raymond Hood

Union Station, Chicago,
Daniel Burnham and Graham,
Anderson, Probst & White

Sir Edwin Landseer Lutyens, Hon. FAIA,
and Bertram Grosvenor Goodhue, FAIA,
received the AIA Gold Medal

Louis Skidmore, FAIA

Richard Guy Wilson, Hon. AIA

The 1957 Gold Medal to Louis Skidmore differed from others in that it recognized an individual's organizational and business talents in creating a successful architecture practice. Through his partnership, Skidmore, Owings & Merrill (SOM), Skidmore crafted what has come to be known as the "full-service firm," which provides design, engineering, interiors, landscaping, and potentially other expertise. His firm also succeeded in making the then-radical, abstract Modern mode acceptable to American corporations and government. SOM created many of the great icons of the mid-20th century—such as Lever House (1949–52) and Manufacturers Hanover Trust (1953–54) in New York; Connecticut General Life Insurance (1954–57) in Bloomfield, Connecticut; and Reynolds Metals Headquarters (1953–58) in Richmond, Virginia—although Skidmore served as business partner, not designer, for these now legendary works.

Skidmore (1897–1962) was born in Indiana, served in World War I, received his architecture training at MIT, worked for Charles D. Maginnis, FAIA, and spent several years in Europe before becoming chief of design for the Century of Progress Exposition to be held in Chicago in 1933. His assistant was his new brother-in-law, Nathaniel Owings, FAIA. Armed with an engaging and persuasive personality, Skidmore gained expertise in both management and construction and experience in convincing clients during the depths of the Depression to embrace new forms of architecture. The fair was a success, and he and Owings founded their firm in 1936 in Chicago. The next year, Skidmore moved to New York, where he opened a branch office and hired a talented team that included Gordon Bunshaft, FAIA, as a lead designer. Engineer John Merrill joined in 1939. The firm prospered during World War II, designing many military bases around the world in addition to Oak Ridge National Laboratory in Tennessee, where the atom bomb was constructed.

After World War II, the firm expanded its services and sought out corporate clients. Skidmore and Owings developed a "team method" in which a designer and a partner-in-chief worked with the client, a project manager handled the business aspects of the project, and staff members from other specialties, such as engineering, landscaping, and interiors, represented their particular disciplines. Such a method was subsequently adopted by many other architecture practices. In 1950 the Museum of Modern Art in New York accorded SOM an exhibition, the first ever devoted to the work of a firm rather than an individual. A model of Lever House dominated the exhibit, and the firm was praised for its "organizational methods" and "discipline of modern architecture."

The buildings produced by SOM in those years exhibited exquisite detailing, perpetual newness, modern materials and construction methods, and accessories that included modern paintings, sculpture, and furniture. Over the years, the firm has opened offices in other cities and has explored other idioms. The work of the Skidmore-led New York branch, however, remains the quintessential image of post–World War II American corporate Modernism.

Under the skillful management and persuasive talents of Skidmore, SOM designed many of the iconic buildings of the mid-20th century, including Manufacturers Hanover Trust (1953–54) on Fifth Avenue in New York (above) and Connecticut General Life Insurance (1954–57) in Bloomfield, Connecticut. *Ezra Stoller/©Esto*

César Pelli, FAIA

Kristen Richards

César Pelli / Peter Freed, courtesy Pelli Clarke Pelli Architects

From New York and London to Kuala Lumpur and Hong Kong, city skylines around the world are graced with skyscrapers designed by César Pelli. What sets a Pelli building apart—be it an office tower, courthouse, retail/entertainment complex, hospital, museum, or library—is how it fits into its surroundings. He is a master of public place making and is a firm believer that buildings should be responsible citizens.

Born in Argentina in 1926, César Pelli immigrated to the United States in 1952 and received his MArch degree from the University of Illinois at Urbana-Champaign in 1954. He immediately began honing his architectural finesse while working as an associate architect at Eero Saarinen & Associates. He later served as director of design at Daniel, Mann, Johnson, & Mendenhall and then as design partner at Gruen Associates. In 1977 he moved to New Haven, Connecticut, where he founded César

Pelli and Associates (now Pelli Clarke Pelli). That same year, he was named dean of the Yale School of Architecture, a post he held until 1984. Pelli and his firm have received more than 100 awards, including the AIA's Architecture Firm Award in 1989. Having selected Pelli as one of the 10 most influential living American architects in 1991, the AIA subsequently honored him with the Gold Medal in 1995.

Today, even with projects as far flung as Spain, Argentina, Qatar, Japan, and Italy, Pelli and his partners Fred Clarke, FAIA, and Rafael Pelli, AIA, practice a hands-on approach to design—and business. The firm limits the number of commissions it accepts to ensure personal involvement by the principals, no matter where a project is located. Their key to success in working from a distance is to form an excellent team of local and foreign architects and engineers and to use the latest technologies and communication

Pelli's Cira Centre, completed in 2005, has already become a landmark in Philadelphia's skyline. ©Jeff Goldberg/Esto

Pelli's Petronas Towers, completed in Kuala Lumpur in 1998, were, until 2004, the tallest buildings in the world. The structures are built of high-strength, reinforced concrete because it is more effective than steel in reducing sway. An inverted, V-shaped arch attached at the center of the two-story sky bridge accommodates the differential movement of the towers. ©Jeff Goldberg/Esto

1926
Dymaxion House,
Buckminster Fuller

Bauhaus,
Dessau, Germany,
Walter Gropius

Los Angeles Central Library,
Bertram Grosvenor Goodhue

GRASS ROOTS

Steed Hammond Paul's Schoolhouse of Quality

James P. Cramer, Hon. AIA

"Stakeholder input," "voice of the customer," and "constituent feedback" are phrases we have all become familiar with. But 16 years ago, when Steed Hammond Paul Inc. of Cincinnati developed the Schoolhouse of Quality planning process, asking for customer input into planning and design was something only major product manufacturers thought to do. At the time, the architecture firm was primarily working with public education clients. The nature of decision making on such projects was changing from a single point of communication to group input, and Steed Hammond Paul recognized the importance of developing a creative planning process built on community values rather than priorities derived from individual wish lists.

Informed by Total Quality Management, which had become popular among business circles, the firm adapted a product development process called Quality Function Deployment to the design of education environments. The result was the Schoolhouse of Quality, a comprehensive systems approach built on the premise that to deliver a product that excites and delights customers, all planning and design decisions must be rooted in client values. To uncover these values, the firm identifies the groups served by a project and randomly selects individuals from each sector to participate in focus groups and in-depth individual interviews. Data gathered from telephone and written surveys is then used to help prioritize the values of the different groups, after which interdisciplinary teams work together to creatively develop design concepts that deliver on them. Visual imagery, sketches, and 3-D models of proposed architectural solutions are developed. When projects are complete, Steed Hammond Paul closes the loop with the client participants by asking them to measure the firm's performance against the values they communicated.

One example of results from the Schoolhouse of Quality process can be seen at the Seven Hills School in Cincinnati, for which Steed Hammond Paul developed a master plan to fulfill long-term curriculum needs. Numerous individuals from a variety of constituent groups participated, including administrators, staff members, students, parents, alumni, and friends of the school. "By listening and getting to the core of what we needed, Steed Hammond Paul gave us buildings and spaces within each building that work. They were a partner with us, working with all of our constituents to deliver the best possible solution," attests Robert Horne, the school's director of finance and operations.

Initially, the Schoolhouse of Quality method was applied specifically to design development in the education marketplace. Over time, however, Steed Hammond Paul has expanded it to services from master planning and fund raising to furniture design, as well as to project types outside the education market, such as libraries and recreation centers. The firm has trademarked its process and provided services using it as a consultant to other architecture firms. Since 1990 Steed Hammond Paul has employed the Schoolhouse of Quality approach on more than $1.5 billion of facilities and included more than 20,000 participants in more than 500 different applications.

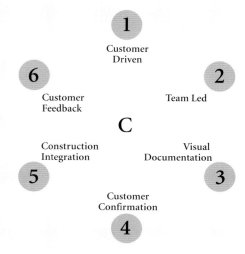

Schoolhouse of Quality
Process Principles

1 Customer Driven

2 Team Led

3 Visual Documentation

4 Customer Confirmation

5 Construction Integration

6 Customer Feedback

C

To develop a master plan for the Seven Hills School in Cincinnati, many stakeholders participated in a planning and development process facilitated by Steed Hammond Paul.
Courtesy Steed Hammond Paul

LS3P's Client Strategies

James P. Cramer, Hon. AIA

The LS3P team of principals: front row, left to right, Jeff Floyd, AIA; Charles Boney Jr., AIA; Mary Beth Branham, AIA; Michael Tribble, FAIA; back row, Thomas Hund, AIA; Frank Lucas, FAIA; Thompson E. Penney, FAIA; and Katherine Peele, FAIA (not pictured: Susan Baker, AIA, and Paul Boney, FAIA). *Douglas Gordon, Hon. AIA*

It has been said that teachers frequently learn more than their students, in part because of the preparation required to be in front of a classroom. Thompson E. Penney, FAIA, chief executive officer of LS3P Associates Ltd., and Paul D. Boney, FAIA, LS3P's chief strategic officer, experienced this firsthand when they served, respectively, as AIA's national president and convention chair in 2003. That year, they led a national discussion with the profession about evidence-based design. In the process, they—and many other practitioners—began to recognize that, through researching client strategies and substantiating, or "proving," the tangible value of good design, architects could provide even greater value to their clients.

This national discussion came home to LS3P. Founded in 1963, the 230-person architecture, interior architecture, and planning firm spans five regional offices and designs corporate/commercial, educational, health care, civic, and federal projects. In its 40th year, the firm decided to refocus on the "proof" of architecture. Specifically, LS3P developed Enhancing Client Strategies® as its mission statement to clearly dispel the notion that architects are only interested in design as an in itself. Staking its future on a value-added, knowledge-based practice, LS3P reorganized itself, from structure to budgeting, to support this vision.

Enhancing Client Strategies consists of three components: understanding clients' markets, potentials, and strategies; informing design decisions based on this research; and advocating for change. To set the groundwork for such a customer-focused approach, LS3P developed its own internal research group, which keeps abreast of the latest technical, economic, and cultural developments in each client's market sector. The data help LS3P's design teams stay current on their clients' concerns and strategies and be responsive to these issues. The research also provides the staff with metrics that demonstrate the relationship between good design and their clients' performance goals, from improvements in workplace productivity to advancements in healing environments and the psychological impact of design.

The type of information gathered varies from client to client and from project to project. The researchers have, for example, compiled studies on the positive effect of daylight in classrooms and on how the location of a store's shopping baskets affects sales. Research projects are investigated jointly by the research staff and market sector experts. Ultimately, LS3P plans to expand, both in size and scope, its research group to study design anthropology (the relationship between human beings and effective design); more fully investigate both existing and new building products; undertake postoccupancy evaluations (in classroom settings, for example); and collaborate with other researchers, from universities to product manufacturers and clients.

The researchers analyze their findings and make them available to the design staff and clients so that the project team can base design decisions on defensible facts rather than vague generalizations or assumptions. As advocates for change, the Enhancing Client Strategies research group has used its data and case studies, for example, to demonstrate to clients the importance of quality school design and to provide public officials with background information to support sustainability tax credits.

A commitment to enhancing client strategies through defensible research has permeated the firm. Since embarking on this journey, the firm has seen revenue increases of more than 81 percent. This strategic direction is clearly resonating with clients.

LS3P's research group provides its findings to the firm's project teams so that they can base design decisions on defensible facts. The open atrium in LS3P's Charleston office (below), which offers visual and physical connections among teams, responds to a 2003 article in *Research Design Connections* on how unplanned, unintended interaction is the single largest facilitator of office collaboration. LS3P created an inviting, open central stair at Johnson & Wales University in Charleston so students at the culinary institute (right) could stay in shape, heeding a Yale study that found walking up and down two flights of stairs daily will keep off six extra pounds of fat per year. *©David Sundberg/Esto, courtesy LS3P*

1927
Gregory Farmhouse,
Santa Cruz,
William Wurster

Howard Van Doren Shaw, FAIA,
received the AIA Gold Medal

Designing an Integrated Practice with Building Information Modeling

Norman Strong, FAIA

Technological evolution and owner demand for better, faster, less costly construction projects are driving change in the construction industry in general and in the practice of architecture in particular. Building information modeling is the technology enabling this transformation. This technology does not replace the critical, innovative thinking that architects bring to every project; rather, it supports and enhances the contributions of architects.

Developed in the 1990s, building information modeling is a nonproprietary computer modeling system founded on open standards for interoperability. The technology is used to create a building information model (BIM)—a 3-D digital representation of a design that embodies its functional characteristics. Such models can serve as a shared knowledge resource for information about a building, offering a reliable basis for decision making throughout the life cycle of a facility. By automatically handling schedules (e.g., door and window schedules), cross-coordination, and "collision avoidance" within construction documents, a BIM frees the architect to spend more time on systems and materials to enrich a design and on the interpersonal relationships so important to the success of a project.

When building information modeling is used from the beginning of a project and across the entire project team, architects can work collaboratively with other project team members to achieve what is termed "integrated practice." At the core of this new form of practice are teams composed of stakeholders from all aspects of the project's life cycle—not only architects and their design consultants but owners, facility managers, end users, contractors, and suppliers—who are all present from the start of the design process and have access to the BIM as it develops. Supported by capabilities of this technology, these teams will be guided by principles of true collaboration, open information sharing, shared risk and reward, and value-based decision making.

This degree of collaboration will make it possible for architects to acquire a full understanding of the long-term environmental and cost ramifications of various design options and better equip the architect to make project-specific decisions. In this way, the profession will be enabled to efficiently deliver higher quality design that is responsive to the needs of clients and communities.

According to the results of the 2006 AIA firm survey, an average of approximately 15 percent of practitioners have purchased building information modeling software, but only about 10 percent employ it for billable work. This average statistic hides, though, the fact that 60 percent of the largest firms use BIM software in their work, while fewer than 7 percent of the smallest firms do.

Since 2003, many leaders in the profession have encouraged architects to embrace integrated practice. However, significant transformations, highlighted in the accompanying chart, are still needed in both architecture education and in architecture practice to fully achieve this vision. Once these changes have been implemented across the board, architects will be able to focus on design again—and the profession promises to be more relevant than ever.

Traditional Practice (Today)		Integrated Practice (Future)
Fragmented, assembled on "as-needed" or "minimum necessary" basis, strongly hierarchical, controlled	Teams	Integrated team composed of all project stakeholders, assembled early in the process, open, collaborative
Linear, distinct, segregated; knowledge gathered as needed; information hoarded	Process	Concurrent, multilevel, integrated; early contributions of knowledge and expertise; information openly shared
Individually managed, transferred to the greatest extent possible	Risk	Collectively managed, appropriately shared
Individually pursued; minimum effort for maximum return; (usually) first-cost based	Compensation/Reward	Team success tied to project success; value-based
Paper-based, two dimensional; analog	Communications/Technology	Digitally based, virtual, four dimensional; building information modeling
Minimum effort for maximum return; minimize or transfer risk; don't share	Agreements	Encourage, foster, promote, and support open sharing and collaboration, full integration
Individually focused, emphasis on composition	Education	Team-based, integrated, collaborative; technologically inclusive; materials and methods focus in addition to composition

Globalization and the Practice of Architecture

James T. Fitzgerald, FAIA

International projects often provide an opportunity to design at a scale not available in the United States. For example, Lotte's department store in Sang-In, Korea, designed by FRCH Design Worldwide, blends minimalism with dramatic features: the exterior iconic tower showcases the store's core services and amenities; metal panels and color lighting highlight the merchandise available on each of the eight retail floors.
Kwang-Sik Kim, courtesy FRCH Design Worldwide

My firm, FRCH Design Worldwide, in Cincinnati, undertook its first international project—a five-star, international-brand hotel for a group of local investors in La Paz, Bolivia—30 years ago, when only a handful of U.S. architecture firms were doing work abroad. Today the number of U.S. firms practicing internationally has increased dramatically.

The first real boom for U.S. architecture firms occurred in the 1980s in the Middle East, particularly in Saudi Arabia, with gigantic projects for the Saudi government, the U.S. Army Corps of Engineers, and American oil companies. These enormous and complicated commissions were undertaken primarily by large, big-name American architecture and engineering firms.

Today, U.S. firms of all sizes are designing on all continents. Clients from the Pacific Rim and Latin America to India and Dubai now have the financial resources and the ambition to compete. These clients are seeking out U.S. firms for their experience and ability to handle specific project types, including large shopping centers, hospitals, airports, and museums.

FRCH's first international work resulted from the client's global search for a firm recognized for its industry expertise and award-winning commercial projects. Today, firms get foreign work in a number of ways, such as following current clients as they expand abroad; targeting market leaders in specific overseas locations; responding to inquiries from international clients conducting global searches; and conducting focused business-development efforts, sometimes with the help of the U.S. Department of Commerce or other government agencies.

International projects can be very fulfilling, especially because they often include buildings of significance at a scale not always available in the United States today. For example, because Asian department stores are traditionally larger in size and scope than their U.S. prototypes, FRCH has had the opportunity to develop more challenging planning solutions as well as unique designs. The firm's domestic department-store clients enjoy seeing ideas from these impressive Asian flagship stores.

In addition, overseas clients are sometimes more willing to break with convention, which may explain why some of FRCH's most prestigious awards have been for projects designed for foreign markets. Working on international projects also broadens a firm and its staff: exposure to new ideas, cultures, and approaches can only improve everyday practice at home.

International projects can also be challenging on many fronts. Although the rapid pace of technological advancement has reduced the time and cost to communicate and to transmit documents from point to point, the difficulties of exchanging information across several time zones can never be eliminated completely. Even the most sophisticated telecommunications network cannot replace the benefit of face-to-face contact with a client.

This is especially true of projects in Asia, where FRCH has found that much more socializing is required to establish a personal relationship and a level of trust before business can be conducted. Factoring in the cost and physical strain of international travel, many firms quickly see the value of setting up a local office. This demonstrates long-term commitment and facilitates rapid response to client needs and new opportunities.

Language differences can also be a barrier, even though English is typically the language of choice in international business. Translators can be problematic because they often are not well versed in service-contract and industry-specific terms. Having a staff member who speaks the client's language is invaluable. Sketches, which fortunately are part of an architect's repertoire, can help overcome some of these hurdles.

Addressing the language barrier is critical in the initial stages of a project. A clear, mutual understanding of the scope of work, contract details, and payment structure ensures project success, financial success, and an ongoing professional relationship. It is also critical that U.S. firms have a fundamental understanding of local building codes.

Some attempts to establish professional licensing reciprocity between foreign countries and the United States have been successful, but many firms are not willing to take the risk of practicing architecture overseas. Instead, many U.S. practices confine their role to front-end planning and design and rely on a firm based in the other country to navigate its laws, execute the documents, and obtain the required certifications.

Despite these logistical complexities, the benefits of international projects outweigh their challenges, as competition from a level, global playing field translates into an exciting future for the practice of architecture.

1928
Chrysler Building,
New York City,
William Van Alen

Founding of CIAM
(Congrès Internationaux
d'Architecture Moderne)

Philadelphia Museum of Art, Horace
Trumbauer & Associates and Zantzinger,
Borie & Medary

Columbia-Presbyterian Medical Center,
New York City,
James Gamble Rogers

VIEWPOINT

A Return to Design-Build Delivery

Martin Sell, AIA

The etymology of the word *architect*, according to *Merriam-Webster's Collegiate Dictionary*, goes back to the Greek *archi + tekton*, for principal builder or carpenter. From classical times until the Renaissance, the same person was responsible for both design and supervision of construction. Since the Italian Renaissance, however, architects have focused on design, divesting themselves of responsibility for construction. This change can be traced to the Renaissance polymath Leone Battista Alberti (1404–72), who supported the notion of architect as scholar and artist. According to Anthony Grafton's 2000 biography, Alberti believed the architect should remain apart from the mason and other craftsmen who physically produced the building, and he recommended that architects avoid taking sole responsibility for construction of projects, lest they incur all blame for errors and delays.

Following in Alberti's footsteps, the original founders of the AIA—wary of construction produced by "package dealers" of the day—formed a design-focused organization in the hope of limiting the role of nonprofessional masons, carpenters, bricklayers, and other members of the building trades. Builders eventually formed their own associations: the Associated General Contractors of America was established in 1918 and the Associated Builders and Contractors of America in 1950. The separation of design and construction did not suit everyone, however, and in the second half of the 20th century more and more owners began to ask for a single source for both design and construction. In response to this changing market, the Design-Build Institute of America was formed in 1993 "to advocate a single source of project delivery within the design and construction community."

AIA acceptance of design-build delivery has come about gradually. For most of the Institute's history, the AIA code of ethics insisted that member architects avoid design-build, fearing that architects could not manage both design and construction while maintaining the interests of owners above their own. In 1975, however, the Institute commissioned a task force to look into the issue, and in 1978 the AIA softened its position, allowing its members to practice design-build if they maintained the AIA's traditionally high ethical standards. By 1991, AIA policy supported design-build in public projects, and in 1995 a design-build professional interest area (now termed a knowledge community in accordance with current parlance) was organized. In 1996 the first series of AIA design-build documents was published. *The Architect's Guide to Design-Build Services*, edited by G. William Quatman II and Ranjit Dhar and published by John Wiley & Sons in association with the AIA, was released in 2003 and followed up with a revised series of design-build documents in 2004. As of 2005, the Institute's position statement on alternative project delivery methods states that "an architect is most qualified to lead alternative project delivery systems," including design-build.

Single-source project delivery has come full circle, from ancient master builder to modern-day designer-builder. The design-build group is now one of the AIA's largest knowledge communities. Nearly half of all nonresidential design and construction projects today are produced using this delivery method, and increasingly AIA members are assuming leadership roles in these efforts. A continuing commitment by the AIA to educate and support architects who practice design-build and other alternative project delivery methods is crucial for architects to retain leadership roles in the design and construction industry.

Market Penetration of Major Project Delivery Systems

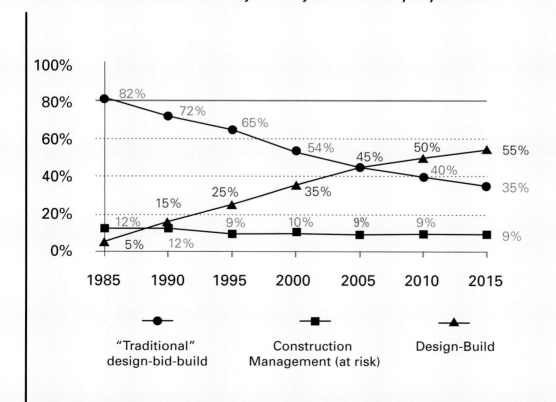

"Traditional"
design-bid-build

Construction
Management (at risk)

Design-Build

Over time, a larger portion of nonresidential design and construction in the United States has been accomplished by the design-build method of delivery. The Design-Build Institute of America developed this chart from limited member surveys, reviews of *Engineering News Record* and Zweig White surveys, and anecdotal evidence. Because federal and state governments do not track projects by delivery method, exact figures are difficult to obtain.
Courtesy Design-Build Institute of America

1929

German Pavilion, Barcelona
International Exposition,
Ludwig Mies van der Rohe

Health House (for Dr. Philip Lovell),
Los Angeles,
Richard Neutra

Milton Bennett Medary, FAIA,
received the AIA Gold Medal

10

Residential Architecture
Shaping Our Homes and Communities

Michael Pyatok, FAIA
Ralph Bennett, AIA

Housing is our most ubiquitous building type. It occurs in every context from the densest cities to the most open landscapes. It is the expression of ourselves and our aspirations, and for architects it continues to be the forum for addressing a wide range of enthusiasms and concerns, including style, technology, social values, and personal expression.

The design of housing in the United States provides built statements about the most fundamental American social issue—the tension between the individual and the collective. The agrarian cottage on a private lot is the animating myth of the American housing market, even today. At the same time, cities endure and require complex housing arrangements to deal with dwelling at higher densities. Architects serve the myths and the realities—their diverse contributions to the design of home in all its situations provide a notable tribute to an inventive profession.

(Opposite) The 27-story Solaire (2003), designed by Cesar Pelli & Associates, is New York City's first LEED-certified residential tower. Among its many green features are a storm-water retenton system, a vegetated roof (on both levels), and photovoltaics.
©Albert Vecerka/Esto

The Single-Family House

The individual house on a self-sufficient farm plot was advocated and represented most vividly by Thomas Jefferson, the genius architect of Monticello, sadly now removed from the back of the nickel but prominent among the icons of American domestic architecture. By building Monticello in arcadian isolation, Jefferson tacitly joined those critics of urban life whose advocacy of even ersatz rurality as an ideal for family life continues to fuel suburbia and bring tensions to metropolitan planning. Monticello was an aspiration toward the genteel values of English country living—a quality of life seemingly available to many, or even all, in view of the limitless horizons of the New World.

Realization of the dream of single-family homeownership was helped by the availability of copious woodlands in undeveloped North America. The building culture centered on the material, producing post-and-beam framing, the balloon frame, and the continuing refinement of wood construction for housing up to four stories. The construction industry has also pursued more industrial methods, such as prefabrication and panelization, to remove some of the vagaries of field construction.

The style of U.S. domestic architecture has generally been independent of the technology employed to build it. Early on, houses reflected Classical styles, with their strictly interpreted elements and massing based on both Greek and Roman precedents, which had been deemed appropriate for the public buildings of the new republic. Later in the 19th century, a broader palette of styles emerged, including Gothic, Romanesque, and the less pure, more inventive and picturesque Victorian. Bungalows, introduced in the early 20th century, remained enormously popular for smaller houses until World War II. In the interwar years, some architects and industrial designers began exploring Art Deco, while others, like Royal Barry

Even as interest in Modernism grew in the period between 1930 and 1950, the popularity of historical house styles continued in the United States. Boston architect Royal Barry Wills became known in this period for his many Colonial Revival house designs, although his firm also produced Modern-style houses.
Courtesy Royal Barry Wills Associates

Frank Lloyd Wright's Usonian houses were an attempt to create affordable single-family housing that was simple yet beautiful. Many of Wright's contributions to Modernism — clean, horizontal lines; unity with nature; and fluid, open space — can be found in the 1,200-square-foot Pope-Leighey House (1939) in Alexandria, Virginia.
Ezra Stoller/©Esto

(Above) The Gropius House in Lincoln, Massachusetts, built in 1937 for the architect's family, combined traditional New England building materials (clapboard and brick) with such Modern details as glass block, cork flooring, and chromed steel banisters.
©Roger Straus III/Esto

(Opposite) The Eames House (1949), Pacific Palisades, was designed as part of the Case Study House program initiated by *Arts and Architecture* magazine just after World War II. The goal of the program was to design quality houses at affordable prices.
©Tim Street-Porter/Esto

Wills of New England, championed American Colonial. Concurrently, picturesque English Tudor and Spanish clay tiles and stucco walls remained popular in the South and West.

Although European Modernism was slow to reach this country — in part because of America's enthusiasm for historical styles — a few forward-looking architects and clients took the opportunity to explore this new direction through the design of single-family homes. In fact, many icons of American Modern architecture are houses. Frank Lloyd Wright contributed both urban and rural examples in the Robie House and Fallingwater, while his Usonian house established the idea of reasonably priced designer houses for owners of more modest means. Wright — followed by European architects including Bauhaus refugees Ludwig Mies van der Rohe, Walter Gropius, and Marcel Breuer — built an enthusiastic following for progressive domestic design enabled by new technologies, from sliding glass doors to central heating and, after World War II, air-conditioning. According to Modernists, these technologies demanded new forms, and the image of simple, abstract, open plan, light-filled houses had broad public exposure through both the architectural and the popular press. Meanwhile, energized by visions of industrial production and futuristic technology, architects such as Buckminster Fuller used the domestic program to propose better houses for more people at lower prices. A case in point is Fuller's Dymaxion house (see page 135). The house as metaphor for new technology found expression in many ways.

After World War II, driven by government programs such as the GI Bill and the Interstate Highway program, the suburbs exploded, offering new opportunities for Modern design. *Arts and Architecture* magazine in California initiated the Case Study House program, which

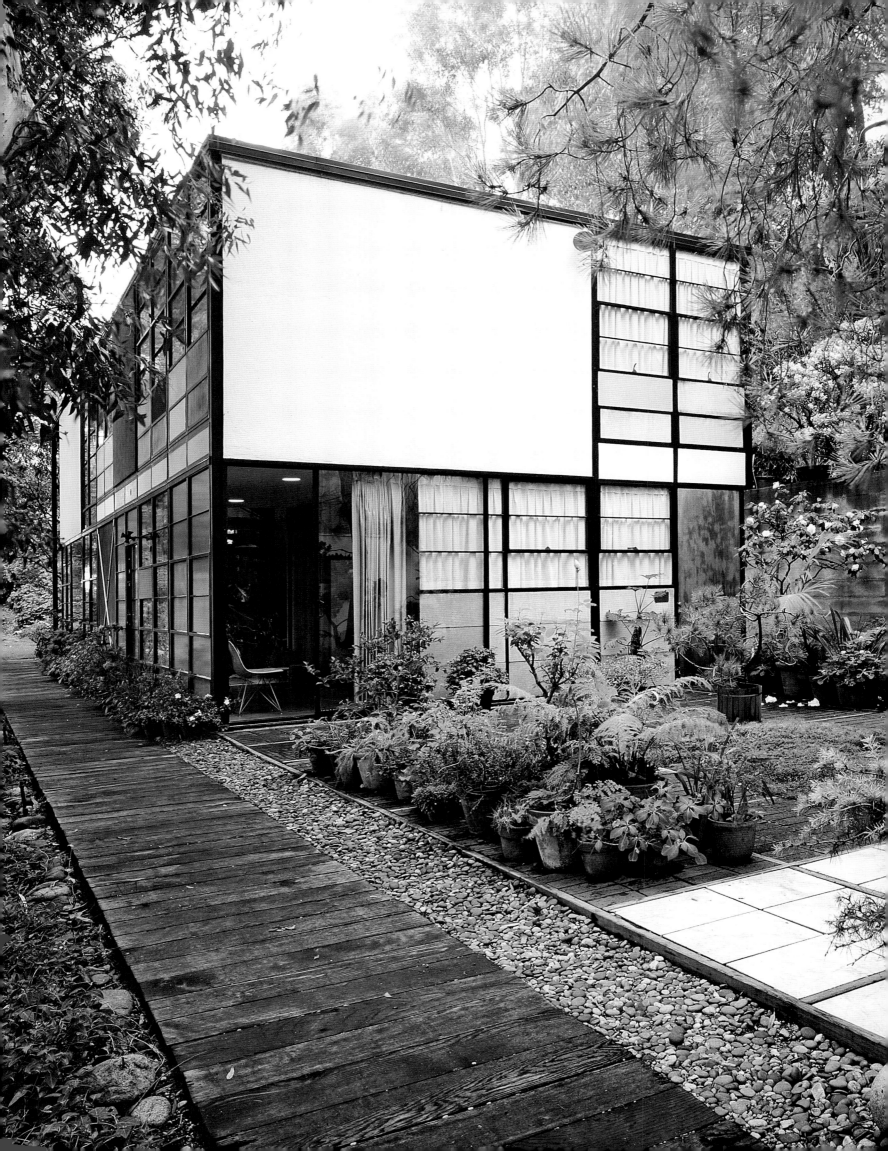

1931
Empire State Building,
New York City,
Shreve, Lamb and Harmon

Philadelphia Savings Fund Society Building,
Philadelphia,
Howe and Lescaze

Phipps Garden Apartments,
Queens, New York,
Clarence Stein

Villa Savoye,
Poissy, France,
Le Corbusier

showcased light, transparent, open plan houses by young designers. Among the most memorable was the Pacific Palisades house designed by Charles and Ray Eames, who combined Modern design with the use of off-the-shelf building parts like steel joists and factory glazing. Walter Gropius's design for the Lustron house, which had a prefabricated steel panel system, had a short run in the 1950s. Carl Koch's Techbuilt houses in New England and the Eichler houses in the San Francisco area give an idea of the national appeal of Modern housing design.

In the late 1960s, with housing production made affordable by industrial methods, the U.S. Department of Housing and Urban Development introduced Operation Breakthrough to encourage innovations in housing design, materials, and construction techniques that could help address low-income housing needs. The program attempted to apply the methods of the automobile industry (from which then-HUD Secretary George Romney came) to housing construction. The program failed simply because these methods could not be employed in a construction industry which has been described as the purest example of the free market—labor intensive, atomized, flexible, nimble, and comprised of small, minimally capitalized entrepreneurs. However, the ideas on which the program was based live today as part of an industry that factory builds stylish Modern designs or historically inspired designs with equal facility. *Architecture* (now *Architect*) magazine's 2006 House of the Year is a prefabricated, stand-alone house of simple, boxlike massing that sits on point foundations, suggesting it can be constructed on any site anywhere.

Modern minimalism is also enjoying popularity through publications like *Dwell*, which showcases minimalist domesticity for young householders of modest means. Taking this a step farther is Empyrean International, the successor firm to Deck House Inc. and Acorn Structures, which is marketing a series of factory-built designer houses in the Modern style, called Dwell Homes.

In response to the urgent need for affordable housing for returning World War II veterans, the Lustron Corporation began producing prefabricated porcelain steel houses in 1948. Although the houses never required painting and could be washed down with a hose, the steel-and-glass boxes never caught on with the public. Some 2,500 Lustron houses were produced before the company folded in 1950.
Martha Holmes/Time & Life Pictures/Getty Images

Studio 804's design-build program at the University of Kansas
School of Architecture and Urban Design gives third-year students
hands-on experience in design and construction, generally of a
house. This house, built of prefabricated modular parts, won the
Architect magazine House of the Year Award in 2006.
Courtesy Dan Rockhill, Studio 804

1932
First edition of
Architectural Graphic Standards
published

Philip Johnson and
Henry-Russell Hitchcock curated
the International Style exhibition,
Museum of Modern Art

Nebraska State Capitol,
Lincoln,
Bertram Grosvenor Goodhue

House designs reminiscent of historical American styles remain popular in the early 21st century. Even the so-called Katrina cottages, introduced by architect Marianne Cusato to replace FEMA trailers after the devastating hurricane of fall 2005, reflect historic Mississippi styles. Lowe's hardware and building supply stores began selling kits for the cottages in fall 2006.
Lowe's Companies Inc./PRNewsFoto/Newscom

Nonetheless, the competition between traditional and Modern styles remains lively today. Strong market interest in historical styles is driving a certain kind of regionalism, for which architects provide inventive and up-to-date interpretations. Named Postmodernism by historian Charles Jencks, this tendency is simply the reemergence into the architecture culture of the popular domestic imagery that always remained strong in the public mind, oblivious of the high-brow architecture style wars. The domestic architecture of the first half of the 20th century provides continuing inspiration for many architects and their colleagues in today's New Urbanism movement, who are happy to provide complementary settings for historically reminiscent houses. Modern architecture and its contemporary revivalists have been much less successful at providing distinctive and successful towns and neighborhoods. Thus, neo-Modern architects focus on the house as object, depicting it in isolated settings rather than as parts of streets or towns.

Multifamily Housing

While the isolated, rustic refuge has long been the animating myth for much of the American housing market, the higher density city has always been a pragmatic necessity, an engine of economic activity. Indeed, John W. Reps, the well-known city planning scholar, argued that even in the pioneer West, cities and towns were needed to provide staging areas for settlement of the wilderness. Most of these cities and towns survive today as desirable places to live.

Indeed, the revival of existing towns and the making of new ones has become a major arena for architectural activity at the beginning of the 21st century. As Douglas Kelbaugh, dean of the College of Architecture and Urban Planning at the University of Michigan, notes in his essay (page 357), architects have led a renewed focus on physical design as a critical component of planning—a focus abandoned in the land-rich, super-subsidized, gasoline-fed planning of post–World War II America.

The pragmatic, builder-designed row house originated in industrializing cities of 18th-century England but found its place in America as well. Architects provided larger versions of the type for clients of means. With the perfection of the elevator, the apartment house grew alongside the high-rise office building. Potential densities were greatly increased, and apartment living emerged in cities to accommodate a middle class for whom the single-family house was out of reach.

Modern architects seized the opportunities presented by tall buildings of all types. Corbusier's Ville Radieuse found its American expression in projects like the affordable Stuyvesant Town, opened in New York in 1947, and Mies's upscale Lake Shore Drive Apartments in Chicago, constructed in 1951. Modern architects also invented new typologies for higher density housing. Freed from historic precedent, apartment buildings like Corbusier's Unité d'Habitation in Marseilles (see page 374) proposed entirely new arrangements in which apartments with two exposures, allowing through-circulation and multiple views, could be connected to corridors on alternate floors, simultaneously improving efficiency and amenity. The American version of this idea can be found in the Married Student Dormitories (1962–64)

VDL Research House,
Los Angeles,
Richard Neutra

Folger Shakespeare Library,
Washington, D.C.,
Paul Cret

in Cambridge, Massachusetts, by Josep Lluis Sert, the émigré Catalan architect who was dean of the Harvard Graduate School of Design from 1953 to 1969.

Toward the end of the 20th century, the idea of mixed uses reemerged. Combining housing with retail and commercial activity, a 19th-century commonplace, had been ruled out of post–World War II planning by Euclidean zoning, but its obvious merits were rediscovered and demonstrated by architects across the country.

Affordability

The United States has arguably the best housed population in the world; 69 percent of its housing is owned by individuals. As well, American houses have become relentlessly larger: The average size of the American dwelling, including apartments, is 1,875 square feet, nearly twice that of the European average of 976 square feet. This could not have happened without a complex system of direct and indirect public subsidies. The federal mortgage interest tax deduction supports an active housing market and an efficient construction industry whose vast collective assets form a significant part of the American economy. The mortgage deduction benefits homeowners of all incomes, providing opportunities for architects to design individual houses, renovations, and additions as well as production designs for builders. The emergence of condominium ownership extended the benefit to multifamily housing for all incomes. The more expensive the house, the greater the benefit.

Stuyvesant Town (1947), designed by Irwin Clavan and Gilmore D. Clarke on Manhattan's East Side, provided affordable housing for middle-class families, especially World War II veterans.
©Bettmann/Corbis

1933
Radio City Music Hall,
New York City,
Edward Durell Stone and
Donald Deskey

Sanatorium,
Paimio,
Alvar Aalto

Beginning in 1993, the U.S. Department of Housing and Urban
Development has run the HOPE VI program to address the problem
of distressed public housing in American cities. Goals for projects
funded through the program include developing mixed-income
communities that include public housing and empower lower
income residents. The Boston-based firm of Goody Clancy
designed the Riverview Hope VI Redevelopment Plan, Cleveland,
shown here. *Courtesy Goody, Clancy and Associates*

New York Hospital–Cornell Medical
Center, New York City, Coolidge
Shepley Bulfinch and Abbott

Radburn,
New Jersey,
Clarence Stein and Henry Wright

Ragnar Östberg, Hon. FAIA,
received the AIA Gold Medal

Low-income-housing tax credits and funding from the City of
San Diego made possible the construction of Lillian Place, an
affordable housing complex for families with children. Designed
by Studio E Architects of San Diego, the complex offers family-
oriented amenities in a downtown location.
Courtesy Studio E Architects

Since the Great Depression and the beginning of federal involvement in affordable housing, the provision of housing to low-income Americans has been a subject of continuing debate and uneven success. The Housing Act of 1935 created public housing that the federal government built, owned, and managed through local housing authorities in participating jurisdictions. During World War II, government programs built military and war worker housing across the country, much of it designed by eminent architects. The most successful recent application of the direct funding approach has been the HOPE VI program, an urban revitalization strategy that replaces aged public housing with new, mixed-income developments in an attempt to repair the urban infrastructure that was damaged by the superblock planning of the 1950s and 1960s. New Urbanist architects have developed the methodology for this program, which includes resident involvement, reestablishment of preexisting street patterns, specific design review, and housing design that reflects its context.

Critics of direct government housing development prefer programs that help the private sector provide housing through rent supplements that make up the difference between what private landlords charge and what low-income families can pay. One such program, originally called the Section 8 program and recently renamed the Housing Choice Voucher Program, over the years has produced thousands of low-income housing units for families, seniors, and persons with special needs. Such housing subsidy programs have provided work for architects willing to develop quality housing design with limited resources and complex regulations.

Less direct incentives are offered through the successful Low Income-Housing Tax Credit program, initiated by HUD in 2000. This program permits developers to raise money by selling tax credits in exchange for providing housing at reduced rents for a guaranteed period of time. Tens of thousands of affordable housing units have been provided through this program, all in mixed-income developments designed by architects.

Safe and adequate housing for all Americans is still an unmet promise. Homeless shelters first emerged as a building type in the 1980s, and the need for them has continued to increase. Inventive and committed architects elevate low-income people into clients and owners through advocacy and participatory design processes.

The recent housing boom has emphasized housing problems for low-income families. The term "workforce housing" describes accommodation of families earning from 80 percent to 120 percent of area median income—a population far from poor and previously thought able to house themselves without direct subsidy. While federal assistance has leveled, state and local governments have initiated a wide variety of affordable housing programs, from inclusive zoning to direct subsidies. Inventive financing arrangements and local integration of many income levels in the same developments will encourage a future with fewer concentrations of poverty.

Pyatok Architects and Stickney Murphy Architects designed
the YWCA Family Village (1995) in Redmond, Washington. This
transitional housing, supported by the Stewart B. McKinney
Homeless Assistance Act, features low-income apartments above
offices and facilities for child care and social services.
Courtesy Pyatok Architects

The Metropolitan in suburban Bethesda, Maryland, designed by WDG Architecture of Washington, D.C., exemplifies the effort to include affordable housing in mixed-income housing projects. The project was developed by the Montgomery County Housing Opportunities Commission with local money but offers federal rent subsidies to low-income residents. *Courtesy WDG Architecture*

Designer Michelle Kaufmann's eco-friendly, prefab Breezehouse™ responds to the desire for innovative Modern design that is also sustainable. *Courtesy Michelle Kaufmann Designs*

Emerging Trends

After access to housing, sustainability has emerged as the greatest coming influence on building design. Architects have long led innovation in this area, and housing has been a compelling demonstration platform. The oil embargo of the early 1970s produced significant active and passive solar house designs. Identification of global climate change has combined with economic and strategic considerations to bring new life to these ideas and to move the AIA to advocate for carbon neutrality by 2030—a very aggressive policy.

Housing can provide solutions in all its forms. The stand-alone house offers a model for self-sufficiency, as it always has, and numerous small, high-tech dwellings are offered as custom or production choices. Size matters; architect Sarah Susanka has started a popular smaller house movement that concentrates on efficient site and space use, using mostly Craftsman-style ingredients. Multifamily prototypes for sustainable construction include Colorado Court (2002), a midrise, small-unit project in Santa Monica, designed by Pugh Scarpa Kodama, that is 100 percent energy neutral, and a luxury condominium development in Manhattan, the Solaire, designed by Cesar Pelli & Associates, that incorporates many green features, including photovoltaics, a geothermal system, and gray-water reuse for toilets and outside irrigation.

The increasing population will find more and more architects working on higher density projects in new and old urban situations—itself a sustainability strategy, as large houses become more difficult to maintain and higher density development inevitably stems from rising land prices. As developing technologies affect the way housing works, housing form will continue to be the subject of debate between those who believe new forms are mandated by new technology and those committed to the cultural continuity of traditional forms that absorb new technologies.

In response to changes in society and increases in population, architects will continue to meet the pragmatic challenges of emerging mandates, but they will do so by taking built positions on all manner of issues, providing variety and surprise in housing suited for its many American settings. ●

Colorado Court (2002), a single-room-occupancy project designed by Pugh Scarpa Kodama in Santa Monica, combines affordable housing with a 100% energy neutral building. Blue photovoltaic panels are integrated into the façade and roof. The project achieved a LEED Gold rating. *Marvin Rand, courtesy Pugh Scarpa Kodama*

Frank Lloyd Wright

Anthony Alofsin, PhD, AIA

Frank Lloyd Wright (1867–1959), a towering figure in modern architecture, left an indelible mark on contemporary culture during seven decades of practice. Born in rural Richland Center, Wisconsin, he had a peripatetic upbringing and limited professional architectural training, with a short stint at the University of Wisconsin, until Louis Sullivan became his mentor in Chicago. Starting an independent practice in 1893, Wright began his experiments in residential design that would revolutionize how people lived and experienced architecture. His integration of interior and exterior spaces, along with the concept of total design, was based on extensive knowledge of building as well as a theory and a philosophy that he defined as organic architecture.

Although Wright designed a broad range of building types, from the well-known Guggenheim Museum in New York City to little-known factory projects, office buildings, and entire communities, such as Broadacre City, he became most recognized for his residential designs. His houses defined the periods of his career, representing cumulative experience, and provided constant opportunities for innovation and experimentation. The breakthrough toward organic architecture crystallized with the Ward W. Willets House (1901–03) in Highland Park, Illinois. A subsequent series of houses articulated by differing roof configurations—gabled, pitched, and even flat—as well various materials—brick, board and batten, and concrete—defined the first great phase of his work, the Prairie period, from 1900 to 1910. It included great ensembles such as the Susan Lawrence Dana House (1902) in Springfield, Illinois, and the Avery Coonley House (1907) in Riverside, Illinois.

Personal perturbations and fatigue with practice terminated this period around 1909, and Wright's career was conventionally, but erroneously, characterized then as entering a fallow phase. The so-called Lost Years from the early 1910s through the 1920s were in fact filled with innovation and experimentation, particularly in the use of archetypal motifs of geometry and complex patterns of ornament. Wright retained his interest in the pattern languages of ornament when he proposed a method of casting concrete blocks known as his textile block system. Intended as an economical means of construction for middle-class housing,

examples included the Charles Ennis and John Storer houses, both built in 1923 in Los Angeles.

By the 1930s, realizing that the Depression had not only recast economic conditions but also social structure, Wright reconsidered the models of the middle-class American dwelling to produce what he called the Usonian home. He removed servants' quarters, provided carports, transformed the kitchen into a workplace, and used inexpensive materials with simple techniques of economic construction. The Usonian house became the vehicle for Wright's solution to single-family living throughout the rest of his career. Built examples range from the modest, including the first Jacobs House (1936), Madison, Wisconsin, to large and elaborate versions, such as the John A. Gillin residence (1950) in Dallas.

After 1945 and throughout the postwar period, Wright's influence in America ascended. His Usonian designs and such monumental works as Fallingwater (1936) in Bear Run, Pennsylvania, the Johnson Wax Administration Building (1936) in Racine, Wisconsin, and the Guggenheim (1943–59) had cemented his position as a major historical figure in Modern architecture. While historians published and republished Wright's Prairie period houses, with emphasis on Chicago's Robie House (1908–10), his booming practice, supported by his student apprentices known as the Taliesin Fellowship, entered its most influential period. Shelter magazines, notably *House Beautiful*, widely distributed his designs. Many of the Usonian versions of his organic architecture began to influence and commingle with other developments in the design and construction of the modern American home.

At the peak of his postwar period, the AIA awarded Wright, at age 82, its Gold Medal. A lifelong critic of the status quo and convention, Wright saw the AIA as representing the Establishment that he long reproached. However, his outsider position did not prevent him from accepting the medal at the annual meeting held in March 1949 in Houston. After the award and during the last decade of his life, he continued to experiment with hybrid geometries, often combining circular and rectilinear plans, as seen in the John L. Rayward residence (1955), New Canaan, Connecticut, and in his last residential design, the Lykes residence (1959), Phoenix.
©*Anthony Alofsin*

The Storer House was one of several Los Angeles–area houses designed by Wright in the 1920s using his concrete textile block system.
Courtesy the Frank Lloyd Wright Foundation, Taliesin West, Scottsdale

The Lykes House (1959), Phoenix, was Wright's last residential design before his death in 1959.
Courtesy the Frank Lloyd Wright Foundation, Taliesin West, Scottsdale

1935
Fallingwater,
Bear Run, Pennsylvania,
Frank Lloyd Wright

U.S. Supreme Court,
Washington, D.C.,
Cass Gilbert

GOLD MEDALIST, 1991

Charles W. Moore, FAIA

Avigail Sachs

Courtesy Centerbrook Architects

Charles Willard Moore was, in equal measure, an architect, educator, and author. Born in 1925 in Benton Harbor, Michigan, Moore earned his BArch at the University of Michigan in 1947 and a PhD from Princeton in 1957, where he was an assistant teacher for Louis Kahn.

Recruited by William Wurster, Moore joined the faculty of the University of California, Berkeley, in 1959, where he taught and served as chair of the department of architecture from 1962 to 1965. During this period, Moore formed the first of several partnerships, MLTW (Moore, Lyndon, Turnbull, Whitaker). With this firm, he designed his most widely acclaimed project, the Sea Ranch Condominium I (1965) on the Pacific Coast, north of San Francisco. Critic Paul Heyer described Sea Ranch as "the California wood tradition projected into a mid-sixties leaner sensibility and aesthetic." When the project received the AIA's Twenty-five Year Award in 1991, the jury noted that Sea Ranch had "formed an alliance of architecture and nature that has inspired and captivated a generation of architects."

In 1965 Moore became chair (and later dean) of Yale University's School of Art and Architecture, where he remained for 10 years. As part of his transformation of the school's philosophy, Moore founded the Yale Building Project in 1967 to teach first-year students about the construction process as well as the social responsibility of architecture. The program recently marked its 40th anniversary. In New Haven, he founded Charles W. Moore Associates and in 1975 became a partner in the firm known today as Centerbrook Architects.

He returned to California in the mid-1970s as a founding partner of Moore Ruble Yudell in Santa Monica and head of the architecture program at UCLA. From 1984 until his death in 1993, he held the O'Neil Ford Centennial Chair in Architecture at the University of Texas, Austin. In addition to practicing and teaching, Moore wrote or cowrote many influential books, including *Water and Architecture* (1994) and *The Place of Houses* (1974). He was honored with numerous design and teaching awards, including the Topaz Medallion for Excellence in Architectural Education in 1989.

Moore's Sea Ranch Condominium I (1965), located about 100 miles north of San Francisico, perfectly captures the partnership of buildings with the landscape.
©*Donald Corner & Jenny Young/GreatBuildings.com*

Antoine Predock, FAIA

Kristen Richards

Born in 1936 in Lebanon, Missouri, and educated at the University of New Mexico and Columbia University in New York City, Antoine Predock was taken by the American Southwest early on. In 1967 he founded his eponymous firm in Albuquerque. Three years later, his design for La Luz, a 500-acre, master planned community of adobe townhouses and common areas set in an open expanse outside the city limits, put him on the architecture map—where he has remained ever since.

The desert Southwest sharpened Predock's architectural sensibilities toward the land, light, and air—and humankind's place among these elements. His personal and place-inspired vision of architecture is evident in all of his work, regardless of scale—from the famed Turtle Creek House (1993) in Dallas built for bird enthusiasts to the

Tang Teaching Museum and Art Gallery (2000) at Skidmore College, to a new ballpark for the San Diego Padres that reinvents the concept of a stadium as a garden rather than a sports complex.

Despite his affinity for the American Southwest, Predock has worked across the country and around the world (for example, his design for the National Palace Museum Southern Branch in Taiwan is scheduled for completion in 2010). And his architecture is in no way limited to one regional vernacular. He has often said that "my 'regionalism' is portable." Every project is a response to its geographic site and cultural context, and to the people who will inhabit it. In that sense, everything Predock designs—from his houses to his institutional and civic projects—is a form of public architecture.

(Right) The Highlands Pond House (2006), in Colorado, settles into the landscape as if it had simply displaced stone fragments on the site. Abundant windows and a titanium-clad roof and façade capture the fluctuating light of the high mountain valley.
©Timothy Hursley

(Below left) Predock's design of the Turtle Creek House (1993), Dallas, was a response to the client's passion for bird watching. Sited at the convergence of two major continental flyways on the Turtle Creek watershed, the house features a "sky ramp" that projects from the entrance up to the surrounding canopy of trees.
©Robert Reck

(Below right) The Logjam House (2006), Rio Blanco, Colorado, is nestled among a spectacular grove of ponderosa pine trees and surrounded by mountain peaks. Large expanses of glass provide ever-changing views, and deep overhangs keep the snow at bay.
©Robert Reck

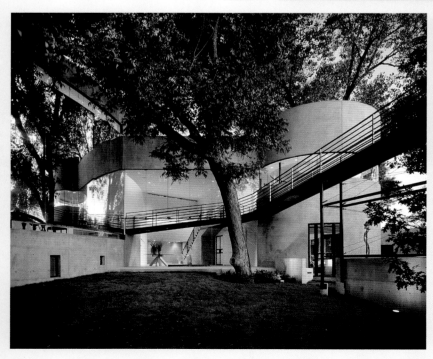

The Social Art of Architecture: Good Design for All

Kira Gould, Assoc. AIA

Single-room occupancy hotels (SROs) were prevalent in large American cities in the late 1800s and early 1900s, serving single workers of various economic classes. As upper classes departed for the suburbs, however, these facilities became associated with the poor. In the 1970s and 1980s, San Diego, like many other municipalities across the country, tore down its SROs or converted them to other uses as part of "redevelopment" efforts, leaving many people homeless. "They thought of these places as flea-bag hotels, but they were home to many people," recalls local architect Rob Wellington Quigley, FAIA. "Every city needs some housing of this type," he adds, noting that they serve people from all walks of life, including those who are new to a community and those who are working there temporarily.

Sensing a viable but untapped market, San Diego developer Chris Mortenson bought a downtown parcel to implement what seemed at the time to be a renegade idea: "He wanted to build a brand new SRO, which hadn't happened in this country for about a half-century," says Quigley, who was asked by Mortenson to design the project. The result, in 1987, was the Baltic Inn, credited by many as the first in a wave of new SROs to spread across the country after others recognized its success.

The Baltic has 204 rooms that range from 120 to 160 square feet in size. Light wells within the building help brighten and ventilate both the common areas and private units. A lean tower with a neon sculpture gives the building a strong identity, and an arched entryway and multiple porches create a lively, interactive connection between the building and the street.

Unlike some other types of affordable housing, SROs are not subsidized; they are private ventures—with tight budgets. "The budget prompted us to think about things in new ways," Quigley says. The developer and the architect also had to negotiate with the building department because, at the time, the city's code did not recognize SROs as a type. Ultimately, this led to new regulations, which Quigley's firm helped to write; similar changes have been adopted in other cities as well.

Quigley designed two more SROs in downtown San Diego for Mortenson. The J Street Inn was completed in 1990 with 221 rooms on four floors. The presence of this SRO did nothing to discourage the subsequent building of high-rise luxury condominiums across the street, helping to silence concerns about adjacent property values. The 202 Island Inn followed in 1992 and earned accolades from *Time* magazine.

Even on the heels of these successes, negative perceptions and NIMBYism are still a challenge in the initial phases of an SRO project. After projects are completed, however, there is often a quick turnaround of opinion, which Quigley attributes in part to the fact that the designers keep security firmly in mind. "We believe in 'eyes on the street,' " he says. They also believe in incorporating innovative strategies and technologies where budgets permit: the Opportunity Center—a project completed in 2006 in Palo Alto, California, for the Housing Authority of Santa Clara County—includes both SRO units and apartments and features energy-efficiency systems that surpass the state's high-performance standards.

Katherine Austin, AIA, 2007 chair of the AIA Housing Committee and a practitioner in Sebastopol, California, credits Quigley with reviving the SRO as a building type. "He gave it panache," she says. "He helped turn around a derelict area of San Diego. Rather than displacing the population, he gave them a dignified place to live."

Rob Wellington Quigley and staff, including office mascot Jackson (springer spaniel, front row). *Courtesy Rob Wellington Quigley, FAIA*

(Left) The Quigley-designed Opportunity Center of the Midpeninsula lives up to its name, providing low-cost housing and social services to the citizens of Palo Alto. *Courtesy Rob Wellington Quigley, FAIA*

Quigley's landmark Baltic Inn in downtown San Diego started a national trend in single-room occupancy hotels. The project received an honor award from AIA San Diego in 1987.
Arthur Ollman, courtesy Rob Wellington Quigley, FAIA

1937
Golden Gate Bridge opened

Main Building,
University of Texas, Austin,
Paul Cret

Gropius House,
Lincoln, Massachusetts,
Walter Gropius

Taliesin West (1937 onward),
Scottsdale,
Frank Lloyd Wright

11

Innovation in Office Design

Vivian Loftness, FAIA

For 150 years, architects have led corporate and federal America in the reinvention of the workplace to match the aspirations and needs of ever-changing economic, technical, and cultural conditions. Although this country began as an agrarian nation and grew prosperous through industrialization, for the past century a large percentage of Americans have worked in jobs that involve going to "the office." While it is not possible to do justice to the extensive accomplishments of professionals and historians on this subject, this essay attempts to highlight the contributions of the architecture profession to the evolution of office design.

(Opposite and below) Frank Lloyd Wright's Larkin Building (1904), Buffalo, New York, was a cutting-edge example of a new building type—a "factory" for the new breed of worker, the office worker. *AIA Archives*

Beyond the Assembly Line

The earliest office buildings were designed to accommodate a new generation of desk and paper-based work that supported the primary business of farming and manufacturing. Not surprisingly, early office architecture evolved from the high-bay spaces that originally brought light and air to blue-collar workers toiling on assembly lines below. The new office was, in essence, a factory for white-collar workers. To ensure order and supervision of linear production, the design and layout reflected the scientific management approach of American engineer Frederick Taylor. Large open plans were densely filled with workstations positioned under the watchful eye of supervisors overhead.

Rising above the utilitarian, these vaulted spaces inspired architects to explore the potentially grand scales and expressiveness of a new building type. At the beginning of the 20th century, Frank Lloyd Wright inspired the nation with the Larkin Building (1904) in Buffalo, New York. Corporate strength and unity was reflected by a large central work space, filled with emerging technologies and furniture freshly designed for the educated, white-collar worker. Architectural innovator Francis Duffy of DEGW exclaims, "It was probably the most advanced office of its time, with perhaps the most perfect relationship between architectural invention and organizational innovation that has ever been achieved. In the messages expressed to employees—through its overpoweringly disciplined architectural form, in the paternalistic homilies carved into the spandrel panels of the galleries, in the centrally controlled environmental services, and in the hierarchically ordered layout—it reinforced the managerial culture of its time."

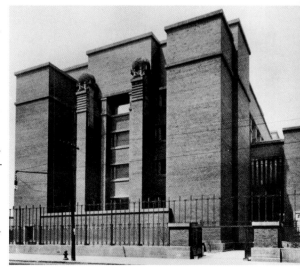

As the importance of white-collar work grew, so did the value of urban centers and commercial real estate. New York, Chicago, and Boston began to emerge as hubs for new and increasingly lucrative enterprises, from financial trading and insurance to marketing. Advances in elevator design and mechanical systems made it possible to build high-rise offices around shared vertical cores for transport and conditioning. With rationalized access and services, the multiple floors of these buildings could be flexibly subdivided and easily rented to a growing number of new businesses. This basic template allowed architects to focus on dramatic building heights, streetscapes, and roofscapes, and on the design of grand lobbies and executive suites that symbolized the growing power and wealth of the commercial building owner. Built to international acclaim, New York City's Rockefeller Center (1929–40; see page 359), Chrysler Building (1930; see page 42), and Empire State Building (1931) all exemplify this era. The Empire State Building was the tallest in the world for 41 years and remains one of New York City's most distinctive buildings today. Filling a city block, the commanding building rises 102 stories. Art Deco details give its crown and observation deck an elegance that withstands the passing of time—indeed challenged only by the silvery Chrysler Building.

A collaborative study titled "Revaluing Buildings," sponsored by office-furniture manufacturer Steelcase in 1993, identified the characteristics of these landmark buildings that have allowed them to continue to support the changing nature of work. These include well crafted and detailed facades, lobbies, and surfaces; high ceilings and wide corridors capable of absorbing distributed service spaces and new vertical and horizontal plenums; high ceilings and operable windows that offer effective daylighting; individual workstation access to windows and outdoor spaces; manageable distances from service cores; substantial structure and durable finishes; and pedestrian, mixed-use contexts. Indeed, these characteristics are being reincorporated into new commercial construction today because of their flexibility and timeless appeal.

Egalitarian and Collaborative Strategies

The end of World War II marked the beginning of the Modern movement for office design. Driven by a desire to move away from an elitist and hierarchical society that ignored the welfare of the common man, architects such as Mies van der Rohe and Walter Gropius and firms such as Skidmore, Owings & Merrill pursued a minimalist, honest, and "democratic" office style. The investment of resources was given not to executive suites, grand lobbies, or ornate roofs and finishes but to providing egalitarian workplaces for all employees.

Represented most eloquently by the Seagram Building (1958; see page 46) in New York City, the Modern movement championed carefully detailed and ordered structural, enclosure, and interior systems. Designed by Mies van der Rohe in collaboration with Philip Johnson, this office building presents a timeless contribution to both the city and the workplace. Its flexible, open floors and spatial clarity absorb an ever-changing set of client demands. Its aesthetic, clean lines continue to inspire new generations of architects.

As the industrialized nations emerged from postwar, get-back-to-work economies, the contribution of individuals to organizational success became a growing force in design. A new focus on personalization, comfort, and individual productivity was combined with the creation of collaborative, organizational places to retain the invaluable "gold collar" worker.

Architect Kevin Roche's 12-story Ford Foundation Headquarters (1968) in New York, for example, introduced clusters of individual, personalized workplaces around a central atrium landscaped by Dan Kiley. The atrium was vast and transparent—an internalized urban park in the dense city. By making such a costly shift from the central-core office planning that was common at the time, the designers of this award-winning building were recognizing the value of the individual to the organization and investing in this human resource. Equally committed to supporting personalized work spaces within the collective, Benjamin Thompson designed the Design Research Headquarters (1969) in Cambridge, Massachusetts, with a transparent and articulated collection of individualized workplaces.

In the landmark Centraal Beheer building, built in 1970 in Apeldoorn, Netherlands, architect Herman Hertzberger introduced an amazing complex of personalized work spaces into an open plan. The result was a dynamic village of offices connected visually and spatially by "main street" and "side street" corridors that are daylit from above. Employees were able to personalize furniture, art, and plants, thereby creating their ideal workplace and representing their strengths to the organization. This emphasis on a completely personalized and humanized workplace within a strong organizational setting catalyzed a rethinking of the modern office.

(Opposite) The increasing number of white-collar workers and advances in elevator and mechanical design made possible high-rise office buildings, which were designed with penthouse suites and other amenities for wealthy business owners. An early and enduring example is the Empire State Building in New York City designed by Shreve, Lamb and Harmon and completed in in 1931. *©Carol Highsmith Photography*

Benjamin Thompson conceived his Design Research Headquarters (1969), Cambridge, Massachusetts, as a "three-dimensional show window." The concrete floor plates seem to float behind the frameless glass walls. *Ezra Stoller/©Esto; AIA Archives*

Visually and spatially connected work spaces reflect the personality of the individual worker in the open plan layout of the 1970 Centraal Beheer building in the Netherlands, designed by Herman Hertzberger. *Lifchez Collection, Architecture Visual Resources Library, University of California, Berkeley*

Linking Productivity to the Indoor Working Environment

In direct response to the organizational thinking that recognized the value of the individual in corporate success, the research community began to study in earnest the importance of ergonomics, comfort, and privacy. In addition, an increase in a variety of symptoms—including headaches, dizziness, and fatigue—among office workers in the 1970s and 1980s led to better understanding of and prevention strategies for what is now known as "sick building syndrome." As a result, the relationship between indoor environmental and spatial quality to worker health and productivity has been transforming the design of both workstations and office buildings.

In 1971, for example, the General Services Administration launched its "Peach Book" to define the performance specifications needed to ensure acoustic, thermal, air, lighting, and spatial/ergonomic quality for both the individual and the work group. The development of high-performance design standards for work environments continues today in the agency's Workplace 20.20 program, incorporating significant before-and-after studies on the impact of workplace quality on measured results.

Beginning in the 1980s, Ole Fanger, director of the Danish Technology Research Institute, along with David Wyon and others, built the proof sets linking temperature control and worker performance at a range of tasks. At Lawrence Berkeley National Laboratory, Bill Fisk and Mark Mendell amassed research that proved the importance of delivering greater quantity and quality of outside air. In their landmark Westbend study, researchers at Rensselaer Polytechnic Institute demonstrated that user control of indoor environmental quality was related to task performance. Alan Hedge and his team at Cornell showed gains in task performance with ergonomic furniture that supported the musculoskeletal system. Meanwhile, building on studies in environmental science and zoology, environmental psychologist Judith Heerwagen, then at the University of Washington, wrote extensively on the importance of human contact with nature, contributing to the biophilia movement of E.O. Wilson at Harvard University and Steven Kellert at Yale. And architects Lisa Heschong and Doug Mahone buoyed this approach with field studies that linked student test scores, retail sales, and call-center productivity to individual access to views and daylight. These are only a few of the researchers who have helped to connect the quality of the workplace to worker productivity and health.

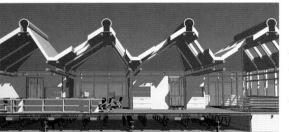

The Intelligent Workplace, a "living laboratory" that opened at Carnegie Mellon in 1997, consists of various building subsystems that permit workers to individualize their space, including the level of enclosure and the location and density of furniture, telecommunications, HVAC, and lighting. *Carnegie Mellon University*

The Intelligent Workplace

With the emergence of distributed computing and desktop computers, new "information technology consultants" joined architects across the United States in the re-creation of offices to support emerging computational tools. At first, the "smart" or "intelligent" building had been defined by the introduction of a long list of the latest products in telecommunications, electronics, security, automation, and building control systems. It soon became evident, however, that the building infrastructure itself—in the form of mechanical, electrical, telecommunications, and interior systems—would have to shift from fixed to flexible to accommodate the rapidly changing organizational and technological requirements set in motion by these changing products. Increasing investments in desktop technology affected space requirements and demands for data, power, and voice connectivity. Work tasks focused on keyboards, and screens changed lighting requirements and the musculoskeletal demands for ergonomic workstation design. The new technologies created other environmental concerns as well, as they generated additional noise and heat plus local changes in airflow patterns.

After completing a series of international studies of innovative office buildings, the Center for Building Performance at Carnegie Mellon argued for buildings with dynamic, user-based infrastructures that allow workers to individually reconfigure their spatial, environmental, and technological services. The Carnegie Mellon team promoted a definition of smart buildings that went beyond a voracious assembly of advanced technology: "Intelligent buildings will support on-going organizational and technological dynamics in appropriate physical, environmental, and organizational settings to enhance individual and collective performance and human health, comfort, and motivation." The team went further to define the type of building infrastructures that are critical to the evolving high-tech workplace and subsequently built a living laboratory to demonstrate the approach: Opened in 1997, the Intelligent Workplace consists of a constellation of building subsystems that permit each individual to set the location and density of HVAC, lighting, telecommunications, and furniture, and the level of work space enclosure.

These researchers, along with leading practitioners and developers, believe that user-based infrastructures that are modular, reconfigurable, and expandable for all key services—including ventilation air, thermal conditioning, lighting, and data/voice and power networks—are critical to avoiding frequent failures in environmental quality and long-term obsolescence. Even for the leased Owens Corning Headquarters (1996) in Toledo, designed by César Pelli, the Hines Partnership invested in raised-floor technologies that support individually reconfigurable services for air, thermal control, light, and, of course, networking. The result was a headquarters that could rapidly absorb a workforce growth from 1,000 to 1,300, with overnight reconfiguration, and the highest level of user-based services.

Cesar Pelli's Owens Corning World Headquarters (1996), Toledo, is an assemblage of component parts linked together by glass-enclosed connectors. The virtually transparent envelope of the "workplace" component follows the curving riverfront and provides natural daylighting to much of the interior. *©Timothy Hursley*

Multidisciplinary Invention

In the meantime, architects and interior designers, in collaboration with the furniture industry, were integrating the demands of technology with the latest results from research on productivity to invent totally new modular kits for the dynamic organization. While technology remained central, the industry came to recognize that people were still critical to today's continuous organizational reengineering for productivity and innovation. Indeed, office design began to focus on the balance of people, place, and technology. Environmental psychologists such as Heerwagen and Cornell's Franklin Becker and Bill Sims, and architects such as Michael Brill of the Buffalo Organization for Social and Technological Innovation (BOSTI) articulated the importance of people and place in the definition of the innovative workplace. Discussions began to shift to motivational buildings, which were defined as those that provide environmental performance at a level that consistently and reliably ensures health, comfort, security, and financial effectiveness, while supporting high levels of productivity amidst continuing organizational and technological change.

The design profession and the furniture industry responded immediately. The dot-com generation drove one of the most inventive periods in interior design for offices, exploring layers of ownership, multiple work environments, ergonomic support for both shared and individual work processes, layers of workstation closure and mobility, and layers of personalization. Architects were creating work environments that spoke to both the individual and the collaborative nature of work, as exemplified by TBWA/Chiat/Day's Los Angeles headquarters (1998) and Google's headquarters (2005) in Mountain View, California, both designed by Clive Wilkinson Architects.

The dot-com boom at the end of the 20th century inspired the development of creative, flexible work environments that encourage both individual and collaborative work, such as the 2005 Google Headquarters designed by Clive Wilkinson Architects.
Benny Chan/Fotoworks

1939
*Pope-Leighey House,
Alexandria, Virginia,
Frank Lloyd Wright*

*University of Colorado at Boulder
(1921–39), Charles Z. Klauder*

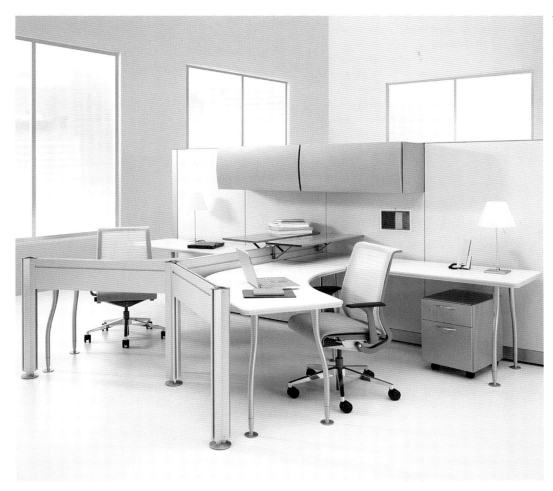

To accommodate the mixed individual and collaborative work environment of the early 21st century, furniture manufacturers such as Steelcase offer small, personal workstations that can be clustered near shared spaces for group efforts. *Steelcase*

Once the lid had been lifted off the Dilbert box, office architecture began to take on a more playful and dynamic character. With new design trends, such as "hot desking," "touchdown workstations," and "free address," workers traded in their personal workstations for better shared places, better technology, and, in some cases, better paychecks because of real estate savings. In the best of the nonterritorial offices, the creative class arrived each morning in search of the right work setting for the task at hand—a library, a fireplace, a porch swing, a figurative sandbox. Residential and resort imagery crept into office building design and into major interior renovations. Michael Brill described the new office as a "red carpet club" of opportunities for collaborative and creative work.

Yet the loss of a personal workstation had its drawbacks: The importance of references and work tools was underestimated; personalization and pride of place were undermined; and the sheer confusion of where your colleague or work team might be was very real. In *Workplace by Design: Mapping the High-Performance Workscape*, Franklin Becker and Fritz Steele argue for "caves and commons"—small, personal workstations clustered near diverse, shared-work environments—as the best of both worlds. Furniture manufacturers again responded quickly. Steelcase, for example, came out with Personal Harbors, followed by the Pathways line, to create each individual's cave in a dynamic cluster of commons.

In *The New Office*, Francis Duffy of DEGW elaborates on the need for diverse workplaces to support the range of individual and collaborative tasks in various organizations. He highlights the differences between what he calls "hive, cell, den, and club" work tasks: "Hives are characterized by individual, routine-process work with low levels of interaction and low autonomy," such as data entry, telesales, or banking operations. "Cell offices accommodate individual, concentrated work with little interaction," such as the work of accountants, lawyers, and computer scientists. "Den offices are associated with group work, typically highly interactive but not necessarily highly autonomous," such as design, advertising, and media work. Finally, club organizations are for "open-ended problem-solving," requiring "constant access to a vast array of shared knowledge . . . work that is both highly autonomous and highly interactive," such as creative advertising, media technology development, and management consulting.

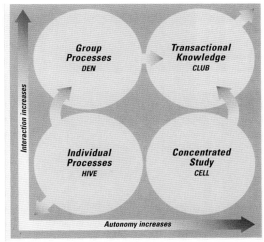

Francis Duffy of DEGW promotes inclusion of diverse work spaces—hive, cell, den, and club settings—in an office building to support a range of individual and collaborative tasks. *Courtesy Francis Duffy, DEGW; reprinted with permission from* The New Office *(Conran Octopus, 1997)*

1940
Federal government
requisitioned the new AIA
headquarters building behind
the Octagon; the building was
returned to the AIA in 1948

Founding of the Society of
Architectural Historians

Crow Island School,
Eliel & Eero Saarinen and Perkins,
Wheeler & Will

Rockefeller Center (1932–40),
New York City,
planned by Raymond Hood

The Triple Bottom Line

While the business community has become increasingly aware of the importance of thinking beyond the bottom line to embrace both the individual and the collaborative productivity of people, it has only just begun to address the triple bottom line, which links profit, people, and planet. In the past several decades, the architecture community has become increasingly active in promoting sustainable strategies in the design and construction industries, from the formation of the AIA's Committee on the Environment in 1990 to the Institute's call, in 2005, for all new and renovated buildings to be carbon neutral by 2030. The imperative for a carbon-neutral architecture to reduce our impact on our planet's life-support systems—its air, water, and soils—has never been more evident.

Architect Ken Yeang argues that environmentally sound high-rises are critical to the future of our growing population centers, and that climate responsive innovation is key. In his book, *Green Skyscraper*, he outlines the delight possible in those built around daylight, natural ventilation, and the vertical regeneration of landscape. One of the most striking success stories in this pursuit is the Commmerzbank (1997) in Frankfurt, Germany, designed by Foster + Partners and Arup. The design team introduced a series of stacked, six-story atriums with wind-protected openings to the outside to provide each office worker in this 56-story building with fresh air, daylight, and windows that open onto a garden. This building, which also features reconfigurable underfloor networking and displacement ventilation, demonstrated that a high-rise office need not be sealed and pressurized.

New solutions to building shapes and skins have resulted from the pursuit for greater daylighting and more effective thermal systems. The Hoffman-LaRoche Building (1996) in Nutley, New Jersey, by the Hillier Group, and the new New York Times Building (2007) by Renzo Piano reveal the power of daylighting strategies as image generators and place makers. The Gap headquarters (1997) in San Bruno, California, by William McDonough + Partners captures the importance of the fifth façade—the roof—in ensuring multidirectional daylighting

(Opposite) Foster + Partners and Arup designed the 1997 Commerzbank building in Frankfurt, Germany, to incorporate access to gardens, natural ventilation, and daylight in every office in the high-rise building. The structure is a striking example of the rising interest in green design. *Nigel Young, courtesy Foster + Partners*

The green roof of the 1997 Gap Headquarters, San Bruno, California, designed by William McDonough + Partners, admits daylight and moderates cooling loads and runoff. *©William McDonough + Partners*

1941
National Gallery of Art,
Washington, D.C.
John Russell Pope

The Octagon *published*
Elisabeth Coit's landmark
study of public housing

without glare or overheating but with quality views for all. The Gap's undulating green roof also moderates storm-water runoff. Dynamic mirrors mounted on the roof of the Genzyme Center (2003) in Cambridge, Massachusetts, by Behnisch, Behnisch & Partner, track the sun and drive daylight deep into the building's atrium so that more than 75 percent of all employees are able to work with natural light alone. Moreover, Genzyme's double-skin façade supports natural ventilation and the highest level of thermal insulation possible in a curtain wall building. And Lloyd's of London (1986) by Sir Richard Rogers was one of the earliest examples of airflow windows, in which overheated indoor air is drawn through the façade for heat dissipation before returning to the mechanical plant. As a result, the waste heat from the core creates a thermally neutral façade, thereby eliminating the need for perimeter heating.

(Opposite) At the Genzyme Center (2003) in Cambridge, Massachusetts, designed by Behnisch, Behnisch, & Partner, roof-mounted mirrors track the path of the sun and drive daylight into the atrium, making it possible for most of the occupants to work using only natural light. *©Anton Grassi/Esto*

Advances in technology have made possible new methods by which buildings can more efficiently modulate their interior temperatures. Sir Richard Rogers designed a triple-glazed façade for Lloyd's of London (1986) that doubles as an air plenum: heat from the return air dissipates through the exterior cladding.
Romilly Lockyer/Getty Images (interior); ©Joe Fletcher/Esto (exterior)

The use of cascading energy systems, in which energy from a variety of sources is transferred within a building to meet its energy needs, can significantly reduce the energy required to run an office building, as demonstrated in the 4 Times Square Building (1999) Fox and Fowle Architects designed for the Durst Organization.
©Jeff Goldberg/Esto, courtesy FXFOWLE Architects

Leading designers are pursuing "ascending environmental conditioning strategies." Beginning with the fundamental principles of "architecture unplugged," building form, orientation, shading, and mass are optimized to minimize the cooling loads and maximize the number of months for which no cooling would be needed. Then, passive strategies—such as cross-ventilation, stack ventilation, fan-assisted ventilation, and night ventilation—are introduced. This is followed only as necessary by evaporative or desiccant cooling, in which the humidity of the air is moderated to keep temperatures comfortable at lower energy demands. Only as outdoor temperatures or indoor heat loads exceed the capability of these systems are absorption cooling and the more energy-intensive refrigerant cooling introduced. The last stage of this ascending conditioning system is the task-ambient, central-system refrigerant cooling that is pervasive today throughout the United States.

One gutsy new project pursuing mixed mode and ascending HVAC strategies is HOK's National Oceanic and Atmospheric Administration building (scheduled for occupancy in 2011) in Hawaii. An inventive, adaptive use of old hangars linked by a new facility, the architectural HVAC system will rely on wind scoops to pull in fresh air; filter, dehumidify, and hydronically cool without fans; and feed the conditioned air directly to the individual workstations through underfloor plenums. The resulting building will be a landmark both for its architectural quality and for its zero energy goals.

A complement to "ascending" energy strategies is the introduction of "cascading" energy systems, in which small fuel cells, biomass or gas turbines, wind towers, and photovoltaics might be bundled for the building's power generation. The waste steam from power generation would then be used to drive the desiccant, then absorption, and then refrigerant air conditioning systems; and finally the resulting waste heat from cooling systems would be used for space heating and hot water. FXFOWLE Architects' 4 Times Square Building (1999) for the Durst Organization used energy cascades to dramatically reduce the 70 percent energy losses that are typical today.

The focus on the triple bottom line has encouraged many nonprofit organizations to pursue a host of environmental strategies in the design of their new headquarters. The Natural Resources Defense Council (1989) and Audubon Society (1993) buildings in New York City, both by the Croxton Collaborative Architects, retained existing structures instead of building new ones, thereby recognizing the value of the energy embodied in the materials and assemblies and the craftsmanship of historic buildings. Celebrating high ceilings and windows, high-quality materials, and mixed-use urban neighborhoods, these two historic renovations created rejuvenating places to work and catalyzed the commitment of the nonprofit world to environmentally smarter revitalization instead of new construction.

Croxton Collaborative Architects' environmentally friendly retrofits of the 1989 National Resources Defense Council headquarters (far left) and the 1993 National Audubon Society headquarters, both in New York City, are seminal projects in the movement toward sustainable architecture.
©Otto Baitz/Esto, courtesy Croxton Collaborative Architects (far left)
©Jeff Goldberg/Esto, courtesy Croxton Collaborative Architects

The SmithGroup's design for the Philip Merrill Environmental Center (2000) in Annapolis employs a number of design techniques and technologies to reduce fresh water consumption.
Courtesy SmithGroup

Other nonprofits, motivated by their underlying mission, have approached the design of their offices as an opportunity to demonstrate sustainable watershed planning and water-use efficiency. One such example is the SmithGroup's Philip Merrill Environmental Center (2000), headquarters of the Chesapeake Bay Foundation in Annapolis, Maryland. A host of measures, from composting toilets to roof forms and large cisterns that collect rainwater, results in a 90 percent reduction of fresh water use as compared to a conventional office building of similar scale. Attention is equally focused on landscape water conservation and runoff water quality, with low-water planting (xeriscaping), permeable surfaces, and bio-retention storm-water treatment to ensure filtration of site water before it meets the Chesapeake Bay. This first LEED platinum office building also achieves outstanding lighting, thermal, and indoor air quality and the highest level of user satisfaction among offices across the United States.

Offices of the Next Generation

As this short history demonstrates, architects have continually and proactively responded to the changing needs of the workforce over time. They have led ongoing innovations in design for the "gold collar" employee, creating work environments that support individual productivity, health, motivation, and comfort. They have created visionary work settings for the high-tech generation, celebrating exposed, flexible infrastructures designed for change and invention. They have created environments for multidisciplinary collaboration in socially and technologically dynamic spaces. And they have led the march toward a carbon-neutral society, with innovations in building form and surface, in passive conditioning integrated with active systems, in historic rediscoveries, and most critically in the rediscovery of the importance of design in the context of regional climates, watersheds, transit, and mixed-use communities. As we go forward, architects are well positioned to lead multidisciplinary teams—from collateral designers, engineers, manufacturers, and building managers to biologists, ecologists, and other research scientists—early in any design process to ensure that the breadth of design issues is met so that the next generation of workplaces will maximize a business's profits while truly supporting its people and the planet as a whole. ●

Louis Henri (Henry) Sullivan, FAIA

Richard Guy Wilson, Hon. AIA

Louis Henry Sullivan/Art Institute of Chicago

The decision to award the Gold Medal to Louis Sullivan in 1944 (the war prevented its actual presentation until 1946) — 20 years after his death — indicates a major revision in thinking about what was important in American architecture. The citation honored him for his originality and rebellious spirit and for his contributions to commercial architecture. To architects, critics, and historians, Sullivan's major works were those of the 1880s and 90s, including the Wainwright Building (1890) in St. Louis and the Guaranty Building (1894–95) in Buffalo, both office high-rises, and the large Carson Pirie Scott Department Store (1896–1902) in Chicago. By the 1940s, these buildings had become icons of genuine American architecture, praised for their clarity of structure and avoidance of historical styles. According to some, Sullivan had invented the skyscraper. His intricate ornamental system, which covered many of his building surfaces, did not receive the same acclaim in this period of Modernism.

Louis Henry (he later changed it to the French "Henri") Sullivan was born in 1856 in Boston and learned architecture through the apprentice system in several offices, including those of Frank Furness of Philadelphia and William Le Baron Jenney of Chicago. He briefly attended the Ecole des Beaux-Arts in Paris. Although a critic of the school's Classicism, he adopted its compositional methods. Back in Chicago, Sullivan entered in partnership with Dankmar Adler and prospered, designing a host of large commercial buildings that received high praise in the architecture press of the time. He also began to write and speak on architecture, coining famous phrases such as "form follows function."

Sullivan began to slip after Adler left the partnership in 1896. His high-handed imperial manner, depressive moods, and excessive drinking scared away clients and, from 1903 onward, his work was largely confined to a few small, rural town banks in the Midwest. The Farmers' National Bank (1906–1908) in Owatonna, Minnesota, is his finest "jewel box," heavily loaded with ornament and decoration inside and out.

Sullivan had always aspired to be an architectural theorist, and he increasingly devoted himself to articles and books such as *Kindergarten Chats* (1901–02), *Autobiography of an Idea* (1924), and *A System of Architectural Ornament According with a Philosophy of Man's Powers* (1924). Henry Whitaker, editor of the *AIA Journal* at the time, supported several of these. Hence, Sullivan remained known to the architecture community even though he had little work and was an anathema to most clients. He died in poverty in 1924.

Sullivan's rehabilitation emerged in the 1930s and 1940s, when he was identified as the progenitor of a new American commercial high-rise architecture and entered into the history books. His elaborate and sinuous ornamentation, which he viewed as one of his most important contributions, was devalued and considered an interesting mistake at best. Likewise, the small-town banks were considered an inconsequential afterthought. But times change and today Sullivan's ornament is admired as one of his most important elements, and his small-town bank is recognized as unique and bringing art to rural America. Frequently the most impressive structure in a small town, Sullivan's banks helped create and maintain a quintessential image of "Main Street USA."

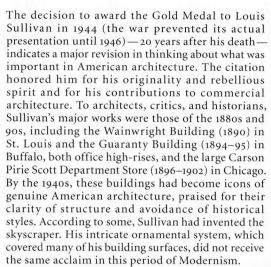

Sullivan spent his last years designing banks for small, rural towns. Perhaps the best of these buildings is the Farmers' National Bank, Owatonna, Minnesota.
Historic American Buildings Survey, Library of Congress

GOLD MEDALIST, 1992

Benjamin Thompson, FAIA

Andrew Brodie Smith, PhD

Benjamin Thompson (1918–2002) was one of the original eight architects who founded The Architects Collaborative (TAC) in Cambridge, Massachusetts, in 1945. For more than 20 years, he was an integral force in TAC, a firm dedicated to the principle that the combined efforts of a design team are greater than the sum of the contributions of individual members, even though many of its members, including Walter Gropius, were internationally recognized figures in their own right. Thompson left TAC in 1966 to establish his own firm, Benjamin Thompson & Associates (BTA), also in Cambridge. The firm's Design Research Headquarters (1969) in Cambridge was the 2003 recipient of the AIA's Twenty-five Year Award. Thompson designed the building to house the home-furnishing retail store he founded to promote the idea that "art is everywhere."

Thompson is best known for his creation and re-creation of grand, vibrant, urban "festival marketplaces." Working with the Rouse Company, the now legendary developer, BTA oversaw the restoration and revitalization of Harborplace (1974) in Baltimore, Faneuil Hall (1978) in Boston, South Street Seaport (1983) in New York, Bayside Marketplace (1987) in Miami, and Jacksonville Landing (1987) in Jacksonville, Florida. Working with other developers, BTA was also responsible for the revitalization of two Washington, D.C., historic landmarks, Union Station and the Old Post Office. By introducing new retail and entertainment spaces to previously neglected historic districts, these projects energized the urban experience of their respective cities. They demonstrate Thompson's belief that "architecture is not pure structure or sculpture, but a setting for an enriched way of life."

Boston's Faneuil Hall Marketplace, designed by Benjamin Thompson & Associates, became a model of adaptive historic rehabilitation for many cities. ©*Steve Rosenthal*

Kevin Roche, FAIA

Andrew Brodie Smith, PhD

Kevin Roche immigrated to America from Ireland in 1948 after having received a BArch degree from the National University of Ireland. He enrolled in a graduate course at the Illinois Institute of Technology, where he met Ludwig Mies van der Rohe and Eero Saarinen. Roche joined Saarinen's firm in 1950. From 1954 until Saarinen's death in 1961, Roche was the firm's principal associate in design. With the help of Joseph Lacy and John Dinkeloo, Roche completed 10 major projects that were unfinished at the time of Saarinen's death, including the St. Louis Arch and Dulles International Airport.

Roche and Dinkeloo went on to establish a model and highly prolific partnership of their own. Roche was the designer, and Dinkeloo focused on the technologies of construction. One of the partnership's best regarded projects is the Ford Foundation Headquarters (1968) in New York City, an office complex of glass, granite, and steel designed around a dramatic 12-story atrium. The building received the AIA's Twenty-five Year Award in 1995. In its letter of nomination, the AIA Design Committee called the building "seminal in its reversal of the 'tower-in-a-plaza' convention that had previously been established by the Seagram Building." The Roche-Dinkeloo partnership was particularly successful in attracting commissions for corporate headquarters, including those for John Deere, Union Carbide, General Foods, J.P. Morgan, Conoco, and Deutsche Bank.

Roche was awarded the Pritzker Architecture Prize in 1982. Critic Paul Goldberger called the 1993 Gold Medalist "one of the most creative designers in glass that the 20th century has produced."

President Bill Clinton presented the AIA Gold Medal to Kevin Roche at the White House.

At the Ford Foundation Headquarters (1968), New York City, windows open to the 12-story atrium from all floors.
Courtesy Kevin Roche John Dinkeloo and Associates

Meet Me in Downtown St. Louis

Jen DeRose

AIA St. Louis teamed up with 14 local firms to launch the Washington Avenue Windows Project. In front of the large storefront windows of the chapter's renovated headquarters are, left to right, Michelle Swatek, executive director; Debra Boussum, business and bookstore manager; and Peggy Johnson, administrative assistant. *Courtesy AIA St. Louis*

Bond & Wolfe Architects filled the 15-foot-tall windows of the 555 Washington Avenue building with historic photographs and sketches of the Eads Bridge construction. The installation remained up for months. *Courtesy AIA St. Louis*

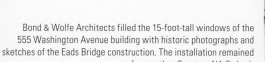

"You're on the air," said Charles Brennan, host of KMOX radio station in St. Louis. He had just announced the upcoming May 2004 home tour of the Washington Avenue Loft District and was now taking a call from AIA St. Louis Executive Director Michelle Swatek. The chapter had recently moved from the mezzanine to the street level of the historic 1898 Lammert Building on Washington Avenue. Committed to downtown, where their headquarters had been located since 1956, the chapter had engaged the local firm of Ottolino Winters Huebner to reconfigure part of the ground floor into an inviting, modern interior with large storefront windows.

The space has become a "landmark" for members, where they can enjoy lectures and receptions, meet up with colleagues before heading off to a business lunch, or simply browse through architecture publications in the chapter's bookstore. Tourists can pick up free maps of downtown to help them explore the burgeoning district, and local law firms and public advocacy groups take advantage of the bright and cheery conference room.

But Swatek was not calling the radio station to revel in the AIA's new digs, which Brennan praised as an example of the revitalization effort underway downtown. Instead, she wanted to offer additional support. The local AIA pledged to refurbish the district's window displays in time for the tour, just three weeks away. Live, and with the city listening, the Washington Avenue Windows Project was born. While the tour highlighted loft apartments that had been converted from abandoned garment warehouses, a number of the storefronts in the 10-block district remained neglected. Unused spaces included a wholesale shoe manufacturer, a residential building under development, and the back area of a restaurant.

AIA St. Louis teamed up with 14 local firms to install art that would reflect the Gateway City's history and architecture in these and other windows.

With $5,000 secured from Downtown STL, a nonprofit organization working toward the city's revitalization, AIA staff and volunteers began by visiting local businesses and real estate agents to secure permission and access. The team quickly cleaned up windows, installed lighting, and took measurements and photographs. By the end of the first week, each firm was given the documentation, $250 dollars per project, and the remaining two weeks to create an installation for one or more windows.

The 30 finished windows stretched for eight blocks and remained up for weeks. In one window, Bond & Wolfe Architects reconstructed the 1874 Eads Bridge that spans the Mississippi. In another, architects at Christner depicted the pavilions and playgrounds of Forest Park, which was the site of the 1904 World's Fair. In a third, Hellmuth Obata + Kassabaum installed a series of photographs of passersby from the knees down.

"The project added energy and excitement to the street-level experience, generating even greater interest in our ongoing downtown development," says St. Louis Mayor Francis G. Slay.

For the chapter's own window display, the staff showcased books on residential and loft construction and hung a welcome sign—something they couldn't have done in their previous location. Those wandering past could also read the words of Winston Churchill, permanently etched in the storefront glass. Speaking to AIA St. Louis's mission, and perhaps to the rebirth of downtown, it reads, "First we shape our buildings. Thereafter, they shape us."

1944
AIA membership reached 5,000

Louis Henri Sullivan, FAIA,
received the AIA Gold Medal
(posthumously)

With the advent of the third millennium, the office takes on a less dominant role as work begins to attach itself to people more than place. The workplace is now more mobile and connected to a global network of creation, production, and logistics. To compete on a global scale, companies arm their employees with mobile tools such as cell phones, laptops, and wireless e-mail devices. The advancement in handheld and small network devices has created a workforce that communicates in ways never seen before. Virtual people networks, a new language using instant paging, and a proliferation of data management devices have freed workers from their desktop computers. The workplace of today is more about access to data than access to their desks.

As work has attached itself more to people than place, companies such as Starbucks have created a third place where work happens. It is an ironic return to the predecessor of the contemporary office—the 18th-century coffeehouse culture of London. The "third place" is not the office, not the home, but everywhere in between. The most successful of these are active, engaging places that leverage the migration of work in a more social direction. Third places have shown up in the office as coffee bars; in between as coffee shops, Internet cafes, and airport hot-desks; and in unexpected spaces, such as religious facilities that want to attract the next generation of workers.

The lines between work, play, and life continue to be blurred, and our workplaces have been blurred along the way. The workplace of the future will continue to change and react to generations that become more tied to virtual rather than physical workplaces. Successful models will be those that drive innovation by turning information into knowledge. The engine for the knowledge economy will be the worker who competes in a complex global arena and works with teams that cross time, space, and communication boundaries. The new workplaces of the future will be virtual environments where workers create virtual identities and work on projects that may never physically exist.

Third Spaces

Roy Abernathy, AIA, and Clark Malcolm

Today's workplace is more about access to people and data than to a traditional office. Third spaces—from Internet cafes to airport hot-desks—are not the office, not the home, but everywhere in between. ©*Comstock Select/Corbis*

12

America on the Move

David A. Daileda, FAIA

Transportation in all its modes embodies the uniquely American ideal of Manifest Destiny, which in the mid-19th century was seen as an obligation to expand west across North America. Families and other migrants set out in wagons, enduring hardship, in search of fertile land or following rumors of gold. By the late 19th century, the transcontinental railroad connected both coasts and changed the American perception of time and distance. Then, in the early 20th century, mass production of the automobile facilitated migration away from cities and their rail hubs. Finally, air travel made distance a completely manageable obstacle. Today, transportation is still a driving force in the U.S. economy as well as a linchpin in the economies of all industrial nations.

While transportation itself focuses on movement, architecture related to transportation marks the points of arrival and departure. Initially, structures were built at these locations primarily to maintain vehicles and store cargo awaiting transit. However, as the number of passengers grew and modes of travel expanded, so did the need for buildings that could process, control, protect, and serve travelers. From the single-room train depots of the 19th century to the increasingly complex airport terminals of today, architects have created facilities to accommodate the needs of the traveling public and the nation as a whole.

In the process, transportation structures have become some of the best-known forms in the country, often serving as symbols of their communities: We immediately associate the Golden Gate Bridge with San Francisco. The tensile-fabric peaks of Denver International Airport's roof mimic the Rocky Mountains. And who doesn't know that Grand Central Terminal is in New York City?

On the Rails

Rail travel emerged as the first convenient, dependable system of public transportation. As the country expanded, the transcontinental railroad became its life blood, carrying people and goods coast to coast, and rail stations soon appeared in almost every town. Because of the railroad's importance to the community, these buildings were often at the core of the town's activity and thus centrally located. As a result, development of other commercial activities grew up around terminals, creating what has become known as "downtown."

(Opposite) Architects Irving F. Morrow and his wife, Gertrude C. Morrow, are largely responsible for the design of San Francisco's Golden Gate Bridge, which opened for traffic in 1937. *Justin Sullivan/Getty Images*

A translucent, tensile membrane roof covers the atrium of the Denver International Airport's Jeppesen Terminal (1995), designed by Fentress Bradburn Architects. *©Carol Highsmith Photography*

As the railroad depot was the major point of entry for most travelers—giving them their first, and lasting, impression of the town—railroad companies and their architects strove to create images that would impress and attract visitors. In the heyday of rail travel, cities became known by the size and style of their railroad depot. The 1894 Romanesque terminal by Theodore Link became a nationally recognized symbol of St. Louis, as did the 1925 Neoclassical station in Chicago, completed by Graham, Anderson, Probst & White after the death of the original architect, Daniel Burnham. The grand architecture and increasingly bold engineering combined to create some of the nation's largest and most elegant buildings, and the passengers who used them became participants in the celebration of travel. "In catching or meeting a train, one became part of a pageant—actions and movements gained significance while processing through such grand spaces," writes Richard Guy Wilson in his 1983 book, *McKim, Mead & White Architects*. This New York firm designed Pennsylvania Station (see page 61) in that city, considered by many to be one of the nation's most impressive terminals.

Support buildings for storage and maintenance also began to appear in towns and cities around the country. Many of the railroads hired architects to design prototypes for such facilities. These were typically sturdy brick structures, architecturally detailed with ornamental cornices and molded brick window jambs that gave them an air of richness and permanence. These secondary structures were often among the best designed and maintained facilities in the community.

(Opposite) The St. Paul firm of Reed and Stern bested more prominent architecture firms to win the 1903 design competition for New York City's Grand Central Terminal (1913). Reed and Stern later teamed up with the New York firm of Warren and Wetmore to complete the design. Grand Central has twice survived plans to demolish it, and in 1978 the U.S. Supreme Court upheld its designation as a landmark by the city's Landmarks Preservation Commission. *©Carol Highsmith Photography*

Local architect Theodore Link modeled the St. Louis Union Station (1894) after Carcassone, a walled, medieval city in southern France. *©Carol Highsmith Photography*

Construction of Chicago's Union Station began in 1913 but was not completed until 1925. World War I, strikes, and labor shortages delayed the project originally designed by Daniel Burnham and completed by the firm of Graham, Anderson, Probst & White upon Burnham's death. *©Bettmann/Corbis*

On the Road

While railroads could only directly serve cities and towns that grew up along its tracks, bus and automobile transportation was far less constrained. By the 1930s, sleek buses had become a popular means of transportation, and the Moderne bus depot, which symbolized this new era, served as an eye-catching advertisement for the new service. With rounded shapes, porthole windows, and shiny metal walls, the Art Deco flavor of many such depots conjured up a feeling of movement and freedom. Wischmeyer, Arrasmith & Elswick of Louisville, Kentucky, applied this design vocabulary to a number of depots in the East and Midwest.

The ultimate form of road travel, however, is the automobile, an invention that feeds the American desire to go wherever and whenever we want. This country's love affair with the automobile drove the rapid development of the state and federal highway systems. As these systems grew, the idea of a system of national "superhighways" took shape, culminating in the plan for the Interstate Highway System. Construction of this dedicated network of high-speed routes connecting all regions of the continental United States began in 1956.

As a marvel of engineering, the interstate system continues to be more about function than form. However, its designers have often added subtle touches that transform an otherwise literal expression of structure into sculptural expressions of strength and confidence. This is visible in the carved shapes, inlaid patterns, and ornamental details of many bridge and roadway piers, retaining and acoustical abatement walls, and railing members. As well, the designs of many critical features, such as tunnels or major bridges, celebrate the freedom made possible by the highway system. Boston's Leonard P. Zakim Bunker Hill Bridge (2002), conceived by Swiss bridge designer Christian Menn and engineered by Theodore Zoli of HNTB, is a striking example.

1946
Kaufmann House,
Palm Springs,
Richard Neutra

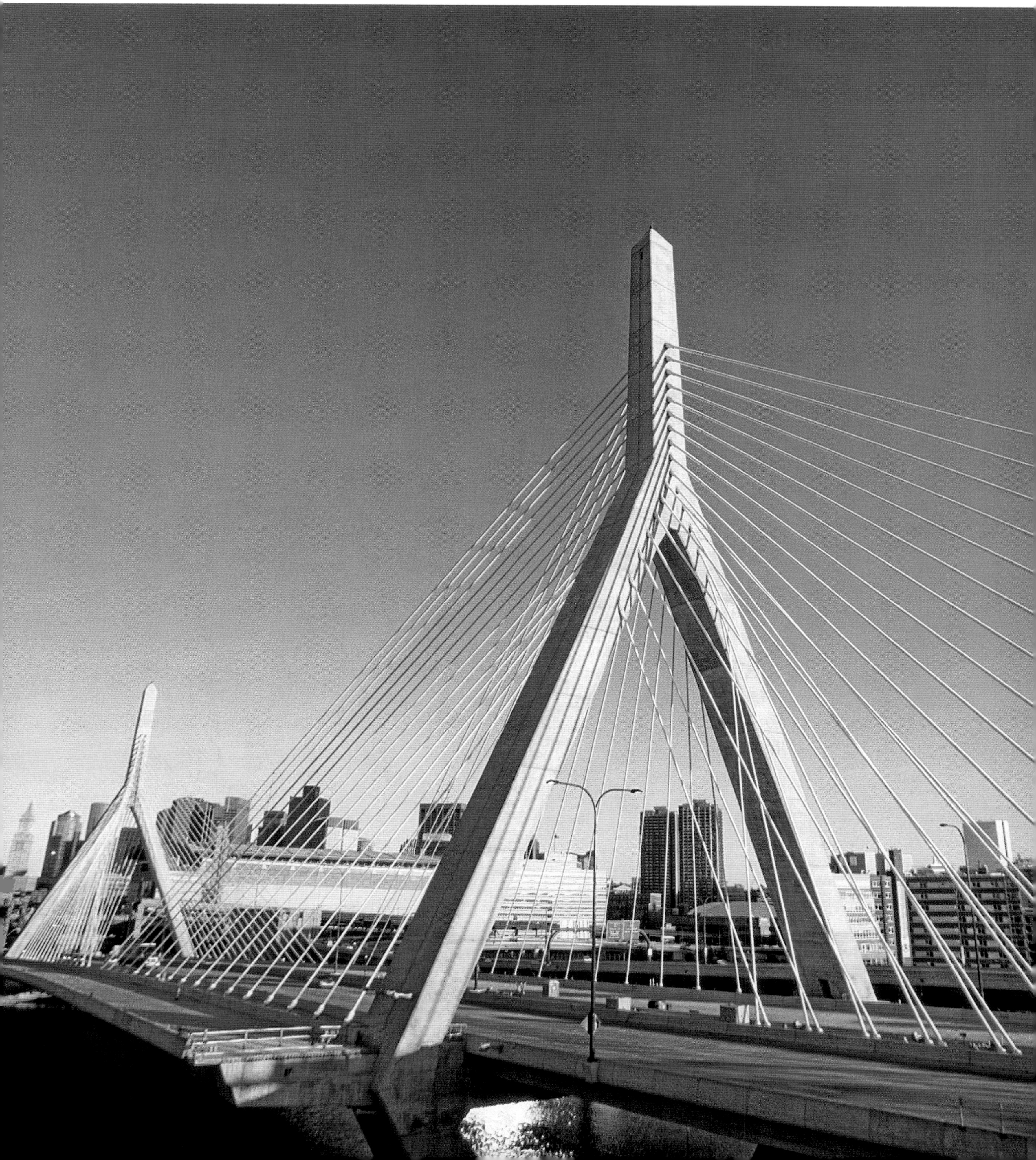

The pedestrian tunnel in Helmut Jahn's United Airlines Terminal One (1987) at O'Hare International Airport in Chicago features a moving walkway and a neon light sculpture titled *Sky's the Limit*, by artist Michael Hayden. *©Carol Highsmith Photography*

A mile-long avenue of retail shops and eateries lines the central circulation spine of Ronald Reagan Washington National Airport (1997), designed by César Pelli. *Courtesy Metropolitan Washington Airports Authority*

1947
Hearst Castle,
San Simeon,
Julia Morgan

Delano Hotel,
Miami Beach,
B. Robert Swartburg

Stuyvesant Town,
New York City,
Irwin Clavan and
Gilmore D. Clarke

Eliel Saarinen, FAIA,
received the AIA Gold Medal

In the Skies

In contrast to the railroads' beginnings, air travel very quickly focused on the passenger as its primary concern. Advances in aircraft design made during World War II were rapidly incorporated into the production of larger, more efficient passenger airplanes. These air ships joined (before they replaced) the glamorous ocean liner as symbols of American modernity and prosperity. As they designed airports to accommodate travelers, architects began to draw on the shapes and materials of flight to glorify the experience of travel. Forms mimicking airfoils, sleek metal skins, and round windows were all major parts of the vocabulary of early airport buildings. Glamour permeated terminal interiors, which featured elegant and highly stylized restaurants and lounges.

With the introduction of the jet engine in the early 1960s, air travel reached the peak of its sophistication, motivating airport architects to respond in kind. Arguably the most famous symbol of the thrill of flight is Eero Saarinen's TWA terminal at JFK International Airport in New York, completed in 1962. "This is surely one of the world's most dramatic airline terminals. Few straight lines here: approached head on, its curving contours uncannily suggest a bird in flight. Inside, the main lobby's soaring, swooping walls; its carefully modeled staircases; seating areas; and many other features are a blend of graceful sculptural forms selected to suggest the excitement of the trip," writes Sylvia Hart Wright in her 1989 *Sourcebook of Contemporary North American Architecture: From Postwar to Postmodern*.

In his design for Dulles International Airport outside of Washington, D.C., which opened in 1962, Saarinen did more than utilize the terminal's form to portray the idea of flight. He redeveloped the entire passenger experience, reinforcing a sense of elegance and sophistication. Following check-in, passengers gathered in "mobile lounges" docked at the terminal. At flight time, instead of walking through the concourse, across the tarmac, and up the mobile stairs, passengers rode in the lounge, which delivered them directly to the airplane. Air travel had reached its golden age.

As the 20th century moved toward its fourth quarter, rapid advancements in aircraft technology and size opened the door to more and more air travelers. Flying was evolving from a luxury to a necessity, forcing terminals to become more efficient and focus on processing passengers rather than on the overall traveler experience. Architects concentrated on function, sacrificing iconic symbolism in the name of efficiency. The truly spectacular buildings of this era were the huge hangar buildings designed to house the new jumbo jets.

In 1987, however, Chicago architect Helmut Jahn brought new life to the airport terminal. His design for United Airlines Terminal One at O'Hare International Airport combined the efficiency of the modern terminal with an exposed steel structure and a soaring barrel vault, thereby creating a dramatic, light-filled gallery that returned the feelings of grandeur and style to air travel. Witnessing the success of Terminal One, airlines combined forces with airports to produce a series of passenger-oriented terminals at other major airports, from New York to St. Louis to Los Angeles.

As with the railroad depots of the last century, communities began to see the airport terminal as an important economic and cultural asset. Communities wanted their airports to be welcoming and make a positive impression on visitors. Louisville, Kentucky, made a redesign of its outdated 1960s airport terminal a critical element in the city's broader plan to transform its image to attract high-tech business. Gensler's 2002 renovation featured a central ceiling light diffuser, glass holdrooms, added amenities, and updated finishes.

Today, mounting passenger volume, coupled with added security measures, means that passengers spend increasingly longer periods in the terminal, a reality that has required transportation authorities to incorporate a variety of amenities—from food courts and shopping malls to cultural offerings—in passenger terminals. In Pittsburgh, the 1992 terminal by Tasso Katselas Associates was dubbed the "air mall" because of the quantity and variety of its retail stores. Here the traveler is greeted by a multistory collection of shops and restaurants, which spreads from the central hub at the intersection of the concourses to multiple gateside locations throughout the terminal. Shops and restaurants line the gathering areas and surround the circulation nodes of Denver International Airport's Jeppesen Terminal (1995), designed by Fentress Bradburn Architects. Similarly, the César Pelli–designed terminal at Ronald Reagan Washington National Airport, which opened in 1997, includes a mile-long avenue of retail shops along its central, dome-covered circulation spine.

After the events of 9/11, the magnitude of security requirements has placed an added strain on the designer's ability to create facilities that are open, elegant, and pleasing, while simultaneously safe and secure. New terminals currently being developed in New York by Gensler and in Indianapolis by HOK will be among the first to deal with these new constraints.

Across Town

As cities grew and suburbs began to appear, the need for people to move into, out of, and around their hometown increased. These transportation needs were initially met primarily through trolleys and streetcars, then buses, run by private companies. In the late 1850s and 1860s, rail lines running on elevated tracks began to appear in larger cities. As the suburbs grew, commuter rail and, later, bus lines were established to carry people to and from the city. Around the turn of the 19th century, as congestion got worse, private entrepreneurs in cities such as Boston and New York began burying their rail lines underground, and subways were born. In many places, all these elements were eventually consolidated into municipal transit systems controlled by the local government.

Santiago Calatrava's popular design for the PATH station at Ground Zero is a central element of the plan to rebuild the World Trade Center site. *Courtesy Lower Manhattan Development Corporation*

1948
Founding of the International
Union of Architects,
Lausanne, Switzerland

Equitable Building,
Portland, Oregon,
Pietro Belluschi

Tremaine House,
Montecito,
Richard Neutra

Charles Donagh Maginnis, FAIA,
received the AIA Gold Medal

The numerous stations built along aboveground rail lines began as simple platforms and sheds, but as the systems developed and modernized, the stations expanded to include waiting rooms and other amenities. As subway ridership grew, the design of the underground stations became more elaborate. In New York, the underground network of tunnels not only connected travelers to the platforms but also to an increasing number of shops and services. In the late 1960s, as Washington, D.C., began to plan a subway system, President Lyndon B. Johnson called for one that was "attractive as well as useful" and that included architecturally significant stations. To comply with this request, architect Harry Weese created an overall architectural vocabulary that is employed for all the system's facilities. The coffered vault of the underground stations is the highlight of this award-winning design and has been an inspiration for other systems throughout the world.

Subway stations have often proved to be a catalyst for development in their immediate vicinity. Like the railroad terminals of yesteryear, they became hubs of activity within the larger city. And, as with other transportation structures, these facilities are now seen as representative of the larger community. In New York, for example, the PATH subway station below the World Trade Center site in New York is currently being redeveloped with architect Santiago Calatrava. His design for the underground platforms and service areas penetrates the surface through a sculptural skylight that evokes open wings, representing what Calatrava calls "the hole in the sky" created by the loss of the twin towers. This new transportation hub will be a key commuter portal to lower Manhattan and, hopefully, a stimulus to rebirth at Ground Zero.

Combining access to both intercity and intracity transportation systems, intermodal facilities are now increasing in numbers across the country. Initially, these facilities linked bus and commuter rail terminals in a single facility to enable passengers to pass easily from one to the other. This concept has continued to grow and expand. The redeveloped lower Manhattan PATH terminal will connect commuters not only to several subway lines and local buses but to a ferry terminal as well. Similarly, a new facility currently planned for Miami International Airport will connect airline passengers to rental car facilities, as well as to the city's bus and commuter rail system.

St. Louis Union Station is typical of a trend toward adaptive use of older transportation buildings. It ceased operation as a train terminal in 1978 and, after extensive renovations, reopened in 1985 as a mixed-use complex of shops, offices, restaurants, and a hotel.
©Richard Cummins/SuperStock

1949
Founding of the
National Trust for
Historic Preservation

Baker House Dormitory,
MIT,
Alvar Aalto

Glass House,
New Canaan, Connecticut,
Philip Johnson

Eames House,
Pacific Palisades, California,
Charles and Ray Eames

Frank Lloyd Wright
received the AIA Gold Medal

All Aboard

More and more, Americans see transportation elements woven with commercial, retail, and service functions in multiuse facilities. Are these transportation buildings with commercial amenities, or commercial buildings with a transportation component? In reality, they are both.

Meanwhile, as modern facilities are brought on line, older transportation buildings are finding new life as well. Because of their generous size and prominent location in the community, old railroad buildings have been turned into retail, commercial, and entertainment facilities. Two famed Union Station buildings, in St. Louis and Washington, D.C., provide excellent examples of this phenomenon. In 1985 Union Station in St. Louis reopened as a mixed-use complex, including offices, shops, restaurants, and a hotel. Through implementation of a public/private partnership, Union Station in Washington, D.C., was restored and redeveloped in 1988. The revitalized facility includes a shopping mall and a host of dining venues, as well as stations to serve both Amtrak and the city's Metro system.

But what of the future? Rising energy costs coupled with increased concern for the environment are two of society's greatest long-term challenges. Many solutions to these problems must come from the transportation industry itself—more fuel-efficient vehicles, better mass transit, and alternative sources of energy. Transportation architecture will have to respond to these challenges as well. The current trend in integrated facilities will grow, allowing people to use their time and energy more efficiently, and intermodal facilities will increase in both number and size, making mass transit more convenient and more efficient. Already, sustainable ideas are being integrated into the design of many transportation facilities. One of note is the 2006 Terminal A project at Boston's Logan International Airport, designed by HOK, which has received LEED certification.

The resource and environmental challenges of the future will not change our ingrained need to travel. But as new methodologies are developed that permit us to keep moving without polluting, architects will create facilities that support these modes, while celebrating the communities these iconic structures will undoubtedly come to represent. ●

(Opposite) After years of decline, including a roof collapse caused by rain damage, Daniel Burnham's Union Station (1907) in Washington, D.C., was restored as a mixed-use retail and transportation center, which opened in 1988. *©Carol Highsmith Photography*

HOK's Terminal A (2006) at Logan International Airport, Boston, is the first airport terminal in the United States to receive LEED certification. *Assassi Productions, courtesy HOK*

GOLD MEDALIST, 1962

Eero Saarinen, FAIA

Jayne Merkel

The construction of large-scale models was an integral part of Saarinen's design process. In the photo, Saarinen (left) and Kevin Roche work on a model of the TWA Terminal.

Saarinen described his design for Dulles International Airport (1962), Chantilly, Virginia, as a "huge, continuous hammock suspended between concrete trees." The building received the AIA's Twenty-five Year Award in 1988. *Ezra Stoller/©Esto*

The soaring, swooping concrete of Saarinen's TWA Terminal (1962) at JFK Airport evoked the romance and excitement of travel and the arrival of the jet age. An icon of Modern design, the terminal was one of Saarinen's last projects. *Ezra Stoller/©Esto*

When he was awarded the Gold Medal in 1962, Eero Saarinen was the youngest architect to receive that honor. Although it was not obvious at the time, Saarinen's death in 1961 at age 51 marked the end of an era. The period of postwar optimism, faith in technology, and dramatic economic growth that his work embodied ended with the disillusion brought on by the Vietnam War and the riots in American cities a few years later.

Rival AIA Gold Medalist Philip Johnson was wont to complain that "Eero has all the best clients." He was pretty much right, partly because Saarinen, who was born outside Helsinki in 1910, had had a head start as the son of Finnish-American early Modernist Eliel Saarinen. On his own, however, he had won a number of competitions, and this and the fact that he was so accommodating brought him many clients.

Saarinen was asked to design buildings for the most powerful, innovative, and prestigious institutions of his time — General Motors; IBM; Bell Laboratories; CBS; Lincoln Center; MIT; Yale; the universities of Michigan, Pennsylvania, and Chicago; and the U.S. government. He participated in three federally sponsored competitions (for the unbuilt Smithsonian Art Gallery in Washington, D.C.; the St. Louis Memorial Arch; and the American Embassy in London), and he won all three. His airport designs — for the TWA Terminal at JFK Airport in New York, the Athens International Airport, and Dulles Airport outside the nation's capital — symbolized the experience of flight when flying was still an adventure. Saarinen also designed one of the few Modern churches that struck a chord with the public: His North Christian Church (see page 327) in

Columbus, Indiana, has been copied (usually badly) perhaps more than any other building of its time.

Eero Saarinen was an aesthetic and technical innovator at a time — before the advent of Postmodernism — when new imagery and technology were still considered thrilling. With the help of his gifted partner, John Dinkeloo, he developed modular systems and neoprene gaskets for curtain walls at the General Motors Technical Center in Warren, Michigan; mirrored glass for Bell Laboratories in Holmdel, New Jersey; Cor-ten steel for a structural frame and shading devices at the John Deere Building in Moline, Illinois; and new vaulting techniques for the Yale Hockey Rink and the TWA Terminal. Every building he designed was different because every building was designed specifically to meet the needs of a particular client and site. As a result, Saarinen never developed a recognizable style and his work was difficult to recognize and classify. This is one reason he was ignored soon after his death. Another was that his work so aptly expressed the spirit of its time that, when times changed, his zealous, lively architecture did not mean as much to people as it had before.

Although Saarinen was only interested in creating architecture that rose to the level of art, he was so committed to serving clients that he would redesign projects as many as half a dozen times, even after construction had begun. He showed the same loyalty to the people in his office, where 60 talented architects from all over the world were willing to work extraordinary hours when nine to five was the norm because, as one employee put it, "He never, simply never, let you down."

Santiago Calatrava, FAIA

Vernon Mays

Almost single-handedly, Santiago Calatrava has revived the notion that public infrastructure can be both highly utilitarian and supremely beautiful. Through a body of work that includes nearly 50 pedestrian and vehicular bridges—flowing structures that evoke both delicacy and strength—he marries structure and form in poetic ways.

Calatrava was born on July 28, 1951, in Valencia, Spain, where he attended primary and secondary schools. In 1974 he earned an architecture degree at the Escuela Tecnica Superior de Arquitectura in Valencia and then pursued graduate study in civil engineering at the Swiss Federal Institute of Technology (ETH) in Zurich. He received his PhD in 1981.

Even before he had built his first bridge, Calatrava was displaying a structural virtuosity that invited comparisons to Robert Maillart, the widely admired, early 20th-century Swiss designer of streamlined bridges and viaducts. Hints of Calatrava's talent emerged in 1985 with his proposal for the Caballeros Footbridge, an asymmetrical structure with a fanlike array of cables. But it was his competition-winning entry for the Bach de Roda Bridge in Barcelona (1987) that thrust him onto the international stage.

Calatrava's reputation was well established by the time he completed the Campo Volantin Footbridge (1997) in Bilbao, Spain, whose single parabolic arch supports a sinuous steel-and-glass deck. Like many of his designs, it transcends mere structural concerns by embracing considerations such as railings, lighting, and connections to pedestrian networks. When Calatrava received the Gold Medal in 2005, it was the sculptural quality of his work—not the engineering—that his peers likened to well-orchestrated music.

Suzanne DeChillo/© The New York Times

(Left) Calatrava's 700-foot long, cable-stayed Sundial Bridge (2004), Redding, California, is paved with granite and translucent glass. A steeply angled, 217-foot-tall pylon supports the deck and also acts as a sundial. Surrounded by mountains and forest, the pedestrian footbridge crosses the Sacramento River. *©Alan Karchmer/Esto*

(Below) The glass-decked Campo Volantin Footbridge (1997), Bilbao, Spain, spans the Nervión River and links the downtown with Frank Gehry's Guggenheim Museum Bilbao.
Barbara Burg + Oliver Schuh/www.palladium.de

1951
Wayfarers Chapel,
Palos Verdes, California,
Lloyd Wright

Lake Shore Drive Apartments,
Chicago,
Mies van der Rohe

Farnsworth House,
Plano, Illinois,
Mies van der Rohe

GRASS ROOTS

Designing the Washington Metro

Zachary M. Schrag

The Metro team: front row, left to right, Harry Weese, National Capital Transportation Agency administrator Walter McCarter, National Capital Planning Commission chair Elizabeth Row; back row, Stanley Allan (in glasses), Bob Reynolds

Visitors to Washington, D.C., are often astonished by the stations of Metro, the rapid transit system serving the nation's capital and its suburbs. Instead of the dense grid of girders and low ceilings that define the older subways of New York, Boston, and Philadelphia, Metro features grand, coffered vaults, soft lighting, and palatial vistas. This design emerged from President John F. Kennedy's call for architecture that could "provide visual testimony to the dignity, enterprise, vigor, and stability of the American Government." In response, the federal National Capital Transportation Agency decided to hire an architecture consultant directly, rather than leave the task to its engineering consultant, De Leuw, Cather. Kent Cooper, Eero Saarinen's project manager at Dulles International Airport, directed the 1966 design competition that selected Harry Weese, a young Chicago architect of growing prominence.

Weese knew little about subways, so on winning the contract, he and two members of his firm, Bob Reynolds and Stan Allan, traveled to Europe and Japan to tour existing systems. Weese returned to advocate for a "public approach," one that would emphasize civic dignity rather than mere utilitarian considerations or advertising opportunities. In July 1966, he produced preliminary sketches that emphasized spacious, vaulted stations. By late 1966, at the prodding of the De Leuw, Cather engineers, he was calling for boxes for the shallow, cut-and-cover stations and Gothic vaults of exposed granite for the deeper stations.

In April 1967, these plans came before the Commission of Fine Arts, which reviews plans for public architecture in Washington. In acrimonious hearings over several months, commissioners Gordon Bunshaft and Aline Saarinen (Eero's widow)

ridiculed Weese's designs as "a refined coal mine shaft" and "awfully folk art." Finally, in September, Bunshaft sketched his idea for a station, a rounded vault similar to Weese's original proposal. Weese acquiesced, letting Bunshaft believe he had suggested something new. With the shape of the stations settled, Weese added coffers to the vault. These appealed to him primarily for structural reasons, but their evocation of classical and neoclassical precedents helped win over critics. Weese hired William Lam to work out the dramatic indirect lighting and Massimo Vignelli to design the system's signage.

The basic design of a prototype station was just the beginning, for each of the system's 83 stations (later expanded to 86) required its own architectural design to fit local conditions. This design work was farmed out to other architecture firms, each receiving guidance from Harry Weese & Associates. Aboveground stations sheltered passengers with a variety of canopies, ranging from concrete gull-wings that evoke the tunnels to peaked glass roofs that recall the colonial architecture of Northern Virginia. Underground stations built during later phases employ a simplified coffer design to reduce shadows, thereby brightening the platforms below.

A handful of stations have dramatic exits, but Weese's hopes for escalators with views of the Washington Monument and the Capitol dome were vetoed by the National Park Service and the Architect of the Capitol, who feared intrusion on their turf. Nevertheless, the stations remain, in the words of the *AIA Journal* of 1975, "awe-inspiring" yet "manageable." Each day, hundreds of thousands of Metro riders enjoy a touch of efficient monumentality, courtesy of Harry Weese and his team.

Harry Weese's coffered ceiling vaults and William Lam's design for indirect lighting create a dramatic effect in the Washington Metro's underground stations.
Larry Levine, courtesy Washington Metropolitan Area Transit Authority

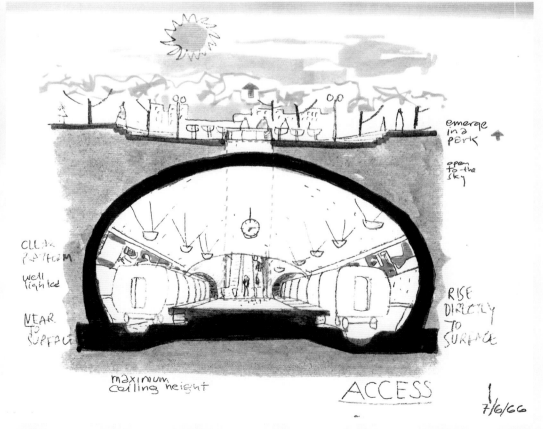

Weese's first design proposal for a Metro station, dated July 1966, emphasized spacious, vaulted stations.
Courtesy Harry Weese and Associates

Caesar Cottage,
Lakeville, Connecticut,
Marcel Breuer

Bernard Ralph Maybeck
received the AIA Gold Medal

The Fort Pitt Bridge Project

Ingrid Spencer

In 2001 the Pennsylvania Department of Transportation (PennDOT) was engaged in an $84 million reconstruction plan for Pittsburgh's Fort Pitt Bridge, opened in 1959 and famed as "the best way to enter an American city." In June 2001 the agency announced it was moving forward with plans to construct a solid concrete safety barrier on the deck of the 1,212-foot-long bridge, which stretches over the Monongahela River and offers views of Pittsburgh's hillsides, rivers, and skyline. The proposed design was blocky and would obscure the views, but this was not an issue for PennDOT, which cared primarily about safety and cost efficiency.

AIA Pittsburgh, the Riverlife Task Force (a public/private advocacy group), and other local organizations and citizens had a different view. With the help of city and Riverlife leaders — and a $93,000 grant from the Heinz Endowments — AIA Pittsburgh executive director Anne Swager, Hon. AIA, assembled a task force of architects, landscape architects, city planners, and PennDOT engineers to design a barrier that would provide an aesthetic solution and also meet the agency's safety standards and budget. Approved in the spring of 2002, the new 50-inch-tall barrier features concrete below and steel railings above. Because this alternate design necessitated a change order, construction for the more attractive barrier was more costly than PennDot had originally budgeted, but the state agency agreed to absorb this increase.

There's an irony here — the process of constructing the barrier, which was completed in September 2003, has broken down the virtual barriers that existed between government agencies and the architecture community in Pittsburgh. A precedent has been set, and city residents can look ahead to more inclusive planning and more thoughtful, aesthetically pleasing public architecture in the years to come.

The view from Pittsburgh's Fort Pitt Bridge would have been severely compromised if PennDOT's barrier proposal had been implemented, as illustrated on the lefthand side of this computer-generated photomontage. The alternative conceptual design, shown on the right, permits sweeping views of the city's skyline.
Tomas Gulisek, AIA, Burt, Hill

13

Design Excellence
Building a Public Legacy

Edward A. Feiner, FAIA
Marilyn Farley, Hon. AIA

During the last quarter of the past century, American architects, both inside and outside government, rediscovered their traditional role as leaders in the ongoing national dialogue about the future of this nation. Whether the subject was environmental protection, historic preservation, accessibility, sustainable design, or the rebuilding of America's infrastructure, architects became active participants in efforts to improve our quality of life as well as our country's competitive standing in the world economy.

(Opposite) Completed in 2000, the Lloyd D. George U.S. Courthouse in Las Vegas was the first federal building designed according to the new security criteria issued by GSA after the 1995 bombing of the Alfred P. Murrah Federal Building in Oklahoma City. Mehrdad Yazdani of Dworsky Associates served as design principal on the project. *©Peter Aaron/Esto. Courtesy GSA Design Excellence Program*

Among these notable efforts, architects in the 1990s began once again to seriously address the important role that the design of public buildings plays in generating the perceptions and attitudes held by citizens toward their government. The Design Excellence Program, established by the U.S. General Services Administration (GSA) in 1994, reflects this greater appreciation for the symbolic power of public architecture.

The Face of a New Nation

Architecture has historically provided physical form to the technology as well as the societal and cultural values of civilizations. Buildings that housed important institutions, whether state or church, expressed the power and prestige of the occupants. The Founding Fathers of the United States—a new nation heralded as the world's first experiment in popular democracy—understood the role of architecture in communicating a strong and positive relationship between the people and their new government, as well as enhancing their mutual respect. These leaders also understood architecture as a medium through which the fledgling government could demonstrate its commitment and permanence to the American people and its legitimacy to foreign countries.

"In the early period of Federal architecture you saw a particular style that embraced certain ideals . . . certain principles of quality, of understanding the human experience and expressing those in a way that really reflects the ideals of our culture," explains Ray Huff, AIA, principal of Huff + Gooden Architects of Charleston, South Carolina. That style, of course, was Classical architecture, which had developed in ancient Greece and Rome alongside the flowering of democracy. The Founding Fathers, several of whom had traveled in Europe, felt this kind of architecture would best represent their far-reaching democratic goals for the new government. Jefferson himself drew heavily on Classical forms and details when he designed the Virginia State Capitol in Richmond and the University of Virginia in Charlottesville.

Through at least the first 150 years of American history, the Federal model became the precedent for design excellence across the nation at all levels of government, from county courthouses to city halls. And, by and large, public officials continued to demand high-quality design and construction for public buildings.

1952
*Formation of the AIA College
of Fellows approved at the
convention*

*Lever House,
New York City,
Gordon Bunshaft/SOM*

*Unité d'Habitation,
Marseilles,
Le Corbusier*

A Period of Pragmatism

After World War II, a new period of technological change ultimately called into question the whole concept of permanence. During the postwar period, the focus of attention shifted away from the development of community to the development of individual welfare and prosperity. As a consequence, priorities in government moved toward nonphysical programs that were designed to provide greater choice for the individual. The government also became more concerned with global competitiveness in technology and science, so national efforts such as the space program became the primary focus of federal funding. Less attention and value were given to cultural and symbolic initiatives, such as art and music appreciation.

Public architecture faltered significantly in this postwar period, as demand floundered for quality and permanence in the design and construction of buildings. Federal agencies adopted a very pragmatic objective: the cheaper and faster, the better. This period was also characterized by suburban sprawl, the decline of America's great cities, and the concept of a "disposable society." It should come as no surprise that many of the more holistic movements that we regard with great respect today, including historic preservation and sustainable design, were born in large part out of a reaction to this period of expediency.

The Robert C. Weaver Federal Building in Washington, D.C., headquarters of the U.S. Department of Housing and Urban Development, was the first federal building in the United States to use precast concrete as the primary structural and exterior finish material. Completed in 1968, it was designed by Marcel Breuer. *Ben Schnall, Smithsonian Archives of American Art, courtesy GSA Center for Historic Buildings*

Yale University Art Gallery,
New Haven,
Louis Kahn

Cerebral Palsy School,
Fresno, California,
David H. Horn and
Marshall D. Mortland

Town Hall,
Säynätsalo, Finland,
Alvar Aalto

Auguste Perret, Hon. FAIA,
received the AIA Gold Medal

Seeds of Change

A few bright moments shone during this otherwise bleak era of public architecture. Some federal buildings, for example, were designed by notable midcentury Modern architects: The John F. Kennedy Federal Building (1966) in Boston, designed by Walter Gropius; the Robert C. Weaver Federal Building (1968) in Washington, D.C., by Marcel Breuer; and the Chicago Federal Center (1974) by Mies van der Rohe are arguably three of the finest works in North America by these legendary architects.

Even more significant, although only on paper, was the penning of "The Guiding Principles of Federal Architecture" in 1962 by Daniel Patrick Moynihan, then a young assistant labor secretary. (Fourteen years later, the citizens of New York elected Moynihan to the U.S. Senate, and he subsequently became America's most recognized advocate for design excellence.) This one-page essay was included in an innocuous "Report to the President by the Ad Hoc Committee on Federal Office Space," which went to President John F. Kennedy. The principles set forth a national design policy through which the federal government would "provide requisite and adequate facilities in an architectural style and form which is distinguished and which will reflect the dignity, enterprise, vigor, and stability of the American National Government."

The principles stated that "major emphasis should be placed on the choice of designs that embody the finest American thought" and that "specific attention should be paid to the possibility of incorporating into such designs qualities which reflect the regional architectural traditions of that part of the nation in which buildings are located." The principles also noted that "where appropriate, fine art should be incorporated in the designs, with emphasis on

The graceful curves and bright red color of Alexander Calder's "Flamingo" sculpture provide a stark contrast to the steel-and-glass design of the Chicago Federal Center by Ludwig Mies van der Rohe, completed in 1974. *Taylor Lednum, GSA Design Excellence Program*

1953
*United Nations building,
New York City, Le Corbusier,
Oscar Niemeyer, Howard
Robertson, et al., with
Harrison and Abramovitz*

*William Adams Delano,
FAIA, received the AIA Gold Medal*

The JFK Federal Building, designed by Walter Gropius of
The Architects Collaborative and completed in 1966, houses several
federal agencies in Boston. *Carol M. Highsmith Photography/GSA,
courtesy GSA Center for Historic Buildings*

Designed by The Miller/Hull Partnership and completed in 1997, the
U.S. Border Station at Point Roberts, Washington, replaced an outdated
1950s-era facility. The exposed structure and ductwork of the current
station reflects the imagery of the sheds and other utilitarian structures
along the Point Roberts waterfront. The first station commissioned under
GSA's Design Excellence Program, it received several design awards,
including an AIA National Honor Award in 2000.
James F. Housel, courtesy GSA Design Excellence Program

the work of living American artists"; "the development of an official style must be avoided"; "design must flow from the architectural profession to the government and not vice versa"; "the government should be willing to pay some additional cost to avoid excessive uniformity in the design of Federal Buildings"; and "the advice of distinguished architects ought to, as a rule, be sought prior to the award of important design contracts." The "Guiding Principles" touched broadly on subjects such as accessible design, design competitions, landscape architecture, and urban design and planning.

GSA, which at the time held the lion's share of federal real estate and the associated construction programs, did attempt to implement many of these concepts. Most notably, GSA's Art in Architecture Program became a national model for every level of government across the nation. Cities such as Chicago, Seattle, and New York supported the use of public funds to commission public art. As for architecture, however, the nuances of Moynihan's principles were never fully understood, let alone consistently applied through an established and clearly defined government program.

During the 1970s, the National Endowment for the Arts, in conjunction with GSA, convened the National Design Assemblies, and GSA also established its first design awards program. The assemblies brought together notable designers and government officials to discuss ways of improving the quality of design in the federal government. As a result, GSA formed advisory panels of private-sector architects to assist the government in the architect-selection process. These panels, however, eventually faded from view as the participants realized that their impact was severely compromised. The value of the panels was also diminished by government procurement rules that prevented the distinguished architects who served on these panels from competing for federal building commissions. In addition, GSA's design awards program was discontinued after a short period for lack of interest.

The next real glimmer of hope came in 1985, almost a quarter of a century after Moynihan drafted his principles. This time, the emphasis was placed on interior design to achieve a high-quality workplace. Attempts were also made to take advantage of new technologies to improve both design and building performance.

Travelers must stop at the checkpoint below a 600-foot-long arc of glass and metal at the U.S. Customs and Immigration Center at Rainbow Bridge in Niagara Falls, New York. The concave side, which faces Canada, echoes elements of the bridge; the convex side faces a park on U.S. soil. The curved span is supported on either end by base buildings constructed of the same bluestone that forms the ledge of the falls. Designed by Hardy Holzman Pfeiffer, the project was completed in 1998 and earned a Federal Design Achievement Award from the National Endowment for the Arts in 2000. *©Michael Moran*

The sweeping, concave glass wall of Boston's John Joseph Moakley U.S. Courthouse embraces HarborWalk, a public waterfront promenade. Art by Ellsworth Kelly provides extra drama in the 108-foot-high, skylit rotunda and other interior spaces. Henry N. Cobb and Ian Bader of Pei Cobb Freed & Partners were the lead designers on the project, which was dedicated in 1998. It received a Federal Design Achievement Award from the National Endowment for the Arts in 2000.
©1998 Steve Rosenthal, courtesy GSA Design Excellence Program and the Honorable Douglas P. Woodlock, Judge, U.S. District Court of Massachusetts

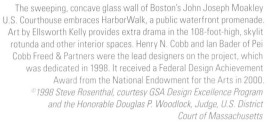

Design Awards Program Reawakened

In 1988 the executive office of the president initiated a government-wide program that called for all agencies to develop strategic plans to define their mission and tactical initiatives to support the plans. Independently, the judicial branch of the government subsequently announced that it required all federal courthouses across the country to be rebuilt over a period of five years due to a dramatic increase in the courts' workload and an assessment that existing facilities were insufficient in terms of security and technology. It was most opportune that this important GSA client was demanding excellent design and construction.

In 1990, in response to this large new building program and the expressed interest of the judicial branch in design quality, a few of the career professionals at GSA felt it was time for change. As a first step, they wanted to assess the results of the earlier, albeit minimal, efforts to encourage good design. To accomplish this, they reestablished the GSA Design Awards Program, which had been dormant for more than 17 years. The awards program recognized completed projects by GSA in several design categories, including historic preservation and new construction. Through the awards program, the GSA staff, which included architects and other design professionals, hoped to raise the profile of quality design in the agency and indelibly associate the subject with the political leadership of the agency. Many leaders and members of the American Institute of Architects, along with other design professionals, participated in the design awards juries and subsequent public ceremonies.

The first two jury chairs—Hugh Hardy, FAIA, in 1990, and Eugene Kohn, FAIA, in 1992—were not impressed with the design submissions for the new buildings. "There was little to choose from," says Hardy. And in his report to the GSA leadership, Kohn noted that the new projects "looked too commercial" for public buildings. In general, the juries believed that the designs were too rooted in the past. As a result, most of the projects recognized by the first two juries focused on historic preservation.

The jurors for the 1990 and 1992 Design Awards felt strongly that architects have a higher responsibility to deliver excellent design for public buildings than for any other building type, because these structures represent some of the most important functions of society and are meant to last hundreds of years. Yet authentic contemporary architecture was not being explored for these projects. The leaders of the GSA Design Program questioned whether this was because public clients were reluctant to leave the comfort of traditional architecture or because talented architects lacked interest in government projects.

The glass and aluminum frame curtain wall and massive interior atrium of the Sandra Day O'Connor U.S. Courthouse in Phoenix allow abundant light into the building and extend the public space of the entry plaza into the courthouse itself. The building, completed in 2000, was designed by Richard Meier & Partners. *©Scott Frances/Esto, courtesy GSA Design Excellence Program*

1954
AIA presented a stained glass
window, designed by Francois
Lorin, to Chartres Cathedral, as a
tribute to the builders of the great
French cathedrals

*Octagon stable modified to serve
as the AIA's library*

*Publication of two seminal books
on architects and architecture:
The Architect at Mid-Century,
ed. by Turpin Bannister, and
Conversations with Architects, ed.
by Francis R. Bellamy*

Crafting a New Vision

Many professionals inside and outside of government already understood that a different process of procurement—the manner in which architecture and engineering services are obtained—was key to facilitating change. Architects were selected based on the credentials and experiences of the entire design team rather than on the talent of the lead designer. Recognizing this, the design and procurement offices of GSA jointly sponsored a "procurement workshop" in 1993 to identify alternative strategies. Representatives from the AIA and the National Endowment for the Arts participated, as well as more than 30 of the nation's foremost design leaders from the private sector. Margaret McCurry, FAIA, who attended the workshop, recalled in an interview 10 years later that "those were very exciting, hopeful times."

The major reforms that came out of this fruitful workshop became the basis for the Design Excellence Program. This new approach to the selection of architects and engineers and to the review of proposed designs places high value on creativity and innovation. In addition, the new procurement process first examines the "design talent" of the lead designers and their respective firms before evaluating the entire team. It also streamlines the application process by drastically reducing the amount of paperwork. Both GSA and the firms benefit from the subsequent reduction in preparation and review efforts. This, in turn, has attracted a broader and more diverse talent pool to the program, and, for the first time, women and minority architects have been selected to lead the design of a significant number of federal buildings.

In addition, highly valued design professionals can now serve as peers for government projects while competing for other federal projects where there is no conflict of interest. In fact, much of the success of the Design Excellence Program can be attributed to its National Register of Peer Professionals. As of 2005, GSA's peer registry listed more than 530 private-sector professionals, including distinguished architects, engineers, designers, public arts administrators, design educators, and critics from across the nation. The range of disciplines represented attests to the holistic approach of the program. Peers are appointed for two-year terms by GSA's commissioner of Public Buildings Service, who is responsible for all GSA public buildings nationwide. The peers take on many critical roles as educators, advocates, provocateurs, consensus builders, and communicators. Their advice and insights are invaluable to those responsible for the design of the projects. Given the large number of participants on the registry, conflicts of interest rarely occur, and the workload is spread widely among the peers.

In 1996, with the support of AIA officials and the ongoing interest of Senator Moynihan, the commissioner of Public Buildings Service established the position and authority of the "chief architect" within GSA. A civil servant, the chief architect is charged with advocating for design excellence in the federal building program, developing design policies and standards that enhance the federal presence in communities, and recommending the approval of designs of all new GSA federal projects to the agency's leadership.

(Opposite) In the October 9, 2000, issue of the *New Yorker*, architecture critic Paul Goldberger described the Alfonse M. D'Amato Courthouse and Federal Building in Central Islip, New York, as a "building that bears not the slightest resemblance to a classical courthouse yet has the formality and public grandeur that we associate with classical architecture." The project, designed by Richard Meier & Partners, was completed in 2000.
©Scott Frances/Esto, courtesy GSA Design Excellence Program

Natural light for all of the offices and laboratories was critical to the design of the Harvey W. Wiley Federal Building, home of the U.S. Food and Drug Administration's Center for Food Safety and Applied Nutrition in College Park, Maryland. The project, by Kallmann McKinnell & Wood Architects, was completed in 2001 and received a GSA Design Award in 2002.
Robert Benson Photography, courtesy GSA Design Excellence Program

From Vision to Reality

The implementation of Design Excellence initiatives sparked renewed interest among design professionals to work on public buildings. "What interested me," says New York architect Richard Meier, FAIA, who received the Pritzker Architecture Prize in 1984 and the AIA Gold Medal in 1997, "was the recognition that this was a program that clearly looked to architects to achieve excellence in design . . . There was an intention to create buildings in which the government could be proud and which symbolized a change of attitude [toward] the building of government buildings." Today, a wide range of firm types—from small, signature design firms to some of the largest architecture practices in the nation—vie for the chance to design federal buildings and courthouses. Underscoring this dramatic turn of events in public architecture, George Hellmuth, FAIA, president of HOK, observed in the video *Of Our Time* that, today, young talented designers are "scurrying" to work on federal projects because they know the work will be interesting.

In addition to attracting top architects, the Design Excellence Program has fostered an ongoing, thoughtful discourse among designers on the desired qualities of public architecture. For example, New York architect and GSA peer Laurie Hawkinson says that "public projects should be something that make us look twice . . . be surprising . . . lift our spirits . . . sing . . . and give us something back." Joan Goody, FAIA, principal of Goody Clancy in Boston, a juror in the 1990 Design Awards Program and an active peer participant, spoke about the new direction in public buildings this way: "Striving for a spirit of openness and dignity is enormously important. It's what really gives us pride and makes landmarks." Describing his view of public buildings and courthouses in particular, Henry Cobb, FAIA, founding partner of Pei Cobb Freed & Partners in New York, says that "every building should have a freshness to it,

1955
Trenton Bath House,
Ewing, New Jersey,
Louis Kahn

Notre-Dame-du-Haut,
Ronchamp,
Le Corbusier

Bavinger House,
Norman, Oklahoma,
Bruce Goff

Kresge Chapel,
MIT,
Eero Saarinen

Willem Marinus Dudok, Hon. FAIA,
received the AIA Gold Medal

With most of its office space two stories underground, this satellite operations facility (2006) for the National Oceanic and Atmospheric Administration, Suitland, Maryland, designed by Thom Mayne of Morphosis, blurs the distinction between building and landscape. The underground work area features garden courtyards and is daylit by 21 skylights. *©Maxwell MacKenzie, courtesy GSA Design Excellence Program*

and if you get that, then you communicate to the American people that the federal government is evolving and these buildings are here to serve people, not to overawe them or make them feel small and insignificant."

By 2005 GSA managed more than 300 million square feet of space located in every state and territory of the nation. It is estimated that, to date, more than 100 federal building projects have been developed or renovated under the Design Excellence Program, a few of which are illustrated on these pages. Every one of these projects has become a symbol of the federal government's commitment to rebuilding cities and their central business districts.

Success breeds success: The mayor of New York City recently announced New York's own Design Excellence Program, based on many of the precepts pioneered by the federal program. Other states, cities, and international governments are recognizing the newly rediscovered value of quality public architecture and how it can enhance and, in some cases, restore a positive relationship between a community and its respective government.

The Design Excellence Program has introduced a new era in public building, thanks to the many architects and other private-sector professionals who are creating a new architectural legacy that Americans—both today and in the future—can point to with great pride. ●

The 138-foot-long great hall of the U.S. Courthouse (2002) in Hammond, Indiana, is designed to reflect the tradition of great public spaces but with a modern spirit. Glass walls at both ends of the building fill the hall with natural light. Henry N. Cobb and Ian Bader of Pei Cobb Freed & Partners led the design. *Jon Miller at Hedrich Blessing, courtesy GSA Design Excellence Program*

(Opposite) The new Federal Building (2006) in San Francisco, designed by Thom Mayne of Morphosis, is GSA's first naturally cooled building. *Taylor Lednum, courtesy GSA Design Excellence Program*

1956
Founding of the American Institute of Architecture Students (then called the National Architectural Student Association)

Architectural Record named Louis Sullivan's Wainwright Building and Carson Pirie Scott as two of the most significant buildings in the development of architecture

GOLD MEDALIST, 1986

Arthur C. Erickson, Hon. FAIA

Andrew Blum

The Canadian Modernist architect Arthur C. Erickson, Hon. FAIA, is a listener—to landscapes, materials, and the public. "We must be attentive to voices other than our own and seek to learn from them," he writes.

Born in Vancouver in 1924 into an artistic family deeply connected to the city's intellectual life, Erickson wanted to be a painter. As a teenager his work was exhibited at the Vancouver Art Gallery. During World War II, he studied Japanese in the Canadian Intelligence Corps and was posted to India and Southeast Asia, beginning a lifetime of travel. After studying architecture at McGill University, he stretched a one-year travel fellowship into a two-and-a-half-year journey "to the far corners of the earth, looking deeply into the heart of the human condition," as stated in his 1986 AIA Gold Medal citation, the first awarded to a Canadian.

Erickson's career has since been defined by his sense of cultural awareness embodied in inspiring forms. He was first launched onto the international scene in 1963 by his competition-winning entry (with Geoffrey Massey) for Simon Fraser University in British Columbia. The student unrest there in the late 1960s was a source of pride for Erickson, who saw it as proof that the architecture "turned the student body inward and made them socially conscious."

Erickson's architecture has helped define for Canada a new, cosmopolitan national identity that simultaneously embraces global cultures and local landscapes—an idea visible in the megastructure of the University of Lethbridge in Alberta, which hugs the prairie coulees; the aboriginal long house–inspired forms of the Museum of Anthropology in Vancouver; and, most publicly, in the quiet grandeur of the Canadian Chancery in Washington, D.C.

Arthur Charles Erickson / Courtesy Arthur Erickson Architectural Corporation

Arthur Erickson's Canadian Chancery (1990) in Washington, D.C., seamlessly blends Modernism and Neoclassicism, reflecting both I.M. Pei's East Building of the National Gallery of Art and other, more traditional federal buildings in the surrounding area.
©Paul Warchol Photography

Crown Hall,
Illinois Institute of Technology,
Ludwig Mies van der Rohe

Socony-Mobil building,
New York City,
Harrison and Abramovitz

Hiroshima Peace Center,
Japan,
Kenzo Tange

Price Tower,
Bartlesville, Oklahoma,
Frank Lloyd Wright

Clarence S. Stein, FAIA,
received the AIA Gold Medal

VIEWPOINT

Engaging the Public, One Person at a Time

Randi Greenberg

When U.S. District Judge Michael Hogan first filed a petition in 1989 for the construction of a new courthouse in Eugene, Oregon, he knew he had to go through the General Services Administration (GSA), which manages all construction and renovation of civilian-based federal buildings. At that time, however, the GSA's Design Excellence Program had not yet been established, so Hogan had no idea what kind of personal renaissance awaited him.

The selection of an architect for the new federal courthouse began with a six-person committee, of which Hogan was one, to whittle 30 submitted design portfolios down to five. From these, a panel of three—a dean of an architecture school and two architecture journalists—met in 1999 and made a unanimous decision: Thom Mayne of the Santa Monica–based firm Morphosis. Hogan was outraged, having assumed Mayne's unorthodox portfolio and his penchant for creating unconventional geometries of glass, concrete, and steel would be dismissed by the peer review. For more than four hours, the judge cross-examined the panel: "I wanted to understand what they saw. None of Thom's ideas remotely resembled what I believed was a courthouse."

Further research on Mayne's career did not improve Hogan's negative opinion of the Pritzker Prize–winning architect. The conservative judge discovered that the press routinely cast Mayne as the bad boy of L.A. architecture who was, self-admittedly, not keen on "pandering to clients" and was "committed to the autonomy of authority in architecture."

During their first meeting in a Washington, D.C., restaurant, Mayne recalls that something intuitive took place between himself and the judge over the night's spirited discourse. "This was the beginning of a process to let Mike know who I was," the architect explains. "I purposefully was provocative. I overemphasized my independence and capitalized

on my radical interests and philosophies." Hogan was refreshed by Mayne's approach, and both men left that evening feeling they had met a worthy collaborator.

The two professionals spent many weekends over the course of six years (the time it has taken to see the courthouse to fruition) discussing architecture—where it is currently and how it got there. For their first weekend together, Mayne, Hogan, and key members of their respective staffs met in a cabin on the Willamette River in Oregon. Mayne was armed with more than a thousand slides that showed the emergence of his career along with detailed explanations that articulated the logic of his work.

Hogan's architectural tutorials subsequently focused on the design development of courthouses. The judge originally—and predictably—believed any new courthouse should resemble the U.S. Supreme Court building, replete with columns, grand staircases, and stone statues. Mayne—who succinctly summarizes the conflicting principles of their respective careers with the observation, "Judges look at precedents; architects look to the future"—was undeterred. With guidance from Mayne, in the form of visits to Morphosis and excursions to courthouses abroad, including projects by Jean Nouvel and Richard Rogers, and explorations of design history on his own, Hogan's appreciation of Modern architecture grew.

In the course of designing the Wayne Lyman Morse Courthouse (2006) in Eugene, Mayne and Hogan jointly investigated the core ideas of what constitutes this building type and agreed on innovations that upheld respect for the institution of law. The resulting 270,000-square-foot structure, with its two-story glass plinth and three concrete volumes, will no doubt become a destination that does justice to both architecture and jurisprudence.

Judge Michael Hogan (left) and Thom Mayne, FAIA
Taylor Lednum, GSA Design Excellence Program

The Wayne L. Morse U.S. Courthouse (2006), in Eugene, Oregon, designed by Morphosis with the DLR Group, earned a Gold LEED® certification from USGBC and was chosen as an AIA/COTE Top Ten Green Project in 2007.
Courtesy GSA Design Excellence Program

14

Building the Foundations for Education

C. C. Sullivan

From little red schoolhouses with slates and chalk to today's laptop-ready classrooms, the physical form of U.S. education has evolved in tandem with changes in social ideals and government policies. The path, however, has not been linear. Sometimes the transformations were quick and dramatic, at other times they appeared more gradually; in some instances, the modifications hearkened back to earlier approaches, although at a more sophisticated level. Throughout much of this history, architects have had an important role in shaping our country's educational framework.

(Opposite) The University of Virginia embodied the democratic ideas of the new nation, particularly the importance of public education. Thomas Jefferson's design for an "academical village" centered around "The Lawn" became a model for numerous other colleges and universities. *Dan Addision, University of Virginia News Service*

European and American Precedents

An early exemplar of architecture for education in the United States is Thomas Jefferson's design for the University of Virginia (chartered 1819). Jefferson employed the European educational model and associated classical motifs he had seen on his travels. Palladian architecture allowed him to encode Western democratic ideals in brick and limestone at the university he founded, which began construction in 1817. By the time the Morrill Land-Grant Acts brought university systems to every state in 1862—making higher education more accessible—Jeffersonian Neoclassicism was virtually synonymous with excellence in learning. The main campuses of such universities as Vanderbilt (1910s) and Rice (1930s) were given shape and image by Jefferson's vision.

A less worldly outlook prevailed in colonial period schools, which were viewed as little more than places for Bible study and preparation for apprenticeship in the trades. By the early 19th century, however, the British-inspired Sunday School Movement spurred the creation of privately run Protestant schools with uniform lesson plans, mainly located in existing churches and private homes. The notion that a well-educated citizenry was vital to a growing democracy began to take root, leading by the 1840s to even more standardized and less class-oriented "Common Schools." Championed by American educator Horace Mann, these were the first government-sponsored schools in the modern sense. Lessons covered civic rather than religious topics in the first buildings dedicated solely to education for the primary grades.

In the latter half of the 19th century, two- and three-story brick school buildings served urban centers and their growing immigrant populations. The facilities were spare and utilitarian, many containing immense classrooms with as many as 65 students crammed on wooden benches breathing stale air and straining to see under dim lights. Late in the century, leaders of the Progressive Movement, seeking to cure the ills of industrialization, decried such "factories of learning." As a result, architects got their first real chance to help shape what was now being called the public school.

1957
AIA celebrated its centennial

Plaque placed at 111 Broadway, New York City, site of the first AIA meeting on February 23, 1857

U.S. Post Office issued a stamp honoring the AIA's centennial

National Gallery of Art exhibition, "One Hundred Years of Architecture in America"

Two Gold Medals were awarded: one to Louis Skidmore, FAIA, founder of SOM, the other to Ralph Walker, FAIA, for service to the profession. Walker's medal was a special design labeled the Centennial Gold Medal.

Albert Lane Technical High School, designed by Dwight Perkins and completed in 1910 in Chicago, exemplified a new approach to school design. Natural light and air were admitted through large windows, and auditoriums and gymnasiums that could also be used by the community were incorporated for the first time.
Chicago History Museum

The Beaux-Arts style was prominently used on many college campuses in the early 20th century, including the Main Building (1937) at the University of Texas at Austin, designed by Paul Cret.
Courtesy University of Texas at Austin

Publication of The AIA's First
Hundred Years, *by Henry Saylor*

*Paul Revere Williams became the
first African-American elected to
the AIA College of Fellows*

*Connecticut General Life Insurance,
Bloomfield, Connecticut,
Skidmore, Owings & Merrill*

*Monastery of St.-Marie de La
Tourette, Eveux-sur-l'Arbresle,
France, Le Corbusier*

*First Lutheran Church,
Boston,
Pietro Belluschi*

Changes in Style and Substance

The turn of the century brought new ideas in K–12 architecture, conceived by such architects as Chicago's Dwight H. Perkins. Trained at Burnham and Root and later head of his own firm, Perkins was named to lead his city's school architecture department, where he oversaw a serious reassessment of the conditions of the day. By 1910 new schools like Tilton Elementary and Albert Lane Technical High School treated pupils to modestly scaled, simply detailed buildings featuring natural materials and bright, airy classrooms with large operable windows. Perkins incorporated large auditoriums and gymnasiums into his plans as well, allowing schools to serve the broader community when school was not in session—an idea that influences facility planners to this day.

At the university level, Jefferson's "academical village" remained the dominant mode of planning well into the 20th century for private as well as some public institutions. Grounds were often divided into quadrangles bounded by residential and academic buildings. Architectural styles grew more eclectic, although still with historical references. Structures designed according to the Beaux-Arts style—a form of Neoclassicism—became the signature image for many established schools for years to come, including the 1917 Peabody College library by Edward L. Tilton for Vanderbilt University and the 300-foot tower of the Main Building at the University of Texas at Austin, designed by Paul Phillipe Cret in 1937. Other schools— including Bryn Mawr College, Duke University, and Notre Dame—adopted the Gothic style associated with Oxford and Cambridge. The resulting iconic look, dubbed "Collegiate Gothic" and forever associated with Charles Z. Klauder's work at Princeton, became virtually synonymous with top-notch academics. Schools in the western states explored Mediterranean vernacular styles that seemed better suited to their locales and climate. When faced with a massive expansion in 1917, for example, the University of Colorado at Boulder resisted pressure to adopt the East Coast's popular Collegiate Gothic; instead, Klauder proposed what resembled a rural Italian village set in the foothills of the Rockies. Other schools adopting similar imagery included the University of California at Los Angeles in the late 1920s.

When it expanded in 1917, the University of Colorado at Boulder (1921–39) chose not to use the Collegiate Gothic style popular in the East. Instead, the school accepted architect Charles Klauder's proposal for a campus resembling a rural Italian village.
Andi Fabri, UC Bolder

While these stylistic options are easy to discern, other less obvious but more profound changes—many of which laid the groundwork for the modern university—were beginning to take shape in the late 19th and early 20th centuries. The very concept of a "campus," for example, arose in describing Princeton's grounds, and quickly became universal. The idea of the research university was emerging as well. Modeled on the German pedagogical tradition, Johns Hopkins University was the first institution of higher learning dedicated primarily to scientific investigation. Its buildings supported functionally distinct academics merged with research, and the clock tower of 1915 Gilman Hall, designed by Douglas Thomas of Parker, Thomas & Rice, became an icon of this new model.

Advent of Modernism

Stirrings of deep change emerged in the 1940s and 1950s as colleges embraced the ideals of open, broad-based, and nonsectarian inquiry. At the same time, new ideas in architecture arrived—in some places like spaceships landing on campus and at others as the basis for entirely new campuses and quads. Master plans by Eero Saarinen, such as those for Drake University in Des Moines in the 1940s and Brandeis University in Waltham, Massachusetts, in the 1950s, aimed to codify these liberal underpinnings with broad strokes.

At most schools, Modernism arrived in a more limited way, often imbued with some symbolic intent. At the Massachusetts Institute of Technology (MIT), the clean lines and expressive shapes of Alvar Aalto's 1949 Baker House dormitory intended to offer returning war veterans "order, peace and beauty" to restore their interrupted lives. By contrast, other

(Opposite) The clock tower atop 1915 Gilman Hall at Johns Hopkins University in Baltimore, designed by Parker, Thomas & Rice, came to symbolize the new concept of the research university. *©Gaja Snover/123RF*

Alvar Aalto's 1949 design for Baker House, a dormitory at MIT, was intended to provide a place of "order, peace and beauty" for war veterans returning to school. *Ezra Stoller/©Esto*

Harvard's Carpenter Center for the Visual Arts (1963) is Le Corbusier's only building in North America. Josep Lluis Sert, dean of Harvard's Graduate School of Design from 1953 to 1969, urged McGeorge Bundy, dean of the Faculty of Arts and Sciences, to offer the commission to Le Corbusier. *Ezra Stoller/ ©Esto*

Peabody Terrace, graduate housing at Harvard designed by Sert, Jackson & Gourley and constructed in 1964, was designed to connect the campus to the community, but the high-rise towers and numerous smaller structures instigated controversy about Modernist approaches to campus design. *©Wayne Andrews/Esto*

modern gestures suggested a rejection of conformity and tradition. For example, Eero Saarinen's windowless and abstract 1955 Kresge Chapel at MIT stood out starkly against the school's Beaux-Arts originals. At nearby Harvard, the angled concrete planes of Le Corbusier's 1963 Carpenter Center for the Visual Arts interrupted the local Georgian fabric. Similarly, the Air Force Academy Cadet Chapel (1956–62; see page 325) in Colorado Springs, by Skidmore, Owings & Merrill, caused a fervent debate over whether Modern design was suitable for U.S. military tradition. In the end, the nonsectarian chapel became emblematic of American spirituality, ensuring the triumph over "godless communism."

Flush with such achievements, Modernist designs morphed into less successful experiments, including the campus "megastructures" created by architects like Arthur Erickson at Simon Fraser University in 1963 and Gunnar Birkerts at Tougaloo College in 1965. These novel environments of sprawling, interconnected buildings with repetitive exteriors were bold and audacious—but also costly and stultifying. They ultimately fell out of favor.

The tasteful, medium-scale insertion of European-inspired Modernism into a classical milieu, on the other hand, became practically de rigueur. Many such additions intended to open the college campus to the community, as Sert, Jackson & Gourley attempted with the 1964 Peabody Terrace for Harvard. With its open plazas and public pathways, the housing complex for married graduate students connected with its neighbors and reflected existing patterns of use. But at 22 stories, its three towers loomed high above the district, and the adjacent smaller structures—meant to ease the transition to the high-rises—gave it the feel of a megablock. Questions about clean-slate modern master plans were already being raised across the country, and Peabody Terrace became a lightning rod in a debate pitting legacy-minded alumni and trustees against future-focused professors and students. This clash, mediated by architects and their university clients, would last for decades, fading only fleetingly during the Postmodern era of the 1970s and 1980s.

First Presbyterian Church,
Stamford, Connecticut,
Wallace Harrison

UNESCO Headquarters, Paris,
Marcel Breuer, Pier Luigi Nervi,
and Bernard Zehrfuss

Ingalls Ice Arena,
New Haven,
Eero Saarinen

Westmoor High School,
Daly City, California,
Mario J. Ciampi

John Wellborn Root II, FAIA,
received the AIA Gold Medal

By the 1930s, some public schools at the K–12 level displayed a stripped-down aesthetic and elements of European Modernism. Giving form to the ideals of philosopher John Dewey and other Progressivists who rejected authoritarian schooling approaches, architects explored flexible class settings and designed to the scale of a child. Radical at the time, these ideas are exemplified in Crow Island School in Winnetka, Illinois, a 1940 collaboration of Eliel and Eero Saarinen and Perkins, Wheeler & Will, the Chicago firm run by D. H. Perkins's son, Lawrence. This innovative, child-centered environment spawned other types of specialized schools for children with unique needs, such as the 1952 Cerebral Palsy School in Fresno, California, by David H. Horn and Marshall D. Mortland.

Unfortunately, such design innovations often fell victim to the pressures of growth. Swelling immigrant numbers and a tenfold increase in high school enrollment between 1900 and 1940 left schools bulging at the seams and straining to adapt during wartime. With scarce resources, architects experimented with new construction methods, such as steel framing, to build schools faster and cheaper. By the late 1950s, interest in bigger facilities and class sizes ultimately overshadowed student-centered designs. Responding to the demographic challenges of the baby boom and the psychological impetus of the Soviet threat, school districts planned schools of record size. Architects delivered, unveiling many-winged complexes for populations of up to 500 students, three to four times the previous norm. Noteworthy examples sprouted throughout fast-growing California, including Mario J. Ciampi's 1958 Westmoor High School in Daly City, with its extensive windows that brought daylight and natural ventilation into classrooms. Novel construction methods emerged as well; a leading example was Paul Rudolph's 1962 Sarasota High School in Sarasota, Florida, a structure remarkable for its use of light steel tubes, flat concrete slabs, and metal window walls.

In the 1930s Progressivist ideas about education began to show up in the design of some schools. At the end of the decade, Eliel & Eero Saarinen and Perkins, Wheeler & Will designed Crow Island School (1940), Winnetka, Illinois, which embodied such concepts as flexible class settings and child-centered design. Eero Saarinen designed the bonded plywood furniture used throughout the school. *Ezra Stoller/©Esto (exterior); ©Cranbrook Academy (interior)*

But the gains in student performance brought by daylighting and outdoor views were not widely understood, and in a few years "schools without windows" became an unfortunate truism. Glass-free walls helped cut maintenance and air-conditioning costs, and they were also thought to reduce vices such as vandalism and daydreaming. Ironically, at the same time they were shutting out the sun, American schools were letting in new pedagogical methods, such as group work and "team teaching," and beginning to accept racial integration.

New Programs, Technologies, and Styles

Civil rights leaders and educators remained relatively aligned in their focus on minority and low income K–12 students during the 1960s. Alternative education programs proliferated, including "freedom schools" and "street academies," some of which laid the groundwork for magnet schools and charter schools a generation later.

As during the postwar boom, school buildings changed in their use and inner workings. Birkerts's Lincoln Elementary School (1969) in Columbus, Indiana, for example, centered on a large, detached multipurpose room for group activities. Elsewhere, open floor plans and movable furniture facilitated team teaching and group activities at the 1970 Butterfield School by Orput Associates in Libertyville, Illinois, and Mitchell/Giurgola Associates' 1972 Columbus East Senior High School in Columbus, Indiana. Larger centralized resources and new media were also incorporated more frequently, such as libraries with microfilm readers and audiovisual rooms with TVs and projectors. Supporting these new learning areas were new kinds of electrical lighting and ventilation systems, which became the rule rather than the exception.

While advances in building systems would remain, interest in alternative schools faltered. By 1980, amid public calls for school reform, a "teachers' movement" sought to restore the traditional, enclosed classroom. Schools like Butterfield, symbols of their times, walled off their open floors into separated classrooms. Educators and architects turned to time-honored and comfortable ideas in schooling and design, often giving contemporary expression to traditional models. As early as 1972, Louis Kahn combined a humane simplicity with the central halls, balconies, alcoves, and colonnades of a classical floor plan in his landmark library at New Hampshire's private Phillips Exeter Academy. Other schools emulated this approach, sometimes with unexpected design ideas or technologies, such as the domestic quality of the

Paul Rudolph's design for new construction at Sarasota High School (1962), Florida, was one of the first examples of the use of materials such as light steel tubes, flat concrete slabs, and metal window walls in school construction.
Ezra Stoller/©Esto

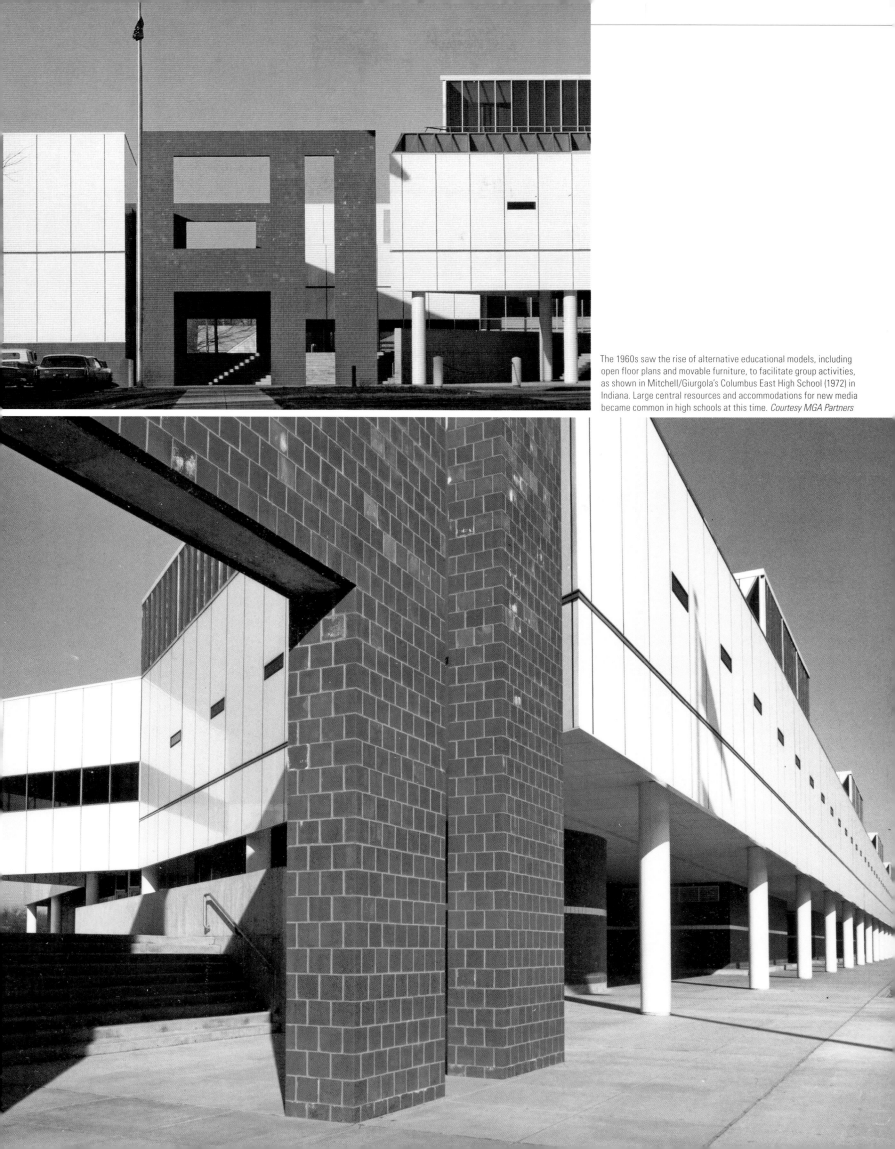

The 1960s saw the rise of alternative educational models, including open floor plans and movable furniture, to facilitate group activities, as shown in Mitchell/Giurgola's Columbus East High School (1972) in Indiana. Large central resources and accommodations for new media became common in high schools at this time. *Courtesy MGA Partners*

1959

Guggenheim Museum,
New York City,
Frank Lloyd Wright

Palazzetto dello Sport,
Rome,
Pier Luigi Nervi

Lykes House,
Phoenix,
Frank Lloyd Wright

Stahl House
(Case Study House #22),
Los Angeles,
Pierre Koenig

Walter A. Gropius, FAIA,
received the AIA Gold Medal

Garfield School (1981) by Joseph Esherick in San Francisco or the environmentally conscious features of Tai Soo Kim's Middlebury Elementary School (1985) in Connecticut.

For universities seeking a middle ground between classical ideals and current attitudes, this fusion seemed an effective remedy. Many of the new building designs also proved cheaper to build than their neotraditional alternatives, which relied on skilled crafts and costly materials. Architects like Ezra D. Ehrenkrantz brought industrialized construction to schools like Harvard as early as 1974. Other designs explored literal representations of historical messages and forms, as did Venturi, Rauch and Scott Brown in Princeton's Gordon Wu Hall (1983). While clinging to their Jeffersonian roots as a moral anchor, many universities found a means to advance in the Postmodernist movement.

Contemporary Complexities

The Postmodern solution was not for everyone, however. Scores of universities, especially in the South, have maintained their tradition-bound sensibilities to the present day. Established schools have preserved and adapted historic landmarks and commissioned master plans that extend and replicate centuries-old campus designs. Recent works of this sort extend from master plans by Ayers/Saint/Gross for Emory University and Duke to the replication of a Beaux-Arts quad (1990–99) at Carnegie-Mellon University by Michael Dennis, Jeffrey Clark Associates. Like Pittsburgh's Carnegie-Mellon, many other northern schools have reverted to the styles of their earliest buildings as a way to establish credibility with donors and to burnish an esteemed institutional "brand." Examples include new Collegiate Gothic dormitories by Demetri Porphyrios and others for Princeton, and Robert A. M. Stern's creation in high Georgian Revival style of the Spangler Campus Center (2000) for the Harvard Business School. Even brand-new institutions have sought the commanding patina of neohistorical architecture, most recently at the 2007 Ave Maria University and town center in Naples, Florida, a Catholic institution conceived by Looney Ricks Kiss and EDAW for pizza magnate Thomas S. Monaghan.

Yet other schools strive for an approach that reflects current trends. At a time of rapid building to accommodate the rising enrollments of the "echo boom" generation—which promises the largest freshman class ever in 2009—innovative, contemporary styles have flourished in new science buildings and arts centers. Examples range from Antoine Predock's serene Nelson Fine Arts Center (1990; see page 306) at Arizona State to the University of

(Opposite) By 1980, educators were refocusing on more traditional educational models, and school designs of the time reflected this but often still in a Modernist style. This trend was foreshadowed in 1972 by Louis Kahn's combination of a classical floor plan with the simplicity of modern architecture in his library for Phillips Exeter Academy, Exeter, New Hampshire. *Barbara Hobson*

The design of Princeton University's Gordon Wu Hall (1983), by Venturi, Rauch & Scott Brown, brings a modern perspective to the campus's historical forms. The building received a national Honor Award for Architecture in 1984.
Tom Bernard, courtesy Venturi, Scott Brown and Associates, Inc.

Robert A. M. Stern's Georgian Revival design for the Spangler Campus Center (2000) at the Harvard Business School respects McKim, Mead and White's 1927 master plan for the campus and complements the red brick and limestone palette of nearby buildings.
©*Peter Aaron/Esto*

Iowa's futuristic Advanced Technologies Laboratory (1992) by Frank Gehry. New and exuberant living quarters followed, with Internet connections and unusual common areas, as at David Baker's lively Manville Student Apartments at Berkeley (1997) and Steven Holl's uncanny Simmons Hall (2002) at MIT.

Many new university buildings proclaimed the universal triumph of technology, even for mundane programs like the University of Pennsylvania's elliptical chiller plant by Leers Weinzapfel (2000). Others lent novel expression to such timeless elements as quads, gates, and residences, as at the new Student Life Center for the University of Cincinnati (2004) by Moore Ruble Yudell Architects & Planners and glaserworks. Still others proclaimed the regional heritage of their institutions, such as the Miller/Hull Partnership's 1999 Olympic College in Shelton, Washington.

Public school districts also grew in population in the final years of the 20th century, but new needs sapped already dwindling budgets, which had been hobbled by tax-averse public sentiment and shrinking federal aid. Violent attacks at schools such as Columbine High School in 1999 led districts to retrofit facilities with guard stations, metal detectors, and bulletproof glass, even in suburban enclaves considered safe. Much financing went to "clicks"—network wiring or laptop computers—rather than bricks. Architecture even became irrelevant for some types of education, as the Internet and videoconference systems became fixtures of distance learning and computer-assisted instruction. At-home learning gained new and forceful advocates in religious and intellectual circles. And the No Child Left Behind Act of 2001, with its focus on national testing standards and performance-based federal funding, further directed resources away from school building.

Where the government was seen as failing its students, private forces had already begun to intercede, bringing novel financing schemes and public/private alliances that considered architectural creativity as central to the efforts. To encourage bond issues, municipalities borrowed D. H. Perkins's concept for joint-use "community schools" that hosted adult education or bingo after daytime classes ended. Many architects, such as Carol Ross Barney, became student and community advocates. Barney's designs for Little Village Academy (2001) and Cesar Chavez Multicultural Academic Center (1993) in Chicago espoused the ideals of multiculturalism and diversity.

(Opposite) Innovative contemporary styles have flourished on some campuses as colleges rush to build dormitories to accommodate an influx of "echo boom" students. Robert Campbell, architecture critic for the *Boston Globe*, described MIT's Simmons Hall (2002), designed by Steven Holl of New York, as a "daring, serious, memorable building." *©Peter Aaron/Esto*

The 2004 Student Life Center at the University of Cincinnati, by Moore Ruble Yudell and glaserworks, provides a new form for traditional collegiate design elements such as quads and gates. *Lisa Ventre, University of Cincinnati*

Carol Ross Barney's design for the Cesar Chavez Multicultural Academic Center (1993) in Chicago emphasized the ideals of diversity and multiculturalism and of connecting the school to the community. *Steve Hall/Hedrich Blessing, courtesy Ross Barney Architects*

1960
National Park Service
established the National Historic
Landmarks program

Ludwig Mies van der Rohe,
FAIA, received the AIA Gold Medal

Other social values have recently become important factors in the location and design of schools. The antisprawl, smart-growth movement called into question greenfield school planning; preservationists and New Urbanists alike asked, "Why can't Johnny walk to school?" in 2001. A new wave of adaptive use and smaller neighborhood schools resulted. Sustainable design also became a core precept, leading to "high-performance schools" that incorporate daylight, environmentally benign materials, and flexible, technology-responsive classrooms. And, to address the public demand for smaller schools, many architecture firms devised separate themed academies within larger existing structures and in new buildings with innovative layouts. An early and iconic example is the 2000 Diamond Ranch High School in Pomona, California, by Morphosis. The design attracted global attention by breaking down a large high school into assorted communal and learning spaces, creating a novel educational setting amid striking forms.

Lessons for the Future

The intimate connection between architecture and education in the United States is reflected in the history of the past 150 years. Never have changes in educational approach been without an institutional or building type that embodied the new ideal. In fact, in some instances, school facilities have been constructed with overt didactic functions built right in, so that students can see examples of what they are learning.

The past 150 years have brought great changes in education—including who is educated, to what degree, and by whom. As knowledge advances, we not only have more information to transmit to the next generation but also new ways of transmitting it. We have also developed a better understanding of how knowledge can best be conveyed, recognizing that people learn in different ways. Architecture, too, is an evolving process, incorporating new planning concepts, new technologies, and new stylistic solutions over time.

Older approaches—in both education and architecture—can be valid and serve their purpose. Nonetheless, this brief history of the building type demonstrates that, when observant of new conditions and open to new information, the two disciplines work well together to create new ways to serve the ever-changing needs and conditions of students, teachers, and society at large. ●

The 21st-century ideas of dividing large schools into smaller communities and using a sustainable design philosophy are exemplified in the 2000 Diamond Ranch High School in Pomona, California, designed by Morphosis.
©Timothy Hursley

Eliel Saarinen, FAIA

C. C. Sullivan

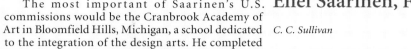

Eliel Saarinen (1873–1950) bridged cultures and continents. His works merged elements of Finnish farm vernacular with British Gothic Revival, Jugendstil, and Art Nouveau. Yet the architect's simplified, heavy forms also link his work with Minimalism. He was awarded the Gold Medal in 1947 for his work in architecture, planning, and education.

After studying painting and architecture at Helsinki Polytechnic, Saarinen opened a firm in 1897 with two schoolmates. Several remarkable buildings resulted, including the Finnish National Museum and the Helsinki Railway Station, in a style later known as Finnish National Romanticism.

In 1922 the arc of his career changed radically: Saarinen earned second place in a closely watched international competition for the Chicago Tribune Tower. Though he did not win, his design earned wide praise. Invitations to build several American projects followed, and he moved to the United States in 1923. (His tower scheme was eventually built—in Houston in 1929, as the Gulf Building.)

The most important of Saarinen's U.S. commissions would be the Cranbrook Academy of Art in Bloomfield Hills, Michigan, a school dedicated to the integration of the design arts. He completed the master plan in 1925 and subsequently designed several of the buildings, which incorporated sculptures, custom-designed furnishings, and other crafts. In 1927 Saarinen began teaching and designing furniture there, profoundly influencing such students as Charles and Ray Eames, Harry Bertoia, and Ralph Rapson. In 1932 Saarinen was named president of the academy.

Saarinen continued to practice and, in 1937, partnered with his son, Eero. The firm's innovation in form and materials was matched by pioneering social and humanistic concepts. For example, the modernist 1940 Crow Island School in Winnetka, Illinois, with its free-form arrangement of simple, rectilinear masses and child-scaled spaces, became a foremost influence on a generation of school buildings.

Eliel Saarinen designed most of the buildings for the Cranbrook Academy campus in Bloomfield Hills, Michigan, including the Academy of Art Library and Museum (1942). Wolf von Eckhardt, former architecture critic for the *Washington Post*, called Cranbrook the "most enchanted and enchanting setting in America."
©Balthazar Korab/Cranbrook Archives

Saarinen's entry in the 1922 competition for the Chicago Tribune headquarters came in second to the Neo-Gothic building by Raymond Hood and John Mead Howells. Nevertheless, his design was widely praised, and the building's spare façade and vertical fenestration helped change ideas about the design vocabulary of skyscrapers. *Atelier Apollo/©Cranbrook Archives*

1961
*Publication of The Death and Life
of Great American Cities,
by Jane Jacobs*

*St. John's Abbey,
Collegeville, Minnesota,
Marcel Breuer*

*Haystack Mountain School of Crafts,
Deer Isle, Maine,
Edward Larrabee Barnes*

GOLD MEDALIST, 1985

William Wayne Caudill, FAIA

Andrew Brodie Smith, PhD

Courtesy CRS Center, Texas A&M University

Bill Caudill's firm, CRS, designed many successful university buildings, including Roy E. Larsen Hall (1965) on the Harvard University campus.
Courtesy CRS Center, Texas A&M University

Sometimes called the Will Rogers of architecture for displaying the same sense of humor, propensity for self-deprecation, and folksy manner as his fellow Oklahoman, William (Bill) Caudill was an educator, researcher, writer, practitioner, theorist, and entrepreneur. He was a strong proponent of team design: "The day of the prima donna approach to designing buildings has passed," he wrote. The client was a critical part of the team effort as he saw it. To ensure client participation, Caudill pioneered a technique he called "squatting," whereby he and his colleagues would travel to the client's location and camp out.

After graduating from MIT in 1939 with an MArch, Caudill spent six years as a professor at Texas A&M University. Later, he directed the School of Architecture at Rice University. In 1946 he and fellow teacher John W. Rowlett, FAIA, founded the firm that would become CRS (Caudill Rowlett Scott). The modest partnership grew into a highly regarded design and construction management company particularly known for its education facilities. The firm received commissions for elementary schools, high schools, colleges, and universities in 26 states and eight foreign countries. Among many other award-winning projects, CRS designed the Olin Hall of Science at Colorado College (1961); the original Cypress College campus (1970) in Cypress, California; and the U.S. Embassy (1981) in Riyadh, Saudi Arabia.

Caudill's energy and joie de vivre were legendary. To better serve his clients in remote areas of Texas, for example, Caudill learned to pilot an airplane. At the age of 60, he earned his sea-plane rating. "Flying an amphibian," he wrote, "is like practicing architecture. We architects are amphibians. We practice on the beach where the world of science and engineering overlaps with the world of arts and humanities. Our danger lies in becoming too obsessed with only one world, forgetting how to operate in the others." Bill Caudill, who died in 1983, received the AIA Gold Medal posthumously.

Palos Verdes High School,
Richard Neutra

Olin Hall of Science,
Colorado College,
William Caudill/CRS

Arena Stage,
Washington, D.C.,
Harry Weese

Le Corbusier (Charles-Édouard Jeanneret),
Hon. FAIA, received the AIA Gold Medal

While many children attend schools designed by architects, more and more youngsters are getting the opportunity to learn about history, planning, design, and engineering from these design professionals as well. AIA chapters at state and local levels across the country have developed education programs, led by their members, which they offer to local public and private schools.

One longstanding and very active model can be found at Minneapolis-based AIA Minnesota. More than two decades ago, a group of its members expressed interest in educating people of all ages about architecture and the profession. Eventually, the chapter formed the Architecture in the Schools Committee. Consisting of six to ten members, this core group coordinates a long list of architect volunteers who enjoy sharing their knowledge with school children throughout the state. These are committed professionals, points out former committee member Mary Shaffer, AIA: "charter members who have since retired still actively participate." Shaffer herself has contributed her time and energy for some 17 years.

Programs are generally created for a fifth-grade level but can be easily adapted to different age groups (they've made presentations to kids in kindergarten through college, and even to adults at Rotary clubs). Some of the curriculum takes only one class period to present; others require multiple sessions.

One project, "World Architecture," a PowerPoint presentation created in conjunction with the University of Minnesota chapter of AIAS, acquaints the young audience with the history of architecture. Another activity, "Mouse House," asks students to create a diagram of a cabin for a mouse on a nearby lake. In this exercise, the children begin to learn about program, scale, and materials. Another popular offering is "DoodleOpolis—Adventures in Urban Architecture," which teaches students about architecture while explaining the formation of cities and the principles of urban planning. DoodleOpolis engages participants in multiple ways, from in-class discussions and activities to field trips that allow students to test their new skill sets. "Sometimes we would set up scavenger hunts at the St. Paul campus of the University of Minnesota," recalls Shaffer. "They'd have to find particular details of buildings, a focal point, or an area of compression and release."

On occasion teachers will ask the designers to integrate architecture topics into their more conventional lesson plan. For example, explains Shaffer, "If teachers want to discuss math, we can go in and discuss scale, proportion, or cost estimation. If they're discussing art in the classroom, we can introduce renderings or perspective drawing."

The synergy of the volunteer architects helps to generate new and timely projects. The Architecture in the Schools Committee decided, for example, to celebrate the AIA's 150th anniversary by arranging for 150 architects to visit classrooms throughout Minnesota during one week in May 2007. The goal of their presentations was to introduce students to the design process and the 10 principles of livable communities. By sparking the imagination of school-age children, AIA Minnesota hopes to engage the next generation of citizens in shaping the future.

From Mouse House to DoodleOpolis: Architecture in the Schools

Randi Greenberg

The Washington Architectural Foundation sponsors the Architecture in the Schools (AIS) program, now in its 15th year, in the Washington, D.C., metropolitan area. Here, a 5th-grade student at Bunker Hill Elementary School works on a "city of the future" for her science class. *Courtesy the Washington Architectural Foundation*

Fifth-grade students at a school in Northern Virginia build a model of the Parthenon for their history class, with help from volunteer architect Andrew Y. Cheng, AIA (not pictured). *Courtesy the Washington Architectural Foundation*

Under the direction of AIA/DC member Stephen J. Vanze, AIA, students formed guilds and collaborated on the building of this Gothic cathedral. *Courtesy the Washington Architectural Foundation*

15

A Model of Health

Robin Guenther, FAIA

Numerous building types constructed today—from gymnasiums to hospitals—have the expressed goal of achieving, restoring, or maintaining human health. But what does this mean? The World Health Organization defines health as a state of physical, mental, and social well-being, but the American writer and cultural critic Wendell Berry perhaps summed it up best in *Another Turn of the Crank*, when he wrote that the word *health* comes from the same Indo-European root as "heal," "whole," and "holy." Literally speaking, to be healthy is to be whole.

For humans to be truly healthy, then, all aspects of their lives, from psychological state to lifestyle choices, must be tended to. Positive outlook, regular exercise, and healthy diet, for example, are frequently cited by the media as important factors in maintaining health. In addition, current research suggests—and anecdotal evidence has long insisted—connections to nature are equally important. This holistic ideal has not always been made manifest, however, in the buildings where we seek healing. Rather, health care architecture has varied over time in response to the health care systems it houses and to society's perceptions of disease.

Advancements in medical education, care, and technology have shaped what has come to be considered the primary building form for healing in modern society—the hospital. Unfortunately, in the 20th century the modern hospital became disconnected from nature in the quest to accommodate rapid and chaotic changes in demographics, delivery of medical care, and medical and construction technologies. In the 21st century, architects and others involved in the design of health care facilities are looking to return health care architecture to its roots.

Among the earliest known examples of architecture for health in the Western world were the Greek Asklepieia, open halls where priests in the 5th century BCE prescribed therapeutic regimens that included medication, diet, and exercise. Operating as both spa and hospital, these "wholesome" places were located according to the orientation of the sun and the direction of prevailing winds. Similarly, the spas, retreats, and wellness centers of today reflect a holistic form of architecture for health that evolved from the baths of ancient Greece.

Although such alternative forms of health care have been dwarfed—literally and figuratively—by the modern hospital, their naturalistic approach retains and nurtures seeds of hope for a more patient-centered form of health care design in the 21st century. In architectural historian Cor Wagenaar's *The Architecture of Hospitals*, Mels Crouwel, state architect of the Netherlands, says that places in health facilities designed for patient comfort offer "compensatory strategies for the less healthy effects of modern life, notably lack of exercise and stress." The concept of human spaces—coupled with growing lifestyle choices and increased awareness of mind/body connections, and supported by green-building design research and advances in medical technology—is helping to transform the hospital into an institution that successfully blends holistic and high-tech to advance wellness in the fullest sense. Many of these same issues are also making planners and architects more aware of how the placement and design of all building types—whether for medical purposes or not—have a direct effect on public health.

(Opposite) The new main entrance to Bellevue Hospital Center in New York City connects one of the older pavilion buildings (1906–16) by McKim, Mead and White with a new 210,000-square-foot ambulatory care facility, providing the medical setting with architectural drama and natural light. The new facility, plus 125,000-square-feet of renovated space in the existing hospital, was undertaken by Pei Cobb Freed & Partners and completed in 2005. *©Paul Warchol Photography*

1962
The Octagon was designated a
National Historic Landmark

AIA presented the first
Architecture Firm Award to
Skidmore, Owings & Merrill

Rachel Carson's Silent Spring
helped inspire the environmental
movement

TWA Terminal,
JFK Airport,
Eero Saarinen

Dulles International Airport,
Chantilly, Virginia,
Eero Saarinen

Hospital Precedents from Europe

The earliest hospitals grew from religious acts of mercy and were often associated with monasteries. For the most part, care was directed at the classes who lacked social or economic support. By the early 17th century, large, formally symmetrical ward buildings arranged around courtyard gardens, such as the Ospedale Maggiore in Milan, could be found throughout Europe. In 18th-century France, the bourgeoisie constructed the massive, 2,600-bed Hôtel Dieu in Paris. Although physically connected to a religious building, it is considered the first major "civic" hospital building. The Hôtel Dieu retained a basic connection to light and air by necessity, but its sheer size and scale overwhelmed its ability to use nature as a healing element.

Subsequently, the growing mercantile class throughout Europe began to construct secular, philanthropically funded hospitals to care for the expanding, increasingly urban labor force. These buildings tended to resemble the palaces or châteaux of their benefactors, complete with landscaped gardens. At the same time, a completely separate set of military hospitals emerged in response to the conflict and unrest that continually engulfed the region. This was an era of neoclassical revival architecture, and the hospital structures reflected the symmetry and axial configurations characteristic of classical styles.

By the late 18th century, lack of utilities and sanitary infrastructure amid growing urbanization was beginning to be recognized as a major issue for the health of Europe's citizens. Clean air and water were also seen as essential in hospital settings. Florence Nightingale reinforced this point of view in her *Notes on Hospitals*, published in London in 1859, in which she outlined prescriptive design measures (including dimensions for a ward and sizes of windows) to provide for abundant daylight and fresh air in patient care areas. To deprive the sick of pure air "is nothing but manslaughter under the garb of benevolence," she wrote. To respond to this vision, hospitals had to be reconfigured, which led to the development of the "pavilion hospital."

As the name implies, pavilion hospitals were often situated on large land parcels far from the dense urban environment. Here, abundant light and clean air and water were readily available. Initially, pavilion designs were limited to about three stories. The multibed wards, traversed by nurses, were narrow and featured high ceilings. These facilities provided highly efficient, naturally lighted and ventilated patient wards in buildings arranged in a formal symmetrical relationship to nature. As urbanization continued throughout the 19th and 20th centuries, however, many of these hospitals were eventually engulfed by the cities from which they had escaped.

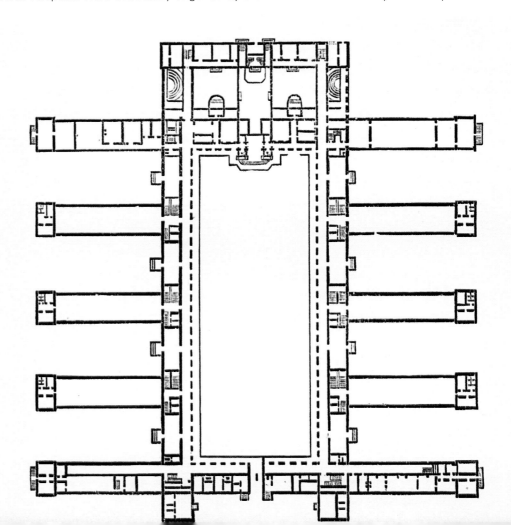

The Hospital Lariboisière, designed by Pierre Gauthier and built between 1846 and 1854 in Paris, was the first pavilion hospital. Narrow, open wards provided patients with daylight and natural ventilation. *Courtesy the collection of John M. Currie, AIA*

Air Force Academy Chapel,
Walter Netsch/SOM

Sarasota High School,
Florida,
Paul Rudolph

Eero Saarinen, FAIA, received the
AIA Gold Medal (posthumously)

Early American Hospitals

Three of the first hospitals in the United States—Pennsylvania Hospital (1755), New York Hospital (1775), and Massachusetts General (1821)—were founded as secular, philanthropic institutions in rapidly expanding eastern cities. Hospitals at this time were built on sites along rivers or on the outskirts of development to maintain their connection to clean water and air. Like their European contemporaries, they were clothed in a Neoclassical architecture resembling wealthy houses or civic buildings. U.S. hospitals were keen from the beginning to offer upgraded accommodations to anyone willing to pay for them (unlike Europe, where the wealthy did not go to hospitals until surgery became more common in the late 17th century). Throughout the 19th century, there was a noticeable difference between the beautifully appointed private "pay-patient" rooms that catered to those with resources and the open wards that accommodated the dying poor.

Built in New York City in 1775, New York Hospital was one of the first hospitals erected in the United States. It first served wounded colonial soldiers, then opened its doors to civilians in 1791. U.S. hospitals offered upgraded rooms for those who could pay for them.
Courtesy Medical Center Archives of NewYork-Presbyterian/Weill Cornell

By the end of the Civil War, massive casualties had necessitated the construction of enormous "barrack" and "tent" hospitals, the design of which was informed by Nightingale's writings. The success of these buildings, coupled with the emergence of Joseph Lister's germ theory of disease, transformed U.S. hospital design, leading to adoption of the European pavilion prototype. In 1873 Johns Hopkins bequeathed a major gift to build the best hospital in the world in Baltimore, Maryland, and librarian and surgeon John S. Billings subsequently produced a model pavilion plan building. This innovative building featured a complex natural ventilation system, relying on chimneys and roof ventilators to "flush" the building. As American cities grew, hospitals continued to seek large sites at the urban edge, alongside rivers, or at higher elevations to maximize natural light and fresh air for their expansive pavilion campuses.

The original Johns Hopkins Hospital building, now called the Billings Administration Building, was designed by librarian and surgeon John Shaw Billings according to the European pavilion plan. It features a Victorian dome. The Baltimore hospital opened in 1889.
Courtesy Johns Hopkins Medical Institutions

1963
Demolition began on
New York City's Pennsylvania
Station, designed by McKim,
Mead and White

Yale University Art and
Architecture Building,
New Haven, Paul Rudolph

Pan American Building,
New York City,
Walter Gropius/TAC

Carpenter Center for the Visual Arts,
Harvard University,
Le Corbusier

Built in 1896 in the Morningside Heights section of New York City, Saint Luke's Hospital was designed by Ernest Flagg, who had studied at the Ecole des Beaux-Arts in Paris. His plan called for nine five-story pavilions linked to a central building. Two of the pavilions were never built. *New York Public Library, Pageant of America Photo Archive*

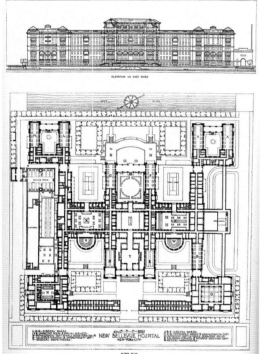

McKim, Mead and White's interlocking pavilion master plan for Bellevue Hospital (1906–16) in New York City replaced an older, chateau-like structure along the East River. Founded as an almshouse in 1736, Bellevue is the nation's oldest public hospital. *Reprinted from* The Architecture of McKim, Mead & White in Photographs, Plans and Elevations *(Dover Publications, 1990)*

By the late 19th century, advances in diagnosis, anesthesia, and infection control were transforming the disciplines of medicine and surgery. At the same time, environmental issues, such as lighting and ventilation, still governed much of the physical arrangement in hospitals. Architect Ernest Flagg, for example, placed an operating theater with natural lighting over a chapel to form the centerpiece of New York's St. Luke's Hospital (1896). In addition, he deliberately staggered adjacent inpatient pavilion floors by a half story to prevent potential cross-contamination of patient rooms. During this period, another, albeit short-lived, advantage of the pavilion plan came to light: as medical specialization emerged, pavilions could be designated for different purposes—such as obstetrics or pediatrics—making it easier to respond to the particular medical needs of patients.

In 1906, in response to the massive influx of new immigrants, a McKim, Mead and White interlocking five-pavilion master plan replaced an older, chateau-like Bellevue Hospital on the banks of New York City's East River. However, even before the phased construction of either St. Luke's or Bellevue was completed, multiple changes in medicine rendered the pavilion plan obsolete.

The Monumental Block Hospital

By the second decade of the 20th century, a better understanding of bacteria had resulted in dismissal of the earlier assumption that elaborate natural ventilation systems were needed for asepsis. In addition, the increase in specialty medical and surgical services led to an expansion in facilities for paying patients, which increased the need for private-patient accommodations. Given the narrow footprint of early pavilion buildings, converting open-ward buildings proved challenging. Another factor leading to change in hospital design was the introduction of the elevator in 1889. This facilitated a vertical dimension to hospital structures, considered necessary in urban areas where the city block constrained campus expansion.

But the biggest driver of change in the 20th-century hospital was undoubtedly the proliferation of new technology. "Technology was to be the weapon with which disease and illness would be vanquished," says educator and cultural critic Neil Postman in his 2003 work *Technopoly: The Surrender of Culture to Technology*. The proliferation of innovative and expensive medical technology, including the X-ray machine, required centralization of capital investment in larger, more complex buildings with more sophisticated systems. The concentration of medical knowledge within the hospital gave rise to diagnostic and treatment

Guthrie Theater,
Minneapolis,
Ralph Rapson

Philharmonie,
Berlin,
Hans Scharoun

First Unitarian Church,
Rochester, New York,
Louis Kahn

John Deere & Company,
Moline, Illinois,
Eero Saarinen

Alvar Aalto, Hon. FAIA,
received the AIA Gold Medal

departments and required the movement of bedridden patients around the hospital. The frenzied speed of change in medical technology also forced hospitals to place greater emphasis on specialization. Medical services—from anesthesia and surgery to emergency medicine and trauma treatment—were emerging and changing faster than buildings could be constructed.

All told, by the 1920s these changes had resulted in the development of a "skyscraper" or "block" hospital type. Architect James Gamble Rogers's plan for Columbia-Presbyterian Medical Center (1928; now New York-Presbyterian Hospital) and the design for New York Hospital–Cornell Medical Center (1933) by the architecture firm Coolidge Shepley Bulfinch and Abbott are two examples of centralized, monumental block hospitals. Each rises nearly 20 stories, with relatively narrow, articulated footprints still determined by the requirement for natural light and ventilation. These buildings celebrated the "machine age" and its technical prowess. Any intentional ground-level connection between nature and healing was erased as the buildings increased in height. Access to the outdoors was minimal, often remaining only in small solaria and at the ends of the wings.

It would be years before people would begin to see the darker side of the emphasis on accommodating technology in health care facilities. As Postman wrote in *Technopoly*, "Like some well-known diseases, the problems that have arisen as a result of the reign of medical technology came slowly and were barely perceptible at the start. Through it all, the question of what was being *undone* had a low priority if it was asked at all."

The proliferation of medical subspecialties and the emergence of the technology-driven hospital also led to specialization in the field of architecture. Prior to the 20th century, generalist architects designed the hospital building. By 1930, "hospital design" firms had formed to consolidate the technical knowledge required to manage the requirements of increasingly complex processes and equipment.

James Gamble Rogers designed the first building for Columbia-Presbyterian Medical Center in New York in 1928. He opted for a skyscraper, or block, typology, believing it would be more efficient than a low, sprawling building. *Archives and Special Collections, Health Sciences Library, Columbia University*

The monumental scale of New York Hospital (1933), designed by Coolidge Shepley Bulfinch and Abbott, signaled the arrival of the "machine age" and the end of the connection between nature and healing. *Courtesy Shepley Bulfinch Richardson and Abbott*

The Modernist Hospital

The tremendous policy and demographic changes in the United States during the 1930s and '40s ultimately shaped the direction of health care for the remainder of the 20th century. Social Security and employer-sponsored health insurance, which emerged as part of the country's new safety net, provided the underpinnings of a social revolution in entitlement. This, in turn, opened high-technology medical services to large segments of the population that previously could not afford them. In addition, the end of World War II and the return of the GIs marked the beginning of the baby boom. The result was a major expansion of acute care hospitals in the United States. The beginning of suburban development provided the infrastructure and land to facilitate this massive boom in hospital construction, and the federal government provided funding through the Hospital Survey and Construction Act (1946), also known as the Hill-Burton Act. By expanding services such as maternity and outpatient care to meet these new market demands, hospitals began to provide greater access to the growing middle class. From a public policy perspective, the Hill-Burton Act also galvanized the assignment of monetary resources to access to treatment rather than to preventive care.

In *The Architecture of Hospitals*, Wagenaar recounts that this era of building "epitomized the promise of science, the victory of technology, and the prospect of a successful battle against old and new diseases. What better way to express the new era than by employing the International Style?" The International Style was modern, free of references to an earlier era. Situated in suburban and rural areas, hospitals built at this time had the land and "clean slate" to reintroduce a connection to nature, part of the appeal of suburban living. Patient wards were based on double-loaded corridors with semiprivate rooms. Separate diagnostic and treatment buildings were provided to accommodate future expansion and technological modifications without affecting the bed units.

The mechanical ventilation systems that emerged in the 1950s and 1960s made possible the larger and deeper horizontal floorplates that, in turn, facilitated the hospital type that remains most prevalent today: inpatient towers above a deep diagnostic and treatment base. Industrial systems thinking applied to hospital design led to a detailed assessment of travel distances, adjacencies, and the emergence of the discipline of medical planning as maximum "plan efficiency" was pursued for each functional building component. This systems thinking led to new nursing unit configurations, such as circular or triangular layouts.

By the early 1970s, high-tech architectural style coupled with expressive building forms and systems yielded modernist hospitals across America. The most notable of these endeavors is Eberhard Zeidler's McMaster University Health Sciences Centre (1972) in Hamilton, Ontario. Each floor plate of this hospital comprises 10 acres, the mechanical system is expressed, and the circulation is organized around a major atrium. The four-story building (with four interstitial spaces), located in a small-scale residential neighborhood, was the first North American hospital with interstitial space—floors for mechanical services interspersed between occupied levels—an idea intended to address the increased demand for flexibility in research and diagnostic space. Critics questioned the overwhelming scale and lack of "humanity" in the expressive machine form of the facility. These massive buildings, they argued, were a physical manifestation of the centralization of power in hospital-based health care.

Many hospitals in the mid-20th century, including the 1968 Stamford Hospital in Connecticut by Perkins & Will, were designed in the International Style, which seemed to visually express the medical profession's faith in technology at that time.
Courtesy Perkins & Will

1964
Competition announced for design
of new AIA headquarters

Peabody Terrace,
Harvard,
Sert, Jackson & Gourley

Vanna Venturi House,
Philadelphia,
Robert Venturi

An Alternative Approach

While the hospital model of health care swelled in size and stature, another form of treatment took its own, more modest course. Whether termed a bath, spa, or retreat, throughout history such alternative environments have, by and large, aimed to restore and rejuvenate individuals through intense contact with the senses. These facilities have retained the powerful and potent connection to "prevention of disease" that was lost in the development of the acute care hospital. Architect Barbara Crisp explains in her 1998 book *Human Spaces*, "The retreat encourages the release of one's body armor and the opening of the psyche to the moment, letting go of time and place."

The Sanctuary of Asklepios at Epidaurus was the most celebrated healing center of the ancient world. Named for the most important healer-god of antiquity, the sanctuary enjoyed enormous financial prosperity in the 6th–4th centuries BCE. The building program progressed from construction of monumental places of worship to development of a series of secular buildings, including a theater, baths, and palaestrae (gymnasia/exercise facilities). Ill people went to Epidaurus seeking cures, and it is said, while they slept, Asklepios advised them in their dreams about what they should do to regain their health. The sanctuary was located near mineral springs, which may also have been used as part of the healing rituals. From the beginning, such "sacred" healing spaces were placed in sacred physical locations.

Numerous cultures have continued the Greek tradition, regarding bathing as a ritual as well as a social experience. In ancient Rome, baths included palaestrae, libraries, and reading rooms. Often, they were performance sites. By the 6th century CE, Rome contained more than 900 baths. The broad reach of the Roman Empire left a legacy of ritual baths and healing spaces as far north as Bath, England (named for the ancient baths that remain in the town's midst).

As the Industrial Revolution progressed and medicine created hospitals for care of the seriously ill, a countervailing health-based movement was always present. In the mid-19th century, a resort spa movement emerged in the United States to recapture the therapeutic aspect of nature for those stressed by the industrial economy. The wealthy routinely retreated to resort spas, seeking respite from the epidemics and pollution of rapidly growing cities. Berkeley Springs, in West Virginia, claimed the title of "first spa in North America" based on a natural warm spring that had been frequented by Native Americans prior to colonization. By the late 1880s, more than 800 spas and resorts dotted the United States.

The ancient baths of Bath, England, fed by a natural hot spring, reflect the broad reach of the Roman Empire's legacy of ritual baths and healing spaces.
©age fotostock/SuperStock

Despite their common ancestry, the hospital and spa models had little in common. While the hospital became increasingly focused on technology, resort spas and related facilities encouraged connection with authentic nature. Straddling the two movements was the tuberculosis sanatorium, a type conceived in the mid-19th century to address the TB epidemic, which was associated with unhealthy air in industrializing urban environments. Thomas Mann's 1924 novel *The Magic Mountain* is a well-known exposition on lost humanism. The story takes place at an elegant tuberculosis sanatorium, modeled on the one at Davos-Clavadel, Switzerland, where Mann's protagonist spends seven years "taking the cure" in nature. Real-life patients were able to do the same at Alvar Aalto's Paimio Sanatorium (1929–33) in Paimio, Finland. This facility comprised a series of connected structures oriented to capture sun and views of the surrounding forest. Patients spent long hours on the rooftop sundecks or walking in the gardens or along the trails. At the end of each patient unit, a large solarium gave the building occupants direct contact with the mountain air and view. When advances in treatment brought an end to the hospitalization of TB patients, Paimio was converted to a hospital and remains in use today. TB sanatoriums in the United States were frequently located in areas known for their resort spas, such as the Adirondacks and the Catskills.

Just as advances in medicine rendered the TB sanatorium obsolete, advances in public health improved living conditions in cities, obviating the need to escape urban epidemics. In addition, the national park system provided Americans with a new way to experience wilderness and nature, and air travel increased the number of leisure travel destinations. Resort spas began to reinvent themselves as "retreats," places for privacy and engagement in individual therapeutic regimens. Modern-day spas have proliferated, attesting to the appeal of this model. Whether urban or rural, they reconnect the individual to nature through numerous design strategies, including natural materials, water features, and the careful sequencing of space and lighting. Urban and suburban spa environments focus inward on intricately designed interiors that evoke authentic nature, while those located in unique natural settings focus outward. Retreats, whether ecocamps or spiritual centers, are typically situated in a remote environment where visitors have the opportunity to experience nature and reflect on the deepest aspects of what it means to be human, while engaging in healthy eating, exercise, and cultivation of spiritual values.

Modern-day spas, such as Clodagh Design's Sasanqua Spa on Kiawah Island in South Carolina, reconnect the individual to nature through material selection, earthy colors, and proximity to nature. Completed in 2002, this spa provides a tranquil getaway for its visitors. *Daniel Aubry, courtesy Clodagh Design*

Redefining the Healing Environment

By the end of the 20th century, a body of research had begun to appear supporting the importance of nature in health care settings. In particular, early studies demonstrated the therapeutic importance of views of nature. Related work on "wayfinding"—the concept that architecture can help individuals find their way through a building or complex—showing that contact with the exterior can help orient occupants of a building, gave additional credence to the notion that health care facilities should increase their connection with nature. Concurrently, the public has become more familiar with alternative approaches to maintaining or restoring health, from exercise, diet, and homeopathic treatments to a better appreciation of the relationship between mind and body. This more holistic outlook, on the part of at least some members of the public and the scientific community, has helped to lay the groundwork for a radical new vision of health care and, consequently, of health care architecture.

Parallel to this change in outlook, E. O. Wilson, the famed entomologist at Harvard University, coined the term "biophilia" to describe the inherent human inclination to affiliate with nature. Building on Wilson's work, Stephen Kellert, social ecologist at Yale University, subsequently proposed the concept of "biophilic design," stressing the importance of buildings and constructed landscapes that foster a positive connection between people and nature. Drawing on a broad range of scientific studies of perception and preferences, Kellert and his colleagues have charted biophilic principles to inform the design of the built environment.

A change in management structure has also affected the physical form of health care organizations. This began in the early 1970s, when the Hill-Burton Act refocused grants from capital construction to provision of services and the private insurance industry broadened to include health maintenance organizations. As a result, the hospital of the 20th century began to transform to a "business model," competing for private financing for its physical structures. As this major change in financing occurred, author John D. Thompson of the Yale School of Public Health observed, "The old idea of one hospital to satisfy all needs is a thing of the past. We'll always need some healthcare factories for efficient, short-term intensive-care stays, but we'll need others where humanity won't have to overcome the technical apparatus."

1965
*Founding of the International
Council on Monuments and Sites
(ICOMOS)*

The 108,000-square-foot Ambulatory Services Building (1988), designed by KMD Architects for Brigham & Women's Hospital in Boston, includes a multilevel lobby that serves as a new campus entry. With interior planters and abundant natural light, this hotel-like atrium adds warmth and visual stimulation to the hospital experience. *KMD Architects*

Salk Institute for Biological Studies,
La Jolla,
Louis Kahn

Sea Ranch Condominium I,
Charles Moore/MLTW

Gateway Arch,
St. Louis,
Eero Saarinen

Richards Medical Research Building,
Philadelphia,
Louis Kahn

Roy E. Larsen Hall,
Harvard University,
William Caudill/CRS

By the early 1980s, hospitals, which had historically been governed by medical professionals, began hiring people with degrees and experience in business to manage their strategic and economic planning. Competition between health care systems intensified as hospitals focused on improving efficiency, reducing length of inpatient stays, and increasing market share for the more lucrative aspects of health care delivery. In step with these changes, the quality of the built environment became a larger focus of these institutions.

This business mindset produced a "medical mall" vision of the hospital with a large, theatrical atrium that often linked an immense ambulatory care center with the "hotel" and medical functions of the traditional acute care setting. At the same time, the diagnosis and treatment of certain diseases required further centralization of high-technology medicine within specialty settings. Morphosis used an atrium to channel daylight into the below-grade waiting areas for radiation therapy in the most notable project of this period, the Cedars-Sinai Comprehensive Cancer Center (1987). Architecture critics noted that the introduction of daylight into this setting acquired a spiritual dimension, an important "wake-up call" in the gradual shift back to reconnecting nature with healing.

In 1993 designer Wayne Ruga founded the Center for Health Design to invigorate a critical dialogue that would finally give a much higher priority to Postman's "question of what was being *undone*" in the reign of technology. Ruga, like many others at this point, believed the poor environmental quality of 20th-century hospitals was having a negative effect on health

In the late 1980s, Morphosis introduced daylighting into below-grade floor levels at Cedars-Sinai Comprehensive Cancer Center in Los Angeles, where patients wait for radiation therapy. The project dramatically focused architectural attention on the medical community's increasing awareness of the value of nature in the healing process. ©*Grant Mudford*

1966
JFK Federal Building,
Boston,
Walter Gropius/TAC

Whitney Museum of American Art,
New York City,
Marcel Breuer and Hamilton P. Smith

Publication of Complexity and
Contradiction in Architecture, by
Robert Venturi

Passage of the National Historic
Preservation Act

Kenzo Tange, Hon. FAIA,
received the AIA Gold Medal

outcomes. Recognizing that technology, insofar as it represented "objective, measurable data," had the front seat in building design, the center was determined to deliver the same kind of objective data by measuring the effect of changes in the built environment on a patient's overall hospital experience and medical outcome.

The center first gathered a coalition of researchers in environmental design to define "evidence-based design" (a term borrowed from the lexicon of evidence-based medicine) in support of life-enhancing environments that promote health and healing. In 1999 the center launched an environmental research program, the "Pebble Projects," to begin to collect data on the role of the physical environment on medical outcomes. Shepley Bulfinch Richardson and Abbott's Bronson Methodist Hospital (2000) in Kalamazoo, Michigan—which features a central garden atrium to organize access to medical offices, outpatient care, and acute care—was the setting for the first major Pebble project.

In 2003 the Center for Health Design completed a "Fable Hospital" study, a business analysis of the economic cost/benefit of constructing a hypothetical, 300-bed hospital using evidence-based principles. In this study, reported in an article titled "The Business Case for Better Buildings" in *Frontiers of Health Services Management*, a series of building improvements implemented and studied through individual Pebble Projects were synthesized into a single, hypothetical building. Aggregate costs and benefits based on the individual Pebble data were calculated for factors ranging from single-bed rooms, an increased number of windows, and wider toilet-room doorways to program enhancements such as meditation rooms and gardens. In total, these improvements increased the construction cost by more than 10 percent, but a combination of improvements in market share, staff retention, staff performance, and safety demonstrated a payback of less than one year. In 2006 many of these evidence-based principles were introduced as recommended practices for the environment of care in the appendix language of *Guidelines for Design and Construction of Health Care Facilities*, the regulatory standard that governs the majority of health care construction in the United States.

(Opposite) Designed by Shepley Bulfinch Richardson and Abbott and completed in 2000, the Bronson Methodist Hospital in Kalamazoo, Michigan, features a central skylit atrium with various amenities, such as a food court, library, and pharmacy. It was selected by the Center for Health Design as one of the first Pebble Projects, an ongoing evidenced-based research initiative to measure the effects of the built environment on medical outcomes. ©Peter Mauss/Esto, courtesy Bronson Methodist Hospital

The Patrick H. Dollard Discovery Health Center in Harris, New York, was designed by Guenther 5 Architects and completed in 2003. It reflects the health care industry's growing interest in sustainable solutions. The architects introduced daylighting, specified operable windows and low-emitting materials, and employed other approaches to significantly reduce energy consumption. *David Alee*

Early in the design process, the architects at NBBJ learned from current residents of an existing nursing home run by the Washington State Department of Veterans Affairs that they wanted to be able to operate their own windows. The replacement skilled nursing facility in Retsil, Washington, completed in 2005, met their needs, becoming the first naturally ventilated nursing home in this era. *Matt Milios/NBBJ ©2005*

Linking Human and Ecological Health

In 1996 growing awareness of environmental degradation caused by industrial production in the United States led the U.S. Environmental Protection Agency to categorize medical waste incineration as the second largest source of airborne dioxin and the fourth largest contributor to mercury emissions. In response to this challenge, a coalition of hospitals, health care systems, and environmental organizations founded Health Care Without Harm to, as its Web site notes, "transform the health care sector so it is no longer a source of harm to people and the environment."

In 2000 a landmark conference, "Setting Healthcare's Environmental Agenda," convened by Kaiser Permanente, Catholic Healthcare West, and Health Care Without Harm, expanded the vision of the health care sector, leading the design and construction industry toward health-based green-building standards. As recorded in the conference proceedings, Lloyd Dean, president and CEO of Catholic Healthcare West, made this statement: "We will not have healthy individuals, healthy families, and healthy communities if we do not have clean air, clean water, and healthy soil." The challenge to respond to this concern extended beyond health care operations to include the design and construction of the built health care environment.

Drawing on environmental medicine, public health, and the emerging discipline of ecological medicine, industry leaders developed the first health-based green-building tool, the "Green Guide for Health Care." Based on the LEED® framework developed by the U.S. Green Building Council, this guide for the sustainable design, construction, and operation of health care facilities is used by design professionals, hospitals, and health systems as a best practices tool for improving environmental performance. It also provides a strong health basis for the continued development of green-building tools for other markets. Kaiser Permanente, the largest nonprofit health care provider in the United States, has been active in developing the Green Guide, piloting its use in a major hospital rebuilding program.

Early sustainable building efforts in health care include the LEED-certified Boulder Community Foothills Hospital (2002), designed by Oz Architects and Boulder Associates, and the Patrick H. Dollard Discovery Health Center (2003) in Harris, New York, designed by Guenther 5 Architects. The ambulatory care Discovery Center exhibits a strong bioregional connection that resulted from incorporation of sustainable design considerations. The project also reduced energy demand by 42 percent, specified low-emitting materials, introduced daylighting and operable windows, and reconsidered traditional mechanical design approaches for ambulatory care facilities.

Legacy Salmon Creek Hospital by Zimmer Gunsul Frasca Architects opened in 2005 in Vancouver, Washington. The project takes advantage of multiple connections to the natural world. The building is oriented to maximize views and includes both outdoor terraces and a healing garden. Patient access and orientation were also carefully considered. *Eckert & Eckert*

1967
Regional/Urban Design
Assistance Teams established
to help communities identify
challenges and develop a vision
for the future

Charles W. Moore, dean of
the Yale School of Art and
Architecture from 1965 to 1970,
founded the Yale Building Project

Joseph Papp Public Theater
(adaptive use of the former
Astor Library), New York City,
Giorgio Cavaglieri

Wallace Kirkman Harrison, FAIA,
received the AIA Gold Medal

NBBJ's Washington State Veterans' Home (2005), a LEED Gold-certified, long-term care facility in Retsil, overcame tremendous regulatory challenges to become the first naturally ventilated nursing home in this era. Drawing from the language of spa architecture and hospitals of an earlier period, its multiple buildings point the way to a new 21st-century vision of health care.

Legacy Salmon Creek Hospital (2005), designed by Zimmer Gunsul Frasca Architects in Vancouver, Washington, reflects a fundamental recalibration of the hospital building, one that celebrates connection to the natural world, daylight, healthy materials, and improved air quality. Located on a site bounded by a forest, the hospital is oriented to maximize views. It includes outdoor terraces for both patients and staff and a healing garden.

Now in the early stages of design for a new hospital for Palomar Pomerado Health, Anshen + Allen of San Francisco is pioneering a closer connection between landscape and the built environment through extensive gardens that begin on the journey from parking to entrance and are replicated throughout the building with generous outdoor terrace areas.

Scheduled to open in Escondido, California, in 2011, the planned Palomar Pomerado hospital by Anshen + Allen hopes to be a model of patient-centered health care. The design calls for extensive landscaping, healing gardens, and abundant natural light.
Courtesy CO Architects

A Healthier Future

The link between our health and built environment has never been clearer. We are now aware that certain materials, such as asbestos and lead paint, can lead to lifelong disabilities; poor mechanical systems can lead to Legionnaires' disease and contribute to sick-building syndrome; and plasticizers added to building materials may trigger asthma. More recent research suggests that an increase in certain chronic diseases—such as diabetes, obesity, and asthma—may be linked to the more sedentary, automobile-oriented lifestyles encouraged by our built environment.

At the same time, ever-escalating health care costs are challenging the medical system's focus on disease rather than prevention. Never in the history of the United States has there been an era with so much possibility for the transformation of the physical form of health care architecture through the application of evidence-based design and sustainable design principles. And never before has there been such an imperative to apply knowledge of disease prevention to other building types as well. Architects—working with members from the planning, public health, and medical professions—are being challenged to think ecologically and empathically to create a built environment that promotes health in all walks of life. ●

1968
Speaking at the AIA convention in Portland, Oregon, civil rights leader Whitney M. Young Jr. challenged the profession to assume its responsibility to the cause of civil rights

Passage of the Architectural Barriers Act

Robert C. Weaver Federal Building, Washington, D.C., Marcel Breuer

Ford Foundation Headquarters, New York City, Kevin Roche and John Dinkeloo

The Cannery, San Fransisco, Joseph Esherick

GOLD MEDALIST, 1963

Alvar Aalto, Hon. FAIA

William Morgan

Kolmio, with permission of the Alvar Aalto Foundation

Alvar Aalto had built only one building in the United States when the American Institute of Architects awarded him the Gold Medal in 1963, and only intrepid architectural pilgrims who had trekked to far-off Finland had seen his other works firsthand. Nevertheless, Aalto was an influential figure whose achievements in design, housing, furniture, and planning placed him in modern architecture's pantheon alongside Frank Lloyd Wright and Le Corbusier.

Finland was part of czarist Russia when Aalto was born in the small village of Kourtane in 1898; his life and that of Finland are inextricably linked. He was a student at the technical university in Helsinki during the declaration of independence and the subsequent civil war. After service in World War II, Aalto led the planning and rebuilding of war-torn towns and cities and oversaw the relocation of thousands of refugees. Before his death in 1976, he had achieved near godlike status among the architecturally literate Finns.

The Paimio tuberculosis sanatorium (1929–33) near Turku—for which Aalto won the design competition when he was only 31—was a watershed work that established him as both a significant talent and the leading proponent of the International Style in Finland. At first glance, the white Cubist composition in the woods appears to be a northern interpretation of the Bauhaus. But Paimio is more than a factory for healing. The hospital's three main wings fan out from the building's fulcrum at other than right angles, sited to make maximum therapeutic use of light and air. There are sinuously curved walls, roofs, and railings, as well as splashes of bright color.

Each patient was given draft-free windows, access to outdoor decks, and long views of forest landscape. The eponymous Paimio chair was raked at an angle to help pulmonary patients breathe more easily. Like much of the affordable laminated wood furniture designed by Aalto and his wife, Aino, the Paimio chair remains a touchstone of modernism.

After World War II, Aalto taught architecture at the Massachusetts Institute of Technology, where he designed Baker House (see page 261), a dormitory notable for its concern with comfort rather than polemical statement. The building's unique undulating façade allowed almost of its residents to have river views. Admirers were taken aback by the use of clinker brick and warm wood detailing, as if somehow the low-tech Aalto had betrayed European Functionalism. Yet Aalto's humanistic approach to institutional housing was a further refinement of Paimio, while the dormitory's characteristic "wave" configuration was foretold in his 1936 signature free-form design now known as the Savoy vase.

The seeds of Aalto's so-called organic phase were planted at Paimio and blossomed at the town hall at Säynätsalo (1949–52), the architect's masterpiece. Again using the humble yet tactile materials of brick and wood, Aalto imbued a domestically scaled complex with a dignified civic presence, echoing medieval Italian city squares as well as the Finnish near-pagan symbiosis with the forest. The ceremonial grass entrance steps at Säynätsalo, the most iconic image of Aalto's career, serve as a metaphor for the temporal state of mankind's building in the face of nature.

Aalto's plan for Paimio can be seen on the wall of the director's office.
Courtesy William Morgan

The Paimio tuberculosis sanatorium (1929–33) established Aalto as the leading proponent of the International Style in Finland.
Gustaf Welin, Alvar Aalto Museum

Stamford Hospital,
Connecticut,
Perkins & Will

New National Gallery,
Berlin,
Mies van der Rohe

Everson Art Museum,
Syracuse, New York,
I. M. Pei

Boston City Hall,
Kallmann, McKinnell & Knowles

Marcel Lajos Breuer, FAIA,
received the AIA Gold Medal

Oakland, California–based Kaiser Permanente occupies a unique niche in the health care community: This nonprofit organization, which offers health insurance to 8.4 million members, owns and operates scores of health care facilities in nine states and Washington, D.C. "We manage 63 million square feet of space in California alone," says John Kouletsis, AIA, director of strategy, planning, and design for Kaiser Permanente's facilities group. Throughout its history, Kaiser has devoted significant resources to improving the health of the communities it serves, reasoning it's not only the right thing to do but also more economical to keep people healthy than treat them when ill. For the past several years, the company has extended that logic to its facilities, taking a leadership role in developing sustainable practices for health care design.

Kouletsis's team includes a standards group composed of several architects and engineers who map out sustainability policies, share best practices, and review outside green design guidelines to gauge their applicability. They work closely with the company's environmental stewardship council, whose participants range from in-house financial officers to representatives from outside firms that design and build Kaiser's health care facilities. "We look for strategies that offer improved patient, worker, and environmental safety with a reasonable payback period—typically no more than three to five years," says Kouletsis.

Among other policies, Kaiser Permanente often eschews the standard three-duct HVAC system for health care (two ducts for supply and return air with some return air reused as supply, plus a third duct to supply only fresh air to isolation areas housing highly infection-prone patients) in favor of a two-duct system using 100 percent fresh intake air throughout the entire hospital. This strategy works best in moderate climates, where air doesn't need as much conditioning or dehumidification. Kaiser also favors rubber over vinyl flooring because it is less hazardous to manufacture and easier to maintain, and Kaiser has found it reduces slips and leg fatigue among health care workers. Through its sheer size

and strategic partnerships with outside designers and building product manufacturers, Kaiser has provided enough incentives to encourage development of green alternatives, which can be implemented widely and cost-effectively within the health care industry.

In recognition of Kaiser Permanente's longstanding commitment to researching and improving health care design, the AIA College of Fellows awarded the 2005 Latrobe Fellowship to the health care provider and two of its longtime collaborators, Chong Partners Architecture of San Francisco and the University of California at Berkeley. The $100,000 grant funded a two-year study to assess if and how elements of architectural design—such as natural light and color palette—affect healing rates and recovery of patients from different cultures. "The study will include literature reviews, physiological evidence, in-facility observations, and interviews," says Gordon Chong, FAIA, principal of Chong Partners and past president of the AIA. "We'll be able to learn a great deal by analyzing the data that Kaiser has been collecting about its facilities and how their patients fare in them."

Kaiser Permanente's expertise in both evidence-based design and sustainable design has extended beyond its walls to engage the broader health care community. A member of Kaiser's standards group sits on the steering committee for the "Green Guide for Health Care," a best practices manual developed to encourage sustainable design in health care facilities. And in June 2006, the nonprofit opened the Sidney R. Garfield Health Care Innovation Center in Oakland. Named for the company's founding physician, this 37,000-square-foot center will allow health care workers to sit side-by-side with architects and designers to test new equipment, technologies, materials, and designs. The company sees all its research efforts as commonsense measures, especially given the rise of environmentally triggered illnesses like asthma and allergies. "As a health care provider, we have an obligation to make sure our buildings are not adding to the problem," Kouletsis says.

The Logic of Green: Sustainable Practices in Health Care Design

Deborah Snoonian

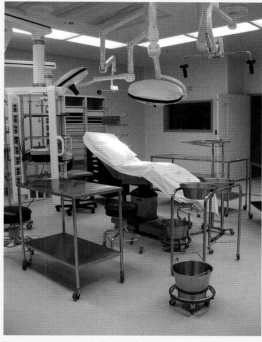

The operating room at the Garfield Center is electronically equipped to enable full-scale surgical simulations; windows allow filming and photographing during simulation exercises. Materials in the OR are sustainable and low in volatile organic compounds.
Courtesy Kaiser Permanente

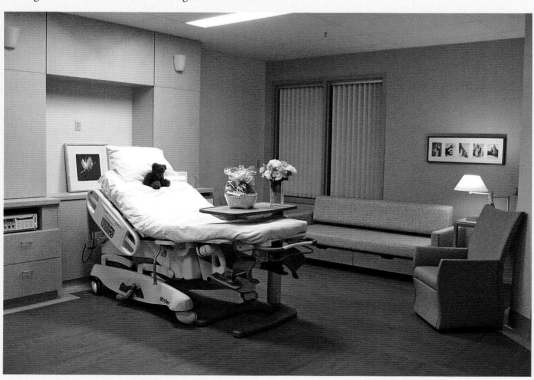

Like other mockup spaces at the Garfield Center, the labor and delivery room features sustainable design strategies and materials. Windows let in natural light, walls are covered with eco-friendly paint, and the designers chose energy-saving lights and low-flow, hands-free faucets. *Courtesy Kaiser Permanente*

1969
Presentation of the AIA's first
Twenty-five Year Award, to
Rockefeller Center

Design Research Headquarters,
Cambridge, Massachusetts,
Benjamin Thompson

Lincoln Elementary School,
Columbus, Indiana,
Gunnar Birkerts

Lincoln Center for the Performing
Arts (1962–69), New York City,
Max Abramovitz, Pietro Belluschi,
Gordon Bunshaft/SOM, Wallace
Harrison, Philip Johnson, and
Eero Saarinen

William Wilson Wurster, FAIA,
received the AIA Gold Medal

16

Architecture for Arts' Sake

John Morris Dixon, FAIA

Performing and visual arts have been part of every culture since humans appeared, but specific architectural settings were not always needed. Through most of history, the arts were dispersed in public squares and places of worship or in private dwellings and palaces. But when a society's arts became distinct from its religious rituals, separate architectural settings were often designed for them.

(Opposite) Adler & Sullivan's Auditorium Building (1887–90) in Chicago remains one of the largest performing arts spaces in the country. It was one of the first theaters in the United States to be lighted with electricity. *Henry Groskinsky/Time Life Pictures/Getty Images*

Historic Precedents

Architecture for the performing arts emerged first. As early as about 600 BCE, the Greeks were building theaters with semicircles of banked seating facing a space for the actors, a design later elaborated in Hellenistic and Roman examples to include a raised stage and an architectural backdrop with portals for entrances and exits. By the 14th century in Japan, the typical theater for Noh drama had taken shape, with a stage in the form of a simple pavilion, standing in a graveled courtyard surrounded by colonnades for audience seating. Shakespearean plays were performed in facilities such as the 1599 Globe Theatre in London, with a portico-sheltered stage at one side and several stories of seating forming a many-sided polygon around an unroofed "pit" for the less affluent audience.

The form of most of the world's theaters and opera houses today can be traced to a horseshoe-shaped type established in Renaissance Italy. Exemplified by the so-called Scientific Theater in Padua (1769), designed by Antonio Bibiena, these structures had tiers of boxes around an orchestra floor and a proscenium arch separating the audience from the stage. The prototypical concert hall—spatially comparable to the theater but without a proscenium arch—developed apace with the symphony orchestra and was well established by the late 19th century.

Toward the end of that century, the American Wallace Clement Sabine founded the science of acoustics, still evolving today, which has placed the acoustician on an equal footing with the architect in the design of performance halls. The first hall to which Sabine applied his scientific method was Boston Symphony Hall (1901), designed with McKim, Mead and White. For all its technical justification, this venue largely confirmed the acoustical effectiveness of the "shoebox" configuration found in other much-admired halls, such as the Concertgebouw (1888) in Amsterdam, The Netherlands, designed by Adolf Leonard van Gendt.

1970
AIA secured appointment of
George White, FAIA, as Architect
of the Capitol, the first practicing
architect to hold the position in
70 years

First Earth Day is celebrated,
April 22

Ada Louis Huxtable, architecture critic
for the New York Times, received the
first Pulitzer Prize for Criticism

La Luz,
Albuquerque,
Antoine Predock

Centraal Beheer,
Apeldoorn, The Netherlands,
Hermann Hertzberger

Many additions have been built around the Metropolitan Museum of Art's original building (1880), on Fifth Avenue in Central Park, designed by Calvert Vaux and Jacob Wrey Mold. Richard Morris Hunt designed the Beaux-Arts main entrance to the museum, shown here, which opened in 1902. McKim, Mead and White designed north and south additions (1911–26), and in the 1970s and 1980s Kevin Roche John Dinkeloo and Associates added six additional wings.
©Peter Mauss/Esto

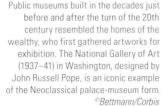

Public museums built in the decades just before and after the turn of the 20th century resembled the homes of the wealthy, who first gathered artworks for exhibition. The National Gallery of Art (1937–41) in Washington, designed by John Russell Pope, is an iconic example of the Neoclassical palace-museum form.
©Bettmann/Corbis

One of America's greatest performing arts venues, in terms of both size and design distinction, remains the Auditorium Building (1887–90) in Chicago, by architects Adler & Sullivan. Containing 4,200 seats for a wide variety of musical and theatrical events, its vast volume is unified by a series of arched forms spanning its width and by consistent relief ornament closely coordinated with the exposed bulbs of its then-novel electric lighting.

Architecture for the visual arts began much later than that for the performing arts. Initially, private collections of paintings and sculpture were displayed in mansions and palaces for the enjoyment of their owners and the owners' guests. Gradually, many palaces, including the Louvre in Paris and the Hermitage in St. Petersburg, became public museums. Structures designed specifically to house visual arts did not emerge until the first half of the 19th century. Setting the pattern for purpose-built museums were John Soane's Dulwich Gallery near London (1814) and Friedrich Schinkel's Altes Museum in Berlin (1830). The new museums were typically laid out with palacelike galleries illuminated from above with light monitors or skylights. Palace imagery also characterized their exteriors, particularly during the worldwide spate of museum building of the late 19th and early 20th centuries brought about to meet the cultural ambitions of the world's burgeoning cities and fueled by capitalist philanthropy.

These palace museums reached their apogee in institutions such as the Metropolitan Museum of Art (1880–1926) in New York, designed by Richard Morris Hunt and McKim, Mead and White, among others, and the Philadelphia Museum of Art (1919–28), by Horace Trumbauer's firm. Brilliantly recapping this movement was the National Gallery of Art (1937–41) in Washington, D.C., by John Russell Pope. After this period, however, most museum design has purposely diverged, often radically, from such Neoclassical models.

New Venues

By the first half of the 20th century, the world of the performing arts appears to have split into three modes: the elite world of symphony, opera, and ballet; the popular manifestations of vaudeville, musical theater, jazz, and pop; and, straddling the other two, live theater.

Of these, popular culture was the first to generate a novel architectural genre—the movie palace. Although based on the Italian Renaissance model used to house theater productions, the structures built to screen movies introduced grand lobbies, enlarged halls with varied and

John Hancock Center,
Chicago,
Bruce Graham/SOM

Butterfield School,
Libertyville, Illinois,
Orput Associates

StageCenter
(formerly Mummers Theater),
Oklahoma City,
John Johansen

Richard Buckminster Fuller, FAIA,
received the AIA Gold Medal

imaginative décor (from Egyptian and Baroque to Art Deco), and new approaches to interior lighting. Bold signs and marquees provided visual drama on the exterior of these buildings, which were often wedged in among other commercial fronts.

The most architecturally ambitious movie palace anywhere in the world is Radio City Music Hall. This 6,200-seat setting for movies and lavish musical reviews opened in 1933. The Music Hall was a key component of New York's multiblock Rockefeller Center, all elements of which—offices, retail, restaurants, open spaces, gardened rooftops—were meticulous in their design and execution. The design of the complex was overseen by an architectural team that included AIA Gold Medalist Wallace Harrison and Raymond Hood, and the Music Hall itself was created by architect Edward Durell Stone with interior designer Donald Deskey. The focus of the huge interior is a kind of abstract sunrise—a composition of concentric arcs and radiating wedges—all unabashedly gilded and glowing in indirect lighting, an innovation at that time.

Radio City Music Hall in New York City, opened in 1933 as part of Rockefeller Center, was a grand example of the movie palace—a new form of architecture for the arts. The innovative indirect lighting in the theater made the stage glow. ©Bettmann/Corbis

1971
Weyerhaeuser Headquarters,
Federal Way, Washington, SOM

John F. Kennedy Center for the
Performing Arts, Washington, D.C.,
Edward Durell Stone

Louis Isidore Kahn, FAIA,
received the AIA Gold Medal

StageCenter (formerly Mummers Theater), designed by architect John Johansen and completed in 1970 in Oklahoma City, houses two theaters, an art gallery, and support space. The building—three concrete pods connected by steel tunnels and bridges—received a national AIA Honor Award in 1972. ©Balthazar Korab Ltd.

It was not until the 1960s that theater design for live performances strayed from the familiar Italian-Renaissance form. Paralleling a shift away from illusionistic staging, a strong movement arose to reorganize the theater interior. Alternative forms, including the arena ("theater in the round") and the slightly less radical thrust stage, were explored in new theaters such as Arena Stage (1961) in Washington, D.C, by Harry Weese; the Guthrie Theater (1963) in Minneapolis by Ralph Rapson; and StageCenter (formerly Mummers Theater; 1970) in Oklahoma City by John Johansen.

Parallel innovations in concert hall design began to appear around 1960, as architects and their clients sought to bring performers and audiences into closer relationship. Hans Scharoun's Philharmonie in Berlin (1963) led the way as the first major hall to position the orchestra roughly in the midst of the audience. Acoustically, this arrangement demanded substitutes for reliable walls to reinforce sound; arrays of reflectors, which acousticians were now able to configure with some confidence, were installed above the orchestra. At Boettcher Hall (1978) in Denver, designed by Hardy Holzman Pfeiffer, the orchestra was located at the center of an arena-like space. Pei Cobb Freed's design for the well-regarded Meyerson Symphony Center (1989) in Dallas moved the orchestra somewhat forward from the back wall, with tiers of seats behind to be occupied either by a chorus or audience members. Frank Gehry did the same in his recently completed Walt Disney Concert Hall (2003) in Los Angeles.

(Opposite) Frank Gehry's Walt Disney Concert Hall, opened in Los Angeles in 2003, continues the design trend of the second half of the 20th century of moving the orchestra closer to the audience. ©Lara Swimmer/Esto

Building as Sculpture

As soon as major arts institutions began to embrace Modernism—beginning in the 1940s—they began to sponsor some of the most adventurous and memorable landmarks of the movement. Many arts clients not only grasped the potential of exceptional design to raise public recognition of their institutions, they also began to see support of innovative architecture as part of their mission. A leading example is Frank Lloyd Wright's design for the Guggenheim Museum in New York, conceived initially in 1943 and completed in 1959, shortly after Wright's death. The museum's continuous spiral of exhibition space around a skylit atrium was a radical departure from previous museum design, providing an exhilarating spatial adventure, and the resulting sculptural form of the building's exterior became an instant urban landmark.

In 1957 an international design competition for the Sydney Opera House, actually a complex of several halls, yielded Jørn Utzon's stunningly sculptural landmark (completed in 1973), which the world quickly recognized as the symbol for Sydney, if not the whole of Australia. The building's complex set of volumes, based on segments of spheres and surfaced with white tiles, suggests a huge array of sails advancing into the Sydney harbor.

Arts commissions continued to yield notable accomplishments. Marcel Breuer and Hamilton Smith's Whitney Museum (1966) in New York made a bold sculptural statement on its confined site, with granite-clad volumes advancing toward the street as they rose floor by floor. Mies van der Rohe's New National Gallery (1968) in Berlin was a large-scale embodiment of his restrained, classically inspired design. At the Kimbell Art Museum (1972) in Fort Worth, Texas, Louis I. Kahn displayed his virtuosity in shaping a concrete vault roof system that diffuses daylight into the galleries.

After World War II, art museums began to recognize innovation in architecture as part of their mission. For the Guggenheim Museum (1959), New York, Frank Lloyd Wright dispensed with traditional ideas about museum design, creating a continuous spiral of exhibition space around a skylit atrium. *Ezra Stoller/©Esto*

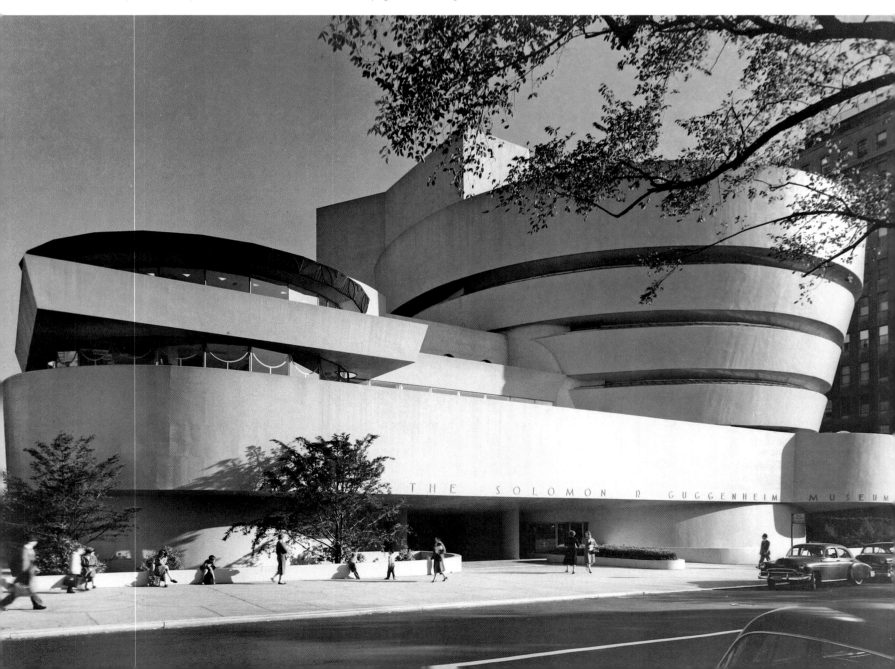

Danish architect Jørn Utzon designed the Sydney Opera House, completed in 1973 and now recognized around the world as the symbol of Australia. Utzon spent years resolving the complex engineering problems involved in building the sail-like roof.
©Alex Bartel/Esto

The concrete vault roof system of Louis Kahn's 1972 Kimbell Art Museum, Fort Worth, admits diffused daylight to the interior.
©Roberto Schezen/Esto

More recent arts buildings memorable for their accomplishments in form include Steven Holl's Kiasma Museum (1998) in Helsinki, a composition of surfaces with complex curvature that yields highly varied interiors; Zaha Hadid's Contemporary Arts Center (2002) in Cincinnati, which stacks subtly angular volumes on a tight downtown site; and the De Young Museum (2006) in San Francisco by Herzog & de Meuron, where a lacy skin of perforated copper wraps low-rise galleries and an identifying tower twists as it rises. Bold urban landmarks for the performing arts are exemplified by Frank Gehry's writhing, stainless-steel-clad volumes for the Disney Concert Hall and Rafael Vinoly's Tokyo International Forum (1996) and Kimmel Center for the Performing Arts (2001) in Philadelphia. Both Vinoly projects feature prominent, glass-enveloped lobby-circulation volumes.

Additions to existing institutions have also provided opportunities for bravura displays of form. Perhaps the most prominent of these is Pei Cobb Freed's East Building of the National Gallery (1978) in Washington, D.C., which received the AIA's Twenty-five Year Award in 2004. The exterior is a remarkable response to its site and its venerable neighbor, Pope's original gallery building. Pei's walls are clad in the same marble as the earlier building, applied here to minimalist geometric volumes that are close in scale and proportion to those of the older structure. Inside, the galleries are clustered around a vast skylit atrium that serves as a kind of indoor plaza for the entire museum. At the Louvre in Paris, Pei produced an equally memorable landmark by adding a modestly scaled glass-and-steel entry pyramid (1989) set between the museum's sprawling wings. The pyramid has become a widely known image, tending to overshadow the firm's more painstaking interior renovations of the huge complex.

(Opposite) The Contemporary Arts Center (2002) in downtown Cincinnati is Zaha Hadid's first U.S. building. Its stacked, angular volumes take advantage of a tight urban site. *©David La Spina/Esto*

I.M. Pei's design for the East Building (1978) of the National Gallery of Art, Washington, D.C., comprises two complementary triangles (an isosceles and a right) to house exhibition and office space. The 16,000-square-foot atrium ties the two together and serves as an indoor plaza for the entire museum. *Ezra Stoller/©Esto*

1972
Robert J. Nash received the first
Whitney M. Young Jr. Award

Publication of Learning from Las
Vegas, by Robert Venturi, Denise
Scott Brown, and Steven Izenour

Phillips Exeter Academy Library,
Exeter, New Hampshire,
Louis Kahn

Columbus East High School,
Indiana,
Mitchell/Giurgola

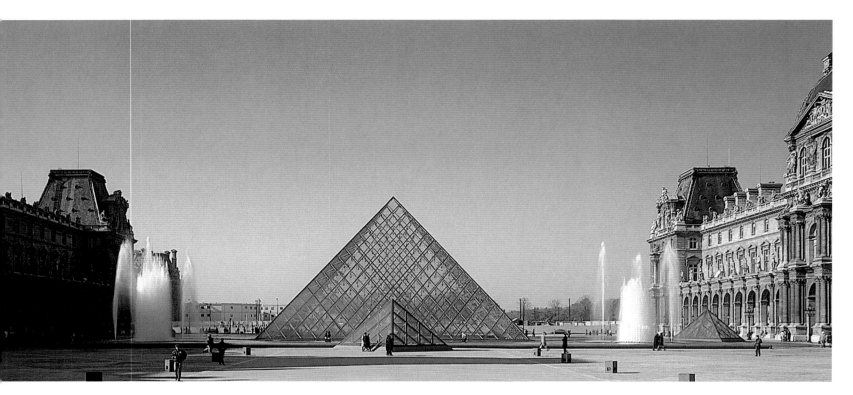

I. M. Pei's design for the Grand Louvre in Paris, a glass-and-steel pyramid (1989) that serves as the entrance portico to the museum's galleries, has become a well-known symbol of the museum and the city. ©*Serge Hambourg*

The façade of the Sainsbury Wing (1991) at London's National Gallery takes its cues from the original 1832 building but with a Postmodern twist, designed by Venturi, Scott Brown and Associates. Inside, the stately, well-proportioned galleries are lit by indirect natural light.
Matt Wargo, courtesy Venturi, Scott Brown and Associates

Transamerica Pyramid,
San Francisco,
William Pereira

McMaster University Health
Sciences Centre, Hamilton,
Ontario, Eberhard Zeidler

Kimbell Art Museum,
Fort Worth,
Louis Kahn

Pietro Belluschi, FAIA,
received the AIA Gold Medal

Postmodernism's most impressive contribution to arts facilities was undoubtedly the Sainsbury Wing addition (1991) to London's National Gallery by Venturi, Scott Brown and Associates . With characteristic irony, the architects applied fragments of the original gallery's classical ornament to their façade, and inside they used some oddly distorted classical details. There is no irony, however, in the stately, axial sequence of the addition's well-proportioned, skylit galleries. Striking, idiosyncratic forms can be seen in two museum additions completed in 2006: Herzog & de Meuron's extension of the Walker Art Center in Minneapolis and Daniel Libeskind's annex to the Denver Art Museum.

The impact of the Sydney Opera House on its city was not equaled until 1997, when Frank Gehry's sculptural Guggenheim Museum made a household name of the hitherto obscure city of Bilbao, Spain. Its swirling, titanium-clad forms, spread along the city's riverfront and seen in enticing fragments from downtown streets, present an image of cultural audacity that was immediately understood around the world. Another, slightly more modest example of what became known as the Bilbao effect is Santiago Calatrava's expansion of the Milwaukee Art Museum (2002), where the architect produced an architectural pilgrimage point that altered the image of its city. Commissioned to design a highly visible entry and lobby, plus visitor amenities, for a museum whose galleries already existed in the podium of the city's War Memorial, Calatrava produced a steel-and-glass pavilion that suggests a huge bird about to take flight over Lake Michigan. The design incorporates huge sunshades that move in response to sun and wind conditions, mimicking bird wings. And although Los Angeles was on the map before Gehry's Disney Concert Hall appeared in 2003, its downtown area was in serious need of memorable landmarks, and this structure is the most prominent of several recently completed or planned to bolster the district.

Inside Daniel Libeskind's titanium-clad addition to the Denver Art Museum (2006), a grand staircase spirals up through a four-story, skylit lobby. ©Momatiuk-Eastcott/Corbis

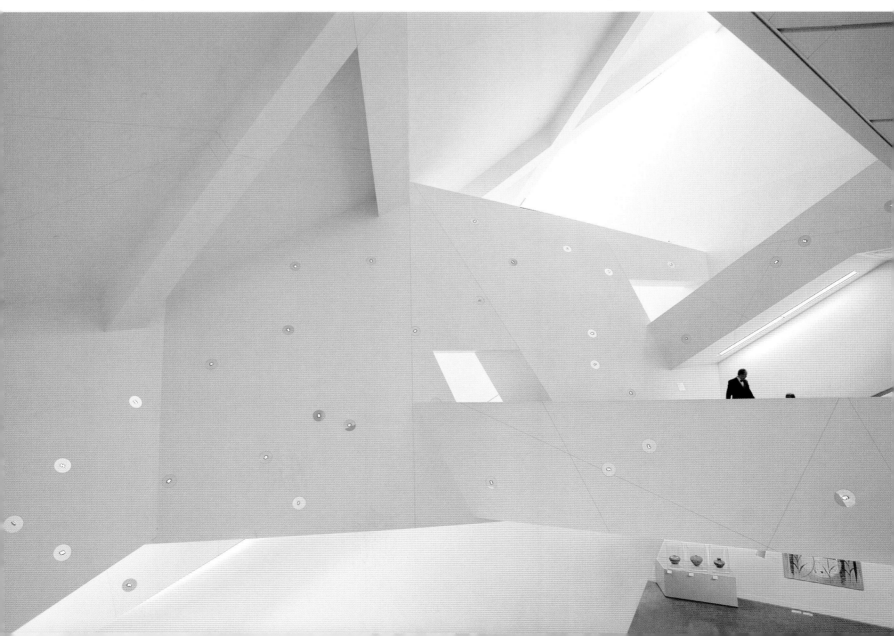

Art Complexes in the City and on Campuses

The 1950s nurtured the concept of combining a number of performing arts venues in one "center." This idea fulfilled a key strategy of the urban renewal movement—to replace an area of urban "decay" with a cluster of prominent buildings around one or more plazas. The center might focus on one function, as in Boston's Government Center (1962–73), or a mix of uses, as in Baltimore's Charles Center (1960–86). The quintessential performing arts center was New York's Lincoln Center (1962–69; see page 366), built to house several world-ranking institutions. Initiated at a time when Modernists were searching for appropriate ways to deal with monumentality, this vast project—still the largest of its kind—drew upon the talents of a team that included four architects who were or would become AIA Gold Medalists: Wallace Harrison, Pietro Belluschi, Philip Johnson, and Eero Saarinen. For Lincoln Center, the all-star team came up with a type of diluted Classicism that influenced other arts buildings for the next several years.

Not long afterward, Edward Durell Stone designed a huge performing arts center in Washington, D.C., intended to upgrade the capital's modest cultural image. Employing a similar kind of stripped-down Classicism, already his trademark, Stone put three major halls (for theater, opera and ballet, and concerts) under one vast roof at the Kennedy Center (1971; see page 151). A single lobby, longer than a Major League home-run hit, provided access to all three halls. The idea of assembling a critical mass of performing arts facilities to stimulate activity in the urban core has persisted ever since.

Expansion or updating of performing arts spaces usually requires new buildings on new sites, making it possible to gather them in a new "center." Museums, on the other hand, tend to become identified with their location, where they often evolve through additions. Although they may be strung along a monumental axis, as on Philadelphia's Benjamin Franklin Parkway or the National Mall in Washington, visual arts facilities have rarely been gathered into any kind of "center." The Getty Center (1997) in Los Angeles is the most ambitious effort to date to aggregate a number of visual arts functions, in this case all under the Getty aegis. Richard Meier

(Opposite) Frank Gehry's Guggenheim Museum (1997) in Bilbao, Spain, became an instant symbol of that city, similar to the impact of the Sydney Opera House almost a quarter century earlier. *©Jeff Goldberg/Esto*

The birdlike shape of Santiago Calatrava's addition for the Milwaukee Art Museum, completed in 2002, has become a focal point on that city's skyline. *©Alan Karchmer/Esto*

The Getty Center, constructed in Los Angeles in 1997, was designed by Richard Meier to house a variety of visual arts functions, including a museum and a conservation center. It is one of only a few such facilities in the world. *©Carol Highsmith*

1973
AIA convention approved a study
of the status of women in the
architecture profession

Dedication of the new AIA
headquarters building,
designed by TAC

Sydney Opera House,
Jørn Utzon

Colleges and universities have sponsored the design of a number of distinctive facilities for the arts in the last half century. A particularly ambitious project is the Nelson Fine Arts Center (1990) at Arizona State University, Phoenix, by Antoine Predock. *©Timothy Hursley*

designed a museum, research center, conservation center, and other facilities in the form of a hilltop acropolis. A group of independent museums recently built in Vienna's Museum Quarter is one other example of an effort to assemble multiple venues for the visual arts.

Complexes that combine both visual and performing arts facilities have also rarely appeared. San Francisco's Yerba Buena development contains a theater by James Stewart Polshek and a visual arts building by Fumihiko Maki (both 1993). The presence of these two buildings, along with the center's plazas and gardens, attracted the San Francisco Museum of Contemporary Art (1995) to build a structure by Mario Botta on an adjoining site. The original plan for the redevelopment of New York's World Trade Center site also included both performing and visual arts buildings, although this may not come to pass.

Some of the architecturally most distinctive arts facilities in the United States have been built on college and university campuses. For the campus of Wesleyan University in Connecticut, Roche Dinkeloo designed a cluster of buildings (1965–73) for both visual and performing arts, which is modest in scale but impressive for its minimalist, seemingly timeless, marble-walled volumes. For Ohio State University, Peter Eisenman won a design competition for the Wexner Center for the Arts (1989; see page 51), which weaves together new and existing arts facilities in a form that challenges the visitor's perceptions. One of the most ambitious and successful of these campus arts centers is the Nelson Fine Arts Center (1990) by Antoine Predock at Arizona State University, where distinct building parts, such as the theater's fly tower and the museum's unusual stepped roof, complement each other in an assemblage recalling a village or pueblo.

Art Revivals

Arts organizations have always occupied space in preexisting buildings. It was not until the 1960s, however, that adaptive use of existing space was widely viewed as a subject for serious architectural effort—and a source of pride and praise for the firms that carried it out. Arts facilities were among the first to generate distinguished examples of reuse, and they have continued to do so, often stimulating the revival of old neighborhoods or even whole towns.

Among the early architecturally notable arts facilities in adapted space was the Joseph Papp Public Theater (1967) in New York City. Designed by pioneering adaptive-use architect Giorgio Cavaglieri, it was constructed in the former Astor Library. By creating an effective home for a repertory theater company, including multiple venues, rehearsal halls, and offices, in a mid-19th-century Classical Revival landmark, Cavaglieri set an example for arts groups and preservationists nationwide. At about the same time, art galleries were beginning to open in the then-shabby loft district of Manhattan that came to be known as SoHo. While the galleries

Architect Giorgio Cavaglieri converted New York's Astor Library into the Joseph Papp Public Theater (1967). Cavaglieri's many adaptive-use projects helped launch the city's architectural preservation movement. *©Robert Holmes/Corbis*

usually required minimal design intervention, they provided welcome commissions for some architects, particularly emerging ones. SoHo's art scene was so successful that posh stores, dot-com offices, and affluent residents inflated rents, forcing most of the galleries to move to underutilized light-industrial spaces in other districts. The same process has since brought art galleries, accompanied by small museums and theaters, into former industrial districts in older cities all over the world.

Beginning in the 1960s, adaptive use of existing buildings for the arts has spawned numerous creative facilities. One example is the conversion of an abandoned factory complex into the Massachusetts Museum of Contemporary Art (1999), or MASS MoCA, in North Adams, by Bruner Cott & Associates. *Nicholas Whitman/nwphoto.com*

Other notable examples of adaptive use for arts facilities include the Warhol Museum (1994) in Pittsburgh, simply and elegantly converted from a factory by architect Richard Gluckman. More recently, Bruner Cott & Associates imaginatively adapted a factory complex in North Adams, Massachusetts, to house the Massachusetts Museum of Contemporary Art, or MASS MoCA (1999). A conversion on a more spectacular scale occurred in London, where a monumental former power plant became the Tate Modern (2000) following designs by Herzog & de Meuron. Also in London, the seemingly weightless glass-and-steel canopy over the British Museum's Great Court (2001) by Foster + Partners has transformed that venerable institution without adding a single gallery. The firm has designed a similar canopy (2007) for the courtyard of the Smithsonian American Art Museum and National Portrait Gallery, housed in the adapted 19th-century Patent Office Building in Washington, D.C.

The conversion of old movie palaces into theaters and concert halls began to gather momentum in the 1970s, and by now almost every city and town has one or more examples. Reinforcing existing urban centers, these reused buildings would otherwise have been demolished or carved up to accommodate the now ubiquitous multiplex cinemas.

Innumerable small arts organizations operate in modest adapted facilities. Alternatively, one of these creative groups occasionally finds a way to build an architecturally distinctive home. Probably the finest work of the noted architect and 2007 AIA Gold Medalist Edward Larrabee Barnes is his Haystack Mountain School of Crafts (1961) on the coast of Maine. Barnes subtly merged Modern minimalism with the traditional materials and proportions of the locale, distributing structures reminiscent of fishing sheds across a steep seaside site. With its design for the Atlantic Center for the Arts (1997) near the Florida coast, the firm of Thompson & Rose created a bold architectural setting for another small-scale, rural arts education facility with modest means. Here, too, functions are dispersed in modestly scaled, wood-framed structures treading lightly on the natural setting, in this case a lush subtropical grove. An urban example of a distinctive new structure for nonprofit performing arts companies can be seen in the New 42 Studios building (1999) in New York by Platt Byard Dovell White. Designed as a kind of multistory lantern, it is illuminated in various colors reflecting the signage of its Times Square district.

1974
Sears Tower,
Chicago,
Bruce Graham/SOM

Chicago Federal Center,
Ludwig Mies van der Rohe

Edward Larrabee Barnes, recipient of the AIA's 2007 Gold Medal, designed the Haystack Mountain School of Crafts (1961) in Deer Isle, Maine. The shingled cottages of the minimalist Modern complex blend into their coastal Maine site. The campus received the AIA Twenty-five Year Award in 1994. *Diana and Dennis Griggs*

Like the design of the Haystack Mountain campus, the Atlantic Center for the Arts (1997), New Smyrna Beach, Florida, by Thompson & Rose, houses the facility's functions in a complex of small buildings on a rural site. *©Chuck Choi*

Benefits to Society

Arts facilities such as those described have contributed immensely to our society by making the arts accessible to more and more people. Technical expertise and design inspiration have played equal roles in creating effective settings for the visual and performing arts. Such facilities have also contributed greatly to the economic health of our urban centers, attracting and holding an interested public. In addition, the adaptive use of existing buildings for arts purposes has often set an example, leading to adaptive use for other kinds of occupancies.

Building for the arts has contributed mightily to the art of architecture, accounting for many of our landmark accomplishments. It has become commonplace to say that museums are the cathedrals of our age—not just in the sense that artworks are today's objects of veneration but that the buildings housing them have become our aesthetic landmarks.

As well, design for the arts has contributed to advancing building technology, albeit less conspicuously than, say, office buildings or sports facilities. Starting in the late 19th century, performance halls were the sites where the science of acoustics was developed. In the late 20th century, buildings such as Kahn's Kimbell Museum and Pei's East Building of the National Gallery presented extraordinary refinements in the structural forms and finishes of concrete. Pei's pyramid at the Louvre and Norman Foster's courtyard canopy at the British Museum demonstrated unprecedented economy and refinement in the use of glass and steel. In recent decades, Gehry's Bilbao museum and Los Angeles concert hall have stretched the potential of computers to achieve formerly impossible complexity of form in design and construction.

The beginning of the 21st century has seen concern expressed that advances in electronics and computer technology will make it unnecessary to leave home—or unplug our iPods—to fully experience the visual and performing arts. But the public never seems to lose its passion for seeing and hearing the real thing, and today computers are supporting the arts with up-to-the-minute programs and online ticket sales. The boom in arts facilities continues, and the work of architects continues to be an incredible part of that boom. ●

(Opposite) Lighting effects on the metal-and-glass façade of the 11-story New 42 Studios (1999), a performing arts facility designed by Platt Byard Dovell White Architects in New York, provide an ever-changing wash of color. *©Elliott Kaufman Photography*

Ieoh Ming Pei, FAIA

Nancy B. Solomon, AIA

Bing Lin, courtesy Pei Partnership Architects

Having bridged continents, cultures, pedagogical styles, and professional disciplines, I.M. Pei has capitalized on his vast education and experiences to create a diverse portfolio of buildings for many kinds of clients across the globe, from residential towers and town houses in Philadelphia to bank headquarters and office towers in Hong Kong. But his business acumen does not come at the expense of his artistry. "His buildings—whether dedicated to living, learning, science, commerce, or the enjoyment of art—are themselves works of art to be enjoyed," states the citation that accompanied the presentation of his Gold Medal. He received the Pritzker Architecture Prize in 1983.

Born in 1917 in Canton (now Guangzhou), China, Pei came to the United States in 1935 to study architecture. He graduated in 1940 with a BArch degree from MIT at a time when Beaux-Arts pedagogy still ruled, but subsequently earned his master's in 1946 at Harvard's Graduate School of Design, which was on the forefront of Modernism in America. Two years later, in 1948, he was hired by New York real estate mogul William Zeckendorf to serve as director of architecture at his development company Webb & Knapp. Although the design community discouraged close ties between architects and builders at that time, this cross-disciplinary collaboration offered fertile ground for Pei's professional growth as it exposed him to the larger socioeconomic and political context of design. Pei went on to establish I.M. Pei & Associates in New York in 1955, which became I.M. Pei & Partners in 1966 and then Pei Cobb Freed & Partners in 1989. With a current staff of about 100, the firm itself

has received numerous awards, including the AIA's Architecture Firm Award in 1968 and the Lifetime Achievement Award from the New York Society of Architects in 1992.

Although Pei's accomplishments can be found across building types, art museums have played a particularly important role in his long and respected career. One of his first significant commissions was the Everson Art Museum (1968) in Syracuse, New York. Built of poured-in-place concrete with local granite aggregate, the museum's interior elements—including stairs and balcony—became sculpture in their own right within the boxy shell. The museum, which clearly reflects Pei's Modernist bent, earned an AIA National Honor Award in 1969. Pei is probably best known to the public for two later museum projects—the East Building (1978) of the National Gallery of Art in Washington, D.C., and the two-phase addition and renovation (1989, 1993) to the Louvre in Paris. In both cases, Pei introduced a Modern vocabulary into a historic setting in a way that delights in the new while respecting the old.

It seems only fitting that, after Pei officially retired in 1990, he was enticed into designing yet three more art museums in three very diverse locales: Musée d'Art Moderne (2006) in Kitchberg, Luxembourg; Suzhou Museum (2006) in the city of Suzhou, where his ancestors had lived for more than six centuries; and the Museum of Islamic Art in Doha, Qatar (scheduled to open in 2008). Through art and for art, he has never ceased to cross boundaries to find new meaning and to help forge ties between disparate worlds.

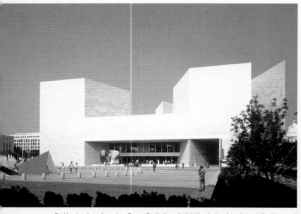

Pei's design for the East Building (1978) of the National Gallery of Art, Washington, D.C., had to harmonize with John Russell Pope's West Building (1941); fit on the irregular, trapezoidal-shaped site; and conform to the monumental scale of the National Mall. The East Building received the AIA's Twenty-five Year Award in 2004. *Ezra Stoller/©Esto*

The gray and white palette of Suzhou Museum (2006), designed by I. M. Pei Architect and Pei Partnership Architects in the 2,500-year-old city of Suzhou, Jiangsu Province, People's Republic of China, reflects the city's "primary" colors, which provide a backdrop for its world-famous gardens (some of which have been named UNESCO World Heritage Sites). *Kerun Ip, courtesy Pei Partnership Architects*

Richard Meier, FAIA

Fred Bernstein

After receiving a BArch degree from Cornell University in 1957 and working for Skidmore, Owings and Merrill and Marcel Breuer, Richard Meier opened his own office in 1963. In the 1960s and '70s, he designed a series of ever-more-elaborate houses in which strict forms inspired by the Bauhaus gave way to complex compositions. Often, he countered dramatic curves with gridded backdrops. But while geometric effects proliferated, colors did not. As Meier explained, "It is against a white surface that one best appreciates the play of light and shadow, solids and voids."

Of the architects known as the Whites, or the New York Five, Meier probably stayed closest to his Modernist roots, even as his buildings became far more lavish. For Atlanta's High Museum of Art (1983), he grouped a series of rectilinear galleries around a curving, four-story atrium, providing the public with a dramatic gathering place without upstaging the art on display. In the late 1980s, Meier received what some considered the commission of the century—the mammoth Getty Center in Los Angeles. Completed in 1997, the series of low buildings, grouped around courtyards, provided countless opportunities for creating sculpture from the interplay of forms. Uncharacteristically, Meier used panels of rough beige travertine for many of the exterior surfaces in response to neighbors' concerns about potential reflections from his customary white enamel.

Meier received the Pritzker Prize in 1984—becoming the youngest architect to do so—and the AIA Gold Medal in 1997. His most recent museums include the Frieder Burda Museum (2004), a white-on-white gem in Baden-Baden, Germany, and the Ara Pacis Museum (2006), a rare Modernist insertion in Rome's historic center.

©Luca Vignelli, courtesy Richard Meier + Partners Architects

Meier has likened the design of the Frieder Burda Museum (2004), Baden-Baden, Germany, to that of a large villa. Louvered skylights allow natural light into interior spaces but protect the artwork. The building received a 2006 Institute Honor Award for Architecture.
©Frieder Burda Museum

Ricardo Legorreta, Hon. FAIA

Luis E. Carranza

Legorreta's Papalote Children's Museum (1993), Mexico City, is one of the largest of its type in the world. It features a five-story maze. Clad in traditional Mexican blue tiles, the complex was built on the site of an old glass factory on the edge of the city's central park. *AIA Archives*

Ricardo Legorreta was born in 1931 in Mexico City and received his professional education at the School of Architecture of the Universidad Nacional Autónoma de México (UNAM), from 1948 to 1952, a time when the university was embarking on construction of a new campus. As a consequence, students of architecture became immersed in polemical debates about the role of art, its integration into Modern architecture, and the legacy of the muralist movement of the 1920s. In his work, Legorreta would resolve these and many other theoretical questions about the function and role of art in architecture.

After founding Legorreta Arquitectos in Mexico City in 1963, the architect began collaborating with Mathias Goeritz, a Mexican sculptor of German origin. Goeritz's notion of Emotional Architecture— an expressive architecture with abstract sculptural qualities intended to arouse the emotions of its users—were evident in their joint efforts on the Automex Towers (1964) in Toluca and the Hotel Camino Real (1968) in Mexico City.

Legorreta learned from Goeritz and his friend Luis Barragán to abstract forms from local history, context, and art and balance them with the vocabulary of the International Style. The results can be seen in the 1994 City of the Arts master plan and the School of Visual Arts in Mexico City, which employs the contrast of bright colors highlighted by natural light, the use of large-scale sculptural elements, and the application of historical forms, such as domes and pyramidal-shaped spiral stairs.

He is the first Latin American to receive the AIA Gold Medal. The AIA noted his ability to connect "the past to the future of architecture using his own inventive and innovative approach."

Legorreta's command of space, light, and color is evident in his design of the College of Santa Fe Visual Arts Center (1999), Santa Fe. Courtyards and porticos link the five-building complex. Exterior walls are of synthetic stucco painted in reds and oranges; interior courtyards are painted lavender, purple, and fuschia. *AIA Archives*

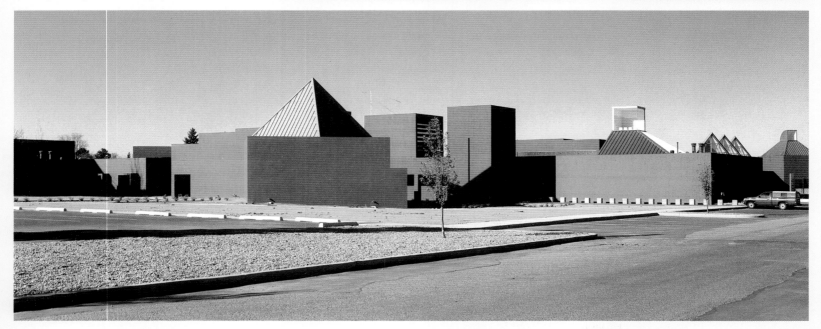

1976
*Jean Labatut received the first
Topaz Medal, for excellence in
architecture education*

*Washington, D.C., Metro,
Harry Weese*

Canstruction:
An Architectural Feast

Jen DeRose

A metallic city skyline soars upward. A cobra stands ready to strike. A sailboat glides underneath a bridge. These installations, like any other architecture project, began with brainstorming and CAD drawings and, like fine art, rely on techniques such as color, scale, and proportion. The difference lies in their medium—the works are made using only the tin can.

Reminiscent of Pop Art, the sculptures are created for the annual international competition Canstruction. Organized by local chapters of the American Institute of Architects and trademarked by the Society for Design Administration (SDA), engineers, architects, interior designers, and students come together to fight against hunger. Once awards are given, the canned goods are donated to local food banks. Last year 1.5 million pounds of food were distributed to those most in need.

"We want to show that architects are caring and active members of the community," says President and Executive Director Cheri C. Melillo, who runs the program with Associate Director Michelle M. Browne. The pair should know. Melillo's an Honorary AIA and full-time employee at New York's Butler Rogers Baskett Architects, while Browne worked for years at Looney Ricks Kiss Architects in Nashville.

The directors and Deborah Gill, the current president of SDA, incorporated Canstruction as a nonprofit in 1998, but it actually began in 1993 when the New York chapters of SDA and AIA, inspired by similar events held by SDA chapters in Denver and Seattle, sponsored a competition at the New York Design Center. The following year, a second competition held at the Decoration & Design Building received national news coverage when John F. Kennedy Jr., whose family owned the company that managed the venue, announced the winners. Thirteen years later, teams in 80 cities around the world are projected to complete more than 500 structures in 2007.

While planning for each project takes weeks, actual building time averages five hours. (Although some dedicated teams pull all-nighters.) At the local level, teams compete for recognition in four categories—jurors' favorite; structural ingenuity; best use of labels; and best meal—and two are given honorable mentions. The selected projects are then sent, via slideshow, to the simultaneously held SDA and AIA national conventions, where design experts from the host city choose the winners.

"It's about the industry giving back to the communities we build," Melillo says. Each team must be led by a design professional. The students—as young as 10 years old—learn about geometry, structure, design development, construction, and teamwork. "The kids run around in hard hats and are just so excited to see how the cans fit together," Melillo says.

And of course there's the occasional topple and a healthy dose of competitive spirit. Rival schools and architecture firms go head-to-head. Taking home the 2006 Best Meal award was Frederick J. Bielefield elementary school in Middletown, Connecticut. Mentored by Bianco Giolitto Weston Architects, the piece features a rabbit, whose eyes of yam and spaghetti are fixed on an eight-foot-tall mixed-vegetable and creamed-corn carrot sprouting from a field of applesauce containers.

NK Architects of Morristown, New Jersey, won that same year for a special category—Most Cans—with "Time to End Hunger." In the shape of an alarm clock, complete with ticking minute hand, it's an artwork that even Andy Warhol would approve of—all 19,103 cans were donated by the Campbell Soup Company.

New York's Platt Byard Dovell White Architects used 3,200 sardine cans to create "Manhattan CAN Chowder," a giant shell sculpture and the 2005 Structural Ingenuity winner. *Kevin Wick*

A feast for the eyes, "An American Classic" by New York's Butler Rogers Baskett Architects took home the 2005 National Jurors' Favorite award with 6,394 cans. The hot dog's mustard stripes are individual "to-go" packets. *Kevin Wick.*

1977
*Centre Pompidou, Paris,
Richard Rogers and Renzo Piano*

*Richard Josef Neutra, FAIA,
received the AIA Gold Medal
(posthumously)*

17

Architecture for the Spirit

Michael J. Crosbie, PhD

Most in the United States would no doubt mention "freedom" as the country's bedrock value, with the assumption that they refer to political freedom. But America was founded as a haven for religious freedom. The religious freedom guaranteed by the U.S. Constitution has encouraged the growth of a great variety of religious denominations, sects, belief systems, and what some might even describe as cults. As wave upon wave of immigrants have come to America, the array of religious observance has grown. Today, the fastest-growing religion in the United States is Islam.

Given this historical context, religious buildings have occupied an important place in the history of American architecture. Yet, over the course of American history, most religious buildings have not been designed by architects. Even today, in the midst of a construction boom of religious buildings, most houses of worship do not benefit from the involvement of an architect (many are "packaged" buildings available from large prefab and construction companies). Nonetheless, much outstanding religious architecture, as exemplified on these pages, has been created by gifted architects working with visionary clients.

A century-and-a-half ago, the best religious buildings and memorials were modeled on European precedents—not unlike other important buildings constructed across the county. Great creativity was shown in interpreting these traditions to give them an American flavor. This was particularly true around the turn of the 20th century, when creative architects such as Bernard Maybeck and Frank Lloyd Wright created fresh, new models for houses of worship that broke away from European patterns. These architects were also interested in experimenting with new materials and structural systems. Later in the century, Modernism further challenged the notion that legitimate religious spaces must rely on centuries-old iconography and traditional materials. Memorial design also took a new turn during this period, as seen in Maya Lin's use of abstraction to capture the scars of war in her Vietnam Veterans Memorial in Washington, D.C. By the end of the 20th century, America had even created a new form of worship space—the megachurch—which reflected the growth of evangelical Christianity in the United States, with its emphasis on community, entertainment, and fundamentalism. The early European precedents were never fully shaken, however, as evidenced by architect Friedrich St. Florian's neoclassical World War II Memorial, which was dedicated in 2004 in Washington, D.C.

(Opposite) St. Patrick's Cathedral on New York's Fifth Avenue is for many the face of Catholicism in the United States. Designed by James Renwick, it is a mix of various Gothic styles and took 20 years to complete, opening for services in 1879.
©age fotostock/SuperStock

The Affirmation of Classicism: 1857–1900

No religious building in the United States better exemplifies the influence of past architectural precedents at the time the American Institute of Architects was founded than James Renwick's St. Patrick's Cathedral on Fifth Avenue in New York City. Construction on St. Patrick's commenced in 1858, and the cathedral was opened for services in 1879. The Lady Chapel at the east end, which is the design of Charles T. Matthews, was finished in 1908. Renwick, one of the foremost architects of his time, also designed the Corcoran Gallery of Art in Washington, D.C., and the Smithsonian Institution Building on the National Mall. In the mid-19th century, architects and congregations valued the weight of tradition in religious buildings. Renwick, well versed in church design, used a mixture of French, English, and German Gothic styles in the cathedral's architecture and decoration.

The exuberance and facility of architects in commanding traditional architecture for contemporary uses can also be seen in another religious landmark of this period, the Plum Street Temple in Cincinnati, designed by James Keyes Wilson (who was also the first president of the Cincinnati AIA chapter) and completed in 1866. The Moorish Revival style of the vibrant, red-brick temple is reminiscent of synagogues constructed in Central Europe at the time, with an arch-framed façade and minarets suggesting the flavor of Muslim architecture of medieval Spain during the flowering of the Jewish faith in that country. In this case, architecture was used to recall the traditions of an ancient religion and its building precedents in Europe.

A similar approach is found in the Central Synagogue on Manhattan's Lexington Avenue (only a few blocks from St. Patrick's). Completed in 1872, the Central Synagogue is the work of architect Henry Fernbach, a Jewish architect born in Germany who immigrated to the United States in 1855. Fernbach designed many synagogues, but none equaled the Moorish Revival richness of the Central Synagogue. The tall, thin central nave is surmounted on either

(Opposite) New York's highly ornamented and colorful Central Synagogue, designed by Henry Fernback and completed in 1872, was gutted by fire in 1998 and was restored to its former glory in 2001 by Hugh Hardy, FAIA. In 2006 it won a Faith & Form Award for restoration. *©Peter Aaron/Esto*

Plum Street Temple in Cincinnati, designed by James Keyes Wilson, was completed in 1866 and restored in 1994–95. Wilson trained in New York with James Renwick and later served as the first president of the Cincinnati chapter of the AIA. *©Jeff Graves/GrayMatter Images*

side by 122-foot-tall octagonal minarets crowned with onion domes. Inside, the central nave, side aisles, iron columns, bimah (dais), and ark are lavishly stenciled and painted in bright blue, ochre, yellow, brown, gold, green, and maroon. Destroyed in a devastating fire in 1998, Central Synagogue was restored in 2001 to its previous glory by New York architect Hugh Hardy.

In Boston's Trinity Church (see page 36), H. H. Richardson took a step away from traditional church architecture by conceiving of the worship space as a generous stage that allowed the congregation and celebrants to better see each other. Trinity is perhaps the greatest example of "Richardson Romanesque" and a spatial tour de force. Completed in 1877, it was included several years ago on the AIA's list of the 10 best buildings in America. Richardson jettisoned the idea of a tall, narrow nave and instead designed a church with a Greek cross plan, broad and welcoming. The chancel fans back across the breadth of the apse, creating a sweeping, luminous gold stage for worship. The 211-foot central tower looms above the heads of worshipers and is filled with light. Trinity was recently restored by the Boston firm Goody Clancy, which also added much-needed space below grade while honoring Richardson's original vision. The renovation was a marriage of preservation and green-building technology: a geothermal system is buried underground to provide modern-day heating and cooling without disturbing the original roofline or picturesque façade.

As the 19th century drew to a close, a new cathedral began to take shape in New York, and it reflects the continuing ease of blending styles by architects of that time. The Cathedral of St. John the Divine's ambitious design was the work of the New York firm Heins & Lafarge. The scheme was Romanesque Byzantine in style. Work proceeded slowly after the cornerstone laying of 1892: by the time of Heins's death in 1907, only the east end of the cathedral was completed. That same year, a new architect, Ralph Adams Cram, was hired. He revised the cathedral's design in the Gothic style, and the interior of the nave was finally completed in 1941 to his 1907 design. For 32 years construction was halted, but when it resumed in 1973, the cathedral reached out to the community by creating a school to teach various building crafts to unemployed people in the neighborhood. About a third of the cathedral is yet to be built: the towers, transepts, the great crossing, and the choir roof. Simultaneously, preservation efforts are now underway for the portions that have been built over the past century.

Goody Clancy's restoration and expansion of H. H. Richardson's Trinity Church (1877), Boston, included the transformation of a shallow storage cellar into a 22,000-square-foot undercroft used for meetings and other activities. The project was completed in 2005.
Courtesy Goody Clancy

The heart of Anglicanism in New York City, St. John the Divine has been under construction for more than a century. During the 1970s, the cathedral became the site of a training program for the disadvantaged in the stone-carving arts. ©*Carol Highsmith*

1978
Louis de Moll became the first
American elected president of the
International Union of Architects

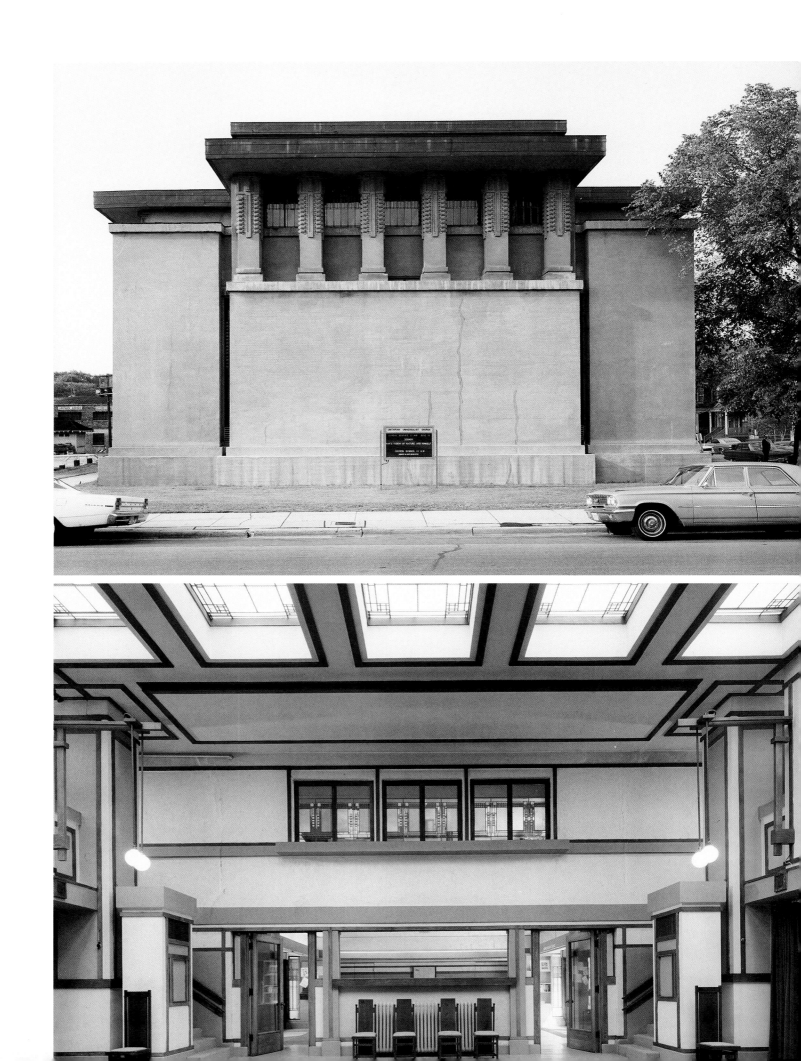

East Building,
National Gallery of Art,
I. M. Pei

Faneuil Hall Marketplace,
Boston,
Benjamin Thompson & Associates

Gehry House,
Santa Monica,
Frank Gehry

Boettcher Concert Hall,
Denver,
Hardy Holzman Pfeiffer

Philip Johnson, FAIA,
received the AIA Gold Medal

The Rise and Flowering of Modernism: 1901–1957

In sharp contrast to St. John's, Frank Lloyd Wright's Unity Temple of 1906 in Oak Park, Illinois, signaled the radical departure from Beaux-Arts classicism that religious and memorial architecture would begin to take in the 20th century. It offered an approach to religious architecture that was different from anything inherited from Europe and was in many ways uniquely American. Wright believed that people should be the focus in this religious space, so he designed a central meeting room around which the temple unfolded. On the exterior, the tall, central meeting hall is expressed as a cubic volume carved away from a solid mass, with deep overhangs shading tall, vertical windows. Inside, the design further disintegrates the exterior geometry. Congregants enter from a lower level and rise into the worship space near its center, lifted into the light. The decorative banding further breaks down the mass of the walls so that the space appears to be in flight—evocative of soaring spirits.

At nearly the same time that Unity Temple rose, California architect Bernard Maybeck designed the incredibly ethereal First Church of Christ, Scientist (1910) in Berkeley. Maybeck was architecturally eclectic, and in this church he melds Gothic influences with the California Arts and Crafts style, particularly in the polychrome concrete columns and elaborate wooden roof structure. Maybeck also possessed a modern fascination with new materials in his use of steel industrial windows and cement-asbestos insulation panels on the exterior.

With Modernism gathering force, Beaux-Arts classicism responded with a more simplified sense of ornament. Bertram Grosvenor Goodhue's St. Bartholomew's Church on New York's Park Avenue, completed in 1918, shows a more contemporary approach to the building's massing of simple rectangular forms. An even more stripped down, simplified version of Byzantine church architecture is seen in the National Shrine of the Immaculate Conception in Washington, D.C., designed by accomplished church architect Charles Donagh Maginnis in 1922. The largest Catholic church in the Western Hemisphere, the shrine is rendered in limestone with simple bas-relief sculpture.

(Opposite) The century-old Unity Temple by Frank Lloyd Wright is considered one of his most important early works (the architect was 39 when it was completed in 1906). The exterior is concrete and stucco, with high windows to maintain privacy in the sanctuary. The reception hall leads to a sanctuary that visitors enter from below, rising into the space. The interior decoration dissolves the sense of enclosure and makes the wall planes appear to float.
Historic American Buildings Survey, Library of Congress

AIA Gold Medalist Bernard Maybeck created an incredibly rich architecture for First Church of Christ, Scientist (1910) in Berkeley, California, that combined the aesthetic traditions of Gothic with the California Arts and Crafts movement.
Bancroft Library, University of California, Berkeley

The Lincoln Memorial (designed in 1910 and completed in 1922) marks a high point in late Beaux-Arts architecture in the United States. The memorial, designed by Henry Bacon, takes the form of a simple Greek peripteral temple turned lengthwise to face the Reflecting Pool and the Washington Monument. The memorial beautifully terminates the axis of the National Mall, extending west from the U.S. Capitol, and provides a majestic setting for Daniel Chester French's statue of a pensive President Lincoln. A year after its completion, Bacon was presented with the AIA Gold Medal by President Warren G. Harding at the Lincoln Memorial, borne on a torch-lit barge floated down the Reflecting Pool.

It was a fitting finale for a style that would eventually fade, to some extent, from memorial architecture and, to a greater extent, from architect-designed religious buildings. The 1930s mark a transition in the design of religious buildings from predominantly classical to greater experimentation with the abstract. Bruce Goff's 1923 design of the Boston Avenue Methodist Church in Tulsa, Oklahoma, manages to use both Gothic and Modern in equal measure. The building, based on sketches by artist Adah Robinson, is an Art Deco masterpiece of astonishing ornamental complexity. The 225-foot-tall tower joins an enormous, semicircular auditorium. The tower is crowned with copper and glass finials that appear as hands lifted in prayer.

In 1942 a Modern religious landmark by Eliel Saarinen was constructed in Columbus, Indiana, and commenced that city's role as a haven for Modern masters. The First Christian Church is a severe brick, concrete, and limestone rectangular volume, marked on the skyline by an asymmetrical, 166-foot-tall brick campanile. The elements—church and campanile—are traditional but their design is inventive. The entrance faces a shallow courtyard for congregational gatherings. The church interior—a long, basilica-like space—is also asymmetrical, with soft natural light from the right and a sanctuary wall dominated by a simple

The work of one of the most prolific church architects of his day, Charles Donagh Maginnis's National Shrine of the Immaculate Conception (1922), Washington, D.C., shows Modernism's influence on the simplification of ornament. *Courtesy the Basilica of the National Shrine of the Immaculate Conception*

1979
Philip Johnson received the first
Pritzker Architecture Prize

Piazza d'Italia,
New Orleans,
Charles Moore

Atheneum,
New Harmony, Indiana,
Richard Meier

Ieoh Ming Pei, FAIA,
received the AIA Gold Medal

Considered one of the first significant Modern religious buildings
in the United States, Eliel Saarinen's First Christian Church (1942)
in Columbus, Indiana, also marked the beginning of that city's
cultivation of contemporary architecture.
©Wayne Andrews/Esto

Lloyd Wright's all-glass Wayfarers Chapel (1951) prefigured the
great glass religious structures to come more than 20 years later,
such as Philip Johnson's Crystal Cathedral and E. Fay Jones's
Thorncrown Chapel. ©Wayne Andrews/Esto

(Opposite) Walter Netsch's Air Force Academy Chapel (1956–62),
composed of stainless steel and forms that suggest aircraft wings,
draws the viewer's eyes toward the heavens, following in the
tradition of Gothic architecture. ©Carol Highsmith

metal cross on white brick. The cross is illuminated by a concealed skylight, heightening the spirituality of the space.

More religious buildings of startling simplicity followed. The Central Lutheran Church in Portland, Oregon, designed in 1948 by Pietro Belluschi, seems a further abstraction of Saarinen's "church as box." Composed as a wooden slat box on a red brick base, the church is joined by a partially open wooden tower. The interior is distinguished by a curved apse with side lights that wash the interior in soft illumination.

The use of glass to make the religious building virtually disappear is seen in architect Lloyd Wright's Wayfarers Chapel of 1951, built on a bluff in Palos Verdes, California. Wright, the son of Frank Lloyd Wright, turned his back on thousands of years of masonry religious architecture to achieve a delicate enclosure that allows the surrounding landscape to define the sacred space.

The Air Force Academy Chapel (1956–62) in Colorado Springs, Colorado, is distinctive in abstract illusions to sacred building, such as its pointed fins that echo Gothic architecture. Composed of aluminum triangular panels that suggest jet aircraft wings, the Air Force Chapel rises on the desert floor like Chartres from the fields beyond Paris. Designed by Walter Netsch of Skidmore, Owings & Merrill, the chapel interior is a mysterious realm of blue and red light, emitted from slender stained-glass windows fitted between the aluminum bays (and barely discernible on the exterior). The chapel can hold nearly 2,000 people and includes separate areas for Jewish, Catholic, and Protestant worship.

1980
Norma Merrick Sklarek, FAIA,
became the first African-
American woman elected to the
College of Fellows

M. Rosaria Piomelli became
first woman dean of a U.S.
architecture school, at the City
College of New York

Crystal Cathedral,
Garden Grove, California,
Philip Johnson

Thorncrown Chapel,
Eureka Springs, Arkansas,
E. Fay Jones

Lady Bird Johnson became
an honorary AIA member and
was presented with a medal
recognizing her as an "individual
who has inspired and influenced
the architectural profession"

The nave of Wallace Harrison's First Presbyterian Church (1958), Stamford, Connecticut, is flooded with light from 20,000 chunks of inch-thick stained glass, designed by Frenchman Gabriel Loire. *G.E. Kidder Smith, courtesy of Kidder Smith Collection, Rotch Visual Collections, MIT*

Wallace K. Harrison's First Presbyterian Church, completed in 1958 in Stamford, Connecticut, is similar in spirit to the design of the Air Force Academy Chapel but with a narrative power that one rarely sees in Modern architecture. Harrison created a fishlike form covered with slate "scales." The plan of the church is a fish shape as well, and from the interior one can behold the breathtaking French stained-glass windows by Gabriel Loire, which appear as webs of color between the bones of the "Fish Church," as it has come to be known. Harrison's wonderful church is a portent of the symbolic power of architecture that would be discovered by late Modern and Postmodern designers.

Late Modernism and the Advent of Pluralism: 1958–2007

The last building of Eero Saarinen, North Christian Church in Columbus, Indiana, was completed in 1964 (three years after his death). Soaring into the sky, North Christian also burrows into the ground. Visitors approach the church through a landscape designed by Dan Kiley and then descend below the structure's hovering roof. They emerge into the sanctuary near its center, surrounded by seating on five of the plan's six sides (there is no way to sneak into the sanctuary—a design feature that must discourage latecomers).

Louis Kahn used a Modern idiom to capture the essence of Unitarian religious beliefs. Commissioned in 1959 to design the First Unitarian Church in Rochester, New York, Kahn started with a simple diagram of a question mark surrounded by a circle. This parti was, for Kahn, the core of Unitarianism—always questioning the tenets of belief. The question mark evolved into a central sanctuary, surrounded by a ring of classroom spaces that seemed to suggest the layers that could be peeled back to get to the essence of truth. In the resulting building of brick, poured concrete, and cinder block, the square sanctuary holds the center of the complex, with light flooding the four corners of the space from towers that rise above the roof. This building offered an identity for Unitarianism that could never be derived from Classical architectural precedents.

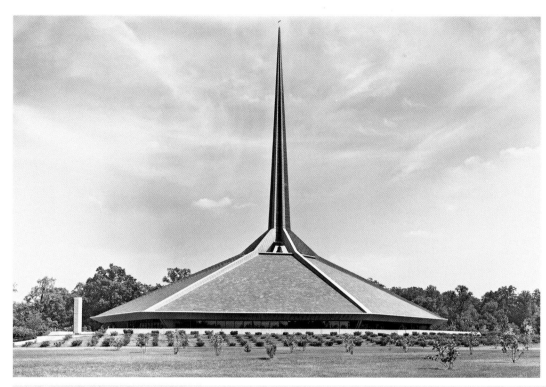

Eero Saarinen's North Christian Church (1964) in Columbus, Indiana, is an arresting object set within a landscape designed by Dan Kiley. The spire is a counterpoint to the below-grade sanctuary.
©Wayne Andrews/Esto

Louis Kahn used humble materials to create the First Unitarian Church (1959–63), Rochester, New York. Reflecting the Unitarian belief in arriving at truth through the constant questioning of assumptions, Kahn's initial parti was a question mark. Light from towers floods the corners of the square central sanctuary.
©Wayne Andrews/Esto

1981
Construction began on Seaside,
designed by New Urbanists
Andres Duany and Elizabeth
Plater-Zyberk

Garfield School,
San Francisco,
Joseph Esherick

Josep Lluis Sert, FAIA,
received the AIA Gold Medal

The poetry of Marcel Breuer's Saint John's Abbey (1961) in
Collegeville, Minnesota, is expressed in the architect's favorite
material: concrete. The campanile takes on the anthropomorphic
form of a man with his face turned toward God.
©Wayne Andrews/Esto

The expressive use of concrete in church architecture was also explored by Marcel Breuer in his design for the Saint John's Abbey in Collegeville, Minnesota, completed in 1961. While many of Breuer's other concrete buildings are abstract, at Saint John's the material achieves an anthropomorphic power, particularly in the campanile, which appears as a robust man, standing on two legs, his face toward God. Connected to the church is a library whose structure mimics a sheltering arbor, suggesting the tree of knowledge.

As Lloyd Wright did decades earlier at Wayfarers Chapel, Philip Johnson eschewed the heavy materials of Breuer, Kahn, and a very long tradition of religious architecture when he designed the Crystal Cathedral in 1978 for a site in Garden Grove, California. This landmark house of worship is perhaps one of the best known in America, thanks to its starring role on Reverend Robert Schuller's "Hour of Power" television program. With more than 10,000 pieces of glass set within a white-painted space frame, the Crystal Cathedral is the first of America's megachurches—structures that contain vast amounts of space for thousands of worshipers yet contain few overtly religious symbols. The interior seats nearly 3,000, and two multistory wall sections near the pulpit swing open so that the minister can preach to people sitting in their parked cars (Schuller started his church on this site of a former drive-in movie theater).

The Crystal Cathedral's theme of light as God's presence and the use of nature as a symbol of the divine are echoed in Thorncrown Chapel (1980) by E. Fay Jones. For this chapel, sited in a dense forest in Eureka Springs, Arkansas, Jones designed a lacy structure so that no element was too large for two men to carry into the woods. He cited Sainte-Chapelle in Paris as design inspiration and described his creation as "Ozark Gothic." This diminutive building

Television preacher Robert Schuller selected Philip Johnson to design his Crystal Cathedral (1980), in Garden Grove, California, so named because of its thousands of glass panels. The building has become the star of Schuller's international TV program, "Hour of Power."
Courtesy Crystal Cathedral (exterior); ©Carol Highsmith (interior)

1982
Vietnam Veterans Memorial,
Washington, D.C.,
Maya Lin with
Cooper-Lecky Partnership

Portland Public Service Building,
Oregon,
Michael Graves

AIA celebrated its 125th anniversary

Romaldo Giurgola, FAIA,
received the AIA Gold Medal

(less than 1,500 square feet and only 48 feet tall) gives the illusion of being much larger, primarily because the surrounding trees lend it a cathedral-like stature. Thorncrown received the AIA's 2006 Twenty-five Year Award, honoring projects completed 25–35 years ago that have withstood the test of time.

By the mid-1980s, Maya Lin's competition-winning design for the Vietnam Veterans Memorial in Washington, D.C., completely changed the conception of memorial architecture in America. Jettisoning the figural content that had dominated memorials since the founding of the country, Lin marshaled the power of abstraction and spatial engagement for the visitor to memorialize a controversial war. The design is a deceptively simple, black granite wall bearing the names of those who gave their lives, listed in the chronological order in which they fell. The full power of the memorial is discovered in moving through it. One slowly descends along two walls that form a V at their apex, at which point the visitor has joined those listed on the wall beneath the ground. In reading the names, one becomes aware of one's own reflection in the polished wall. The site is one of pilgrimage for veterans and others, some of whom trace the names of loved ones and leave mementoes at the foot of the wall. The AIA's Honor Awards for Architecture jury chose Lin's memorial for the 2007 Twenty-five Year Award.

For his 1985 design of the Gates of the Grove Synagogue in East Hampton, New York, architect Norman Jaffe drew upon imagery new and old, modern and ancient. The shingled exterior of the synagogue alludes to the style of wooden synagogues in Europe from hundreds of years ago, as well as to the agrarian architecture one finds in rural Long Island. Within this shingled shell, Jaffe created a sun-filled setting for worship, framed by "gates" of light cedar interspersed with clear glass. The gates grow in size as they approach the bimah, while the floors of irregularly shaped pink limestone lend lightness to the ground plane.

Reflecting the growth of Islam in America, the New York Mosque and Islamic Cultural Center in New York City, completed in 1991, seems to bridge traditional decorative design with Modernism. Architect Michael McCarthy of Skidmore, Owings & Merrill used a geometric logic to organize the mosque's plan and elevations. The design is successful on two levels: the reliance on

(Opposite) Arkansas-based architect E. Fay Jones described his delicate Thorncrown Chapel (1980) as "Ozark Gothic." The chapel was one of the most popular buildings among architects in the late 20th century. ©*Greg Hursley*

The walls of the abstract yet powerful Vietnam Veterans Memorial (1982), designed by Maya Lin in Washington, D.C., align with the Washington Monument to the east and the Lincoln Memorial to the west, taking in the full measure of American history and the sacrifice of those who lost their lives. The memorial received the AIA's Twenty-five Year Award in 2007.
Historic American Buildings Survey, Library of Congress

simple geometry echoes the geometric systems used in traditional mosque design; at the same time, the square geometry articulates the building with a contemporary architectural language.

Architect Steven Holl's design for the Chapel of St. Ignatius at Seattle University, completed in 1997, is pregnant with mystery and meaning. This small building is masterful in the way it captures light. Holl uses an assortment of slit windows to bring sunlight into the chapel, where it falls on colored walls, which in turn illuminate white plaster surfaces with reflected hues. The curved plaster walls describe a womblike interior, while pendant candles hover like spirits over the heads of worshipers.

The plan of Rafael Moneo's Cathedral of Our Lady of the Angels, completed in 2002 in Los Angeles (with the firm of Leo A Daly as executive architect), is unique in that one enters from the front, traverses a long ambulatory, and then turns to face the main altar from the back of the nave. Light is admitted through walls of translucent alabaster. The structure is almost entirely of poured concrete, and the cathedral was constructed on base isolators, making it one of the safest places to be during an earthquake (for more than just spiritual reasons).

As if coming full circle in the history of American architecture, the World War II Memorial dedicated in 2004 is controversial for its classically inspired design. Inserted between the Lincoln Memorial and the Washington Monument on the National Mall in Washington, D.C., it has proven to be one of the most visited sites in the nation's capital. Designed by architect Friedrich St. Florian, the memorial is an unadulterated tribute to the "Greatest Generation." Taking a completely different tack than Maya Lin's Vietnam Veterans Memorial, St. Florian's design recalls memorials from more than a generation earlier, which used classicalism as the language of memorial architecture. This work is evidence that the meaning of such memorials continues to be pliable and pluralistic.

(Opposite) The design of the New York Mosque and Islamic Cultural Center (1991), by Skidmore, Owings & Merrill, used geometric patterns to link ancient Islamic and Modern architecture. *©Wolfgang Hoyt/Esto*

Steven Holl described his vision for the Chapel of St. Ignatius (1997) at Seattle University as a "gathering of different lights." Soft light in different colors, emitted through irregularly placed skylights, suffuses the spare, unadorned chapel. *©Peter Aaron/Esto*

1983
High Museum of Art,
Atlanta,
Richard Meier

Sher-e-Bangla Nagar,
Bangladesh,
Louis Kahn

New Inspirations

The concrete of Rafael Moneo's Cathedral of Our Lady of the Angels (2002) is a warm terra-cotta color, suggesting the Spanish influence in Los Angeles culture and the cultural diversity of Roman Catholicism in California's largest city. ©Lara Swimmer/Esto

Our sacred places and memorials reflect American cultural values in all of their diversity. Today, for example, more congregations are building religious buildings not only to serve the faith community but also to express a belief in earth stewardship. Congregations are joining a global fellowship committed to the conservation of natural resources and nonrenewable energy. The Unitarian Universalist Fellowship Hall in Reno, Nevada, designed by Pfau Architecture and completed in 2002, and the Temple Bat Yahm Torah Center in Newport Beach, California, designed by Lehrer Architects and completed in 2003, point the way to a future of sustainable sacred spaces. Architects such as these are helping congregations make responsible environmental choices.

At the same time, plans for memorials to the 9/11 attacks, particularly the one in New York City, continue to be debated, reconsidered, and revised. It is likely that they will never be built according to the designers' original concepts. Perhaps these events are too politically charged to be properly memorialized today. We are still too close to the horrendous events and lack the historical perspective necessary to achieve coherent designs. After all, Lincoln had been dead for nearly 60 years before Henry Bacon completed his stunning memorial on the National Mall. And Maya Lin, designer of the Vietnam memorial, was a young college student far removed from the East Asian battlefields when she won the design competition. It may fall to the next generation, with greater historical insight and less emotion, to design and construct memorials that duly honor the dead, and touch the hearts and spirits of the living.

The Neoclassical design of Friedrich St. Florian's World War II Memorial, dedicated in 2004 in Washington, D.C., recalls the language of memorial architecture from an earlier generation. ©Richard Latoff 2007

Transco Tower,
Houston,
Philip Johnson

Gordon Wu Hall,
Princeton University,
Venturi, Rauch & Scott Brown

Nathaniel Alexander Owings, FAIA,
received the AIA Gold Medal

Many Gold Medals recognize a person's entire career, but a few focus on a single building. Such was the case for Henry Bacon, who received the award in 1923 for his design of the Lincoln Memorial in Washington, D.C.

Bacon (1866–1924) was born in Watseka, Illinois, grew up in Wilmington, North Carolina, and received some architectural training at the University of Illinois. Between 1888 and 1897 he worked for McKim, Mead and White, where he served as Charles McKim's assistant for projects such as the Boston Public Library, the World's Columbian Exposition, and the Rhode Island State House. He left McKim in 1897 for a short-lived partnership; in 1903 he began an independent practice.

McKim had proposed the Lincoln Memorial as part of the McMillan Plan (1901–02). The Commission of Fine Arts, chaired by Daniel Burnham, in conjunction with the Lincoln Memorial Commission subsequently selected Bacon as the architect. Daniel Chester French, who had succeeded Burnham as chair, resigned that post in 1915 when Bacon chose him as the sculptor for the project.

For the memorial, Bacon employed traditional forms in new ways: he rotated a classical temple so one entered from its long side; replaced its pediment with an attic; and inserted seals of American states in its entablature. Bacon viewed the building as a container for the allegorical murals of unity and emancipation by Jules Guerin and the marble, larger-than-life statue of Abraham Lincoln by French.

Perhaps no American monument has the evocative power of the memorial. It portrays the greatness and character of Lincoln while serving as a symbolic and actual backdrop for some of the greatest political dramas in recent history.

GOLD MEDALIST, 1923

Henry Bacon, FAIA

Richard Guy Wilson, Hon. AIA

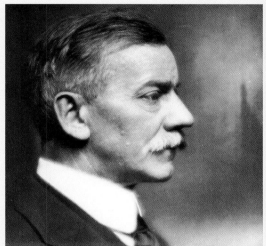

AIA Archives

Henry Bacon's Lincoln Memorial (1911–22) anchors the west end of the National Mall, opposite the U.S. Capitol. Inside, Daniel Chester French sculpted the statue of a pensive Lincoln, and Jules Guerin painted the allegorical murals.
Historic American Buildings Survey, Library of Congress

GOLD MEDALIST, 1990

E. Fay Jones, FAIA

Allen Freeman

Courtesy University of Arkansas

For more than four decades, [E. Fay Jones] has created an exquisite architecture of gentle beauty and quiet dignity that celebrates the land and embraces the American spirit. Complex yet delicate, grand in vision yet human in scale, bound firmly to the earth yet soaringly spiritual, his work strikes an emotional chord that touches the soul of all who encounter it. Humble, original, intelligent, and uncompromising, he embodies everything that architecture can and should be.
— Gold Medal citation, 1990

Born in 1921 in Pine Bluff, Arkansas, Euine Fay Jones studied civil engineering and architecture at the University of Arkansas. He first taught architecture at the University of Oklahoma, where he was mentored by Bruce Goff, and then apprenticed with Frank Lloyd Wright in Wisconsin and Arizona. Saying he missed the hills, Jones accepted a faculty position at his alma mater in 1953 and soon established a shoestring practice with the help of his wife, Gus. Maurice Jennings, a former Jones student, joined him in 1973 and became his partner in 1986. Jones taught at the university until 1988, practiced until 1998, and died in Fayetteville in 2004.

Unlike the many Wright disciples who merely borrowed externalities—such as pinwheel plans, cantilevered terraces, and geometric decorations—from their mentor, Jones absorbed Wright's material

and spatial principles and made them his own. This is evident even in his first building—a modest, two-story house that he designed in the mid-1950s for his family in Fayetteville. Stone retaining walls and vertically applied redwood siding wed the house to its wooded hillside; interlocking, flowing spaces visually enlarge and integrate the interior.

Although the majority of Jones's projects were houses, it was his religious buildings—most notably Thorncrown Chapel (1980) in Eureka Springs, Arkansas, and the Mildred B. Cooper Memorial Chapel (1988) in Bella Vista, Arkansas—that brought him world attention. Tall, transparent, and cross-braced with slender wooden arms, Thorncrown is a woodland temple. Cooper Chapel employs a more complicated system of bent steel I-beams that form Gothic arches. When Thorncrown was selected to receive the AIA's Twenty-five Year Award in 2006, the jury described it as a "truly inspiring work of art and architecture."

Jones consistently espoused architectural principles and eschewed architectural fashion. Accepting the Gold Medal in 1990, he challenged architects to create "new forms in the landscape . . . that will illuminate and will nourish and will poetically express our human qualities at their spiritual best."

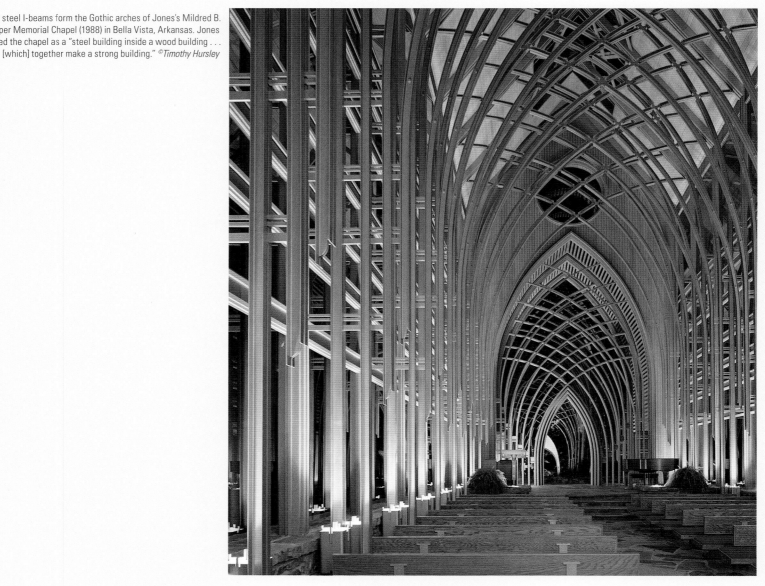

Bent steel I-beams form the Gothic arches of Jones's Mildred B. Cooper Memorial Chapel (1988) in Bella Vista, Arkansas. Jones described the chapel as a "steel building inside a wood building . . . [which] together make a strong building." ©Timothy Hursley

PPG Place,
Pittsburgh,
Philip Johnson

AT&T (Sony) Building,
New York City,
Philip Johnson

Monterey Bay Aquarium,
California, Joseph Esherick/
Esherick Homsey Dodge and Davis

GRASS ROOTS

Partners for Sacred Places, Texas Regional Office

Ingrid Spencer

With their emphasis on the moral, ethical, and spiritual, religious communities do not always have the resources to put into the physical. But the reality is that we all need a safe haven before we can work toward those higher goals. For architect James Nader, AIA, president of Nader Design Group and formerly president of the Texas Society of Architects, seeing the deterioration of church buildings in his home city of Fort Worth seemed an incredible shame. Spearheading an all-day conference in June 2005 for architects, preservationists, community developers, city officials, and congregational leaders of all faiths, Nader introduced the local participants to the Philadelphia-based Partners for Sacred Places. This nonprofit, nonsectarian organization began in 1989 to accomplish exactly what Nader had in mind for Texas—bringing resources to congregations that wished to preserve and renovate their historic but deteriorating buildings. In October 2006 Nader officially inaugurated the Texas regional office of Partners for Sacred Places in Fort Worth, the parent organization's first branch office.

"I've been doing pro-bono work for several disadvantaged churches in Fort Worth for years," says Nader. "A lot of older urban churches need help—they have recreation facilities that need upgrading, they aren't handicapped accessible, or they are so old that they just aren't up to code, among other problems."

Nader knew that Fort Worth had a strong faith community, having served on the boards of the Central Texas Methodist Foundation, the Committee on Church Finance and Administration, and the Metropolitan Board of Missions, as well as on the board of directors for the Fort Worth Chamber of Commerce. He assembled a team of religious, community, historic, and design organizations to create the Fort Worth office. Through his efforts, several philanthropic foundations and agencies—including a fund started by Nader and his wife in honor of her parents—pledged financial support, and the vision came to life.

The office in Fort Worth has an advisory board of community leaders and is connected to a group of experts from the community ministry and construction professions, including architects, contractors, and historic preservationists who volunteer their time and services or offer lower rates to disadvantaged congregations. Nader expects that, in the first five years, 160 congregations in Fort Worth and the surrounding environs will receive support for congregational renewal, strategic development of community ministries, and the restoration of sacred places. Training, direct technical assistance or help in getting those services, and an extensive resource library will be available to congregations of any faith that have historical buildings in need of repair.

Even before its official inauguration, the Fort Worth office of Partners for Sacred Places held the first session of its training program, called New Dollars/New Partners. The graduated class includes members of St. Andrews United Methodist Church, which has been working with Nader for several years to obtain the funding and expertise necessary to renovate its gymnasium.

As executive developer of the new regional office, Nader's vision is large: once the Fort Worth program is securely in place, he intends to expand his efforts to other areas of central Texas, and then beyond.

Left to right, Mike Moncrief, mayor, Fort Worth; the Reverend Carol Gibson, pastor, St. Andrews UMC Fort Worth; and James R. Nader, AIA, executive developer, Partners for Sacred Places, Texas Regional Office, on the occasion of the October 20, 2006, opening of the Texas Regional Office of Partners for Sacred Places, headquartered in Fort Worth. *Courtesy James R. Nader, AIA*

1985
Great Britain's Prince Charles
invited AIA/AAF leaders and
others to begin dialogue on urban
revitalization

AIA Design-Build contract
documents introduced

Humana Building,
Louisville,
Michael Graves

Middlebury Elementary School,
Connecticut,
Tai Soo Kim

William Wayne Caudill, FAIA,
received the AIA Gold Medal
(posthumously)

18

Creating Community in the Midst of Diversity

David Dixon, FAIA

America is entering a new era of urban renaissance. Interest in urban living has reached levels rarely imagined a decade ago. People of widely different incomes, backgrounds, ages — and often races — are moving into older urban neighborhoods that, until very recently, had been experiencing disinvestment for decades. These new residents are spurring a phenomenon that extends beyond the revival of well-known historic cities, such as Boston, Chicago, and San Francisco, to include the transformation of a much wider variety of municipalities — places as different from each other in size and setting as Providence, Rhode Island; Jackson, Mississippi; Nashville, Tennessee; Columbus, Ohio; and Kansas City, Missouri. This phenomenon is even taking hold in the traditional icons of low-density living, such as Denver, Houston, Los Angeles, and Miami.

High-end condominium towers and trophy museums rising up within once-forgotten urban cores may be the most visible (and monumental) symbols of this renaissance, but its most profound effects are being felt in the neighborhoods that constitute the background fabric of urban life. To appreciate the impact of neighborhood changes, one must first understand that, for more than two centuries, America built its cities and, later, its suburbs around largely homogeneous groups of people. Local churches, schools, and main streets became the physical structure within which people of common backgrounds created their sense of community. While people were proud of the diverse cities they shared, they felt at home in — and cherished — their respective homogeneous neighborhoods. Today, individual neighborhoods are becoming as diverse as the cities they comprise.

Because of this growing diversity, neighbors are less likely to share life's everyday activities — and the sense of community that such associations foster. Increasingly, neighbors do not worship in nearby churches, do not have kids (or dogs) to take to the local park, and choose to shop at Target or through the Internet rather than at the corner store. So, while the icons of older neighborhoods — the churches, parks, and main streets — are still beloved, these traditional forms, by themselves, have come to represent only the body but not the soul of community.

(Opposite) In 1968 the Hall family, founders of Hallmark Cards, initiated Crown Center to revive downtown Kansas City. The center, designed by leading U.S. architects, consisted of more than 5 million square feet of office buildings and hotels clustered around a shopping mall and plaza. In 2006 the Crown Center Development Corporation hired Boston-based Goody Clancy to create a plan to overlay a significant new dimension — a neighborhood consisting of 2,000 housing units along with new, mixed-use squares.
Courtesy Goody, Clancy & Associates

Denver-based urban designer Ron Straka, FAIA, joined with John Anderson, FAIA, and other architects to articulate a compelling vision for Denver's Lower Downtown (LoDo), which developed around Union Station. The station was transformed into a mixed-use development, and nearby century-old warehouses that had fallen into disrepair in the 1980s became sought-after lofts. In the process, LoDo has emerged as one of Denver's liveliest neighborhoods.
Courtesy Sean O'Keefe Professional Imaging

At a community visioning charrette held in Decatur, Illinois, in 2001, the author, a principal at Goody Clancy, worked with elected officials, developers, and residents of public housing and surrounding neighborhoods to help Goody Clancy plan the city's first new urban neighborhood in five decades.
Courtesy Goody, Clancy & Associates

Ironically, the same neighborhoods that, for decades, symbolized the greatest social, racial, and cultural divides in American life are now demonstrating how to create community in the midst of diversity. To make this dream a reality, architects are stretching beyond their traditional design responsibilities and taking on the additional role of facilitator. Working with both new and longtime residents, practitioners are designing the next generation of development in existing neighborhoods—and, in some cases, entirely new neighborhoods—by exploring concepts that in previous decades had been largely unmentionable (density), unfeasible (mixed-use development), or unbelievable (mixed-income living).

A Brief History of American Community

While a few early cities like Philadelphia, Washington, D.C., and Savannah were planned, most of America's oldest neighborhoods grew incrementally as speculators bought up tracts of land. These neighborhoods are still visible along the streets of such early port cities as Salem, Massachusetts, and Charleston, South Carolina; in the "quaint" sections of Old Town in Philadelphia and the West Village in New York; and surrounding the original plazas of Albuquerque and other Spanish-American settlements. Speculators laid out street grids and sold lots to builders—generally craftsmen, surveyors, or engineers—who often developed one or two blocks of houses that replicated European styles. (These builders were the forebears of America's architecture profession, which was not formally established in this country until the founding of the AIA in 1857. The country's first formal school of architecture, the Massachusetts Institute of Technology, did not open its doors until 1868.)

Although most American cities grew at a modest pace until the Industrial Revolution took hold after the Civil War, seeds of change were sown at the end of the 18th century. What would eventually become a dramatic explosion in urban living (while America claimed four cities with more than 200,000 people in 1850, the country had 40 such cities on the eve of the Depression) can be largely attributed to innovative methods in textile production that were based on new, water-powered technology introduced in 1789 in Pawtucket, Rhode Island, by English émigré Samuel Slater. The new technology quickly spread through Rhode Island and Massachusetts. Initially, farmers worked in the mills for extra income. By 1810, mill owners began to build new neighborhoods—including housing, stores, schools, and even churches—within walking distance of the mills.

One of the best known of these early "company towns" was Lowell, Massachusetts, which was far larger than its predecessors. Francis Cabot Lowell had improved upon the technology for converting cotton into cloth and founded the Boston Manufacturing Company in 1813. In 1822 the company moved its operations to the Merrimack River, and the new city of Lowell took form as the company built mills, housing, shops, and churches. Row houses for the workers framed views of the monumental mill buildings; detached houses for upper management resembled Greek temples. Canals, carrying the water that powered the looms, crisscrossed the city. Red brick textile mills spread across New England, creating the signature complexes that still distinguish cities like Fall River, Massachusetts; Manchester, New Hampshire; and Providence.

Industrial growth became much more rapid after the Civil War, transforming the relatively small cities and towns of the pre–Civil War era into bustling metropolises. Between the Civil War and the Depression, more than 30 million immigrants disembarked on America's shores, drawn by the young country's economic promise. Most of them settled into rapidly growing urban neighborhoods. While these neighborhoods did foster a rich sense of community, most of them also suffered deprivations. By the end of the 19th century, crowding in New York City would reach 300,000 people per square mile (roughly five times the density in America's most crowded cities today). Most of the tenement housing built in these hastily developed neighborhoods "did not represent even the hygienic standards of its own day," noted architectural historian Lewis Mumford.

The introduction of streetcars in the 1870s and 1880s exponentially increased the area available for development, triggering the construction of row houses, semidetached houses, and closely spaced single-family houses in new "streetcar neighborhoods" that today still make up large parts of American cities. As was the case before the appearance of streetcars, speculators would lay out streets and sell parcels to small-scale builders, who would often develop only one or two blocks of houses. While most of these neighborhoods served working-

These views of a quiet neighborhood street and bustling King Street, both taken in 1910 in Charleston, South Carolina, provide a glimpse into a community that had been a major American city a century earlier. Architectural styles range from Federal to Victorian. The streetcar tracks, now long gone, are the most modern element in both photographs. After many years of economic decline, the city has revived its economy by building on the attraction of its intact historic character. *Library of Congress*

The Pawtucket Canal in Lowell, Massachusetts, is flanked by former textile mills built between the 1840s and 1900s, which today have been redeveloped for residential and commercial uses. The City of Lowell has received several proposals from developers around the country who want to transform nearby vacant mill buildings and 15 acres of adjacent land into a new mixed-use urban neighborhood. This project symbolizes the resurgence of Lowell and other industrial New England cities, which were still in economic decline in the early 1990s.
Courtesy the City of Lowell, Massachusetts

class residents, developers also created distinct communities for an emerging middle class and for the newly rich—such as Mount Vernon in Baltimore and Westmoreland Place in St. Louis—that today represent some of America's most admired urban neighborhoods.

As immigration patterns changed, so did America's neighborhoods. At any given point, however, homogeneity remained a constant. For example, as East Boston's population grew from a few thousand before the Civil War to more than 60,000 in the 1920s, waves of immigrants from Ireland, Europe's Jewish ghettos, Italy, Latin America, and elsewhere washed through its various neighborhoods, transforming their ethnic character again and again. After each transition, however, these neighborhoods re-emerged as highly homogeneous communities whose residents lived in a web of connection formed by their particular churches, schools, and cultural organizations. The *Boston Globe* chronicled the intertwined nature of neighborhood and community when it reported the pride that surrounded the inauguration of Saint Mary's Church in one East Boston neighborhood and of Temple Ohel Jacob in another.

Architects began to play a more visible role toward the end of the 19th century. The "company town" of Pullman, outside Chicago, was designed by the architect Solon S. Berman and landscape architect Nathan Barrett and built between 1880 and 1884. Confident in his contributions, Berman is reputed to have asked his client, George Pullman, if the town could bear the name "Berman." Pullman's reputed answer: "Sure, we'll take the first half of my name, and the second half of yours."

A period of steady neighborhood development ground to a halt with the Depression and World War II. The America that emerged from that war was very different from the country that had entered the Depression. A significantly larger share of the population had access to automobiles, and a century of explosive industrial expansion drew to a close. Developers, who by now often employed architects, continued into the 1960s to build urban neighborhoods that emulated the earlier ones but on a smaller scale. The era of large-scale urban neighborhood development was now over.

During the late 1800s and early 1900s, Baltimore's developers were busy constructing row-house neighborhoods, such as this block in West Baltimore (above), to house a growing working-class population, which was attracted by jobs in the city's new factories and busy port. Upper-class neighborhoods such as Mt. Vernon Square (left) clustered around a new park and monument to George Washington. *Library of Congress*

1986
Lloyd's of London,
Sir Richard Rogers

Hong Kong and Shanghai Bank,
Hong Kong,
Norman Foster

Arthur Erickson, Hon. FAIA,
received the AIA Gold Medal

Mid-Century America

In the early 1950s, without a depression or a war to discourage renewed growth, mayors and chamber of commerce leaders spoke of an exciting future for American cities. But for most cities, this optimism proved to be premature. Instead, a perfect storm of overlapping economic, technological, and social forces was brewing—with a dramatic and rapid force few people foresaw—that literally reshaped the American landscape.

America's economy had begun a 50-year migration to the suburbs and beyond. To some extent this migration reflected the at-first gradual, and then much more rapid, transition to a postindustrial economy. The new economy no longer needed the mills and factories that gave birth to the Industrial Revolution and provided a livelihood for urban residents. In addition, by the 1950s, access to a car was almost universal. Together with the federal government's national highway-building program and the rapid growth in mortgage financing, the automobile spawned a new mass-market housing industry that converted vast tracks of land outside cities into low-density suburbs. And finally, in what must be described as one of the ugliest chapters in American history, whites began to move out of urban neighborhoods as many blacks moved in during the large-scale African-American migration from southern farms to jobs in northern cities. As a result of these multiple forces, the population of America's suburbs increased by almost half between 1950 and 1956, while its cities stopped growing. By 1970, more Americans lived in suburbs than cities or rural settlements.

To make matters worse, a national initiative to break down racial segregation—however well intended—resulted in the destruction of a lively, neighborhood-based African-American urban culture that is little acknowledged today. Before so-called urban renewal projects bisected them with freeways or totally uprooted them to make way for public housing, many neighborhoods of color were surprisingly diverse economically. Doctors and patients, merchants and customers, artists and laborers, musicians and shipyard workers all lived side by side. This mix supported vital Main Streets, music clubs, churches, and other institutions that nurtured a cherished sense of community in Harlem and other historically black urban neighborhoods across the country.

In the meantime, the neighborhoods that formed the building blocks of America's suburbs were as homogeneous as the urban neighborhoods left behind. Across the country, residents of many urban neighborhoods relocated in large numbers to the same suburban developments, so that by the mid-1960s many suburbs were known as Jewish, Irish, Italian, or African American.

Today's Niches and Riches

Since the late 1990s, America has been experiencing another perfect storm that is again reshaping its housing markets and, hence, where and how Americans live. This shift is launching a new period of neighborhood building that is very different from any in the past. For the first time in its history, America no longer has a "mass housing market," which historically had encouraged "one-size-fits-all" neighborhoods. According to the Urban Land Institute, America has rapidly become "a nation of niches": Younger, older, and childless households now control a much greater share of housing dollars, and many of these "niche" markets are sinking their dollars into urban neighborhoods.

In recent years, rising frustration with increasingly long commutes has reinforced this trend. The Boston region's Metropolitan Area Planning Council reported that during the 1990s, hours lost to traffic congestion increased by more than 50 percent, reflecting a pattern seen in many parts of the country. In 2004 the Environmental Protection Agency indicated that regions with well-developed mass transit systems would need to double the amount of housing near stations to meet the expected market demand over the next two decades. And, in 2005, the *Boston Globe* reported that 79 percent of respondents in a national poll indicated, "a shorter commute would be a primary factor in choosing their next house." The desire for proximity to transit has turned into a powerful market force.

Is this renewed interest in urban living a bubble? In an October 2005 report, the *Wall Street Journal* said no. Noting that the average price of a condominium has surpassed that of a single-family house, the *Journal* suggested that "for many, an urban condo is now more luxurious than a . . . yard." The report went on to state that this trend is due to a fundamental shift in demographics that should last for several decades. Because the households moving into cities are smaller and richer, increased urban affluence is far outpacing urban population growth. *USA Today* reported on this phenomenon in April 2006, noting significant recent gains in the share of regional wealth (as measured by household income and housing values) held by slow-growing central cities such as Pittsburgh, Cleveland, and Boston—gains of as much as 10 percent in just five years.

(Opposite) The confluence of forces that fueled rapid suburban growth after World War II has begun to dissipate. In response to the dramatic increase in traffic congestion during the 1990s, more and more Americans report in polls that they would prefer a short commute instead of a suburban lawn.
Courtesy Alex S. MacLean/Landslides

ILLUSTRATIVE PLAN

PHASE II SENIOR HOUSING

FIRE STATION

EDMONDSON VILLAGE SHOPPING CENTER

GIANT SUPERMARKET

PHASE III REDEVELOPMENT SITE

EDMONDSON

TECH SCHOOL

NORTH ATHOL AVE

HIGH SCHOOL

SINGLE-FAMILY | DUPLEX | ROWHOUSE | MANSION-ETTE | MANSION | MULTI-FAMILY | SENIOR HOUSING

Former Baltimore Mayor Martin O'Malley called The Uplands, a new neighborhood with 735 units of mixed-income housing planned by Goody Clancy, "the city's most exciting development in 50 years." Working with a task force of leaders from adjacent neighborhoods, the firm responded to concerns about density and income mix by demonstrating how a wide range of housing options could be integrated with buildings that are comfortably scaled and rich in architectural character.
Courtesy Goody, Clancy & Associates

1987
Baltic Inn,
San Diego,
Rob Wellington Quigley, FAIA

United Airlines Terminal One,
O'Hare International Airport,
Helmut Jahn

Cedars-Sinai Comprehensive
Cancer Center, Los Angeles,
Morphosis

Gates of the Grove Synagogue,
East Hampton, New York,
Norman Jaffe

The reversal of fate for the Uplands neighborhood in West Baltimore tells this story at a neighborhood level. The Uplands was developed in the 1950s as a middle-class community of more than 900 garden apartments. Part of a city that saw its population drop from 950,000 to 650,000 between 1950 and 2000, the 52-acre development was bankrupt by the late 1990s. After deciding to take ownership of the failed development, the city's housing agency hired Goody Clancy to work with the surrounding neighborhoods to create a master plan for a new, mixed-income neighborhood.

Leaders from surrounding neighborhoods—which themselves conformed to historical patterns of economic and physical homogeneity—were stunned to learn that a 2004 market study demonstrated demand for more than 1,000 housing units on the site at price levels three to five times greater than prevailing prices for most nearby houses. Perhaps even more surprising for a city that had traditionally built entire neighborhoods of almost identical row houses (and which today holds neighborhood-based ethnic fairs on its waterfront), this demand came from people identified as black and white, young and old, gay and straight, white- and blue-collar, and more likely to be single than heading a household with children. These people sought everything from single-family houses of varying sizes to row houses, apartments, and lofts. The one common denominator: everyone wanted to live in the same new neighborhood.

This phenomenon is not limited to the largest cities. Returning to New England, the city of Providence, which numbers fewer than 100,000 people, hired Duany Plater-Zyberk (DPZ) in 1993 to create a plan to revive the city's proud, but dying, downtown into a dynamic, mixed-use urban neighborhood. The Miami-based firm has been a leader in "new urbanism," a movement of architects, developers, planners, and others who seek to reassert traditional neighborhood character in the design of new developments. Previously known for creating new neighborhoods on green-field sites such as Seaside, a "neotraditional" seaside village of closely spaced bungalows clustered near a walkable Main Street along the Florida panhandle, DPZ's work in Providence reflects an early effort to bring housing into a downtown. A decade later, the downtown boasts a thriving loft movement, and a second condominium tower is scheduled to rise among new shops and restaurants along a downtown street that was virtually deserted a few years ago.

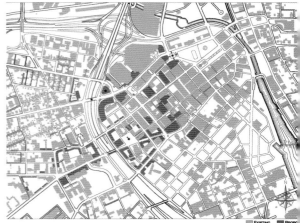

The Miami-based firm of Duany Plater-Zyberk (DPZ) was one of the founders of the New Urbanism movement, which emphasizes walkable streets over the automobile in its planning and a sense of community over stand-alone buildings in its architecture. In the early 1990s DPZ led a charrette that created a vision to revitalize downtown Providence (top) by transforming it into a mixed-use district that accommodates a variety of urban neighborhoods.
Courtesy Duany Plater-Zyberk

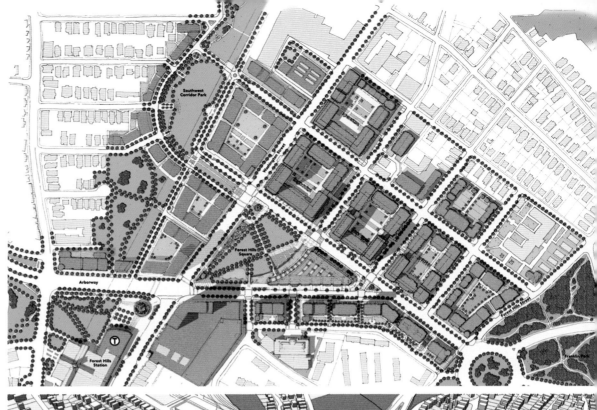

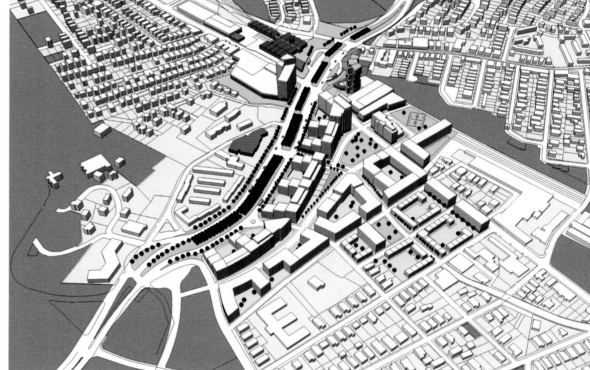

At a 2005 conference titled "Reinventing the Urban Village," three urban designer/developer teams prepared visions for a 21st-century transit-oriented neighborhood in Boston. The Goody Clancy/Avalon Bay proposal (top) illustrates how a variety of building types, ranging from row houses to mid-rise lofts and slender towers framing a new village square, can be used to create a diverse urban neighborhood. The proposal by Icon Architects/Trinity Financial (middle) illustrates that a higher density neighborhood can also be a greener neighborhood by organizing blocks of mid-rise housing around a series of parks that connect to Boston's Olmsted park system. Stull Lee Architects/Urban Edge (bottom) proposed a lively new "main street" to celebrate cultural diversity and create a sense of community. *Courtesy Goody Clancy/Avalon Bay; Icon Architects/Trinity Financial; and Stull and Lee, Inc. Architects and Planners/Urban Edge*

1988
Founding of DOCOMOMO
(Documentation and Conservation of
Buildings, Sites and Neighborhoods
of the Modern Movement)

AIA Committee on the
Environment formed

"That Exceptional One" exhibition
celebrated the centennial of
Louise Blanchard Bethune's
election as the first woman AIA
member

Mildred B. Cooper Memorial Chapel,
Bella Vista, Arkansas,
E. Fay Jones

The Los Angeles firm Roschen Van Cleve was asked by the city's planning department and a developer to work with Hollywood neighborhood leaders to create an urban design vision for a controversial site one block from the fabled intersection of Sunset and Vine. With Nakada & Partners, Roschen Van Cleve translated this vision into a bold design that preserves and incorporates the façade of the 1950s modern ABC Headquarters building. Finished in 2004, the development has served as a model for community-based design for large mixed-use developments in neighborhood settings.
Courtesy Roschen Van Cleve

In nearby Lowell, city planners with a strong interest in new urbanism have adapted the movement's principles to help revitalize the Hamilton Canal mill complex. These officials recently issued a request for proposals from developers to transform the historic mill complex and adjacent land into Lowell's first new urban neighborhood in more than a century, with 1,000 units of housing and new shops and cafés lining two of the city's now historic canals.

Designing Community in the 21st Century

As new people bring new wealth into the city, the icons of neighborhood—the row houses, Main Street shops, and other building forms that historically constituted the "civic infrastructure" of community—are no longer sufficient. But what constitutes a new civic infrastructure? A group of Boston-based urban designers, working with the AIA's Regional and Urban Design Committee, the AIA's Center of Communities by Design, and the Federal Reserve Bank of Boston (one of the country's 12 Reserve Banks, which finance most American housing development) organized a charrette and conference in Boston in 2005 to answer this question.

This event, "Reinventing the Urban Village," began with visionary presentations for a hypothetical 21st-century urban neighborhood next to Boston's Forest Hills transit station by three teams, each of which consisted of a Boston-based architecture and urban design firm and a prominent developer or community development corporation: Goody Clancy/Avalon Bay, Icon /Trinity Financial, and Stull Lee/Urban Edge. Their concepts were then considered by the approximately 200 conference participants, who included neighborhood leaders, architects and planners, academicians, developers, and directors of development, planning, and urban design departments from several prominent American cities. The discussions focused on the six building blocks that are critical to creating a new generation of civic infrastructure:

Civic engagement

Diverse neighborhoods need more public process than homogeneous neighborhoods to build consensus around new projects. Bill Roschen, AIA, principal of the firm Roschen Van Cleve and a recent appointee to the Los Angeles Planning Commission, has built his career around working with residents of diverse neighborhoods to determine how development can create community. Brought in to help a development team respond to strong neighborhood opposition to a large-scale, transit-oriented housing proposal, named Sunset + Vine in honor of its proximity to the historic epicenter of the film industry, Roschen spent many nights bringing longtime residents, preservation and affordable-housing advocates, developers, and others to the same table to talk about the future of the neighborhood they shared. He drew his inspiration from their comments and produced a plan that won wide acclaim, despite the fact that it introduced greater density, by adding lively retail space, providing affordable housing, creating innovative public spaces, and preserving the historic ABC Television Headquarters building.

Mixed-Use Main Streets

Nothing strikes a deeper chord in meetings with neighborhood residents than the proposal to bring back a vital, walkable Main Street. Sometimes known as "third places," the tree-lined sidewalks, cafés, coffee shops, and local stores along neighborhood Main Streets are treasured places where neighbors connect with one another. Architects are designing exciting mixed-use developments that reinvigorate Main Streets by combining these uses with housing, offices, and even hotels and other programmatic functions on upper floors. Five years ago, developers in Columbus, Ohio, deemed South Campus Gateway Center "unbuildable," because its retail space lined High Street, then in a depressed university district, rather than clustering around a more conventional, internal mall. Today, the 500,000-square-feet mixed-use development, designed by architects Elkus Manfredi of Boston and completed in 2005, attracts new residents to the district with an arts cinema, restaurants, bookstore, food market, bars, and music venues at street level. Housing, offices, and university facilities are situated on upper floors.

Density

In 2000 Goody Clancy undertook a study with Pam McKinney, a nationally respected real-estate economist based in Boston, to determine how many additional housing units are required to spur development of one block of new Main Street retail (30,000 to 50,000 square feet). The answer: 1,000 to 2,000 units within a 10- to 15-minute walk, depending on disposable income levels and the economics of local retail development.

Adding this much new housing involves reintroducing the kinds of densities traditionally found in urban neighborhoods (50 to 100 units or more per acre). While existing residents are often initially concerned about these higher ratios, local support can grow when well-designed presentations demonstrate the many advantages of density. The Chicago office of the national landscape architecture firm JJR and Goody Clancy worked with residents of Chicago's Cabrini-Green public housing development to create an urban design vision for rebuilding the complex of low-income towers as a mixed-income and mixed-use neighborhood with a wide variety of housing types. Most participants initially wanted to lower density from the existing level of 40 units per acre. They subsequently changed their minds, however, when they realized that a mix of building types and densities—including row houses, lofts, and mid-rises that, together, achieved 50 or more units per acre—could be designed at a very human scale and oriented along neighborhood streets, and that this higher density would support new retail, provide a greater range of housing choices, and help offset the costs of creating new parks and other neighborhood amenities.

The mixed-use neighborhood of NorthPoint replaced a rail yard
located roughly one mile from downtown Boston. CBT and
Greenberg Consulatants designed the buildings to frame and
clearly define tree-lined streets. *Courtesy CBT*

Church of the Light,
Tadao Ando

Nelson Fine Arts Center,
Arizona State University,
Antoine Predock

Founding of the Center for
Universal Design,
North Carolina State University

Morton H. Meyerson
Symphony Center, Dallas,
Pei Cobb Freed & Partners

Joseph Esherick, FAIA,
received the AIA Gold Medal

Housing choices

One reason Cabrini-Green residents came to accept higher densities was because they began to recognize that significantly fewer of them lived in families with children than had been the case even ten years before. Similarly, Seattle, which is now returning to its 1960 population of 600,000 (up roughly 20 percent since 1980), needs 35 percent more housing units to accommodate the same number of people in households that are smaller and more varied. In a city with a tradition of single-family neighborhoods, roughly 80 percent of housing permits over the past five years have been for multifamily housing, often with 50 or more units. The city's urban designer, John Rahaim, AIA, is working with various architecture firms to design the next generation of urban neighborhood housing, including mixed-use buildings that often include four or more floors of lofts over retail space.

Public realm

Residents in Eastern Cambridge, Massachusetts, put in place a moratorium in 2002 to block higher density development, in part because they said the large new buildings undermined the quality of their traditional neighborhoods. Goody Clancy worked with a broad-based task force to create guidelines that would ensure that additional private development would also enhance the quality of life for its neighbors. Two years later, these same residents argued for new zoning that restored all 12 million square feet blocked by the earlier moratorium, but this time stipulating that the development had to fund new parks and orient new buildings along neighborhood streets. Using these same guidelines, Boston-based CBT designed the new neighborhood of NorthPoint, which replaces a former rail yard with over six million square feet of mixed-use development oriented around a large new public park and along a network of new, landscaped streets. The result is a community connected to adjacent, established, mixed-income neighborhoods via a lively public realm.

Mixed-incomes

Ultimately, one of the most exciting opportunities facing America today is the ability to achieve the dream of mixed-income communities. The unprecedented demand by middle- and upper-income residents to live in urban neighborhoods is setting the stage, as people with the resources to live anywhere are investing their dollars in mixed-income areas. Lexington Terrace (2000) in Baltimore by the firm of Torti Gallas, based in Silver Spring, Maryland; Park DuValle (2006) in Louisville, by Urban Design Associates, based in Pittsburgh; and Cabrini Green, cited above, represent examples of public housing reimagined as vibrant, mixed-income neighborhoods. These projects were funded by the federal government's HOPE VI program, launched in 1992 to help underwrite the cost of transforming public housing into mixed-income neighborhoods. A new generation of mixed-income neighborhoods is now taking shape without federal assistance. One such example can be found in Norfolk, Virginia, where Goody Clancy is currently working with local residents of the downtown Saint Paul's public housing development to transform its 600 units into a higher density neighborhood. It will include more than 1,200 units of mixed-income housing together with new shops, parks, and community facilities.

Park DuValle in Louisville, planned by Ray Gindroz, FAIA, of Pittsburgh-based Urban Design Associates in collaboration with David Lee, FAIA, of Boston-based Stull Lee, and others, transformed a large public housing development (top) into a mixed-income neighborhood in which a variety of housing types line new neighborhood streets. Despite initial concerns, Park DuValle demonstrates that moderate- and higher-income households can be attracted to a well-designed, mixed-income neighborhood. *Courtesy Urban Design Associates*

Looking Ahead

America has often been called a "melting pot," but historically the pot's ingredients never really blended together. Today, however, diversity is finally becoming a reality in neighborhoods across America. Consider Boston: 96 percent white and one of America's poorest major cities in 1960, it is now less than 50 percent white and one of America's wealthiest. African-Americans are moving into Irish South Boston. Whites are moving into African-American Roxbury. Hispanics are moving into Italian East Boston. White-collar families are moving into blue-collar Dorchester. Straight families are dotting the gay South End. And gay couples with kids are putting down roots in traditional, family-oriented West Roxbury. Architects are working with these, and many other Americans, to build—for the benefit of all—what was once only a dream: neighborhoods that celebrate their diversity and foster a new generation of community. ●

The new fountain in Chicago's Millennium Park represents one of America's most significant investments in creating community— a new city park that invites kids of all ages and races to play together in the heart of a great American city. *Courtesy Sam Assefa*

1990
Passage of the Americans with
Disabilities Act

Science Complex,
University of Oregon,
Ratcliff Architects

Canadian Chancery,
Washington, D.C.,
Arthur C. Erickson

E. Fay Jones, FAIA,
received the AIA Gold Medal

GOLD MEDALIST, 1956

Clarence S. Stein, FAIA

Allen Freeman

Clarence S. Stein (left) received the Gold Medal from George Bain Cummings, FAIA, 1955–56 president of the AIA.

No famous building can be attributed to architect Clarence S. Stein. Instead, he was awarded the Gold Medal because of his significant contribution to innovative community and regional planning and, in particular, a development of middle-class houses called Radburn, built 16 miles from Manhattan in Bergen County, New Jersey, between 1927 and 1933. Keeping automobiles in their place was the driving force behind the design of this so-called New Town.

Stein, the son of a successful casket manufacturer in Rochester, New York, was born in 1882. The family moved to New York City in 1890. He studied architecture at the Ecole des Beaux-Arts in Paris and returned to New York in 1912, where he worked for architect Bertram Grosvernor Goodhue on the design of St. Bartholomew's Church in Manhattan and buildings for the Panama California Exposition of 1915–16 in San Diego. In the early 1920s, Stein set out on his own as an architect and was drawn into a circle of intellectuals who directed their energies toward regional planning and affordable housing. Among his associates were Benton MacKaye, who fathered the Appalachian Trail, the critic Lewis Mumford, and the architect Henry Wright. These four men studied Ebenezer Howard's English Garden Cities at Letchworth and Welwyn, seeking to adapt the concepts to America.

Stein and Wright—along with real estate developer Alexander Bing and others—demonstrated these ideas at Sunnyside Gardens (1924) in Queens, New York. Here, they placed modest town houses along the perimeter of each urban block so that residents could share the large, undivided green spaces within the interior instead of being limited to just a sliver of a backyard. The plan called for several apartment buildings as well.

Stein and Wright went on to design Radburn and then Chatham Village (1929) in Pittsburgh.

The center of Radburn is a bucolic greensward with footpaths surrounded by houses. Cars are relegated to perimeter roads and a series of cul-de-sacs that serve the houses from the back. Children play on the central commons and walk to nearby schools and recreation facilities using underpasses and bridges that separate cars from pedestrians. Construction of Radburn was halted during the Great Depression, and a majority of the land was sold to meet financial obligations. Later, when postwar construction resumed in America's suburbs, housing developers there, as elsewhere, largely ignored what has come to be known as the Radburn Plan. Today, the portion that was built—a charming cluster of small brick houses in a mature landscape—survives and functions much as the original designers intended.

Stein also consulted with the federal government on the New Town plan of Greenbelt (1937), Maryland, in suburban Washington and later lobbied Congress not to sell off lands acquired for other Greenbelt towns. In the 1950s he helped plan Kitimat, a small town in northwestern British Columbia, and he wrote *Toward New Towns for America* (1951). Soon after Stein died in 1975 at the age of 93, Lewis Mumford wrote in the *AIA Journal* that the central core of Stein's character was "his modesty, his hospitality to other talents, [and] his sensitive respect for human individuality" directed by "a strong drive toward an open society."

Stein's design for the New Jersey development of Radburn (right), with its emphasis on common green space and a system of footpaths, offered a different vision of suburbia for America. The Phipps Garden Apartments, built in Queens, New York, in 1931 by a nonprofit housing development corporation, offers rental units overlooking a central courtyard. ©*Frederick Charles (Radburn)*; *Clarence S. Stein Papers, Division of Rare and Manuscript Collections, Cornell University Library (Phipps Garden)*

Five Points Community Revitalization Charrette

Gregory Walker, AIA

The Norfolk, Virginia, community of Norview is typical of many post–World War I suburban neighborhoods. Anchored by a small central business district of Depression-era commercial storefronts, the surrounding streets consist primarily of single-family homes built in the early- to mid-20th century. By the late 1980s, population shifts to newer suburbs had reduced the older community to a shell of its former self. Vacant homes and neglected properties, plus rising crime rates, left many longtime residents feeling disaffected.

To address these problems, local residents and business and community leaders formed the Five Points Partnership, a community-based action group. This grassroots coalition, formed in 1996, consists of a five-member board of governors representing five facets of the neighborhood: citizens, businesses, schools, churches, and public safety.

Soon after forming, the partnership approached the local AIA component, Hampton Roads, to obtain assistance. Ten members of the chapter's Young Architects Forum (YAF) became the core group of volunteers for the AIA effort: Robert Bell, Assoc. AIA; Tom Beverly, AIA; David Levy, AIA; Dinna Magno, Assoc. AIA; Lisa Moritz; Ted Sawruk, Assoc. AIA; Cary Simmons, AIA; John Sivils; Shelly Sulik; Joy Thorpe; and Charles Woods.

The YAF group—in conjunction with partnership coordinator Bev Sell and other community leaders—developed a series of questionnaires that were distributed throughout the community to collect information about the neighborhood's physical properties and the residents' psycho-geographical perceptions of its condition. In the first survey, residents were asked to describe what they liked best and least about the community's physical attributes and to qualitatively imagine the community's potential. The physical attributes were graphically recorded and the resulting map was distributed to residents as part of a second survey. This time, respondents were asked to place color-coded dots on the map to indicate, for example, where they lived, where they felt unsafe, and which areas made them most proud of their neighborhood.

A few months later, in June 1997, 11 YAF members facilitated an all-day charrette at Norview High School for 50 community leaders and citizens. The visioning session explored how to make the neighborhood safer—the partnership's primary concern—by examining the central business district, local recreational opportunities, and the physical connections between various neighborhood sectors.

Out of these efforts came a written report, titled "The Five Points Partnership: Proposals for Revitalization," that outlined several ways in which the streetscapes could be improved. The document also provided a comprehensive inventory of architecturally significant Depression-era buildings, identified areas that should be targeted for community investment, and defined a "recreation corridor" that would connect the central business district and public buildings with a system of parks.

Perhaps most important, the final report became a critical tool for local leaders to convey to Norfolk city officials how they wanted to reimagine their neighborhood. In 2004, building directly on YAF's efforts, the city of Norfolk prepared a comprehensive Five Points Community Streetscape master plan and overlay district. Streetscape improvements are currently underway, a new high school has been built, and a farmers' market is now thriving.

Members of the Young Architects Forum of AIA Hampton Roads (Virginia) volunteered to help plan the revitalization of the Norfolk community of Norview, which by the 1980s was plagued with crime, vacant properties, and other woes associated with the postwar flight to suburbia. The Norview Theater, shown here, was once the center of the community. The photo above shows Norview as it looked when the YAF began its study of the community in 1996–97. *Courtesy Lisa Moritz*

1991
Architectural Record *poll named*
Frank Lloyd Wright's Fallingwater *the*
best building of the past century

Sainsbury Wing,
National Gallery, London,
Venturi, Scott Brown and Associates

New York Mosque and
Islamic Cultural Center,
New York City,
Michael McCarthy/SOM

Charles W. Moore, FAIA,
received the AIA Gold Medal

19

City Limits

Douglas Kelbaugh, FAIA

Cities are arguably the greatest of humanity's accomplishments and the most human of its great accomplishments. They have been the birthplace, engine, and repository of civilization, as well as its collective soul. Societies coalesce, grow, and thrive with the exchange of ideas, goods, and services that occur within their orbit. Yet, while cities provide the opportunity for the chance encounters and productive frictions that give rise to creativity and nourish culture, their size and intensity often make them difficult to manage—and therefore susceptible to crime, disease, social dysfunction, and unrest. This inherent tension has played a pivotal role in the evolution of cities, particularly in the United States where plentiful land, a relatively small population, an emphasis on individual rights, and ever-more advanced technologies have afforded its political leaders, entrepreneurs, and designers the opportunity to explore and experiment with a variety of settlement patterns. These forms of urbanism have included traditional cities, garden cities, suburbia, new towns, megastructures, edge cities, transit villages, and neotraditional towns and neighborhoods, as well as urban renewal and redeveloped urban cores and suburbs. American architects—Thomas Jefferson, Daniel Burnham, Frank Lloyd Wright, and Louis Kahn, among them—have been actively engaged not only in the theoretical discourse on human settlement but also in the design of buildings, complexes, neighborhoods, districts, and entire cities, all of which have influenced the evolution of urbanism.

(Opposite) One of the great public spaces of the world, St. Mark's Square in Venice is surrounded by the seats of religious, political, economic, and cultural power in a tour de force of urban design that evolved over many centuries. It continues to delight millions of tourists each year. ©*Yann Arthus-Bertrand/Corbis*

1992
L. Jane Hastings, FAIA, became the first woman chancellor of the AIA College of Fellows

Susan A. Maxman, FAIA, became the first woman president of the AIA (1992–93)

Founding of Auburn University's Rural Studio by Samuel Mockbee with D. K. Ruth

AIA President Cecil Steward, FAIA, convened a Task Force on Diversity

Benjamin Thompson, FAIA, received the AIA Gold Medal

Basic Patterns of Human Settlement

Human beings are social, as well as vulnerable, creatures. Traditionally, people have lived in families, tribes, villages, and towns for a host of reasons—from basic survival and commerce to culture, recreation, and religion. For thousands of years, the location and success of human settlements were closely allied with the natural environment and, by necessity, exhibited relatively informal, organic growth. People made their homes near sources of water (springs, oases, rivers, lakes, or seas) for drinking, transportation, and trade, on high ground that offered protection from animals and enemies, and near places that could be hunted. Communities also were often located where trails and trade routes intersected or crossed rivers. They were generally supported by an agricultural hinterland, although historians debate whether agricultural surplus first gave rise to towns or vice versa.

As some villages and towns developed into commercial, religious, military, political, or cultural centers of considerable size and complexity, their configuration and morphology tended to become more formal. They were centroidal, linear, scattered, or some combination of these basic patterns. Many marked their boundaries with walls and fortifications, which tended to concentrate and densify their development. Some marked their centers with a marketplace, souk, forum, palace, temple, church, synagogue, or mosque. Wells, fountains, pools, and structures for ritual were also often located in central public places. Parks and gardens—private or open to the townsfolk—sometimes adjoined royal residences or religious structures. Especially in Europe and America, towns frequently had commons and greens at their center or edge for the public grazing of livestock. Uses were typically mixed, with housing above or behind shops that abutted other private and public buildings lining streets and lanes, which were generally wider in American towns and cities than in other parts of the world.

As civilizations advanced, many towns grew into cities. Some, such as London and Paris, continued to evolve organically. Generally speaking, the architects of the day primarily focused on individual buildings or complexes for royal, religious, and wealthy secular patrons. Sometimes these structures, such as the cathedral and palace in many Italian cities, fronted and defined active public squares, thereby enhancing the lives of not only the ruling class but all citizens. These outdoor living rooms, popular the world over, are among the most potent devices of urban design. A more contemporary exemplar of an urban center with a lively public space is Rockefeller Center in New York City.

Political and religious capitals were often laid out by the designers of the day in more formal patterns to glorify seats of power, often with grand, symmetrical axes and complexes, such as the Champs-Elysées in Paris or the National Mall in Washington, D.C. None were larger in scale or more axial than Angkor Wat in Cambodia, the Forbidden City in Beijing, the Avenue of the Dead in Teotihuacan, Mexico, or the Kings Way in New Delhi, and none more refined than the Mughal city of Fatehpur Sikri and the Taj Mahal tomb complex in India. Other cities were planned and built in grids, with early examples in ancient Greece, China, and medieval Japan. Although it was easier to build these more geometrically formal cities from scratch, sometimes they were, like Chicago, created retroactively after a great fire or flood, or by edict, such as the draconian case of Baron Haussmann's slicing through medieval Paris to create wide, straight boulevards and avenues.

(Opposite) Rockefeller Center, designed by a host of architects and built during the Great Depression, is one of New York's and the country's most successful and admired urban ensembles. Soaring buildings surround a central open space, animated by restaurants, a skating rink, flags, and a seasonal Christmas tree. *©Peter Aaron/Esto*

Baron Haussmann, commissioned by Napolean III in the mid-19th century to "modernize" Paris, is responsible for the design of the city's wide, straight boulevards and avenues, shown here from the Place de l'Etoile. *©Yann Arthus-Bertrand/Corbis*

1993
U.S. Green Building Council formed

AIA President Susan Maxman,
FAIA, and Olufemi Majekodunmi,
president of the UIA, signed the
Declaration of Independence for a
Sustainable Future

U.S. Holocaust Memorial Museum,
Washington, D.C.,
James I. Freed

Cesar Chavez Multicultural Academic
Center, Chicago,
Carol Ross Barney

Frederick R. Weisman Art Museum,
University of Minnesota,
Frank Gehry

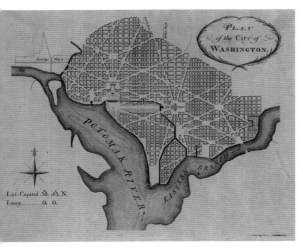

L'Enfant's plan for Washington mixed open spaces, ceremonial spaces, monumental axes, and wide, radial boulevards, all superimposed over a grid system of streets. *Library of Congress*

Colonial America

Although an indigenous population had occupied North America for thousands of years and created settlements as impressive as the magnificent Mayan and Aztec religious centers of pre–Columbian Mexico and the rock dwellings of the Anasazi peoples in the American Southwest, the Europeans who conquered these cultures brought their own ideas of human settlement to their "New World" from England, France, Holland, Portugal, and Spain. The Spanish colonizers built their colonial cities according to the Law of the Indies, which, for reasons of climate, called for street grids rotated 45 degrees from the cardinal points and, for reasons of legitimating and celebrating secular and religious power, built central plazas fronted by the most important religious, civic, and commercial buildings. Many of their settlements, such as Los Angeles and San Francisco, were built in conjunction with mission churches. They and other Europeans mixed Christian proselytizing with imperial conquest or colonization, although the others were not always as formal or methodical in their planning of colonies founded for religious, political, and commercial freedom.

In colonial America, the three largest cities of the 13 British colonies were Boston, Philadelphia, and New York, founded in that order during the 17th century. Boston was settled by the Puritans in an organic pattern at the mouth of the Charles River on a series of islands that were later joined to the mainland with landfill. Philadelphia, the capital of the Quaker colony of Pennsylvania, was laid out between the Schuylkill and Delaware rivers in a formal grid by its founder, the Englishman William Penn. New York was the capital of the former Dutch trading colony that was founded on the southern tip of Manhattan, where the East River empties into the Hudson. This port city grew in a relatively haphazard pattern, later to adopt a rigid grid of streets and avenues with Broadway, its famous diagonal exception that followed a Native American trail.

Savannah was planned in 1733 as the capital of the Georgia colony by its first governor, James Oglethorpe. Cut out of the forest on the banks of the Savannah River, 18 miles from the Atlantic Ocean, the city was also laid out on a grid but with public squares of several sizes and configurations at frequent intervals that give it—to this day—a unique urban character. Other important colonial cities, such as Charleston, South Carolina, and Baltimore, Maryland, evolved informally. Both were important seaports, the former at the mouth of a river and the latter near the top of the Chesapeake Bay, which gave it easier access to the colony's agricultural interior. All these colonial towns and cities contained handsome public and private buildings, typically designed in the Georgian style of architecture that dominated the American colonies.

A Young Nation

No city was more ambitiously planned and designed than the nation's capital, Washington, D.C. After the 13 colonies won their independence from Britain, they agreed to build the city near the center of the fledgling nation in the new and politically neutral District of Columbia. In 1791 Pierre L'Enfant, a French volunteer in the American army, boldly laid out a plan that was Baroque, a style of simple but dramatic clarity and powerful spatial sequences that were ironically associated with absolutist thinking in Europe. Over the last two centuries, many architects have designed impressive government and institutional buildings for the nation's capital, mostly in the classical style. Benjamin Latrobe's U.S. Capitol was among the first, largest, and most notable.

Thomas Jefferson may have influenced L'Enfant's plan, but he was nonetheless wary of cities, which he considered a necessary evil, associated as they were with moral corruption and decadence. He believed the young democracy of farmers (at the time, 98 percent of the country's population was involved in agriculture) should eschew urban temptations and vanities in favor of universal citizenship based on enlightened agrarian values. An accomplished architect himself, he designed the University of Virginia's "academical village" and his rural estate, the Neo-Palladian and inventive Monticello. In 1803 Jefferson was also instrumental in the Louisiana Purchase, which added much of the vast territory west of the Mississippi River, and the super-imposition of the Cartesian grid on it. The continental-scaled Jeffersonian grid was to later shape much of the nation's settlement of the West and its cadastral system of land boundaries and speculation.

The nation's capital was designed in a very formal and monumental style that mirrored foreign cities such as Paris, Vienna, and Beijing. However, the rest of the country generally opted for a less grand urbanism—just as Americans favored laissez-faire capitalism and representative democracy over the more authoritarian economic and political systems they had both fled and fought a war over. Although they dispensed with the formality, Americans

Founding of the Design-Build Institute of America

Turtle Creek House, Dallas, Antoine Predock

Audubon Society Headquarters (renovation of historic building), New York City, Croxton Collaborative Architects

Papalote Children's Museum, Mexico City, Ricardo Legorreta

Kevin Roche, FAIA, and Thomas Jefferson (posthumously) received the AIA Gold Medal

maintained Europe's abiding respect for the city center as a place of public gathering and exchange. Indeed, there were village greens and town commons in New England and courthouse squares in Midwestern county seats, as well as impressive boulevards, squares, and parks within the gridiron of larger cities. And public and major institutional buildings, such as city halls and churches, were often accorded the more central or conspicuous sites — but business, housing, and other institutions jockeyed for land in a universal grid of blocks that was more open and egalitarian than the stratified and hierarchical cities of Europe.

From the start, Americans, including the young army officer and surveyor George Washington, engaged in land speculation — a practice that has remained fundamental to real estate development and urbanism in this country. Indeed, the form and character of its cities has been the result of market forces and private investment as much as public planning, urban design, and abundant land. Towns and cities across the country were typically subdivided, platted primarily into residential lots and incrementally developed by speculative builders who competed for the growing middle class of home buyers. Some developers built private tram and trolley lines to their new subdivisions on the outskirts of cities, which the municipalities frequently annexed in subsequent years.

This country's "national" public square extends some two miles between the Capitol and the Lincoln Memorial, and its axis extends across the Potomas River to Arlington National Cemetery in Virginia. The city's generous scale, which expressed the heroic aspirations and natural grandeur of a vast young country, exceeded Baroque Rome and the Paris of Louis XIV. *©Dean Conger/Corbis*

1994
The three model code groups
formed the International Code
Council, which led to the first
International Building Code

Warhol Museum
(adaptive use of factory building),
Pittsburgh,
Richard Gluckman

Sir Norman Foster, Hon. FAIA,
received the AIA Gold Medal

Industrialization and Rapid Growth

Philadelphia and New York City, both busy ports and robust industrial centers, were already important cities of the world by the middle of the 19th century. As the West became more settled and served by an extensive network of railways, dusty cities like Kansas City, Missouri, boomed on cattle and Denver on mining, but few grew as spectacularly as San Francisco during the California Gold Rush of 1849. These cities were typically laid out on flat land with the road network shifting along river and lake frontages to accommodate the topography, although the streets of San Francisco and Seattle climb straight up their steep hills.

After the Civil War, which slowed development in the North and actually devastated southern cities like Atlanta, U.S. cities grew more rapidly. The sometimes explosive growth was spurred by new waves of immigrants from southern and eastern Europe, who were escaping poverty and lured by the promise of fortune in America but, unlike many colonial settlers, were not as estranged from city life. The growth was also fueled by rapid industrialization that attracted workers from farms, where mechanization was making them redundant, to gritty factory towns.

In these fast-growing cities, architects were called on to design city halls, courthouses, railroad stations, churches, banks, office buildings, clubs, and mansions, which variously signified civic aspiration, commercial success, and social status. These buildings were typically located "downtown," often on "Main Street"—two distinctly American contributions to the urban lexicon. They were usually substantial masonry buildings symbolically designed in classical architectural styles of European derivation. However, new American architectural types and styles were also invented, most notably the Chicago steel-frame, high-rise elevator building with its simpler detailing that made fewer references to historical antecedents. These "skyscrapers" allowed for much denser "central business districts"—two other American urban coinages.

Nonetheless, neither Chicago nor the rest of the country was ready to fully shed its classical connections. The city was the site of the World's Columbian Exposition of 1893, also known as the "White City" because its edifices were sheathed and decorated with white plaster. This federally sanctioned exhibition celebrated the 400th anniversary of Columbus's "discovery" of the Americas with a very ambitious and grand array of monumental buildings in the Neoclassical style. The chief designer and planner, Daniel Burnham, assembled a large and talented team of designers and artists who shared his vision of civic splendor. Among others, he brought in the cosmopolitan East Coast firm of McKim, Mead and White to design some of the major buildings, and the father of American landscape architecture, Frederick Law Olmsted, to lay out the overall grounds and picturesque gardens.

This popular and financially successful World's Fair was largely responsible for the preeminence of Beaux-Arts design that was to dominate architecture and urbanism in the United States until the middle of the 20th century, when Modernism would take hold. It also inspired the City Beautiful movement, which turned the centers of many American cities from muddy cow towns and squalid factory towns into places with picturesque parks, public plazas, and grand boulevards. These civic spaces were punctuated with elegant, Neoclassical government buildings, as well as museums, libraries, pavilions, and band shells, all artfully sited in public gardens and among fountains, lakes, and lagoons.

Also following on the heels of the World's Fair—and reaffirming the Jeffersonian ideals of rural America—was the Garden City Movement. It began in England as an antidote to both overcrowded cities and newly spreading suburbs and migrated to this continent at the turn of the century. Its philosophy and principles were to mix the beauty and peacefulness of rural living with the culture and energy of town life through a central garden city surrounded by towns and an agricultural greenbelt. The movement influenced Lewis Mumford and Clarence Stein, two major figures in the American movement for regional planning, and three model towns were subsequently built by the U.S. government as part of President Franklin D. Roosevelt's New Deal: Greenhills, Ohio; Greendale, Wisconsin; and Greenbelt, Maryland. But garden cities were never fully adopted in the United States or Great Britain. Instead, our suburbs became watered-down versions of these visionary attempts to harmoniously integrate town and country, urban and rural.

(Opposite) The Lake Shore Drive Apartments, designed by Mies van der Rohe in Chicago and completed in 1951, are a canonical example of the Modernist high-rise building first developed in Chicago in the 1880s and later taken to new heights in New York City. High-rise towers quickly became the signature of urban skylines around the world. These vertical cities, sometimes rising 100 stories or more, could house as many as 5,000 people, the number of citizens in an ideal classical Greek city. *Ezra Stoller/©Esto*

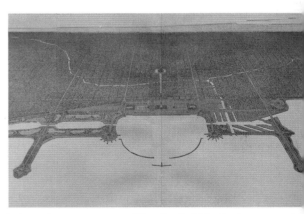

No Beaux-Arts plan was more ambitious than Daniel Burnham's 1909 plan for Chicago, which attempted to recast American architecture and urbanism in a grand Neoclassical style, inspiring the City Beautiful movement that was soon to elegantly transform many U.S. cities. The plan's ongoing legacy is the lakefront string of parks, piers, and marinas, including public buildings, which continue to delight the public to this day. *Chicago History Museum*

The Rise of Modernism and Suburbia

Modernism, which began in Europe as a revolutionary movement in the fine arts before World War II, became a conscious force in American architecture after the war. The movement was about more than modernization per se: it envisioned a brave, new world where science, technology, and a new social order would replace the ancient regime of eclectic art and handcraft, class and economic inequities, and the former imperial political order—all of which were emphatically rejected as decadent and obsolete. Le Corbusier, along with Walter Gropius, Mies van der Rohe, and Alvar Aalto, proposed a radically new architecture based on new technology and expressed in the machine aesthetic. In 1922 Le Corbusier put forward Radiant City, a radically new urbanism meant to completely erase and replace everything that preceded it. Equally modern but diametrically opposed in form and intent, Broadacre City was proposed by Frank Lloyd Wright in the 1930s as his idealized version of the city.

In America, the Modernist city was ushered in at the 1939 World's Fair in New York by General Motors' Futurama Exhibit, which promised a new world of clean, modern design and a life style freed of drudgery by new technology, especially the automobile. Indeed, the automobile industry was wildly successful in incorporating the private motorized vehicle into the American Dream. By then the ubiquitous streetcar system was in crisis. Sometimes these systems—most blatantly in Los Angeles—were actually purchased and shut down by the big auto manufacturers themselves. The automobile—from freeways to parking garages—was to radically transform our cities, as much or more than steam power and railroads had in the previous century. During the Depression, New York City's czar of planning and development, Robert Moses, built a network of parkways out to Long Island and Westchester County. These early, limited-access highways formed linear parks that curved through the bucolic countryside beyond the city and were intended for both commuting and for leisurely Sunday drives with the family. Soon parkways and freeways were built in many American cities, along rivers and lakefronts, through parks, and into the suburban countryside. Indeed, the federal Interstate Highway system, which cut through most large towns and cities, became the largest public works project in history.

Le Corbusier's vision for the Radiant City (below) was distinctly rational, with high-rise "towers in the park," mass-produced social housing, and superblocks with vehicles and pedestrians separated. Diametrically opposed in form and intent, Frank Lloyd Wright's Broadacre City (right) of the 1930s was a low-density, pastoral settlement that proposed an acre of productive land for every American family. The two models embodied and fed the country's love-hate relationship with cities. *Le Corbusier, "Ville Contemporaine," ©2008 Artists Rights Society, NY/ ADAGP, Paris/FLC; Frank Lloyd Wright, "Broadacre City," ©2008 Frank Lloyd Wright Foundation, Scottsdale/Artists Rights Society, NY*

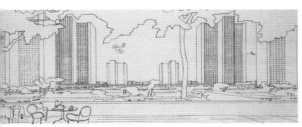

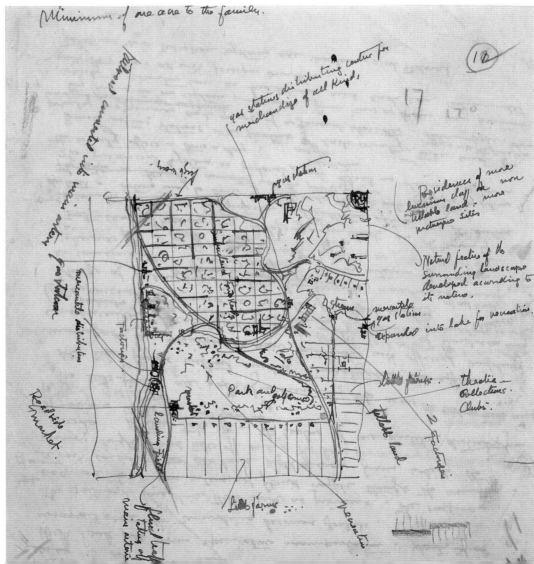

1995
YWCA Family Village,
Redmond, Washington,
Pyatok Architects and
Stickney Murphy Architects

Denver International Airport,
Fentress Bradburn Architects

César Pelli, FAIA,
received the AIA Gold Medal

Norman Bel Geddes's Futurama exhibit for General Motors was a smash hit among corporate displays at the 1939 World's Fair in New York. The futuristic city of wide freeways, sleek cars, and modernist high-rises captured the imagination of the American public. *Margaret Bourke-White, Norman Bel Geddes Collection, Harry Ransom Humanities Research Center, University of Texas at Austin*

(Opposite) Boston City Hall (1968), the product of an international design competition won by Kallman, McKinnell & Knowles, is the centerpiece of an urban renewal plan for the city's Government Center designed by I. M. Pei & Associates. The muscular icon sits on an oversized civic space, typically empty except for public events. *©Joseph Sohm/Visions of America/Corbis*

Lincoln Center for the Performning Arts, a 15-acre complex with buildings designed by many of the leading architects of the mid-20th century, was part of Robert Moses's urban renewal program for the west side of Manhattan in the 1960s. *©Jeff Albertson/Corbis*

Baltimore's Harborplace (1980) revitalized a dormant and decaying inner city with a coordinated redevelopment plan that included a "festival marketplace" by AIA Gold Medalist Benjamin Thompson, as well as an aquarium and new office and residential towers. *©Joseph Sohm/Visions of America/Corbis*

The American dream of self-sufficiency, privacy, and landownership manifested itself most pervasively after World War II in suburbanization, which hastened the decline of many inner cities. Early suburbs in metropolitan New York, Philadelphia, and Chicago, among others, were built in the late 19th and early 20th centuries, many along commuter railroad lines. After World War II, returning veterans could buy homes with government-backed, low-interest mortgages, which favored the purchase of single-family homes in the new suburban subdivisions that were sprouting up like weeds, especially in sunny California cities such as Los Angeles. The detached, single-family house has deep roots in the American ideal of agrarian democracy and has resulted over the last half-century in an unprecedented pattern of low-density metropolitan settlement. This historical trajectory is remarkable and ironic in light of the fact that only 2 percent of the country's population is involved in agriculture now, as opposed to the 98 percent in Jefferson's time.

The industrialization and modernization that had brought new prosperity to our cities enabled them to grow much larger, with many metropolitan areas of a million or more people and several of more than five million by 1950. The unintended consequences of "progress" were also becoming obvious. Air and water pollution and traffic congestion—on top of crime and racial and ethnic tensions—became untenable urban problems. In the 1950s and 1960s, the federal government implemented an ambitious urban renewal program that was meant to remove urban blight and replace it with modern, efficient commercial and residential development. Poor inner-city neighborhoods were razed for the construction of limited access highways and other projects that split the city asunder and displaced residents, especially African Americans. Many "slums" were cleared under the power of eminent domain for new development that, for better or worse, never came to fruition.

As the rescue of ailing central cities failed, the flight to suburbia hastened and, by the country's bicentennial in 1976, they were home not only to more residents but also to more jobs than the city itself. Single-use zoning, which became pervasive after World War II, kept different land uses apart and created large areas of monotonous, monocultural built environments; single-family zoning also kept densities low and vehicular usage high. Between declining central cities and sprawling suburbs and exurbs, the American metropolis found itself in need of repair.

Revitalizing Urban Life

Fortunately, the central city was not totally abandoned. Historic preservation as a national movement was born in the middle of the 20th century (Charleston, South Carolina, helped lead the way by establishing its historic district as early as 1931). It was a reaction to the wholesale abandonment and demolition of buildings, districts, and neighborhoods that were important to the local history and character of our cities. Citizens from all walks of life, amateur and professional alike, joined together to save thousands of structures of architectural merit from the wrecking ball. One of the most memorable episodes was the attempt to rescue New York's monumental Penn Station in the early 1960s. Although the protest, led by activists like Jane Jacobs and Philip Johnson (later to become an AIA Gold Medalist), were unsuccessful in saving McKim, Mead and White's majestic gateway to the city, it was an early and galvanizing campaign for the national movement. This grassroots effort gradually rippled across virtually every city and town in the country, thereby increasing these communities' awareness of not only their architectural heritage but also the importance of protecting whole neighborhoods and districts. This movement, however, was not an unalloyed success; although it architecturally preserved and enhanced our inner cities, many poor neighborhoods were passed over or gentrified.

Other movements, which began percolating in the latter half of the 20th century in reaction to the unforeseen problems associated with robust growth and prosperity, also saw the value of more traditional notions of architecture and urbanism. The environmental movement began in the 1960s as a reaction to increased air and water pollution and, soon after, to concerns about the declining supply of fossil fuels and other natural resources. Proponents of energy conservation gradually recognized that greater density and closer adjacencies among land uses are essential to the reduction of energy consumption and greenhouse gas emissions by both buildings and vehicles.

Since the 1970s, architects have played an important role in trying to address these issues, individually and through the American Institute of Architects. The AIA's Livable Cities initiative and the smart growth movement are examples of planning and development approaches that grew out of these environmental concerns. In addition, the Congress for the New Urbanism (CNU) was organized by architects in the 1990s to promote a return to more traditional forms of compact, mixed-use, walkable urbanism, as well as transit-oriented development. The movement attempts to promote dense, diverse, sustainable communities on greenfield and grayfield sites on the urban fringe and on brownfield and infill sites in the city. Well-publicized greenfield examples are Seaside, a resort town in the Florida panhandle, and Kentlands in the Maryland suburbs of Washington, D.C., both planned by Duany Plater-Zyberk & Company. The conversion of Denver's former Stapleton Airport into a large, mixed-use community is an example of a New Urbanist brownfield/grayfield development. Henry Horner Homes, an example of a HUD Hope VI project, is an infill redevelopment that converted the high-and mid-rise apartment towers of a Chicago public housing project into a low-rise, street-oriented mix of subsidized and market-rate townhouses.

Charleston's historic preservation district (top), established in 1931, was the first in the country. The city's urban core has flourished with successful commercial districts and residential neighborhoods. Decades later, Miami Beach established a historic district in South Beach (bottom). Its mixed-use urban streets lined with Art Deco buildings present a rare and refreshing combination of traditional, street-oriented urbanism and modern architecture of its era. ©*Kevin Fleming/Corbis (Charleston); ©Nik Wheeler/Corbis (South Beach)*

Jane Jacobs (second from left) and Philip Johnson (right) were among those who gathered in 1963 to protest the demolition of New York's Penn Station. They were unsuccessful in saving the building, but their efforts helped galvanize support nationwide for historic preservation. *Walter Daran/Hulton Archive/Getty Images*

Nationale-Nederlanden,
Prague,
Frank Gehry

Yancey Chapel,
Sawyerville, Alabama,
Rural Studio

Publication of Building Community:
A New Future for Architecture
Education and Practice, *by Ernest
Boyer and Lee Mitgang*

Owens Corning World Headquarters,
Toledo,
César Pelli

(Above) The resort of Seaside (1984–1991), in Florida's Panhandle,
has become a poster child of New Urbanism, a movement that
strives to build compact, mixed-use, walkable communities on
vacant urban and suburban land. Many award-winning architects
have been commissioned to design public and private buildings in
this small town founded by Robert Davis and planned by DPZ.
Alex S. MacLean/Landslides

To counter sprawl, more real estate developers are building denser
communities. Forest City Enterprises has commissioned several
architecture and planning firms, including Calthorpe Associates,
to convert the 4,700-acre site of Denver's former airport into an
expansive, mixed-use, ecologically green community.
Courtesy Calthorpe Associates

1997
Guggenheim Museum,
Bilbao,
Frank Gehry

Commerzbank,
Frankfurt,
Foster + Partners

Getty Center,
Los Angeles,
Richard Meier

Chapel of St. Ignatius,
Seattle University,
Steven Holl

Gap Headquarters,
San Bruno, California,
William McDonough + Partners

Challenges and Opportunities, Here and Abroad

The first cities were founded some 6,000 years ago. And current archeological evidence suggests that these nascent urban centers were more widespread than once thought. The Middle East's Tigris-Euphrates Valley—sometimes referred to as the cradle of civilization—is often cited as the very first area to develop villages that grew into cities, including the fabled Babylon. Yet some of the earliest cities emerged in east and south Asia as well, such as the ancient cities of Xian in China and Benares in India. Ancient Athens and Rome are better known to Westerners, but many Asian and European cities were in full bloom before the city of Rome had an estimated one million inhabitants at the height of its empire in the first centuries CE.

Human settlement remained overwhelmingly rural, however, until the Industrial Revolution nearly two centuries ago. In 1800, London had a population of more than one million. Today, 326 cities have reached that number, including 180 in developing countries. Urbanization has led to a tripling of the population living in cities since 1950. Very recently, the planet's human population has become half urban and is expected to be two-thirds urban by 2030. This accelerating pace of urbanization is one of the defining and dramatic phenomena of our time, with global cities exploding on several continents. In search of jobs, education, and other opportunities or fleeing oppressive conditions, massive influxes of people from the countryside are swelling and stressing existing cities, turning some into teeming agglomerations of more than 10, 15, and even 20 million people. Fifteen of the 20 largest urban metropolitan areas in 2015 are expected to be in developing countries. Cities now embody, animate, and, in many ways, symbolize the global civilization that envelops the entire planet.

Ironically, as cities elsewhere have been intensifying in recent decades, many American cities have been decanting residents and jobs to suburbs and exurbs. These low-density developments have been leapfrogging across the metropolitan hinterland in an unprecedented, auto-centric pattern, typically referred to as "sprawl." Originally bedroom suburban communities for commuters, this carpet of low-rise buildings is increasingly home to a wide range of office, retail, and institutional uses, typically providing more jobs outside than inside the city limits. Sometimes this light scrim of suburban development bunches into denser knots that are somewhat like traditional cities but different enough to be called "edge cities."

Shanghai (bottom), Mumbai, Delhi, Sao Paolo, Lagos, and Mexico City are growing as populous as New York, and more populous than Paris or London. Tokyo is expected to remain the world's largest city for the foreseeable future. In Ixtapaluca, Mexico (top), more than 10,000 nearly identical dwelling units have been built at densities greater than American suburbia but without the mixed uses of the city or the generous yards of the suburb.
Courtesy Douglas Kelbaugh, FAIA (Shanghai); C.O. Ruiz (Ixtapaluca)

Campo Volantín Footbridge,
Bilbao, Spain,
Santiago Calatrava

Ronald Reagan Washington
National Airport,
Washington, D.C.,
Cesar Pelli

U.S. Border Station at Point Roberts,
Washington,
Miller/Hull Partnership

Atlantic Center for the Arts,
New Smyrna Beach, Florida,
Thompson & Rose

Richard Meier, FAIA,
received the AIA Gold Medal

The leafy suburbs of the midcentury were often close enough to downtown jobs that the breadwinner of a nuclear family household, then typically the father, could easily drive to work. By the end of the century, suburbs extended as far as the eye could see, with longer commutes and smaller households that now often have multiple jobholders. In Las Vegas (left), one of the fastest growing U.S. metropolitan areas, sprawl carpets the desert with houses (and rental storage units) that are built in large numbers at one time, which makes developments more placeless and repetitive than previous generations of suburbia. ©Brooks Kraft/Corbis

Even though recent trends suggest that young professionals and empty-nesters are less enthralled with suburban life styles and are beginning to repopulate many central cities, more Americans now live in suburbs than in either central cities or rural areas. Suburbanization is also happening in Europe, Australia, and elsewhere, but until the combination of plentiful, inexpensive energy and land has abated, North America will remain the poster child of sprawl.

It is becoming painfully clear that energy is a major global issue for the foreseeable future. As the planet runs out of cheap, abundant oil, there will be a desperate need to find alternatives to support the estimated 9 to 12 billion people on the planet by the end of this century (at least 6 to 9 billion of whom are expected to be living in cities). Cities act to decrease the need for vehicular trips by moving people closer together. Compact, mixed-use, walkable urbanism, coupled with regional bus and rail transit, can reduce automobile dependence, while providing healthier, cleaner, safer mobility that is more convivial and less expensive in economic and environmental terms to both the individual citizen and society as a whole. Dense urbanism means more compact and fewer freestanding buildings, which typically translates into less energy to heat and cool them. For these two reasons, cities require on average less energy per capita than suburban or rural communities. Accessibility—the ability to be where you need and want to be—is emerging as the sustainable transportation paradigm for cities, rather than mobility and speed. Indeed, as cities around the world become gridlocked with vehicular traffic and overburdened with aging roads, bridges, and tunnels, the old transportation mantra—more system capacity for more cars running at higher speeds—no longer suffices.

The most vexing and potentially devastating of the unwanted consequences of a carbon-based energy system is the change in climate exacerbated by human production of greenhouse gases. Rising air and sea temperatures, especially at the planet's poles, will continue to produce—perhaps more rapidly than originally estimated—rising sea levels and more violent weather, both of which are sure to wreak urban havoc. The compounding consequences of deteriorating ecosystems are more complex to visualize than flooding, but their impacts may be more difficult to correct or adapt to. Cities, many of which are located in low-lying coastal areas, will bear much of the brunt of these potent and pervasive natural forces. Not only will

their physical environment be severely tested but also their more fragile social and political systems. Indeed, as geopolitical tensions are exacerbated by ecological disasters around the world, social unrest, terrorism, and military conflict become more likely. In the meantime, reliably providing clean water, electricity, and other public utilities, not to mention clean air, healthy food, and all other staples of life, will be challenging enough for the urbanized world. If these basic needs are difficult to meet for much of the world's population now, they will become even more burdensome as energy becomes less plentiful and more expensive and as industrialized societies struggle to support their already huge ecological footprints.

Americans consume four or five times their per capita share of energy and natural resources and produce a commensurate amount of greenhouse gases and solid waste, much of it a result of auto dependence and life styles of excessive consumption. They will no doubt be held more and more accountable by the rest of the world for their excessive levels of consumption and pollution, resulting in more political and moral pressure to live more sustainably within more environmentally benign patterns of settlement. All the more reason for American architecture, planning, and engineering firms, which are being commissioned to design large projects around the world, to apply the latest thinking and highest standards in green buildings and sustainable urban design.

Coming Full Circle: The Link between Cities and the Environment

The earliest cities formed in relationship to nature—adjacent to water bodies, on hilltops that could be easily defended, and in climates that were conducive to hunting and farming. As cities developed, particularly during the Industrial Revolution, their relationship to nature became more tenuous and strained. Today's designers are beginning to understand that human society needs to establish a different relationship with nature—one in which nature again informs and permeates our built environment in a more holistic way. Rising concerns about social justice, gentrification, the aging baby-boomer generation, energy consumption, and global climate change have caused architects and planners to reconsider how and where we build. Indeed, a commitment to ecologically sustainable buildings and socially equitable communities seems to be emerging as the most widely and deeply supported mandate for our cities.

The building sector consumes more than a third of the nation's energy output—by one estimate as high as 40 percent for building operations, plus 8 percent for building materials and building construction. The transportation sector consumes a third, with the industrial sector consuming the balance. Although architects have little impact on industry and only an indirect impact on transportation (by designing for less automobile dependency), they have an immense impact on the amount of energy buildings embody and utilize (both directly in the buildings that they design and indirectly by influencing the design of vernacular buildings, which is the bulk of the built environment). Architects can design more energy-efficient structures by specifying green and recycled materials, employing more climate-responsive site planning strategies, installing active and passive solar heating and cooling systems, improving the configuration and insulation of building envelopes, and designing smaller buildings. The

1998
AIA Committee on the Environment
launched its Top 10 Green Projects
awards program

Petronas Towers,
Kuala Lumpur,
Cesar Pelli

U.S. Customs and Immigration
Center at Rainbow Bridge,
Niagara Falls, New York,
Hardy Holzman Pfeiffer

John Joseph Moakley U.S.
Courthouse, Boston,
Pei Cobb Freed & Partners

Kiasma Museum of Contemporary Art,
Helsinki,
Steven Holl

AIA has already established a goal of a 50 percent reduction in energy consumption and greenhouse gas emissions for new buildings by 2010, with the ambitious intention of achieving carbon-neutral buildings by 2030. With appropriate techniques, architects can also reduce water consumption, storm-water runoff and pollution, the urban heat-island effect, and light pollution in our urbanized areas. And they can also design ecologically sustainable neighborhoods, as illustrated at BedZed in London.

The professional charge to architects has traditionally been to protect health, safety, and welfare. These responsibilities are slowly being recalibrated by new imperatives. While "health" originally referred to the prevention of the infectious diseases that plagued the 19th-century city, now it more aptly applies to environmental health, including the provision of clean air and water. Likewise, "safety" has gone beyond issues of structural failure and fire to include the protection of life and property from terrorism and crime, as well as keeping pedestrians safe from speeding vehicles. Safety also includes helping cities survive emergencies and rebuild after severe storms, flooding, and earthquakes, as so vividly illustrated by the role architects played along the Gulf Coast in the aftermath of Hurricane Katrina. And "welfare" now applies more than ever to the provision of well-designed, livable, and affordable places for people of differing races, incomes, and ages to live and work, as well as places for education, recreation, and culture. Architects are also in the position to help alleviate racial and economic inequities by getting involved in community-based planning and design.

A post-petroleum economy will produce a different city, one that is difficult to envision now because of the complexity and pace of technological change and its unintended consequences. Science and technology, especially digital media and communications, will continue to alter the nature of our lives and our realities in unpredictable ways. And the global forces that endanger our planet's ecosystems and carrying capacity will both threaten and empower local community and culture in new and unexpected ways. No one, however, is better equipped and qualified than architects to visualize and help bring to life sound urban paradigms and models, both old and new. Moreover, they have the enviable opportunity to help make new and existing buildings and cities that not only function well but are also livable and delightful places—so much so that they will be loved and therefore cared for and, ultimately, sustained. Designing functional, beautiful, just, sustainable buildings and cities—the architecture profession could not have a more noble goal and a more timely mission.

BedZED, a sustainable neighborhood redevelopment outside London designed by Bill Dunster Architects and completed in 2002, uses solar energy to provide heat and electricity, as well as natural ventilation and daylight, to a compact array of south-facing townhouses served by public transit.
©*Raf Makda/VIEW*

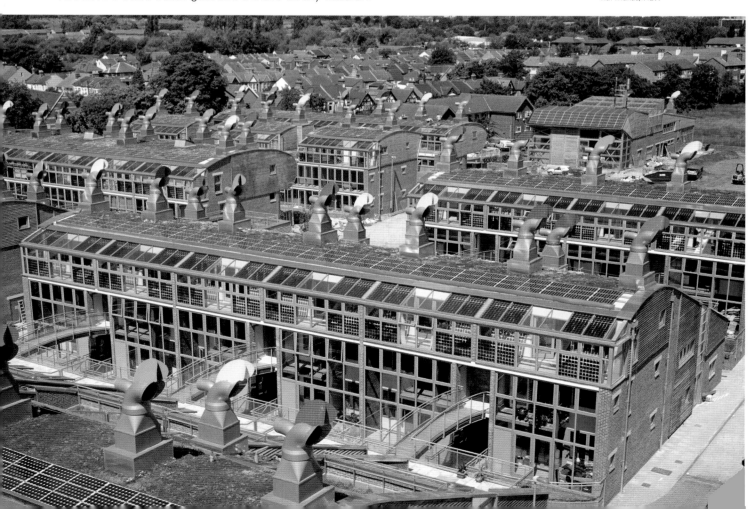

1999
College of Santa Fe Visual Arts Center,
Ricardo Legorreta

4 Times Square,
Fox and Fowle Architects

Arthur & Yvonne Boyd Education Center,
New South Wales,
Glenn Murcutt, Wendy Lewin,
and Reg Lark

Cameron Sinclair and Kate Stohr
founded Architecture for Humanity

Reichstag (dome and remodeling of
original building), Berlin, Norman
Foster/Foster + Partners

GOLD MEDALIST, 1961

Le Corbusier, Hon. FAIA
(Charles-Édouard Jeanneret)

William Richards

Le Corbusier (left) and Walter Gropius

Le Corbusier's Unité d'Habitation (1946–52), Marseilles, built in response to the severe postwar housing shortage in France, incorporates hundreds of apartment units with commercial and communal spaces and civic amenities. *Ezra Stoller / ©Esto*

Le Corbusier left an indelible mark on the history of urbanism. Born Charles-Édouard Jeanneret in the small town of La Chaux-de-Fonds, Switzerland, the architect, painter, and planner has been hailed, derided, cast, and recast as both a genius and a malediction. Certainly no other figure has so greatly affected the ways in which public and private spaces are conceived. For better or for worse, Le Corbusier has become the point of departure for urban polemicists who seek to solve the timeless questions of the city and identify new ones. For this and many other reasons, Le Corbusier received the AIA Gold Medal on April 27, 1961, in Philadelphia.

For Le Corbusier (1887–1965), the fabric of the city should be a coherent system that is organized and efficient. These ideas were advanced by him and others through the Congrès International d'Architecture Moderne (CIAM) at a time when the European city needed to be rebuilt and reappointed, and its citizens housed quickly, decisively, and sensibly after World War II. At the core of Le Corbusier's proposals was the relationship between the community and the individual. His La Ville Contemporaine (1922), Plan Voisin (1925), the "Obus" plan for Algiers (1932), and La Ville Radieuse (1933) organized people within a comprehensive physical and social infrastructure. After the war, the spirit of these proposals was realized at the Unité d'Habitation (1946–52) in Marseilles, France, but on a much smaller scale.

Commissioned by the government in 1945, the Marseilles Unité was a complete city in the air. Hundreds of apartment units—representing 23 different configurations to serve a diverse population—were unified by commercial space, communal space, civic amenities, and various circulation systems in much the same way that a traditional town in the landscape might self-organize over time. Despite the acontextual elements of its artifice, such as its use of béton brut, its brise-soleil applications, and its pilotis footprint, the Unité d'Habitation demonstrates a particular relationship with the landscape in which the land is largely spared and the city is contained.

A later project, the Monastery of La Tourette (1953–57) at Eveux-sur-l'Arbresle, France, speaks tangibly about the relationship between man-made structure and nature. La Tourette, like the Unité, is about abstract form in space. More concretely, it is about community and the spirit of collaboration that is fundamental to any account of Le Corbusier and to any urban proposal. Working with the Dominican brotherhood, an urban order whose cloisters were historically places of repose within the city, Le Corbusier transposed the program at La Tourette so that the cloister became an urban proposition within the countryside.

For Le Corbusier, the ordering principles of life, as the agent of civilization, should be adjudicated by architecture in accordance with nature. It is certainly debatable whether his earlier, theoretical urban proposals achieved this harmony. But Le Corbusier's realized projects, such as the Unité and La Tourette, evoke a unique balance between the built environment and the landscape.

Freedom by Design program
started in Denver

Massachusetts Museum of
Contemporary Art (adaptive use of
a factory complex), North Adams,
Bruner Cott & Associates

New 42 Studios,
New York City,
Platt Byard Dovell White

Founding of the China-U.S. Center
for Sustainable Development

Frank O. Gehry, FAIA,
received the AIA Gold Medal

China–U.S. Center for Sustainable Development

Deborah Snoonian

In April 1999, Chinese premier Zhu Rongji met with Vice President Al Gore in Washington, D.C., to discuss the double-edged sword of rapid development. With cities and buildings sprouting up at a blinding pace, China was creating new jobs and raising the standard of living for many of its citizens. But its air and water pollution were getting worse, and vital resources, such as arable farmland, were disappearing. The United States was struggling with many of the same problems. Could the world's fastest-developing country work alongside the most developed one to address these challenges?

Out of Rongji and Gore's conversations grew the China-U.S. Center for Sustainable Development, a nonprofit organization with secretariats in Beijing and Portland, Oregon. The center promotes cooperative efforts in both countries that aim to make urban centers and rural areas productive, profitable, and clean. Renowned green architect William A. McDonough, FAIA, was tapped to lead the U.S. side of the board of councilors that advises the center; his counterpart in China is Madame Deng Nan, China's vice minister of science and technology. McDonough's cradle-to-cradle design principles have become the basis for the center's initiatives. "Our strategy is to engage leaders and citizens from both countries in commercial projects that illustrate the ways in which sustainable design and development serve nature, the marketplace, and human communities," said McDonough.

One of the center's main activities has been the formation of teams of Chinese and American professionals to design model sustainable villages in China. The first one was for Huangbaiyu, a rural village of some 1,400 residents who survive on subsistence farming. It is located in northeastern China near Benxi City, where air pollution is so thick it blots out the city on satellite images. A master plan for the village was created by a team that included staff from Tongji University in Shanghai, nearby Benxi Urban Planning Design and Research Institute, and William McDonough + Partners of Charlottesville, Virginia, plus planner and China-U.S. Center councilor John Miller of Salem, Oregon.

Under the new plan, residential areas will be centralized and made denser to maximize the land's productivity; buildings will be constructed of local, renewable materials; and solar energy will replace the burning of cornhusks or coal. "The residents of Huangbaiyu were directly involved in these planning decisions," said Rick Schulberg, executive director of the International Sustainable Development Foundation, the Portland-based nonprofit that serves as the center's U.S. secretariat. "Engaging citizen participation is an important part of all the center's projects." In addition to Huangbaiyu, international teams, working with the center and the China Housing Industry Association, have completed master plans and prototypes for new urban townships in Zhejiang Province, Shandong Province, and Beijing. The plans will be constructed as funds and capacity become available.

Supported by an impressive roster of businesses, government agencies, nonprofits, and academic organizations, the center seems well poised to make environmentally productive growth the rule instead of the exception. "China and the U.S. have mutual opportunities and responsibilities for putting the entire world on a more sustainable path," says Schulberg. Or, as McDonough insists, "We must reach for nothing less than the magnificent re-evolution of human enterprise."

Madame Deng Nan and William A. McDonough, FAIA, at the first joint board of councilors meeting of the China-U.S. Center for Sustainable Development, 2002.
Courtesy China-U.S. Center for Sustainable Development

Ringed by mountains, Huangbaiyu is home to fertile farmland and a unique underground river once famous for its clarity.
Courtesy China-U.S. Center for Sustainable Development

Locally sourced, energy-efficient straw bale was used for wall infill for a model home in Huangbaiyu.
Courtesy China-U.S. Center for Sustainable Development

The goal of transforming Huangbaiyu is to create an intergenerational community of people who are engaged in restorative commerce.
Courtesy China-U.S. Center for Sustainable Development

A committee of Huangbaiyu residents, including leader Dai Xialong (left), helped refine the master plan to reflect the region's traditions and life styles.
Courtesy China-U.S. Center for Sustainable Development

The master plan for Huangbaiyu calls for dense housing and efficient use of farmland. The sustainable village is based on cradle-to-cradle design principles.
Courtesy China-U.S. Center for Sustainable Development

20

The Experience of Place

Diane Georgopulos, FAIA

German polymath Johann Wolfgang von Goethe called architecture "frozen music." The goal of this book was to capture the many voices of the American Institute of Architects over the past 150 years and create a work that captured that polyphony. We invited more than 70 writers from practice, academia, and journalism to share their perspectives with us. In turn we provided the reader with material enough to ponder where the profession has been and to consider what note it must now sound to cross the threshold into the next 150 years.

The AIA has collected an impressive repertoire that resonates through 150 years of practice. The richness of these variations — played out on the American landscape — heightens our appreciation for the vision, discipline, and courage of architects to stir our hearts and minds through built form. The many viewpoints presented demonstrate that our history is sometimes a symphony and sometimes a cacophony of approaches, experiments, and commitments to great design in response to society's ever-changing demands. We applaud the singular vision of Thomas Jefferson, perhaps the first American architect; the new American vernacular created by Louis Sullivan; the Modernist rigor of Mies van der Rohe and Walter Gropius; the poetics of Tadao Ando and Santiago Calatrava; the inspiration of Pier Luigi Nervi and both Saarinens; the humanism of Alvar Aalto; the pragmatic genius of Benjamin Thompson; the exuberance of Frank Gehry; and the fearlessness of Thom Mayne and Zaha Hadid. The work of these and the many other architects portrayed on these pages speaks to the experience of place, with all the joyousness and messy contradictions engendered by the man-made world. *(Opposite) StockTrek/Getty Images*

2000
Tate Modern, London,
Jacques Herzog and
Pierre de Meuron

Spangler Campus Center,
Harvard Business School,
Robert A. M. Stern

Diamond Ranch High School,
Thom Mayne/Morphosis

Mason's Bend community center,
Alabama, Rural Studio

Experience Music Project,
Seattle, Frank Gehry

Tang Teaching Museum and
Art Gallery, Skidmore College,
Antoine Predock

But what does "experience of place" mean in today's world, when our daily lives are increasingly dominated by wireless technologies that create seemingly limitless virtual space and when we can communicate from anywhere in the world with an ease once unimaginable? Although we certainly take advantage of these technologies, we recognize that such electronic connections cannot replace face-to-face interactions between people, let alone the actual sights, sounds, and essences of a culture or a community. Humans are physical beings and, therefore, need physical signposts to help find their bearings in a world—a universe—that literally expands beyond our comprehension. What better way to feel grounded than through our buildings, which make manifest the patterns of our daily lives. Each structure represents a unique location with a particular blend of climate, geography, and topography and reflects the knowledge and values of a culture at a specific point in time. In concert, then, architecture offers the potential for infinite and wonderful variations on a theme.

Today, as many of these essays attest, we are keenly aware of—and perhaps more sensitive to than ever—the boundary between what we know and what we don't know in our universe. We are mindful that wherever building occurs—in other words, wherever humans settle—the landscape is the place where natural and man-made systems meet to engage, overlap, support, or compete. To continue the musical analogy, the natural landscape is the staff upon which sit all the notes of our symphony. Done properly, an architect's designs enhance the human experience of both the built and natural world. One of the book's essayists reminds us of a long-forgotten classical tradition in which citizens swore to pass on the city to posterity in a form that was greater and more beautiful than they had inherited. We must reapply this notion but at a larger scale—to our most remarkable planet as a whole. As architects practicing today, our challenge is to carefully master that zone between our artificial systems and nature's complex vastness to ensure longevity for all.

Against the backdrop of the unknown, architects apply patterns and rules, ratios and proportions—not unlike the predictable rhythms and harmonies of music—that use reference standards and scale to ensure our physical safety and comfort. Although these patterns and rules may change over time as our knowledge expands or our values progress, they are knowable in any given period. These patterns can be technical, ranging from an understanding of regional traffic flow and density requirements in a walkable city to the sizing needs of a particular structural system. They can also be theoretical or stylistic, ranging from the formulas of Vitruvius and the manifestos of the Modernists to Derrida's writing on deconstruction and the principles of New Urbanism.

Throughout history, architects have employed technical knowledge and theoretical principles to inform the myriad decisions they must make about how to approach a design problem. The resulting visual and spatial effects often echo, and sometimes foreshadow, the cultural and aesthetic values of the society at large. Although simplistic adherence to principles alone may not result in great architecture or music, exceptional works do breathe life into such principles. When we celebrate the genius of Louis I. Kahn's Salk Institute, E. Fay Jones's Thorncrown Chapel, or Frank Lloyd Wright's Fallingwater, we are aware of something that is impossible to articulate in words but has been made manifest through the incredible power of design. It is as though we understand something about humanity and our place in the universe.

And, moving to yet another level, architects use personal themes to complement these idealized patterns and rules. The result produces a new melody that underscores the human condition. The practical and emotional complexities of our lives fine-tune the structure to both serve and delight us as we progress through our life journeys. As seen in this compilation, American architects have produced extraordinary buildings in service to corporations, medical research, religion, justice, and education, among other building types. Through technical and artistic innovation, architects work toward improving the human experience in all these places—not just by attending to the specific needs of the client organization but also to the occupants and public at large. Architects have introduced natural features, such as abundant daylight and healing gardens, into the hospital in an effort to improve medical outcomes of patients. They have developed new urban planning strategies to better unite our increasingly diverse population. And they have produced a portfolio of excellent new federal buildings that are encouraging citizens to directly reconnect to the collective experience once again. These sensitive touches—the pianissimo and forte of music—add the emphases that create the textures of real life. These notes resonate deeply within us, creating visceral experiences that cannot be adequately recorded in a virtual world.

Philip Merrill Environmental
Center, Annapolis, SmithGroup

Lloyd D. George U.S. Courthouse,
Las Vegas, Mehrdad Yazdani

Sandra Day O'Connor U.S.
Courthouse, Phoenix, Richard
Meier & Partners

Alfonse M. D'Amato Courthouse
and Federal Building,
Central Islip, New York,
Richard Meier & Partners

Bronson Methodist Hospital,
Kalamazoo, Michigan, Shepley
Bulfinch Richardson and Abbott

Ricardo Legorreta, Hon. FAIA,
received the AIA Gold Medal

More than ever, the skills of the architect are needed to orchestrate a holistic vision for a flourishing civilization. A profound human experience is to see oneself in others, to understand the world as others do. Architecture reminds us that humanity is a family to which we all belong. As architects, we must strive for designs that allow each person to feel that magical connection, to appreciate our place within the larger family of man on our precious, living planet Earth. Goethe wrote: "Whatever you can do or dream you can do, begin it. Boldness has genius, power and magic in it." And so let us begin our next 150 years.

Philip Merrill Environmental
Center, Annapolis, SmithGroup

Lloyd D. George U.S. Courthouse,
Las Vegas, Mehrdad Yazdani

Sandra Day O'Connor U.S.
Courthouse, Phoenix, Richard
Meier & Partners

Alfonse M. D'Amato Courthouse
and Federal Building,
Central Islip, New York,
Richard Meier & Partners

Bronson Methodist Hospital,
Kalamazoo, Michigan, Shepley
Bulfinch Richardson and Abbott

2001
September 11 terrorist
attack on the World Trade
Center towers, designed by
Minoru Yamasaki

Gordon Chong, FAIA,
became the first Asian-
American to serve as
president of the AIA
(2001–02)

AIA College of Fellows
established the
Benjamin Latrobe
Research Fellowship

Maison Hermès,
Tokyo,
Renzo Piano

Michael Graves, FAIA,
received the AIA Gold Medal

Endnotes

Chapter 1

The Need for Architecture

1   Vitruvius, *The Ten Books on Architecture*, trans.
    Morris Hicky Morgan
    (Cambridge: Harvard University Press, 1926).
2   William Gass, "House VI,"
    Progressive Architecture 58 (June 1977): 64.
3   Friedrich Nietzsche,
    Menschliches, Allzumenschliches, I, 218.
4   Robert Venturi, Denise Scott Brown, Steven Izenour,
    Learning From Las Vegas, rev. ed.
    (Cambridge: MIT Press, 1977).
5   Nietzsche, *Menschliches, Allzumenschliches*.
6   Paul Valéry, *The Art of Poetry*, trans.
    Denise Folliot (New York: Vintage, 1961), 192.
7   Frank Lloyd Wright, "Organic Architecture," in
    *Programs and Manifestoes on 20th-Century
    Architecture*, ed. Ulrich Conrads, trans. Michael
    Bullock (Cambridge: MIT Press, 1975), 25.
8   Friedrich Nietzsche, "Streifzüge eines
    Unzeitgemässen," *Götzen-Dämmerung* 11.
9   [Walter] Gropius, [Bruno] Taut, and [Adolf] Behne,
    "New Ideas on Architecture," in *Programs and
    Manifestoes*, p. 31.
10 See Denis Hollier, *Against Architecture*
    (Cambridge: MIT Press, 1989).
11 *The Best Short Stories of Dostoevsky*, trans. D.
    Magarshack (New York: Random House, 1955), 139.
12 Hundertwasser, "Mould Manifesto against
    Rationalism in Architecture," in *Programs and
    Manifestoes*, 157.
13 Cf. Hans Sedlmayr, *Verlust der Mitte*
    (Frankfurt: Ullstein, 1959), 77.
14 Juhani Pallasmaa, *Animal Architecture*
    (Helsinki: Museum of Finnish Architecture, 1995), 11.
15 Paul Weiss, *Nine Basic Arts* (Carbondale: Southern
    Illinois University Press, 1961), 69.
16 Ibid., p. 84.
17 Walter Benjamin, "On Some Motifs in Baudelaire," 188.
18 Jean Baudrillard and Jean Nouvel, *The Singular
    Objects of Architecture*, trans. Robert Bononno,
    foreword by K. Michael Hays (Minneapolis: University
    of Minnesota Press, 2002), 50.
19 Ibid., 4.
20 Ibid., 13, 20–21.

Chapter 2

Architecture as a Reflection of Evolving Culture: The American Experience

Viewpoint:
History of the Preservation
Movement in the United States

1   Melissa Houghton et al.,
    *Architects in Historic Preservation: The Formal
    Role of the AIA, 1890–1990* (AIA, 1990), 2.
2   William Murtagh, *Keeping Time*,
    The History and Theory of Preservation in America
    (Preservation Press, 1997), 11.

Chapter 3

Engaging the Public, Seeking Common Ground

1   David W. Orr, *Earth in Mind: On Education,
    Environment, and the Human Prospect* (Washington,
    D.C.: Island Press, 1994).
2   Samuel Bowles and Herbert Gintis, *Democracy
    and Capitalism: Property, Community, and the
    Contradictions of Modern Social Thought*
    (New York: Basic Books, Inc., 1986).
3   William M. Sullivan, *Work and Integrity: The Crisis and
    Promise of Professionalism in America*
    (San Francisco: Jossey-Bass, 2005).
4   Paul Boyer, *Urban Masses and Moral Order in America,
    1820–1920* (Cambridge: Harvard University Press,
    1978); Daphne Spain, *How Women Saved the City*
    (Minneapolis: University of Minnesota Press, 2001).
5   Robert Lewis, "Frontier and Civilization
    in the Thought of Frederick Law Olmsted,"
    American Quarterly 29 (autumn 1977): 385–403.
6   Bonnie Ellen Blustein, review of *The Papers of
    Frederick Law Olmsted. Volume IV: Defending
    the Union: The Civil War and the U.S. Sanitary
    Commission, 1861–1863*, Jane Turner Censer, ed., *Iris*
    78 (December 1987): 642–43.
7   Laura Wood Roper, "Frederick Law Olmsted in the
    'Literary Republic,'" *Mississippi Valley Historical
    Review* 39 (December 1952): 459–82.
8   Blustein, review of *Olmsted*.
9   Geoffrey Blodgett, "Frederick Law Olmsted:
    Landscape Architecture as Conservative Reform,"
    Journal of American History 62 (March 1976):
    869–89.
10 Ibid.; Boyer, *Urban Masses*.
11 Blodgett, "Olmsted."
12 Lewis, "Frontier."
13 Blodgett, "Olmsted."
14 Boyer, *Urban Masses*; Blaine A. Brownell, "The
    Commercial-Civic Elite and City Planning in Atlanta,
    Memphis, and New Orleans," *Journal of Southern
    History* 41 (August 1975): 339–68;
    Thomas S. Hines, "The Imperial Mall: The City
    Beautiful Movement and the Washington Plan
    1901–1902," *Studies in the History of Art* 30 (1991):
    78–99; Spain, *How Women Saved the City*.
15 Boyer, *Urban Masses*; Sullivan, *Work and Integrity*.
16 Spain, *How Women Saved the City*.
17 Boyer, *Urban Masses*.
18 Brownell, "Commercial-Civic Elite"; E.S. Taylor, "The
    Plan of Chicago in 1924 with special reference to the
    traffic problems and how they are being met," *Annals
    of the American Academy of Political and Social
    Science* 116 (November 1924): 224–31.
19 Boyer, *Urban Masses*.
20 Hines, "Imperial Mall."
21 Executive Committee of AIA New York Chapter,
    FAIA submission for Elisabeth Coit, AIA Archives,
    Washington, D.C., 1953.
22 Boyer, *Urban Masses*; Lewis Mumford,
    The Culture of Cities (New York: Harcourt Brace, 1938).
23 H. Ehrenreich, *The Altruistic Imagination:
    A History of Social Work and Social Policy in the
    United States* (Ithaca: Cornell University Press,
    1985); W.H. Ledbetter Jr., "Public Housing: A Social
    Experiment Seeks Acceptance,"
    Law and Contemporary Problems 32
    (summer 1967): 490–527.
24 Executive Committee, Coit; Susana Torre, ed.,
    *Women in American Architecture: A Historic and
    Contemporary Perspective* (New York: Whitney Library
    of Design, 1977).
25 H. W. Smith, "Architecture in the Public Service,"
    National Association of Housing Officials 102 (March
    1939): [unnumbered].

26 Ehrenreich, *Altruistic Imagination*.
27 Buckminster Fuller [http://en.wikipedia.org/wiki/Buckminster_Fuller]
28 P. N. Youtz, review of *R. Buckminster Fuller*, by John McHale, in *Journal of Architectural Education* 17, no. 4 (March 1963): 105–6.
29 Fuller (wikipedia).
30 Youtz, review of *Fuller*.
31 Fuller (wikipedia).
32 A. F. Snyder and V. Vesna, "Education Automation on Spaceship Earth: Buckminster Fuller's Vision More Relevant Than Ever" 31, no. 4, *Leonardo* (1998): 289–92.
33 Fuller (wikipedia).
34 Feuerstein, interview with Susana Torre, undated [http://www.arch.vt.edu/CAUS/Newsletters/asp/Uploads/torre.pdf].
35 Ehrenreich, *Altruistic Imagination*.
36 Ada Louise Huxtable, "Architecture View: The Last Profession to be 'Liberated' by Women," *New York Times*, March 13, 1977, 25, 33; Torre, *Women in American Architecture*.
37 Marita O'Hare, foreword to *Women in American Architecture: A Historic and Contemporary Perspective*, ed. by Susana Torre (New York: Whitney Library of Design, 1977), 6–7.
38 Women in architecture, author's personal files, undated; Torre, *Women in American Architecture*.
39 Lewis Davis, FAIA submission for J. Max Bond, AIA Archives, 1994; Eric Pace, "J. Max Bond Sr., 89, an American Who Headed Liberian University," *New York Times*, December 18, 1991 [online archives].
40 Robin Finn, "Public Lives: Breaking Molds, and Then Designing New Ones," *New York Times*, April 21, 2004 [online archives].
41 Davis, FAIA submission for Bond.
42 Tom A. Dutton, "Architectural Education and Society: An Interview with J. Max Bond Jr.," in *Voices in Architectural Education: Cultural Politics and Pedagogy*, ed. Tom A. Dutton (New York: Bergin & Garvey, 1991), 83–95.
43 J. Max Bond Jr., FAIA (undated) [http://www.tcaup.umich.edu/facultystaff/visitingfaculty/bond.html]; Davis, FAIA submission for Bond.
44 Craig E. Barton, "Max Bond on Building," *Point* (spring 1984): 4–5 (Columbia University Graduate School of Architecture and Planning, New York).
45 Margalit Fox, "Ruth C. Bond Dies at 101; Her Quilts Had a Message," *New York Times*, November 13, 2005 [online archives].
46 Barton, "Max Bond."
47 Dutton, "Architectural Education and Society."
48 David W. Dunlap, "Minority Firm Joins Davis Brody Architects," *New York Times*, October 21, 1990 [online archives].
49 Mitch Gipson, interview with author, July 24, 2006; Tracie Rozhon, "Research Park Rising on Site of Audubon Ballroom," *New York Times*, June 11, 1995 [online archives].
50 Gipson, interview.
51 Ibid.
52 Rozhon, "Research Park."
53 Gipson, interview.
54 Rick Sundberg, FAIA submission for Peter Steinbrueck, AIA Archives, Washington, D.C., 2005; Peter Steinbrueck, interview with author, August 18, 2006.
55 Steinbrueck, interview.
56 Sundberg, FAIA submission for Steinbrueck.

57 Philip Dawdy, "Time to Grow Up," *Seattle Weekly*, August 10, 2005 [http://www.seattleweekly.com/news/0532/050810_news_density.php]; Jennifer Langston, "Vancouver Offers Tips on Vibrant Urban Living," *Seattle Post-Intelligencer*, August 4, 2005. [http://seattlepi.nwsource.com/local/235217_vancouver04.html].
58 Dawdy, "Time to Grow Up."
59 Bob Young, "Seattle Downtown Plan Needs Adjusting, Report Says," *Seattle Times*, August 9, 2005 [http://archives.seattletimes.nwsource.com/].
60 Langston, "City Seeks Cut of Profits of High-Rises for Public: Developers Could Afford to Pay More, Study Says," *Seattle Post-Intelligencer*, January 12, 2006; Bob Young, "High High-Rise Fee Proposed," *Seattle Times*, January 12, 2006 [http://archives.seattletimes.nwsource.com/].
61 Steinbrueck, interview.
62 Seattle City Council, Adopted Downtown Livability Legislation, 2006 [http://www.seattle.gov/council/issues/height_density.htm#overview].
63 Doug Kelbaugh, interview with author, August 23, 2006; Douglas S. Kelbaugh, FAIA, dean and professor of architecture and urban planning, no date [http://sitemaker.umich.edu/kelbaugh] (hereafter cited as Kelbaugh, no date).
64 Kelbaugh, no date.
65 Doug Kelbaugh, "Student/Academic Charrettes at the Universities of Michigan and Washington," in *Charrette Handbook: The Essential Guide for Accelerated, Collaborative Community Planning*, ed. Bill Lennertz (Chicago: American Planning Association, 2006), 22.
66 Kelbaugh, "Student/Academic Charrettes"; Kelbaugh, no date.
67 Kelbaugh, "Student/Academic Charrettes"; Kelbaugh, interview.
68 Mark Puls, "Stadium Plans Scaled Back: Architects Say Original Designs Were too Costly," *Detroit News*, January 12, 2000 [online archives].
69 University of Michigan News and Information Services (Ann Arbor), "Designers Go to Bat for Detroit Neighborhoods" (press release), January 4, 2000.
70 At Trumbull: Turning the Corner: 2000 Detroit Design Charrette and Studios, A. Alfred Taubman College of Architecture and Urban Planning, Ann Arbor, 2000.
71 Ibid.
72 Kelbaugh, interview with author.
73 Kelbaugh, "Student/Academic Charrettes."
74 Kelbaugh, interview.
75 Vernon Reed, Honorary AIA submission for Ginny Graves, AIA Archives, Washington, D.C., 1989; CUBE, Building Kids, Building Community, Building the Future, undated [http://www.cubekc.org/].
76 Andrea Oppenheimer Dean, "Why Is This Woman Smiling?" *Historic Preservation* (September-October 1993): 54–59, 100; Ginny Graves, interview with author, August 3, 2006.
77 Reed, Honorary AIA submission for Ginny Graves; CUBE, Building Kids; Dean, "Why Is This Woman Smiling?"
78 Dean, "Why Is This Woman Smiling?"
79 Box City, A Neighborhood Plan Created by the Washington Wheatley Neighborhood (unpublished report), June-September 1996; Michael Mansur, "Cardboard Buildings, Concrete Dreams: Residents along Prospect Avenue Erect a Sprawling Model of the Ideal Neighborhood," *Kansas City Star*, August 15, 1996, 10.
80 Ibid.

Grass Roots: Discovering the Power of Youth

1 See S.E. Sutton, "The Role of Creative Expression and Inter-dependency" (PhD diss., City University of New York, 1982), iv.
2 S.E. Sutton, S.P. Kemp, L. Gutiérrez, and S. Saegert, *Urban Youth Programs in America: A Study of Youth, Community, and Social Justice Conducted for the Ford Foundation* (Seattle: University of Washington, 2006).
3 Ibid.
4 C. Cahill, "Defying Gravity? Raising Consciousness through Collective Research," *Children's Geographies* 2, no. 2 (August 2004): 273–86; R.A. Hart, *Children's Participation: The Theory and Practice of Involving Young Citizens in Community Development and Environmental Care* (London: Earthscan, 1997); S.E. Sutton, "Enabling Children to Map Out a More Equitable Society," *Children's Environments* 9, no. 1 (1992): 37–48.
5 S.E. Sutton, "A Social Justice Perspective on Youth and Community Development: Theorizing the Processes and Outcomes of Participation," *Children, Youth, and Environments* (2006), http://www.colorado.edu/journals/cye.

2002
Quadracci Pavilion,
Milwaukee Art Museum,
Santiago Calatrava

Publication of William
McDonough and Michael
Braungart's Cradle to Cradle:
Remaking the Way We
Make Things

Cincinnati Contemporary Arts
Center, Zaha Hadid

Simmons Hall, MIT,
Steven Holl

Unitarian Universalist
Fellowship, Reno,
Pfau Architecture

Monolith,
Lake Murten, Switzerland,
Jean Nouvel

U.S. Department
of Energy held the
first Solar Decathlon,
Washington, D.C.

Chapter 5

Education and Practice:
The Architect in the Making

1   See, especially, F.H. Bosworth Jr. and Roy
    Charles Jones, *A Study of Architectural Schools*
    (New York: Charles Scribner's Sons, 1932);
    Turpin C. Bannister, ed., *The Architect at Mid-
    Century: Evolution and Achievement* (New York:
    Reinhold, 1954); Robert L. Geddes and Bernard
    P. Spring, *A Study of Education for Environmental
    Design: The "Princeton Report"* (Washington,
    D.C.: American Institute of Architects, December
    1967; reprinted June 1981); William L. Porter and
    Maurice Kilbridge, *Architecture Education Study,
    Volume I: The Papers* (MIT Study; New York:
    Andrew Mellon Foundation, 1981); Robert Gutman,
    Architectural Practice: A Critical View (New York:
    Princeton Architectural Press, 1988); AIA Special
    Education Task Force, "Architectural Education
    Initiative: 1987–1989 Report" (American Institute
    of Architects, 1989); Dana Cuff, *Architecture:
    The Story of Practice* (Cambridge, Mass.: MIT
    Press, 1992); Ernest L. Boyer and Lee D. Mitgang,
    *Building Community: A New Future for Architecture
    Education and Practice* (Boyer Report; Stanford,
    Calif.: Carnegie Foundation for the Advancement
    of Teaching, 1996).
2   Boyer and Mitgang, *Building Community*, 20.
3   Ibid, 19.
4   Garry Stevens, "Angst in Academia: Universities,
    the Architecture Schools and the Profession,"
    Journal of Architectural and Planning Research 15,
    no. 2 (summer 1998): 162.
5   Michael Crosbie, "The Schools: How They're
    Failing the Profession," *Progressive Architecture*
    (September 1995): 47–52, 94–96; Reed Kroloff,
    "How the Profession Is Failing the Schools,"
    Architecture 85 (August 1996).
6   Stevens, "Angst in Academia," 155.
7   Stephen Kieran and James Timberlake,
    Refabricating Architecture (McGraw-Hill, 2004).
8   Boyer and Mitgang, *Building Community*, 19.
9   Kate Holliday, "'Build More and Draw Less':
    The AIA and Leopold Eidlitz's Grand School
    of Architecture," *Journal of the Society of
    Architectural Historians* 65, no. 3 (September
    2006).
10 Boyer and Mitgang, *Building Community*, 4.

Chapter 6

Reflections on Architectural
Research

1   Bernard Cache, "Sollertiae ac rationis pro portione,"
    Hunch 9 (2005), 56–65.
2   Alan Riding, "Glimpses of a Genius
    Who Blazed His Paper Trail," *New York Times*,
    September 26, 2006, B9.
3   A. Latour, *Louis I. Kahn: Writings, Lectures,
    Interviews* (New York: Rizzoli, 1991).
4   Richard L. Hayes, AIA, "Research Initiatives
    Program Business Plan" (internal AIA memo to the
    Board Knowledge Committee), 2005.
5   Amos Rapoport, *House Form and Culture*
    (Englewood Cliffs, N.J.: Prentice-Hall, 1969) and
    *Human Aspects of Urban Form: Towards a Man-
    Environment Approach to Urban Form and Design*
    (New York: Oxford; Pergamon Press, 1977).
6   Stephen Kieran and James Timberlake,
    Refabricating Architecture (New York: McGraw-
    Hill, 2004), and John P. Eberhard, Academy of
    Neuroscience for Architecture Web site
    (http://www.anfarch.org/2006/index.html;
    accessed October 2006).
7   Ernest D. Boyer and Lee D. Mitgang,
    *Building Community: A New Future for Architecture
    Education and Practice* (Princeton: Carnegie
    Foundation for the Advancement of Teaching,
    1996).
8   S. Allen and J. Corner, "Urban Natures," in
    *The State of Architecture at the Beginning of the
    21st Century*, ed. by Bernard Tschumi and Irene
    Cheng (New York: Monacelli Press and Columbia
    Books of Architecture, 2003), 16–17.
9   P. G. Bernstein and J. H. Pittman, *Barriers to the
    Adoption of Building Information Modeling in the
    Building Industry*, 2004 (http://images.autodesk.
    com/adsk/files/BIM_Barriers_WP_Mar05.pdf).
10 P. Thorne and N. Ballard, "The AEC Industry,
    Building Information Modeling and the 3 Rs," 2004
    (http://www.cambashi.co.uk/research/articles/
    AEC_ind_3Rs_Mar04.htm; accessed December
    2005).

Chapter 8

The Design Process:
Catching the Third Wave

1   For a more extensive discussion of these
    disruptive trends and other ideas presented in
    this chapter, see Kyle V. Davy and Susan L. Harris,
    *Value Redesigned: New Models for Professional
    Practice* (Atlanta: Greenway Communications–
    Ostberg, 2005).
2   Michael Schrage, *Serious Play: How the World's
    Best Companies Simulate to Innovate* (Boston:
    Harvard Business School Press, 2000).
3   Mildred Friedman, ed., *Gehry Talks: Architecture +
    Process* (New York: Universe, 2002).
4   Stephen Kieran and James Timberlake,
    Refabricating Architecture
    (New York: McGraw-Hill, 2004).
5   B. Joseph Pine II and James H. Gilmore,
    The Experience Economy (Boston: Harvard
    Business School Press, 1999).
6   Robert I. Sutton and Thomas A. Kelley, "Creativity
    Doesn't Require Isolation: Why Product Designers
    Bring Visitors Backstage," *California Management
    Review* 40 (fall 1997).
7   William McDonough and Michael Braungart,
    Cradle to Cradle (New York: North Point Press,
    2002).
8   Ronald A. Heifetz, *Leadership Without Easy
    Answers* (Cambridge: Harvard University Press,
    Belknap Press, 1994).
9   To learn more about "living systems theory" and
    how it is affecting leadership and management
    theories, see Margaret J. Wheatley, *Leadership
    and the New Science: Discovering Order in a
    Chaotic World* (San Francisco: Berrett-Koehler,
    1999); Roger Lewin, *Life at the Edge of Chaos*
    (New York: MacMillan, 1992); Steven Johnson,
    *Emergence: The Connected Lives of Ants, Brains,
    Cities, and Software* (New York: Scribner, 2001);
    Richard T. Pascale, Mark Milleman, and Linda Gioja,
    Surfing the Edge of Chaos (New York: Crown
    Business, 2000); Janine M. Benyus, *Biomimicry:
    Innovation Inspired by Nature* (New York: Quill
    William Morrow, 1997).

Colorado Court,
Santa Monica,
Pugh Scarpa Kodama

Leonard P. Zakim
Bunker Hill Bridge,
Boston, Christian Menn

U.S. Courthouse,
Hammond, Indiana,
Pei Cobb Freed & Partners

Cathedral of Our Lady
of the Angels, Los
Angeles, Rafael Moneo
with Leo A Daly

BedZED, near London,
Bill Dunster Architects

Tadao Ando, Hon. FAIA,
received the AIA Gold Medal

Stanley Abercrombie, FAIA, worked in the office of Marcel Breuer from 1962 to 1965. He has been an editor of several architecture and design magazines, including the former *AIA Journal*, and is the author of 13 books, including monographs on Gwathmey Siegel, Ulrich Franzen, and George Nelson. Now retired, he lives in Sonoma, California.

Roy Abernathy, AIA, is the president, CEO, and managing principal of Jova/Daniels/Busby in Atlanta, a progressive architecture, design, and planning firm begun in 1966. In addition to leading the firm's design practice, Abernathy also heads its Strategy Practice, which focuses on helping clients make more informed decisions about where they live, work, and play. Before joining Jova/Daniels/Busby, Roy worked for Accenture, the global consulting company, AT&T, and MediaOne, now Comcast.

Stan Allen, AIA, is an architect and dean of the School of Architecture at Princeton University. His current work includes single-family houses in New York and the Philippines, urban design work on multiple scales, and a 240-acre eco-resort in Cartagena, Colombia. His urban projects have been published in *Points and Lines: Diagrams and Projects for the City* and his theoretical essays in *Practice: Architecture, Technique and Representation*.

Anthony Alofsin, PhD, AIA, is an architect, art historian, author, and exhibition curator. Recipient of the Frank Lloyd Wright Building Conservancy's Wright Spirit Award in 2006, he is one of the world's leading experts on Frank Lloyd Wright and a specialist in modern architecture. His most recent book is *When Buildings Speak: Architecture as Language in the Habsburg Empire and its Aftermath, 1867–1933*. His architecture practice is based in Austin, where he is Roland Roessner Centennial Professor of Architecture at the University of Texas.

Kathryn H. Anthony, PhD, is a professor at the University of Illinois at Urbana-Champaign. She is the author of *Designing for Diversity: Gender, Race, and Ethnicity in the Architectural Profession; Design Juries on Trial: The Renaissance of the Design Studio;* and more than 100 other publications. She received the 2005 Achievement Award from the Environmental Design Research Association and a 2003 Institute Honor for Collaborative Achievement from the AIA.

Jonathan Bahe, Assoc. AIA, was the 2006–07 president of the American Institute of Architecture Students. An Iowa native, he received his BS degree in architecture from the College of Architecture and Landscape Architecture, University of Minnesota, in 2006. He plans to attend graduate school when his AIAS term ends. While at Minnesota, he was active in the college and AIA Minnesota, serving on various boards, committees, and task forces as an advocate for students and the future of the profession.

Ralph Bennett, AIA, is a professor of architecture at the University of Maryland. He is president of Bennett Frank McCarthy Architects, which specializes in residential architecture. His publications include *Settlements in the Americas: Cross Cultural Perspectives* (editor), 10 pages in *Architectural Graphic Standards* on housing design, and a chapter on design for the *Affordable Seniors Housing Handbook*. Bennett is a guest cocurator of "Affordable Housing: Designing an American Asset," an exhibition now touring the United States.

Fred Bernstein studied architecture at Princeton, where his professors included Michael Graves. He has written about architecture and design for many American and British publications, including *Blueprint, Architectural Record, Metropolis,* the *Wall Street Journal,* and, most frequently, the *New York Times*. As a columnist for *Oculus*, the journal of the New York chapter of the AIA, he reviews buildings from 10 to 100 years after their construction.

Andrew Blum, a contributing editor at *Metropolis* and *Wired* magazines, writes about architecture, design, art, technology, and travel for other publications, including the *New York Times, Architectural Record, BusinessWeek,* and *Dwell*. A New York City native, he studied English and architecture history at Amherst College and human geography at the University of Toronto. He lives in Brooklyn.

Lauren Weiss Bricker, PhD, is associate professor of architecture at California State Polytechnic University, Pomona, and director of the archives and special collections in the College of Environmental Design. She was a member of the State Historical Resources Commission in California from 2001 to 2005. Bricker is the author of *The Mediterranean House in America* and a forthcoming study on the pragmatists, supported by the Clarence S. Stein Institute of Urban and Landscape Studies, Cornell University.

2003

Genzyme Center,
Cambridge, Massachusetts,
Behnisch, Behnisch & Partner

Pulitzer Foundation for the Arts,
St. Louis,
Tadao Ando

Walt Disney Concert Hall,
Los Angeles,
Frank Gehry

AIA San Diego created
the Academy of Neuroscience
for Architecture

McCormick Tribune Campus Center,
Illinois Institute of Technology,
Rem Koolhaas

Lance Jay Brown, FAIA, teaches at and recently completed two terms as chair of the School of Architecture, Urban Design and Landscape Architecture at the City College of New York, where he was named ACSA Distinguished Professor. Brown started his award-winning private architecture and urban design consulting practice in 1972. Recently he has been a professional adviser to the International World Trade Center Site 9/11 Memorial, and he codirected the AIA's Learning from Lower Manhattan conference in 2004.

Brad Buchanan, FAIA, is a principal with Buchanan Yonushewski Group, a 50-person, single-source architecture, construction, and development services firm in Denver. BYG has extensive experience designing and building mixed-use, urban infill projects and is a leader nationally in architect-led design-build. Buchanan is the founder of Freedom by Design, a nonprofit organization providing design and construction services for the disabled community.

Robert Campbell, FAIA, is the Pulitzer Prize–winning architecture critic for the *Boston Globe* and writes a regular column for *Architectural Record*. A graduate of Harvard College and the Harvard Design School, he has practiced as an architect since 1975 and as a consultant to cultural institutions and cities. He has been artist-in-residence at the American Academy in Rome. In 2004 he received the annual Award of Honor of the Boston Society of Architects. He is co-author of *Cityscapes of Boston: An American City through Time* (1992).

Luis E. Carranza is associate professor of architecture at Roger Williams University. He earned a BArch from the University of Southern California and a PhD in architectural history and theory from Harvard University. He has published and lectured extensively on Mexican and Latin American art and architecture and serves on the editorial board of *AULA* magazine. He is currently completing a book on the Mexican architectural avant-garde.

Helen Castle is editor of *Architectural Design* and the executive commissioning editor of the John Wiley & Sons architecture list in London. As well as editing *AD*, she is a regular contributor to the journal and to other architecture publications. She studied art and architectural history at the University of East Anglia and has an MSc in the history and theory of Modern architecture from the Bartlett School of Architecture, University College London. She has worked in architectural publishing for 15 years.

Tony Costello, FAIA, is the Irving Distinguished Professor Emeritus of Architecture at Ball State University and principal of Costello + Associates. He pioneered the integration of university-based, urban design education and public service when he established Ball State's Community-Based Projects Program in 1969 and the Muncie Urban Design Studio in 1980. Costello has directed award-winning projects focusing on citizen participation, downtown revitalization, affordable housing, and historic preservation.

James P. Cramer, Hon. AIA, CAE, is chairman and CEO of the Greenway Group, a consulting and research firm for design firms and related organizations. A former AIA executive vice president/CEO, Cramer is founder of the Design Futures Council and founding editor of *DesignIntelligence*. He is the author of *Design + Enterprise*, executive editor of the annual *Almanac of Architecture & Design*, and coauthor of *How Firms Succeed* and *The Next Architect: A New Twist on the Future of Design*.

Michael J. Crosbie, PhD, is a licensed architect and editor-in-chief of *Faith & Form*, the quarterly interfaith journal on religion, art, and architecture. He is also the author of three best-selling books on religious architecture: *Architecture for the Gods*; *Architecture for the Gods, Book II*; and *Houses of God: Religious Architecture for a New Millennium*. He has lectured on emerging design trends in religious buildings, including presentations at the AIA national convention and the Yale Institute of Sacred Music.

David Allen Daileda, FAIA, is a principal and director of operations for the Arlington, Virginia, office of DMJM Design. He has more than 30 years of experience in the design and management of major facility development programs nationwide. His principal involvement over the last 15 years has been in the management of major airport development projects and programs. Daileda holds a BArch degree from the University of Arizona and was elected to the AIA College of Fellows in 1991. He has served in numerous AIA leadership rolls, including the national AIA Board of Directors.

Kyle V. Davy, AIA, established his consulting practice in 1992 to help architecture and engineering firms develop the leadership and management capacities they need to thrive in an increasingly turbulent business environment. A principal faculty member of the American Council of Engineering Companies' Senior Executive Institute, he earned an MBA from the Stanford Graduate School of Business. He is coauthor of *Value Redesigned: New Models for Professional Practice* (2005).

Andrea Oppenheimer Dean is coauthor, with photographer Timothy Hursley, of *Rural Studio: Samuel Mockbee and an Architecture of Decency* (2002) and *Proceed and Be Bold: The Rural Studio after Samuel Mockbee* (2005) She authored *Bruno Zevi: On Modern Architecture* (1983), is a former executive editor of *Architecture* magazine, and freelances for *Architectural Record*, among other publications.

Jen DeRose is a writer living in Brooklyn. A staff member at *Interior Design* magazine, she is the founding creative director of homegurls.com.

David Dillon has been the architecture critic for the *Dallas Morning News* since 1983. He has a PhD in literature and art history from Harvard University and was a Loeb Fellow at its Graduate School of Design from 1986 to 1987. He has written 10 books, including *The Architecture of O'Neil Ford: Celebrating Place*. He is a contributing editor to *Architectural Record*, *Landscape Architecture*, and other professional journals.

David Dixon, FAIA, is a principal of Goody, Clancy & Associates, where he leads the firm's planning and urban design division and often writes and speaks about creating community. His work to revitalize and create new urban communities has won more than a dozen national planning and urban design awards. As 2003 president of the Boston Society of Architects, Dixon chaired the first national density conference, "Density: Myth & Reality." He holds degrees from Wesleyan University, the University of Pennsylvania, and Harvard University.

John Morris Dixon, FAIA, was chief editor of *Progressive Architecture* magazine from 1972 to 1996. More recently, he has written for such publications as *Architecture*, *Architectural Record*, *Competitions*, *Domus*, and *Places*. He is now at work, with a Graham Foundation grant, on a book tracing the evolution of Modern architecture from the 1950s to the present. Dixon is an architecture graduate of MIT.

Martin Luther King Jr. Library,
San Jose,
Anderson Brulé Architects

Solaire,
New York City,
César Pelli

Patrick H. Dollard Discovery Health Center,
Harris, New York,
Guenther 5 Architects

Temple Bat Yahm Torah Center,
Newport Beach, California,
Lehrer Architects

Salt Lake City Public Library,
Moshe Safdie

John Eberhard, FAIA, has served as director of research of the Sheraton Hotel Corporation and director of the Institute for Applied Technology at the National Bureau of Standards. He has been dean of the School of Architecture and Environmental Design at SUNY-Buffalo and head of the department of architecture at Carnegie Mellon University. He received the 2003–05 Latrobe Fellowship from the AIA College of Fellows on behalf of the Academy of Neuroscience for Architecture. Eberhard earned a BArch from the University of Illinois and a master's degree in industrial management from MIT.

Marilyn Farley, Hon. AIA, helped launch the U.S. General Services Administration's (GSA) award-winning Design Excellence Program and served as its first director. She helped lead the renaissance in federal architecture by engaging some of America's most respected architects to participate in the program. She previously was program manager for GSA's Art in Architecture Program.

Edward A. Feiner, FAIA, is director of the Washington, D.C., office of Skidmore, Owings & Merrill. He previously served as chief architect of the U.S. General Services Administration. He provided national leadership for the design and construction activities of the agency, which included federal courthouses and office buildings. Under Feiner's leadership, GSA developed the Design Excellence Program. He received the AIA's Thomas Jefferson Award for Public Architecture in 1996.

Thomas Fisher is dean of the College of Design at the University of Minnesota. He is the author of numerous book chapters and journal articles, and he has written three books: *In the Scheme of Things: Alternative Thinking on the Practice of Architecture*, *Salmela Architect*, and *Lake/Flato: Buildings and Landscapes*. He currently serves on the advisory board of the AIA's Committee on the Environment and is at work on two books on ethics and architecture.

James T. Fitzgerald, FAIA, is founder and chair of FRCH Design Worldwide, an international architecture and design firm. Established in 1968, FRCH has served clients across the globe in the retail, entertainment, restaurant, corporate office, and hospitality markets. In addition to serving as chair of the AIA's International Committee and its International Honorary Fellows Jury, Fitzgerald received the AIA Ohio Gold Medal Award in 2003 for his achievements and contributions to the advancement of the architecture profession.

Harrison S. Fraker Jr., FAIA, is the William W. Wurster Professor and dean of the College of Environmental Design at the University of California, Berkeley. Educated as an architect and urban designer at Princeton and Cambridge universities, he has pursued a career that bridges innovative architecture education and award-winning professional practice. He has helped implement new models of education and research that build strategic partnerships between the college and design professionals.

Allen Freeman was the managing editor and staff photographer at *Architecture* from 1976 to 1989. He was senior editor for *Preservation* from 1990–2002 and for *Landscape Architecture* from 2002–04. He edited *Fay Jones* (1992), by Robert Adams Ivy, and Andrea Oppenheimer Dean's two recent books about Samuel Mockbee and the Rural Studio. Currently he is advisory editor for *The American Scholar*, published by the Phi Beta Kappa Society.

Daniel S. Friedman, PhD, FAIA, is dean of the College of Architecture and Urban Planning at the University of Washington. He writes on professional education, public architecture, and ethics, and recently edited two publications for the AIA: "Report on University Research" (2005) and "Report on Integrated Practice" (2006). He completed his PhD in architectural theory at the University of Pennsylvania.

Diane T. Georgopulos, FAIA, is an architect at MassHousing, where she has managed thousands of units of rehabilitation and new construction of multifamily development and administered complex resident participation programs. Her work in the public sector has been honored by the Ford Foundation and the AIA Thomas Jefferson Award. She is a graduate of MIT and an active member of the Boston Society of Architects, where she was recently elected president.

Paul Goldberger, Hon. AIA, is the architecture critic for *The New Yorker*, where since 1997 he has written the magazine's celebrated "Sky Line" column. He also holds the Joseph Urban Chair in Design and Architecture at The New School in New York. He began his career at the *New York Times*, where his architecture criticism was awarded the Pulitzer Prize in 1984. He is the author of several books, most recently his chronicle of the process of rebuilding Ground Zero, *Up from Zero: Politics, Architecture and the Rebuilding of New York*.

Kira Gould, Assoc. AIA, works for Gould Evans, the 230-person, seven-office design firm cofounded by her father, and writes about architecture and sustainability for *Metropolis*, *Architectural Record*, and other publications. She is a national advisory group member of the AIA's Committee on the Environment. She is coauthor, along with Lance Hosey, of *Women in Green: Voices of Sustainable Design* (2006).

Randi Greenberg began writing about design at *Architectural Record*, where she served as editor of archrecord.com and spearheaded the magazine's coverage of young and emerging designers. Currently, as the editor of metropolismag.com, the online companion to *Metropolis* magazine, she supervises a Web site that examines contemporary life through design. She lives in Brooklyn.

Robin Guenther, FAIA, is founding principal of Guenther 5 Architects, a 20-person health care design firm in New York. Her work has been published in magazines such as *The Architectural Review*, *Interior Design*, *Contract*, *Architectural Record*, and *Healthcare Design*. In 2005 she was awarded the Center for Health Design's Changemaker Award for her efforts to improve and support change in the healing environment.

Karsten Harries, PhD, is professor of philosophy at Yale University. He is the author of more than 180 articles and reviews and five books: *The Meaning of Modern Art*; *The Bavarian Rococo Church: Between Faith and Aestheticism*; *The Broken Frame: Three Lectures*; *The Ethical Function of Architecture*; and *Infinity and Perspective*. Architecture has allowed him to explore the question of the legitimacy and limits of that objectifying reason that presides over our science and technology and the significance of the aesthetic.

Sara Hart is a New York–based freelance writer and former senior editor at *Architectural Record*. She is also a contributing editor to Princeton Architectural Press.

Robert Ivy, FAIA, has led *Architectural Record* as editor-in-chief since 1996; the magazine has become the world's most widely read architecture journal. In 2003 it received the National Magazine Award for General Excellence. A widely published author, Mr. Ivy is a frequent speaker. Three times Ivy has served as the commissioner of the U.S. Pavilion at the Venice Biennale for architecture. He holds an MArch from Tulane University and a bachelor's degree from the University of the South.

Douglas Kelbaugh, FAIA, is dean and professor of architecture and urban planning at the Taubman College of Architecture and Urban Planning, University of Michigan. He has practiced, taught, and written and lectured on architecture for 35 years since receiving his BA and MArch degrees from Princeton University. Kelbaugh has won a score of design awards and competitions, spoken at more than 100 conferences, served on 35 design juries, and authored *Common Place: Toward Neighborhood and Regional Design* and *Repairing the American Metropolis: Common Place Revisited.*

Vivian Loftness, FAIA, is University Professor of Architecture at Carnegie Mellon and senior researcher/author in the Center for Building Performance and Diagnostics. In 2005 she served as chair of the AIA's Committee on the Environment. She is on the national board of the U.S. Green Building Council (USGBC) and a member of the Federal Energy Management Advisory Council and Turner Construction's Sustainable Advisory Board. She received the National Educator Award from the American Institute of Architecture Students in 2002 and the USGBC Sacred Tree Award in 2003.

John Loomis, FAIA, is director of communications and development for the CyArk 3D Heritage Archive project of the Kacyra Family Foundation. He is also a consulting associate professor at Stanford University. Loomis is the author of *Revolution of Forms: Cuba's Forgotten Art Schools* and many articles on architecture and urban issues. He has been a visiting scholar at the Getty Research Institute, a Loeb Fellow at Harvard University, and chair of architecture at the California College of the Arts.

Clark Malcolm has written, edited, and coauthored books on leadership, management, architecture, and design. He is senior writer and editor for Herman Miller, Inc., where he has worked for more than 20 years.

Thom Mayne, FAIA, founded Morphosis in 1972 in Los Angeles, as an interdisciplinary practice involved in rigorous design and research that yield innovative, iconic buildings and urban environments worldwide. Mayne received his BArch from the University of Southern California in 1968 and his MArch from Harvard University in 1978. He was a founder of the Southern California Institute of Architecture, and he currently holds a tenured faculty position at the UCLA School of the Arts and Architecture. Mayne's distinguished honors include the 2005 Pritzker Architecture Prize.

Vernon Mays is curator of architecture and design at the Virginia Center for Architecture in Richmond. He is the founder and current editor of *Inform*, a regional design journal published by the Virginia AIA chapter. He has been an architecture critic for the *Hartford Courant* and senior editor for *Progressive Architecture* magazine. Mays, who studied journalism at the University of North Carolina at Chapel Hill and architecture at Virginia Polytechnic Institute, writes frequently for national design magazines.

Christine McEntee is executive vice president and CEO of the AIA. She was previously the CEO of the American College of Cardiology and has held senior leadership positions at the American Hospital Association and AARP. She holds a master's degree in health administration from George Washington University and a bachelor's degree in nursing from Georgetown University and is a graduate of the Advanced Executive Program at the Kellogg School of Management at Northwestern University.

Michael James Meehan, AIA, practices architecture with BWBR Architects in St. Paul, Minnesota. An advocate for recently licensed architects, he was the 2007 chair of the Young Architects Forum. Meehan earned a BArch from Iowa State University in 1994. He worked on intern issues through AIA Minnesota, where he was cochair of the IDP Committee. He also teaches ARE review seminars.

Jayne Merkel is the author of *Eero Saarinen* and is a New York–based contributing editor to *Architectural Design/AD* magazine in London. She also writes for the *Architect's Newspaper* and *Architectural Record*. Previously, she edited the AIA New York chapter magazine, *Oculus*, worked as architecture critic of the *Cincinnati Enquirer*, and taught writing and art history at various colleges and universities.

William Morgan is an architectural historian who has written extensively on Finnish architecture. He edited the monograph on the Helsinki firm of Heikkinen and Komonen and was twice a visiting lecturer at Åbo Akademi, the Swedish-language university in Turku.

Barbara A. Nadel, FAIA, principal of New York City–based Barbara Nadel Architect, specializes in planning and designing justice, health, and institutional facilities. She is editor-in-chief of *Building Security: Handbook for Architectural Planning and Design.* She was the 2001 AIA national vice president, chair of the Advertising Committee, and 2002 chair of the AIA Academy of Architecture for Justice. In 2006 the White House appointed her as an expert security panelist to the Preserve America Summit.

Dietrich Neumann is a professor for the History of Modern Architecture at Brown University and Vincent Scully Visiting Professor at Yale University. He trained as an architect in Munich and London. His publications concentrate on 19th- and 20th-century European and American architecture, including *Film Architecture*, *Architecture of the Night*, *Luminous Buildings*, and others. He is currently finishing a book on Ludwig Mies van der Rohe.

Susan Piedmont-Palladino, PhD, is an architect, an associate professor at Virginia Tech's Washington/Alexandria Architecture Center, and a curator at the National Building Museum. She is the former national president of Architects/Designers/Planners for Social Responsibility. She has lectured and written on design-build, sustainability, and the design process. She served as a consultant to the Department of Energy on the development of the rules and regulations for the Solar Decathlon.

Wolfgang F. E. Preiser, PhD, is a professor of architecture at the University of Cincinnati. He holds a PhD from Pennsylvania State University and MArch degrees from Virginia Polytechnic Institute and State University and the Technical University of Karlsruhe, Germany, as well as the First State Exam from the Technical University in Vienna, Austria. As a researcher and international building consultant, he has worked on topics ranging from universal design to facility programming, building performance assessments, health care facilities, and intercultural design in general. His most recent books are *Assessing Building Performance*, *Improving Building Performance*, and *Universal Design Handbook.* Preiser has received many honors, awards, and fellowships, including the *Progressive Architecture* Applied Research Award and Citation.

Solar Umbrella House,
Venice, California,
Pugh + Scarpa

30 St. Mary Axe, London,
Norman Foster/Foster + Partners

Sundial Bridge,
Redding, California,
Santiago Calatrava

Frieder Burda Museum,
Baden-Baden, Germany,
Richard Meier

Samuel "Sambo" Mockbee, FAIA,
received the AIA Gold Medal
(posthumously)

Michael Pyatok, FAIA, has been an architect and professor of architectural design for 38 years and is a graduate of the architecture schools of Harvard University and Pratt Institute. His practice focuses on building market-rate and affordable housing. Since opening his office in 1984, he has designed more than 30,000 units of affordable housing for lower-income households in the United States. In 1983 Harvard University appointed him a Loeb Fellow; he explored strategies for affordable housing in this age of shrinking public involvement.

Jack Pyburn, FAIA, is an award-winning historic preservation architect in private practice in Atlanta, who works throughout the southeastern United States and the Caribbean. He was the 2007 chair of the AIA Historic Resources Committee Advisory Group and chair of the HRC's Preservation Architectural Education Initiative, which promotes preservation values in professional architecture education. Mr. Pyburn is a director of DOCOMOMO/US, an organization advocating the documentation and conservation of Modern movement buildings, sites, and neighborhoods.

Kristen Richards is founder and editor-in-chief of the international Webzine and daily newsletter, archnewsnow.com. She also is editor of Oculus magazine and e-Oculus, publications of the AIA New York chapter. She has been writing about the architecture/engineering industry for almost 20 years as a journalist and photographer, including 10 years as news editor/feature writer for Interiors. She is the author of Retail & Restaurant Spaces: An International Portfolio.

William Richards is a doctoral student in art and architectural history at the University of Virginia. He has written for the magazines Competitions, Art New England, and Future Anterior.

Avigail Sachs is a practicing architect from Israel. Currently a PhD candidate at the University of California at Berkeley, she is completing a dissertation on the history of architecture education in the United States.

Zachary M. Schrag is an assistant professor of history at George Mason University. His book, The Great Society Subway: A History of the Washington Metro, examines the politics, planning, engineering, architecture, finance, and operations of the nation's second largest rail transit system. Schrag received the 2003 John Reps Prize from the Society for American City and Regional Planning History.

Martin (Marty) Sell, AIA, is an architect, design-build practitioner, author, educator, and architectural leader. He practices design-build in the hospitality and recreation industries as managing partner of Horizon in Madison, Wisconsin. He authored the introductory chapter to The Architect's Guide to Design-Build Services (John Wiley & Sons) and has been published in numerous architecture journals. He teaches architecture history and real estate development at the Milwaukee School of Engineering. He was the 2007 president of AIA Wisconsin and the Wisconsin AIA150 Blueprint for America champion. Nationally, he is a member of the Design-Build Knowledge Community Advisory Committee.

Judith Sheine is chair of and a professor at the Department of Architecture at California State Polytechnic University, Pomona. She has won several prizes in design competitions and an Architectural Record House Award in 1995 for the Sarli house. She was coeditor of R. M. Schindler: Composition and Construction and author of R. M. Schindler: Works and Projects and R. M. Schindler.

George Skarmeas, AIA, is an national expert in historic preservation. He has been the lead architect on such nationally recognized projects as Independence Hall, the Virginia Capitol, and the U.S. Supreme Court Building. The founding principal of Hillier's historic preservation practice, he holds a BArch from the National Technical University of Athens, an MArch and MCRP from Ohio State University, and a PhD from the University of Pennsylvania. He publishes and lectures widely on historic preservation.

Andrew Brodie Smith, PhD, holds a PhD in history from the University of California, Los Angeles. He has conducted oral histories of Los Angeles–area architects and written widely on American cultural history, including the book Shooting Cowboys and Indians: Silent Westerns, American Culture, and the Birth of Hollywood. He works as a freelance writer and researcher and nonprofit consultant.

Deborah Snoonian, a writer and former engineer, is an expert on sustainable design and eco-friendly living. For five years she was a senior editor at Architectural Record, where she covered design, green building, and technology and helped conceive GreenSource, McGraw-Hill's magazine for the sustainable design community. Now a senior editor at Plenty, a lifestyle magazine, she writes about eco-friendly homes and design and appears regularly on TV and radio to discuss environmental issues.

Nancy B. Solomon, AIA, is a freelance architecture journalist. She has been a contributing editor to Architectural Record since 1997. Her prior work experience includes a year as editor of the AIA's Environmental Resource Guide and several years as senior editor for technology and practice at Architecture magazine. She earned an MArch degree from Columbia University and a bachelor's degree in physics and philosophy from Yale University.

Susan G. Solomon, PhD, is founding president of Curatorial Resources & Research, an independent research and consulting firm. Trained as an art historian with a concentration on 20th-century architecture, Solomon has extensive experience as a curator, educator, and speaker. She is the author of Louis I. Kahn's Trenton Jewish Community Center and American Playgrounds: Revitalizing Community Space. Solomon received a PhD from the University of Pennsylvania in 1997.

Michael Sorkin is the principal of the Michael Sorkin Studio in New York City, a design practice with a special interest in the city and in green architecture. He is the director of the Graduate Urban Design Program at the City College of New York. He lectures and publishes widely and is currently contributing editor at Architectural Record and Metropolis. For 10 years, he was the architecture critic of The Village Voice. Sorkin received his architecture training at Harvard and MIT.

Ingrid Spencer is a contributing editor at Architectural Record and a Web editor of archrecord. com. In 2004 she left New York City and her post as Record's managing editor to live and write in Austin, Texas. Previously she was managing editor of Contract magazine. She has a bachelor's degree in journalism and English from San Diego State University.

James Steele, PhD, has taught at the School of Architecture at the University of Southern California since 1991. He also taught at King Faisal University in Saudi Arabia and was a senior editor of Architectural Design magazine in London. His books include Los Angeles Architecture: The Contemporary Condition, Architecture Today, and Ecological Architecture. Steele earned a bachelor's degree in English from Lafayette College, BArch and MArch degrees from the University of Pennsylvania, and PhD in urban planning from the University of Southern California.

2005
AIA position statement called
for 50% reduction by 2010 of
the current consumption level of
fossil fuels used to construct and
operate buildings

Jeff Stein, AIA, an architect, teacher, and author, directs the architecture program at Boston Architectural College. A frequent contributor to *Architecture Boston*, he is also architecture critic for the newspaper *Banker + Tradesman*, where his work garnered an award from the New England Press Association. He lectures widely and recently completed editing and translating an American edition of the Swiss architecture text *The Ecological Aspects of Building*, with art historian Emilie Altemose.

Robert A.M. Stern, FAIA, a practicing architect, teacher, and writer, is dean of the Yale School of Architecture and founder and senior partner in the firm of Robert A.M. Stern Architects in New York. He coauthored a series of books documenting the development of New York City's architecture and urbanism, and he hosted *Pride of Place: Building the American Dream*, a documentary television series that first aired on PBS in 1986.

RK Stewart, FAIA, was the 2006–07 president of the AIA. He is a principal at Gensler's San Francisco office, where he is responsible for the development and implementation of forward-looking strategies for project delivery across the 1,850-member firm. He has held numerous leadership positions at the local, state, and national levels of the AIA, focused on advocacy, emerging professionals and the Intern Development Program, and sustainability. Stewart earned a bachelor's degree in environmental design from the University of Kansas and an MArch degree from the University of Michigan.

Norman Strong, FAIA, is the managing partner of The Miller/Hull Partnership, a 60-person architecture firm in Seattle. Established in 1977, the firm has been recognized for innovative design and has received more than 140 design awards, including 80 AIA awards, and the 2003 AIA national Architecture Firm Award. He is also an elected AIA vice president focused on implementing the AIA's strategic plan for integrated practice and sustainability.

C.C. Sullivan, a consultant and author, has served as editor-in-chief of such magazines as *Architecture* and *Building Design & Construction*. Principal of his own marketing communications company and a director of a5 Group, Sullivan contributes regularly to *Interior Design* and other architecture-related publications. Previously he worked with architects Tai Soo Kim, Angel Fernandez Alba, and Emery Roth & Sons. Sullivan speaks frequently on design trends, media strategy, and building technology. He studied architecture at Yale University.

Sharon E. Sutton, PhD, FAIA, teaches at the University of Washington. An architecture educator since 1975, she has also held positions at Pratt Institute, Columbia University, the University of Cincinnati, and the University of Michigan. Sutton has degrees in music, architecture, psychology, and philosophy. Her fine art has been exhibited and collected widely, and she has played in the orchestras of several Broadway hits and the Bolshoi Ballet.

Richard Swett, FAIA, is a civic leader who has served as a U.S. ambassador and member of Congress. A licensed architect and author of *Leadership by Design: Creating an Architecture of Trust*, he is president of Swett Associates, a consulting business that provides development and management services, leadership and management training, and alternative energy and energy-conservation development services.

Thomas Vonier, FAIA, RIBA, was the founder and first president of AIA Continental Europe, which began in Paris and currently has members in 28 countries. A member of its International Committee, he was AIA liaison delegate to the Architects' Council of Europe in Brussels. He led groundbreaking research on the security of U.S. foreign mission buildings and serves on the board of the Institute for Research and Study in Urban Security in Europe.

Gregory Walker, AIA, is a founding partner of Houser Walker Architecture, an Atlanta-based architecture and design firm that focuses on cultural buildings and the culture of building. A graduate of Auburn University and Harvard University's Graduate School of Design, he currently serves as an adjunct instructor at the Georgia Institute of Technology and on the national advisory board of the Young Architects Forum. In 2004 he received AIA Georgia's Young Architect Award.

Richard Guy Wilson, Hon. AIA, holds the Commonwealth Professor's Chair in Architectural History at the University of Virginia. A frequent lecturer and television commentator, he has also published many articles and books on various aspects of American and Modern architecture, including *The American Renaissance* (1979), *McKim, Mead & White, Architects* (1982), *The AIA Gold Medal* (1983), *Machine Age in America* (1986), *Campus Guide: University of Virginia* (1999), and *The Colonial Revival House* (2004).

Tony P. Wrenn, Hon. AIA, a writer, architectural historian, and photographer, was the first trained archivist to serve the AIA. During his tenure, from 1980 to 1998, the AIA Archives became one of the nation's best-known sources on American architects and architecture practice. In his most recent work for the AIA, he traced its 150-year history a decade at a time.

AIA formed Sustainable Design
Assessment Teams to help
communities frame sustainable
policies and design solutions

Google Headquarters,
Mountain View, California,
Clive Wilkinson Architects

Cira Centre,
Philadelphia,
César Pelli

Legacy Salmon Creek Hospital,
Vancouver, Washington,
Zimmer Gunsul Frasca

Santiago Calatrava, FAIA,
received the AIA Gold Medal

AIA Presidents, 1857–2007

Richard Upjohn, FAIA	1857–1876	William Marshall Jr., FAIA	1974–1975
Thomas U. Walter, FAIA	1877–1887	Louis de Moll, FAIA	1975–1976
Richard M. Hunt, FAIA	1888–1891	John McGinty, FAIA	1976–1977
Edward H. Kendall, FAIA	1892–1893	Elmer Botsai, FAIA	1977–1978
Daniel H. Burnham, FAIA	1894–1895	Ehrman B. Mitchell Jr., FAIA	1978–1979
George B. Post, FAIA	1896–1898	Charles E. Schwing, FAIA	1979–1980
Henry Van Brunt, FAIA	1899–1900	R. Randall Vosbeck, FAIA	1980–1981
Robert S. Peabody, FAIA	1900–1901	Robert Lawrence, FAIA	1981–1982
Charles F. McKim, FAIA	1902–1903	Robert Broshar, FAIA	1982–1983
William S. Eames, FAIA	1904–1905	George M. Notter, FAIA	1983–1984
Frank Miles Day, FAIA	1906–1907	R. Bruce Patty, FAIA	1984–1985
Cass Gilbert, FAIA	1908–1909	John A. Busby Jr., FAIA	1985–1986
Irving K. Pond, FAIA	1910–1911	Donald J. Hackl, FAIA	1986–1987
Walter Cook, FAIA	1912–1913	Ted P. Pappas, FAIA	1987–1988
R. Clipston Sturgis, FAIA	1913–1915	Benjamin E. Brewer Jr., FAIA	1988–1989
John Lawrence Mauran, FAIA	1915–1918	Sylvester Damianos, FAIA	1989–1990
Thomas R. Kimball, FAIA	1918–1920	C. James Lawler, FAIA	1990–1991
Henry H. Kendall, FAIA	1920–1922	W. Cecil Steward, FAIA	1991–1992
William B. Faville, FAIA	1922–1924	Susan A. Maxman, FAIA	1992–1993
Dan. Everett Waid, FAIA	1924–1926	L. William Chapin II, FAIA	1993–1994
Milton B. Medary, FAIA	1926–1928	Chester A. Widom, FAIA	1994–1995
C. Herrick Hammond, FAIA	1928–1930	Raymond Post Jr., FAIA	1995–1996
Robert D. Kohn, FAIA	1930–1932	Raj Barr-Kumar, FAIA	1996–1997
Ernest John Russell, FAIA	1932–1935	Ronald Arthur Altoon, FAIA	1997–1998
Stephen F. Voorhees, FAIA	1935–1937	Michael J. Stanton, FAIA	1998–1999
Charles D. Maginnis, FAIA	1937–1939	Ronald L. Skaggs, FAIA	1999–2000
Edwin Bergstrom, FAIA	1939–1941	John D. Anderson, FAIA	2000–2001
R.H. Shreve, FAIA	1941–1943	Gordon H. Chong, FAIA	2001–2002
Raymond J. Ashton, FAIA	1943–1945	Thompson E. Penney, FAIA	2002–2003
James R. Edmunds Jr., FAIA	1945–1947	Eugene Hopkins, FAIA	2003–2004
Douglas William Orr, FAIA	1947–1949	Douglas L Steidl, FAIA	2005–2006
Ralph Walker, FAIA	1949–1951	Katherine Lee Schwennsen, FAIA	2005–2006
A. Glenn Stanton, FAIA	1951–1953	RK Stewart, FAIA	2006–2007
Clair W. Ditchy, FAIA	1953–1955	Marshall E. Purnell, FAIA	2007–2008
George Bain Cummings, FAIA	1955–1956		
Leon Chatelain Jr., FAIA	1956–1958		
John Noble Richards, FAIA	1958–1960		
Philip Will Jr., FAIA	1960–1962		
Henry Lyman Wright, FAIA	1962–1963		
J. Roy Carroll Jr., FAIA	1963–1964		
Arthur Gould Odell Jr., FAIA	1964–1965		
Morris Ketchum Jr., FAIA	1965–1966		
Charles M. Ness Jr., FAIA	1966–1967		
Robert L. Durham, FAIA	1967–1968		
George E. Kassabaum, FAIA	1968–1969		
Rex Whitaker Allen, FAIA	1969–1970		
Robert F. Hastings, FAIA	1970–1971		
Maximilian O. Urbahn, FAIA	1971–1972		
S. Scott Ferebee Jr., FAIA	1972–1973		
Archibald C. Rogers, FAIA	1973–1974		

2006
AIA Sustainability Task
Force was established to
recommend policies on
environmental sustainability
to the AIA Board of Directors

Hearst Tower,
New York City,
Norman Foster/Foster + Partners

Frederic C. Hamilton Building,
addition to Denver Art Museum,
Daniel Libeskind

Highlands Pond House,
Colorado,
Antoine Predock

Opportunity Center of the
Midpeninsula, Palo Alto,
Rob Wellington Quigley, FAIA

U.S. Courthouse,
Brooklyn,
César Pelli

Bureau of the Census headquarters,
Suitland, Maryland,
SOM

AIA Honors and Awards AIA Gold Medal Recipients, 1907–2007

Sir Aston Webb, RA, Hon. FAIA	1907
Charles Follen McKim, FAIA	1909
George Browne Post, FAIA	1911
Jean Louis Pascal, Hon. FAIA	1914
Victor Laloux, Hon. FAIA	1922
Henry Bacon, FAIA	1923
Sir Edwin Landseer Lutyens, Hon. FAIA	1925
Bertram Grosvenor Goodhue, FAIA	1925
Howard Van Doren Shaw, FAIA	1927
Milton Bennett Medary, FAIA	1929
Ragnar Östberg, Hon. FAIA	1933
Paul Philippe Cret, FAIA	1938
*Louis Henri Sullivan, FAIA	1944
Eliel Saarinen, FAIA	1947
Charles Donagh Maginnis, FAIA	1948
Frank Lloyd Wright	1949
Sir Patrick Abercrombie, Hon. FAIA	1950
Bernard Ralph Maybeck	1951
Auguste Perret, Hon. FAIA	1952
William Adams Delano, FAIA	1953
William Marinus Dudok, Hon. FAIA	1955
Clarence S. Stein, FAIA	1956
Ralph Walker, FAIA	1957
Centennial Medal of Honor)	
Louis Skidmore, FAIA	1957
John Wellborn Root, FAIA	1958
Walter Gropius, FAIA	1959
Ludwig Mies van der Rohe, FAIA	1960
Le Corbusier (Charles-Édouard Jeanneret), Hon. FAIA	1961
*Eero Saarinen, FAIA	1962
Alvar Aalto, Hon. FAIA	1963
Pier Luigi Nervi, Hon. FAIA	1964
Kenzo Tange, Hon. FAIA	1966
Wallace K. Harrison, FAIA	1967
Marcel Breuer, FAIA	1968
William Wilson Wurster, FAIA	1969
Richard Buckminster Fuller, FAIA	1970
Louis I. Kahn, FAIA	1971
Pietro Belluschi, FAIA	1972

*Richard Joseph Neutra, FAIA	1977
Philip Cortelyou Johnson, FAIA	1978
Ieoh Ming Pei, FAIA	1979
Joseph Luis Sert, FAIA	1981
Romaldo Giurgola, FAIA	1982
Nathaniel A. Owings, FAIA	1983
*William Wayne Caudill, FAIA	1985
Arthur Erickson, Hon. FAIA	1986
Joseph Esherick, FAIA	1989
E. Fay Jones, FAIA	1990
Charles W. Moore, FAIA	1991
Benjamin Thompson, FAIA	1992
*Thomas Jefferson	1993
Kevin Roche, FAIA	1993
Sir Norman Foster, Hon. FAIA	1994
César Pelli, FAIA	1995
Richard Meier, FAIA	1997
Frank Gehry, FAIA	1999
Ricardo Legorreta, Hon. FAIA	2000
Michael Graves, FAIA	2001
Tadao Ando, Hon. FAIA	2002
*Samuel "Sambo" Mockbee, FAIA	2004
Santiago Calatrava, FAIA	2005
Antoine Predock, FAIA	2006
*Edward Larrabee Barnes, FAIA	2007

*honored posthumously

National Oceanic and
Atmospheric Administration,
satellite operations facility,
Suitland, Maryland,
Thom Mayne/Morphosis

Federal Building,
San Francisco,
Thom Mayne/Morphosis

Wayne L. Morse U.S. Courthouse,
Eugene, Oregon,
Thom Mayne/Morphosis

De Young Museum,
San Francisco,
Herzog & de Meuron

Suzhou Museum,
Jiangsu Province,
People's Republic of China,
I. M. Pei Architect and
Pei Partnership Architects

Ara Pacis Museum,
Rome,
Richard Meier

Antoine Predock, FAIA,
received the AIA Gold Medal

Architecture Firm Award Recipients, 1962–2007

Skidmore, Owings & Merrill	1962
The Architects Collaborative	1964
Wurster, Bernardi & Emmons	1965
Hugh Stubbins and Associates	1967
I.M. Pei & Partners	1968
Jones & Emmons	1969
Ernest J. Kump Associates	1970
Albert Kahn Associates	1971
Caudill Rowlett Scott	1972
Shepley Bulfinch Richardson and Abbott	1973
Kevin Roche John Dinkeloo and Associates	1974
Davis, Brody & Associates	1975
Mitchell/Giurgola Architects	1976
Sert Jackson and Associates	1977
Harry Weese & Associates	1978
Geddes Brecher Qualls Cunningham	1979
Edward Larrabee Barnes Associates	1980
Hardy Holzman Pfeiffer Associates	1981
Gwathmey Siegel & Associates, Architects	1982
Holabird & Root	1983
Kallmann McKinnell & Wood Architects	1984
Venturi, Rauch and Scott Brown	1985
Esherick Homsey Dodge & Davis	1986
Benjamin Thompson & Associates	1987
Hartman-Cox Architects	1988
César Pelli & Associates	1989
Kohn Pedersen Fox Associates	1990
Zimmer Gunsul Frasca Partnership	1991
James Stewart Polshek and Partners	1992
Cambridge Seven Associates	1993
Bohlin Cywinski Jackson	1994
Beyer Blinder Belle	1995
Skidmore, Owings & Merrill	1996
R. M. Kliment & Frances Halsband Architects	1997
Centerbrook Architects and Planners	1998
Perkins & Will	1999
Gensler	2000
Herbert Lewis Kruse Blunck Architecture	2001
Thomas, Ventulett, Stainback & Associates	2002
The Miller | Hull Partnership	2003
Lake | Flato Architects	2004
Murphy | Jahn	2005
Moore Ruble Yudell Architects and Planners	2006
Leers Weinzapfel Associates	2007

Twenty-five Year Award Recipients, 1969–2007

Rockefeller Center, New York City Reinhard & Hofmeister; Corbett, Harrison & MacMurray	1969
Crow Island School, Winnetka, Ill. Perkins, Wheeler & Will; Eliel & Eero Saarinen	1971
Baldwin Hills Village, Los Angeles Reginald D. Johnson; Wilson, Merrill & Alexander; Clarence S. Stein	1972
Taliesin West, Paradise Valley, Ariz., Frank Lloyd Wright	1973
Johnson and Son Administration Building Racine, Wis., Frank Lloyd Wright	1974
Philip Johnson's Residence ("The Glass House"), New Caanan, Conn., Philip Johnson	1975
860-880 North Lakeshore Drive Apartments, Chicago, Ludwig Mies van der Rohe	1976
Christ Lutheran Church, Minneapolis Saarinen, Saarinen & Associates; Hills, Gilbertson & Hays	1977
Eames House, Pacific Palisades, Calif. Charles and Ray Eames	1978
Yale University Art Gallery New Haven, Conn., Louis I. Kahn, FAIA	1979
Lever House, New York City Skidmore, Owings & Merrill	1980
Farnsworth House, Plano, Ill. Ludwig Mies van der Rohe	1981
Equitable Savings and Loan Building Portland, Ore., Pietro Belluschi, FAIA	1982
Price Tower, Bartlesville, Okla. Frank Lloyd Wright	1983
Seagram Building, New York City Ludwig Mies van der Rohe	1984
General Motors Technical Center Warren, Mich., Eero Saarinen and Associates with Smith, Hinchman & Grylls	1985
Solomon R. Guggenheim Museum New York City, Frank Lloyd Wright	1986
Bavinger House, Norman, Okla. Bruce Goff	1987
Dulles International Airport Terminal Building, Chantilly, Va. Eero Saarinen and Associates	1988
Vanna Venturi House, Chestnut Hill, Pa. Robert Venturi, FAIA	1989
Gateway Arch, St. Louis Eero Saarinen and Associates	1990

Sea Ranch Condominium I Sea Ranch, Calif., Moore Lyndon Turnbull Whitaker	1991
Salk Institute for Biological Studies La Jolla, Calif., Louis I. Kahn, FAIA	1992
Deere & Company Administrative Center, Moline, Ill. Eero Saarinen and Associates	1993
Haystack Mountain School of Crafts Deer Isle, Maine, Edward Larrabee Barnes	1994
Ford Foundation Headquarters New York City, Kevin Roche, John Dinkeloo and Associates	1995
Air Force Academy Cadet Chapel Colorado Springs, Skidmore, Owings & Merrill	1996
Phillips Exeter Academy Library Exeter, N.H., Louis I. Kahn, FAIA	1997
Kimbell Art Museum, Fort Worth Louis I. Kahn, FAIA	1998
John Hancock Center, Chicago Skidmore, Owings & Merrill	1999
Smith House, Darien, Conn., Richard Meier & Partners	2000
Weyerhaeuser Headquarters Federal Way, Wash., Skidmore, Owings & Merrill	2001
Fundació Joan Miró, Barcelona Sert Jackson and Associates	2002
Design Research Headquarters Building Cambridge, Mass., BTA Architects (formerly Benjamin Thompson & Associates)	2003
East Building, National Gallery of Art Washington, D.C., I.M. Pei & Partners, Architects	2004
Yale Center for British Art New Haven, Conn., Louis I. Kahn, FAIA; completed by Pellecchia & Meyers, Seattle	2005
Thorncrown Chapel Eureka Springs, Ark., E. Fay Jones, FAIA	2006
Vietnam Veterans Memorial Washington, D.C., Maya Lin with Cooper-Lecky Partnership	2007

Conferred on projects completed 25–35 years ago in recognition of architectural design of enduring significance

AIA150 Capital Campaign Donors

Norman L. Koonce, FAIA, and Ronald Skaggs, FAIA, served as cochairs of the national AIA150 Capital Campaign.

Founders Circle ($1,000,000)
McGraw-Hill Construction *Official Media Sponsor*
Autodesk *Official Software Sponsor*

Gold ($500,000–$999,999)
HKS, Inc.
NBBJ

Silver ($250,000–$499,999)
AIA Board of Directors
Deltek, Inc.
DLR Group, Inc.
Haworth, Inc.
Hellmuth, Obata + Kassabaum, Inc.
Perkins+Will
RTKL Associates, Inc.
Satellier
Thompson Ventulett Stainback & Associates, Inc.
Victor O. Schinnerer & Company, Inc.
SHW Group LLP
Zimmer Gunsul Frasca Partnership

Bronze ($100,000–$249,999)
Bank of America
Bentley Systems, Inc.
Stephen B. & Lisa S. Bonner
Clark Construction Group, LLC
Cooper Carry Charitable Foundation, Inc.
Ellerbe Becket
Hanley Wood, LLC
HGA
HMC Architects
Helmut Jahn, FAIA
Little
OWP/P Architects, Inc.
Pei Cobb Freed & Partners Architects, LLP
SmithGroup, Inc.
Swanke, Hayden, Connell Architects, LLP

Granite ($50,000–$99,999)
ADD, Inc.
BWBR Architects, Inc.
Cannon Design
FreemanWhite, Inc.
Reed Construction Data

Marble ($25,000–$49,999)
AIA Trust
Craig Beale, FAIA, FACHA
Nunzio DeSantis, AIA
Brian Dougherty, FAIA, & Betsey Dougherty, FAIA
GBBN Architects, Inc.
GSBS Architects
Gund Partnership, Inc.
H. Ralph Hawkins, FAIA, FACHA
John J. Hoffmann, FAIA
Norman Koonce, FAIA, & Suzanne Koonce, Hon. AIA
Lord, Aeck & Sargent Architecture
Miller | Hull Partnership
Munger Munger Architecture
Shepley Bulfinch Richardson and Abbott, Inc.
Ronald L. Skaggs, FAIA, FACHA
Victor F. Trahan III, FAIA
R. Randall Vosbeck, FAIA, & Phoebe Vosbeck
TRO Jung | Brannen
WHR Architects, Inc.

Friends of the AIA ($10,000–$24,999)
Altoon + Porter Architects
Anderson Mason Dale Architects, PC
John Anderson, FAIA, & Flodie Anderson
Noel Barrick, AIA
Barron, Heinberg & Brocato
Bobby Booth, AIA
Michael Broshar, FAIA, & Mary Broshar
Joe Buskuhl, FAIA
E. Davis Chauviere, AIA
Tommy Cowan, FAIA, & Ann Cowan
Louis de Moll, FAIA
Helene Combs Dreiling, FAIA
James H. Eley, FAIA
Eskew + Dumez + Ripple, Studio EDR
Glenn Fellows, AIA
GouldEvans
Marion L. Fowlkes, FAIA
FRCH Design Worldwide
Ron Gover, AIA
Donald J. Hackl, FAIA
Ernest Hanchey, AIA
Heller Manus Architects, Inc.
Dan Jeakins, AIA
Chuck Means, AIA
Mike Menefee, AIA
Morris Architects
Dan Noble, FAIA, FACHA
Marshall Purnell, FAIA
Freddy Roberts, AIA
Miguel Rodriguez, AIA, & Lourdes Rodriguez, AIA
Kate Schwennsen, FAIA, & Barry Jones, AIA
Joseph Sprague, FAIA
Steed Hammond Paul, Inc.
Douglas L Steidl, FAIA, & Sue Steidl
Norman Strong, FAIA, & Susan Strong
Bryce A. Weigand, FAIA
Enrique A. Woodroffe, FAIA/Woodroffe Corporation Architects

2007
Marshall Purnell, FAIA, became
the first African-American to
serve as president of the AIA
(2007–08)

Empire State Building ranked #1
in AIA public poll of "America's
Favorite Architecture"

AIA celebrated its
sesquicentennial

AIA membership reached 82,000

Edward Larrabee Barnes, FAIA,
received the AIA Gold Medal
(posthumously)

Special Donors (up to $10,000)

Roy L. Abernathy, AIA
Henry C. Alexander Jr., FAIA
Anderson Brulé Architects, Inc.
Architecture by Norbert Peiker, LLC
Newell Arnerich, AIA
Arrowstreet, Inc.
Edward Abeyta, AIA
Ronald Arthur Altoon, FAIA
Peter J. Arsenault, AIA
Jim Atkins, FAIA, KIA
Danny P. Babin, AIA
Donald R. Barsness, AIA
Ronald J. Battaglia, FAIA, & Sandra Battaglia
Lee Palmer Bearsch, FAIA
Ronald P. Bertone, FAIA
William Beyer, FAIA
Robert R. Billingsley, AIA
Elmer Botsai, FAIA
David Bowen, FAIA
Jay and Michelle Brand
Leon Bridges, FAIA
Thomas D. Briggs, AIA
Robert Broshar, FAIA
David J. Brotman, FAIA
John A. Busby Jr., FAIA
H. Kennard Bussard, FAIA
Joan Capelin, Hon. AIA
Richard E. Carroll, AIA
Stephan Castellanos, FAIA
Lorenzo Castillo, AIA
L. William Chapin II, FAIA
Matthew Clear, AIA
CMSS Architects P.C.
David S. Collins, FAIA
Douglas J. Compton, AIA
Donald M. Comstock, FAIA
Laura Cordero-Agrait
Jess Raymond Corrigan, Jr., AIA
Anthony J. "Tony" Costello, FAIA
David Crawford
Sylvester Damianos, FAIA
Edgardo de Lara
Ronald W. Dennis, AIA, ACHA
Frank F. Douglas, FAIA
George Dove, FAIA
Brian J. Eason, AIA
Jeremy Edmunds, Assoc. AIA
Elliott + Associates
Robert J. Farrow, AIA
S. Scott Ferebee, FAIA
Robert D. Fincham, AIA
Jonathan L. Fischel, AIA, LEED AP
Ford, Powell, & Carson, Inc.
John P. Franzen, AIA
T.E. Garduque, FAIA
Francisco G. Gonzalez, AIA
B. Todd Gritch, FAIA

Grooters Leapaldt Tideman Architects
Roy L. Gunsolus, AIA
Maureen Guttman, AIA
Walter Hainsfurther, AIA
Anna M. Halpin, FAIA
Thomas E. Harvey, Jr., AIA, FACHA
Jeffrey K. Haven, AIA
Helix | Architecture + Design
James G. Herman, AIA
John Hesseler, AIA
Jeff Hill, AIA
William E. Hinton, AIA
Michael Hoagland
Kerry J. Hogue, AIA
Thomas R. Holt, AIA
Clifford H. Horsak, AIA
M. Teresa Hurd, AIA
John M. Hutchings, AIA
Paul Hyett, Hon. AIA
IMRE Communications
Dick Jackson
Jeffrey K. Jensen, AIA
J.K. Roller Architects
Bruce E. Johnson, AIA
Danie A. Johnson, FAIA
Larry A. Johnson, PE
Richard D. Johnston, AIA
Mark Jones, AIA
Leevi Kiil, FAIA
Tim Konganda
Leonard Koroski, AIA
KPS Group, Inc.
Kirk J. Krueger, AIA
Sylvia Kwan, FAIA
Joseph P. Laakman, AIA, NCARB
Brian F. Larson, AIA
Jeff LaRue, AIA
Robert Lawrence, FAIA
Rick James Lee, Assoc. AIA
Robin Lee, Hon. AIA
Larry D. Le Master, CPA
Michael Lischer, AIA, RIBA
Clark Llewellyn, AIA
Stephen K. Loos, AIA
Marvin Malecha, FAIA & Cindy Malecha
Clark D. Manus, FAIA
Elizabeth Bell Martin
Robert T. Martineck, AIA
John M. Maudlin-Jeronimo, FAIA
Susan Maxman, FAIA
Linda McCracken-Hunt, AIA & Thomas Hunt
Owen E. McCrory, AIA
Christine W. McEntee
Connie S. McFarland, FAIA
Brian McFarlane, AIA
John McGinty, FAIA
Adam Melis

Elizabeth Mitchell, Hon. AIA
Norman T. Morgan, AIA
Rodney W. Morrissey, AIA
Mortar Net USA, Ltd.
Robin L. Murray, AIA PP
Barbara A. Nadel, FAIA
Celeste Novak, AIA
Gregory Palermo, FAIA, and Olivia Madison
Gordon Park, AIA
Raymond G. Post Jr., FAIA
Jack D. Price, Jr., AIA
David Proffitt, AIA
David E. Prusha, AIA
Marvin Ragland, Jr.
Ratio Architects, Inc.
Remson-Haley-Herpin Architects
John H. Richardson, PE
Terry R. Richter, AIA
Christopher Rose, AIA
Jeffrey Rosenblum, AIA
Harry R. Rutledge, RIBA, FAIA
James A. Scheeler, FAIA
Charles E. Schwing, FAIA & Jerry Schwing
Scott & Goble Architects
Linda Searl, FAIA
John C. Senhauser, FAIA
Oliver B. Stark II, AIA
Greg Staskiewicz, Assoc. AIA
RK Stewart, FAIA & Barbara Lyons, AIA
Craig R. Stockwell, AIA
Jeffrey C. Stouffer, AIA
James M. Suehiro, AIA, LEED AP
Anne-Marie Taylor
T.H. Teasdale, FAIA
B. Kirk Teske, AIA
Leslie J. Thomas, AIA, and Steven J. Bracy
James D. Tittle, FAIA
Bryan K. Trubey, AIA
Larry J. Tuccio, AIA
Nicholas E. Vlattas
Jeffrey D. Vandersall, AIA
Mark Vander Voort, AIA
Edward J. Vidlak, AIA
The Vinyl Institute, Inc.
Jane Wolford and Arol Wolford, Hon. AIA
Michael Wayne Vela, AIA
David Vincent, AIA, ACHA
Craig Williams, AIA
Penelope J. H. Wright, AIA
Eric Zaddock, Assoc. AIA
Andrew J. Zekany

Index

Aalto, Alvar, 13, 290, 290*f*
    Baker House dormitory, MIT, 261, 261*f*
    Paimio Sanatorium, 283
Abercrombie, Leslie Patrick, 13
Abercrombie, Stanley, 170
Abernathy, Roy, 223
Academy of Neuroscience for Architecture
    (ANFA), 139
access issues, 91, 100, 100*f*
    See also universal design
Acorn Structures, 192
acoustics, 293
ACSA. *See* Association of Collegiate Schools
    of Architecture
activist architects, 64–85
    contemporary, 70–76
    contributions of, 77
    historical, 65–70
adaptive work, 167–168
Adler, Dankmar, 219
Adler and Sullivan, 15, 292*f*, 294
Advisory Council on Historic Preservation, 59
AEG Turbine Factory, 19*f*
AFH. *See* Architecture for Humanity
African-American architects, 63, 63*f*
    AIA Gold Medal and, 13
    Bond, 70–71, 71*f*
    and education, 115*f*
AIA. *See* American Institute of Architects
AIA150 Blueprint for America, 81, 81*f*
AIA Gold Medal, 2, 12–13, 12*f*
    Aalto, 290
    Ando, 154
    Bacon, 335
    Breuer, 170
    Calatrava, 237
    Caudill, 272
    Erickson, 254
    Esherick, 56
    Foster, 98, 98*f*
    Fuller, 135
    Gehry, 171
    Graves, 119
    Gropius, 118
    Jefferson, 10
    Johnson, 55
    Jones, 336
    Kahn, 32
    Le Corbusier, 374
    Legorreta, 312
    Meier, 311
    Mies van der Rohe, 31
    Mockbee, 79
    Moore, 201
    Nervi, 134
    Neutra, 97
    Pei, 310
    Pelli, 182
    Perret, 153

    Predock, 202
    Roche, 221
    Saarinen, Eero, 236
    Saarinen, Eliel, 271
    Skidmore, 181
    Stein, 354
    Sullivan, 219
    Thompson, 220
    Wright, 200
    Wurster, 78
AIA Journal, 16
AIAS. *See* American Institute of Architecture
    Students (AIAS)
Air Force Academy Cadet Chapel, 262, 324, 325*f*
airplane hangers, by Nervi, 134, 134*f*
airports, 230*f*, 231
Alberti, Leone Battista, 127, 187
Alcoa Building, 150
Alessi kettle, 119, 119*f*
Alfred P. Murrah Federal Building, 103, 103*f*
Algiers, Obus plan for, 374
Allan, Stanley, 238, 238*f*
Allen, Stan, 139
Alofsin, Anthony, 200
alternative medicine, architecture for, 275,
    282–283, 282*f*–283*f*
Altes Museum, Berlin, 294
aluminum sheet-metal technology, 150
American Institute of Architects (AIA)
    Blueprint for America initiative, 81
    Board Knowledge Committee, 113
    code of ethics, 89
    College of Fellows, 11
    Committee on the Environment (COTE), 91,
        99
    and design-build, 187
    Disaster Response Committee, 82;
        and education, 113
    headquarters of, 16–17, 16*f*–17*f*
    Historic Resources Committee, 59
    history of, 14–17
    international connections, 11
    Kemper Award, 82
    Langley Scholarship, 68
    Livable Cities initiative, 368
    Research Corporation, 132
American Institute of Architecture Students
    (AIAS), 120, 125, 125*f*
American Red Cross, 88
American Society of Heating, Refrigerating, and
    Air-Conditioning Engineers, Inc., 91
Americans with Disabilities Act, 91, 100–101, 130
anarchitecture, 23–25, 23*f*
Anderson, John, 339*f*
Anderson, MacVickar, 15
Anderson Brulé Architects, 166*f*, 167
Ando, Tadao, 13, 30*f*, 154, 154*f*
ANFA. *See* Academy of Neuroscience for
    Architecture

Anshen + Allen, 289, 289f
Anthony, Kathryn H., 63
apprenticeship model, 105
Arad, Michael, 84, 84f
Ara Pacis Museum, 311
architect
    and HSW issues, 96
    as rebel, 60
    responsibility of, 28–30, 87
    role of, history of, 2, 6, 9, 80, 160, 378
    term, 2, 187
Architects Renewal Committee of Harlem
        (ARCH), 70
Architectural Barriers Act, 91
Architectural League of New York, 70
Architectural Research Centers Consortium,
        130
architectural thinking
    and design, 159
    and diversity, 102
    and politics, 85
    studio education and, 121
    and sustainable design, 96
    teachers and, 108
architecture
    definition of, 19, 28
    history in U.S., 34–63
    need for, 18–33
    architecture education, 104–125
    accreditation of, performance-based
            criteria for, 124
    current directions in, 114–115
    faculty in, 108–109
    on security issues, 103
Architecture for Humanity (AFH), 33, 80
Architecture in the Schools program, 273, 273f
Archive of Women in Architecture, 70
arcology, 57
Arcosanti, 57, 57f
Arena Stage, 296
Arizona State University, Nelson Fine Arts
        Center, 267, 306, 306f
Art Deco style, 42f, 43, 207
    Boston Avenue Methodist Church, 322, 323f
arts
    architecture for, 292–313
    complexes for, 305–306
Arts and Crafts movement, 40f, 41
Arup, 91f, 96, 139, 157, 161, 162f
    Commerzbank, 212, 213f
Asklepieia, 275, 282
Association for Computer Aided Design in
        Architecture, 130
Association of Collegiate Schools of
        Architecture (ACSA), 105, 124
Astor Library, 306, 306f
atelier model, 104f, 105, 121, 160, 160f
Athens, 370
    International Airport, 236

Atlantic Center for the Arts, 307, 308f
AT&T Building, 51, 55
Auditorium Building, 292f, 294
Audubon Ballroom, 71, 71f
Audubon Society, 217, 217f
aura, 20, 29–30
Austin, Katherine, 203
Austrian Postal Savings Bank, 20f
Automex Towers, 312
automobiles
    and architecture, 228, 229f
    and cities, 364, 365f
    and suburbs, 345
    and urban renewal, 354
Avalon Bay, 348f, 349
Ave Maria University, 267
avian flu, 92f, 93
Ayers/Saint/Gross, 267

Babylon, 370
Bach de Roda Bridge, 237
Bacon, Francis, 25
Bacon, Henry, 12, 16, 322, 335, 335f
Bader, Ian, 246f, 252f
Bahe, Jonathan, 125
Baillie Scott, Mackay Hugh, 41
Baker, David, 269
Baker, Susan, 184
Ballard Library and Neighborhood Service
        Center, 99f
Baltic Inn, 203, 203f
Baltimore, MD, 342, 343f, 360
    Harborplace, 366f
    Lexington Terrace, 353
    Uplands, 346f, 347
Ban, Shigeru, 84f
Bandits' Roost, 88f
Banham, Rayner, 152
Barnes, Edward Larrabee, 307, 308f
Barney, Carol Ross, 269
Barnsdall, Aline, 44
Barragán, Luis, 312
Barr-Kumar, Raj, 63, 63f
Bartholomew, George, 146
Barton House, 79
Bataille, George, 23
Bath, England, 282, 282f
Baudrillard, Jean, 30
Bauhaus, 4, 22, 31, 46
    buildings of, 118, 118f
    and education, 121
Bay Area regional style, 78, 78f
Bayside Marketplace, 220
Beach, Victoria, 33, 33f
beauty, architecture and, 19–22, 29
Beaux-Arts, 36
    and architecture education, 105, 121
    and cities, 363
    and design process, 160

    Kahn and, 32
Beaux-Arts Institute of Design, 105
Becker, Franklin, 210–211
Beck Group, 173, 173f
Becquerel, Antoine-César, 121
BedZED, 373, 373f
Behnisch, Behnisch, & Partner, 214f, 215
Behnisch, Stefan, 27f
Behrens, Peter, 19f, 118
Beijing National Aquatic Center, 157
Bel Geddes, Norman, 365f
Bell, Bryan, 33
Bell, Robert, 355
Bell, Victoria Ballard, 33
Bellevue Hospital, 274f, 278, 278f
Bell Laboratories, 236
Belltown, 72f
Belluschi, Pietro, 13, 118f, 305
    Central Lutheran Church, 324
    Equitable Building, 149f
Benares, 370
Benjamin, Walter, 20, 29
Benjamin Thompson & Associates, 220
Bennett, Ralph, 188–199
Berkebile, Robert, 75–76, 77f, 99
Berkeley fire station, 172f
Berlin Free Zone, 23f
Bermak House, 56f
Berman, Solon S., 342
Bernhard, Karl, 19f
Bernstein, Fred, 134, 154, 311
Berry, Wendell, 275
Bessemer process, 143
Bethune, Louise Blanchard, 16f, 63
Bethune, Robert Armour, 63
Beverly, Tom, 355
Beyer Blinder Belle, 84
Bianco Giolitto Weston Architects, 313
Bibiena, Antonio, 293
Bilbao effect, 303
Bill Dunster Architects, 373f
Billings, John Shaw, 277, 277f
Biloxi Model Home Fair, 9f, 80f
BIM. See building information modeling
Bing, Alexander, 354
biophilia, 208, 283
biophilic design, 283
biorealism, 96
Birkerts, Gunnar, 262, 264
Bitter, Karl, 16f
Blacker House, 41
Blashfield, Edwin W., 12
Blueprint for America, 81, 81f
Blum, Andrew, 78, 254
Boettcher Concert Hall, 296
Bogardus, James, 38
Bohlin Cywinski Jackson Architects, 99f
Bolus, Jay, 136
Bond, J. Max, Jr., 70–71, 71f, 84f

Bond & Wolfe Architects, 222, 222f
Boney, Charles, 184f
Boney, Paul D., 184
Border Station, Point Roberts, 244f
Boston, 353, 360
    City Hall, 367f
Boston Architectural College, 111f
Boston Avenue Methodist Church, 322, 323f
Boston Symphony Hall, 293
Botta, Mario, 306
Boulder Associates, 288
Boulder Community Foothills Hospital, 288
Boussum, Debra, 222f
Box City, 75–76, 76f
Boyd Education Center, 26f
Boyd Ryder, 71
Boyer, Ernest L., 121, 132
Boyer Report, 105, 113, 121, 132
branch offices, 186
brand differentiation, 176
Brandeis University, 261
Branham, Mary Beth, 184f
Braungart, Michael, 136, 163
Breezehouse, 164, 198f
Brennan, Charles, 222
Breuer, Marcel, 13, 61, 170, 170f
    St. John's Abbey, 328, 328f
    Weaver Federal Building, 242f, 243
    Whitney Museum, 298
Breuer House, 170
Bricker, Lauren Weiss, 97
bridges, 228, 229f
    Calatrava and, 237, 237f
    Fort Pitt Bridge Project, 239, 239f
    Golden Gate Bridge, 224f, 225
Brigham & Women's Hospital, 284f
Brill, Michael, 210–211
Britco, 165–166
British Museum Great Court canopy, 307
Broadacre City, 57, 364, 364f
Bronson Methodist Hospital, 286f, 287
Brooklyn Courthouse, 251f
Brown, Glenn, 16, 17f
Brown, Lance Jay, 74f, 141–152
Browne, Michelle M., 313
Brunelleschi, Filippo, 2, 127, 128f
Bruner Cott & Associates, 307, 307f
Buchanan, Brad, 120
Buchanan Yonushewski Group, 120
Buffalo Organization for Social and
        Technological Innovation, 210
building codes
    future of, 94
    history of, 87, 89, 91
    security issues and, 103f
building composition, dynamic versus static, 132
building information modeling (BIM), 6, 131f,
        133, 176–177
    education on, 114

and integrated practice, 185
Building Officials and Code Administrators, 89
building performance, education on, 114
buildings
    versus architecture, 19
    complete, 22
Bulfinch, Charles, 35
Bundy, McGeorge, 262f
bungalows, 189
Bunker Hill Bridge, 228, 229f
Bunker Hill Elementary School, 273f
Bunshaft, Gordon, 46, 47f, 238
Burke, Patrick, 119
Burnham, Daniel Hudson, 15–16, 67, 335
    and cities, 363
    and Columbian Exposition, 145
    Flatiron Building, 148f, 149
    Union Station, Chicago, 227f
    Union Station, D.C., 234f, 235
Burnham and Root, 39, 39f
    Monadnock Building, 147f, 149
    Reliance Building, 149
Bush, George H. W., 100
business district, 363
bus stations, 228, 228f
Butler Rogers Baskett Architects, 313f
Butterfield School, 264

Caballeros Footbridge, 237
Cabrini Green, 350, 350f
Cache, Bernard, 127
Caesar Cottage, 170, 170f
Calatrava, Santiago, 4, 4f, 13, 28f, 237, 237f
    Milwaukee Art Museum addition, 303, 304f
    and World Trade Center, 84, 232f, 233
Calder, Alexander Milne, 43, 243f
Calthorpe Associates, 369f
Campbell, Robert, 62, 268f
Campo Volantin Footbridge, 237, 237f
Canadian Chancery, 254f
The Cannery, 56
Canstruction, 313, 313f
Capitol, U.S., 360, 361f
    construction of, 35
    dome of, 14, 14f
Caracas, Venezuela, 92f
carbon dioxide emissions, 93
Carlyle, Thomas, 41
Carnegie Mellon University, 115f, 117f, 122, 267
    Intelligent Workplace, 208f, 209
Carnegie Technical Schools, 106f
Carpenter Center for the Visual Arts, Harvard,
        262, 262f
Carranza, Luis E., 312
Carrier, Willis, 152
Carroll, Stewart, 173f
cars. See automobiles
Carson Pirie Scott Department Store, 38, 38f,
        41, 219

Carter, Jimmy, 82
Cary, John, 122
Case Studies Initiative, 122f
Case Study House program, 190–192, 191f
Castle, Helen, 98
Castle Farms, 58f
cathedrals, 2, 2f, 22, 51, 273f
    Lincoln, 18f, 19–20
    Our Lady of the Angels, 333, 334f
    St. John the Divine, 318, 319f
Catholic Healthcare West, 288
CATIA, 152, 171
Caudill, William Wayne, 13, 272, 272f
Cavaglieri, Giorgio, 306, 306f
CBT, 352f, 353
Cedars-Sinai Comprehensive Cancer Center,
        285, 285f
cell work tasks, 211, 211f
Census Bureau Headquarters, 250f
Centerbrook Architects, 201
Center for Building Performance at Carnegie
        Mellon University, 208f, 209
Center for Health Design, 285, 287
Center for Understanding the Built Environment
        (CUBE), 75, 77f
Center for Universal Design, 100
Centraal Beheer building, 207
Central Lutheran Church, Portland, 324
Central Park, 64f, 86f, 87
Central Synagogue, 316–318, 317f
Cerebral Palsy School, 263
César Pelli & Associates, 188f, 198
Cesca chair, 170
CFA. See Commission of Fine Arts
Chace, Clyde, 44
Channel Heights Housing, 97
Chapel of St. Ignatius, 333, 333f
Chapin, L. William, II, 98
Charles Center, Baltimore, 305
Charleston, SC, 340, 341f, 360, 368, 368f
charrette, academic design, 74–75
Chartres cathedral, 2f
Chatham Village, 354
Chavez (Cesar) Multicultural Academic Center,
        269, 269f
Chesapeake Bay Foundation, 218
Chicago
    urban planning in, 362f–363f
    and urban renewal, 350, 350f, 353, 353f
Chicago Federal Center, 243, 243f
Chicago frame, 149
Chicago Tribune Tower, 271, 271f
Chicago window, 38
Childs, David, 4f, 84, 250f
China
    Beijing National Aquatic Center, 157
    Center for Sustainable Development, 375,
        375f
Chong, Gordon H., 63, 63f, 291

Chongming, 372f
Chong Partners Architecture, 291
Christensen, Clayton, 159
Christner Architects, 222
Chrysler, Walter, 43
Chrysler Building, 42f, 43, 207
church architecture, 314–337
Churchill, Winston, 222
Church of Light, 154, 154f
Ciampi, Mario J., 263
Cira Centre, 182f
cities, 356–375
    education on, 114
    and office architecture, 207
    universal design and, 101
    See also New Urbanism; urban renewal
City Beautiful movement, 15–16, 67, 363
Civil Rights Act, 70
Clarke, Fred, 182
Clarke, Gilmore D., 195f
Classical architecture
    houses, 189
    in public works, 241
    and religious architecture, 316–318
Clavan, Irwin, 195f
Clèrisseau, Charles-Louis, 10
client strategies, 184
climate change. See global warming
climate control, 152
Climatroffice, 98
Clinton, Bill, 85, 85f, 221f
Clive Wilkinson Architects, 210, 210f
Clodagh Design, 283f
club system, and architecture education, 105,
    111f
club work tasks, 211, 211f
Cobb, Henry N., 246f, 250, 252f
Codman, Henry Sargent, 67
coffeehouses, 223
Coit, Elisabeth, 68, 68f
Coleman House, 78f
collaboration
    architecture education and, 107
    environment for, 160
    and integrated practice, 185
    office design and, 211
    and research, 139
College of Santa Fe Visual Arts Center, 312f
Collegiate Gothic, 259, 267
Colonial Revival houses, 189–190, 189f
Colorado College, Olin Hall of Science, 272
Colorado Court, 198, 199f
Columbia-Presbyterian Medical Center, 279,
    279f
Columbus East Senior High School, 264, 265f
Commercial Club of Chicago, 67f
Commerzbank, 95f, 98, 212, 213f
Commission of Fine Arts (CFA), 16, 238, 335
commodity, 141

community design, 70, 75–76, 77f, 338–355
computer numerical control, 152
concrete
    Ando and, 154
    pavement, 146
    reinforced, 140f
Congress for the New Urbanism, 368
Congressional Accountability Act, 85
Connecticut General Life Insurance, 181, 181f
Contemporary Arts Center, Cincinnati, 300f, 301
Cook House, 79
Coolidge Shepley Bulfinch and Abbott, 279, 279f
Coonley (Avery) House, 200
Cooper, Kent, 238
Cooper (Mildred B.) Memorial Chapel, 336,
    336f
Cooper Union, 109, 109f
Cornell University, 15, 121f
Costello, Anthony J., 81
COTE. See American Institute of Architects,
    Committee on the Environment
courthouses, 240f
Cox, Maurice, 9f
cradle-to-cradle design, 136
Cram, Ralph Adams, 318, 319f
Cramer, James P., 174–180
Cranbrook Academy of Art, 271, 271f
Cranbrook Teachers Seminar, 113
Cret, Paul Phillipe, 13, 56, 258f, 259
Crisp, Barbara, 282
Critical Planet Rescue, 99
criticism, of architecture: and research, 130
    role of, 62
Crosbie, Michael J., 112, 314–334
Crouwel, Mels, 275
Crow Island School, 263, 263f, 271
Crown Center, 338f
Crown Hall, 108f
Croxton Collaborative Architects, 217, 217f
CRS, 272
Crystal Cathedral, 328, 329f
Crystal Palace, 142f, 143
CUBE (Center for Understanding the Built
    Environment), 75, 77f
Cummings, George Bain, 354f
Cunningham, Ann Pamela, 61
curtain wall construction, 149, 149f–150f
Cusato, Marianne, 194f
Customs and Immigration Center, Niagara Falls,
    245f
Cypress College, 272

Daileda, David A., 224–235
Dailey, Gardner, 56
Dai Xialong, 375f
Daly, William, 350f
D'Amato (Alfonse M.) Courthouse and Federal
    Building, 248f
Dana Building, 90f–91f

Dana (Susan Lawrence) House, 200
da Vinci, Leonardo, 126f, 127
Davis, Mike, 92
Davis, Robert, 369f
Davis Brody + Associates, 71
Davy, Kyle V., 158–169
daylighting strategies, 212, 213f–214f, 215
    and arts institutions, 298, 299f
    and hospital design, 276, 276f, 285, 285f
    and religious institutions, 326, 326f
Dean, Andrea Oppenheimer, 79
Dean, Lloyd, 288
decision making, Swett on, 85
Deck House Inc., 192
Deconstructivism, 23, 51
degrees in architecture, 106
De Leuw, Cather, 238
delight, 141
delivery methods
    design-build, 173, 173f, 177, 180f, 187
    market penetration of, 187f
del Monte, Betsy, 173, 173f
del Monte, Rick, 173
DeMars, Vernon, 107f
Deng Nan, 375, 375f
Dennis, Michael, 267
density, 371
    and urban renewal, 350
Denver, CO, 339, 339f
Denver Art Museum, 303, 303f
Denver International Airport, Jeppesen
    Terminal, 225, 225f, 231
den work tasks, 211, 211f
Department of Housing and Urban
    Development, 192, 196f, 197
    Weaver Federal Building, 242f, 243
DeRose, Jen, 222, 313
Derrida, Jacques, 23, 51, 51f
Descartes, René, 19, 25
design
    cradle to cradle, 136
    evidence-based, 130
    evolution of, 159, 159f
    Graves and, 119, 119f
    power of, 1–17
    process, 158–173
    research and, 127
design-build, 173, 173f, 177, 187
    best practices for, 180f
Design Corps, 33
Design Excellence Program, GSA, 240–255
Design Foundations, 33
Design Research Headquarters, 207, 207f, 220
desk, electroluminescent, 163, 163f
Deskey, Donald, 295
Destini, 173
Dewey, John, 263
De Young Museum, 301
Dhar, Ranjit, 187

diagrid pattern, 5f, 6
Diamond, Jared, 94
Diamond Ranch High School, 270, 270f
digital technology, 54
    and construction, 173, 173f
    and design, 159, 161
    and education, 114
    and materials, 152
    and research, 139
Dillon, David, 173
Dinkeloo, John, 221, 236
disabilities, people with, 91.
    See also universal design
disaster response, architects and, 82, 82f, 99
disease, future issues in, 93
Disney (Walt) Concert Hall, 171, 171f, 296,
    297f, 301, 303
diversity in architecture, 63, 102
    AIA Gold Medal and, 13
Dixon, David, 338–353, 340f
Dixon, John Morris, 292–309
DLR Group, 255
Dollard (Patrick H.) Discovery Health Center,
    287f, 288
DoodleOpolis, 273
Dostoevsky, Fyodor, 23
DProfiler, 173
Drake University, 261
Duany, Andrés, 52f
Duany Plater-Zyberk, 347, 347f, 368, 369f
Dudok, Willem, 13
Duffy, Francis, 205, 211f
Duke University, 267
Dulles International Airport, 221, 231, 236, 236f
Dulwich Gallery, 294
DuPont, 6, 137
Durst Organization, 217
Dwell Homes, 192
Dymaxion House, 135, 135f, 190
dynamic building composition, 132

Eames House, 191f, 192
Earth Day, 91
Eastern Cambridge, MA, 353
East River Waterfront Esplanade and Piers
    Project, 139f
Eberhard, John P., 139
École des Beaux-Arts. *See* Beaux-Arts
EDAW, 267
Eden Project, 157, 157f
edge cities, 370–371
education. *See* architecture education;
    school design
Egyptian style, 43
Ehrenkrantz, Ezra D., 267
Eichler houses, 192
Eidlitz, Leopold, 117
Eisenman, Peter, 19, 51, 51f, 79, 84, 306
elevators, 38, 145f, 194

and office architecture, 207
Elkus, Howard, 17f
Elkus Manfredi, 350
Emerging Professional's Companion (EPC),
    113, 122
Emerson, Ralph Waldo, 41
Emory University, 267
Emotional Architecture, 312
Empire State Building, 43, 206f, 207
Empyrean International, 192
energy codes, 91, 94
energy issues
    and cities, 371–373
    materials and, 152
    and office architecture, 217
engineers, and design process, 161
Ennis (Charles) House, 200
Environmental Design Research Association, 130
Environmental Protection Agency,
    Environmental Research Center,
    177, 178f–179f
Environmental Resource Guide, 99
EPC. *See Emerging Professional's Companion*
Equitable Building, 149f
Erickson, Arthur C., 13, 254, 254f, 262
Esherick, Joseph, 13, 56, 56f, 107f, 267
Esherick, Wharton, 56
Esherick Homsey Dodge and Davis, 56
ethics, code of, AIA, 89
ethylenetetrafluoroethylene (ETFE), 157
Evans, Robin, 23
Everson Art Museum, 310
evidence-based design, 130, 287
experience economy, 166
Experience Music Project, 171
exurbs, 370

Fagus Factory, 118, 118f
Fallingwater, 44, 45f, 190, 200
Faneuil Hall Marketplace, 220, 220f
Fanger, Ole, 208
fantastic architecture, 25
Farley, Marilyn, 240–253
Farmers' National Bank, 219, 219f
Farnsworth House, 31, 46, 46f
fast architecture, 177
Faville, William, 12
Federal Emergency Management Agency
    (FEMA), 82
Federal style architecture, 241
Feiner, Edward A., 240–253
female architects, 63, 63f
    AIA Gold Medal and, 13
    Bethune, 16f
    Coit, 68
    and education, 114f
    Torre, 70
Fentress Bradburn Architects, 225, 225f, 231
Fernandez, John, 157

Fernbach, Henry, 316–318, 317f
Ferris wheel, 144f, 146
ferrovitreous construction, 142f, 143, 143f
finance, 176
Finnish National Museum, 271
fire codes, history of, 87
firmness, 141
First Christian Church, Columbus, 322, 324f
First Church of Christ, Scientist, Berkeley, 321,
    321f
First National Tower, 122f
First Presbyterian Church, Stamford, 326, 326f
First Unitarian Church, Rochester, 326, 327f
Fisher, Thomas, 86–96
Fisk, Bill, 208
Fitch, James Marston, 141, 146
Fitzgerald, James T., 186
Five Points Partnership, 355, 355f
Flagg, Ernest, 278, 278f
Flatiron Building, 148f, 149
Fletcher, Norman, 17f
Floyd, Jeff, 184f
Ford, Jack, 81
Ford Foundation Headquarters, 207, 221, 221f
Ford Motor Company: Rotunda Dome, 135;
    Rouge River plant, 165
Forest City Enterprises, 369f
Fort Pitt Bridge Project, 239, 239f
Foster, Norman, 13, 84, 98, 98f
Foster + Partners, 95f, 96, 212, 213f, 307
4 Times Square Building, 216f, 217
Fraker, Harrison S., Jr., 104–117, 122
Frampton, Kenneth, 154
France, Anatole, 62
Franklin (Benjamin) Elementary School, 138f
FRCH Design Worldwide, 186, 186f
freedom, and architecture, 22–25
Freedom by Design, 120, 120f
Freedom Tower, 177
Freeman, Allen, 336, 354
French, Daniel Chester, 12, 322, 335, 335f
Frieder Burda Museum, 311, 311f
Friedman, Daniel S., 126–133
Friedrichstrasse building, 31f
Fuller, Richard Buckminster, 13, 69, 69f, 135,
    135f
    and Foster, 98
    and houses, 190
Furness, Frank, 219
furniture, office, 210–211
Futurama, 364, 365f
Futurism, 55
FXFOWLE Architects, 216f, 217

Gamble House, 40f, 41
Gandhi, Mohandas, 94
Gang, Jeanne, 80f
Gantt, Harvey, 63
Gap headquarters, 177, 212–213, 212f

Garden City movement, 363
Garfield School, 267
Garfield (Sidney R.) Health Care Innovation
        Center, 291, 291*f*
Gass, William, 19, 28
Gates of the Grove Synagogue, 331
Gauthier, Pierre, 276*f*
Gehry, Frank O., 4, 13, 84, 171, 171*f*
    Advanced Technologies Laboratory,
        267–269
    on computers, 54
    and digital technology, 152, 161
    Disney (Walt) Concert Hall, 171*f*, 296, 297*f*,
        301, 303
    Grand Avenue district, 372*f*
    Guggenheim Museum, 303, 304*f*
    on Mockbee, 79
    Nationale-Nederlanden building, 28*f*
    Weisman Art Museum, 21, 21*f*
General Electric, 145*f*
General Motors: Futurama Exhibit, 364, 365*f*
    Technical Center, 236
General Services Administration (GSA)
    chief architect, 249
    Design Excellence Program, 240–255
Gensler, 231
Genzyme Corporation headquarters, 27*f*, 214*f*,
        215
geodesic dome, 69, 135, 135*f*
George (Lloyd D.) Courthouse, 240*f*
Georgopulos, Diane, 376–379
German Pavilion, International Exposition, 31, 31*f*
Germany
    and Bauhaus, 46
    and Modernism, 19*f*, 44
    Nazi architecture, 22
Getty Center, 4, 305–306, 305*f*, 311
Ghirardo, Diane, 63
Gibling, Sophie, 44
Gibson, Carol, 337*f*
Gill, Deborah, 313
Gillin (John A.) House, 200
Gilman Hall, Johns Hopkins University, 260*f*,
        261
Gilmore, James, 165
Gindroz, Ray, 353*f*
Giurgola, Romaldo, 13
glaserworks, 269, 269*f*
glass
    curtain wall construction, 149–150,
        149*f*–150*f*
    and iron, 142*f*, 143, 143*f*
    Modernism and, 46
    technology and, 156, 156*f*
Glass House, 46, 55, 55*f*
Glidehouse, 164, 165*f*
globalization, 186
global warming, 93, 93*f*, 371–372
Globe Theatre, 293

Gluckman, Richard, 307
Glymph, Jim, 171
Goeritz, Mathias, 312
Goethe, Johann Wolfgang von, 377, 379
Goff, Bruce, 322, 323*f*
Goldberger, Paul, 221
    D'Amato (Alfonse M.) Courthouse and
        Federal Building, 248*f*
Golden Gate Bridge, 224*f*, 225
Goodhue, Bertram Grosvenor, 12–13, 321, 354
Goody, Joan, 250
Goody Clancy
    Crown Center, 338*f*
    Riverview Hope VI Redevelopment Plan, 196*f*
    Trinity Church, 318, 318*f*
    Uplands, 346*f*, 347
    and urban renewal, 340*f*, 348*f*, 349–350,
        350*f*
Google
    Earth, 81
    Headquarters, 210, 210*f*
Gordon, Harry, 99
Gore, Al, 375
Gothic style: Collegiate, 259, 267
    Ozark, 328–331, 330*f*
Gould, Kira, 80, 99–100
Government Center, Boston, 305
Grafton, Anthony, 187
Graham, Anderson, Probst & White, 227*f*
Grand Avenue, 372*f*
Grand Central Station, 61, 225, 226*f*, 227
Grant, Bradford, 63
Graves, Dean, 75
Graves, Ginny, 75–76, 76*f*
Graves, Michael, 4*f*, 13, 50*f*, 51, 119, 119*f*
    and World Trade Center, 84
Gray, Christopher, 150
Great Exhibition, 142*f*, 143
Greenbelt, MD, 354, 363
Greenberg, Randi, 255, 273
Greenberg Consultants, 352*f*
Greendale, WI, 363
green design. *See* sustainable design
Greene, Charles and Henry, 40*f*, 41
Greenhills, OH, 363
Greenway Group, 178, 180*f*
Greenwich Village, 59
Gregory Farmhouse, 78, 78*f*
Grimshaw, Nicholas, 157, 157*f*
Gropius, Walter, 13, 118, 118*f*, 374*f*
    and Breuer, 170
    on complete architecture, 22
    and education, 121
    Kennedy Federal Building, 243, 244*f*
    and Modernism, 44, 46
    and residential design, 192
Gropius House, 190*f*
Grossman, Marc, 85
Ground Zero. *See* World Trade Center

Gruzen Samton, 109*f*
GSA. *See* General Services Administration
Guaranty Building, 57, 219
Guenther, Robin, 274–289
Guenther 5 Architects, 287*f*, 288
Guerin, Jules, 12, 67*f*
Guggenheim Museum (Bilbao), 4, 171, 303, 304*f*
Guggenheim Museum (New York), 200, 298,
        298*f*
Gulf Building, 271
Guthrie Theater, 296
Gutman, Robert, 112
Gwathmey, Charles, 51, 84

Haag, Richard, 73*f*
Haas, Richard, 111*f*
Hadid, Zaha, 63, 63*f*, 84, 300*f*, 301
Hamilton Canal mill complex, 349
Hammond Courthouse, 252*f*
Haney, Gary, 250*f*
Harborplace, 220
Harding, Warren G., 12, 322
Hardy, Hugh, 247, 317*f*, 318
Hardy Holzman Pfeiffer, 245*f*, 296
Harper, Charles, 82, 82*f*
Harper Perkins Architects, 82
Harries, Karsten, 18–30
Harris, Susan, 167
Harrison, Wallace K., 13, 295, 305, 326, 326*f*
Harrison and Abramovitz, 150
Hart, Sara, 58, 137, 156–157
Harvard University, 262, 262*f*, 267
    Larsen (Roy E.) Hall, 272*f*
    Married Student Dormitories, 194–195
    Spangler Campus Center, 267, 267*f*
Hastings, L. Jane, 63, 63*f*
Haussmann, Georges-Eugène, baron, 358, 358*f*
Hawkinson, Laurie, 250
Hay Bale House, 79*f*
Hayden, Michael, 230*f*
Hayden, Sophia, 63, 63*f*
Haystack Mountain School of Crafts, 307, 308*f*
health, safety, and welfare (HSW), 86–103
    and cities, 373; history of, 87–91
health care, architecture for, 274–291
Health Care Without Harm, 288
Hearst, William Randolph, 36*f*
Hearst Castle, 36, 37*f*
Hearst Tower, 5*f*, 6, 98, 98*f*
Hedge, Alan, 208
Heerwagen, Judith, 208, 210
Hegel, G. W. Friedrich, 22
Heifetz, Ronald, 167
Heins & Lafarge, 318, 319*f*
Hejduk, John, 51, 109
Hellmuth, George, 250
Hellmuth Obata + Kassabaum (HOK), 222
    Environmental Research Center, 177,
        178*f*–179*f*

National Oceanic and Atmospheric Administration, 217
Terminal A, Logan International Airport, 235, 235f
Helsinki Railway Station, 271
Henry Horner Homes, 368
Hermitage, 294
Hertzberger, Hermann, 207
Herzog & de Meuron, 301, 303, 307
Heschong, Lisa, 208
Heyer, Paul, 201
Highlands Pond House, 202f
High Museum of Art, 311
Hill-Burton Act, 280, 283
Hillier Group, 212
Hines, Gerald, 55
Hines Partnership, 209
Historic American Buildings Survey, 17, 59
Hitchcock, Henry-Russell, 46, 55
hive work tasks, 211, 211f
Hoban, James, 35, 35f
Hoffman-LaRoche Building, 212
Hogan, Michael, 255, 255f
HOK. See Hellmuth Obata + Kassabaum
Holabird and Roche, 38, 147f
Holl, Steven, 84, 301
    Chapel of St. Ignatius, 333, 333f
    Simmons Hall, MIT, 268f, 269
Hollyhock House, 44
Home Insurance Building, 146f, 149
homeless shelters, 197, 197f
Hong Kong and Shanghai Bank, 98
Hood, Raymond, 43, 43f, 271f, 295
HOPE VI program, 196f, 197, 353, 368
Hopkins, Johns, 277
Horn, David H., 263
Hospital Lariboisière, 276f
hospitals, 274–291
Hotel Camino Real, 312
Hôtel Dieu, 276
housing, 188–203
    affordability and, 195–197
    multifamily, 194–195, 195f
    single-family, 189–194
    and urban renewal, 353
Housing Choice Voucher Program, 197
Howard, Ebenezer, 354
Howe, George, 32, 43, 56
Howells, John Mead, 271f
HSW. See health, safety, and welfare
Huangbaiyu, 375, 375f
Huff, Ray, 241
Hugo, Victor, 22
Huichól community, 155, 155f
Humana Building, 119, 119f
Hund, Thomas, 184f
Hundertwasser, Friedensreich, 24f, 25–26
Hundertwasser Haus, 24f
Hunt, Richard Morris, 15, 16f

atelier of, 105
and Columbian Exposition, 145
Metropolitan Museum of Art, 294, 294f
Huxtable, Ada Louise, 62, 62f, 134, 171
HVAC
    and hospital design, 280, 291
    and materials, 146, 152
    and office architecture, 215–217
HyperTrack, 177
Hypo Alpe-Adria Bank, 60f

Icon Architects, 348f, 349
IDEO, 165
IDS Center, 55
Illinois Institute of Technology, Crown Hall, 108f
Independence Hall, 61
indoor environment, and office design, 208
Industrial Revolution
    and architecture, 36
    and cities, 340, 363
    and materials, 143–145
    reaction to, 41
integrated practice, 185
Intelligent Workplace, 208f, 209
International Building Code, 91
International Conference of Building Officials, 89
international practice, 11, 175, 186
International Style, 46, 55
    and hospital design, 280, 280f
    Legorreta and, 312
International Union of Architects, 11
Intern Development Program, 113
internships, university education and, 110
iron, and glass, 142f, 143, 143f
Island Inn, 203
Ivy, Robert, 1–9, 80
Ixtapuluca, 370f
Izenour, Steven, 49

Jacksonville Landing, 220
Jacobs, Jane, 59, 59f, 368, 368f
Jacobs House, 200
Jaffe, Norman, 331
Jahn, Helmut, 230f, 231
Japan
    temples, 2f
    and Wright, 41
JCDecaux, 100f
Jeanneret-Gris, Charles-Édouard. See Le Corbusier
Jefferson, Thomas, 10, 10f, 13, 35
    and cities, 360
    and public architecture, 241
    and residential architecture, 189
    and school architecture, 256f, 257
Jeffrey Clark Associates, 267
Jencks, Charles, 194
Jenney, William Le Baron, 15, 38, 38f

and Columbian Exposition, 145
Home Insurance Building, 146f, 149
and Sullivan, 219
Jennings, Maurice, 336
Jeppesen Terminal, 225, 225f, 231
JJR, 350f
Johansen, John, 296, 296f
John Deere Building, 236
Johns Hopkins Hospital, 277, 277f
Johns Hopkins University, 260f, 261
Johnson, Lyndon B., 233
Johnson, Peggy, 222f
Johnson, Philip Cortelyou, 13, 48, 55, 55f
    Crystal Cathedral, 328, 329f
    Lincoln Center, 305
    and preservation, 368, 368f
    and Saarinen, 236
    Seagram Building, 46, 46f, 207
Johnson & Wales University, 184f
Johnson Wax Administration Building, 200
Jones, E. Fay, 13, 328–331, 330f, 336, 336f
J Street Inn, 203

Kahn, Louis I., 12, 32, 32f, 129
    First Unitarian Church, 326, 327f
    Kimbell Art Museum, 298, 299f
    and Modernism, 48–49, 48f
    and Moore, 201
    Phillips Exeter Academy Library, 264, 267f
Kaiser Permanente, 288, 291
Kallman McKinnell & Knowles, 367f
Kallman McKinnell & Wood Architects, 249f
Kansas City, MO, 338f, 339, 363
Katrina, Hurricane, 6, 8f, 52, 80
    cottages, 194f
Kaufmann, Michelle, 164, 165f, 198f
Kaufmann House, 97
Kelbaugh, Douglas, 74–75, 74f, 194, 356–373
Kellert, Steven, 208, 283
Kelly, Ellsworth, 246f
Kennedy, John F., 238
Kennedy, John F., Jr., 313
Kennedy, Sheila, 155, 155f
Kennedy (John F.) Airport, TWA Terminal, 231, 236, 236f
Kennedy (John F.) Center for the Performing Arts, 150, 151f, 305
Kennedy (John F.) Federal Building, 243, 244f
Kennedy & Violich Architecture, 155, 163, 163f
Ken Smith Landscape Architects, 139f
Kentlands, MD, 368
Kiasma Museum, 301
Kieran, Stephen, 6, 113, 137, 164
KieranTimberlake Associates, 6, 94f, 137, 137f, 164, 164f
Kiley, Dan, 207, 326, 327f
Kim, Tai Soo, 267
Kimbell Art Museum, 32f, 298, 299f
Kimmel Center for the Performing Arts, 301

King, Richard, 121
King (Martin Luther, Jr.) Library, 166f, 167
Kings Road House, 44, 44f
Kitimat, 354
Klauder, Charles Z., 259, 259f
KMD Architects, 284f
knowledge-based practice, 130
Knowles, Edward F., 21f
Knowlton School of Architecture, 112f
Koch, Carl, 192
Kohn, Eugene, 247
Kolbe, Georg, 31
Koolhaas, Rem, 156, 156f, 163f
Kouletsis, John, 291
Krawina, Joseph, 24f
Kresge Chapel, MIT, 262
Kroloff, Reed, 112

Lacy, Joseph, 221
Lake Shore Drive Apartments, 31, 194, 362f
Laloux, Victor, 13
La Luz, 202
Lam, William, 238
Lane (Albert) Technical High School, 258f, 259
Langhorne Pavilion, 21f
language differences, and international practice,
    186
Larkin Building, 204f, 205, 205f
Lark, Reg, 26f
Lasker Biomedical Building, 71
Las Vegas, 371f
Las Vegas Springs Preserve and Desert Living
    Center, 168, 168f
La Tourette Monastery, 374
Latrobe, Benjamin, 35, 360
Latrobe Prize (Research Fellowship), 113, 132,
    137
leadership
    and design, 167–168, 172
    and practice, 178–180
LEAP, 178, 180f
Le Corbusier, 13, 44, 48, 51, 374, 374f
    Carpenter Center for the Visual Arts,
        Harvard, 262, 262f
    Unité d'Habitation, 194
    United Nations Building, 150f
    Ville Radieuse (Radiant City), 194, 364,
        364f, 374
LEDs, 155
Lee, David, 353f
Lee, Laura, 122, 122f
LEED. See United States Green Building
        Council, Leadership in Energy and
        Environmental Design rating system
Leers Weinzapfel, 269
Legacy Salmon Creek Hospital, 288f, 289
Legorreta, Ricardo, 13, 312, 312f
Le Havre, France, 153f
Lehrer Architects, 334

Leiter Buildings, 38, 38f
L'Enfant, Pierre-Charles, 10, 16
Leo A Daly, 122f, 333, 334f
Lescaze, William, 43, 56
Lever House, 46, 47f, 150, 181
Levin, Carl, 74f
Levy, David, 355
Lewin, Wendy, 26f
Lewis, Carl, 74f
Lexington Terrace, 353
Libeskind, Daniel, 4, 4f, 84, 109
    Denver Art Museum, 303, 303f
life-cycle design, 177
light-emitting diodes (LEDs), 155
Lillian Place, 197f
Lin, Maya, 315, 331, 331f
Lincoln Cathedral, 18f, 19–20
Lincoln Center for the Performing Arts, 305,
        366f
    Plaza, 55
Lincoln Elementary School, 264
Lincoln Memorial, 322, 335, 335f
Lindsey, Gail, 99
Link, Theodore, 227, 227f
Lister, Joseph, 277
Little Village Academy, 269
living systems theory, 169
Lloyd's of London, 215, 215f
load-bearing structural skeleton, 146f, 149
Loeb, Albert, 58f
Loftness, Vivian, 204–218
Logan International Airport, Terminal A, 235,
        235f
Logjam House, 202f
Loire, Gabriel, 326
London, 370
Loomis, John A., 122
Looney Ricks Kiss, 267
Loos, Adolf, 20f
Los Angeles, 366, 372f
Lotte's department store, 186f
Louisiana Purchase, 360
Louisville airport, 231
Louvre, 294, 301, 302f, 310
Lovell, Phillip, 97
Lovell Health House, 97
Lowell, Francis Cabot, 340
Lowell, MA, 340, 342f, 349
Lower Manhattan Development Corporation, 84
low-income housing, 195–197, 196f–197f
LS3P, 184, 184f
Lucas, Frank, 184f
Lucchesi, Ray, 168
Lucchesi Galati, 168, 168f
Lustron House, 192, 192f
Lutyens, Edwin Landseer, 12–13
Lykes House, 200, 200f
Lynn, Greg, 84

Mace, Ronald F., 100, 100f

MacKaye, Benton, 354
Mackintosh, Charles Rennie, 41
Mack Scogin Merrill Elam Architects, 112f
Madison Square Garden, 61
Maginnis, Charles Donagh, 12, 181, 321, 322f
Magno, Dinna, 355
Mahlum Architects, 138f
Mahone, Doug, 208
Maiden, Doug, 173f
Maillart, Robert, 237
Main Street, 363
    mixed-use, 350
Maison Hermès, 161, 162f
Majekodunmi, Olufemi, 99
Maki, Fumihiko, 84, 306
Malcolm, Clark, 223
mall style
    and airport design, 231
    and hospital design, 285
Mann, Horace, 257
Mann, Thomas, 283
Manufacturer's Hanover Trust Building, 150,
        181, 181f
Manville Student Apartments, Berkeley, 269
marketing, 176
Marshall Field Warehouse, 36
masonry load-bearing wall construction, 147f
Mason's Bend Community Center, 54f
Massachusetts General Hospital, 277
Massachusetts Institute of Technology, 15
    Baker House dormitory, 261, 261f, 290
    Kresge Chapel, 262
    Simmons Hall, 268f, 269
Massachusetts Museum of Contemporary Art,
        307, 307f
Massey, Geoffrey, 254
mass transit systems, 232–233, 345
materials, 141–157
    and design process, 163–165
    indigenous, 141
Matta-Clark, Gordon, 23, 25
Matthews, Charles T., 316
MATx, 155, 163, 163f
Maxman, Susan, 63, 63f, 99
Maybeck, Bernard, 13, 41, 321, 321f
Mayne, Thom, 60, 109
    Morse (Wayne Lyman) Courthouse, 255,
        255f
    National Oceanic and Atmospheric
        Administration satellite operations
        facility, 252f
    San Francisco Federal Building, 253f
Mays, Vernon, 135, 171, 237
MBDC, 136, 163
McCarter, Walter, 238f
McCarthy, Michael, 331–333, 332f
McCormick Tribune Campus Center, 156, 156f
McCurry, Margaret, 249
McDonough, William, 136, 163, 375, 375f

McDonough Braungart Design Chemistry, 136
McKibben, Bill, 94
McKim, Charles Follen, 12–13, 15–16, 145, 335
McKim, Mead and White, 15, 363
    Bellevue Hospital, 274f, 278, 278f
    Boston Symphony Hall, 293
    Metropolitan Museum of Art, 294, 294f
    Pennsylvania Station, 61, 61f, 368
McKinney, Pam, 350
McMaster University Health Sciences Center,
        280, 281f
McMillan Commission, 16
McMillan Plan, 335
MechoShade, 136, 136f
Medary, Milton, 13
Meehan, Michael James, 118
megachurches, 315, 328, 329f
Meier, Richard, 4, 84, 250, 311, 311f
    Getty Center, 305–306, 305f
    and Modernism, 51
Melillo, Cheri C., 313
memorials, 84, 315, 334
    Lincoln Memorial, 322, 335, 335
    Vietnam Veterals Memorial, 331, 331f
    World War II Memorial, 333, 334f
Mendell, Mark, 208
Mendelsohn, Erich, 97
Menn, Christian, 228, 229f
Mercutt, Glenn, 26f
Merkel, Jayne, 236
Merrill, John, 181
Merrill (Philip) Environmental Center, 218, 218f
methods
    and design process, 163–165
    indigenous, 141
Metropolitan, 198f
Metropolitan Museum of Art, 294, 294f
Metro system, D.C., 233, 238, 238f
Meyer, Adolf, 118
Meyerson Symphony Center, 296
Miami Beach, FL, 368f
Michael Graves & Associates, 119
Michelangelo, 2
Michigan Central Depot, 74–75, 74f–75f
Middlebury Elementary School, 267
Mies van der Rohe, Ludwig, 13, 31, 31f, 46, 46f,
        55
    Chicago Federal Center, 243, 243f
    Crown Hall, 108f; and education, 121
    Lake Shore Drive Apartments, 194, 362f
    on material, 152
    and Modernism, 44, 46
    New National Gallery, 298
    Seagram Building, 46f, 207
Miller, John, 375
Miller/Hull Partnership, 244f, 269
Mills, Robert, 59
Mills College Music Building, 172f
Milwaukee Art Museum, 303, 304f

minimalism, 46
Mitchell/Giurgola Associates, 17, 17f, 264, 265f
Mitgang, Lee D., 121, 132
MLTW, 201
Moakley (John Joseph) Courthouse, 246f
Mockbee, Samuel "Sambo," 13, 54, 54f, 79, 79f
Moderne bus stations, 228, 228f
Modernism, 19f, 22, 44–46, 46f, 48–49
    and arts institutions, 298–303
    and cities, 364–366
    education on, 114
    Esherick and, 56
    and hospital design, 280
    Kahn and, 32
    Meier and, 311
    Mies van der Rohe and, 31
    and office design, 207
    versus Postmodernism, 51
    and preservation, 59, 61
    and religious architecture, 321–326
    and residential design, 190–192, 190f–191f
    and school design, 261–263
    Skidmore and, 181
modular houses, 165–166, 166f, 193f
Moholy-Nagy, Laszlo, 121
Mold, Jacob Wrey, 294f
Monadnock Building, 38, 147f, 149
Monaghan, Thomas S., 267
Moncrief, Mike, 337f
Moneo, Rafael, 333, 334f
Monolith, 29f
Monterey Bay Aquarium, 56f
Monticello, 10, 10f, 35, 35f, 189
Moore, Charles W., 13, 201, 201f
Moore Ruble Yudell Architects & Planners, 172,
        201, 269, 269f
Morgan, Julia, 36, 36f, 41, 63
Morgan, William, 290
Moritz, Lisa, 355
Morphosis, 109f
    Cedars-Sinai Comprehensive Cancer Center,
        285, 285f
    Diamond Ranch High School, 270, 270f
    Hypo Alpe-Adria Bank (Udine, Italy), 60f
    National Oceanic and Atmospheric
        Administration satellite operations
        facility, 252f
    San Francisco Federal Building, 253f
Morris, William, 41
Morrow, Irving F. and Gertrude C., 224f, 225
Morse (Wayne Lyman) Courthouse, 255, 255f
Mortenson, Chris, 203
Mortenson, Wayne, 120
Mortland, Marshall D., 263
Moses, Robert, 59, 364, 366f
Mount Vernon, 342, 343f
Mount Vernon Ladies' Association of the Union,
        59, 59f, 61
Mouse House, 273

movie palaces, 294–295, 295f
    conversion of, 307
Moynihan, Daniel Patrick, 243, 249
multifamily housing, 194–195, 195f
Mumford, Lewis, 16, 62, 62f, 340, 354, 363
Mummers Theater, 296, 296f
Musée d'Art Moderne, 310
Museum of Islamic Art, 310
Museum of Modern Art, 181
    Garden, 55
Muthesius, Hermann, 44

NAAB. See National Architectural Accrediting
        Board
Nadel, Barbara A., 82, 103
Nader, James, 337, 337f
Nakada & Partners, 349, 349f
National Airport, D.C., 230f, 231
National Architectural Accrediting Board
        (NAAB), 110, 113, 124
National Board of Fire Underwriters, 87
National Center for Preservation Technology
        and Training, 59
National Council of Architectural Registration
        Boards (NCARB), 110, 113
National Endowment for the Arts, 245
Nationale-Nederlanden building, 28f
National Gallery (London), Sainsbury Wing,
        302f, 303
National Gallery of Art, 294, 294f
    East Building, 301, 301f, 310, 310f
National Historic Preservation Act, 59, 91
national identity, architecture and, 35
National Mall, 10, 16, 305
National Oceanic and Atmospheric
        Administration, 217
    satellite operations facility, 252f
National Palace Museum Southern Branch, 202
National Park Service: National Historic
        Landmarks program, 59
    Technical Preservation Services, 58
National Register of Historic Places, 59
National Shrine of the Immaculate Conception,
        321, 322f
National Trust for Historic Preservation, 59
Natural Resources Defense Council, 217, 217f
nature, and architecture, 25–28, 25f
NBBJ, 288f, 289
NCARB. See National Council of Architectural
        Registration Boards
Nelson Fine Arts Center, 267, 306, 306f
Neoclassical style
    National Gallery of Art, 294, 294f
    World War II Memorial, 333, 334f
Nervi, Pier Luigi, 13, 134, 134f
Netsch, Walter, 324, 325f
Neumann, Dietrich, 31
neuroscience, and architecture, research on,
        139, 139f

Neutra, Richard J., 13, 44, 96, 97, 97f
New 42 Studios, 307, 308f
New National Gallery, Berlin, 298
New Urbanism, 52, 52f, 194, 347, 347f, 368
    and multifamily housing, 197
    and school design, 270
New York, 360; World's Fair, 364, 365f
New York Hospital, 277, 277f, 279, 279f
New York Mosque and Islamic Cultural Center,
        331–333, 332f
New York-Presbyterian Hospital, 279, 279f
New York State Theater, 55
New York Times Building, 212
Niemeyer, Oscar, 150f
Nietzsche, Friedrich, 20, 22
Nightingale, Florence, 276
NK Architects, 313
Norfolk, VA, 353, 355, 355f
North Christian Church, Columbus, 236, 326,
        327f
NorthPoint, 352f, 353
Norview Theater, 355f
Notre Dame du Raincy, 153, 153f
Nouvel, Jean, 29, 29f

Oak Park House, 41, 41f
Oak Ridge National Laboratory, 181
Obus plan for Algiers, 374
O'Connor (Sandra Day) Courthouse, 247f
Octagon House, 16, 16f, 59
office architecture, 204–223
Office for Metropolitan Architecture, 163, 163f
Oglethrope, James, 360
O'Hare International Airport, United Airlines
        Terminal One, 230f, 231
Ohio State University: Knowlton School of
        Architecture, 112f
    Wexner Center for the Arts, 51, 51f, 306
Old Post Office, 220
Olmsted, Frederick Law, 15–16
    and activism, 64f, 65–67, 65f
    and cities, 363
    and Columbian Exposition, 145
    and HSW, 87, 87f, 88
Olsen, Donald, 107f
Olympic College, 269
O'Malley, Martin, 346f
Operation Breakthrough, 192
operations, 176
Opportunity Center, 203, 203f
Orput Associates, 264
Orr, Douglas William, 13f
Ospedale Maggiore, 276
Östberg, Ragnar, 13
Otis, Elisha, 145f
Otis elevator, 38, 145f
Ottolino Winters Huebner, 222
Owens Corning World Headquarters, 209, 209f
Owings, Nathaniel, 13, 181

Oz Architects, 288

Paimio Sanatorium, 283, 290, 290f
Palazzetto dello Sport, 134
Pallasmaa, Juhani, 26
Palomar Pomerado Hospital, 289, 289f
Palos Verdes High School, 97
pandemics, 93
Panelite, 156
Papalote Children's Museum, 312f
Papp (Joseph) Public Theater, 306, 306f
Paris, 358, 358f
    exposition, 43
Park, Sharon C., 58, 58f
Park DuValle, 353, 353f
Parker, Thomas & Rice, 260f, 261
participatory action research, 84
Partners for Sacred Places, 337
Pascal, Jean, 13
Pataki, George, 84
pavilion hospitals, 276, 276f, 278, 278f
Paxton, Joseph, 142f, 143
Peabody & Stearns, 15
Peabody Terrace, Harvard, 262, 262f
Pebble Projects, 287
Peddle Thorp Walker, 157
Peele, Katherine, 184f
Pei, I. M., 12–13, 310, 310f
    Louvre, 301, 302f
    National Gallery of Art, East Building, 301,
        301f
Pei Cobb Freed & Partners, 296, 310
    Bellevue Hospital, 274f
    National Gallery of Art, East Building, 301,
        301f
Pelikan, Peter, 24f
Pelli, César, 13, 182, 182f
    Brooklyn Courthouse, 251f
    Owens Corning World Headquarters, 209,
        209f
    Reagan (Ronald) Washington National
        Airport, 230f, 231
Pelli Clarke Pelli Architects, 182
Pelli, Rafael, 182
Penn, William, 360
Penney, Thompson E., 184, 184f
Pennsylvania Hospital, 277
Pennsylvania Station, 61, 61f, 227, 368, 368f
Pennzoil Place, 55
Pereria, William, 48
performance-based criteria, 124
performing arts, architecture for, 292–313
Perkins, Dwight H., 258f, 259, 269
Perkins, G. Holmes, 48–49
Perkins, Wheeler & Will, 263, 263f
Perkins & Will, 280f
Perret, Auguste, 13, 153, 153f
Peterson, Charles, 17, 61
Peterson, John, 33

Peterson Littenberg, 84
Petronas Towers, 182f
Pevsner, Nikolaus, 19
Pfau Architecture, 334
Philadelphia, 360
Philadelphia Museum of Art, 294
Philadelphia Savings Fund Society building, 43
Philadelphia School, 48–49
Philharmonie, Berlin, 296
Phillips Exeter Academy, 49, 264, 267f
Phipps Garden Apartments, 354f
photovoltaics (PVs), 155
Piano, Renzo, 161, 162f, 212
    Building Workshop, 176
Piazza del Campidoglio, 2, 3f
Piedmont-Palladino, Susan, 121
Pine, Joseph, 165
Pittsburgh Plate Glass Company, 55
place, sense of, 376–379
Plan Voisin, 374
plastics, 157, 157f
Plater-Zyberk, Elizabeth, 52f
Platt Byard Dovell White, 307, 308f, 313f
play, and design process, 161
Plum Street Temple, 316, 316f
Pluralism, 326–333
Polanyi, Michael, 121
politics, architects in, 85
Polshek, James Stewart, 306
polymers, 157, 157f
Pope, John Russell, 294, 294f
Pope-Leighey House, 190f
Poplar Forest, 10
population growth, 91f, 92
    and cities, 370
    and residential design, 198
Porphyrios, Demetri, 267
Portable Light Project, 155, 155f
Portland Building, 119
Portland Public Service Building, 50f, 51
Post, George Brown, 12–13, 15, 145
Postman, Neil, 278–279
Postmodernism, 49, 194
    and arts institutions, 303
    Graves and, 119
    versus Modernism, 51
Postparkasse, 20f
poststructuralism, and education, 115
poverty, 94
Powell, Colin, 85
practice, 174–187
    architecture education and, 112–113
    factors affecting, 176, 176f
    integrated, 185
    knowledge-based, 130
    research based in, 139
    trends in, 176–177
Prada, 163, 163f
Prairie Style house, 41, 41f, 200

Predock, Antoine, 13, 13*f*, 202, 202*f*
    Nelson Fine Arts Center, 267, 306, 306*f*
Preiser, Wolfgang F. E., 101
preservation movement, 61
    and cities, 368, 368*f*
    history of, 59
    laws and codes of, 91
    NPS and, 58
Princeton University, 259, 261, 267
    Wu (Gordon) Hall, 267, 267*f*
Pritzker Architecture Prize, 63, 154, 171, 221,
        250, 255, 310, 311
Pritzker (Jay) Pavilion, 171
professional services, 176
Providence, RI, 347
Public Architecture, 33
public architecture, 240–255
public good, architecture and, 64–85
    contemporary leaders in, 70–76
    contributions of, 77
    historical leaders in, 65–70
public schools, architecture of, 256–273
public spaces, 356*f*, 358, 360
Pugh + Scarpa, 52, 53*f*
Pugh Scarpa Kodama, 198, 199*f*
Pugin, A. W. N., 41
Pulitzer Foundation for the Arts building, 30*f*
Pullman, IL, 342
Purnell, Marshall, 63, 63*f*
PVs. *See* photovoltaics
Pyatok, Michael, 188–199
Pyatok Architects, 197*f*
Pyburn, Jack, 59
pyramids, 2*f*

quality, schoolhouse of, 183, 183*f*
Quarterly Bulletin, 16
Quatman, G. William II, 187
Quigley, Rob Wellington, 203, 203*f*
Quinn Evans Architects, 91*f*

Radburn, NJ, 354, 354*f*
Radiant City (Ville Radieuse), 194, 364, 364*f*,
        374
Radio City Music Hall, 295, 295*f*
Rahaim, John, 353
railroad architecture, 225–226
    adaptation of, 234*f*, 235, 235*f*
Rapoport, Amos, 130
Rapson, Ralph, 296
Ratcliff, Christopher (Kit), 172
Ratcliff, Robert, 172
Ratcliff, Walter H., 172
Ratcliff Architects, 172
Rayward (John L.) House, 200
RDG Planning & Design, 163–164
Reagan (Ronald) Washington National Airport,
        230*f*, 231
rebars, 140*f*

Redefining Progress, 93
Reed and Stern, 226*f*, 227
regionalism, 194, 202
Regional/Urban Design Assistance Team
        (R/UDAT), 81–82
Rehabilitation Act, 91
Reichstag, 98
Reilly, Bill, 99
reinforced concrete, 140*f*
Reinventing the Urban Village, 348*f*, 349
Reliance Building, 38, 39*f*, 149
Reliance Controls Factory, 98
religion, architecture for, 314–337
Renwick, James, 314*f*, 316
Reps, John W., 194
Republic Bank, 55
research, architectural, 126–139
    collaborative, 139
    highlights of, 132–133
    institutions and organizations for, 130–132
    mechanics of, 130; nature of, 127–129
research model, of architecture education, 105
residential architecture, 188–203
resorts, 282–283
Reynolds, Bob, 238, 238*f*
Reynolds Metal Headquarters, 181
Rice University, 110, 257
Richard Meier & Partners, 247*f*–248*f*
Richards, Kristen, 119, 182, 202
Richards, William, 153, 374
Richards Medical Research Building, 48*f*, 49
Richardson, Henry Hobson, 36, 36*f*, 318, 318*f*
    atelier of, 105, 105*f*
Richardsonian Romanesque, 36*f*, 318
Riis, Jacob, 88*f*
Rita, Hurricane, 6
Riverlife Task Force, 239
Riverview Hope VI Redevelopment Plan, 196*f*
Robertson, Howard, 150*f*
Robie House, 190, 200
Robinson, Adah, 322
Robinson House, 170
Roche, Kevin, 12, 207, 221, 221*f*, 236*f*
Roche-Dinkeloo, 294*f*, 306
Rockefeller Center, 43, 43*f*, 207, 295, 358, 359*f*
Rogers, James Gamble, 279, 279*f*
Rogers, Richard, 84, 98, 215, 215*f*
Rome, 370
Romney, George, 192
Roosevelt, Franklin Delano, 68, 363
Roosevelt, Theodore, 12, 16
Root, John Wellborn II, 13, 15, 67, 129
Roschen, Bill, 349
Roschen Van Cleve, 349, 349*f*
Rotondi, Michael, 79
Rouse Company, 220
Rousseau, Jean-Jacques, 350
Row, Elizabeth, 238*f*
Rowlett, John W., 272

Royal Institute of British Architects, 14
R & R Partners, 168
R/UDAT. *See* Regional/Urban Design
        Assistance Team
Rudofsky, Bernard, 23
Rudolph, Paul, 48, 263, 264*f*
Ruga, Wayne, 285–287
Rural Heritage Center, 9*f*
Rural Studio, 54, 54*f*, 79, 79*f*
Ruskin, John, 41
Ruth, Dennis K., 54, 79
Ryan, William, 79
Ryder, Don, 71

Saarinen, Aline, 238
Saarinen, Eero, 12, 236, 236*f*, 271, 305
    Dulles International Airport, 231
    North Christian Church, 326, 327*f*
    and Roche, 221
    and school design, 261–263, 263*f*
    TWA Terminal, 231
Saarinen, Eliel, 13, 236, 271, 271*f*
    Crow Island School, 263, 263*f*
    First Christian Church, 322, 324*f*
Sabine, Wallace Clement, 293
Sachs, Avigail, 201
St. Bartholomew's Church, 321, 354
St. Florian, Friedrich, 315, 333, 334*f*
Saint Gaudens, Augustus, 16
St. John's Abbey, 328, 328*f*
St. Louis, 342
    Arch, 221, 236
    Union Station, 227, 227*f*, 233*f*
    Washington Avenue Windows Project, 222,
        222*f*
St. Luke's Hospital, 278, 278*f*
St. Mark's Square, Venice, 356*f*
St. Patrick's Cathedral, 314*f*, 316
Salk Institute, 48*f*, 49
sanatoriums, 283, 290, 290*f*
San Diego Padres Stadium, 202
San Francisco, 363
San Francisco Federal Building, 253*f*
San Francisco Museum of Contemporary Art,
        306
Santa Maria del Fiore, dome of, 2, 127, 128*f*
Sarasota High School, 263, 264*f*
Sasanqua Spa, 283*f*
Savannah, GA, 360
Sawruk, Ted, 355
Säynätsalo town hall, 290
Scharoun, Hans, 296
Schiller, Freidrich, 28
Schindler, Rudolf M., 44, 44*f*
Schinkel, Friedrich, 294
school design, 256–273
    Benjamin Franklin Elementary School, 138*f*
    Palos Verdes High School, 97
    Seven Hills School, 183*f*

Shaw (P. A.) School, 33, 33f
  Sidwell Friends Middle School, 94f
Schoolhouse of Quality, 183, 183f
School of Visual Arts, 312
schools of architecture, 15, 104–125
  Weiss on, 28–29
Schrage, Michael, 161
Schulberg, Rick, 375
Schuller, Robert, 328
Schuyler, Montgomery, 62
Schwartz, Frederick, 84
Scientific Theater, 293
Scott Brown, Denise, 49, 51
Scully, Vincent, 59f
SDAT. See Sustainable Design Assistance Team
Seagram Building, 31, 46, 46f, 207
Sea Ranch Condominium, 201, 201f
Seaside, FL, 52f, 368, 369f
Seattle: Steinbrueck and, 72–73, 72f
  urban renewal in, 351f, 353
security issues, 103, 103f
  and airports, 231
  and cities, 373
  and school design, 269
seismic codes, history of, 89f, 91
Sell, Martin, 187
Semper, Gottfried, 129
September 11, 2001, 4f, 9, 25
  memorials to, 334
  and security issues, 103, 231
serious play, and design process, 161
Sert, Jackson & Gourley, 262, 262f
Sert, Josep Lluis, 13, 195, 262f
settlement, patterns of, 358
Seven Hills School, 183f
Shaffer, Mary, 273
Shanghai, 370f
Sharples Holden Pasquarelli (SHoP), 139f
Shaw, Howard Van Doren, 13
Shaw (P. A.) School, 33, 33f
Shays, Chris, 85
sheet-metal technology, 150
Sheine, Judith, 97
Shepley Bulfinch Richardson and Abbott, 286f,
  287
Sher-e-Bangla Nagar, 49, 49f
Shreve, Lamb and Harmon, 43, 206f, 207
sick building syndrome, 208
Sidwell Friends Middle School, 94f
Silverstein, Larry, 4f, 84
Simmons, Cary, 355
Simmons Hall, MIT, 268f, 269
Simon Fraser University, 262
Simpson, Scott, 176
Sims, Bill, 210
Sinclair, Cameron, 33, 80
single-family houses, 189–194
single-room occupancy hotels (SROs), 203, 203f
Singleton, James, 74f

Sivils, John, 355
Skarmeas, George C., 61
Skidmore, Louis, 12–13, 181, 181f
Skidmore, Owings & Merrill (SOM), 46, 47f, 84,
  158f, 181
  Air Force Academy Cadet Chapel, 262, 324,
    325f
  Census Bureau Headquarters, 250f
  Chongming, 372f
  Freedom Tower, 177
  Lever House, 47f, 150
  Manufacturer's Hanover Trust Building, 150
  New York Mosque and Islamic Cultural
    Center, 331–333, 332f
  and practice-based research, 139
Sklarek, Norma Merrick, 63, 63f
skyscrapers, 38, 38f–39f, 46f–47f
  and cities, 362f, 363
  definition of, 149
  and hospital design, 279
  Mies van der Rohe and, 31, 31f
  origins of, 148f, 149–150, 149f–150f
  Sullivan and, 219
Slater, Samuel, 340
Slay, Francis G., 222
slums, 91f, 92–93
Smart Growth, 59, 270, 368
smart windows, 156
SmartWrap, 6, 7f, 137, 137f
Smith, Andrew Brodie, 56, 220–221, 272
Smith, Hamilton, 298
Smith, Ken, 83f
SmithGroup, 218, 218f
Smithsonian American Art Museum courtyard,
  98, 307
Snelson, Kenneth, 69
Snohetta, 84
Snoonian, Deborah, 136, 155, 291, 375
Soane, John, 294
socially responsible architecture, 9, 33, 54
  and arts institutions, 308
  Canstruction, 313, 313f
  Freedom by Design, 120, 120f
  and residential design, 203, 203f
  and school design, 269
Society for Design Administration, 313
Society of Beaux-Arts Architects, 105
Socony-Mobil Building, 150
Solaire, 188f, 198
Solar Decathlon, 121, 121f
Solar Umbrella House, 53f
Soleri, Paolo, 57, 57f, 84
Solomon, Nancy B., 310
Solomon, Susan G., 32
SOM. See Skidmore, Owings & Merrill
Sorkin, Michael, 102
South Campus Gateway Center, 350
Southern Building Code Conference
  International, 89

South Street Seaport, 220
Spangler Campus Center, Harvard, 267, 267f
spas, 282–283, 283f
species loss, 94
Speer, Albert, 22
Spencer, Ingrid, 239, 337
spirit, architecture for, 314–337
sprawl, 370–371, 371f
squatting, term, 272
SROs. See single-room occupancy hotels
StageCenter, 296, 296f
Stainer, Christian, 33
Stamford Hospital, 280f
Stapleton Airport, Denver, 368, 369f
Starbucks, 223
starchitects, 62
Stata Center, 171
static building composition, 132
Steed Hammond Paul, 183
steel, 143, 145
  sheet-metal technology, 150
Steelcase, 207, 211, 211f
Steele, Fritz, 211
Steele, James, 34–54
Stein, Clarence S., 13, 16, 354, 354f, 363
Stein, Jeff, 57
Steinbrueck, Peter, 72–73, 72f–73f
Steinbrueck, Victor, 72
Stern, Robert A. M., 55, 267, 267f
Stickney Murphy Architects, 197f
Stohr, Kate, 33, 80
Stone, Edward Durell, 150, 151f, 295, 305
Stonorov, Oscar, 32
Storer (John) House, 200, 200f
Straka, Ron, 339f
streetcar neighborhoods, 340, 364
Strong, Norman, 185
Stubbins Associates, 176–177
Studio 804, 193f
Studio Daniel Libeskind, 84f
Studio E Architects, 197f
studio model, of architecture education, 121, 160
Stull Lee Architects, 348f, 349, 353f
Stuyvesant Town, 194, 195f
suburbs, 344f, 345, 364–366, 370, 371f
  and residential architecture, 190–192
subway systems, 232–233
Sulik, Shelly, 355
Sullivan, C. C., 256–270
Sullivan, Louis H., 13, 16, 57, 219, 219f
  Carson Pirie Scott Department Store, 38,
    38f, 41
  Transportation Building, 143f, 145
  and Wright, 200
Sundial Bridge, 237f
Sunnyside Gardens, 354
Sunset + Vine, 349, 349f
Susanka, Sarah, 198
sustainable design, 6, 26, 28, 94f

AIA and, 11, 81, 99
China-U.S. Center for Sustainable
        Development, 375, 375f
and churches, 318
and cities, 372–373, 373f
development of, 91, 94
education on, 114
Fuller and, 69
and hospital design, 287f, 288–289,
        288f–289f, 291, 291f
Kelbaugh and, 74
McDonough and, 136
Neutra on, 96
and office architecture, 212–216, 212f–213f
and practice, 177, 178f–179f
and research, 133
and residential architecture, 198
and school design, 270
Solar Decathlon, 121, 121f
Steinbrueck and, 72
and transportation architecture, 235, 235f
Sustainable Design Assistance Team (SDAT),
        81
Sutton, Sharon Egretta, 64–77, 70f, 83
Suzhou Museum, 310, 310f
Swager, Anne, 239
Swan and Dolphin Resort, 119
Swatek, Michelle, 222, 222f
Swett, Richard N., 85, 85f
Swiss Re Building, 98, 98f
Sydney Opera House, 298, 299f
Sygar, Janet, 70f
systems thinking, education on, 114
Szenasy, Susan, 80

TAC. See The Architects Collaborative
Taft, William Howard, 12, 16
Taliesin Fellowhip, 4, 200
Tange, Kenzo, 13, 13f
Tang Teaching Museum and Art Gallery, 202
Tasso Katselas Associates, 231
Tate Modern, 307
tax issues
    for historic preservation, 58–59
    and housing, 195
Taylor, Frederick, 205
TBWA/Chiat/Day Headquarters, 210
Team 4, 98
Team Disney Building, 119
Techbuilt houses, 192
Technical Preservation Services (TPS), 58
technology
    and arts institutions, 308
    and cities, 373
    and hospital design, 278–279
    and materials, 141–157
    and office architecture, 210–211
    performance life cycle of, 159, 159f
    and public architecture, 242

and residential architecture, 189
and school design, 269
and sense of place, 378
Temple Bat Yahm Torah Center, 334
Tenement House Act, 88–89, 88f
tenure issues, 108–109
Terminal A, Logan International Airport, 235,
        235f
termite mounds, 25f
terrorism, 94
Texas regional office, Partners for Sacred
        Places, 337
textile block system, 200
The Architects Collaborative (TAC), 17, 17f, 118,
        220
theory: death of, 52–54
    and design, 169
    and research, 130
THINK, 84, 84f
thin stone veneer, 150, 151f
third spaces, 223, 223f, 350
third wave, definition of, 159, 159f
30 St. Mary Axe, 98, 98f
Thomas, Douglas, 260f, 261
Thompson, Benjamin, 13, 207, 207f, 220, 220f,
        366f
Thompson, John D., 283
Thompson & Rose, 307, 308f
Thorncrown Chapel, 328–331, 330f, 336
Thornton, William, 16f, 35
Thorpe, Joy, 355
Tiger Stadium development, 74–75, 74f–75f
Tilton, Edward L., 259
Tilton Elementary School, 259
timber, 141, 141f
Timberlake, James, 6, 113, 137, 164
Tokyo International Forum, 301
Top Ten Green Projects, 99, 99f, 138f
Torre, Susana, 70, 70f
Torti Gallas, 353
Total Quality Management, 183
Tougaloo College, 262
TPS. See Technical Preservation Services
Transco Tower, 55
transportation, architecture and, 224–239
Transportation Building, 143f, 145
Tremaine House, 97, 97f
Trenton Bath House, 32, 32f
Tribble, Michael, 184f
Trinity Church, 36, 36f, 318, 318f
Trinity Financial, 348f, 349
triple bottom line, 212.
        See also sustainable design
Troost, Paul Ludwig, 22
Trumbauer, Horace, 294
tuberculosis sanatoriums, 283, 290, 290f
Turning Torso building, 28f
Turtle Creek House, 202, 202f
Twain, Mark, 85

TWA Terminal, JFK Airport, 231, 236, 236f
Twin Towers. See World Trade Center
Tyng, Anne, 32

underground transportation systems, 232–233
UNESCO headquarters, 170, 170f
Union Station, Chicago, 227f
Union Station, D.C., 220, 234f, 235
Union Station, Denver, 339f
Union Station, St. Louis, 227, 227f, 233f, 235
Unitarian Universalist Fellowship Hall, 334
United Airlines Terminal One, 230f, 231
Unité d'Habitation, 194, 374, 374f
United Nations Building, 150f
United States, history of architecture in, 34–63
United States Embassy
    London, 236
    Riyadh, 272
United States Green Building Council,
        Leadership in Energy and
        Environmental Design (LEED) rating
        system, 72, 91, 98, 177, 288
United States Sanitary Commission, 87f, 88
Unity Temple, 320f, 321
universal design, 91, 101
    Graves and, 119
    Mace and, 100, 100f
    principles of, 101
    term, 101
universities
    architecture education in, 105–107
    faculty in, 108–109
University of California, Berkeley, 291
    College of Environmental Design, 78, 107,
        107f
    Manville Student Apartments, 269
University of California, Los Angeles, 259
University of Cincinnati, 110
    Student Life Center, 269, 269f
University of Colorado, 121f
University of Colorado at Boulder, 259, 259f
University of Illinois, 15
University of Iowa, Advanced Technologies
        Laboratory, 267–269
University of Maryland, 113
University of Oregon, Science Complex, 172,
        172f
University of Pennsylvania, 48–49, 269
University of Texas at Austin, tower, 258f, 259
University of Virginia, 10, 10f, 256f, 257
Upjohn, Anna Milo, 14f
Upjohn, Richard, 14, 14f
Upjohn, Richard M., 59, 104f
Uplands, 346f, 347
Urban Architecture, 173
Urban Design Associates, 353, 353f
Urban Edge, 348f, 349
Urban Land Institute, 345
urban renewal, 338–355, 368, 368f–369f

art complexes and, 305–306
See also cities
Usonian house, 190, 19   0*f*, 200
Utzon, Jørn, 298, 299*f*

Valéry, Paul, 22
Van Alen, William, 42*f*
van Berkel, Ben, 84
Van Brunt and Howe, 15
Vanderbilt University, 257
        Peabody College Library, 259
Van der Leeuw, C. H., 97*f*
van Gendt, Adolf Leonard, 293
van Ginkel, Blanche Lemco, 63
Vanna Venturi House, 49, 49*f*
Vaux, Calvert, 87, 294*f*
VDL Research House, 97, 97*f*
ventilation, 215, 215*f*
        See also HVAC
Venturi, Rauch & Scott Brown, 267, 267*f*
Venturi, Robert, 49, 49*f*, 51
Venturi, Scott Brown and Associates, 302*f*, 303
Vietnam Veterans Memorial, 315, 331, 331*f*
Vignelli, Massimo, 238
Villa Savoye, 44
Ville Contemporaine, 374
Ville Radieuse (Radiant City), 194, 364, 364*f*,
        374
Vinoly, Rafael, 84, 301
Viollet-le-Duc, Eugène, 129
Virginia State Capitol, 10
visionary architecture, 57
visual arts, architecture for, 292–313
Vitruvius, 127, 141
von Eckhardt, Wolf, 271*f*
Vonier, Thomas, 11

Wagenaar, Cor, 275, 280
Wagner, Otto, 20f
Wainwright Building, 57, 219
Walker, Gregory, 355
Walker, Peter, 84, 84*f*
Walker, Ralph, 12
Walker Art Center, 303
Walter, Thomas U., 14, 15*f*
Ware, William, 117
Warhol Museum, 307
Warren and Wetmore, 226*f*, 227
Washington, D.C., 360–361, 360*f*–361*f*
        Metro system, 233, 238, 238*f*
        National Mall, 10, 16, 305
Washington, George, 361
Washington Avenue Windows Project, 222,
        222*f*
Washington State Veterans' Home, 288*f*, 289
Wassily chair, 170
Wayfarers Chapel, 324, 324*f*
wayfinding, 283
WDG Architecture, 198*f*

Weaire-Phelan structure, 157
Weaver (Robert C.) Federal Building, 242*f*, 243
Webb, Aston, 12–13, 13*f*, 16
Webb & Knapp, 310
Weese, Harry, 233, 238, 238*f*, 296
Weinman, A. A., 12
Weisman, Winston, 149
Weisman Art Museum, 21, 21*f*
Weiss, Paul, 28–29
Werkbund, 44, 46
Wesleyan University, 306
Western Association of Architects, 15
Westmoor High School, 263
Westmoreland Place, 342
Wexner Center for the Arts, 51, 51*f*, 306
Whitaker, Henry, 219
White City, 15, 66*f*, 67, 129, 129*f*, 145, 363
White House, 16, 35, 35*f*
Whites versus Grays, 51
Whitney Museum, 170, 298
Wichita House, 135, 135*f*
Wiley (Harvey W.) Federal Building, 249*f*
Willets (Ward W.) House, 200
William McDonough + Partners, 91*f*, 165, 177,
        212–213, 212*f*
Williams, Paul Revere, 63, 63*f*
Wills, Royal Barry, 189–190, 189*f*
Wilson, E. O., 208, 283
Wilson, James Keyes, 316, 316*f*
Wilson, Richard Guy, 10, 12–13, 181, 219, 227,
        335
Wischmeyer, Arrasmith & Elswick, 228
wood, 141, 141*f*
Woods, Charles, 355
Woods, Lebbeus, 23, 23*f*
workforce housing, 197
workplace architecture. *See* office architecture
World Bank, 93
World Green Building Council, 11
World's Columbian Exposition, 15, 41
        and cities, 363
        and materials, 144*f*, 145, 145*f*, 146
        and public good, 66*f*, 67
        and research, 129, 129*f*
World's Fair, New York, 364, 365*f*
World Trade Center, 4*f*, 9, 25, 30, 103, 103*f*
        PATH station, 232*f*, 233
        rebuilding, 84, 84*f*
World War II Memorial, 315, 333, 334*f*
Wrenn, Tony P., 14–17
Wright, Frank Lloyd, 4, 4*f*, 97, 200, 200*f*
        and AIA Gold Medal, 12–13, 13*f*
        Broadacre City, 364, 364*f*
        Fallingwater, 44, 45*f*
        Guggenheim Museum, 298, 298*f*
        Larkin Building, 204*f*, 205, 205*f*
        Oak Park House, 41, 41*f*
        and organic architecture, 22
        and residential design, 190, 190*f*

Unity Temple, 320*f*, 321
        and visionary architecture, 57
Wright, Lloyd, 324, 324*f*
Wright, Sylvia Hart, 231
WSA Studio, 112*f*
Wu (Gordon) Hall, Princeton, 267, 267*f*
Wurster, William Wilson, 13, 56, 78, 78*f*, 201
Wurster Hall, 56, 107*f*
Wyon, David, 208

X, Malcolm, 71
xeriscaping, 218
Xian, 370

Yadzani, Mehrdad, 240*f*
Yale University
        Art Gallery, 32*f*
        Building Project, 201
        dormitories, 164, 164*f*
        Hockey Rink, 236
Yamini, A. Hakim, 75–76
Yancey Chapel, 79*f*
Yeang, Ken, 212
Yerba Buena, 306
Yoshida, Joanne B., 70*f*
Young, Leslie, 100
Young Architects Forum, 355
youth, and architecture, 83, 83*f*
YWCA Family Village, 197*f*

Zakim (Leonard P.) Bunker Hill Bridge, 228, 229*f*
Zeckendorf, William, 310
Zeidler, Eberhard, 280, 281*f*
Zhu Rongji, 375
Zimmer Gunsul Frasca Architects, 288*f*, 289,
        351*f*
Zoli, Theodore, 228
zoning, 366